5 STEPS TO A 5

AP U.S. History

2016

Daniel P. Murphy
Stephen Armstrong

McGraw Hill Education

New York   Chicago   San Francisco   Athens   London   Madrid
Mexico City   Milan   New Delhi   Singapore   Sydney   Toronto

Copyright © 2015, 2013, 2011, 2010, 2007, 2002 by McGraw-Hill Education. All rights reserved. Printed in the United States of America. Except as permitted under the United States Copyright Act of 1976, no part of this publication may be reproduced or distributed in any form or by any means, or stored in a database or retrieval system, without the prior written permission of the publisher.

1 2 3 4 5 6 7 8 9 0   RHR/RHR   1 2 1 0 9 8 7 6 5 (book alone)
1 2 3 4 5 6 7 8 9 0   RHR/RHR   1 2 1 0 9 8 7 6 5 (Cross-Platform edition)

ISBN 978-0-07-184667-7 (book alone)
MHID 0-07-184667-0
ISSN 1935-6374

ISBN 978-0-07-184692-9 (Cross-Platform edition)
MHID 0-07-184692-1

e-ISBN 978-0-07-184668-4 (e-book alone)
e-MHID 0-07-184668-9

e-ISBN 978-1-259-58793-1 (Cross-Platform edition)
e-MHID 1-259-58793-2

Trademarks: McGraw-Hill Education, the McGraw-Hill Education logo, *5 Steps to a 5*, and related trade dress are trademarks or registered trademarks of McGraw-Hill Education and/or its affiliates in the United States and other countries and may not be used without written permission. All other trademarks are the property of their respective owners. McGraw-Hill Education is not associated with any product or vendor mentioned in this book.

AP, Advanced Placement Program, and *College Board* are registered trademarks of the College Entrance Examination Board, which was not involved in the production of, and does not endorse, this product.

The series editor was Grace Freedson, and the project editor was Del Franz.
Series design by Jane Tenenbaum.

McGraw-Hill Education products are available at special quantity discounts to use as premiums and sales or for use in corporate training programs. To contact a representative, please visit the Contact Us pages at www.mhprofessional.com.

CONTENTS

Preface xi
Introduction: 5-Step Program xiii

STEP 1 Set Up Your Study Program

Chapter 1 What You Need to Know About the AP U.S. History Exam 3
Advanced Placement Program 3
AP U.S. History Exam 5
Taking the AP U.S. History Exam 6

Chapter 2 Preparing for the AP U.S. History Exam 8
Getting Started 8
Three Plans for Test Preparation 10

STEP 2 Determine Your Test Readiness

Chapter 3 Take a Diagnostic Exam 17
How to Use the Diagnostic Exam 17
When to Use the Diagnostic Exam 18
Conclusion (After the Exam) 18
AP U.S. History Diagnostic Exam 21
Answers to the Diagnostic Exam 34
Explanations for the Multiple-Choice Questions 35
Explanations for the Short-Answer Questions 38
Explanation for the Document-Based Question 42
Explanations for the Long-Essay Questions 43

STEP 3 Develop Strategies for Success

Chapter 4 Mastering Skills and Understanding Themes for the New Exam 49
New Approach to the AP U.S. History Exam 49
Historical Analytical Skills, Historical Themes, and Exam Questions 51

Chapter 5 Strategies for Approaching Each Question Type 54
Multiple-Choice Questions 55
Short-Answer Questions 57
Document-Based Question (DBQ) 57
Long-Essay Question 58
Using Primary Source Documents 59

STEP 4 Review the Knowledge You Need to Score High

Chapter 6 Settling of the Western Hemisphere (1491–1607) 65
Native Americans 66
European Exploration of the Americas 66
Chapter Review 67

Chapter 7 Colonial America (1607–1650) 70
The French in Canada 70
The English in the Americas 71

‹ iii

Effects of English, French, and British Settlement 73
Chapter Review 74

Chapter 8 British Empire in America: Growth and Conflict (1650–1750) 76
Impact of Mercantilism 77
African Slavery in the Americas 78
Continued Unrest in New England 79
Salem Witch Trials 79
Wars in Europe and Their Impact on the Colonies 79
Growth of the Colonial Assemblies 80
Era of "Salutary Neglect" 80
Great Awakening 81
Chapter Review 81

Chapter 9 Resistance, Rebellion, and Revolution (1750–1775) 84
Problems on the Frontier 85
Additional Conflicts Between the British and Their Colonial "Allies" 85
Policies of George Grenville 86
A Sense of Crisis: The Stamp Act 87
More Protest: The Townshend Acts 87
Continued Tension in Massachusetts 88
Calm Before the Storm: 1770–1773 88
Boston Tea Party 89
Intolerable Acts 89
First Continental Congress 89
Chapter Review 90

Chapter 10 American Revolution and the New Nation (1775–1787) 92
American Revolution 93
Second Continental Congress 93
Declaration of Independence 94
Outbreak of the Revolution: Divisions in the Colonies 94
Strategies of the American Revolution 95
Washington as Commander 95
War Moves to the South 96
Treaty of Paris 97
Establishment of Governmental Structures in the New Nation 97
Articles of Confederation 97
Northwest Ordinances 98
Shays's Rebellion 98
Chapter Review 99

Chapter 11 Establishment of New Political Systems (1787–1800) 101
Desire for a Stronger Central Government 102
Government under the New Constitution 102
Issue of Slavery 103
Ratification of the Constitution 103
Presidency of George Washington 103
Bill of Rights 104
Competing Visions: Alexander Hamilton and Thomas Jefferson 104
French Revolution 105
Foreign Policy and Jay's Treaty 106
Washington's Farewell Address 106
Presidency of John Adams 106

        Alien and Sedition Acts   107
        Chapter Review   107

Chapter 12   Jeffersonian Revolution (1800–1820)   110
        Election of 1800   111
        Reform of the Courts   111
        Westward Expansion   112
        Political Tensions and the Strange Case of Aaron Burr   113
        European Wars Spill Over to America (Again)   114
        War of 1812   114
        American System   115
        Missouri Compromise   116
        Chapter Review   116

Chapter 13   Rise of Manufacturing and the Age of Jackson (1820–1845)   119
        Growth of the Factory   120
        Monroe Doctrine   121
        Policy Toward Native Americans   121
        Second Great Awakening   121
        Political Reform: The Jacksonian Era (1829–1841)   122
        Election of 1824   123
        1828 Presidential Election   123
        Jackson as President   123
        Nullification Controversy   124
        Bank Crisis   124
        Whig Party: A Challenge to the Democratic-Republicans   125
        Chapter Review   125

Chapter 14   Union Expanded and Challenged (1835–1860)   128
        Ideology of Manifest Destiny   129
        "Remember the Alamo!"   130
        Pivotal Election of 1844   130
        War with Mexico   131
        Political Challenges of the 1850s   132
        Effects of the Compromise of 1850   133
        Presidency of Franklin Pierce   133
        Return of Sectional Conflict   134
        "Bleeding Kansas": Slave or Free?   134
        Dred Scott Decision   135
        Lincoln-Douglas Debates   135
        John Brown's Raid   135
        Presidential Election of 1860   136
        Chapter Review   136

Chapter 15   Union Divided: The Civil War (1861–1865)   139
        Advantages of the North and South in the War   140
        Attack on Fort Sumter and the Beginning of the War   141
        War Aims and Strategies   141
        Developments in the South and in the North   143
        Emancipation Proclamation   144
        1863: The War Tips to the North   144
        War Weariness in the North and the South   145
        End of the Confederacy   145
        Chapter Review   145

Chapter 16 Era of Reconstruction (1865–1877) 148
    Lincoln's Plans for Reconstruction 149
    Andrew Johnson's Plan for Reconstruction 150
    Reconstruction Programs of the Radical Republicans 151
    Period of Radical Reconstruction 151
    Impeachment of Andrew Johnson 152
    Radical Reconstruction Reinforced 152
    End of Reconstruction 153
    Chapter Review 153

Chapter 17 Western Expansion and Its Impact on the American Character (1860–1895) 156
    Federal Legislation Encourages Western Settlement 157
    Farming on the Great Plains 158
    Transformation of Agriculture on the Plains 158
    Women and Minorities on the Plains 159
    Mining and Lumbering in the West 159
    Ranching in the West 160
    Plight of Native Americans 160
    Organization of the American Farmer and Populism 161
    Impact of the West on American Society 163
    Chapter Review 164

Chapter 18 America Transformed into the Industrial Giant of the World (1870–1910) 166
    Growth of Industrial America 167
    Changing Nature of American Industry 168
    Consolidation of Businesses 169
    Growth of Labor Unions 170
    Improved Standard of Living? 171
    Impact of Immigration on American Society 172
    Transformation of the American City 173
    Politics of the Gilded Age 174
    Cultural Life in the Gilded Age 176
    Chapter Review 176

Chapter 19 Rise of American Imperialism (1890–1913) 180
    Period of Foreign Policy Inaction 181
    Sign of Things to Come: Hawaii 182
    The 1890s: Reasons for American Imperialism 182
    Spanish-American War 183
    Role of America: Protector or Oppressor? 185
    Debate over the Philippines 185
    Connecting the Pacific and the Atlantic: The Panama Canal 186
    Roosevelt Corollary 186
    Chapter Review 187

Chapter 20 Progressive Era (1895–1914) 190
    Origins of Progressivism 191
    Goals of Progressives 192
    Urban Reforms 192
    Progressives at the State Level 193

Women and Progressivism   193
Reforming the Workplace   194
Square Deal of Theodore Roosevelt   194
Progressivism under William Howard Taft   195
1912 Presidential Election   196
Progressive Legacy of Woodrow Wilson   196
Did Progressivism Succeed?   197
Chapter Review   197

Chapter 21   United States and World War I (1914–1921)   200
American Response to the Outbreak of War   201
Increasing American Support for the Allied Powers   202
America Moves Toward War   202
America Enters the War   203
Impact of the American Expeditionary Force   203
Home Front During World War I   204
Keeping America Patriotic   204
Woodrow Wilson and the Treaty of Versailles   205
United States and the Middle East   206
Treaty of Versailles and the U.S. Senate   207
Consequences of American Actions After the War   207
Chapter Review   207

Chapter 22   Beginning of Modern America: The 1920s   210
Decade of Prosperity   211
Republican Leadership in the 1920s   212
Presidency of Warren G. Harding   212
Scandals of the Harding Administration   213
Presidency of Calvin Coolidge   214
Election of 1928   214
Urban vs. Rural: The Great Divide of the 1920s   215
Culture in the 1920s   217
The Jazz Age   217
The Lost Generation   218
Chapter Review   219

Chapter 23   Great Depression and the New Deal (1929–1939)   222
American Economy of the 1920s: Roots of the
    Great Depression   224
Stock Market Crash   225
Social Impact of the Great Depression   226
Hoover Administration and the Depression   226
1932 Presidential Election   227
First Hundred Days   228
Second New Deal   229
Presidential Election of 1936   230
Opponents of Franklin Roosevelt and the New Deal   231
Last Years of the New Deal   232
Effects of the New Deal   232
New Deal Culture   233
Chapter Review   233

Chapter 24   World War II (1933–1945)   236
    American Foreign Policy in the 1930s   237
    United States and the Middle East in the Interwar Era   238
    Presidential Election of 1940 and Its Aftermath   239
    Attack on Pearl Harbor   239
    America Enters the War   240
    Role of the Middle East in World War II   242
    War Against Japan   243
    Decision to Drop the Atomic Bomb   243
    Home Front During the War   244
    Discrimination During the War   245
    Chapter Review   246

Chapter 25   Origins of the Cold War (1945–1960)   249
    First Cracks in the Alliance: 1945   251
    The Iron Curtain   251
    Marshall Plan   252
    Berlin: The First Cold War Crisis   253
    1949: A Pivotal Year in the Cold War   253
    Middle East in the Early Years of the Cold War   254
    Cold War at Home   255
    Heating of the Cold War: Korea   257
    Rise of McCarthyism   257
    Cold War Policies of President Eisenhower   258
    Dangerous Arms Buildup   259
    Chapter Review   260

Chapter 26   Prosperity and Anxiety: The 1950s   263
    Economic Growth and Prosperity   264
    Political Developments of the Postwar Era   265
    Civil Rights Struggles of the Postwar Period   266
    Conformity of the Suburbs   267
    Chapter Review   269

Chapter 27   America in an Era of Turmoil (1960–1975)   272
    1960 Presidential Election   273
    Domestic Policies Under Kennedy and Johnson   274
    Struggle of Black Americans: From Nonviolence
       to Black Power   275
    Rise of Feminism   277
    Cold War in the 1960s   278
    Vietnam War and Its Impact on American Society   278
    Chapter Review   281

Chapter 28   Decline and Rebirth (1968–1988)   284
    Presidency of Richard Nixon   285
    Watergate Affair   287
    Presidency of Gerald Ford   289
    Presidency of Jimmy Carter   290
    Election of 1980   291
    Presidency of Ronald Reagan   291
    Chapter Review   293

Chapter 29   Prosperity and a New World Order (1988–2000)   296
        1988 Election   297
        Presidency of George H. Bush   297
        1992 Election   298
        Presidency of Bill Clinton   299
        2000 Presidential Election   301
        Chapter Review   301

Chapter 30   Threat of Terrorism, Increase of Presidential Power, and Economic Crisis (2001–2014)   304
        9/11 and Its Aftermath   305
        Events Leading Up to the American Invasion of Iraq   305
        Operation Iraqi Freedom   306
        Effects of the War at Home   306
        Victory of Conservatism in the Bush Era   307
        United States in Transition: 2007–2008   308
        Obama Presidency   309
        Election of 2012   310
        Chapter Review   311

Chapter 31   Contemporary America: Evaluating the "Big Themes"   314

STEP 5 Build Your Test-Taking Confidence
        AP U.S. History Practice Exam 1   323
        AP U.S. History Practice Exam 2   351

Glossary   377
Bibliography   413
Websites   415

PREFACE

So, you have decided to take AP U.S. History. Prepare to be continually challenged in this course: this is the only way you will attain the grade that you want on the AP exam in May. Prepare to read, to read a lot, and to read critically; almost all students successful in AP U.S. History say this is a necessity. Prepare to analyze countless primary source documents; being able to do this is critical for success in the exam as well. Most important, prepare to immerse yourself in the great story that is U.S. history. As your teacher will undoubtedly point out, it would be impossible to make up some of the people and events you will study in this class. What really happened is much more interesting!

This study guide will assist you along the journey of AP U.S. History. The chapter review guides give you succinct overviews of the major events of U.S. history. At the end of each chapter is a list of the major concepts, a time line, and review multiple-choice questions for that chapter. In addition, a very extensive glossary is included at the back of this manual. All of the **boldface** words throughout the book can be found in the glossary (it would also be a good study technique to review the entire glossary before taking the actual AP exam).

The first five chapters of the manual describe the AP test itself and suggest some test-taking strategies. There are also two entire sample tests, with answers. These allow you to become totally familiar with the format and nature of the questions that will appear on the exam. On the actual testing day you want absolutely no surprises!

In the second chapter, you will also find time lines for three approaches to preparing for the exam. It is obviously suggested that your preparation for the examination be a year-long process; for those students unable to do that, two alternative calendars also appear. Many students also find that study groups are very beneficial in studying for the AP test. Students who have been successful on the AP test oftentimes form these groups very early in the school year.

It should also be noted that the AP United States History test that you are taking is different from the one that your older brother or sister took in the past. There are even some new things in the test that your teacher has not prepared students for before. We will outline the new AP U.S. History exam in detail in the first several chapters. Do not use old study guides or review sheets that were used to prepare for prior tests—these do not work anymore!

We hope this manual helps you in achieving the "perfect 5." That score is sitting out there, waiting for you to reach for it.

INTRODUCTION: 5-STEP PROGRAM

The Basics

This guide provides you with the specific format of the AP U.S. History exam, three sample AP U.S. History tests, and a comprehensive review of major events and themes in U.S. history. After each review chapter, you will find a time line and several review questions.

Reading this guide is a great start to getting the grade you want on the AP U.S. History test, but it is important to read on your own as well. Several groups of students who have all gotten a 5 on the test maintain that the key to success is to *read* as much as you possibly can on U.S. history.

Reading this guide will not guarantee you a 5 when you take the U.S. History exam in May. However, by carefully reviewing the format of the exam and the test-taking strategies provided for each section, you will definitely be on your way! The review section that outlines the major developments of U.S. history should augment what you have learned from your regular U.S. history textbook. This book won't "give" you a 5, but it can certainly point you firmly in that direction.

Organization of the Book

This guide conducts you through the five steps necessary to prepare yourself for success on the exam. These steps will provide you with many skills and strategies vital to the exam and the practice that will lead you toward the perfect 5.

In this introductory chapter we will explain the basic five-step plan, which is the focus of this entire book. The material in Chapter 1 will give you information you need to know about the AP U.S. History exam. In Chapter 2 three different approaches will be presented to prepare for the actual exam; study them all and then pick the one that works best for you. Chapter 3 contains a practice AP U.S. History exam; this is an opportunity to experience what the test is like and to have a better idea of your strengths and weaknesses as you prepare for the actual exam. Chapter 4 describes historical skills and themes emphasized in the exam. Chapter 5 contains a number of tips and suggestions about the different types of questions that appear on the actual exam. We will discuss ways to approach the multiple-choice questions, the short-answer questions, the document-based question (DBQ), and the long-essay question. Almost all students note that knowing how to approach each type of question is crucial.

For some of you, the most important part of this manual will be found in Chapters 6 through 31, which contain a review of U.S. history from the European exploration of the Americas to the reelection of Barack Obama in 2012. Undoubtedly, you have studied much of the material included in these chapters. However, these review chapters can help highlight certain important material that you may have missed or forgotten from your AP History class. At the end of each chapter, you will also find a time line of important events discussed in the chapter and multiple-choice review questions.

After these review chapters you will find two complete practice exams, including multiple-choice questions, short-answer questions, and essays. Correct answers and explanations for these answers are also included. Take one of the exams and evaluate your success; review any material that you had trouble with. Then take the second exam and use the results to guide your additional study. At the back of the manual is a glossary that defines all of the **boldface** words found in the review chapters. Use this to find the meaning of a specific term you might be unfamiliar with; some students find reviewing the entire glossary a useful method of reviewing for the actual exam.

Five-Step Program

Step 1: Set Up Your Study Program

In Step 1, you will read a brief overview of the AP U.S. History exam, including an outline of the topics that might be covered on the test itself. You will also follow a process to help determine which of the following preparation programs is right for you:

- Full school year: September through May
- One semester: January through May
- Six weeks: Basic Training for the Exam

Step 2: Determine Your Test Readiness

Step 2 provides you with a diagnostic exam to assess your current level of understanding. This exam will let you know about your current level of preparedness and on which areas and periods you should focus your study.

- Take the diagnostic exam slowly and analyze each question. Do not worry about how many questions you get right. Hopefully the exam will boost your confidence.
- Review the answers and explanations following the exam, so that you see what you do and do not yet fully know and understand.

Step 3: Develop Strategies for Success

Step 3 provides strategies and techniques that will help you do your best on the exam. These strategies cover the multiple-choice, short-answer, and the two different essay parts of the test. These tips come from discussions with both AP U.S. History students and teachers. In this section you will:

- Learn the skills and themes emphasized in the exam.
- Learn how to read and analyze multiple-choice questions.
- Learn how to answer multiple-choice questions, including whether or not to guess.
- Learn how to respond to short-answer questions.
- Learn how to plan and write both types of essay questions.

Step 4: Review the Knowledge You Need to Score High

Step 4 makes up the majority of this book. In this step you will review the important names, dates, and themes of American history. Obviously, not all of the material included in this book will be on the AP exam. However, this book is a good overview of the content studied in a "typical" AP U.S. History course. Some of you are presently taking AP courses that cover more material than is included in this book; some of you are in courses that cover less. Nevertheless, thoroughly reviewing the material in the content section of this book will significantly increase your chance of scoring well.

Step 5: Build Your Test-Taking Confidence

In Step 5, you will complete your preparation by taking two complete practice exams and examining your results on them. It should be noted that the practice exams included in this book do not include questions taken from actual exams; however, these practice exams do include questions that are very similar to the "real thing."

Graphics Used in This Book

To emphasize particular skills and strategies, we use several icons throughout this book. An icon in the margin will alert you that you should pay particular attention to the accompanying text. We use three icons:

The first icon points out a very important concept or fact that you should not pass over.

The second icon calls your attention to a problem-solving strategy that you may want to try.

The third icon indicates a tip that you might find useful.

Boldface words indicate terms that are included in the glossary at the end of the book. Boldface is also used to indicate the answer to a sample problem discussed in the test. Throughout the book, you will find marginal notes, boxes, and starred areas. Pay close attention to these areas because they can provide tips, hints, strategies, and further explanations to help you reach your full potential.

STEP 1

Set Up Your Study Program

CHAPTER **1** What You Need to Know About the AP U.S. History Exam
CHAPTER **2** Preparing for the AP U.S. History Exam

CHAPTER 1

What You Need to Know About the AP U.S. History Exam

IN THIS CHAPTER

Summary: Learn about the test, what's on it, how it's scored, and what benefits you can get from taking it.

Key Ideas

✪ Most colleges will award credit for a score of 4 or 5. Even if you don't do well enough on the exam to receive college credit, college admissions officials like to see students who have challenged themselves and experienced the college-level coursework of AP courses.
✪ The exam in 2015 will have a new format. The new exam de-emphasizes the simple memorization of historical facts. Instead, you have to demonstrate an ability to use historical analytical skills and think thematically across time periods in American history.
✪ In addition to multiple-choice and short-answer questions, the test contains a DBQ (document-based question) and one long-essay question.

Advanced Placement Program

The Advanced Placement (AP) program was begun by the College Board in 1955 to administer standard achievement exams that would allow highly motivated high school students the opportunity to earn college credit for AP courses taken in high school. Today there are 34 different AP courses and exams, with well over 3.5 million exams administered each May.

There are numerous AP courses in the social studies besides U.S. History, including European History, World History, U.S. Government and Politics, Comparative Government, Psychology, and Micro and Macro Economics. The majority of students who take AP courses and exams are juniors and seniors; however, some schools offer AP courses to freshmen and sophomores (AP U.S. History is usually not one of those courses). It is not absolutely necessary to be enrolled in an AP class to take the exam in a specific subject; there are rare cases of students who study on their own for a particular AP examination and do well.

Who Writes the AP Exams? Who Scores Them?

AP exams, including the U.S. History exam, are written by experienced college and secondary school teachers. All questions on the AP exams are field tested before they actually appear on an AP exam. The group that writes the history exam is called the AP U.S. History Development Committee. This group constantly reevaluates the test, analyzing the exam as a whole and on an item-by-item basis.

As noted in the preface, the AP U.S. History exam has undergone a substantial transformation that will take effect beginning with the 2015 test. The College Board has conducted a number of institutes and workshops to ensure that teachers across the United States are well qualified to assist students in preparing for this new exam.

The multiple-choice section of each AP exam is graded by computer, but the free-response questions are scored by humans. A number of college and secondary school teachers of U.S. History get together at a central location in early June to score the free-response questions of the AP U.S. History exam administered the previous month. The scoring of each reader during this procedure is carefully analyzed to ensure that exams are being evaluated in a fair and consistent manner.

AP Scores

Once you have taken the exam and it has been scored, your raw scores will be transformed into an AP grade on a 1-to-5 scale. A grade report will be send to you by the College Board in July. When you take the test, you should indicate the college or colleges that you want your AP scores sent to. The report that the colleges receive contains the score for every AP exam you took this year and the grades that you received on AP exams in prior years. In addition, your scores will be sent to your high school. (Note that it is possible, for a fee, to withhold the scores of any AP exam you have taken from going out to colleges. See the College Board website for more information.)

As noted above, you will be scored on a 1-to-5 scale:

- 5 indicates that you are extremely well qualified. This is the highest possible grade.
- 4 indicates that you are well qualified.
- 3 indicates that you are qualified.
- 2 indicates that you are possibly qualified.
- 1 indicates that you are not qualified to receive college credit.

Benefits of the AP Exam

If you receive a score of a 4 or a 5, you can most likely get actual college credit for the subject that you took the course in; a few colleges will do the same for students receiving a 3. Colleges and universities have different rules on AP scores and credit, so check with the college or colleges that you are considering to determine what credit they will give you for a good score on the AP History exam. Some colleges might exempt you from a freshman-level course based on your score even if they don't grant credit for the score you received.

The benefits of being awarded college credits before you start college are significant: You can save time in college (by skipping courses) and money (by avoiding paying college tuition for courses you skip). Almost every college encourages students to challenge themselves; if it is possible for you to take an AP course, do it! Even if you do not do well on the actual test—or you decide not to take the AP test—the experience of being in an AP class all year can impress college admissions committees and help you prepare for the more academically challenging work of college.

AP U.S. History Exam

Achieving a good score on the AP U.S. History exam will require you do more than just memorize important dates, people, and events from America's history. To get a 4 or a 5 you have to demonstrate an ability to utilize specific historical analytical skills when studying history. In addition, you will be asked to demonstrate your ability to think thematically and evaluate specific historical themes across time periods in American history. You'll find more information about these analytical skills and historical themes in Chapter 4. The good news is that every question on the AP U.S. History exam is rooted in these analytical skills and historical themes; there is no need to remember material not related to the stated historical analytical skills or historical themes.

As far as specific content, there is material that you need to know from nine predetermined historical time periods of U.S. history. For each of these time periods, key concepts have been identified. You will be introduced to a concept outline for each of the historical periods in your AP course. You can also find this outline at the College Board's AP U.S. History website. These concepts are connected to the historical themes and analyzed using historical analytical skills. Again, there is good news: you will not have to know any historical content that is not included in the concept outline.

To do well on this exam you have to exhibit the ability to do much of the work that "real" historians do. You must know major concepts from every historical time period. You must demonstrate an ability to think thematically when analyzing history, and you must utilize historical thinking skills when doing all of this. The simple memorization of historical facts is given less emphasis in the new exam. This does not mean that you can ignore historical detail. Knowledge of historical information will be crucial in explaining themes in American history. Essentially this exam is changing the focus of what is expected of AP U.S. History students. It is asking you to take a smaller number of historical concepts and to analyze these concepts very carefully. The ability to do this does not necessarily come easily; one of the major functions of this book is to help you "think like a historian."

Periods of U.S. History

As noted earlier, U.S. history has been divided into specific time periods for the purposes of the AP course. The creators of the AP U.S. History exam have established the following nine historical periods and have also determined approximately how much of the year should be spent on each historical era:

- **Period 1: 1491 to 1607.** Approximately 5 percent of instructional time should be spent on this period.
- **Period 2: 1607 to 1754.** Approximately 10 percent of instructional time should be spent on this period.
- **Period 3: 1754 to 1800.** Approximately 12 percent of instructional time should be spent on this period.

- **Period 4: 1800 to 1848.** Approximately 10 percent of instructional time should be spent on this period.
- **Period 5: 1844 to 1877.** Approximately 13 percent of instructional time should be spent on this period.
- **Period 6: 1865 to 1898.** Approximately 13 percent of instructional time should be spent on this period.
- **Period 7: 1890 to 1945.** Approximately 17 percent of instructional time should be spent on this period.
- **Period 8: 1945 to 1980.** Approximately 15 percent of instructional time should be spent on this period.
- **Period 9: 1980 to present.** Approximately 5 percent of instructional time should be spent on this period.

On the actual AP test that you will take:

- 5 percent of the exam will relate to issues concerning Period 1.
- 45 percent of the exam will relate to issues concerning Periods 2, 3, 4, and 5.
- 45 percent of the exam will relate to issues concerning Periods 6, 7, and 8.
- 5 percent of the exam will relate to issues concerning Period 9.

Many students are worried when their AP class doesn't get to the present day. As you can see, only 5 percent of the test is on material after 1980; therefore, making it all the way to Barack Obama will not have a major impact on your score.

Structure of the AP U.S. History Exam

The actual test has two sections, each of which contains two parts:

Section I
- Part A: 35 to 40 multiple-choice questions—35 minutes
- Part B: Four short-answer questions—50 minutes. These questions will address one or more of the themes that have been developed throughout the course and will ask you to utilize historical thinking when you write about these themes.

Section II
- Part A: One document-based question (DBQ)—60 minutes. In this section you will be asked to analyze and utilize a number of primary source documents as you construct a historical argument.
- Part B: One long-essay question—35 minutes. You will be given a choice between two long-answer questions in this section. It will be critical to utilize historical thinking skills when writing your response.

There will be much more discussion of the different components of the exam later in this book.

Taking the AP U.S. History Exam

Registration and Fees

If you are enrolled in AP U.S. History, your teacher or guidance counselor is going to provide all of these details. However, you do not have to enroll in the AP course to take the AP exam. When in doubt, the best source of information is the College Board's website: www.collegeboard.com.

Students who demonstrate financial need may receive a refund to help offset the cost of testing. There are also several other fees required if you want your scores rushed to you or if you wish to receive multiple score reports.

Night Before the Exam

Last minute cramming of massive amounts of material will not help you. It takes time for your brain to organize material. There is some value to a last-minute review of material. This may involve looking at the fast-review portions of the chapters or looking through the glossary. The night before the test should include a light review and various relaxing activities. *A full night's sleep is one of the best preparations for the test.*

What to Bring to the Exam

Here are some suggestions:

- Several pencils and an eraser that does not leave smudges.
- Several black pens (for the essays).
- A watch so that you can monitor your time. The exam room may or may not have a clock on the wall. Make sure you turn off the beep that goes off on the hour.
- Your school code.
- Your driver's license, Social Security number, or some other ID, in case there is a problem with your registration.
- Tissues.
- Something to drink—water is best.
- A quiet snack.
- Your quiet confidence that you are prepared.

What *Not* to Bring to the Exam

It's a good idea to leave the following items at home or in the car:

- Your cell phone and/or other electronic devices.
- Books, a dictionary, study notes, flash cards, highlighting pens, correction fluid, a ruler, or any other office supplies.
- Portable music of any kind (although you will probably want to listen as soon as you leave the testing site!).
- Panic or fear. It's natural to be nervous, but you can comfort yourself that you have used this book and that there is no need for fear on your exam.

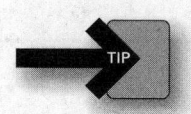

Day of the Test

Once the test day has arrived, there is nothing further you can do. Do not worry about what you could have done differently. It is out of your hands, and your only job is to answer as many questions correctly as you possibly can. The calmer you are, the better your chances are of doing well.

Follow these simple commonsense tips:

- Allow plenty of time to get to the test site.
- Wear comfortable clothing.
- Eat a light breakfast and/or lunch.
- Think positive. Remind yourself that you are well prepared and that the test is an enjoyable challenge and a chance to share your knowledge.
- Be proud of yourself!

CHAPTER 2

Preparing for the AP U.S. History Exam

IN THIS CHAPTER

Summary: The right preparation plan for you depends on your study habits and the amount of time you have before the test. This chapter provides some examples of plans you can use or adapt to your needs.

Key Ideas

○ Choose the study plan that is right for you.
○ Begin to prepare for the AP exam at the beginning of the school year. Developing historical analytical skills, evaluating themes in U.S. history, and studying important concepts take far more time and effort than by simply memorizing facts. The sooner you begin preparing for the test, the better.

Getting Started

You have made the decision to take AP U.S. History. Enjoy! You will be exposed to all of the fascinating stories that make up U.S. history. To be successful in this course, you will have to work much harder than you would in a "regular" high school U.S. history course. You will be required to read more, including reading and analyzing a wide variety of primary source documents throughout the year. In addition, you will be required to utilize historical thinking, to analyze history in a thematic way, and to be knowledgeable of specific concepts that help guide the study of American history. It cannot be stressed enough that the examination for this course that you will take in May is not a test that will simply measure what you "know" about U.S. history; instead, it is an examination that tests your ability to analyze major events, concepts, and themes in American history utilizing specific historical analytical skills.

Being able to utilize historical analytical skills, study history thematically, and develop conceptual thinking are not skills that develop overnight. In fact, it is difficult to develop these skills in the context of one specific course. If you are reading this before you are actually enrolled in an AP U.S. History course, you may want to take the most challenging history courses you can *before* you take AP U.S. History. Try to think conceptually in any history course that you take; a *real* study of history of any type is much more than just memorizing facts.

Creating a Study Plan

As has already been noted several times, preparing for this exam involves much more than just memorizing important dates, names, and events that are important in U.S. history. Developing historical analytical skills, evaluating themes in U.S. history, and studying important concepts take far more time and effort than by simply memorizing facts. Therefore, it is strongly suggested that you take a year-long approach to studying and preparing for the test.

However, for some students this is not possible. Therefore, some suggestions for students who have only one semester to prepare for the exam and students who have only six weeks to prepare for the exam are included. In the end, it is better to do *some* systematic preparation for the exam than to do none at all.

Study Groups

Many students who have gotten a 5 on the U.S. History exam reported that working in a study group was an important part of the successful preparation that they did for the test. In an ideal setting, three to five students get together, probably once a week, to review material that was covered in class the preceding week and to practice historical, thematic, and conceptual thinking. If at all possible, do this! A good suggestion is to have study groups set a specific time to meet every week and stick to that time. Without a regular meeting time, study groups usually meet fewer times during the year, often cancel meetings, and so on.

THREE PLANS FOR TEST PREPARATION

Plan A: Yearlong Preparation for the AP U.S. History Exam

STRATEGY → This is the plan we highly recommend. Besides doing all of the readings and assignments assigned by your teacher, also do the following activities. (Check off the activities as you complete them.)

IN THE FALL

_____ Create a study group and determine a regular meeting time for that group.

_____ Coordinate the materials in this manual with the curriculum of your AP U.S. History class.

_____ Study the review chapters in Step 4 of this book that coincide with the material you are studying in class.

_____ Begin to do outside reading on U.S. history topics (either topics of interest to you or topics that you know you need more background in).

_____ In your study group, emphasize historical analysis and thematic and conceptual thinking.

FROM DECEMBER TO MARCH

_____ Continue to meet with your study group and emphasize historical analysis and thematic and conceptual thinking.

_____ Continue to study the review chapters in Step 4 of this book that coincide with the material you are studying in class.

_____ Take the diagnostic test in Step 2 of this book to see what the test will be like and assess your strengths and weaknesses.

_____ Learn the strategies discussed in Step 3 of this book. Practice applying them as you study and review for the AP U.S. History exam.

_____ Carefully study the format and approach to document-based questions (DBQs). You will probably have one on your midterm exam in class.

_____ Using the eras of U.S. history you have studied in class, create your own DBQ for two of the units and try to answer it.

_____ Intensify your outside reading of U.S. history topics.

_____ Take two U.S. history textbooks and compare and contrast their handling of three events of U.S. history. What do these results tell you?

DURING APRIL AND MAY

_____ Continue to meet with your study group and emphasize historical analysis and thematic and conceptual thinking. Many study groups meet at additional times in the weeks leading up to the test.

_____ Continue to study the review chapters in Step 4 of this book that coincide with the material you are studying in class.

_____ Practice creating and answering multiple-choice and short-answer questions in your study group.

_____ Develop and review worksheets of essential historical content with your study group.

_____ Highlight material in your textbook (and in this manual) that you may not understand, and ask your teacher about it.

_____ Write two or three essays as they would appear on the exam under timed questions and have a member of your study group (or a classmate) evaluate them.

_____ Take the practice tests provided in Step 5 of this book. Set a timer and practice pacing yourself.

You are well prepared for the test. Go get it!

Plan B:
One-Semester Preparation for the AP U.S. History Exam

STRATEGY → Besides doing all of the readings and assignments assigned by your teacher, you should do the following activities. (Check off the activities as you complete them.)

FROM JANUARY TO MARCH

_____ Establish a study group of other students preparing in the same way that you are. In your study group you should review essential factual knowledge, but also analyze the essential themes and concepts in the course.

_____ Study the review chapters in Step 4 of this book that coincide with the material you have studied or are studying in class.

_____ Take the diagnostic test in Step 2 of this book to familiarize yourself with the test and assess your strengths and weaknesses.

_____ Learn the strategies discussed in Step 3 of this book. Practice applying them as you study and review for the AP U.S. History exam.

_____ Write two or three document-based and sample multiple-choice questions.

_____ Read at least one outside source (historical essay or book) on a topic that you are studying in class.

_____ In your study group, practice creating and answering short-answer and multiple-choice questions.

DURING APRIL AND MAY

_____ Continue to meet with your study group, and review essential factual knowledge and essential themes and concepts of the course you have taken or are currently taking. Some study groups increase the amount of time that they meet together in the weeks right before the test.

_____ Study the review chapters in Step 4 of this book that coincide with the material you have studied or are presently studying in class. Focus on weak areas you identified in the diagnostic test of Step 2 of this book.

_____ Practice creating and answering sample essays with your study group.

_____ Develop and review worksheets of essential historical content with your study group.

_____ Ask your teacher to clarify things in your textbook or in this manual that you do not completely understand. If you have nagging questions about some specific historical details, get the answers to them!

_____ Take the practice tests provided in Step 5 of this book. Set a timer and practice pacing yourself.

Plan C:
Four- to Six-Week Preparation for the AP U.S. History Exam

STRATEGY Besides doing all of the reading and assignments assigned by your teacher, do the following activities. (Check off the activities as you complete them.)

IN APRIL

_____ Take the diagnostic test in Step 2 of this book to familiarize yourself with the test and assess your strengths and weaknesses.

_____ Study the review chapters in Step 4 of this book that coincide with any weak areas you identified from the diagnostic exam.

_____ Learn the strategies discussed in Step 3 of this book. Practice applying them as you study and review for the AP U.S. History exam.

_____ Write one sample document-based question (DBQ) as modeled by samples in this manual.

_____ Carefully review the sections of this manual that outline the essential content of each historical period.

_____ If possible, create or join a study group with other students to help prepare for the exam.

IN MAY

_____ Many teachers organize study sessions right before the actual exam. Go to them!

_____ With your study group or individually, review essential content from the course and major concepts of each unit.

_____ Complete another sample DBQ essay and analyze your results.

_____ Review the glossary of this manual another time to help review essential content.

_____ Be certain of the format of the test and the types of questions that will be asked.

_____ Take the practice tests provided in Step 5 of this book. Set a timer and practice pacing yourself.

STEP 2
Determine Your Test Readiness

CHAPTER 3 Take a Diagnostic Exam

CHAPTER 3

Take a Diagnostic Exam

IN THIS CHAPTER

Summary: In the following pages, you will find a diagnostic exam whose content and structure closely matches the "real" AP U.S. History exam. Use this test to familiarize yourself with the actual test and to assess your strengths and weaknesses.

How to Use the Diagnostic Exam

Section I of the AP U.S. History exam contains a multiple-choice section and a short-answer section. On the actual test the number of questions may be slightly different (at press time final details of the new test—to be administered for the first time in 2015—were still not determined). Section II contains the document-based question (DBQ) and an essay question—you will need to pick one question to answer out of the two questions you are given.

The purpose of this chapter is to allow you to familiarize yourself with the test and to assess your test readiness in terms of both the skills and the content understanding needed. Try to take this test under testlike conditions; in other words, time yourself and do the test—or at least each section of the test—uninterrupted. Note that in Chapter 5 you will find strategies for each type of question that will allow you to more effectively and efficiently tackle the questions.

When to Use the Diagnostic Exam

This diagnostic test can be helpful to you regardless of whether you are following Plan A, B, or C. Those who chose Plan A should study this exam early in the year so that you will thoroughly understand the format of the test. Look for the types of multiple-choice and short-answer questions early and carefully study the format of the essay questions. Go back and look at this exam throughout the year: Many successful test-takers maintain that knowing how to tackle the questions that will be asked on any exam is just as important as knowledge of the subject matter.

Plan B students (who are using one semester to prepare) should also analyze the format of the exam. Plan B folks: as you begin using this book you might also want to actually answer the multiple-choice and short-answer questions dealing with content you have already studied in class and answer the document-based question and the free-response question and evaluate your results. This will help you analyze the success of your previous preparation for the test.

Plan C students should take this diagnostic exam as soon as they begin working with this manual to analyze the success of their previous preparation for the actual exam.

Conclusion (After the Exam)

After you have studied or taken the diagnostic exam, you will continue to Step 3 of your 5 Steps to a 5. Chapter 5 will provide you with tips and strategies for answering all of the types of questions that you found on the diagnostic exam.

Don't be discouraged and if you answered a lot of questions on the diagnostic exam incorrectly. At this point, the main thing is that you get a feel for the types of questions that you will encounter on the real AP U.S. History exam.

AP U.S. HISTORY DIAGNOSTIC EXAM

Answer Sheet for Multiple-Choice Questions

1.1 Ⓐ Ⓑ Ⓒ Ⓓ	4.4 Ⓐ Ⓑ Ⓒ Ⓓ	8.3 Ⓐ Ⓑ Ⓒ Ⓓ
1.2 Ⓐ Ⓑ Ⓒ Ⓓ	5.1 Ⓐ Ⓑ Ⓒ Ⓓ	8.4 Ⓐ Ⓑ Ⓒ Ⓓ
1.3 Ⓐ Ⓑ Ⓒ Ⓓ	5.2 Ⓐ Ⓑ Ⓒ Ⓓ	9.1 Ⓐ Ⓑ Ⓒ Ⓓ
1.4 Ⓐ Ⓑ Ⓒ Ⓓ	5.3 Ⓐ Ⓑ Ⓒ Ⓓ	9.2 Ⓐ Ⓑ Ⓒ Ⓓ
2.1 Ⓐ Ⓑ Ⓒ Ⓓ	5.4 Ⓐ Ⓑ Ⓒ Ⓓ	9.3 Ⓐ Ⓑ Ⓒ Ⓓ
2.2 Ⓐ Ⓑ Ⓒ Ⓓ	6.1 Ⓐ Ⓑ Ⓒ Ⓓ	9.4 Ⓐ Ⓑ Ⓒ Ⓓ
2.3 Ⓐ Ⓑ Ⓒ Ⓓ	6.2 Ⓐ Ⓑ Ⓒ Ⓓ	
2.4 Ⓐ Ⓑ Ⓒ Ⓓ	6.3 Ⓐ Ⓑ Ⓒ Ⓓ	
3.1 Ⓐ Ⓑ Ⓒ Ⓓ	6.4 Ⓐ Ⓑ Ⓒ Ⓓ	
3.2 Ⓐ Ⓑ Ⓒ Ⓓ	7.1 Ⓐ Ⓑ Ⓒ Ⓓ	
3.3 Ⓐ Ⓑ Ⓒ Ⓓ	7.2 Ⓐ Ⓑ Ⓒ Ⓓ	
3.4 Ⓐ Ⓑ Ⓒ Ⓓ	7.3 Ⓐ Ⓑ Ⓒ Ⓓ	
4.1 Ⓐ Ⓑ Ⓒ Ⓓ	7.4 Ⓐ Ⓑ Ⓒ Ⓓ	
4.2 Ⓐ Ⓑ Ⓒ Ⓓ	8.1 Ⓐ Ⓑ Ⓒ Ⓓ	
4.3 Ⓐ Ⓑ Ⓒ Ⓓ	8.2 Ⓐ Ⓑ Ⓒ Ⓓ	

AP U.S. HISTORY DIAGNOSTIC EXAM

Section I

Part A (Multiple Choice)

Time: 35 minutes

Directions: Each of the following questions refers to a historical source. These questions will test your knowledge about the historical source and require you to make use of your historical analytical skills and your familiarity with historical themes. For each question select the *best* response and fill in the corresponding oval on your answer sheet.

Questions 1.1–1.4 refer to the following cartoon:

Political cartoon from 1807

1.1 This cartoon criticizes which policy of President Thomas Jefferson?
   A. The Louisiana purchase
   B. The Embargo Act
   C. The War with Tripoli
   D. Reductions in government spending

1.2 Jefferson was responding to what situation?
   A. British interference with American shipping and trade
   B. British support for Indians in the West
   C. Aggressive actions by the French Emperor Napoleon
   D. Electoral losses to domestic opponents

1.3 Which of the following reflects how many Americans responded to Jefferson's policy?
   A. Emigrating to other countries
   B. Advocating military involvement in the Napoleonic Wars
   C. Engaging in illicit trade with foreign countries
   D. Moving to the Western frontier

1.4 Which of the following most closely resembles Jefferson's policy?
   A. The Open Door in China
   B. The Good Neighbor Policy with South America
   C. Manifest Destiny of the 1840s
   D. Neutrality Laws of the 1930s

Questions 2.1–2.4 refer to the following quotation:

Yes, let us pray for the salvation of all those who live in that totalitarian darkness—pray that they will discover the joy of knowing God. But until they do, let us be aware that while they preach the supremacy of the State, declare its omnipotence over individual man, and predict its eventual domination of all peoples on the earth, they are the focus of evil in the modern world. … But if history teaches anything, it teaches that simpleminded appeasement or wishful thinking about our adversaries is folly. It means the betrayal of our past, the squandering of our freedom. So, I urge you to speak out against those who would place the United States in a position of military and moral inferiority. … So, in your discussions of the nuclear freeze proposals, I urge you to beware the temptation of pride—the temptation of blithely … declaring yourselves above it all and label both sides equally at fault, to ignore the facts of history and the aggressive impulses of an evil empire, to simply call the arms race a giant misunderstanding and thereby remove yourself from the struggle between right and wrong and good and evil.

—Ronald Reagan, Address to the National Association of Evangelicals, March 8, 1983

2.1 The sentiments in the passage above most directly reflect which of the following?
   A. A religious revival in the 1980s
   B. An intensification of the cold war in the early 1980s
   C. A desire to limit the size of government
   D. A distrust of the American military

2.2 Which of the following would have been most likely to approve the sentiments expressed in the passage?
   A. An antinuclear activist
   B. An atheist
   C. A Democrat
   D. A Republican

2.3 The sentiments expressed in the passage are most closely linked to which of the following policies?
   A. Strategic Defense Initiative (SDI)
   B. Business deregulation
   C. Encouraging prayer in the public schools
   D. Military cutbacks

2.4 The sentiments in the passage best reflect which long-standing concern of American presidents?
   A. Support for civil rights
   B. Promoting the separation of church and state
   C. Containment of communism
   D. Expanding the welfare state

Questions 3.1–3.4 refer to the following quotation:

They were smart and sophisticated, with an air of independence about them, and so casual about their looks and manners as to be almost slapdash. I don't know if I realized as soon as I began seeing them that they represented the wave of the future, but I do know I was drawn to them. I shared their restlessness, understood their determination to free themselves of the Victorian shackles of the pre-World War I era and find out for themselves what life was all about.

—Colleen Moore, movie star, writing about the 1920s

3.1 In this passage, Moore is writing about which of the following?
A. The Ku Klux Klan
B. Prohibitionists
C. Flappers
D. The Model T

3.2 Many young women of the 1920s expressed their freedom through which of the following?
A. Political activism
B. "Mannish" haircuts, new clothing styles, and cosmetics
C. Living amongst the poor in settlement houses
D. Rejection of marriage and child-rearing

3.3 The new freedoms for women in the 1920s were supported by which of the following?
A. Widespread economic prosperity
B. Growth in fundamentalist Christianity
C. A massive movement of women into political offices
D. Moral reforms like the temperance movement

3.4 The passage by Moore most directly reflects which of the following continuities in United States history?
A. Concerns about economic inequality
B. Efforts to expand civil rights
C. Worries about political radicalism
D. Concerns for individual liberty and self-expression

Questions 4.1–4.4 refer to the following quotation.

I am for doing good to the poor, but ... I think the best way of doing good to the poor, is not making them easy in poverty, but leading or driving them out of it. I observed ... that the more public provisions were made for the poor, the less they provided for themselves, and of course became poorer. And, on the contrary, the less was done for them, the more they did for themselves, and became richer.

—Benjamin Franklin, *Autobiography*

4.1 In this passage, Franklin takes a position similar to which of the following?
A. Advocates of a market-driven economy like Adam Smith
B. Supporters of the First Great Awakening
C. Opponents of British rule in America
D. Believers in an extensive social welfare system

4.2 The idea that Franklin expresses in this passage most directly reflects which of the following continuities in U.S. history?
A. Concern about a religious foundation for society
B. Belief in individual self-reliance
C. A distrust of politicians
D. A desire to expand Social Security

4.3 Which of the following helped Franklin justify his position?
  A. Strong class distinctions in colonial America
  B. British efforts to tax Americans
  C. A decline in religious beliefs
  D. Social mobility in colonial America

4.4 Which of the following presidents would be most likely to share Franklin's position?
  A. Barack Obama
  B. Lyndon Baines Johnson
  C. Calvin Coolidge
  D. Franklin D. Roosevelt

Questions 5.1–5.4 refer to the following cartoon:

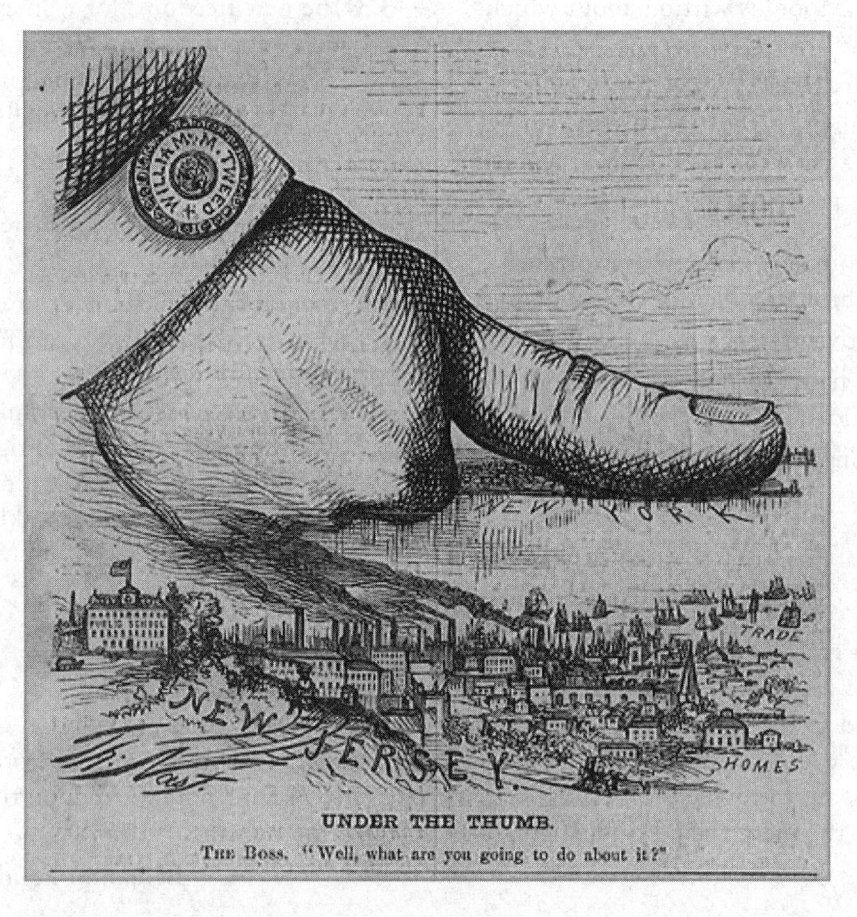

Thomas Nast, *Harper's Weekly*, June 10, 1871

5.1 Which of the following *best* expresses Nast's perspective in this cartoon?
  A. New York City is benefiting from the leadership of Tammany Hall boss William M. Tweed
  B. New Jersey is unfairly exploiting New York City
  C. The federal government is oppressing New York City
  D. Tammany Hall boss William M. Tweed wields too much power in New York City

5.2 Urban political machines like Tammany Hall derived most of their support from which of the following?
  A. Immigrants and lower-class voters
  B. The wealthier classes of society
  C. Patronage from the federal government
  D. Rural voters from outside the city

5.3 Urban political machines endured for many years because they provided which of the following?
- A. Honest and efficient government
- B. Help and services for the poor
- C. Rights and privileges unavailable outside the city
- D. Opposition to the encroachments of the federal government

5.4 Nast's journalistic perspective can *best* be compared to which of the following?
- A. Progressive muckrakers exposing the business practices of the Standard Oil Company
- B. Yellow journalists during the period of the Spanish-American War
- C. Reporters investigating President Richard M. Nixon during the Watergate scandal
- D. Newspaper coverage of World War II

Questions 6.1–6.4 refer to the following quotation:

At last they brought him [John Smith] to Werowocomoco, where was Powhatan, their emperor. Here more than two hundred of those grim courtiers stood wondering at him, as he had been a monster; till Powhatan and his train had put themselves in their greatest braveries. Before a fire upon a seat like a bedstead, he sat covered with a great robe, made of raccoon skins, and all the tails hanging by. On the other hand did sit a young wench of sixteen or eighteen years, and along on each side of the house, two rows of men, and behind them as many women, with all their heads and shoulders painted red, many of their heads bedecked with the white down of birds, but every one with something, and a great chain of white beads about their necks. At his entrance before the king, all the people gave a great shout. … Having feasted him after their best barbarous manner they could, a long consultation was held, but the conclusion was, two great stones were brought before Powhatan; then as many as could laid hands on him, dragged him to them, and thereon laid his head, and being ready with their clubs to beat out his brains, Pocahontas, the king's dearest daughter, when no entreaty could prevail, got his head in her arms, and laid her own upon his to save his from death; whereat the emperor was contented he should live to make him hatchets, and her bells, beads, and copper; for they thought him as well of all occupations as themselves. For the king himself will make his own robes, shoes, bows, arrows, pots; plant, hunt, or do anything so well as the rest.

—John Smith, *The General Historie of Virginia*, 1624

6.1 Which of the following *best* describes the perspective of Captain John Smith?
- A. Powhatan and his followers were a backward people.
- B. Europeans unfairly looked down on Indians.
- C. Indians lacked the vices of the more technologically advanced Europeans.
- D. Indian women were the dominant force in their society.

6.2 Smith's account makes clear which of the following?
- A. The people of Powhatan's Confederacy were divided by strong class distinctions.
- B. Powhatan's people made important decisions by consensus.
- C. Powhatan enjoyed the same sorts of power as a European king.
- D. Powhatan's people lived in poverty.

6.3 Smith's story *best* illustrates which of the following?
- A. Indians were unusually cruel.
- B. Europeans were usually deceitful in dealing with Indians.
- C. The English were foolish to venture into the American wilderness.
- D. Indian-European relations often suffered from misunderstanding and suspicion.

6.4 In the context of this story, Pocahontas can *best* be compared to which of the following women?
- A. Susan B. Anthony
- B. Sally Ride
- C. Jane Addams
- D. Amelia Earhart

Questions 7.1–7.4 refer to the following quotation:

Let us not wallow in the valley of despair, I say to you today, my friends.

And so even though we face the difficulties of today and tomorrow, I still have a dream. It is a dream deeply rooted in the American dream.

I have a dream that one day this nation will rise up and live out the true meaning of its creed: "We hold these truths to be self-evident, that all men are created equal."

I have a dream that one day on the red hills of Georgia, the sons of former slaves and the sons of former slave owners will be able to sit down together at the table of brotherhood.

I have a dream that one day even the state of Mississippi, a state sweltering with the heat of injustice, sweltering with the heat of oppression, will be transformed into an oasis of freedom and justice.

I have a dream that my four little children will one day live in a nation where they will not be judged by the color of their skin but by the content of their character.

I have a *dream* today!

—Martin Luther King, Jr., "I Have a Dream" speech, Lincoln Memorial, August 28, 1963

7.1 Martin Luther King, Jr., in this passage is calling for which of the following?
  A. Economic justice for the poor
  B. Renewed commitment to the cold war struggle against communism
  C. Equal rights for African Americans
  D. Special privileges for African Americans

7.2 In this passage, King points out which of the following?
  A. A contradiction between American ideals and American practice
  B. A need to create new American ideals
  C. The superiority of African-American values
  D. The futility of hoping for change

7.3 At the time of King's speech, which of the following would be likely to oppose King's message?
  A. A Midwestern Republican Senator
  B. A Southern Democratic Senator
  C. A Northern liberal
  D. A member of the Southern Christian Leadership Conference (SCLC)

7.4 In this passage, King is addressing which continuity in U.S. history?
  A. The struggle for greater economic opportunity
  B. A fear of sectionalism in the United States
  C. Concerns about moral decline
  D. The struggle for individual liberty

Questions 8.1–8.4 refer to the following cartoon:

War Department cartoon, 1943
Credit: U.S. Army

8.1 The message of the cartoon can be *best* described by which of the following?
  A. The invasion of Europe is endangered by inferior weapons.
  B. The war is being lost.
  C. Too many American supplies have been given to allied nations.
  D. Civilians play a vital role in the war effort.

8.2 Viewing this cartoon would encourage Americans to do which of the following?
  A. Avoid the wasteful use of metal products
  B. Plant a victory garden
  C. Volunteer for military service
  D. Build fewer ships and construct more tanks

8.3 This cartoon most directly refers to which aspect of the American war effort during World War II?
  A. American efforts to launch a second front in Europe as early as possible
  B. Military operations in the Mediterranean in 1942 and 1943
  C. American industrial production
  D. Efforts to create new and improved weapons systems

8.4 The message of the cartoon for Americans can *best* be compared to which of the following?
  A. The environmental movement of the 1970s
  B. The boycotts of British goods in the 1760s and 1770s
  C. Abolitionism in the nineteenth century
  D. Consumerism in the 1950s

Questions 9.1-9.4 refer to the following quotation:

That whereas your poor and humble Petition(er) being condemned to die, do humbly beg of you to take it into your Judicious and pious considerations that your poor and humble petitioner knowing my own innocence Blessed be the Lord for it and seeing plainly the wiles and subtlety of my accusers by my self can not but Judge charitably of Others that are going the same way of my self if the Lord steps not mightily in I was confined a whole month upon the same account that I am condemned now for and then cleared by the afflicted persons as some of your honors know and in two days time I was cried out upon by them and have been confined and now am condemned to die the Lord above knows my innocence then and likewise does now at the great day will be known to men and Angels I petition your honors not for my own life for I know I must die and my appointed time is set but the Lord he knows it is that if be possible no more Innocent blood may be shed which undoubtedly cannot be avoided In the way and course you go in I Question not but your honors does to the utmost of your Powers in the discovery and detecting of witchcraft and witches and would not be guilty of Innocent blood but for the world but by my own innocence I know you are in the wrong way the Lord in his infinite mercy direct you in this great work if it be his blessed will that no more innocent blood be shed.

—Mary Easty, petition to her judges, Salem, Massachusetts, 1692

9.1 Mary Easty in this passage is asking her judges to do which of the following?
  A. Stop condemning innocent persons to death for witchcraft
  B. Redouble their efforts to find the real witches in Salem
  C. Separate church from state in their deliberations
  D. Stop their oppression of women

9.2 Most historians believe that the Salem Witch Trials were the result of which of the following?
  A. The activities of a coven of witches in Salem
  B. Social tensions in Salem
  C. English efforts to enforce religious conformity in Massachusetts
  D. The ideas of the English political philosopher John Locke

9.3 The religious convictions of Mary Easty and the rest of Salem were shaped by which of the following?
  A. Roman Catholicism
  B. Anglicanism
  C. Quakerism
  D. Puritanism

9.4 Writers and intellectuals have often compared the Salem Witch Trials to which of the following?
  A. The mistreatment of slaves in the South
  B. Anti-immigrant rioting in the nineteenth century
  C. Government actions in the Red Scares of the twentieth century
  D. The suppression of strikers in the late nineteenth century

Part B (Short Answer)

Time: 50 minutes

Directions: Answer the following four questions. Carefully read and follow the directions for each question. Some will refer to historical sources. These questions will require you to make use of your historical analytical skills and your familiarity with historical themes. These questions do *not* require you to develop a thesis in your responses.

Question 1 is based on the following two passages:

I think, and shall try to show, that it is wrong; wrong in its direct effect, letting slavery into Kansas and Nebraska and wrong in its prospective principle, allowing it to spread to every other part of the wide world where men can be found inclined to take it.

This declared indifference, but, as I must think, covert real zeal for the spread of slavery, I cannot but hate. I hate it because of the monstrous injustice of slavery itself. I hate it because it deprives our republican example of its just influence in the world; enables the enemies of free institutions, with plausibility, to taunt us as hypocrites; causes real friends of freedom to doubt our sincerity, and especially because it forces so many really good men amongst ourselves into an open war with the very fundamental principles of civil liberty—criticizing the Declaration of Independence, and insisting that there is no right principle of action but self-interest.

—Abraham Lincoln

I will stand by that great principle of States' rights, no matter who may desert it. I intend to stand by it for the purpose of preserving peace between the North and South, the free and slave States. If each State will only agree to mind its own business, and let its neighbors alone, there will be peace forever between us. … I hold that the people of the slaveholding States are civilized men as well as ourselves; that they bear consciences as well as we, and that they are accountable to God and their posterity, and not to us. It is for them to decide, therefore, the moral and religious right of the slavery question for themselves within their own limits. I assert that they had as much right under the Constitution to adopt the system of policy which they have as we had to adopt ours. So it is with every other State in this Union. Let each State stand firmly by that great Constitutional right, let each State mind its own business and let its neighbors alone, and there will be no trouble on this question. If we will stand by that principle, then Mr. Lincoln will find that this Republic can exist forever divided into free and slave States, as our fathers made it and the people of each State have decided.

—Stephen Douglas

1. Based on these passages from the 1858 Lincoln-Douglas Debates, complete the following three tasks.
   A. Briefly explain the main point made by Passage 1.
   B. Briefly explain the main point made by Passage 2.
   C. Explain how one of the two perspectives influenced American politics in the 1850s. Provide at least *one* piece of evidence to support your explanation.

2. U.S. historians have argued that expansionism was a major force in American history.
   A. Choose *one* of the following and explain how it reflected American expansionism. Provide at least *one* piece of evidence to support your explanation.
      - The French and Indian War
      - The Louisiana Purchase
      - The Mexican War
   B. Explain the perspective of someone who opposed the expansionism of the example that you chose. Provide at least *one* piece of evidence to support your explanation.

3. In the years before the American Revolution many colonists began to see themselves less as Englishmen and more as Americans.
   A. Choose *one* of the following, and explain why it was most important in the formation of a distinctively American identity in the colonies. Provide at least *one* piece of evidence to support your explanation.
      - The Great Awakening
      - The French and Indian War
      - Resistance to the Stamp Act and other examples of British taxation
   B. How did your choice influence the American Revolution? Provide at least *one* piece of evidence to support your explanation.

4. Use the image and your knowledge of U.S. history to answer parts A, B, and C.
   A. Briefly explain the subject matter of the image. Provide at least *one* piece of evidence to support your explanation.
   B. Briefly explain the political point of view of this image. Provide at least *one* piece of evidence to support your explanation.
   C. Briefly explain the political perspective of someone opposed to the political point of view expressed by the image. Provide at least *one* piece of evidence to support your explanation.

Question 4 is based on the following image:

Clifford Berryman, 1936

END OF SECTION I

Section II

Part A (Document-Based Question)

Time: 60 minutes

Directions: This question asks you to write a well-constructed essay making use of the following documents and your broader knowledge of U.S. history. You will need to make use of your historical analytical skills and your familiarity with historical themes. You must develop a thesis that answers the question, supporting it with evidence drawn from the documents and from evidence and information outside the documents.

1. To what extent did the Federalist administrations of George Washington and John Adams promote national unity and advance the authority of the federal government?

Document A
Source: George Washington's First Inaugural Address, April 30, 1789

> *I behold the surest pledges that as on one side no local prejudices or attachments, no separate views or party animosities, will misdirect the comprehensive and equal eye which ought to watch over [Congress] so . . . that the foundation of our national policy will be laid in the pure and immutable principles of private morality, and the preeminence of free government be exemplified by all the attributes which can win the affections of its citizens and command the respect of the world.*

Document B
Source: Virginia Resolutions on the Assumption of State Debts, December 16, 1790

> *The General Assembly of the Commonwealth of Virginia . . . represent [that] . . . in an agricultural country like this . . . to perpetuate a large monied interest, is a measure which . . . must in the course of human events produce . . . the prostration of agriculture at the feet of commerce, or a change in the present form of federal government, fatal to the existence of American liberty.*

Document C
Source: Thomas Jefferson's Opinion on the Constitutionality of the Bank, February 15, 1791

> *I consider the foundation of the Constitution as laid on this ground—that all powers not delegated to the United States, by the Constitution, nor prohibited by it to the states, are reserved to the states, or to the people. To take a single step beyond the boundaries thus specially drawn around the powers of Congress, is to take possession of a boundless field of power.*

Document D

Source: Alexander Hamilton's Opinion on the Constitutionality of the Bank, February 23, 1791

> *This restrictive interpretation of the word necessary is also contrary to this sound maxim of construction; namely, that the powers contained in a constitution of government, especially those which concern the general administration of the affairs of a country, its finances, trade, defense, etc., ought to be construed liberally in advancement of the public good.*

Document E

Source: George Washington's Proclamation on the Whiskey Rebellion, August 7, 1794

> *Whereas combinations to defeat the execution of the laws laying duties upon spirits distilled within the United States . . . have . . . existed in some of the western parts of Pennsylvania; and whereas the said combinations, proceeding in a manner subversive equally of the just authority of government and the rights of individuals; . . . it is in my judgement necessary under the circumstances to take measures for calling forth the militia in order to suppress the combinations aforesaid, and to cause the laws to be duly executed.*

Document F

Source: The Sedition Act, July 14, 1798

> *That if any person shall write, print, utter, or publish, any false, scandalous, and malicious writing or writings against the government of the United States . . . with the intent to defame the said government, . . . then such person, being convicted before any court of the United States having jurisdiction thereof, shall be punished by a fine not exceeding two thousand dollars, and by imprisonment not exceeding two years.*

Document G

Source: Kentucky Resolutions, November 16, 1798

> *Resolved, that the several States composing the United States of America, are not united on the principle of unlimited submission to their general government; . . . that [the States] retain to themselves the right of judging how far the licentiousness of speech and press may be abridged without lessening their useful freedom . . . therefore [the Sedition Act], which does abridge the freedom of the press, is not law but is altogether void.*

Part B (Long Essay)

Time: 35 Minutes

Directions: Answer *one* of the following questions. Develop a thesis and support it with appropriate historical evidence. This question will require you to make use of your historical analytical skills and your familiarity with historical themes.

1. Some historians have argued that mobilization for total war during World War I and World War II influenced American political and social development in the twentieth century. Support, modify, or refute this contention using specific evidence.

2. Some historians have argued that the role of the United States as a world power changed dramatically between the Spanish-American War and the coming of the cold war. Support, modify, or refute this contention using specific evidence.

END OF SECTION II

ANSWERS TO THE DIAGNOSTIC EXAM

Multiple Choice

1.1. B	3.2 B	5.3 B	7.4 D
1.2. A	3.3 A	5.4 C	8.1 D
1.3. C	3.4 D	6.1 A	8.2 A
1.4 D	4.1 A	6.2 B	8.3 C
2.1 B	4.2 B	6.3 D	8.4 B
2.2 D	4.3 D	6.4 C	9.1 A
2.3 A	4.4 C	7.1 C	9.2 B
2.4 C	5.1 D	7.2 A	9.3 D
3.1 C	5.2 A	7.3 B	9.4 C

Explanations for the Multiple-Choice Questions

1.1 B. The cartoon criticizes President Thomas Jefferson's 1807 Embargo Act. Following a British naval attack on the American frigate U.S.S. *Chesapeake* that forced the ship to surrender and resulted in removal of four alleged British deserters, many Americans called for war. President Jefferson wanted to avoid war with Great Britain and believed that economic pressure could force the British to change their policy of interfering with American trade and ships. Jefferson persuaded Congress to pass the Embargo Act, which cut off the export of American goods to Europe. The embargo devastated American trade and was very unpopular with many Americans.

1.2 A. President Jefferson was responding to British interference with American shipping and trade. The British were at war with Napoleonic France and were trying to cut off trade with French-controlled parts of Europe. The British seized American ships that they thought were trading with their enemy, and also impressed American sailors to serve in their navy. Americans deeply resented these policies, which showed no respect for American rights or the flag of the United States.

1.3 C. Many Americans responded to Jefferson's Embargo Act by ignoring it and engaging in illicit trade, especially with Canada. Jefferson convinced Congress to pass legislation rigorously enforcing the embargo. This made it even more unpopular.

1.4 D. The Neutrality Laws of the 1930s most closely resemble Jefferson's policy. These laws also regulated American trade to achieve foreign policy objectives. The authors of the Neutrality Laws hoped to keep the United States out of another war by avoiding the conditions that led to American involvement in World War I. The Neutrality Laws stated that once the president recognized the existence of a foreign war, Americans could not make loans to or sell munitions to warring powers, or take passage on belligerent ships.

2.1 B. President Ronald Reagan's "Evil Empire" speech reflected an intensification of the cold war in the early 1980s. Concerned about Soviet actions in the 1970s, such as the 1979 invasion of Afghanistan, Reagan intensified an arms buildup begun by President Jimmy Carter. Convinced of the essential criminality of the Soviet Union's totalitarian system, Reagan believed that the United States needed to wage the cold war from a position of strength.

2.2 D. A Republican would have been most likely to support President Reagan's position. Ronald Reagan was a champion of conservative Republican ideas in both domestic and foreign policy.

2.3 A. The sentiments of the passage are most closely linked to the passage of the Strategic Defense Initiative (SDI), popularly known as the "Star Wars" program. The SDI was a missile defense program proposed by President Reagan and intended to defend the United States by shooting down incoming nuclear missiles. Many critics thought the plan impractical, expensive, and too provocative to the Soviets. President Reagan believed that it offered a way out of the menace of nuclear annihilation. The SDI program, along with Reagan's military buildup, put more pressure on the Soviet Union.

2.4 C. The sentiments in the passage best reflect the long-standing concern of American presidents to contain communism. The containment of communism had been a cornerstone of American foreign policy since the late 1940s. President Reagan was determined to halt and reverse what he believed was an expansion of Communist influence in the 1970s.

3.1 C. In this passage Colleen Moore is writing about flappers. Flappers were young women in the 1920s who cut their hair short in a bobbed style, wore shorter dresses, and often experimented with makeup and cigarettes. The flappers represented the growing freedom of women in the United States in the years after World War I and the passage of the Nineteenth Amendment giving women the vote.

3.2 B. Many young women of the 1920s expressed their freedom through "mannish" haircuts, new clothing styles, and cosmetics. Rather than focusing on politics and social reform, many young women of this period explored their growing independence through an emphasis on social freedoms and self-expression.

3.3 A. The new freedoms for women in the 1920s were supported by widespread economic prosperity. Growing economic security gave many people more leisure time and the opportunity to explore greater personal freedoms. The general prosperity stimulated a vibrant cultural life that opened up new ways for women to express themselves.

3.4 D. The passage by Moore most directly reflects concerns for individual liberty and self-expression. Women in the 1920s took advantage of new opportunities to expand their personal freedoms and express themselves more openly.

4.1 A. In this passage, Benjamin Franklin takes a position similar to advocates of a market-driven economy like Adam Smith. The author of *The Wealth of Nations*, Adam Smith defended the principles of modern capitalism. Like Smith, Franklin believed that individuals operating freely in the market can accomplish more than paternalistic government policies can. Franklin believed that the best way to help the poor is to encourage them to help themselves.

4.2 B. The idea that Franklin expresses in this passage most directly reflects a belief in individual self-reliance. Franklin was himself a self-made man. He articulated the self-reliant ethos that became a long-standing American value.

4.3 D. A high degree of social mobility in colonial America helped Franklin justify his position. Most Americans were farmers, or in the few cities businesspeople or artisans. The ready availability of land and a prospering economy opened up many avenues for social advancement. The absence of a privileged aristocracy, along with plentiful avenues to accumulate wealth, made America a land of opportunity.

4.4 C. The president most likely to share Franklin's position was Calvin Coolidge. A man who rose from modest circumstances to the presidency, Coolidge was a believer in hard work and thrift. He insisted on reducing government expenses and resisted interfering with business and the markets.

5.1 D. In this cartoon, Thomas Nast expresses his conviction that Tammany Hall boss William M. Tweed wields too much power in New York City. As the leader of the Tammany Hall political machine that dominated politics in New York City, Boss Tweed used his power to enrich himself and his cronies. Nast was a longtime opponent of Tweed and helped publicize the political boss's misdeeds through his cartoons. Tweed eventually was sentenced to prison because of his crimes.

5.2 A. Urban political machines like Tammany Hall derived most of their support from immigrants and lower-class voters. When they controlled the political structure of a city, machines prospered through the control of city contracts for improvements like sewers and streets. Machine politicians would pocket kickbacks from contractors eager for the work. This money, in turn, funded a hierarchical machine structure that reached into every neighborhood. Local precinct captains would help turn out the vote on election day, keeping the machine in power.

5.3 B. Urban political machines endured for many years because they provided help and services for the poor. In an era before extensive social services and welfare, urban political machines assisted the poor with gifts of food and shelter, and sometimes jobs. In return, the machines expected these people to vote in their favor.

5.4 C. Nast's journalistic perspective can best be compared to reporters investigating President Richard M. Nixon during the Watergate scandal. Nixon, like Tweed, was accused of misusing his office. As with Nast, reporters like Bob Woodward and Carl Bernstein of the *Washington Post* played a key role in exposing a political leader's wrongdoing.

6.1 A. From the perspective of Captain John Smith, Powhatan and his followers were a backward people. Smith sees the Indians as "barbarous." They wear animal skins and paint, and are cruelly ready to execute Smith. The fact that Powhatan makes his own clothes and tools would also lead Smith to see this as a primitive society.

6.2 B. Smith's account makes clear that Powhatan's people made decisions by consensus. After a feast, Powhatan consults with his people and there is a long discussion about what to do with Smith. When the decision is made to kill Smith, only the determined intervention of Pocahontas saves him.

6.3 D. Smith's story illustrates that Indian-European relations often suffered from misunderstanding and suspicion. Smith did not appreciate the concerns of Powhatan's people, and the Indians clearly were hostile to the newly arrived English. Only Pocahontas in this story attempts to bridge the divide between the Indians and English.

6.4 C. In the context of this story, the peace-making Pocahontas can best be compared to Jane Addams. In addition to being a founder of Hull House in Chicago and a pioneering social worker, Addams was also a vocal peace activist. Addams was awarded the Nobel Peace Prize in 1931.

7.1 C. Martin Luther King, Jr., in this passage is calling for equal rights for African Americans. King gave his "I Have a Dream" speech during the August 28, 1963, march on Washington, when 250,000 people congregated in the nation's capital to express their support for proposed civil rights legislation.

7.2 A. In this passage, King points out a contradiction between American ideals and American practice caused by racial discrimination. Invoking the Declaration of Independence and Constitution of the United States, King in this speech called for all Americans, regardless of their color, to enjoy the inalienable rights of life, liberty, and the pursuit of happiness.

7.3 B. A Southern Democratic Senator would be likely to oppose the message of King's speech. The Democratic party in the South had dominated the region for over a century, and for the most part strongly supported the Jim Crow laws upholding racial segregation. The civil rights laws of the 1950s and 1960s were passed with the overwhelming support of Northern Democrats and Republicans.

7.4 D. In this passage, King is addressing the struggle for greater individual liberty in American history. As King pointed out in his "I Have a Dream" speech, Americans since the founding of the United States have been striving to achieve greater individual liberty for themselves and their families. King saw the civil rights movement as a continuation of that struggle.

8.1 D. The message of the cartoon can be best described as civilians playing a vital role in the war effort. Americans on the home front during World War II were encouraged to see themselves as active participants in the conflict. Food products like meat and sugar and consumer goods like gasoline were rationed. People raised victory gardens and bought war bonds. Many women and African Americans took jobs in war industries. What people did at home was seen as crucial to supporting the fighting men overseas.

8.2 A. Viewing this cartoon would encourage Americans to avoid the wasteful use of metal products. Metals were vital for the manufacture of weapons and ammunition. Civilians collected scrap metal that could be melted down and used for the war effort. Many consumer goods made of metal, most notably new automobiles, were not available during the war as industries focused on war production.

8.3 C. The cartoon most directly refers to American industrial production during World War II. The United States became what President Franklin D. Roosevelt called the "arsenal of democracy" during the war, producing enough weapons and military supplies to equip Americans fighting a global war, while also providing great quantities of Lend-Lease aid to American allies. American industrial output was a major factor in winning World War II.

8.4 B. The message of the cartoon can be best compared to the boycotts of British goods in the 1760s and 1770s. In both cases, Americans were asked to give up goods and make sacrifices to help further a larger cause. In the 1760s and 1770s Americans gave up British goods to exert pressure on British policymakers. In World War II, Americans made sure most metals went to war production to ensure the defeat of Nazi Germany and Imperial Japan.

9.1 A. Mary Easty in this passage is asking her judges to stop condemning innocent people to death for witchcraft. In 1692, a group of girls in Salem, Massachusetts, began acting as if they were possessed. They claimed that they were bewitched. This led to a witch-hunting hysteria that resulted in 20 executions, including the death of Mary Easty. Eventually, the governor of Massachusetts put an end to the witchcraft prosecutions. Years later, the convictions of the people executed and imprisoned during this hysteria were officially overturned.

9.2 B. Most historians believe that the Salem Witch Trials were the result of social tensions in Salem. Massachusetts was undergoing rapid political and social change in the early 1690s. Most of those accused of being witches came from more prosperous families associated with business and trade, while the accusers came from less well-off farming families. Fears about witchcraft probably also reflected anxieties about the shifting social and economic status of people in Salem.

9.3 D. The religious convictions of Mary Easty and the rest of Salem were shaped by Puritanism. Massachusetts was settled in the 1630s by Calvinist Puritans escaping the religious domination of the Anglican Church in England. They saw their new colony as an opportunity to create a truly godly community. Initially only members of Puritan congregations could vote. Concern that people were falling away from strict Puritan belief probably played a part in the Salem witch hysteria.

9.4 C. Writers and intellectuals have often compared the Salem Witch Trials to government actions in the Red Scares of the twentieth century. The investigations of Senator Joseph McCarthy in the early 1950s were often compared to witch hunts. Arthur Miller's play about the events in Salem, *The Crucible* (1953), was a critique of McCarthyism.

Explanations for the Short-Answer Questions

1. A. Abraham Lincoln, the Republican candidate from Illinois for the U.S. Senate in 1858, opposed the extension of slavery into the western territories. He referred to the Kansas-Nebraska Act of 1854, sponsored by Senator Stephen Douglas, that repudiated the 1820 Missouri Compromise and allowed settlers to exercise popular sovereignty on whether or not they wanted slavery in the Kansas and Nebraska territories. This led to bloody fighting between pro- and antislavery settlers in Kansas. Lincoln was also implicitly criticizing the 1857 Supreme Court decision in *Dred Scott v. Sandford*, which ruled that African Americans could not be citizens, and also stated that Congress could not bar slavery in the territories, another blow to the Missouri Compromise. Lincoln argues that slavery hurts the reputation of the United States in the world and forces people to repudiate American ideals, such as the rights listed in the Declaration of Independence.
B. Stephen Douglas, the Democratic candidate for reelection as U.S. senator from Illinois, stands by the principle of states' rights. During the 1850s, he was a leading proponent of popular sovereignty, letting the people in a territory decide whether they would organize a free or slave state. Douglas believed that if the agitation over slavery ceased, the Union would flourish with a mix of free and slave states. This position was a repudiation of Lincoln's argument that "A house divided against itself cannot stand."
C. Stephen Douglas's perspective influenced politics in the 1850s in a variety of ways. Douglas was the author of the 1854 Kansas-Nebraska Act, which by overturning the Missouri Compromise inflamed sectional disputes over slavery. This act also led to fighting in Kansas between pro and antislavery forces. "Bleeding Kansas" accentuated the growing divide between the North and South over slavery. The Dred Scott decision by the Supreme Court angered many Northerners because it seemed to make constitutional the importation of slaves into any part of the country. The sectional discord that followed the passage of the Kansas-Nebraska Act led to the dissolution of the Whig party. The Republican party emerged in the North and West. The Republicans opposed the expansion of slavery into the western territories. They argued that slaves

would constitute unfair competition for white farmers and laborers. A Republican slogan was "Free Soil, Free Labor, Free Men." The Republicans were organized enough to nominate the western explorer John C. Fremont for president in 1856. Fremont lost, but carried 11 Northern states. Lincoln did not win his Senate race in 1858 because the Democrats won more districts in the Illinois legislature, and senators were still elected by state legislatures. Despite this, his strong performance in the debates with Douglas brought him to national prominence and helped win him the Republican nomination for president in 1860.

2. **A.** The French and Indian War began because of British and colonial concerns about French activity in the Ohio Valley and, in particular, the construction of Fort Duquesne on the site of what is now Pittsburgh, Pennsylvania. The British claimed this territory, and many American colonists wanted to develop lands there. Once the French and Indian War was underway, the British leader William Pitt decided to commit resources to the eradication once and for all of French claims in North America. The French in Canada were decisively defeated outside Quebec at the Battle of the Plains of Abraham, on September 13, 1759. At the 1763 Treaty of Paris, France signed away all of its North American lands. The British took control of Canada and all the lands east of the Mississippi River. The British also acquired Florida from Spain. The French and Indian War opened up vast lands for possible American settlement and removed the major military obstacle to moving westward.

The Louisiana Purchase of 1803 greatly expanded the United States. President Thomas Jefferson was very interested in western lands. He envisioned a great republic of independent yeoman farmers. To make this possible, he needed land. When Jefferson learned that the weak government of Spain had transferred the Louisiana Territory to the control of Napoleon's France, Jefferson grew concerned that the French might try to reconstitute a strong empire in America. This disquietude was intensified when Spanish officials closed New Orleans to American trade, threatening the economic well-being of Americans living in the west. Jefferson sent James Monroe to join the American minister in France, Robert Livingston. They were to negotiate the purchase of New Orleans. By this time, Napoleon had decided that Louisiana was a liability. He had lost an army to disease trying to reconquer Haiti, and he assumed that he would be cut off from Louisiana by the British navy once war resumed with Great Britain. Napoleon offered to sell the whole Louisiana Territory to the startled American diplomats. For a purchase price of $15 million dollars, the size of the United States was doubled. Jefferson had some constitutional scruples about the purchase because there was nothing in the Constitution about acquiring territory. He swallowed his scruples, and the Senate quickly ratified the purchase.

The Mexican War took place at a time when many Americans were embracing the ideology of Manifest Destiny and arguing that it was inevitable that American settlements and free institutions would spread throughout North America. President James Polk was elected in 1844 on a platform of American expansionism in Texas and Oregon. Polk negotiated with the British on the Oregon border. Texas was annexed to the United States just before he became president. Mexico broke off diplomatic relations in protest. Polk sent the diplomat John Slidell to Mexico to resolve issues with the Mexicans. He also sent troops under General Zachary Taylor to the disputed border between Texas and Mexico along the Rio Grande. On April 24, 1846, Mexican forces attacked a troop of American soldiers. This began fighting between the United States and Mexico. Congress declared war on May 13. During the Mexican War, the United States won a series of victories that culminated in General Winfield Scott's occupation of Mexico City. In the 1848 Treaty of Guadalupe Hidalgo, Mexico ceded over 500,000 square miles of territory to the United States in return for a payment of $15 million dollars. This included California, Utah, Nevada, New Mexico, and Arizona and set the border of Texas at the Rio Grande.

B. In the French and Indian War the expansionism of American colonists was obviously opposed by the French. Many Indians also opposed this expansionism, which came at their expense. Many Indians allied with the French realized that the defeat of the French would eliminate one of the great restraints on western settlement by the Americans. Following the conclusion of the French and Indian War, the Ottawa leader Pontiac led a brief war against the British, driving them from a number of western outposts. Some opposition to the Louisiana Purchase came from Federalist politicians, unenthusiastic about acquiring more western lands likely disposed to send Democratic Republicans to Congress. Some people, including for a time Jefferson himself, had doubts about the Louisiana Purchase for constitutional reasons, seeing it as an example of federal overreach. The American acquisition of Mexican territory was opposed by the Mexicans, including many settlers in places like California, who did not like seeing their lands overrun by American invaders. There was strong opposition to the Mexican War in the United States. Many Americans believed that the war was unjust and was an excuse to acquire territories for the expansion of slavery. Among the opponents of the war were Congressman Abraham Lincoln and writer Henry David Thoreau, who refused to pay his poll tax, was briefly arrested, and then wrote his essay "Civil Disobedience."

3. **A.** The Great Awakening that began in the 1730s set off several decades of religious revivals in the American colonies. The preachers of the Great Awakening, such as Jonathan Edwards, George Whitefield, and Gilbert Tennent, emphasized the dependence of individuals upon God's grace and the need for the individual to develop a personal relationship with God. Many religious congregations split between the "New Lights" who embraced the revival and "Old Lights" who preferred the traditional religious authorities. The Great Awakening was a phenomenon that united all the colonies. Many Americans contrasted the new religious fervor around them with the less godly state of affairs back in Britain. The French and Indian War saw the American colonies mobilize large forces to assist the British in the war effort. By the end of the war, 20,000 Americans had served in the military. The Americans cooperated in a joint effort that gave many young men like George Washington a more continental sense of American affairs. Following the conflict, Americans saw themselves as an important part of the growing British Empire. The resistance to the Stamp Act and other examples of British taxation was widespread throughout the American colonies. Opposition to the Stamp Act and other actions by Parliament forced the colonies to cooperate as never before. The 1765 Stamp Act Congress saw representatives from nine colonies meet to coordinate measures against the Stamp Act. Over time, organizations like the Sons of Liberty and Committees of Correspondence appeared across the colonies. In the crisis that followed the 1773 Boston Tea Party and the passage of the British Coercive Acts, the First Continental Congress met in 1774, bringing together such leaders as Patrick Henry, Samuel Adams, John Adams, and George Washington. Americans were increasingly thinking of themselves as a united people.

B. The Great Awakening weakened Americans' attachment to traditional religious authorities, making them also more inclined to question British political authority. The sense that Americans were a more religious people than the British also made them more inclined to strike out on their own. The French and Indian War helped prepare the way for the American Revolution by leading to the British financial crisis that led Parliament to attempt to tax the colonies. The defeat of the French removed the major threat to the Americans and made British military protection less important. The political and military lessons learned in the war would be important in shaping the decisions of many American leaders during the War for Independence. George Washington and a number of other American military commanders were veterans of the French and Indian War and used the experience they gained there against the British. The acts of resistance to British taxation led directly to the American Revolution. Between the Stamp Act Congress and the First Continental Congress, Americans across the colonies grew used to coordinating their actions. The First Continental Congress created the "Association," an agreement to cease trading with Great Britain until the Coercive Acts were repealed. It also paved the way for the Second Continental Congress, which began meeting in May 1775. By then, fighting had begun outside Boston. The Second Continental Congress coordinated the American war effort and in July 1776 declared American Independence.

4. **A.** This cartoon concerns the "alphabet soup" of agencies that emerged during President Franklin Roosevelt's New Deal. Early in the New Deal Roosevelt and Congress launched a number of new programs and agencies to promote economic recovery from the Great Depression and provide relief to jobless Americans. Pictured in the cartoon are the AAA, the Agricultural Adjustment Administration, which attempted to raise farm prices by paying farmers to take land out of production, the PWA, the Public Works Administration, which launched a series of public works to provide jobs, and the WPA, the Works Progress Administration, which directly hired unemployed workers and set them to work on projects ranging from construction to the creation of murals and plays.
B. The cartoon is sympathetic to Roosevelt and the New Deal, showing the various "alphabet soup" agencies as happy children dancing around a smiling father-figure president. The early New Deal was popular, leading to Roosevelt's Democratic party winning a victory in the 1934 congressional elections. Despite this, challenges to the New Deal came from both the right and the left in American politics. In 1935, the Supreme Court struck down as unconstitutional the National Recovery Administration (NRA), which had attempted to get industries to cooperate in setting standards on such things as prices and wages. Roosevelt responded with the Second New Deal and the passage of such laws as the Social Security Act (1935), which set up a system to provide pensions to the elderly, and the National Labor Relations Act (1935), which made it easier for workers to organize unions.
C. There were a number of critics of the New Deal. The Supreme Court invalidated some of the legislation of the First New Deal. Only after a bruising political battle in Roosevelt's second term, during which he lost a lot of political support attempting to pass legislation that would have "packed" the court with his supporters, did the Supreme Court begin upholding New Deal legislation. Many conservatives opposed the New Deal. Former Democratic New York governor Al Smith was a member of the Liberty League, which believed that the New Deal undermined property rights. From the left, Louisiana Senator Huey Long did not believe that the New Deal was going far enough. He promoted a "Share the Wealth" plan that would give every American a home and a $2,500 income. The money from this would come from confiscating wealth from millionaires.

Explanation for the Document-Based Question

Although the Federalists intended to unify the nation and strengthen the federal government, their political and economic policies split the nation into rival partisan factions. Students might note that debates over ratification of the Constitution set the stage for the emergence of political parties by the end of the 1790s. They could briefly discuss the supporters and opponents of ratification, the anti-Federalists, and *The Federalist Papers,* particularly *The Federalist,* no. 10. Students should examine the ideological conflict between loose and strict interpretations of the Constitution, as well as federal versus state authority. They should identify the leading Federalists (Washington, Adams, Hamilton) and Republicans (Jefferson, Madison, Randolph). Document A indicates Washington's desire that Congress may set policy without party division. Students may note, however, that friction stemmed from Hamilton's financial program. They should examine his intention to establish a sound financial foundation for the new nation by creating a national bank, addressing the public debt (Assumption Act, Funding Bill), and raising revenue (excise taxes, tariffs). While Hamilton's program strengthened the federal government, it fostered dissent among the Republicans. Document B reflects Virginia's opposition to the assumption of state debts. Students will note that the conflict over the Bank of the United States in Documents C and D reflects Jefferson and Hamilton's interpretations of the "necessary and proper clause" of the Constitution. Students may also contrast the Republican view of an agricultural economy in Document B, with Federalist support for the Tariff of 1789 and Hamilton's Report on Manufactures. They may note that opposition to the excise tax led to the Whiskey Rebellion. In Document E, Washington states his intention to enforce federal law and implement powers granted under the Constitution. Washington demonstrated federal authority by calling forth the militias from three states to suppress the rebellion. Some students may refer to Shays's Rebellion. Students may begin a discussion of diplomatic policy with Washington's Neutrality Proclamation (1793) and Neutrality Act (1794). They may explain how the neutrality policy survived the challenge of "Citizen Genet." However, Great Britain challenged the policy by seizing American ships. Students should discuss partisan perceptions of Jay's Treaty. They may note that it achieved some of its nationalistic goals regarding the Northwest Territory and promoting commerce with Great Britain. However, they should also address Republican views of its shortcomings. Some students may address Pinckney's Treaty. Students should discuss Washington's views on parties in his Farewell Address. They will note how the election of 1796 yielded a Federalist president (Adams) and a Republican vice president (Jefferson). Students will note how the strife in the executive office reflected party differences in the United States. A discussion of the undeclared naval war with France will reveal the pro-British views of Federalists and pro-French sympathies of the Republicans. Students will discuss how opposing perceptions of the war and the XYZ Affair led to the Alien and Sedition Acts of 1798 (Document F). Students will observe how Madison and Jefferson penned the Virginia and Kentucky Resolutions (Document G), which asserted the theory of nullification. They might conclude how the problems of the Adams's administration led to the election of Jefferson in 1800.

Explanations for the Long-Essay Questions

1. You can construct an argument making use of information that can include the following:

   The First World War saw the culmination of the Progressive Era's movement toward greater government regulation of the economy. The federal government took unprecedented steps as it mobilized the American people and the American economy for total war against Imperial Germany. The administration of President Woodrow Wilson and Congress financed the war through the sale of Liberty Bonds to the American people and through steep rises in income taxes and taxes on corporate profits. A War Industries Board (WIB) coordinated the production of war materials, setting prices and allocating resources. A series of war boards supervised different aspects of the economy, such as fuel and railroads, which had come under federal control. Herbert Hoover headed the food board, encouraging Americans to conserve different types of foodstuffs. This organization of the economy had mixed results. Initially there was some confusion and missteps as the government sorted out its programs. The United States was still not producing all the military supplies and weapons that it needed when the war ended in November 1918, but during the brief period of its involvement in the war the United States had made impressive gains in organizing its enormous economic potential. Very important for the future, businessmen and government officials had learned the advantages of working together, establishing a longstanding cooperative relationship between big business and government.

   In addition to organizing the economy, President Wilson attempted to mobilize public opinion during the war. He created the Committee on Public Information (CPI), headed by the journalist George Creel. The CPI worked to educate Americans about the war through books, pamphlets, posters, and movies. Although the original intent was to provide largely factual material, the CPI ended up producing a lot of overt propaganda. The government also acted to repress dissent. The Espionage Act of 1917 and the Sedition Act of 1918 essentially criminalized public opposition to the war. The Socialist leader Eugene Debs was one of many who went to prison for criticizing the war. The government fomented an atmosphere of hysteria that stigmatized all things German, leading to such phenomena as the renaming of sauerkraut as "liberty cabbage," and also promoted the suppression of radical groups like the International Workers of the World (IWW). This search for internal enemies eventually branched into the postwar First Red Scare.

   In large part because of the excesses of this attempt to regiment American opinion, there was a reaction against the wartime policies of Woodrow Wilson that resulted in the election of Warren G. Harding to the presidency in 1920 with his promise of a return to "normalcy." Despite this reaction, elements of the wartime mobilization persisted, especially in the relationship between government and business, fostered in the 1920s by Commerce Secretary Herbert Hoover.

   The New Deal was influenced by the example of World War I. Once again the federal government intervened heavily in the economy. President Franklin Roosevelt and a number of his subordinates, such as General Hugh Johnson, the head of the National Recovery Administration (NRA), were veterans of the First World War mobilization. The NRA, with its attempt to set up industry codes, echoed aspects of the WIB.

   The mobilization of the United States for total war again in World War II unsurprisingly echoed that of World War I. The war was financed through a combination of loans and high taxes. The Office of Price Administration (OPA) worked to prevent inflation by controlling prices and wages. It also supervised an elaborate system of rationing resources and goods important to the war effort such as sugar, meat, rubber, and gasoline. A succession of federal agencies worked to coordinate industrial production. The War Production Board (WPB) was eventually replaced by the Office of War Mobilization (OWM). Despite this bureaucratic experimentation, the government successfully organized the American industrial base to produce massive amounts of war material, becoming the "arsenal of democracy" during the war. Though Roosevelt created the Office of War Information (OWI) to coordinate war information and propaganda, it never took on the importance of Creel's CPI, and the Roosevelt administration studiously avoided launching the sort of political repression seen during World War I. The Roosevelt administration did make one notorious concession to wartime hysteria. In 1942, it rounded up Japanese and Japanese-American people living on the West Coast and sent them to internment camps.

By the end of World War II, after years of expanding federal power, Americans had become used to the government playing an important role in their lives and in the economy. The overall success of the American war effort in World War II would foster a confidence in the abilities of government to meet challenges that would undergird the policies of later presidents such as John F. Kennedy and his New Frontier and Lyndon B. Johnson and his Great Society.

2. Before the Spanish-American War, the United States did not play a prominent role as a great power, despite its burgeoning economic strength. Beginning in the 1880s the United States began building up a modern navy, leading to an interest in coaling stations in places like Pearl Harbor in Hawaii and Pago Pago in Samoa. Despite this, as late as 1893, President Grover Cleveland would refuse an opportunity to annex the Hawaiian Islands. The Spanish-American War of 1898 ushered the United States onto the world stage. After rapidly defeating the obsolescent naval forces of Spain, the United States became an imperial power. Though Cuba, the occasion of the war with Spain, would be given a measure of independence, the United States retained control of Puerto Rico, Guam, and the Philippines. The Philippines, with the magnificent harbor at Manila Bay, were seen as a way station to China, which many Americans hoped would become a major market for American goods. This interest in China led the United States in 1900 to join in the suppression of the antiforeigner Boxer Rebellion. The United States through its "Open Door" notes attempted to keep the Chinese market from being closed by colonial powers. This would be the keystone of American foreign policy in China through World War II.

In the early twentieth century the United States exerted its power in the Western Hemisphere, building the Panama Canal, and, through President Theodore Roosevelt's corollary to the Monroe Doctrine, asserting a right to police the small republics of the Caribbean and Central America. American troops would be repeatedly sent to restore order in countries like Haiti and Nicaragua through the early 1930s.

Under Theodore Roosevelt, the United States was accepted into the club of great powers. Roosevelt won a Nobel Peace Prize in 1906 for helping negotiate an end to the Russo-Japanese War of 1904–1905, and American delegates took part in the 1906 Algeciras Conference. The United States attempted to remain neutral during World War I, while maintaining a profitable trading relationship with Britain and France. Germany's unrestricted submarine campaign brought the United States into the war in 1917. American troops helped turn the tide against Germany on the Western Front.

President Woodrow Wilson's Fourteen Points became for many people around the world a blueprint for a better postwar world, for when the Treaty of Versailles was being negotiated at Paris in 1919, Woodrow Wilson seemed to be the most influential figure in the world. This power evaporated quickly. Wilson did not prevent the imposition of harsh peace terms on the Germans. His League of Nations failed to win ratification in the United States Senate.

The United States did not become isolationist in the 1920s. President Warren Harding hosted the 1921–1922 Washington Disarmament Conference. The 1924 Dawes Plan helped stabilize German and European finances. However, the Great Depression turned the United States inward. President Hoover did little to oppose Japanese aggression in Manchuria in 1931. President Franklin Roosevelt "torpedoed" the London Economic Conference attempting to stabilize the international economy so he could focus on fighting the depression in the United States. Both Hoover and Roosevelt improved relations with Latin America through the Good Neighbor policy, which rejected the role of the United States as "policeman" of the Western Hemisphere. The mid-1930s saw the height of American isolationism with the passage of the 1935, 1936, and 1937 Neutrality Laws, essentially designed to prevent another World War I by forbidding Americans to trade with warring countries or travel on belligerent ships.

During the late 1930s, President Roosevelt became increasingly alarmed at the aggressions of Japan, Italy, and Germany. Following the outbreak of World War II in 1939, he took steps to allow trade with Britain and France and began a major rearming program. This military buildup intensified after the defeat of France in 1940. Roosevelt assisted Britain with the Destroyers for Bases Deal, giving Britain old American destroyers in exchange for leases on British bases in the Western Hemisphere. In 1941, Roosevelt persuaded Congress to pass the Lend-Lease Act, allowing him to give military supplies to Britain and other countries fighting Germany. By late 1941, the United States was waging an undeclared naval war on the Atlantic Ocean, as the United States Navy helped protect British convoys from German submarines.

In the Pacific, Japan launched an all-out war on China in 1937. Following the defeat of France in 1940, the Japanese moved into French Indochina. In 1941, the Japanese established fuller control over Indochina. The United States finally halted its trade in metals and oil with Japan and demanded that the Japanese end the war in China. The Japanese preferred to fight, hoping to conquer the resources they needed in the British and Dutch colonies of Malaysia and Indonesia. To do this safely, they had to neutralize the American fleet at Pearl Harbor. The December 7, 1941, Japanese attack on Pearl Harbor brought the United States into the Second World War. American military and industrial power proved crucial in defeating Japan and Germany.

American policymakers, remembering the failure of Woodrow Wilson at the end of World War I, were determined that the United States would play a constructive role in the postwar world. The United States hosted the new United Nations. The United States played a key role in the 1944 Bretton Woods Conference that laid the foundations of the World Bank, the International Monetary Fund (IMF), and the postwar international economic order.

Complicating a postwar settlement was a growing conflict with the Soviet Union, an ally during World War II but a Communist totalitarian state run by the dictator Josef Stalin. At the end of World War II, the Soviets brutally established their control in Eastern Europe. There was fear that they might try to subvert the pro-American governments of Western Europe. The American policy of containment began to take shape. In 1947, President Harry Truman used a bill to provide support to Greece and Turkey to announce what became known as the Truman Doctrine: the United States would assist any nation threatened by communism, either by external attack or internal subversion. In 1949, after an abortive Soviet attempt to blockade West Berlin, the United States and 11 other countries formed the North Atlantic Treaty Organization (NATO). NATO gave the signatories collective security against a Soviet attack. The United States for the first time since the end of the French alliance in 1800 had entered into an alliance with other countries. The United States was now committed to the defense of Western Europe. This would be a cornerstone of American policy for decades to come.

STEP 3

Develop Strategies for Success

CHAPTER 4 Mastering Skills and Understanding Themes for the New Exam
CHAPTER 5 Strategies for Approaching Each Question Type

CHAPTER 4

Mastering Skills and Understanding Themes for the New Exam

IN THIS CHAPTER

Summary: The new exam emphasizes historical analytical skills and a thematic approach to U.S. history. You will need to familiarize yourself with the specific skills and themes listed in this chapter and then be able to apply these skills and interpret these themes using your knowledge of U.S. history.

KEY IDEA

Key Ideas
✪ Just memorizing facts will not be enough to do well on the new exam.
✪ You should become familiar with nine historical analytical skills.
✪ You should also become familiar with seven historical themes.
✪ All the questions on the new exam will be based on one or more of these skills and themes.

New Approach to the AP U.S. History Exam

If you have taken the diagnostic exam, it should be clear that it is very different from the exam taken by your older brother, sister, or friends. All the questions on the new exam—multiple choice, short answer, document-based question (DBQ), and long essay—require you to think in terms of specific historical analytical skills and historical themes. To do well, it is essential that you have a thorough understanding of the nine historical analytical skills and seven historical themes described in this chapter. You should try to regularly utilize them throughout your study of U.S. history. Your teacher will provide you with many activities that will allow you to work with these skills and themes. Whether you are part of a study group or studying alone, you should find additional opportunities to use them while reviewing major events in U.S. history. These skills and themes are the tools you should use to analyze—not just memorize—the information that you are introduced to in your classwork and reading.

Historical Analytical Skills

Questions on the AP U.S. History exam will all involve one or more of the historical analytical skills in the following list. Be sure you practice these skills as you review for the exam.

1. **Identifying cause and effect.** This involves establishing the relationships between events, determining the ways historical actions and forces influence each other.
2. **Differentiating between change and continuity.** This involves identifying patterns over periods of time and demonstrating how changes and continuities are related to broad historical forces.
3. **Grouping events into periods.** This involves organizing events and historical forces into meaningful stretches of time, distinguishing them from other possible models, and facilitating our ability to better understand the past.
4. **Comparing historical events.** This involves relating and contrasting events across time and space, creating contexts by which to evaluate them.
5. **Connecting events to broader historical trends.** This involves linking specific events to wider historical processes taking place around them, showing how they are related to similar occurrences taking place elsewhere.
6. **Creating and assessing historical arguments.** This involves understanding the components of an effective historical argument, recognizing these in the arguments of others, and utilizing them to craft persuasive arguments of your own.
7. **Evaluating historical data.** This involves assessing the significance of different forms of historical evidence and determining its appropriate value for a historical argument.
8. **Interpreting the past.** This involves understanding the ways that the perspective of historians is shaped by their particular circumstances and recognizing that there can be many models of historical interpretation.
9. **Synthesizing historical evidence.** This involves pulling together a variety of different types of evidence, both primary and secondary, to construct a compelling historical argument.

Historical Themes

All questions on the AP U.S. History exam will relate in some way to the following overarching themes of U.S. History. You'll need to use your historical analytical skills to explain, interpret, and apply these themes of U.S. history.

1. **American identities.** This addresses the development of American nationalism, and within this larger national identity, the emergence of various group identities during the course of U.S. history.
2. **American economies and technology.** This addresses the ways that Americans have structured their economic systems over time, and how technological change has affected economic development in the United States.
3. **American populations.** This addresses the movements to and within the United States by various groups of people.
4. **Political power in the United States.** This addresses the role of government in American history, the understandings Americans have had about the nature of government, and the ways people in the United States have organized themselves to shape the political process.

5. **The United States in world affairs.** This addresses the ways in which the American colonies and the United States interacted with other peoples and governments, in North America and around the world.
6. **The influence of American geography and environment.** This addresses the ways the physical environment and geography of America, including such factors as climate, plants, animals, and natural resources, helped shape the history of the United States.
7. **American culture and conviction.** This addresses the significance of ideas, religious beliefs, and cultural values as formative influences in American history.

Historical Analytical Skills, Historical Themes, and Exam Questions

To illustrate the ways in which the questions on the new exam expect you to make use of these historical analytical skills and historical themes, let's look at a few examples.

Sample Multiple-Choice Questions

Questions on the exam will often begin with a look at some historical document that you will be asked to read, analyze, and interpret. Following the document below, we'll try some sample multiple-choice questions like those you'll find on the actual test.

> Everybody is talkin' these days about Tammany men growin' rich on graft, but nobody thinks of drawin' the distinction between honest graft and dishonest graft. There's all the difference in the world between the two. Yes, many of our men have grown rich in politics. I have myself. I've made a big fortune out of the game, and I'm gettin' richer every day, but I've not gone in for dishonest graft—blackmailin' gamblers, saloonkeepers, disorderly people, etc.—and neither has any of the men who have made big fortunes in politics.
>
> There's an honest graft, and I'm an example of how it works. I might sum up the whole thing by sayin': "I seen my opportunities and I took 'em."
>
> Just let me explain by example. My party's in power in the city, and it's goin' to undertake a lot of public improvements. Well, I'm tipped off, say, that they're goin' to lay out a new park in a certain place.
>
> I see my opportunity and I take it. I go to that place and I buy up all the land I can in the neighborhood. Then the board of this or that makes its plan public, and there is a rush to get my land, which nobody cared for particular before.
>
> Ain't it perfectly honest to charge a good price and make a profit on my investment and foresight? Of course, it is. Well, that's honest graft.
>
> —William Riordan, *Plunkitt of Tammany Hall*, 1905

Let's look at a sample multiple-choice question based on this passage:

1. The perspective of George Washington Plunkitt expressed in the passage above most directly reflected the attitudes of which of the following?
   A. Progressive political reformers
   B. The owners of big businesses and trusts
   C. Supporters of the Social Gospel
   D. Urban machine politicians

The correct answer is D. George Washington Plunkitt was a leader in New York City's Tammany Hall political machine, and his questionable distinction between "dishonest" and "honest" graft is a justification of the fact that, like many machine politicians, he used his position and insider knowledge to make money at the taxpayers' expense. Note that you have to use historical analytical skills to answer the question, including evaluating historical data as you interpret the meaning of the passage, and comparing historical events as you weigh the correct answer against responses reflecting contemporary events, such as the rise of progressivism, the growth of big business, and the efforts of social workers and reformers to ameliorate conditions in the cities, including the Protestant leaders preaching the Social Gospel. The question also asks you to reflect on historical themes, such as political power in the United States, because of its obvious political content, and American populations, because the movement of masses of people into rapidly growing American cities in the late nineteenth century was the essential backdrop to the rise of the great urban political machines.

Let's try another multiple-choice question:

2. Given the perspective expressed by George Washington Plunkitt in the preceding passage, which of the following reforms would he be most likely to oppose?
   A. Civil service reform
   B. Abolitionism
   C. Dechartering the Bank of the United States
   D. Creating Social Security

The correct answer is A. As a machine politician who used his position in the city to feather his nest, George Washington Plunkitt vehemently opposed civil service reform, which would replace machine workers on the city payroll with civil servants who would not owe their livelihood and loyalty to political bosses. A historical analytical skill useful in answering the question is connecting events to broader historical trends, necessary in relating Plunkitt's concerns to the movement for civil service reform in the late nineteenth and early twentieth centuries. Grouping events into periods is essential because the other responses to the question date from other times in American history. Correctly answering the question requires you to connect Plunkitt to what was for him a contemporary reform movement. Historical themes that are important for this question are political power in the United States, because once again we are dealing with politics, and American culture and conviction, because this question asks you to reflect on important social ideas in U.S. history.

Sample Short-Answer Question

Now let's try a short-answer question.

1. The Trans-Mississippi West was rapidly settled in the period 1865 to 1890.
   A. Choose *one* of the following, and explain how it contributed to this rapid settlement. Provide at least *one* piece of evidence to support your explanation.
      - Railroads
      - Cattlemen
      - Farmers
   B. Demonstrate how your choice affected *one* of the other options.

This question asks you to discuss factors in the rapid opening of the West in the period following the Civil War. You can treat the impact of railroads, the emergence of the great open-range cattle empire, and the rise of a new farming frontier. To answer it, you need to use such historical analytical skills as differentiating between change and continuity when you relate one of the options to a broader historical pattern, and identifying cause and effect, as you explore how one of the options affected another. Relevant historical themes are American economies and technology and the influence of American geography and environment as you analyze economic development in the very distinctive climactic environment of the West in the late nineteenth century. The historical theme of American identities would come into play as you discussed the emergence of distinctive cultures among cattlemen and western farmers.

Sample Essay Question

Long-essay questions, including DBQs, can draw on all the historical analytical skills, but they often especially test your skill in (1) creating and assessing historical arguments, (2) interpreting the past, and (3) synthesizing historical evidence. Consider a DBQ that begins with the following statement:

> Historians Stephen Armstrong and Daniel P. Murphy, writing in the early twenty-first century, argue that American military involvement in World War I was a mistake that could have been avoided if the U.S. government had not insisted on an unrealistic understanding of the freedom of the seas.

In an essay dealing with this position, the three historical analytical skills identified above would need to be heavily utilized. Creating and assessing historical arguments and interpreting the past would be important as you weigh the argument of Armstrong and Murphy, putting it into context and evaluating its strengths and weaknesses. Synthesizing historical evidence would be crucial as you shape the documents provided into a persuasive argument of your own. As you do this, you will also rely on the historical theme concerning the United States in world affairs.

In Conclusion

What should be clear by now is that the historical analytical skills and historical themes discussed in this chapter are the intellectual framework of the new exam. You ought to be as familiar with these skills and themes as you are with the facts of U.S. history. Mastery of them will enable you to respond effectively to the questions you will encounter on the test in the spring of 2015.

CHAPTER 5

Strategies for Approaching Each Question Type

IN THIS CHAPTER

Summary: Knowing how to most efficiently and effectively attack each type of question on the test will help you score higher on the exam. Learn the question-answering strategies in this chapter and practice applying them to the test questions.

Key Ideas

Multiple-Choice Questions
- Multiple-choice questions now relate to prompts such as historical texts and images.
- The questions test analytical and interpretive skills as well as factual knowledge.
- Intelligent guessing will improve your score on the test; there is no penalty for guessing.
- There may be more than one possible "right" answer.
- Memorizing the facts is *not* enough.

Short-Answer Questions
- Short-answer questions ask you to make use of your historical analytical skills and thematic knowledge.
- For short-answer questions, it is *not* necessary to develop a thesis statement.

Document-Based Essay Question
- Use an appropriate organizational approach: create a thesis and support it.

- It is not necessary to use every single document to construct your argument.
- It is not necessary to spend the entire time writing your answer.
- There must be logic to your answer.
- Make your essay as readable as possible.
- Make sure to comment on all the quotes you include in your essay.

Long-Essay Question
- Use an appropriate organizational approach: create a thesis and support it.
- Make an outline before you begin to write.
- Pick the question you know the most about.
- Watch your time!

Reading and Interpreting Primary Source Documents
- Be prepared to analyze a variety of primary source documents.

Taking the Exam
- Come to the exam prepared but relaxed.

Multiple-Choice Questions

All multiple-choice questions will be tied to a prompt. These prompts may be primary source texts, secondary source texts, or images. For each prompt there will be two to six questions. These questions will require you to interpret source material and analyze it in conjunction with your broader historical knowledge. Remember, you will have 35 minutes to answer 35 to 40 questions. This does not give you a lot of time to ponder each question.

All questions on the test will have four possible answers. The following question is an example of the format of questions you may encounter on the exam:

> The peace, the freedom and the security of ninety percent of the population of the world is being jeopardized by the remaining ten percent who are threatening a breakdown of all international order and law.... When an epidemic of physical disease starts to spread, the community approves and joins in a quarantine of the patients in order to protect the health of the community against the spread of the disease.... War is a contagion, whether it is declared or undeclared. It can engulf states and peoples remote from the original scene of hostilities. We are determined to keep out of war, yet we cannot insure ourselves against the disastrous effects of war and the dangers of involvement. We are adopting such measures as will minimize our risk of involvement, but we cannot have complete protection in a world of disorder in which confidence and security have broken down.... Most important of all, the will for peace on the part of peace-loving nations must express itself to the end that nations that may be tempted to violate their agreements and the rights of others will desist from such a course. There must be positive endeavors to preserve peace.
>
> —Franklin D. Roosevelt, "Quarantine" Address, October 5, 1937

1. In the passage above, Franklin D. Roosevelt is expressing concern about which of the following?
   A. The economic consequences of the Great Depression
   B. The explosion of the U.S.S. *Maine*
   C. American interventions in Central America and the Caribbean
   D. Aggressive actions by Japan, Italy, and Germany

The correct answer is D. In the "Quarantine" Address, President Franklin D. Roosevelt was warning his fellow Americans about the dangers posed by the military actions taken by Japan in China, Italy in Ethiopia, and Germany in the Rhineland and Spain. Note that to correctly answer this, you have to understand what President Roosevelt is saying in the passage and put it into the historical context of the 1930s, a time when war clouds were gathering because of the aggressions of the totalitarian states.

Sometimes multiple-choice questions will ask you to make connections between the topic discussed by a source and another historical period. Here is an example:

2. The policy being proposed by Franklin D. Roosevelt in the passage above can *best* be compared to which of the following?
   A. The Monroe Doctrine
   B. The containment policy
   C. George Washington's policy of "no entangling foreign alliances"
   D. Isolationism

The correct answer is B. President Roosevelt was calling for a policy in which the "peace-loving nations" combined to "quarantine" the warlike states, dissuading them from further aggressive action. This is similar to the containment policy of the cold war, in which the United States and its allies attempted to halt or "contain" the expansion of communism. Note that the question asks you to compare policies from a wide range of U.S. history.

Useful Hints for the Multiple-Choice Section

- **Guessing:** On the multiple-choice portion of the test, no points are deducted for incorrect responses. Therefore it is to your advantage to guess on every question when you are not sure of the correct answer.
- **There may be more than one possible right answer.** The directions ask you to "select the one that is *best* in each case." Get rid of one or two responses that are obviously incorrect, and focus on the others. For example:

3. Which of the following would be most likely to support the perspective of Franklin D. Roosevelt in the passage above?
   A. A believer in Manifest Destiny
   B. An Isolationist
   C. A supporter of collective security
   D. A Democrat

Looking at the possible answers, let's eliminate those that are obviously incorrect. Manifest Destiny was an ideology of American continental expansionism that flourished in the mid-nineteenth century; it is inapplicable to the situation Roosevelt was describing. Isolationists opposed American interventionism abroad; this runs counter to what Roosevelt was proposing. This leaves C and D. Roosevelt was a Democrat and obviously could normally expect heavy support from members of his party. But a number of Democrats were Isolationists. Supporters of collective security, regardless of party affiliation, believed that the United States should act with other countries to preserve international peace. Therefore, though D is a plausible answer, C is the *best* response.

- **Memorizing the facts is *not* enough.** Although you do need to have a good knowledge of the facts of U.S. history, these questions place a heavy emphasis on analysis and a thematic understanding of the American past.
- **Don't overlook the obvious.** Questions on the AP U.S. History test emphasize major themes in U.S. history. Don't overthink the question. If you think an answer is so obvious that it has to be right, it probably is! The questions in this exam are not designed to test you on obscure trivia.
- **Use a good pencil with a good eraser.** We know that this may seem a little far-fetched, but we have a colleague who is convinced that this is an approach to be emphasized. He maintains that many students get marked off because they don't entirely fill in the bubbles or totally erase when they change their answers. He claims to have proof of this. Don't take this lightly; be sure you don't lower your score just because your eraser left a lot of smudges.

Short-Answer Questions

Short-answer questions require you to prepare brief responses to questions that ask you to address themes in U.S. history and utilize your historical analytical skills. Very important, short-answer questions do *not* require thesis statements. Short-answer questions may relate to prompts similar to those in the multiple-choice questions, or they may ask you to evaluate broad assertions about U.S. history. You will have 50 minutes to complete four short-answer questions.

The following question is an example of the format of questions you may encounter on the exam.

1. Reform movements transformed American life during the late nineteenth and early twentieth centuries.
   A. Choose *one* of the following and explain how it affected this transformation. Provide at least *one* piece of evidence to support your explanation.
      - Populism
      - Progressivism
      - Feminism
   B. Explain how your choice affected *one* of the other options. Provide at least *one* piece of evidence to support your explanation.

Useful Hints for the Short-Answer Section
- **Don't waste time!** You have to answer four of these in 50 minutes. Don't get bogged down with an elaborate response—remember that these are *short*-answer questions.
- **Just answer the question.** You don't have to develop a persuasive argument.
- **Be sure to provide supporting facts.** The directions may ask for "at least *one* piece of evidence," but it would be to your advantage to provide a few more.

Document-Based Question (DBQ)

During this essay section, you are required to analyze a number of documents and to utilize previously learned knowledge to answer a question. *Not all of the information needed to earn a 5 is included in the documents.* You need to bring what you know about the subject of the question to the table as well. In a typical question you might be presented with a political cartoon, a graph, extracts from speeches and letters, and part of an editorial from the 1850s and be asked to discuss the causes of the Civil War. By the time of the AP test your teacher has probably provided you with numerous document-based questions. For a specific example of a DBQ, refer to the DBQ in the diagnostic test in Chapter 3. On the new exam, the DBQ will contain no more than seven documents, and you will have 60 minutes to complete your essay.

Useful Hints for the DBQ

- **Use the standard essay format.** This is the format that you have used for all historical essays. Start off with a thesis and then use analysis of individual documents to prove your thesis. If the documents are presented chronologically, then write about them in the same way.
- **You don't need to use all the documents.** It is not always necessary to use every single document you are given to construct your answer; use as many as possible but make sure that their inclusion in your essay is relevant.
- **You don't need to keep writing on and on.** It is not necessary to spend every second of the 60 minutes writing the essay. Answer the question, including what the documents say and what you can say about them, and be done with it. Remember, some of what you already know has to be included in your answer.
- **There must be logic to your answer.** Organization as well as knowledge is important. Please remember that there is no "right answer" to the DBQ.
- **Spelling:** Many students ask whether spelling counts. The answer is generally, no. Scorers know that you are rushed on these essays; in all probability, if you think your handwriting is bad they have likely seen worse. Nevertheless, do what you can to make your presentation as readable as possible. Avoid writing with a pencil. Avoid messiness—lots of scratch-outs, arrows going off in different directions pointing to material you forgot to insert—as much as is possible under the circumstances. Don't write using extremely small script. We know from personal experience as instructors and scorers that it is hard to give a high score to a student if you can hardly read what the student wrote.
- **Don't waste time with direct quotes from the documents.** It will not help your score to spend time or space including direct quotes from the sources in your DBQ essay. If you are going to quote your sources, it is perfectly acceptable to paraphrase your quote. It is much more important to be sure to comment on any and all quotes that you include in your essay.
- **Answer the question.** This generally involves analysis and interpretation. Simply quoting the documents without analyzing them is not answering the question.
- **Demonstrate your historical knowledge.** To excel on the DBQ you must bring in outside information—the more the better.
- **Watch the time!** Don't get so wrapped up in the DBQ that you forget that you still have to do a long-essay question.

Long-Essay Question

Immediately after writing the DBQ essay, you will have to answer a long-essay question. You will get to choose which of two questions you will answer. The long-essay question asks you to utilize higher-level thinking skills; which means you will be asked to analyze and interpret events and themes of the past rather than simply give some historical facts. You will have 35 minutes to answer the long-essay question.

The following question is an example of the format of questions you may encounter on the exam:

1. Some historians have argued that the development of different economic systems in the North and South was a major cause of the Civil War. Support, modify, or refute this contention using specific evidence.

Useful Hints for the Long-Essay Question

Use the organizational approach that you have probably utilized in answering long-essay questions all year. Specifically this means you should:

- **Create a thesis.** What will your essay say? Decide the position you will take and then clearly state that position.
- **Write an effective opening statement.** This is crucial. Your thesis should be part of your opening statement.
- **Support your opening statement with historical facts.** Don't include facts for the sake of including them: make sure you use the historical facts you mention to support your opening argument.
- **If you can, include a discussion of counterarguments.** This shows that you thoroughly understand the issue at hand. This is usually done after you have supported your opening statement with sufficient evidence. This section often begins with "However, some historians believe …" and discusses and evaluates evidence that contradicts your thesis.
- **Don't forget a conclusion.** An effective conclusion includes a restatement of your thesis.
- **Make a rough outline before you begin to write.** Make sure to answer the question. Don't just go around in circles with information you know about the topic in question.
- **Be sure to pick the question that you know the most about.** We have known students who said they chose a specific question because it "looked easier." Avoid that approach. You'll do your best on the question about which you have the most historical knowledge.
- **Watch your time!** Finally, don't spend too much time on your outline. If you decide to do the long-essay before the DBQ, don't forget that you still have that task before you.

Using Primary Source Documents

As a student of AP U.S. History, you will undoubtedly be spending a lot of time this year analyzing primary source documents. Your teacher will probably give you a number of them to read during the year. The document-based question (DBQ) that is on every AP examination will most likely ask you to read and interpret a number of primary sources and then to make a historical argument based upon them.

Historical documents, accounts, and books can be either primary or secondary sources. A secondary source is an account written after the fact. A chapter in your textbook is a secondary source, as is a biography, for example, of Franklin D. Roosevelt written in 2005. However, when historians write secondary source accounts, their research should include a thorough study of the available primary sources. A primary source is a document from the era or person in question. A primary source relating to George Washington might be a letter that George Washington wrote when he was at Valley Forge, an account on Washington written by someone who knew him personally, or a portrait of Washington that was done when he was alive. Primary sources relating to the 1950s might be a speech made by Senator Joseph McCarthy, a recording of the song "Hound Dog" by Elvis Presley, or an episode of the television show "The Adventures of Ozzie and Harriet." (Note that primary source documents are not limited to written documents.) Secondary source accounts such as your textbook usually have excerpts from various primary source accounts scattered throughout the chapters.

Analyzing primary source documents allows you to study history as a historian does. When you are analyzing, for example, the actual text of a fireside chat given by Franklin D. Roosevelt in 1933, you are the one doing the historical analysis; no other historian or author is doing the work for you.

Types of Primary Source Documents

Types of primary source documents that you will be reading will likely include:

- **Documents published during the time period.** These will include magazine articles, newspaper accounts, official government documents, posters, Supreme Court decisions, novels written during the era, and countless other sources.
- **Resources published after the fact.** These will include letters and diaries written by historical (and nonhistorical) figures that were not originally meant for publication. These can be incredibly revealing; many politicians, for example, are much more honest in their diary entries than they are when they are giving speeches to the public. Oral histories are also very valuable and can be found at many local historical societies. A wonderful primary source, for example, would be the transcript (or audiotape) of a "common person" telling about the effects of the Great Depression on his or her family and community.
- **Visual documents.** Paintings and photographs can provide incredibly revealing details about any time period you may be studying. Recently, the photographs of people waiting for help after Hurricane Katrina told more about the suffering of New Orleans than a thousand-word article could have. In 1945, photographs from recently liberated Nazi concentration camps shocked the world. Newsreel and television footage of historical events can be invaluable.
- **Films.** Movies from any era can provide a fascinating window into the values and beliefs of that period. By watching a film from, for example, the 1980s, you can get an idea of how people talked, what they wore, and what they believed in that era. A 1967 movie, *Bonnie and Clyde*, glorified the lives of Bonnie Parker and Clyde Barrow, two small-time gangsters who continually flouted authority during the Great Depression. Although this film was about the 1930s, it perfectly reflected the disrespect for authority of many young people in the late 1960s.
- **Songs, recordings, etc.** Sources that one can listen to can also be valuable. As with films, songs are very valuable windows into the culture and values of a time period, whether it is "Fight the Power" by Public Enemy or "Masters of War" by Bob Dylan. Listening to speeches given by historical figures can also be a valuable historical tool.

Analyzing Primary Source Documents

It should be remembered that virtually every single primary source document contains some amount of bias. Memoirs written by many historical figures are generally self-serving and do not dwell on mistakes and problems from the writer's past. It is virtually impossible to write about anything without bias; therefore, it is critical to consider this when evaluating primary sources. A source in which an observer discusses the impact that Theodore Roosevelt had on people when he met them would be influenced by preexisting judgments and opinions the author already had about Theodore Roosevelt. As a result, it is necessary to use a number of primary sources when evaluating a historical figure, event, or era.

There are many methods that historians and students can utilize when studying primary source documents. When looking at a document, try to find some information about its producer. What was the relationship of the author to the person or event being described? Did the producer have preexisting biases toward the subject of the document? How far after the events being described was the document written? Another important question is the audience; the historian/student should identify the target group at which the document was aimed, and whether or not this might have influenced what was stated by the author.

Students wanting more specific information on analyzing primary source documents can turn to numerous resources, including the Learning Page of the Library of Congress (http://memory.loc.gov/ammem/index.html). In addition, an excellent analysis of the use of primary sources is available from the Wisconsin Historical Society (http://www.wisconsinhistory.org/turningpoints).

… STEP 4

Review the Knowledge You Need to Score High

CHAPTER 6 Settling of the Western Hemisphere (1491–1607)

CHAPTER 7 Colonial America (1607–1650)

CHAPTER 8 British Empire in America: Growth and Conflict (1650–1750)

CHAPTER 9 Resistance, Rebellion, and Revolution (1750–1775)

CHAPTER 10 American Revolution and the New Nation (1775–1787)

CHAPTER 11 Establishment of New Political Systems (1787–1800)

CHAPTER 12 Jeffersonian Revolution (1800–1820)

CHAPTER 13 Rise of Manufacturing and the Age of Jackson (1820–1845)

CHAPTER 14 Union Expanded and Challenged (1835–1860)

CHAPTER 15	Union Divided: The Civil War (1861–1865)
CHAPTER 16	Era of Reconstruction (1865–1877)
CHAPTER 17	Western Expansion and Its Impact on the American Character (1860–1895)
CHAPTER 18	America Transformed into the Industrial Giant of the World (1870–1910)
CHAPTER 19	Rise of American Imperialism (1890–1913)
CHAPTER 20	Progressive Era (1895–1914)
CHAPTER 21	United States and World War I (1914–1921)
CHAPTER 22	Beginning of Modern America: The 1920s
CHAPTER 23	Great Depression and the New Deal (1929–1939)
CHAPTER 24	World War II (1933–1945)
CHAPTER 25	Origins of the Cold War (1945–1960)
CHAPTER 26	Prosperity and Anxiety: The 1950s
CHAPTER 27	America in an Era of Turmoil (1960–1975)
CHAPTER 28	Decline and Rebirth (1968–1988)
CHAPTER 29	Prosperity and a New World Order (1988–2000)
CHAPTER 30	Threat of Terrorism, Increase of Presidential Power, and Economic Crisis (2001–2014)
CHAPTER 31	Contemporary America: Evaluating the "Big Themes"

CHAPTER 6

Settling of the Western Hemisphere (1491–1607)

IN THIS CHAPTER
Summary: There were several reasons why Europeans became interested in the Americas during this period. Economic and political factors were most important. The Spanish originally viewed the Americas as a barrier to a direct route to the Indies. However, soon they developed a large empire in South and Central America and viewed the region as a potential source of tremendous wealth. Some Native American tribes had developed complex civilizations in the years before the Europeans arrived. The ecosystem of the Americas was drastically altered by the arrival of the Europeans.

Key Concept
On the North American continent, contact among the peoples of Europe, the Americas, and West Africa created a new world.

Keyword
Columbian Exchange: exchange of crops, animals, diseases, and ideas between Europe and colonies of the Western Hemisphere that developed in the aftermath of the voyages of Columbus.

Native Americans

Native Americans Before European Exploration

The Spanish, the French, and the English all encountered well-established tribes of Native Americans when they began to settle in the Western Hemisphere. When the Spanish entered into the central and southern parts of the hemisphere they encountered several prosperous civilizations. The Aztecs developed a civilization centered at Tenochtitlan (near present day Mexico City). The Aztecs were a warrior people and ended up controlling most of central Mexico. The Incas established a highly developed farming civilization in present-day Ecuador, Peru, and Bolivia. By the mid-1500s the Incas had a massive empire that stretched along the Andes Mountains and the Pacific Ocean.

Native Americans of North America

A wide variety of Native American tribes existed east of the Mississippi River. The Hopewell culture developed in the Ohio River Valley and was centered on trade and later the growing of corn. Elaborate burial mounds were built by the Hopewell; it is believed that Hopewell leaders were buried in these mounds. Most other tribes of North America were not as complex as the Hopewell, the Aztecs, or the Incas; most tribes depending on fishing, hunting, or gathering. Tribes of the Far West and the Great Plains were primarily farmers; Native Americans east of the Mississippi were known as Woodland Indians and had the advantage of having excellent resources and crops to farm. Many of the tribes in this region were nomadic; as a result, permanent alliances between different tribes were rare. This would later make it more difficult for Native Americans to challenge the encroachment of European settlers. In time more and more of these tribes began to farm extensively, causing many to establish permanent settlements.

European Exploration of the Americas

There are several important reasons why Europeans were interested in the Americas during this period. Some historians emphasize that only limited economic growth appeared possible in Europe itself: many saw that additional natural resources were needed. European monarchs and entrepreneurs therefore had to look abroad for future profits. Europeans could now travel faster and farther because of better shipbuilding techniques and the perfection of the **astrolabe** and the compass. The **Crusades** had whetted the appetites of Europeans for the luxury goods provided by Asia, further encouraging exploration. In addition, the growth of nation-states (governed by kings) during this period increased the competition for both wealth and territory.

Explorations and Exploitations of Columbus

Europe in the 1400s was expanding: many individuals were migrating into European towns and cities. Europeans were also becoming interested in the world "outside." Prince Henry of Portugal sent expeditions to explore the coast of Africa. New shipbuilding techniques and navigational tools allowed ships to travel farther and safer with less chance of getting lost at sea.

Most students learned at least part of the story of Christopher Columbus when they were in elementary school. The goal of many explorers and other adventurers of the period was to get to the Indies and gain access to all of the riches that could be found there.

According to historical legend, Columbus was the first to ask the question, Why not sail west to get to the Indies? In reality, he was not the first to ask that question, but he was the first to go to the King of Portugal for funding for his voyage. After being turned down, Columbus went to King Ferdinand and Queen Isabella of Spain, who eventually agreed to fund his voyage.

Debate over Columbus

There is tremendous historical debate over the role of Columbus in history. The fact that he is considered a historical hero is incredibly problematic to many. After landing at San Salvador in the Bahamas, Columbus found gold on the island of Hispaniola that he carted back to Spain. He and his soldiers killed many natives and made slaves of thousands of others. Under the **encomienda** system natives were given over to Spanish colonists, who in exchange for their labor, promised to "protect" them. At the same time, Columbus and the explorers that followed him brought diseases that killed countless Native Americans.

It can also be argued that Columbus had a positive effect on world history. Because of the journeys of Columbus, Europeans of several countries began to look to expand outside of Europe for trade and exchange. European foods, animals, ideas, ideologies (as well as diseases) went from Europe to the Western Hemisphere; at the same time animals, plants, gold, and some local customs and ideas came to Europe from the Western Hemisphere; this is called the **Columbian Exchange.**

Spanish colonists found that sugarcane was a very profitable crop to grow as it could be easily sold in Europe for high prices. Harvesting sugarcane required a large number of workers; colonists soon found that there were not enough natives to do the job. As a result, beginning in the 1540s African slaves began to be imported into the region. In the 1500s nearly one million Africans were shipped to the Western Hemisphere. Slaves imported to the Americas would maintain, to the best of their abilities, some of their native cultural heritage.

Conquest of Mexico

In 1519, Hernando Cortes went from Cuba to challenge the Mayas. The Mayas were defeated by armored Spaniards on horseback (as you probably remember from elementary school, the Mayas had never seen horses and bolted in panic). The Aztecs, located in Mexico, initially attempted to appease Cortes and his men with gifts. Cortes was treated as a deity by Montezuma, the Aztec leader; within four days Montezuma was taken hostage by Cortes's soldiers and all of his wealth seized. By 1521, Cortes and his soldiers had completely destroyed the Aztec army and the capital city of Tenochtitlan. After this conquest, the Spanish further extended their economic domination of Mexico, Peru, Central America, and even parts of what is now the United States. The result of Spanish (and Portuguese) settlement in the Americas was the emergence of a racially mixed population, with a mixture of Spanish colonists, Africans, and Native Americans.

Chapter Review

Rapid Review

- Economic difficulties in Europe, the desire for geographic knowledge, the desire to acquire lands, riches, and raw materials, and the desire to spread Christianity all caused Europeans to become interested in the Americas.

- Cortes, Francisco Pizarro, and other Spanish conquistadors entered much of Central America, South America, the southeastern section of North America, and the area now known as Florida, conquering the Aztecs, the Incas, and other Native American tribes. Guns, horses, and diseases brought from Europe all aided the Spanish in their efforts to defeat the native tribes.
- The Columbian Exchange was the exchange of animals, plants, diseases, and ideas that took place between the Western Hemisphere and Europe as a result of initial Spanish and Portuguese exploration.

Time Line

2500 BCE: Migration of Asians to the Americas across the Bering Strait begins
1492: Voyage of Columbus to the Americas
1519: Cortes enters Mexico
1520–1530: Smallpox epidemic devastates Native American populations in many parts of South and Central America, virtually wiping out some tribes
1542: Spanish explorers travel through southwestern United States

Review Questions

1. Which of the following was *not* an initial result of interaction between Spanish explorers and Native Americans?
    A. Diseases that killed many of the Native Americans
    B. Domestication by Native Americans of animals brought by Spanish explorers
    C. Spread of Catholicism among Native Americans
    D. Plants from South and Central America being sent back to Europe

2. Slave labor was brought to the Western Hemisphere by colonists because
    A. the region was lightly populated when the Spanish arrived.
    B. Native Americans were unfamiliar with the tools and methods necessary to harvest sugarcane.
    C. Aztec and Inca leaders had already begun to import slaves even before Spanish explorers arrived.
    D. there was a lack of manpower to do the labor-intensive work of harvesting sugarcane.

3. North American Native American tribes
    A. displayed a uniformity of lifestyle
    B. modeled themselves after tribes from Central America and Mexico
    C. were greatly varied in lifestyle and economic systems
    D. formed alliances on numerous occasions to fight competing tribes

4. One factor *not* responsible for European expansion into the Western Hemisphere was
    A. desire for economic expansion
    B. desire to expand Christianity
    C. democratization of European society
    D. better shipbuilding and navigational tools

5. The very first Americans
    A. were nomadic wanderers
    B. lived in permanent sites
    C. were subsistence farmers
    D. predated Spain's arrival in the New World by only two centuries

> Answers and Explanations

1. **B.** It would take a long time before these animals were used by Native Americans; Native Americans were terrified of them and the Spanish explorers who rode on them.

2. **D.** Harvesting sugar took a massive amount of manpower. Since the Spanish had killed off a large number of native laborers and many more died from European diseases, slaves were needed.

3. **C.** There was a tremendous variety in the lifestyles and economic systems of Native Americans living in North America.

4. **C.** European expansion into the Western Hemisphere was supported and financed by European monarchs; no democratization of society or government was taking place at this time.

5. **A.** Almost all early Native American tribes were nomadic in nature.

CHAPTER 7

Colonial America (1607–1650)

IN THIS CHAPTER

Summary: The French settled in Canada and eventually turned to trapping and fur trading. Overcrowding in England and religious persecution were both factors in driving some Englishmen toward America. In the Jamestown colony indentured servants and the first slaves brought to the Americas made up a majority of the workforce. The Massachusetts Bay Colony was established in 1629 by the Puritans; Governor John Winthrop envisioned the colony as a "city upon a hill." Religious dissent led to the founding of several more New England colonies. The ecosystem of the Americas was drastically altered by the Europeans.

Keywords

Puritans: group of religious dissidents who came to the New World so they would have a location to establish a "purer" church than the one that existed in England.
Separatists: religious group that also opposed the Church of England; this group first went to Holland, and then some went on to the Americas.
Indentured servants: individuals who exchanged compulsory service for free passage to the American colonies.

The French in Canada

The French didn't have any permanent settlements in Canada until 1608, when Samuel de Champlain founded Quebec. Few colonists ever came to the French territory in Canada: the climate was considered undesirable, and the French government provided few incentives for them to leave France. In addition, the dissident **Huguenots** were legally forbidden from emigrating. It should be noted that over 65 percent of all those who did come to Quebec ended up returning to France.

The French also desired to convert Native Americans to Catholicism but used much less coercive tactics than the Spanish had in Central and South America. Samuel de Champlain actually entered into alliances with the Huron and other Native American tribes, largely for protection for his somewhat unstable settlement. The French joined with the Hurons and the Algonquins in a battle against the Iroquois tribe in 1608.

Those settlers who did stay in Quebec turned from farming to trapping and fur trading. French explorers ventured into the interior of North America to develop the fur-trading industry. Jesuit Jacques Marquette and fur trader Louis Joliet reached the Mississippi River, Wisconsin, and Arkansas; Robert La Salle continued to explore along the Mississippi River and named the territory Louisiana (after Louis XIV).

The impact of the French on Native Americans they came into contact with was profound. The diseases they brought wiped out an estimated 30 percent of all tribes they encountered. Many Native American tribes desired to dominate the fur trade desired by the French; this created a series of very bloody wars between these tribes. Jesuit priests were effective in converting thousands of Native Americans to Christianity. **Jesuits** were more successful than the Spanish **Franciscans** in converting natives, largely because natives were also asked to become forced laborers in Spanish territories. When the French fought the British and British colonists in the French and Indian wars in the late seventeenth and early eighteenth centuries, most Native American tribes sided with the French.

In short, the French territories were successful as a fur-trading enterprise and a place where natives were converted to Christianity; the territories were a failure in the sense that large numbers of settlers never took root there.

It should also be noted that during this period the Dutch made their initial entry into the Americas. The Dutch were largely interested in the commercial possibilities that the Americas offered them. In 1609, Henry Hudson discovered and named the Hudson River, and proceeded to establish trading settlements on the island of Manhattan, at Fort Nassau (soon renamed Albany), and in present-day Connecticut, New Jersey, and Pennsylvania. Like the French, the Dutch were unable to attract large numbers of settlers to Dutch territories, and were successful in fur trading. However, the aggression of the Dutch in expanding their territory brought them into bloody conflict with several Native American tribes, thus limiting the success of Dutch economic endeavors.

The English in the Americas

Several factors encouraged English entrepreneurs and settlers to come to America. After 1550, there was huge population growth in England, with high inflation and a decline in wages for many workers. The number of landless laborers increased dramatically; thousands entered London and other English cities. Many observers noted that England appeared to be dangerously overcrowded, and leaders became increasingly convinced that settlement in America could help relieve the population problem. Many English people became increasingly attracted to the possibility of resettlement in the Americas.

In addition, many English **Puritans** were increasingly disenchanted with the **Church of England**, feeling that the church was too close to Catholicism. Puritans, who followed the Protestant teaching of John Calvin, had enjoyed some measure of religious freedom under Elizabeth I. After her death in 1603, the position of Puritans in England became more difficult, with some Puritan clergymen removed from their pulpits. Thus, by the

1630s, many Puritans felt that by moving to the Americas they would be able to practice their religion without interference from either English civil or religious authorities. Another religious group opposed to the Church of England was the **Separatists**. After several of its leading spokespeople were arrested, this group fled to Holland; from here, a percentage of Separatists decided to go to the Americas.

Settlement in Jamestown

The first permanent English settlement in America was the Jamestown colony, founded in 1607 by Captain John Smith. King James I had granted the **London Company** a charter permitting them to establish this colony. The swampy site of the Jamestown colony encouraged disease; in addition, several years of poor harvests created severe food shortages. In addition, early conflict with the **Powhatan Confederacy** of Native Americans placed additional strains on the colony.

Because of a severe shortage of food, John Smith created a trade alliance with the Powhatans; the corn received from the Native Americans kept the colony alive. Pocahontas, the daughter of the Powhatan chief married one of the more influential men in the Jamestown colony, John Rolfe. This marriage helped to temporarily prevent further conflict with Native Americans. Rolfe's main contribution, however, was to begin the cultivation of tobacco in Jamestown. Rolfe's system of cultivation ensured that tobacco would become the main cash crop of Virginia; the demand for tobacco in England helped to ensure the economic success of the colony.

Large numbers of workers were needed in Virginia to harvest the tobacco crop. To meet this demand, **indentured servants** began to arrive in Virginia; many of these men were unemployed, ex-criminals, or both. As an additional measure to meet the demand for labor, the first African slaves arrived in Virginia in 1619, the same year that the first white women arrived there. It should be noted that the Virginia colony created the House of Burgesses in 1619; this was the first representative government in any British colony.

Settlement in Massachusetts

Colonization in New England was different. While economic gain was the major motivation for settlement in Virginia, many religious dissenters settled in New England, thus making religious zeal a primary factor in the colonization of that region.

A group of Separatists received a charter to settle southeast of the Hudson River. The purpose of this journey was to spread the "gospel"; these men saw their journey as a "pilgrimage," and thus became known as Pilgrims. This group, led by William Bradford, encountered a storm as they neared America and landed on Plymouth Rock in Massachusetts. Before landing, they produced the Mayflower Compact (1620), a document that promised that their settlement would have a government answerable to the will of the governed. As in the case of Plymouth, the first year of settlement proved to be very difficult, and the settlers were forced to rely on help from the Native Americans. However, after the first year, the Pilgrims had some amount of economic success; many of the diseases that ravaged the Virginia colony were absent in the colder New England. By 1691, this group joined with the other major settlement in the region, the Massachusetts Bay Colony.

The Massachusetts Bay Colony was established in 1629 by the Puritans. This colony was established as a location on earth where the will of God could be truly manifested; the colony was established as a commonwealth and was based on the Calvinist view of man's relation to God. By 1640, nearly 25,000 English people had migrated to Massachusetts Bay. Nearly half of these were fleeing bad economic times in England; the remainder were Puritans, who used the Bible as their religious and legal guide.

In 1629, John Winthrop was elected governor of the Massachusetts Bay Colony, a position he held for 20 years. Winthrop envisioned the colony as a "city upon a hill," away from the corrupting influences of England. Here, he felt, residents could freely live according to the precepts of God. Church, community, and political participation were all emphasized.

Massachusetts Bay did not have the devastating first several years experienced by other colonies. The colony came to be governed by a "General Court," which was an assembly elected by Puritan males in good standing. Thus, in both Virginia and Massachusetts, representative governments (albeit in a limited form) were established. Additional towns were chartered in the years following the initial arrival of the Puritans near Boston.

It should be noted that there were profound differences between the Virginia and Massachusetts Bay colonies. The slave labor of Virginia never existed in Massachusetts; while many families settled in Massachusetts, Virginia was mostly settled by single men. In Massachusetts, religion and political participation went hand in hand, while land ownership was a necessity for political participation in Virginia.

Development in Massachusetts Bay was steady, but leaders continued to emphasize that the main purpose of the colony was to be a place where God would be served. Religious dissent was simply not tolerated, obviously alienating some within the colony. As a result, four new colonies were created. Roger Williams believed that the Puritans in Massachusetts were still too close to the ways of the Church of England, and he preached on the necessity for the total separation of church and state. (This was obviously not practiced in Massachusetts Bay.) Williams was finally asked to leave Massachusetts, and he settled in Providence, Rhode Island. Thomas Hooker was another dissenter who was hounded out of the colony; he ended up settling near Hartford, Connecticut. Anne Hutchinson claimed to have received special revelations from God; as a result, she was invited to leave and founded Portsmouth near Narragansett Bay. Finally, John Davenport and other Puritans founded a colony in New Haven. In 1662, Hooker's colony combined with Davenport's to create the colony of Connecticut.

Maryland and the Carolinas

By 1640, the English kings began to create proprietary colonies, which were given to a single individual or groups of individuals and not to a stock company. Maryland was settled in 1632 by George Calvert and was designed as a refuge for English Catholics. North Carolina was very similar to Virginia, while planters in South Carolina used slaves from almost the very beginning. Plantation owners found both Native Americans and indentured servants to be good workers; their search for large numbers of workers inevitably made them turn to slavery as a possible solution.

The importation of slaves was to become crucial to the economies of several southern colonies in the seventeenth and eighteenth centuries. It is estimated that over 20 million Africans were brought to the Americas before slavery was outlawed. By the late 1600s, laws had been made in several southern colonies regulating the institution of slavery.

Effects of English, French, and British Settlement

Many effects, intended and otherwise, were created by European settlement in the Americas. Diseases and agricultural products introduced by Europeans dramatically changed the ecosystem of the Americas. As stated above, new crops introduced by the Europeans soon became the lifeblood of the economy in several southern colonies. Settlement fundamentally altered population patterns in Africa (with the loss of slaves) and in the Americas (with the loss of Native American populations). Settlements in the Americas gradually introduced representative government and freedom of religion when these concepts were not popular in much of Europe.

Chapter Review

Rapid Review

To achieve the perfect 5, you should be able to explain the following:
- French settlers in Canada were less oppressive than the Spanish. Jesuit priests converted thousands of Native Americans to Christianity. French settlers became increasingly interested in fur trading.
- Puritans and other religious dissidents came to the Americas because they felt the Church of England was too close to Catholicism.
- The first English settlement in America was the Jamestown colony, founded in 1607. Tobacco became the main crop in Jamestown, and the first slaves arrived in 1619.
- A group of religious Separatists arrived in Plymouth, Massachusetts, in 1620. The first year of settlement was difficult for these Pilgrims, who had to rely on help from the Native Americans to survive.
- The Massachusetts Bay Colony was established in 1629 by the Puritans. This colony was established as a "city upon a hill," where the will of God could be manifested. A limited representative government was established. Religious dissent was not tolerated in this colony: Dissenters were thrown out, and they founded new colonies in Rhode Island, Connecticut, and Portsmouth.
- The ecosystem of the Americas was tremendously altered by European settlement.

Time Line

1534–1535: French adventurers explore the St. Lawrence River
1607: The English settle in Jamestown
1619: Virginia establishes House of Burgesses (first colonial legislature)
1620: Plymouth colony founded
1629: Massachusetts Bay Colony founded
1634: Maryland colony founded
1636: Roger Williams expelled from Massachusetts Bay Colony and settles in Providence, Rhode Island; Connecticut founded by John Hooker
1642: City of Montreal founded by the French

Review Questions

1. Which colonists enjoyed the best relations with the Native Americans?
   A. The Spanish
   B. The French
   C. The Dutch
   D. The English

2. Who of the following was *not* a religious dissenter in Massachusetts Bay?
   A. William Bradford
   B. Roger Williams
   C. Anne Hutchinson
   D. Thomas Hooker

3. A colony designated as a refuge for English Catholics was
   A. Pennsylvania
   B. South Carolina
   C. Maryland
   D. Virginia

4. English people came to the New World because of
   A. their dislike for the Church of England
   B. overcrowding in English cities
   C. economic opportunity
   D. All of the above

5. Most early English colonies were different from those of Spain and France because they
   A. were not directly ruled by the crown
   B. granted rights to Indians
   C. were economic failures
   D. were more sparsely populated

Answers and Explanations

1. **B.** The French were mainly interested in fur trading rather than farming, and so posed less of a threat to Native American lands. French missionaries and fur traders were more respectful of Native American culture.

2. **A.** Bradford was a governor of Massachusetts Bay for 20 years; all of the others left for religious reasons and founded colonies elsewhere.

3. **C.** George Calvert settled this colony in 1632 for exactly that purpose.

4. **D.** The overcrowding of cities was an additional factor in convincing some English people to "try their lot" in the New World.

5. **A.** Most of the early English colonies were governed by companies or proprietors granted charters by the King.

CHAPTER 8

British Empire in America: Growth and Conflict (1650–1750)

IN THIS CHAPTER

Summary: The economic theory of mercantilism, which held that a state should be as economically self-sufficient as possible, helped to motivate England and other European powers to discover and develop colonies, as colonies could provide raw materials. The triangular trade system tied together the economies of Europe, the Americas, and Africa and brought slaves to the Americas. The Salem Witch Trials in Massachusetts were a result of social unrest existing in the Massachusetts colony. Wars between the European powers spilled over into the Americas during this period, with Native American tribes cultivated as allies by either the English or the French.

Keywords

Mercantilism: economic system practiced by European powers in the late seventeenth century stating that economic self-sufficiency was crucial; as a result, colonial empires were important for raw materials.
Navigation Acts (1660): acts passed by the British Parliament increasing the dependence of the colonies on the English for trade; these acts caused great resentment in the American colonies but were not strictly enforced.
Triangular trade system: complex trading system that developed in this era between Europe, Africa, and the colonies; Europeans purchased slaves in Africa and sold them to the colonies, raw materials from the colonies went to Europe, while European finished products were sold in the colonies.
Middle Passage: voyage taken by African slaves on horribly overcrowded ships from Africa to the Americas.

Salem Witch Trials (1692): trials in Salem, Massachusetts, after which 19 people were executed as witches; historians note the class nature of these trials.
Salutary neglect: early eighteenth-century British policy relaxing the strict enforcement of trade policies in the American colonies.

Impact of Mercantilism

The dominant economic philosophy of the period in Europe was **mercantilism**. This theory proclaimed that it was the duty of the government to strictly regulate a state's economy. Mercantilists believed that it was crucial for a state to export more than it imported, since the world's wealth was limited. The possession of colonies (so a nation wouldn't have to rely on other nations for raw materials), tariffs, and monopolies were other mercantilist tactics of the era. The American colonies were more than adequate from a mercantilist point of view, as they could provide crops such as tobacco and rice from the southern colonies and raw materials such as lumber from the colonies of the north.

Charles II came to the throne in England in 1660 and desired to increase British trade at the expense of its main trading rival, the Dutch. Charles influenced the British Parliament to pass the **Navigation Acts** of 1660 and 1663. These bills had great influence on colonial trade. They stated that certain products from the colonies such as sugar, tobacco, and indigo, could only be shipped to England, in an effort to help British merchants. The acts required that all goods going from anywhere in Europe to the American colonies must pass through England first.

Resistance to the Navigation Acts came from both the Dutch and the American colonies. Three commercial wars between the Dutch and the British took place in the late 1600s (with one result being the ending of the Dutch monopoly over the West African slave trade). In New England, many wanted to be able to continue to trade with the Dutch, who offered them better prices for their goods than the British did. Edmund Randolph, the chief British customs official in Massachusetts Bay, noted that colonial officials welcomed non-British traders, and he called upon the British government to "reduce Massachusetts to obedience." In 1684, a British court ruled that Massachusetts Bay Colony had intentionally violated the Navigation Acts (as well as restricted the Church of England). The charter of the colony was thus declared invalid, and the colony was placed under direct British control. The **Dominion of New England** was created that revoked the charters of all the colonies from New Jersey to Maine and placed immense powers in the hands of Sir Edmund Andros, the governor.

Similar feelings of resentment against the Navigation Acts developed in Virginia. The price of tobacco dropped sharply after 1663, with many landowners blaming Royal Governor Sir William Berkeley, who was thought to be profiting greatly from his position in Virginia. Some landowners joined in opposition to Berkeley under Nathaniel Bacon. In a dispute over policy toward Native Americans (specifically, how the government could protect farmers against Native American attacks) and how the colony would be governed, Bacon and his followers took control of the colony and burned the city of Jamestown. Some historians view this revolt as a rebellion of poor western farmers against the "eastern elite." The rebellion ended in October 1676 when Bacon and several of his followers died from dysentery. The results of Bacon's Rebellion were a limitation of the power of the royal governor by the Virginia gentry and an increase in the slave trade. (Some of Bacon's supporters were former indentured servants; the leaders of Virginia believed that African slaves would be much more docile.)

African Slavery in the Americas

For both political and economic reasons, African slavery became widely introduced in the Chesapeake colonies in the 1670s and 1680s. Cultivation of goods such as tobacco required a large number of workers, and by this point fewer and fewer English people were willing to come to Virginia as indentured servants. (With increased prosperity, more workers were remaining in England, while others viewed the economic possibilities of the Middle Colonies as more appealing.) The Portuguese and other European powers had engaged in slave trading as early as the 1440s, and African slaves had been imported to the Spanish possessions in the Americas. The first Africans entered Virginia as workers in 1619; few legal differences existed between white and black workers at that time. By 1662, servitude for blacks in Virginia was a legal fact, and it was stated that a child born to a mother who was a slave was also a slave.

The trading of slaves was a pivotal part of the **triangular trade system** that tied together the economies of North America, South America, the Caribbean, Africa, and Europe in the late seventeenth century. Under this system, finished products from Europe went to Africa and the Americas, while raw materials from various colonies went to Europe. The shipping of slaves from Africa to America became known as the **Middle Passage**, as it served as the foundation of the entire trading system.

Until the 1670s, the financial risk of owning African slaves was too much for most Virginia plantation owners, who still could be guaranteed a supply of British indentured labor. Yet, as that labor force eroded, the desire to own African slaves increased. This desire only expanded when the Dutch monopoly on slave trade ended in 1682, drastically reducing the price of slaves in British colonies. Many landowners in the region who could not afford slaves ended up moving westward.

The Middle Passage or journey of African slaves on European slave ships to the Americas is well documented. Disease and death were common on these ships for both the Africans kept chained under the decks and the European crews of the ships. It is estimated that almost 20 percent of all Africans who began the journey on these ships perished before reaching the Americas.

Until the 1730s, most slaves in the region worked on small farms with two or three other slaves and the plantation owner. Under these conditions, it was difficult to create a unique slave culture. However, slave cultures did slowly develop, combining elements of African, European, and local traditions. African religious traditions were sometimes combined with Christianity to create a unique religious culture. Slaves used various methods to demonstrate their hatred of the slave system that had been thrust upon them. Many owners reported examples of broken tools, stolen supplies, and imagined illnesses.

Slaves were used in other colonies as well. The most oppressive conditions for slaves existed in South Carolina, where they were used to harvest rice. Overwork and mosquito-borne epidemics caused thousands of slaves to die an early death there. Slavery also existed in several northern colonies, such as Connecticut as well.

Slave owners lived in fear of slave revolts, which occasionally did occur. The most famous slave uprising occurred near Charleston, South Carolina, in 1739 and was called the **Stono Rebellion**. Nearly 100 slaves took up arms and killed several plantation owners before they were killed or captured and executed. The effect of the rebellion was that slaves were treated more harshly than they had been before.

Continued Unrest in New England

The New England colonies chafed under the harsh and arbitrary rule of Sir Edmund Andros as governor. In 1688, they saw an opportunity to remove him. The **Glorious Revolution** in England removed James II from the throne and replaced him with William of Orange and Mary, who pledged their support to a parliamentary system. Andros was jailed in Massachusetts; colonists there wrote to the new monarchs pledging their loyalty to them and asking what form of government they should adopt. A Protestant revolt also took place in Catholic Maryland, while a revolt in New York put Jacob Leisler, a military officer, in charge.

The colonists soon discovered that William and Mary, like the Stuart monarchs that preceded them, believed in firm control by Britain over colonial affairs. They sanctioned the rebellion in Maryland because of its religious overtones but ordered Jacob Leisler hanged and again established Massachusetts as a royal colony with a governor appointed by the Crown. However, the authoritarian nature of the Dominion of New England ended, as representative political institutions at the local level were restored.

Salem Witch Trials

The Massachusetts colony underwent great economic and social change in the last half of the seventeenth century. Tensions developed between the Puritan ideals of small, tightly knit farming communities and the developing ideals of a colony based on trade and commerce, with less emphasis on strict Puritan beliefs. These tensions were largely responsible for the **Salem Witch Trials** of 1692.

Several women had been killed earlier in the century in Massachusetts for suspicion of witchcraft, but in 1692 a larger group of women was reported to display strange behavior. Observers testified many had strange fits and experienced "great distress." By the end of August, over 100 people were jailed for suspicion of witchcraft; 19 (18 of them women) had already been executed. The new royal governor of Massachusetts arrived and ended the trials, freeing those in prison. As stated previously, the trials demonstrated the social clashes existing in the colony; almost all of the accusers were members of the older farm communities, while the accused all were part of the newer "secular" class.

Wars in Europe and Their Impact on the Colonies

Beginning in 1689 and continuing through much of the eighteenth century, England and France fought a series of wars to see which of them would be the dominant power of Western Europe. Various other countries also became involved in these wars in Europe; predictably, English and French colonies would also become involved. Both England and France also used Native American tribes as allies during various campaigns in the American continent.

The War of the League of Augsburg (known in American textbooks as **King William's War**) lasted from 1689 to 1697. During this war, troops from New England fought with allies from the Iroquois tribe against French soldiers, who were allied with the Algonquins. The French destroyed the British settlement in Schenectady, New York, while troops made up largely of residents of Massachusetts captured Port Royal (in present-day Nova Scotia). The Treaty of Ryswick ended this war, reaffirming prewar colonial boundaries and allowing the French to maintain control over half of Santo Domingo (now Haiti).

The War of the Spanish Succession (called **Queen Anne's War** in American textbooks) took place between 1702 and 1713; in this war, Spain was also allied with France.

Anticipating an attack by the Spanish from Florida, the British attacked first from South Carolina, burning the settlement at St. Augustine and then arming many Native Americans who had fled the near-slavelike working conditions in the Spanish missions. These Indians attacked the missions, as well as the Spanish settlement at Pensacola. Native Americans allied with the French attacked English settlements in Maine. In 1704, the Iroquois, also allied with the French, attacked Deerfield, Massachusetts, killing 48 settlers there and taking 112 into captivity.

Neither side could conclusively claim victory in several other battles that were to follow, but victories in Europe allowed the British to make sizable gains in the Treaty of Utrecht. In this treaty, France had to give the British Newfoundland, Acadia (Nova Scotia), territory along the Hudson Bay, as well as more access to the Great Lakes region.

Growth of the Colonial Assemblies

After these wars, the British attempted to reform their control of the colonies in general, but failed. Many were royal colonies, with governors appointed by the Crown; other colonies such as Connecticut and Rhode Island elected their own governors and other local officials. Colonies such as the Carolinas, Maryland, and Pennsylvania were **proprietorships**, with residents who owned property-electing assemblies and governors appointed by the proprietors themselves.

One disturbing development during this period for the British was the rise in the independence of **colonial assemblies**. In the 1720s, the Massachusetts assembly resisted on three occasions instructions from the Crown to pay the royal governor a permanent salary; similar acts of resistance took place in other assemblies. These developments should not be seen as a move toward democracy in any way; assemblies were made up of members of the landowning elite in every colony. Nevertheless, popular opinion did begin to be expressed during New England town meetings and in political discussions throughout the colonies. Some colonial legislators perceived that the "power of the purse" could be a powerful tool against the British in the future.

Era of "Salutary Neglect"

British politics during the reigns of George I (1714–1727) and George II (1727–1760) helped to foster a desire for more self-government in the American colonies. During this period of "**salutary neglect**," British policies were most concerned with defending British territory at home and abroad and strengthening British economy and trade. Strict control of political affairs in the colonies was not a priority in this era. Many officials appointed to positions in the Americas during this era were appointed because of political connections and not because of political skill. British politics during this era weakened the British political hold in the Americas.

The British did impose policies in this era that increased their economic control over the American colonies. Under the terms of the Navigation Acts, all "finished products" owned by colonists had to be made in Great Britain. English officials passed additional regulations prohibiting the colonists from producing their own textiles (1699), hats (1732), and iron products (1750). However, the Navigation Acts allowed the colonies to own ships and to transport goods made in the colonies. Colonial ships carried on a lively trade with the French West Indies, importing sugar from there instead of from British colonies producing sugar in the Caribbean. In 1733, Parliament enacted the **Molasses Act**, which tightened British control over colonial trade. By 1750, Charles Townshend and others on the British Board of Trade were convinced that the colonies had far too much economic freedom, and they were determined to bring the era of salutary neglect to an end.

Great Awakening

A great religious revival, the **First Great Awakening**, swept through the American colonies from the 1720s through the 1740s. Ministers of the movement claimed that local ministers were not devoted enough to God and practiced "cold" preaching. Preachers such as Jonathan Edwards preached of the pitiful condition of man and the terrors of hell that most will confront when they die. Entire congregations were stirred to greater religious devotion; thousands turned up to hear Anglican George Whitefield as he toured the colonies in 1740. Some congregations also split over the message and the tactics of the "Awakeners."

The Great Awakening had several major effects on the colonies. Yale, Harvard, Brown, Dartmouth, Princeton, and Rutgers were all founded to train ministers during this period, yet preachers without college degrees preaching during the Great Awakening claimed to "know God" as well; several historians claim that the movement introduced a sense of social equality to the colonies. By challenging the existing religious establishment, the Great Awakening introduced a sense of social rebellion to colonial thought that became amplified in the ensuing years. In addition, some historians maintain that the debate and the questioning of religious authority that took place in the Great Awakening reinforced the idea that the questioning of political authority was also acceptable.

Chapter Review

Rapid Review

To achieve the perfect 5, you should be able to explain the following:

- The dominant economic theory of the era was mercantilism; British mercantilist measures such as the Navigation Acts created resentment in the American colonies.
- The importation of African slaves became increasingly important for the continued economic growth of several southern colonies.
- The Salem Witch Trials demonstrated the social conflict present in the American colonies.
- Eighteenth-century European wars between the British and the French spilled over into the Americas, with British and French colonies becoming involved.

- In the early eighteenth century, colonial assemblies became increasingly powerful and independent in several colonies, including Massachusetts.
- Even during the era of "salutary neglect," the British attempted to increase their economic control over the colonies.
- The religious revival called the Great Awakening caused some colonists to question many of the religious, social, and political foundations on which colonial life was based.

Time Line

1651: First of several Navigation Acts approved by British parliament
1676: Bacon's Rebellion takes place in Virginia
1682: Dutch monopoly on slave trade ends, greatly reducing the price of slaves coming to the Americas
1686: Creation of Dominion of New England
1688: Glorious Revolution in England; James II removed from the throne
1689: Beginning of the War of the League of Augsburg
1692: Witchcraft trials take place in Salem, Massachusetts
1702: Beginning of the War of the Spanish Succession
1733: Enactment of the Molasses Act
1739: Stono (slave) Rebellion in South Carolina
1740: George Whitefield tours the American colonies—the high point of the Great Awakening

› Review Questions

1. The creation of the Dominion of New England
   A. increased democracy in the colonies
   B. increased the power of the governor of the area
   C. allowed New England colonies to discuss common grievances
   D. guaranteed direct control of the king over affairs in the New England colonies

2. A major effect of the Stono Rebellion was
   A. an increase in the number of slaves brought into the Southern colonies
   B. increased fortifications around several southern cities
   C. an attempt by slave owners to lessen the horrors of the Middle Passage
   D. harsher treatment of slaves in many parts of the South

3. The growth of colonial assemblies alarmed the British for all of the following reasons *except*
   A. Assemblies holding the "power of the purse" could ultimately undermine British control.
   B. Assemblies increased democratic tendencies in the colonies.
   C. Assemblies occasionally ignored or resisted instructions from Great Britain.
   D. Governors appointed in Britain had little control over these assemblies in most colonies.

4. For the British, the major economic role of the American colonies was
   A. to produce manufactured goods the English did not want to produce
   B. to produce crops such as tobacco
   C. to produce raw materials such as lumber
   D. B and C above

5. What changes in the slave system of the southern colonies began in the 1730s?
   A. The Dutch lost the monopoly on slave trading, thus increasing the number of slaves being brought into the Americas.
   B. Conditions during the Middle Passage began to slightly improve.
   C. More slaves began to live and work on larger plantations.
   D. A series of slave rebellions created much harsher treatment for slaves.

› Answers and Explanations

1. **B.** This occurred after resistance in Massachusetts to the Navigation Acts, and it gave increased power to Sir Edmund Andros.

2. **D.** Many plantation owners were fearful of additional rebellions and felt that harsh treatment of slaves would prevent rebellious behavior.

3. **B.** These assemblies were in no way democratic, as in every colony they were dominated by the landowning elite.

4. **D.** The role of the colonies under mercantilism was to provide England with crops and raw materials.

5. **C.** Before the 1730s, most slaves worked on small farms. The Dutch lost their monopoly on slave trading back in 1682. The Stono Rebellion was the first major slave rebellion and occurred in 1739.

CHAPTER 9

Resistance, Rebellion, and Revolution (1750–1775)

IN THIS CHAPTER

Summary: Tensions between the British and the French intensified in the 1740s; a result of this tension was the Seven Years' War, in which colonial militias were involved. The French were defeated in this war, essentially ending their political influence on the Americas. During and after this war the British imposed a number of taxes and duties on their colonies, creating unrest. The Stamp Act created great resentment in the colonies. The results of this resentment included the Stamp Act Congress of 1765, the Boston Massacre of 1770, and the Boston Tea Party of 1773. The First Continental Congress met in 1774 and resolved that the colonies would resist efforts to tax them without their consent.

KEY IDEA

Keywords

French and Indian War (1756–1763): also known as the Seven Years' War, a conflict between the British and the French that also involved Native Americans and colonial militias. French defeat in this war greatly decreased their influence in the colonies.

Stamp Act (1765): imposed by the British, this act dictated that all legal documents in the colonies had to be issued on officially stamped paper. This act created strong resentment in the colonies and was later repealed.

Townshend Acts (1767): British legislation that forced colonies to pay duties on most goods coming from England; these duties were fiercely resisted and finally repealed in 1770.

Boston Massacre (1770): conflict between British soldiers and Boston civilians on March 5, 1770; five colonists were killed and six wounded.

Sons of Liberty: radical group that organized resistance against British policies in Boston in the 1760s and 1770s. This was the group that organized the Boston Tea Party.

Committees of Correspondence: created first in Massachusetts and then in other colonies, these groups circulated grievances against the British to towns within their colonies.

Boston Tea Party (1773): in response to British taxes on tea, Boston radicals disguised as Native Americans threw 350 chests of tea into Boston Harbor on December 16, 1773; important symbolic act of resistance to British economic control of the colonies.

First Continental Congress (1774): meeting in Philadelphia at which colonists vowed to resist further efforts to tax them without their consent.

Problems on the Frontier

An energetic traveler going west of the Appalachian Mountains in 1750 would discover a land inhabited by Native American tribes who had no desire to release their territory to colonial or European settlers. The Iroquois and other tribes of the region had traded and allied with both the English and the French, depending on who offered the best "deal" at the time.

Beginning in the 1740s, English and French interests in this region began to come into conflict. Land speculators from Virginia and other colonies began to acquire land in the Ohio Valley, and they tried to broker further treaties with Native Americans who resided there. French colonial officials viewed this with alarm, as their ultimate aim was to connect Canada and Louisiana with a series of forts and settlements through much of the same region.

In 1754, delegates from seven northern and middle colonies met at the **Albany Congress**, at which the colonies attempted to coordinate their policies concerning further westward settlement and concerning Native Americans. While the representatives couldn't agree on several main points, Governor Robert Dinwiddie of Virginia sent a young militia officer to attempt to stop the French construction of a fort at what is now the city of Pittsburgh. The young officer, George Washington, was defeated in battle there. Several Native American tribes, noting the incompetence of Washington and the colonial army, decided to cast their lot with the French. After hearing of this defeat in early 1756, the British sent a seasoned general, Edward Braddock, to stop the French construction of Fort Duquesne. Braddock's army was routed by the French, and he was killed in the battle. When London heard of this, war was officially declared against the French. This was the beginning of the Seven Years' War (called the **French and Indian War** in American textbooks).

Additional Conflicts Between the British and Their Colonial "Allies"

The war went very badly for the British and the colonial Americans in 1756 and 1757. Much of New York was captured by the French, and even the western New England territories appeared to be in jeopardy. Other than the Iroquois, most Native American tribes sided with the French. The British finally put the war in the hands of William Pitt, who sent nearly 25,000 troops to the Americas to fight against the French. The British had had little luck in convincing the colonies to supply many men or much material to the war effort. To get the support of the colonies, Pitt agreed to reimburse them for expenses during the war and put the recruiting of troops totally in local hands (Pitt's willingness to incur large debts for Great Britain to finance the war effort should be noted). As a result, a colonial army of nearly 24,000 joined with the British army to battle the French. The French stronghold at Quebec was defeated in 1759, and Montreal was taken one year later.

The Treaty of Paris, ending the French and Indian War effectively in 1763, also ended French influence in the Americas. Most French territory in the New World was given to the British, who now controlled over half of the continent of North America. France also gave Spain (its ally in the war) the Louisiana territory west of the Mississippi River.

The American colonists and the British both shared a sense of victory in 1763, yet resentments festered between the two. The colonists resented the patronizing attitude that the British had toward them; in addition, many British soldiers had been quartered in the homes of colonists without compensation. Many colonial soldiers viewed with horror the harsh punishments given to British soldiers for trivial infractions. The British felt that the colonists never did their fair share in the war; they also noted that some colonists continued to trade with the French during the first two years of the war.

Policies of George Grenville

George II died in 1760 and was succeeded by his grandson, George III. George III never exhibited even average political skills and was more than willing to give his ministers (whom he frequently replaced) a large amount of political power. In 1763, he selected George Grenville as prime minister.

Grenville faced a difficult financial task. Great Britain had great debt, largely because of the lengthy wars that had taken place both on the European continent and in the colonies. British citizens were already very heavily taxed. Grenville felt that one way to relieve the financial burden facing the Crown would be for the American colonists to pay a greater share for colonial administration. Grenville was convinced that Britain should be making more money than it was in the Americas; he was personally disturbed by the illegal trading carried out by colonists during the Seven Years' War.

Grenville took measures to "reform" the trading relationship between Britain and the Americas. The **Currency Act** of 1764 made it illegal to print paper money in the colonies. Because of the lack of hard currency in the colonies, the impact of this bill was significant. The **Sugar Act** of the same year conceded that the colonies were importing large amounts of French molasses, but it increased the penalties for colonial smuggling and ensured that colonists would pay the British a duty for all molasses brought into the colonies. In the years after the Seven Years' War, colonial economies were already suffering from depression; the Grenville Acts only served to make that depression worse.

Debate over the reforms of Grenville appeared in many colonial newspapers, with many editorials pondering the proper relationship between decisions made in Great Britain and the American colonies.

A Sense of Crisis: The Stamp Act

The act proposed by Grenville that created the greatest furor in the colonies was the **Stamp Act**. This act would require a purchased stamp on virtually all printed material purchased in the colonies: newspapers, wills, dice, official documents, and countless other written documents would require this stamp. This was controversial in the colonies because this was the first time that Parliament would directly tax the colonies; before this, all taxation was self-imposed. Grenville's purpose was twofold: the Stamp Act would raise needed revenue and would uphold "the right of Parliament to lay an internal tax upon the colonies."

For many colonists, the final straw was the **Quartering Act**, which insisted that colonial governments provide food and accommodations for British troops stationed in the colonies.

In several colonies, such as Massachusetts, reaction against the Stamp Act was swift. During July 1765, the **Sons of Liberty** was created in Boston, led by Samuel Adams. Demonstrations by this group forced the stamp agent in Massachusetts, Andrew Oliver, to resign. Similar outbursts in other colonies forced stamp agents to resign. Some politicians also began to speak in state assemblies against the act. Patrick Henry proclaimed in the Virginia Houses of Burgesses that the act demonstrated the tyranny of George III; several members of the assembly demanded that he be arrested for treason. James Otis from Massachusetts and Benjamin Franklin from Philadelphia both proposed that the colonists be directly represented in the British Parliament. In October 1765, nine colonies met together at the **Stamp Act Congress**, where representatives reaffirmed the principle that taxation of the colonies be imposed only from within the colonies.

Repeal of the Stamp Act

The uproar from the colonies may have helped the British Parliament to repeal the Stamp Act. However, the real pressure for repeal came from British merchants, who feared the act would destroy the profits they made by trading with the colonies. Economic boycotts were threatened in numerous colonies. Lord Rockingham, the new prime minister, urged repeal of the bill not for philosophical but for economic and political reasons. Celebration occurred in many colonies when news of the repeal came from Britain. These celebrations became muted when word arrived that Parliament had also passed a **Declaratory Act**, which stated that Parliament had the right to tax and pass legislation regarding the colonies "in all cases whatsoever."

More Protest: The Townshend Acts

In 1766, George III appointed the aging and infirm William Pitt as prime minister. Ill health made him unable to concentrate on his duties concerning the colonies. As a result, Charles Townshend, the **Chancellor of the Exchequer**, had a large hand in creating policy concerning the American colonies. Townshend decided to follow the policies of Grenville and try to extract more income for the government from colonial trade. In 1767, he proposed new duties on glass, paper, and tea. These **Townshend Acts** were different from previous duties on colonial trade; these were for goods produced in Britain. In addition, income from these acts would be used to pay the salaries of certain ranks of British officials in the colonies; colonial assemblies had always authorized these salaries. Townshend also created new courts in the colonies, the Admiralty courts, to try smuggling cases and ordered British soldiers to be stationed in major port cities (to hopefully prevent the protests that had followed the Stamp Act).

The opposition to the Townshend Acts in the colonies was immediate and sustained. Newspaper editorials and pamphlets renounced the acts with vehemence. John Dickinson from Pennsylvania best expressed the colonial position in his *Letters from a Farmer in Pennsylvania* (1767). Dickinson said that Parliament had the right to regulate colonial trade, but not to use that power to raise revenue. By this argument, only duties used to control trade or regulate the affairs of the empire were legal. Benjamin Franklin expressed a different view of the situation. Franklin stated that "Either Parliament has the power to make all laws for us, or Parliament has the power to make no laws for us; and I think the arguments for the latter are more numerous and weighty than those of the former."

In early 1768, Samuel Adams in Massachusetts composed a document opposing the Townshend Acts, proclaiming that "taxation without representation is tyranny." The Massachusetts Assembly voted to approve this document and send it along to other colonial assemblies for approval. The royal governor stated that this **Circular Letter** was a form of sedition, and Parliament suggested abolishing the assemblies that had approved it. Yet, similar resolutions were passed in five other colonies. Boycotting of British goods took place again to protest the Townshend Acts. In 1770, a new prime minister came to power in Britain, Lord North. North repealed all the Townshend Acts except the tax on tea; the tea tax remained to remind the colonists that the British had the right to collect such taxes if they desired to.

Continued Tension in Massachusetts

British customs officials and merchants in Massachusetts continued to clash over the smuggling of goods into Boston Harbor. In 1768, officials seized a vessel belonging to a well-known smuggler, John Hancock; several days later, several customs officials were roughed up. As a result, two regiments of regular British soldiers were assigned to the city. Tension increased notably in Boston; many local workers became incensed when, in their off-duty hours, British soldiers took up jobs that had previously been held by Bostonians. Soldiers were taunted on a regular basis. On March 5, 1770, the event that became known as the **Boston Massacre** took place. A confrontation occurred, with laborers throwing snowballs filled with rocks at the soldiers. The soldiers, acting against orders, finally shot into the crowd, killing five men and wounding eight. Sam Adams and others made much of the "massacre," yet members of the Sons of Liberty opposed uncontrolled violence. Seven soldiers were later put on trial for the "massacre"; five were acquitted, and two were branded on their thumbs and then freed.

Calm Before the Storm: 1770–1773

There was an apparent calm in relations between the British and the colonies between 1770 and 1773. Import duties were collected on a regular basis. The tea tax was still in effect; some colonists boycotted British tea, but some drank it openly. Resistance again occurred first in Massachusetts. Samuel Adams established a **Committee of Correspondence** in Boston. Similar groups were created throughout Massachusetts, Virginia, and other colonies as well. These groups were designed to share information on British activities in the Americas, as well as to share details of demonstrations, protests, and so on. Some historians argue that these committees were the first permanent machinery of protest in the colonies.

Boston Tea Party

The Boston Tea Party occurred because of an effort by the British government to save the near-bankrupt East India Tea Company. American boycotts and smuggled Dutch tea had hurt this company; they asked the government for permission to sell their tea directly to the American colonies without going through English merchants as middlemen. The old tax on tea would remain, but tea would now be cheaper to purchase by the colonists. Lord North and Parliament approved the passage of the **Tea Act** that would legalize these changes.

Colonial leaders were furious. Some pointed out that this measure reaffirmed that Parliament could tax the colonies; others feared a monopoly of the East India Company on all colonial trade. In the fall of 1773, crowds prevented tea from being unloaded in several port cities. Predictably, Boston was the city where resistance was the strongest. On December 16, 1773, in an event called the **Boston Tea Party**, 65 men dressed as Mohawk Indians boarded the tea ships and dumped nearly 350 chests of tea into the harbor.

Intolerable Acts

The British were extremely quick to act in punishing the colonists. The **Intolerable Acts** all took effect by May 1774. The port of Boston was closed except for military ships and ships specifically permitted by British customs officials. The upper house of the Massachusetts Assembly would now be appointed by the king instead of being elected by the lower house. Town meetings could not be held without the governor's consent, and the Quartering Act was again put into effect. Many concerned citizens in other colonies feared that similar actions could easily occur elsewhere. As a result, several colonial legislatures suggested a meeting of representatives from all the colonies to discuss the situation in Massachusetts. The passage of the Quebec Act by the British further alarmed many colonial leaders. Among other things, this act increased the religious freedom of French Catholics. To many Protestants in the colonies, Catholicism was easily equated with the absolutist French monarchy of the eighteenth century.

First Continental Congress

Fifty-six delegates from every colony except Georgia attended the Continental Congress in Philadelphia on September 5, 1774. Some of those present, such as Sam Adams, pushed for a total boycott of British goods; others proposed further negotiations with Parliament. John Adams worked out a compromise entitled the **Declaration of Rights and Grievances**, which stated that the colonists would not object to measures designed to regulate their external commerce. The colonies would, however, resist any measures that taxed them without their consent. The mood of the meeting was even clearer when the **Suffolk Resolves** were adopted. This act stated that colonies would continue to boycott English imports and approve the efforts of Massachusetts to operate a colonial government free from British control until the Intolerable Acts were rescinded. Colonies were also urged to raise and train militias of their own.

Before they adjourned, the Continental Congress sent a petition to George III requesting the repeal of all regulatory acts since 1763 and informing him of the continued boycott of British goods. Colonial leaders returned home, wondering what the response of George III would be to their petition.

Chapter Review

Rapid Review

To achieve the perfect 5, you should be able to explain the following:

- Tensions between the British and the French intensified in the 1740s when land speculators from English colonies began to acquire land in the Ohio Valley.
- The Seven Years' War (the French and Indian War in American textbooks) was between the English and colonial militias and the French; Native Americans fought on both sides.
- The defeat of the French in this war largely ended their influence in the Americas; after the war, the British attempted to make the colonies pay their fair share for the war effort.
- Parliamentary efforts during this era to produce money for Great Britain by imposing various taxes and duties on the colonies resulted in great unrest in the colonies.
- The impact of the Stamp Act on the colonies was great; as a result, nine colonies met at the 1765 Stamp Act Congress and the Sons of Liberty formed in Boston.
- Boston remained a center of opposition to British policy; the Boston Massacre in 1770 and the Boston Tea Party in 1773 helped to create resistance to the Crown in other colonies as well.
- The 1774 Intolerable Acts that closed the port of Boston and curtailed freedom of speech in Massachusetts outraged many in the colonies.
- The 1774 First Continental Congress passed a resolution that firmly stated the colonies would firmly resist measures that taxed them without their consent. At this meeting it was also decided that individual colonies should start to raise and train state militias.

Time Line

1754: Representatives of colonies meet at Albany Congress to coordinate further Western settlement
1756: Beginning of Seven Years' War
1763: Signing of Treaty of Paris ending Seven Years' War
1764: Parliament approves Sugar Act, Currency Act
1765: Stamp Act approved by Parliament; Stamp Act Congress occurs and Sons of Liberty is formed, both in opposition to the Stamp Act
1766: Stamp Act repealed, but in Declaratory Act, Parliament affirms its right to tax the colonies
1767: Passage of the Townshend Acts
1770: Boston Massacre occurs
1773: Boston Tea Party takes place in December in opposition to the Tea Act
1774: Intolerable Acts adopted by Parliament
First Continental Congress held in Philadelphia

Review Questions

1. William Pitt was able to convince the colonies to fight in the Seven Years' War by
   A. threatening military reprisals by the British army
   B. threatening to make the colonists fight the French by themselves
   C. putting the recruiting of troops in the colonies totally in the hands of the colonies themselves
   D. paying colonial soldiers generous bonuses to fight against the French

2. The Stamp Act created great fury in the colonies because
   A. it imposed massive duties on the colonies
   B. it was the first time Parliament had imposed a duty on the colonies
   C. it took badly needed revenue away from colonial legislatures
   D. this was the first time that Parliament imposed a direct tax on the colonies

3. The statement "taxation without representation is tyranny" was first proclaimed by
   A. Benjamin Franklin
   B. John Hancock
   C. Samuel Adams
   D. Patrick Henry

4. After the Seven Years' War, resentment between the British and the colonists existed for all of the following reasons *except*
   A. The British resented the fact that few colonists had actually helped them in the war against the French.
   B. British soldiers had been quartered in colonial homes.
   C. The British resented the fact that some colonists continued to trade with the French at the beginning of the war.
   D. Colonial militiamen felt the British exhibited a patronizing attitude toward them.

5. Most delegates at the First Continental Congress of 1774
   A. felt that there should be a total boycott of British goods by the colonies
   B. felt that the colonies should firmly resist measures to tax them without their consent
   C. felt that it was time to seriously consider military measures against the British
   D. wanted the British to totally refrain from regulating trade to the colonies

Answers and Explanations

1. **C.** Pitt put the recruiting of colonial troops totally in local hands and agreed to reimburse the colonies for all their expenses during the war.

2. **D.** All previous taxation of the colonies had been self-imposed.

3. **C.** This statement was first made by Adams in 1768 in an article he wrote opposing the Townshend Acts.

4. **A.** The colonies contributed nearly 24,000 men to the war effort—while the British contributed 25,000.

5. **B.** Although some, including Sam Adams, wanted a boycott of all British goods, John Adams crafted a compromise that called for the colonies to oppose "taxation without representation."

CHAPTER 10

American Revolution and the New Nation (1775–1787)

IN THIS CHAPTER

Summary: The Second Continental Congress, meeting in May 1775, began to prepare the American colonies for war. The impact of *Common Sense* by Thomas Paine and other documents continued to fan anti-British sentiment in the colonies, although there were still a number of Loyalists who supported British policies. As commander of the colonial army, George Washington practiced a defensive strategy, which, along with invaluable assistance from the French, helped to defeat the British army. The first government of the new nation was established by the Articles of Confederation, which created a weak national government.

Keywords
Second Continental Congress (May 1775): meeting that authorized the creation of a Continental army; many delegates still hoped that conflict could be avoided with the British.
***Common Sense* (1776):** pamphlet written by Thomas Paine attacking the system of government by monarchy; this document was very influential throughout the colonies.
Battle of Yorktown (1781): defeat of the British in Virginia, ending their hopes of winning the Revolutionary War.
Treaty of Paris (1783): treaty ending the Revolutionary War; by this treaty Great Britain recognized American independence and gave Americans the territory between the Appalachian Mountains and the Mississippi River.
Articles of Confederation (ratified 1781): document establishing the first government of the United States; the federal government was given limited power and the states much power.

Northwest Ordinances (1784, 1785, 1787): bills authorizing the sale of lands in the Northwest Territory to raise money for the federal government; bills also laid out procedures for these territories to eventually attain statehood.

American Revolution

Prelude to the Revolution: Lexington and Concord: April 1775

Events in the colonies had little effect on attitudes in Britain. Both George III and Lord North still insisted that the colonies comply with edicts from England. What they failed to realize was that royal authority in the colonies was routinely being ignored. British General Thomas Gage was the acting governor of Massachusetts, and in early 1775 he ordered the Massachusetts assembly not to meet. They met anyway.

Gage also wanted to stop the growth of local militias. On April 19, he sent a group of regular British troops to Concord to seize colonial arms stored there and to arrest any "rebel" leaders who could be found. As you learned in second grade, Paul Revere and other messengers rode out from Boston to warn the countryside of the advance of the British soldiers. At dawn on April 19, several hundred British soldiers ran into 75 colonial militiamen on the town green in **Lexington**. The British ordered the colonists to disperse; in the confusion, shots rang out, with eight colonists killed and ten wounded.

The British marched on to **Concord**, where a larger contingent of militiamen awaited them. The British destroyed military stores and food supplies and were ready to return to Boston when the colonists opened fire, with three British soldiers killed and nine wounded. The British were attacked as they retreated to Lexington; they lost 275 men, compared to the 93 colonial militiamen killed. At Lexington, the British were saved by the arrival of reinforcements.

Several weeks later, Ethan Allen and his Green Mountain Boys captured Fort Ticonderoga from the British. Cannons from the fort were dragged to Boston, where they would be a decisive factor in forcing the British to leave Boston Harbor in March 1776.

Second Continental Congress

The purpose of the **Second Continental Congress**, which met in Philadelphia in May 1775, was clear: to get the American colonies ready for war. It authorized the printing of paper money to buy supplies for the war, established a committee to supervise foreign relations with other countries, and created a Continental army. George Washington was appointed commander in chief of this new army. Washington was chosen because of his temperament, because of his experiences in the Seven Years' War, and because he was *not* from Massachusetts, considered by George III to be the place where the "rabble" were.

The Congress made one final gesture for peace when moderates drafted, and the Congress approved, the sending of the "Olive Branch Petition" to George III. This document, approved on July 5, 1775, asked the king to formulate a "happy and permanent reconciliation." The fact that the king refused to even receive the document strengthened the hand of political radicals throughout the colonies.

Impact of *Common Sense*

The impact of Thomas Paine's ***Common Sense*** on colonial thought was immense. Paine was a printer and had only been in the colonies for two years when his pamphlet was published in January 1776. Virtually every educated person in the colonies read this document: 120,000 copies were sold within three months. Paine proclaimed that "monarchy and hereditary succession have laid the world in blood and ashes" and called George III a "royal brute." Paine attacked the entire system of monarchy and empire, expressing confidence that the colonies would flourish once they were removed from British control. Many saw in Paine's document very sensible reasons why the Americas should break from Britain. When discussing the document, one New York **Loyalist** bitterly complained that "the unthinking multitude are mad for it. . . ."

Declaration of Independence

On June 7, 1776, Henry Lee of Virginia made a motion at the meeting of the Second Continental Congress in Philadelphia. His motion proposed that American colonies be considered independent states, that diplomatic relations begin with other countries, and that a confederate form of government be prepared for future discussion by the colonies. It was decided that the motion would be voted on July 1 (giving delegates time to win the resistant middle colonies over). In the meantime, one committee worked on a potential constitution, while another was appointed to write the declaration of independence. This committee gave the job of writing the first draft to Thomas Jefferson. Jefferson was a perfect choice. He was a student of the thinkers of the **Enlightenment** and other thinkers of the era.

Jefferson's argument maintained that men had certain "unalienable rights" that included "Life, Liberty, and the pursuit of Happiness." Jefferson stated that when a government "becomes destructive of these ends" those who live under it can revolt against it and create a government that gets its "just powers from the consent of the governed." Jefferson also listed many things the British had done that were oppressive to the colonies. Unlike others who had criticized certain ministers or Parliament, Jefferson personally blamed George III for many of these misdeeds. This document was formally approved on July 2, 1776; this approval was formally announced on July 4.

Outbreak of the Revolution: Divisions in the Colonies

The celebrations surrounding the announcement of the Declaration of Independence took place in every colony, but not every citizen living in the Americas took part. Many Loyalists were members of the colonial economic elite and feared the repercussions on their pocketbooks of a break with Great Britain. Other Loyalists saw the legitimacy of Britain's control over the colonies; some Loyalists were also very practical men, who predicted the easy defeat of the colonies by the seemingly immense British army.

Blacks in America greeted the Declaration of Independence with enthusiasm. Many free blacks saw the possible revolution as a chance to improve their position; slaves saw the possibilities of freedom from slavery. (During the war, some slaves managed to escape their masters, and a few even fought on the side of the British.) During the fighting, British troops freed slaves in Georgia and South Carolina. In the North, some slaves fought in colonial militias, winning their freedom through military service. The British courted Native American tribes, but their determination to definitively help the British in battle was never strong.

Strategies of the American Revolution

It is easy to see how the British thought that they would be able to defeat the colonists quickly and decisively. Britain had a strong navy, one of the finest armies of Europe, and considerable support from approximately 150,000 Loyalists in the colonies. In addition, in the first years of the war, the Continental army suffered from poor discipline, frequent desertions, lack of supplies and money, and a virtually nonexistent navy. However, an obviously long supply line (four to six weeks by ship) divided British policies in London, and an army used to fighting the more "formal" European type of war would end up hindering British efforts. The leadership of George Washington, the willingness to use defensive tactics and only attack when needed, and the fact that they were fighting on home territory, all helped aid the colonial military efforts. Washington felt that a lengthy war would assist the colonists, since they were fighting on home ground.

In June 1775, a bloody battle had taken place at **Bunker Hill** in Boston. The colonists were defeated, but at the expense of nearly 1,000 British dead or wounded.

Washington as Commander

The British approach under General William Howe was to slowly move his army through the colonies, using the superior numbers of the British army to wear the colonists down. However, from the beginning things did not go as planned for the British. In March 1776, the British were forced to evacuate Boston. The British then went to New York, which they wanted to turn into one of their major military headquarters. (A large number of Loyalists lived there.) Washington and his troops attempted to dislodge the British from New York in late August 1776; Washington's army was routed and chased back into Pennsylvania.

During November and December 1776, Washington's army faced daily desertions and poor morale. On Christmas night, Washington boldly led the Battle of Trenton against the **Hessian** allies of the British, defeating them. On January 3, Washington defeated a small British regiment at Princeton. These victories bolstered the morale of the Colonial army greatly.

Another tremendous advantage for the colonists was the arms shipments from the French that they began receiving in late 1776. French aid for the colonies did not come from any great trust that developed between the two sides; for over a century, France and Britain had been bitter rivals, and the French saw the American Revolution as another situation that they could exploit for their gain against the British. Massive British naval superiority in the Americas was at least partially counterbalanced by the entry of the French navy into the war.

"British Blunder" of 1777

The British decided on a strategy to strike a decisive blow against the colonists in 1777. Three separate British armies were to converge on Albany, New York, and cut off New England from the rest of the colonies. The British effort is called a blunder because of the poor execution of military plans that might have been effective. An army led by General

Howe headed toward Philadelphia when, for obvious strategic reasons, it should have been heading toward Albany. Howe was intent on taking on Washington's army in Philadelphia and decisively defeating it. The army under "Gentleman Johnny" Burgoyne carried too much heavy equipment, which could be carried in preparation for European battles but not through the forests of North America. On October 17, 1777, Burgoyne was forced to surrender at Saratoga. Some military historians claim this defeat was the beginning of the end for the British. The colonial victory convinced the French to send troops to aid the war effort.

Women became increasingly important to the war effort of the colonies. Women were prominent in the boycott of British goods, provided support services for the Continental army, spied on British troops, and ran numerous households when the "man of the house" was off fighting the British. In a March 1776 letter to her husband John, Abigail Adams reminded him to "Remember the Ladies. . . . Do not put such unlimited power in the hands of the Husbands."

War Moves to the South

After their defeat at Saratoga, the British abandoned their strategy of fighting in New York and New England and decided to concentrate their efforts in the Southern colonies, where they imagined more Loyalists to live. Despite their victory at Saratoga, the winter of 1777–1778 was the low point for the Continental army. The British camped for the winter in Philadelphia, while Washington's army stayed at **Valley Forge**. Cold weather, malnutrition, and desertion severely hurt the army. Morale improved when daily drilling began under the leadership of Baron von Steuben, a Prussian who had volunteered to help the colonists. As a result, the Continental army that emerged in the spring was a much tougher and more disciplined unit.

Nevertheless, initially the British southern strategy was successful. By the summer of 1780, the British captured Georgia and South Carolina. Desertions continued, and General Benedict Arnold went over to the British side.

Things soon turned against the British. A Virginia army under George Rogers Clark defeated a British force and their Native American allies at Vincennes, Indiana, securing the Ohio River region for the colonies. By the summer of 1781, French army forces joined the Continental army as two regiments marched from New York to Virginia. The British southern campaign, now headed by General Cornwallis, was constantly hampered by attacks of bands of "unofficial" colonial soldiers, led by Francis Marion and other rebel leaders.

Cornwallis decided to abandon the southern strategy and went into Virginia, where he was ordered to take up a defensive position at **Yorktown**. Once the British troops began to dig in, they were cut off by a combination of French and continental forces. Cornwallis hoped to escape by sea, but ships of the French navy occupied Chesapeake Bay. For three weeks, Cornwallis tried to break the siege; on October 17, 1781, he finally surrendered. Fighting continued in some areas, but on March 4, 1782, Parliament voted to end the British military efforts in the former colonies.

Treaty of Paris

British, French, Spanish (also allies with the colonists in the war), and American diplomats gathered in Paris in 1783 to make the treaty ending the war. The British and French diplomats were initially not impressed with the diplomatic efforts of the Americans, but soon the American team of John Jay, Benjamin Franklin, and John Adams demonstrated shrewd diplomatic skills. The Americans negotiated separately with the British, and on September 3, 1783, the Treaty of Paris was signed. (Please note that this is a different Treaty of Paris from the one ending the French and Indian War.) By this treaty, Great Britain formally recognized American independence. Britain held on to Canada, but all of the territory they had received from France after the French and Indian War (territory between the Appalachian Mountains and the Mississippi River) was given over to the Americans. The American diplomats also negotiated for fishing rights off the coasts of Newfoundland and Nova Scotia. The British insisted on, and received, promises that British merchants would be free to recover prewar debts and that Loyalists would be treated as equal citizens and would be able to recover property seized from them during the war. (As might be expected, many Loyalists were leaving the Americas during this period.)

Establishment of Governmental Structures in the New Nation

Drafting of State Constitutions

By the end of 1777, 10 new state constitutions had been written. Written into these constitutions were safeguards to prevent the evils that Americans had seen in the colonial governments established by the British. The governor was the most oppressive figure in many colonies; as a result, many new constitutions gave limited power to the governor, who was usually elected by the state assembly. All states except Pennsylvania and Vermont adopted **bicameral legislatures**, with more power usually given to the upper house. Most states also lowered the property qualifications for voting, thus allowing people who had not voted before the Revolutionary War to vote. Many historians comment that writers of these constitutions were making a conscious attempt to broaden the base of American government. Most state constitutions also included some form of a bill of rights.

Articles of Confederation

In the fall of 1777, the Continental Congress sent a proposed constitution out to the individual states for ratification. This document, called the **Articles of Confederation**, intentionally created a very weak national government.

The main organ of government was a **unicameral legislature**, in which each state would have one vote. Executive authority was given to a Committee of Thirteen, with one representative from each state. For both amendment and ratification, the unanimous consent of all 13 state legislatures was required.

The national government was given the power to conduct foreign relations, mediate disputes between states, and borrow money. The weakness of the national government was shown by the fact that it could not levy taxes, regulate commerce, or raise an army.

Because of disputes over land claims in the West, all 13 states didn't ratify the Articles of Confederation until 1781.

Economic Distress

Financial problems plagued the new nation in the years immediately after the war. Many merchants had overextended themselves by importing foreign goods after the war. Large numbers of Revolutionary War veterans had never been paid for their service. The national government had large war debts. By the terms of the Articles of Confederation, the national government could not tax, so the national government began to print a large amount of paper money. These bills, called "**Continentals**," were soon made worthless by inflation. Proposals for the national government to impose import tariffs came three times, and all three times they were defeated. Loans from foreign countries, especially France, propped up the national government during this period.

Northwest Ordinances

The sale of lands in the West was one way that the national government *could* make money, and westward settlement was encouraged. By 1790, nearly 110,000 settlers were living in Kentucky and Tennessee, despite the threat of Native American attack. The **Northwest Ordinances** of 1784, 1785, and 1787 regulated the sale of lands in the Northwest Territory and established a plan to give these settled territories statehood. The 1784 Ordinance provided governmental structures for the territories and a system by which a territory could become a state. The Ordinance of 1785 spelled out the terms for the orderly sale of land in the Northwest Territory. The Ordinance of 1787 stated that any territory with 60,000 white males could apply for statehood, provided a bill of rights for settlers, and prohibited slavery north of the Ohio River. Controversy over whether slavery should be allowed in these territories was a foreshadowing of the bitter conflicts that would follow on the issue of slavery in newly acquired American territories.

Shays's Rebellion

Like farmers in other parts of the colonies, farmers in western Massachusetts were in desperate shape in the years after the Revolution. Many owed large amounts to creditors, inflation further weakened their economic position, and in 1786 the Massachusetts Assembly raised the taxes. Farmers took up arms, closing government buildings and freeing farmers from debtor's prisons. This rebellion was called Shays's Rebellion, after one of its leaders, war veteran Daniel Shays. The rebellion spread throughout Massachusetts and began to gain supporters in other New England states. The rebellion was put down by an army paid for by citizens of Boston and by lowering the taxes. To many, Shays's Rebellion demonstrated that stronger state and national governments were needed to maintain order.

Chapter Review

Rapid Review

To achieve the perfect 5, you should be able to explain the following:

- The first armed resistance to the British army occurred at Lexington and Concord.
- The Second Continental Congress began to prepare the American colonies for war against the British, but by passing the Olive Branch Petition, they tried to accommodate colonial interests with those of the Crown.
- The impact of the message presented in *Common Sense* by Thomas Paine was widespread throughout the colonies.
- Many Loyalists lived in the colonies at the outbreak of the Revolutionary War; many were members of the economic elite.
- Blacks and women played large roles in the war effort of the colonies.
- The defensive tactics of George Washington as leader of the Continental forces proved decisive, since a longer war was disadvantageous to the British army.
- French assistance to the Continental war effort proved invaluable; the French navy proved to be especially critical as the war progressed.
- The Treaty of Paris ended the Revolutionary War. In this treaty, American independence was recognized by the British and large amounts of territory west of the Appalachians became American territory.
- The Articles of Confederation created a weak national government, partially to avoid replicating the "tyranny" of the Crown in England.
- To many colonial observers, Shays's Rebellion demonstrated that a stronger national government was needed.

Time Line

1775: Battles of Lexington and Concord
Meeting of Second Continental Congress
1776: *Common Sense* published by Thomas Paine
Declaration of Independence approved
Surrender of British forces of General Burgoyne at Saratoga
1777: State constitutions written in 10 former colonies
1777–1778: Continental army encamped for the winter at Valley Forge
French begin to assist American war efforts
1781: Cornwallis surrenders at Yorktown
Articles of Confederation ratified
1783: Signing of the Treaty of Paris
1786–1787: Shays's Rebellion in Massachusetts
1787: Northwest Ordinance establishes regulations for settlement of territories west of the Appalachian Mountains

Review Questions

1. The purpose of the Olive Branch Petition was to
   A. rally colonial support for war against Great Britain
   B. petition the king for redress of economic grievances suffered by the colonies
   C. ask the king to craft a solution to end the tensions between Great Britain and the colonies
   D. ask the king to grant independence to the colonies

2. At the beginning of the Revolutionary War, the British were extremely confident of victory because all of the following reasons *except*
   A. They had outstanding generals that would be commanding British forces in the Americas.
   B. There were many Loyalists throughout the American colonies.
   C. The Continental army suffered from poor discipline.
   D. The British had an outstanding navy.

3. All of the following were contained in the Treaty of Paris of 1783 *except*
   A. Territory west of the Appalachian Mountains was ceded to the Americans.
   B. American independence was recognized by Great Britain.
   C. Quebec and the area immediately surrounding it was ceded to the Americans.
   D. Former Loyalists in the colonies could retrieve property seized from them during the Revolutionary War.

4. Women were important in the war effort because they
   A. provided much of the financial backing for the colonial cause
   B. wrote influential articles in colonial newspapers urging the colonies to resist the British
   C. provided clothing and blankets for the frozen troops at Valley Forge
   D. maintained economic stability in the colonies by managing households across the colonies while men were off fighting the British

5. The weakness of the national government created by the Articles of Confederation was demonstrated by the fact that it was *not given the power to*
   A. mediate disputes between states
   B. raise an army
   C. conduct foreign relations
   D. print money

Answers and Explanations

1. **C.** Although the Second Continental Congress began to prepare the colonies for war against Great Britain, the delegates also voted to send this petition to George III, asking him to create harmony between Great Britain and the colonies.

2. **A.** Several of the main generals commanding British troops in the Revolutionary War proved early on to be quite ordinary in tactical and leadership skills.

3. **C.** None of the British territory in Canada was taken from them as a result of the treaty.

4. **D.** Although women assisted the war effort in many ways, they made an important contribution by managing estates and farms while their husbands were serving in the colonial militias or in the Continental army.

5. **B.** The national government was not given the power to issue taxes, regulate commerce, or raise an army.

CHAPTER 11

Establishment of New Political Systems (1787–1800)

IN THIS CHAPTER

Summary: In 1787 the Articles of Confederation were discarded and the Constitution of the United States was created, establishing a stronger federal government. The Constitution established a bicameral legislature, three branches of government, and the division of power between the states and the federal government. The Bill of Rights also established many basic freedoms central to the identity of the United States. During the presidency of George Washington, different visions of America were expressed by Thomas Jefferson and Alexander Hamilton.

KEY IDEA

Keywords
Virginia Plan: during debate over the Constitution, the plan proposing a bicameral legislature with representatives determined by proportional representation.
New Jersey Plan: during debate over the Constitution, the plan proposing one legislative body for the country, with each state having one vote.
Great Compromise: Connecticut plan that stated that one house of the Congress would be based on population (the House of Representatives) while in the other house all states would have equal representation (the Senate).
Electoral College: procedure for electing the president and vice-president of the United States as outlined in the Constitution; electors from each state, and not the popular vote, ultimately elect the president.
Three-Fifths Compromise: as the Constitution was being created, the plan that stated that slaves would be counted as three-fifths of a free person; this was used to determine eventual membership in the House of Representatives.

Federalists: party in the first years of the republic that favored a larger national government; was supported by commercial interests. Federalists were opposed by Jeffersonians, who wanted a smaller national government.
Alien and Sedition Acts: proposed by President John Adams, gave the president power to expel "dangerous" aliens and outlawed "scandalous" publications against the government.

Desire for a Stronger Central Government

Many Americans viewed the flaws of the national government established by the Articles of Confederation with dismay. As Alexander Hamilton stated, the American Revolution had taught those living in the former colonies to think "continentally"; yet the government in existence did not foster continental thought or action. To many, a stronger national government was a necessity.

In 1787, delegates from the 13 states went to Philadelphia to amend the Articles of Confederation. Many of the great men of the age were present at this meeting, including Alexander Hamilton, George Washington, James Madison, and Benjamin Franklin. (John Adams and Thomas Jefferson were both in Europe during this convention.) Debates quickly turned away from reforming the Articles of Confederation to creating a new national government. Most delegates believed that the central government had to be much stronger, with the ability to raise an army, collect taxes, and regulate commerce.

However, some delegates at the convention had doubts about how strong a new central government should actually be. They feared that too much power might fall into the hands of a small group, who would use it to their own advantage. In addition, small states and large states had very different ideas about how representation in a new national legislature should be determined. Smaller states favored the model provided by the Articles of Confederation with one vote per state; larger states proposed that population determine representation. In addition, Southern and Northern states began to view each other suspiciously. Debates also took place over the future relationship of the national government to the various state governments.

Government under the New Constitution

Virginia plantation owner Edmund Randolph presented the **Virginia Plan**, which proposed a bicameral legislature with the number of representatives in each house determined by **proportional representation**. The guiding force behind this plan was James Madison, a 36-year-old scholar and member of the Virginia legislature. Madison also proposed a structure of three branches of government: judicial, legislative, and executive. The importance of the contributions of James Madison in the creation of the Constitution cannot be overemphasized; by proposing branches of government, Madison dispelled the fears held by many critics that, in the new government, too much power would be placed in the hands of a small number of leaders.

Smaller states, while favoring a strong central government, were opposed to Madison's concept of a national legislature, fearing it would be dominated by the larger states. Smaller states supported the **New Jersey Plan**, which proposed a unicameral legislature where every state would receive one vote. This plan was equally unpopular with the larger states. Delegates from Connecticut finally proposed the plan that was ultimately adopted, the **Great**

Compromise. This plan included an upper house, called the Senate, which would have two representatives per state, and a lower house, the House of Representatives, whose members would be elected by proportional representation.

Many representatives remained skeptical of a national government with massive powers. To diminish these fears, it was voted that the chief executive of the national government would be elected by an **Electoral College**, membership to which would be chosen by individual states. In addition, senators would be elected by state legislatures and not by the voters. By the twentieth century, many presidential candidates and their political advisors developed campaign strategies centered on winning enough states to emerge victorious in the Electoral College.

Issue of Slavery

The issue of slavery was discussed several times during the deliberations of the Convention. It was decided that the new national government could not regulate slavery for 20 years. Much debate took place over how slaves should be counted when determining representation for states in the House of Representatives; slave states wanted to count the slaves in their total populations. This issue was resolved by the **Three-Fifths Compromise**, which stated that three-fifths of a state's slave population would be counted when determining representation in the House of Representatives. Southern states applauded the section of the Constitution promising national aid to any state threatened with "domestic violence"; Southern politicians assumed that this meant that federal troops would be utilized to help dispel any future slave revolts.

Ratification of the Constitution

The writers of the new document wanted it to be approved by **ratifying conventions** that would be held in each state. Supporters of the new Constitution began to call themselves **Federalists**, a term used at the time for a supporter of a strong *national* government. Federalists had faith that the elites who would come to dominate both federal and state governments would act in the interest of the entire nation. Those opposed to the new, stronger national government were soon called **anti-Federalists**. Anti-Federalists sometimes equated the potential tyranny they saw in the new government with the tyranny that had been practiced by British monarchs. Anti-Federalists felt that the best protection against the tyranny of a strong central government would be the power of the individual states. In the end, they said that the major problem was that the new government was not based on republican principles and, without a Bill of Rights, was not interested in individual rights. After especially tough fights in New York, Virginia, and Massachusetts, the new Constitution was finally passed by all states (with New York being last) on July 26, 1788.

Presidency of George Washington

Although he did not seek the presidency, the national reputation of George Washington made him the most logical choice to be the first chief executive of the United States of America. For at least the first term of Washington's administration, the future of the United States remained uncertain. Washington felt that it was crucial to establish respect for the office of the president of the United States. Washington believed it was his job to administer the laws and not to make them; he almost never made legislative proposals to Congress.

Bill of Rights

When the Constitution was being written, James Madison opposed including a bill of rights, fearing that such a document might actually limit the rights of citizens. By 1791, he saw the wisdom of such a document, and proposed 12 amendments to the Constitution. Anti-Federalists unanimously supported the addition of a bill of rights; they felt these would be added protections against the tyranny of the federal government. By the end of the year, 10 amendments had been ratified by the individual states. The **Bill of Rights** contains the basic protections that Americans hold dear today; politically, it quieted the anti-Federalists and their fears of authoritarian government. The Bill of Rights guaranteed the right of free speech, ensured freedom of worship, gave citizens the right to bear arms, forbade the quartering of troops in private homes, and said that warrants were needed before searches took place. In addition, persons could not be forced to testify against themselves, citizens were guaranteed a trial by jury, "due process of law" was guaranteed, and "cruel and unusual punishments" were outlawed. The Ninth Amendment stated that these were not the only rights that Americans had; the Tenth stated that any powers not specifically given to the federal government belonged to the states. Some historians point out that the basis of the entire American political system can be found in these ten amendments.

Competing Visions: Alexander Hamilton and Thomas Jefferson

Two of the most brilliant men in the Washington administration were Secretary of State Thomas Jefferson and Secretary of the Treasury Alexander Hamilton. Hamilton was a huge admirer of the British economic system and wanted to turn America, which was still largely agrarian, into a manufacturing society like Britain. Hamilton wanted to institute strong **mercantilist policies** and proposed economic union with Great Britain. Hamilton believed that a strong national government was necessary for economic growth and believed in a broad interpretation of the Constitution. By this interpretation, the federal government had many powers not specifically mentioned in the Constitution and was only denied those powers specifically given to the states.

Jefferson (supported by James Madison) proposed a radically different view of America. He proposed an America that would remain largely agricultural, with industry serving only as "a handmaiden to agriculture." While Hamilton supported the mercantilist policy of high tariffs on foreign goods, Jefferson proposed a system of **free trade** (which would keep prices low). Jefferson came to be influenced by the events of the French Revolution and was fearful of the power of the federal government (emphasizing the importance of state power instead). Jefferson also favored a strict interpretation of the Constitution; by this interpretation, the federal government only had the powers it was specifically given in the Constitution.

From these differences emerged the two-party system in the United States. Hamilton and his supporters called themselves Federalists; mercantilism would impel them to propose a strong government hand in economic affairs. Jefferson and his followers were called Republicans. As stated previously, they favored **laissez-faire economic principles** and the continued vision of America as a largely agricultural nation. The plans of Hamilton were most popular in the commercial cities of the Northeast and the port cities of the South, while the Republican plan was most popular in the Western and Southern sections of the country.

Plan of Alexander Hamilton

Determined to turn the United States into a manufacturing power, Hamilton began a gigantic economic reform of America. In his *Report on the Public Credit*, Hamilton proposed that the United States had the obligation to redeem in full all notes that had been issued by the government established by the Articles of Confederation. In addition, he proposed that the federal government take over all of the debts of the individual states. Hamilton also proposed the chartering of a **national bank** that could provide loans to developing industries. Hamilton proposed that the federal government use subsidies and tax incentives to spur industrial growth. He also proposed that these measures be paid for largely by high tariffs on foreign imports.

Jefferson and Madison opposed these plans on both practical and philosophical grounds. They maintained that the commercial elite would be the ones to benefit from these programs, largely at the expense of the farmer. Most of Hamilton's programs were adopted, although the plan to increase industrial growth was not. Hamilton's economic vision provided a system of public credit and a steady stream of government revenue through tariffs.

French Revolution

The French Revolution broke out as George Washington was taking over as president in 1789. By 1793, a continentwide war pitted revolutionary France against most of Europe. Within months, Washington issued a **Declaration of Neutrality**, which allowed American merchants to prosper by trading with both sides. Many Americans sided with the democratic principles that the Revolution appeared to be based on; Democratic-Republican clubs in many cities carefully followed events in France. Many of the people supporting the Revolution also supported Jefferson and his republican ideals in America. The entire Revolution and especially the violence that was associated with it appalled other Americans; many of these people supported federalism in the United States. Note, however, that some historians maintain that there are strong connections between the American and French revolutions.

Pennsylvania farmers who supported the **Whiskey Rebellion** of 1794 were inspired by the French Revolution (they actually carried signs proclaiming "Liberty, Equality, and Fraternity"). They opposed a tax Alexander Hamilton had placed on distilled alcohol, which reduced the profits on the whiskey that they produced and sold. The tax was necessary because the federal government needed more money. Hamilton's plan of having the federal government take over certain debts of state governments had recently been instituted. Hamilton demonstrated his political skill by taxing whiskey; the grain from which it was made came from Western farmers, most of whom supported Jefferson. Washington raised an army and put the whiskey revolt down; by the time the army was ready to fight, the rebellion had largely ended.

Foreign Policy and Jay's Treaty

The war between France and the rest of Europe continued. By 1794, British officials became concerned that the Americans were trading mostly with the French West Indies during their period of "neutrality." The British began to search, and then to seize, American merchant ships, often demanding that the crews of these ships join the British navy. Washington sent Chief Justice John Jay to negotiate with the British, and the results were mixed at best. Jay was unable to get the British to promise not to undermine American freedom of the seas, and he was forced to comply with the British demand that they had the right to remove French products and materials from American ships. The British did agree to leave some of the forts they still occupied in the Northwest Territory.

Bitter political battles took place in America over **Jay's Treaty**. On the other hand, the treaty negotiated by Thomas Pinckney with Spain was extremely popular; by this treaty, the United States gained navigating rights along the Mississippi River. Farm produce from the South and the West got to markets much quicker as a result of this treaty.

Washington's Farewell Address

Increased political battles between Federalists and Republicans convinced George Washington not to run for a third term as president. In his Farewell Address, Washington spoke against party politics, asking political leaders to work together and not against each other. He also warned America not to "interweave our destiny with any part of Europe" and stated that America should not enter into alliances that would cause them to get involved in foreign wars. Political leaders for the next 200 years would invoke the words of Washington when opposing American plans to ally with foreign nations.

Presidency of John Adams

John Adams had been Washington's vice president, was also a Federalist, and served one term as president (1796–1800). Adams was opposed in the 1796 election by Thomas Jefferson, contesting as a Republican. Adams won, but Jefferson came in second in the Electoral College, thus putting candidates of two different parties in as president and vice president.

Despite recent biographies that suggest otherwise, Adams had four largely unsuccessful years in office. Adams spent a great deal of time back home in Quincy, Massachusetts, thus allowing his cabinet members to make major decisions with little input from the president.

In contrast to Adams, recent historical scholarship has emphasized the extraordinary leadership skills that Washington possessed.

Problems with France

The French were unhappy with a series of American laws and policies that economically favored the British at their expense. For many in France, Jay's Treaty was the last straw. The French impounded several American ships going to England and announced that American sailors doing duty on British ships would be treated as "pirates." A three-member diplomatic delegation went to Paris in 1798 to negotiate with the French. French Minister Talleyrand, through third and fourth parties, informed the Americans that a bribe would have to be paid before negotiations could begin. The American diplomats refused to pay, and word of this caused outrage at home. This affair came to be known as the "XYZ Affair," named for the unnamed "assistants" of Talleyrand who asked for the bribe.

Adams announced the buildup of the American navy in preparation for a potential war against France. Trading with France was temporarily suspended, and American ships were authorized to attack French ships at sea. In 1800, the French and the Americans met again (Napoleon was now in power in France), and tensions decreased. The Convention of 1800 gave the United States compensation for ships that had been seized by the French. In addition, the United States was freed from its diplomatic entanglements with the French.

Alien and Sedition Acts

During the undeclared war against France, the policies of Adams were attacked by some in the press; several pamphlets written by French emigrants were especially vindictive. As a result, Adams and his administration supported several measures that would threaten the rights of Americans. The **Alien Act** gave the president the right to deport any immigrant who was felt to be "dangerous to the peace and safety of the United States." The **Sedition Act** stated that the administration could prohibit any attacks on the president or Congress that were deemed to be "malicious." Twenty Republican journalists and politicians were arrested under the Sedition Act, with some going to jail. State legislatures in Virginia and Kentucky passed the **Kentucky and Virginia Resolves**, proclaiming that states had the right to not enforce laws that were unconstitutional, such as the Sedition Act. This would later be the philosophy of some Southern states in the years leading up to the Civil War and again in the civil rights struggles of the 1950s and 1960s.

The negative publicity generated by the Sedition Act certainly did not help John Adams as he ran for president against Thomas Jefferson in 1800.

Chapter Review

Rapid Review

To achieve the perfect 5, you should be able to explain the following:

- The 1787 meeting on amending the Articles of Confederation turned into a historical session when the Constitution of the United States was drafted.
- The importance of James Madison in the formulation of the Constitution cannot be overemphasized.
- The format of the bicameral legislature, the branches of power established at the federal level, and the division of powers between federal and state governments made the U.S. Constitution a unique document for its time.
- The division between Federalists and anti-Federalists demonstrated that very different visions of America and the scope of the federal government existed in the United States at this time.
- The Bill of Rights established the basic freedoms that Americans cherish today.
- During the Washington administration, very different visions of America were expressed by Alexander Hamilton and Thomas Jefferson. The ideas of Hamilton helped spur American economic growth during the Washington administration.
- The United States had a great deal of trouble convincing the British and the French that the United States was a major power during this era.

- Many critics viewed the Alien and Sedition Acts of John Adams as gross overextensions of the power given to the federal government by the Constitution.

Time Line

1787: Constitutional Convention ratifies U.S. Constitution
1788: U.S. Constitution ratified by states
1789: Washington sworn in as first president
1790: Hamilton issues plans proposing to protect infant U.S. industries
1791: Establishment of First National Bank
Ratification of the Bill of Rights
1793: Democratic-Republican clubs begin to meet
1794: Whiskey Rebellion begins
1795: Jay's Treaty with England/Pinckney's Treaty with Spain
1796: John Adams elected president, Thomas Jefferson, vice president (each from a different political party)
1798: XYZ Affair
Sedition Act of John Adams issued
Kentucky and Virginia Resolves
1800: Convention of 1800
Thomas Jefferson elected president

Review Questions

1. The Connecticut Plan presented to the Constitutional Convention of 1787:
   A. Proposal for a two-house legislature based on proportional representation.
   B. Proposal for a one-house legislature based on proportional representation.
   C. Proposal for a two-house legislature, with one house based on proportional representation.
   D. Proposal for a balance of power between executive, legislative, and judicial branches.

2. The Kentucky and Virginia Resolves
   A. expressed support for the new U.S. Constitution
   B. stated that individual states do not have to enforce laws the states consider unconstitutional
   C. were written to support John Adams's support of the Sedition Act
   D. were written in opposition to the economic policies of Alexander Hamilton

3. Many in America felt that the English and the French failed to treat the United States as a major power in this era. All of the following are evidence of that *except*
   A. the Convention of 1800
   B. Jay's Treaty
   C. the treatment of American ships by the British during the 1790s
   D. the XYZ Affair

4. Thomas Jefferson and Alexander Hamilton had different views on all of the following *except*
   A. the amount of power the federal government should have
   B. the tariff policy of the United States
   C. the importance of a national bank
   D. their belief in the power of the U.S. Constitution

5. Under the Electoral College system
   A. voters directly elect the president of the United States
   B. voters approve electors, who elect the president of the United States
   C. it is possible to win the popular vote and lose the election in the Electoral College
   D. B and C above

Answers and Explanations

1. **C.** The Connecticut Plan, also called the Great Compromise, was ratified by the delegates. Under this plan, representation in the House of Representatives would be by population, while all states would have equal representation in the Senate.

2. **B.** After the passage of the Sedition Act, legislatures in Kentucky and Virginia passed resolutions stating that states do not have to enforce laws they consider to be unconstitutional.

3. **A.** As a result of the Convention of 1800, the French agreed to compensate the United States for ships seized during the previous decade. Events mentioned in all of the other choices demonstrate that the French and English had little respect for American rights in diplomatic matters and on the high seas during this era.

4. **D.** Both believed in the power of the Constitution, although their interpretations of the Constitution were different. Jefferson believed in a strict interpretation of the Constitution, while Hamilton believed in a broad interpretation.

5. **D.** As demonstrated in the presidential election of 2000, it is possible to get the most number of votes nationwide but to lose the presidential election in the Electoral College. This also occurred in the presidential elections of 1876 and 1888.

CHAPTER 12

Jeffersonian Revolution (1800–1820)

IN THIS CHAPTER

Summary: The election of Thomas Jefferson in 1800 was a critical election in American history; Jefferson's view of America differed greatly from that of the Federalists. Alexander Hamilton and other Federalists envisioned America as a future industrial power. For Jefferson, the independence and pride of the yeoman farmer would guide America into the future. During the time when John Marshall was chief justice of the Supreme Court, the power of the federal courts increased. The overall size of America also increased in this era as a result of the Louisiana Purchase. The War of 1812 was fought over continued tensions between the Americans and the British. Many Americans in this era envisioned massive economic growth in the United States; this was the focus of Henry Clay's "American System."

Keywords

***Marbury v. Madison* (1803):** critical Supreme Court decision that established the principle of judicial review, stating that the Supreme Court has the right to review all federal laws and decisions and declare whether or not they are constitutional.

Louisiana Purchase (1803): massive land purchase from Emperor Napoleon of France that virtually doubled the size of the United States.

Lewis and Clark Expedition (1804): expedition that discovered much about the western part of the North American continent and the economic possibilities there.

War of 1812: war between the British and the Americans over British seizure of American ships, connections between the British and Native American tribes, and other tensions. The British sacked Washington, DC, in 1814. The treaty ending the war merely restored diplomatic relations between the two countries.

American System: plan proposed by Senator Henry Clay and others to make America economically independent by increasing industrial production in the United States and by the creation of a Second National Bank.

Missouri Compromise (1820): political solution devised to keep the number of slave states and free states equal; Missouri entered the Union as a slave state and Maine entered as a free state. Potential states in the northern part of the Louisiana territory would also come in as free states in the future.

Election of 1800

John Adams, despite much criticism over the Sedition Act, stood for reelection in 1800. The vice presidential candidate of the Federalists was Charles Pinckney. The candidate for the Republicans was Thomas Jefferson, with Aaron Burr running for vice president. At this point, all candidates were eligible for votes in the Electoral College; Jefferson and Burr each received 73 votes. (The **Twelfth Amendment** of 1804 would change this, stating that the Electoral College could vote for president and vice president separately.) The Constitution in 1800 threw the election to the House of Representatives, where each state received one vote. Federalists supported Burr, and it was only on the thirty-sixth ballot that Jefferson was elected president. Jefferson's victory was only assured when Alexander Hamilton convinced some Federalists to switch their votes to Jefferson, telling them that Burr was "the most unfit man in the United States for the office of president." Some historians term this election the "Revolution of 1800." As previously stated, Jefferson's vision of America had almost no similarity to the views of the Federalists who had been in power since the beginning of the Republic, yet they peacefully gave up power when the balloting was completed in the House of Representatives.

Some historians maintain that Thomas Jefferson was one of the most brilliant men ever to be elected president. Recent biographies and exposés on the life of Jefferson have largely ignored his immense political skills and intellect. Jefferson had been a diplomat, was familiar with European affairs, was a skillful politician, and was a distinguished political philosopher. He implemented Republican policies almost as soon as he took office, with the goal of cutting back on the growth of the federal government that had taken place under Adams. The Alien and Sedition Acts of Adams were not renewed, taxes such as the whiskey tax were eliminated, and Jefferson opposed further expansion of the national debt. On the other hand, Jefferson remained a pragmatist. As a member of Washington's cabinet, he had vigorously opposed the creation of a national bank, yet as president he supported it. (He reasoned that American economic growth was dependent on the existence of the bank.)

Reform of the Courts

When Jefferson was inaugurated in 1801, virtually every justice in the court system was a Federalist, since they had all been appointed by either Washington or Adams. Several weeks before Jefferson took office, the Congress passed the **Judiciary Act**, creating a large number of new federal courts. In a series of "**midnight appointments**" made just hours before he left office, Adams appointed Federalists to all of these positions.

Jefferson's Republican allies in the Congress repealed the Judiciary Act almost immediately and also impeached two Federalist judges. John Marshall was a Federalist who had been appointed chief justice of the Supreme Court by Adams and continued in office during Jefferson's presidency and beyond. Marshall served as chief justice from 1801 to 1835 and served to dramatically improve the prestige and functioning of the federal court system.

Marshall also dramatically increased the power of the Supreme Court itself in the 1803 *Marbury v. Madison* decision. John Adams had appointed William Marbury to be justice of the peace for the District of Columbia in one of his final appointments before leaving office. James Madison, secretary of state under Jefferson, refused to issue the appointment letter signed by Adams. Marbury sued, demanding that the Supreme Court force Madison to release the appointment letter.

Marshall ruled that the Supreme Court did not have the power to force Madison to act. However, the ruling also stated that the Supreme Court did have the right to judge the constitutionality of federal laws and decisions. This began the principal of **judicial review**, making the judiciary an equal branch in every way with the executive and legislative branches.

Westward Expansion

As previously mentioned, Thomas Jefferson had a very different vision for America than had been held by Alexander Hamilton and many other Federalists. While Hamilton had envisioned America as evolving into a mighty industrial power, Jefferson's view of an ideal America was one made up largely of yeoman farmers, who would possess a spirit of fierce independence and pride. To accomplish this end, Jefferson encouraged further expansion westward (into the area between the Appalachian Mountains and the Mississippi River). Over 1 million settlers lived there in 1800; in 1804, it became even easier to purchase land in this territory when it became possible to buy 160 acres of land for a down payment of $80. New settlers streamed into the area, sometimes settling on land legally owned by Native American tribes.

Jefferson publicly stated that the best approach to Native Americans would be to show them the benefits of farming. He felt that if Native Americans could be turned into farmers, they would not need all of their forestlands and they might incorporate themselves as citizens of the United States. However, Jefferson's desire for western settlement far outweighed his desire for fair treatment for Native Americans. The pattern that began under Jefferson and continued for decades was one in which Native Americans were forced to sign treaties in which they gave up more and more of their lands with virtually nothing given in return.

Louisiana Purchase

In secret treaties between France and Spain signed in 1800 and 1801, France regained the Louisiana territory. Americans did not hear of this until 1802 and were worried that Napoleon's France might attempt to reassert its power in the Americas. Napoleon also expressed his desire to place Haiti back under French control. Concerns increased when, in the last two months of their control there, the Spanish refused to allow American ships to store products in New Orleans (which had been common practice).

Jefferson feared war with France and sent Virginia governor James Monroe to France to see if France would sell part of the territory to the United States. Napoleon had been unable to recapture Haiti and needed money to finance his army for his European conquests, so he offered to sell the Louisiana Territory to the United States for $15 million. The **Louisiana Purchase** doubled the size of the United States; for Jefferson this was the perfect opportunity to expand the "empire of liberty." Many Northeastern Federalists were opposed to the Louisiana Purchase, fearing it would decrease their economic and political power. Nevertheless, the purchase was overwhelmingly ratified by Congress in late 1803. Jefferson's pragmatism was also displayed when he approved the Louisiana Purchase. The Constitution did not mention that the federal government had the right to acquire new territory; Jefferson had always interpreted the Constitution strictly, and normally stated that the federal government had no powers that were not specifically mentioned in the Constitution. However, in Jefferson's eyes, the acquisition of the Louisiana territory was absolutely essential for the continued growth of the United States.

Jefferson and many others in America wanted more accurate information about the geography, the peoples, and the economic possibilities of the rest of the continent. In 1804, the **Lewis and Clark Expedition** began. This expedition of nearly 50 men took two years to complete; despite hardships, they crossed the Rockies and eventually made it to the Pacific Ocean. The information they brought back about the possibilities of further expansion in the West intrigued many.

Political Tensions and the Strange Case of Aaron Burr

Federalists feared that the country was being debased by virtually every move that Jefferson made. A group of Federalists called the **Essex Junto** existed in Boston and loudly campaigned against the "decline in public virtue" they saw personified in Jefferson. Thomas Pickering, senator from Massachusetts, saw Jefferson as a "Parisian revolutionary monster." A younger group of Federalists tried to improve the image of the party, although the Federalist candidate, Charles C. Pinckney, received only 14 electoral votes in the 1804 election.

Aaron Burr was vice president, but after the fiasco of the 1800 election, he had no meaningful role during Jefferson's first term. Some New England Federalists had spoken of leaving the Union after the Louisiana Purchase and forming a Northern Confederacy. The group tried to get Alexander Hamilton to join them. After he refused, they tried to recruit Aaron Burr, who, seeing no future role in a Washington run by Thomas Jefferson, was trying to become governor of New York. Hamilton accused Burr of attempting to ruin the United States. At this point, Burr challenged Hamilton to a duel (a practice that had been outlawed in the United States). Hamilton died in the duel, and Burr was indicted for murder.

After ending his term as vice president, Burr moved to the West (probably to avoid jail). While in Louisiana, he met up with General James Wilkinson, the military governor there. The two plotted to turn Louisiana into an independent nation, with Burr as its leader. Burr was betrayed by Wilkinson and arrested. Burr was acquitted, but his actions and the actions of other Federalists demonstrated the deep divisions that were developing in the United States. Federalists had plotted secession; President Jefferson wanted a conviction of Burr at all costs; and Federalist John Marshall, who presided over the trial, made several rulings that helped Burr (possibly to discredit the efforts of Jefferson).

European Wars Spill Over to America (Again)

The Napoleonic Wars of Europe that lasted from 1802 until 1815 had a powerful impact on the United States. America viewed its role in these wars as neutral, yet came into conflict with both France and Great Britain. According to the terms of the Continental System, American ships that traded in Britain were sometimes stopped and seized. British ships also seized ships trading with the French West Indies, made merchants pay heavily to get special licenses to send their ships through the British naval blockade of the continent, and practiced **impressment** (forcing deserted British sailors but also American citizens into the British navy). Jefferson banned British warships from American ports, yet impressment and the stopping and seizing of American ships continued.

Many in America wanted war, but Jefferson thought that economic pressure would cause the British and the French to respect the rights of America as a neutral. He declared the **Embargo of 1807** by which American ships could not enter the seas until England and France stopped their harassment of American shipping. Predictably, the effect on the American economy was disastrous. Exports dropped dramatically, with Northeastern merchants, Southern plantation owners, and even farmers dramatically affected.

The Embargo of 1807 was by far the most unpopular act championed by Jefferson. In the 1808 presidential election, Congressman James Madison was elected president, even though he was one of the architects of the embargo bill.

Seeing that America had actually fallen into economic depression, Madison in 1808 introduced the **Non-Intercourse Act**, which opened trade with all countries except England and France. An 1810 act again threatened to cut trade with any nation that interfered with American ships, which England and France continued to do.

War of 1812

Reasons for the War

Frustrated by the continued British policies of impressment and seizure of ships, Madison formally asked Congress for a Declaration of War against Britain in June 1812. Many Federalists opposed the war. They regarded Great Britain as a potential trading partner and viewed British citizens as people "like themselves." To many Americans, Madison's argument that the country's political and economic rights as a neutral power had been violated was convincing. A younger group of Republicans, personified by Henry Clay of Kentucky, were especially supportive of war. This group, called the "War Hawks," felt that war would enable the United States to acquire more territory in the West, leading to greater economic growth.

Another stated cause for war revolved around connections between the British and Native Americans. In 1812, two members of the Shawnee tribe, Tecumseh and his brother Tenskwatawa, decided the time was right to take a stand against further settlement by whites in the region between the Appalachians and the Mississippi River. Tecumseh joined many tribes together, terrifying settlers in the region. James Madison was convinced by Western political leaders that the Native Americans were being encouraged (and being armed) by the British in Canada. The attack on Tecumseh's village by General William Henry Harrison in late 1811 intensified the conflict that would take place with Native Americans in the region.

Outbreak of War

The United States was totally unprepared for war against Britain when war was first declared. In 1812, the army consisted of 6,000 men, and the entire navy was made up of 17 ships. The first military effort was a three-pronged attack against Canada, with the intent of destroying Indian villages, defeating British troops, and taking Montreal. Military efforts were largely unsuccessful, and American troops soon retreated.

The American navy had some initial successes, but American ships were soon driven back and blockaded in their own ports. The naval victories of 1812 at least boosted the morale of the American nation. Native Americans, including Tecumseh and the Shawnees, were fighting on the side of the British. The first big victory for the Americans came in the summer of 1813 when William Henry Harrison and his force defeated the British and the Native Americans at the Thames River (east of present-day Detroit), killing Tecumseh. In Tennessee, a militiaman, Andrew Jackson, led many victories over Indian forces.

Attack on Washington

Napoleon was finally defeated in 1814. Many Americans rejoiced at the defeat of the French, but also realized that the United States was now Britain's only enemy. The British began an offensive in New York, and, in August 1814, a second British army advanced on Washington. Most Washingtonians (including President Madison) left the city before the British arrived, but the British proceeded to sack the city, including the White House and the Capitol.

Ironically, as the British were burning the Capitol, peace negotiations for ending the war were already in progress in Ghent, Belgium. With the European war over, many of the issues that had driven Britain and America apart, such as blockading and impressment, now appeared to be less important. After sustained battles against Napoleon, public opinion in England did not favor continued military action in the Americas. The strange **Treaty of Ghent**, which ended the war, actually said nothing about impressment or neutral trading rights, but simply restored diplomatic relations between Britain and the United States. Two weeks after peace was declared, Andrew Jackson defeated a large British force at the Battle of New Orleans.

Political Effects of the War

Nine days before the Treaty of Ghent was signed, a group of Federalists met at the **Hartford Convention**. They continued to see the war as disastrous to their interests and viewed with extreme suspicion the growing influence of politicians and military leaders from the West. Proposals regarding **nullification**, and even one concerning **secession**, were debated. When the ending of the war and the victory at New Orleans were announced, the actions of the Federalists appeared foolish. Their influence on political life in America was drawing to an end. With the decline of the Federalists, the United States was more united after the War of 1812 than it had been for years. As a result, the years 1816 to 1823 are called in textbooks the **Era of Good Feelings**, with James Monroe taking over the presidency in 1817.

American System

Henry Clay and other Nationalists in Congress proposed the **American System** in the aftermath of the War of 1812. This plan was supported by James Madison and most fully implemented by James Monroe. The purpose of this plan was to make America less economically dependent on Europe by encouraging the production of goods in the United States that had previously been imported. Important to this economic growth would also be a **Second National Bank**, so that credit would be readily available, and a rather large protective tariff, which would encourage production and interstate commerce.

The **Tariff of 1816** raised tariff rates to nearly 22 percent, providing more than adequate protection for American business interests and revenues for improvements in the internal transportation system of the United States. A second national bank was also chartered in 1816. There was rapid economic growth in the postwar years, as Europeans and others traded for American tobacco, cotton, and grain. Economic growth could not last forever, and a depression gripped America in 1819.

Missouri Compromise

The issue of slavery was one that grew more urgent as more settlers moved westward: would the territories they were moving into be slave states or free? In 1808, the further exporting of slaves was eliminated. Additional states had joined the Union, some slave and some free. By 1819, there were 11 slave states and 11 free states. The issue came to a head that year when Missouri petitioned to join the Union as a slave state. Debate in the Congress and in newspapers around the country was heated; to many Northerners, to have more slave states than free states was unthinkable. In 1820, Speaker of the House Henry Clay engineered the Missouri Compromise, by which Maine entered the Union as a free state, Missouri entered as a slave state, and, in the Louisiana Territory, any states north of 36 degrees, 30 minutes had to come in as free states. Many at the time realized that this solution would only be a temporary one.

Chapter Review

Rapid Review

To achieve the perfect 5, you should be able to explain the following:

- The election of Thomas Jefferson in 1800 is called the "Revolution of 1800," as the new president had a completely different vision of America from the Federalists whom he replaced.
- Thomas Jefferson was one of the most brilliant men ever to serve as president, and he instituted many "Republican" policies during his eight years in office.
- The role of the federal courts was greatly strengthened during the tenure of John Marshall as chief justice of the Supreme Court.
- The Louisiana Purchase more than doubled the size of the United States and allowed the "empire of liberty" to continue to expand.
- The case of Aaron Burr showed the deep political divisions that existed in the United States during this period.
- The Napoleonic Wars greatly impacted the relationship between the United States, England, and France.
- America entered the War of 1812 because President Madison convinced the nation that America's rights as a neutral power had been violated and because many in Congress felt that the British were encouraging the resistance by Native American tribes.

- The American System of Henry Clay and others was proposed after the War of 1812 and outlined a plan for broad economic growth for the United States.
- The Missouri Compromise temporarily solved the issue of the number of slave states versus the number of free states.

Time Line

1800: Thomas Jefferson elected president in "Revolution of 1800"
1801: John Marshall named chief justice of the Supreme Court
Alien and Sedition Acts not renewed
1803: Louisiana Purchase
Marbury v. Madison established federal judicial review
1804: Alexander Hamilton killed in duel with Aaron Burr
Thomas Jefferson reelected
Twelfth Amendment ratified (separate voting for president, vice president)
Beginning of Lewis and Clark expedition
1807: Embargo Act greatly harms foreign trade
1808: James Madison elected president
Further importation of slaves into the United States made illegal
1812: Beginning of the War of 1812
1814: British army sacks Washington
Treaty of Ghent formally ends the War of 1812
Indian removal from Southern territories begins in earnest
1814–1815: Hartford Convention (meeting of Federalists)
1815: Victory of Andrew Jackson at the Battle of New Orleans (after the War of 1812 was officially over)
Henry Clay proposes the American System
1816: James Monroe elected president
1816–1823: Era of Good Feelings
1820: Missouri Compromise

> Review Questions

1. The *Marbury v. Madison* decision
   A. gave powers to the president that the Republicans of Thomas Jefferson claimed he didn't have
   B. gave broad judicial power to the state courts
   C. declared that the Alien and Sedition Acts were constitutional
   D. established the principle of judicial review

2. As a result of the election of Thomas Jefferson in 1800,
   A. more assistance was given to the commercial sector.
   B. American foreign policy became more pro-British.
   C. the federal debt rose dramatically.
   D. federal excise taxes were eliminated.

3. All of the following are reasons why America entered the War of 1812 *except*
   A. the impressment of American naval crews
   B. the existence of a strong American navy ready to demonstrate its capabilities
   C. the relationship between the British and Native American tribes in the western territories of North America
   D. the desire of American leaders to acquire additional western territories

4. The Hartford Convention demonstrated that
   A. the Federalist party had remained a dominant party in American political life.
   B. the War of 1812 brought political union to the United States.
   C. the concept of nullification was not exclusively a Southern one.
   D. the Treaty of Ghent was a controversial treaty.

5. The American System of Henry Clay
   A. favored strong economic growth and a Second National Bank
   B. wanted to make the United States the military equivalent of Great Britain or France
   C. favored lowering tariffs so that more goods could be purchased from abroad
   D. advocated the elimination of slavery

› Answers and Explanations

1. **D.** The decision stated that the Supreme Court had the right to decide on the constitutionality of federal rulings and laws.

2. **D.** All of the remaining answers would have been true if a Federalist had been elected president. Jefferson favored lessening the power of the federal government, and eliminating federal excise taxes was one way in which he did so.

3. **B.** The United States had an army of 6,000 men and 17 ships when war began. All the other choices are reasons why Americans supported the War of 1812.

4. **C.** Kentucky and Virginia spoke of nullification after the Sedition Act. New England Federalists saw the War of 1812 as a disaster and at the Hartford Convention also spoke of nullification.

5. **A.** The American System favored American economic growth, a National Bank, and increased tariffs to protect American businesses and finance new transportation systems within the United States.

> CHAPTER 13

Rise of Manufacturing and the Age of Jackson (1820–1845)

IN THIS CHAPTER

Summary: Large-scale textile production began in the United States during this era of factories in places like Lowell, Massachusetts. As America grew economically, it also began to assert its authority in the Western Hemisphere. The Monroe Doctrine boldly stated that the hemisphere was offlimits to European intervention. Beginning in 1824, the United States began the resettlement of Native American tribes east of the Mississippi. The era of "Jacksonian Democracy" was one where many say that the values of the "common man" reigned supreme. In the 1830s, the Whig party emerged as an opposition party to the Democratic party of Jackson. Several state legislatures began to claim that they could nullify federal laws that were not in the interests of their individual states.

> KEY IDEA

Keywords

Monroe Doctrine (1823): proclamation that countries of the Western Hemisphere "are not to be considered as subjects for future colonization by any European powers."
Removal Act of 1830: Congressional act that authorized the removal of all Native American tribes east of the Mississippi to the west. The Trail of Tears and other forced migrations caused the deaths of thousands.
The Liberator: abolitionist newspaper began by William Lloyd Garrison in 1831.
Spoils system: system used heavily during the presidency of Andrew Jackson whereby political supporters of the winning candidate are given jobs in the government.

Nullification: in reaction to tariff legislation passed in 1828, the South Carolina legislature explored the possibility of nullification, by which individual states could rule on the constitutionality of federal laws. Other Southern legislatures later discussed the idea of nullifying federal laws in their own states.

Whig party: political party that emerged in the 1830s in opposition to the Democratic party; Whigs favored policies that promoted commercial and industrial growth.

Growth of the Factory

Economic growth was a key component of Henry Clay's American System, and measures were taken to expand American industry in the aftermath of the War of 1812. American industries were protected by the Tariff of 1816, which raised import tariffs by 25 percent. At the same time, state governments began improving road, river, and canal transportation systems.

Before 1820, almost all products made in America were completed using a system borrowed from Europe, called the **putting-out system**. Under this system, merchants would buy the raw materials, recruit dozens, or in some cases, hundreds of farm families to do the work, and then sell the finished product. Many shoes in New England were made in this manner; women and children would make part of the shoe, which would be finished by experienced shoemakers.

Beginning in the late 1780s, the textile industry started to use power-driven machines and interchangeable parts. All power in these early factories came from water, so the early factories were all located along rivers. Most were located in New England or the Middle states. In the 1790s, factories like those in Lowell, Massachusetts, began to weave cotton imported from the south. With the introduction of the cotton gin in the same decade, more cotton became available, and production boomed. By 1840, the textile industry employed nearly 75,000 workers, almost half of them women.

The workforce of many of the early factories was hired using the "**Lowell System.**" Young women from surrounding areas were brought in to work. They worked for a pittance in horrible conditions and slept in dormitories provided by the factories. The young women saw this as temporary work, as many went home after several years, after making some money (and in some cases spending it). This constant turnover of workers kept worker demands low, which pleased the factory owners. An economic middle class of manufacturers, bankers, and their families began to grow during this period. Factory towns such as Lowell, Massachusetts, began to grow rapidly in area.

An economic panic hit the United States in 1819, caused by the recovery of European economies after the Napoleonic Wars, by money policies of the National Bank, and by the efforts of officials at several branch banks of the National Bank to enrich themselves through speculation. It was not until the 1830s that worker strikes began; during this era there were also drives to influence state legislatures to shorten the workday. A real **labor movement** did not develop in the textile industry until the 1840s.

Monroe Doctrine

The Monroe Doctrine estimated the fact that America now was beginning to consider itself a major world power, announced by President Monroe in 1823. Many Latin American nations had announced their independence in the Napoleonic Era, and many in Latin America and in the United States felt that the Spanish and the French might send armies to reassert their control of the region. The Monroe Doctrine stated that countries in the Western Hemisphere were now off limits to European control. (These states "henceforth are not to be considered as subjects for future colonization by any European powers.")

Policy Toward Native Americans

In 1824, President James Monroe proposed that all Native Americans be moved west of the Mississippi River. Conflict had continued east of the Mississippi between settlers and various Native American tribes. Even though tribes had signed legal treaties for land, settlement constantly encroached on Native American territories. Monroe claimed that his proposal would benefit the Native Americans, stating that settlers would never bother them as long as they settled west of the Mississippi River. Some tribes such as the Cherokee, adopted systems of government similar to those used in many states, but even that did not stave off the pressure for removal.

The state of Georgia pressured the Cherokee to sell the land they held in that state. The Cherokees felt they held a valid treaty for the lands that they lived on and decided to take their case to the federal court system. In an 1831 decision, ***Cherokee Nation v. Georgia***, Chief Justice Marshall stated that Native Americans had no real standing in court, since they were not a state or a foreign country. Nevertheless, Marshall affirmed that Cherokees had rights to the lands that they possessed.

The Constitution states that it is the job of the executive branch to enforce the laws or decisions of the other two branches. Andrew Jackson was now president, and a large part of his reputation was based on his successful fights against the Indians. Jackson declined to take action to enforce this decision, stating "John Marshall has made his decision: let him enforce it." In his inaugural speech, Jackson affirmed his support for Native American removal. During the War of 1812, Jackson led troops against the Creek tribe. As a result, the Creeks lost over 60 percent of their tribal lands. Congress had already passed and Jackson signed the **Removal Act of 1830**, which authorized the removal of all tribes east of the Mississippi.

Tribes were forced to move beginning in 1831; the horrors of these journeys, sometimes undertaken during winter months, are very well documented. In 1838, the Cherokees were finally marched west at gunpoint in what is now called the **Trail of Tears**; nearly one-third died of disease or exhaustion along the way. Many Native Americans were never able to adjust to the alien environment found west of the Mississippi. Indian resistance continued in Florida until 1841.

Second Great Awakening

The rise of industry, the growing commercialization of cities, and westernization, all fundamentally altered America in the years 1800 to 1830. Transportation was rapidly changing; a national road linked the Potomac and the Ohio rivers, and the Erie Canal was completed in 1825. The lives of vast numbers of ordinary people were being altered as a result of these economic and social changes.

In the midst of these transformations, the **Second Great Awakening** reaffirmed the role of religion in the lives of believers. The movement began in the late 1790s and reached its zenith in the 1830s. Where earlier Calvinist preachers had spoken of predestination, preachers of this era such as Timothy Dwight and Charles Finney proclaimed that one's actions on earth played at least some role in the individual's fate after death. During this period, **revival meetings**, some lasting as long as a week, would cause followers to faint, speak in tongues, or writhe uncontrollably. The Second Great Awakening began as a rural phenomenon, but by the 1820s it spread to the cities as well. Evangelical sects such as the Methodists and the Baptists also grew in popularity.

Women played a significant role in the revivalism of the era. Many women became dedicated Christians and worked as volunteers for Protestant churches. In addition, many of these churches set up "academies" to educate women.

Other Reform Movements

Many individuals involved in the religious fervor of the era wanted to use that enthusiasm to reform society. Many wanted to act to improve the lives of those living in the cities and others with disadvantages. Dorothea Dix campaigned for better treatment of the mentally ill in the 1830s and 1840s. A prison reform movement also developed. In addition, a large **temperance movement** developed in this period, urging the working class to not drink in excess. Individuals such as Horace Mann spoke out for formal education for all children, the expansion of the school year, and the need for rigorous standards of teacher training.

Many Christians, especially in the North, began to speak out forcefully about the treatment of American slaves. In the 1820s and 1830s, the **Abolitionist movement** gained a large number of supporters. Abolitionists considered slavery to be a sin. The most prominent abolitionist was William Lloyd Garrison, who founded *The Liberator*, his antislavery newspaper, in 1831. Some were against slavery for other reasons. The **American Colonization Society**, founded in the South in 1817, opposed slavery on the grounds that it encouraged contact between blacks and whites; members of this organization urged slave owners to free their slaves and return them to Africa.

Frederick Douglass, an ex-slave, was another leader of the abolitionist movement, who in 1845 would write the *Narrative of the Life of Frederick Douglass*, a key text for those who opposed slavery. In 1831, Nat Turner, a slave in Virginia, organized a bloody slave revolt that killed 60 whites. As was the case in the **Stono Rebellion,** the revolt was brutally repressed, and **Black Codes** and other restrictions on slaves in Southern states became more harsh.

Political Reform: The Jacksonian Era (1829–1841)

Alexis de Tocqueville and other visitors from Europe noticed a different spirit in America than what existed in European countries. Tocqueville viewed with wonder the egalitarian system that he observed in virtually all aspects of American life. Many political changes both before and during the presidency of Andrew Jackson accentuated the sense that the "common man" reigned in this era.

Changes were already taking place in how presidential candidates were chosen. In 1800, only five states chose electors to the Electoral College by popular vote. By 1824, 18 out of 24 states chose electors in this manner. By the 1824 campaign, banners, posters, buttons, and hats were commonplace (the 1828 campaign was the first time when these were mass-produced).

In addition, more and more people could vote. By 1824, property qualification, long a method to keep the "rabble" away from the political process, had been eliminated in most states. Blacks (even free blacks in the North) and women were still excluded from the political process.

Election of 1824

In this election, Secretary of the Treasury William Crawford, Speaker of the House Henry Clay, Secretary of State John Quincy Adams, and Tennessee's Andrew Jackson, all ran for president. All of them considered themselves Republicans (the party was now referred to in many newspapers as **Democratic-Republicans**). Jackson won the most popular votes, but only 38 percent of the electoral votes, so the election was turned over to the House of Representatives. Speaker of the House Clay threw his support to Adams, who won in the House and then appointed Clay to the position of secretary of state.

For the next four years, supporters of Jackson did everything they could to sabotage the presidency of John Quincy Adams, constantly reminding themselves of the "corrupt bargain" between Adams and Clay that had decided the 1824 election.

1828 Presidential Election

The 1828 presidential campaign was the model for many political campaigns of the future. Campaign rallies were held by supporters of both Quincy Adams and Jackson. Mudslinging was a daily occurrence during the campaign. Jackson's supporters claimed that Adams stole the 1824 election and gave too many fancy dinners; they also claimed that when he had been envoy to Russia, Adams had helped procure American prostitutes for the Russian tsar. Supporters of Adams said that Jackson was a murderer and an adulterer (the charge was made that his wife was an adulteress as well). Jackson won the election handily; under him, the **Democratic party** became the first real political party of the United States.

Jackson as President

Andrew Jackson had been born in a log cabin, but when he was elected president in 1828, he was a planter and slaveholder. He was the first president from the West and had first achieved fame by fighting Native Americans. Jackson, however, was not naïve in terms of politics; he had been a congressman and a senator from Tennessee, in addition to serving as the territorial governor of Florida. Jackson was personally popular, especially with the common people.

Jackson also expressed loyalty to those who supported him politically. He infrequently consulted with his appointed cabinet, relying instead on his "**Kitchen Cabinet**," the inner circle of his political supporters. Jackson also utilized the **spoils system** to give other political supporters jobs in the government.

Jackson also wanted to return to the Jeffersonian ideal of America as a nation of independent yeoman farmers. He opposed excessive government involvement in economic affairs, fearing that in most cases only wealthy interests benefited from that involvement. In modern terms, Jackson favored "smaller government" and was not afraid to use the power of the presidential veto to stop government programs he thought were excessive. At the end of his presidency, Jackson appointed Roger B. Taney as chief justice of the Supreme Court; the Taney court would validate almost all of Jackson's decisions favoring states rights.

To many of his opponents, Jackson was a paradox. While he spoke of the need to limit the influence of government in society, he increased the power of the presidency. Opponents often referred to him as "King Andrew I." On the issue of slavery, Jackson was no friend of Abolitionists; he was a slave owner and was opposed to reform of the slave system.

Nullification Controversy

Jackson was forced early in his presidency to face the issue of the power of the states in relation to the power of the federal government. In 1828, Congress passed a bill authorizing new tariffs on imported manufacturing of cloth and iron. The cost of these goods rose dramatically, and legislators in South Carolina began to revisit the doctrine of **nullification**, whereby individual states could rule on the constitutionality of federal laws. Jackson's own vice president, John C. Calhoun of South Carolina, stated that the practice of nullification was a necessity to protect states from the potential tyranny of the federal government.

In 1830, a debate in the U.S. Senate over western land sales between Robert Hayne of South Carolina and Daniel Webster of Massachusetts evolved into a debate on nullification. In the **Webster-Hayne Debate**, Daniel Webster argued that if nullification were to proceed, the results would be "states dissevered, discordant, belligerent; on a land rent with civil feuds, or drenched . . . in fraternal blood!" President Jackson was a believer in states' rights but firmly opposed the concept of nullification.

New tariffs were imposed on imported goods, and in November 1832 a specially called convention in South Carolina voted to nullify the law imposing these tariffs. Jackson moved troops and federal marshals to South Carolina to collect the tariff payments there; Congress authorized these decisions when it passed the **Force Act**. John Calhoun resigned as vice president (Jackson suggested privately that he should be hanged). A crisis was avoided when Congress passed a bill, acceptable to South Carolina, that lowered the tariffs to be collected.

Bank Crisis

The second bank of the United States was chartered in 1816 (it was a crucial part of Henry Clay's American System). The bank issued national currency, regulated loan rates, and controlled state banks. The bank had been run since 1823 by Nicholas Biddle. As stated previously, Jackson was suspicious of government involvement in the economy. These suspicions extended to the national bank.

Henry Clay was going to run for president in the 1832 election and wanted to use the Bank as a campaign issue. Clay began pushing to have the Bank rechartered, even though its original charter did not expire until 1836. Clay was convinced that national support of the Bank would swing supporters his way. Jackson vetoed the rechartering proposal, claiming it served special interests and little else. This increased his popularity with the public and helped ensure his reelection in 1832.

Jackson wanted to destroy the national bank, and in 1833, he ordered that money be removed from it and placed in state or local banks (Jackson's political enemies called these his "pet banks"). To keep the national bank going, Biddle increased interest rates and called in loans that had been made to state banks. The results of this **Bank War** would eventually be the **panic of 1837** and a depression that would last into the 1840s.

Whig Party: A Challenge to the Democratic-Republicans

In the 1830s, the **Whig party** emerged as the major opposition party to the party of Jackson. The Whigs and the Democratic-Republicans battled for elections throughout the 1830s and 1840s. Taking their lead from the legacy of Andrew Jackson, the Democrats generally favored a limited government. They saw urbanization and industrialization as necessary evils; the America they favored was still essentially a Jeffersonian one.

The Whigs favored more governmental involvement in commercial activities and favored the national bank and industrial growth. They were opposed to rapid and uncontrolled settlement of the West. Consistent with their view of a more activist government, the Whigs also were more likely to sponsor reformist legislation. Predictably, businessmen from the North and Northeast supported the Whigs, as did Southern planters. The Democrats were generally supported by the "common man," which included small farmers, factory workers, and smaller merchants. A Democrat Martin Van Buren won the 1836 election, but Whig William Henry Harrison was elected in 1840. Harrison died after one month in office and was succeeded by John Tyler. Developments in Texas and American expansionism would become important issues during his presidency.

Chapter Review

Rapid Review

To achieve the perfect 5, you should be able to explain the following:

- A new production system developed in textile mills such as those that existed in Lowell, Massachusetts, in the early nineteenth century.
- The Monroe Doctrine boldly proclaimed that the Western Hemisphere was off limits to European intrusion.
- Beginning in 1824, it was official American policy to move Native American tribes west of the Mississippi; the horrors of many of these relocations are well documented.
- The Second Great Awakening influenced many to become involved in reform movements, including the Abolitionist movement.
- The presidency of Andrew Jackson is celebrated as an era when the "common man" reigned supreme, although Jackson greatly expanded the powers of the presidency.
- The Democratic party of Andrew Jackson was the first real political party in American history.
- Jackson's tariff policy caused a renewal of interest in the policy of nullification in several Southern state legislatures.
- In the 1830s, the Whig party emerged as the major party opposing the Democratic party of Jackson.

Time Line

1790s: Beginning of Second Great Awakening
1816: Second bank of United States chartered
Tariff of 1816 imposes substantial import tariffs
Election of James Monroe
1819: Panic of 1819 (unemployment lasts until 1823)
1820: Missouri Compromise
Reelection of James Monroe
1820s: Growth of New England textile mills
1823: Monroe Doctrine
1824: Proposal by President Monroe to move Native Americans west of the Mississippi River
1825: John Quincy Adams elected president by House of Representatives (no candidate had won a majority in Electoral College)
1828: Andrew Jackson elected president
1830: Passage of Indian Removal Act in Congress
Webster-Hayne Debate
1830s: Growth of the Whig party
1831: Cherokee nation goes to court to defend tribal rights in *Cherokee Nation v. Georgia*
First issue of William Lloyd Garrison's *The Liberator* published
1832: Andrew Jackson reelected
Nullification crisis after nullification of tariffs by South Carolina
1834: First strike of women textile workers in Lowell, Massachusetts
1836: Democrat, Martin Van Buren, elected president
1840: Whig, William Henry Harrison, elected president

> Review Questions

1. President Monroe claimed that westward relocation of Native Americans would be to the advantage of the Native Americans because
   A. they would not be bothered west of the Mississippi
   B. the American military would protect them during the journey
   C. they would be well compensated for the tribal lands that they were leaving
   D. settlers west of the Mississippi were receptive to Native American settlement there

2. The concept of nullification became an issue during this period when
   A. Georgia opposed congressional legislation concerning slavery.
   B. South Carolina nullified congressional legislation concerning the removal of Native Americans.
   C. South Carolina nullified congressional tariff bills.
   D. Southern representatives to the Electoral College switched their votes in the 1824 election.

3. Critics of Andrew Jackson would make all of the following claims *except* that
   A. he was a very common man and not fit to be president
   B. he gave too much power to the presidency
   C. he lacked experience in governmental affairs
   D. he relied too much on his "Kitchen Cabinet"

4. The following are *true* about the textile mills of New England in the early nineteenth century *except*
   A. a large percentage of their workforce was made up of women
   B. they depended on water for power
   C. they used a system called the putting-out system
   D. there was little labor unrest in the mills until the 1830s and 1840s

5. Horace Mann is associated with
   A. abolitionism
   B. the temperance movement
   C. prison reform
   D. educational reform

〉 Answers and Explanations

1. **A.** Monroe stated that Native Americans could not avoid being continually harassed if they lived east of the Mississippi, but that this would not happen after they moved.

2. **C.** Because the tariff bills increased the prices of cloth and iron, the South Carolina legislature first nullified the Tariff of 1828.

3. **C.** All of the other criticisms were often made against Jackson. However, he did have an impressive background: before becoming president, he had served as a congressman and a senator from Tennessee and as the territorial governor of Florida.

4. **C.** It was the putting-out system that these mills replaced.

5. **D.** Horace Mann wrote and spoke about the need to improve schools and to improve teacher training methods.

CHAPTER 14

Union Expanded and Challenged (1835–1860)

IN THIS CHAPTER

Summary: Guided by the principle of "Manifest Destiny," Americans began to stream westward in the 1830s. By the mid-1840s settlers were entrenched in the Oregon and California territories. Adventurers also settled in Texas and helped the Texans defeat the Mexican army in 1836. The Mexican-American War took place between 1846 and 1847. By the terms of the treaty ending this war the United States paid Mexico $15 million dollars; in return the United States acquired the northern part of the Texas territory and New Mexico and California. The pivotal issue for Americans remained whether newly acquired territories would enter the Union as slave states or as free states. Under the Missouri Compromise a line was drawn westward to the Pacific Ocean; all territories north of the line would enter the Union as free states and all territories south of the line would come in as slave states. The issue of whether California would enter the Union as a free or slave state necessitated the Compromise of 1850. The Kansas-Nebraska Act of 1854 stated that settlers living in those territories could vote on whether they would become slave states or free states. The *Dred Scott* Supreme Court decision of 1857 stated that Congress had no right to prohibit slavery in the territories and that even though Scott, an ex-slave, had spent time in a free state and a free territory this did not make him a free man. Tensions between the North and the South remained high. In the 1860 presidential election, Illinois Congressman Abraham Lincoln campaigned on the need to contain slavery in the territories. After his election, representatives of seven Southern states met to create the Confederate States of America, with Jefferson Davis as the first president of the Confederacy.

KEY IDEA

Keywords

Manifest Destiny: concept that became popularized in the 1840s stating that it was the God-given mission of the United States to expand westward.

Mexican-American War: war fought over possession of Texas, which was claimed by both Mexico and the United States; the settlement ending this war gave the United States the northern part of the Texas territory and the territories of New Mexico and California.

Compromise of 1850: temporarily ending tensions between the North and the South, this measure allowed California to enter the Union as a free state but also strengthened the Fugitive Slave Law.

Fugitive Slave Act: part of the Compromise of 1850, legislation that set up special commissions in northern states to determine if accused runaway slaves were actually that. Commissioners were given more money if the accused was found to be a runaway than if he/she was not. Many northern state legislatures attempted to circumvent this law.

Kansas-Nebraska Act (1854): compromise that allowed settlers in Kansas and Nebraska to vote to decide if they would enter the Union as free states or slave states. Much violence and confusion took place in Kansas as various types of "settlers" moved into this territory in the months before the vote in an attempt to influence it.

***Dred Scott* case:** critical Supreme Court ruling that stated that slaves were property and not people; as a result they could not seek a ruling from any court. The ruling also stated that Congress had no legal right to ban slavery in any territory.

Ideology of Manifest Destiny

The idea of **Manifest Destiny** fueled the continued American expansion westward. Americans from the time of the Puritans spoke of America as a community with a divine mission. Beginning in the 1830s, some began to express the view that it was "God's plan" that America expand beyond the Mississippi River. Both political leaders and Protestant missionary organizations fervently supported western expansion. In 1845, Democratic newspaperman John O'Sullivan wrote that the most critical need for America was "the fulfillment of our Manifest Destiny to overspread the continent allotted by Providence for the free development of our yearly multiplying millions."

Americans had begun to settle in Oregon in the 1830s. The six-month, 2,000-mile journey along the **Oregon Trail** brought settlers to the Oregon territory; many of them settled in the Willamette Valley. Many settlers in the Ohio Valley began to catch "Oregon Fever" by 1842; stories of a mild climate and the possibility of fur trading fueled the imaginations of many. Missionaries came to "tame" the Native Americans who lived in the region. By 1845, over 5,000 had streamed into the Oregon territory. A section of Oregon was controlled by the British and a section by America. "Fifty-four Forty or Fight" became the rallying cry for expansionists who wanted all of Oregon to be under American control. The **Oregon Treaty** of 1846 gave most of Oregon to the Americans. The California territory, controlled by Spain, also attracted the interest of American settlers; American settlers first arrived there in the 1830s. The future of expansion in Oregon and California were key issues in the 1844 presidential campaign.

"Remember the Alamo!"

The drive for expansion, which fueled the dreams of many Americans in the first half of the nineteenth century, made eventual conflict with Mexico inevitable. Mexico gained its independence from Spain in 1821 and encouraged the economic development of its northern province of Texas (which consisted of what we now know as the state of Texas and parts of Kansas, Oklahoma, New Mexico, Wyoming, and Colorado). American economic investment was encouraged in the region. American settlers who would agree to become Mexican citizens, become Catholics, and encourage other Americans to come to Mexico were given large tracts of land for next to nothing. These settlers numbered nearly 30,000 by 1836.

Predictably, many Americans who settled in Texas were not diligent in fulfilling their obligations to the Mexican government, causing the Mexican government to act to reassert control over Texas. In 1836, the American settlers and some Mexicans living in Texas revolted against Mexican control of Texas. On March 2, they declared that Texas was an independent state and established a constitution (in which slavery was legal). Led by Davey Crockett and Jim Bowie, 165 Texans were defeated at the Alamo on March 6 by over 3,000 Mexican soldiers, but their cry of "Remember the Alamo!" became the rallying cry for those fighting for the independence of Texas. A declaration of independence was issued in early March 1836 by a convention of Texans opposed to continued Mexican rule.

Many American adventurers eager for land now poured into Texas and helped the Texans defeat the Mexican army on April 21, 1836. An independent Republic of Texas was proclaimed. General Sam Houston, who had led the army that defeated the Mexicans, became president of the Lone Star Republic. Most people living there (the vast majority being Americans) desired to become part of the United States. Andrew Jackson gave stirring speeches favoring the annexation of Texas and offered diplomatic recognition to the Lone Star Republic just before he left office. However, most Whigs were against annexation, fearing it would cause war with Mexico and domestic dissension. Abolitionists in the North were opposed to it, since they feared the entry of another slave state (which Texas would undoubtedly be) into the Union. Jackson feared that the annexation of Texas would hurt the chances of his chosen successor, Martin Van Buren, in the 1836 presidential election. He never acted on the annexation issue, causing the Republic of Texas to turn to Europe for potential allies.

Martin Van Buren also refused to support legislation that would make Texas part of the United States. William Henry Harrison, a Whig, defeated Van Buren in the 1840 presidential election but died after one month in office. Harrison's vice president was John Tyler, a Democrat who had been placed on the ticket to appeal to Southerners. Tyler favored the annexation of Texas and, by mid-1844, had completed negotiations with the Texans on a treaty that would bring Texas into the United States. John C. Calhoun, the secretary of state, wrote a note to the British government concerning the situation in Texas; in the note, he stated that the continuation of slavery would be good for Texas. This was enough to doom the treaty when it went to the Senate for approval.

Pivotal Election of 1844

Democrat James K. Polk was elected president in 1844. Polk was the first American **dark horse candidate** for president, as he was not one of the announced candidates before the Democratic convention of that year. The campaign of that year showed several trends that would be pivotal to American political life in the 1840s and 1850s. The South and Southern interests increasingly influenced and were reflected in Democratic policies, and the Walker Tariff of 1846 established a very low tariff on imported goods, delighting many in the South and disgusting many Northern industrialists.

Abolitionism officially entered presidential politics in 1844. The Liberty party, with James Birney as its presidential candidate, was an Abolitionist party. Although Birney attracted only 62,000 votes, abolitionism, and the sectional divisions it would help to foster, became a permanent part of the political landscape until the Civil War.

The 1844 election also demonstrated that desire for Manifest Destiny was the most important issue facing America at the time. Most historians credit Polk's support of American expansionism as the major reason for his election. Polk was inaugurated in March 1845. By December, Texas had entered the Union. Expansionism and slavery also became increasingly intertwined as a single issue. The status of slavery in each newly acquired territory would have enormous political consequences, as forces in the North and the South were determined that the number of slave and free states remain equal.

War with Mexico

The reasons for the Mexican-American War were numerous. Patriots in Mexico were outraged when Texas joined the United States, as they considered Texas still to be part of Mexico. The war served the economic interests of groups both in Mexico and the United States. However, the main reason for war was the determination of President Polk to fulfill what he perceived to be America's mission, to occupy the lands all the way to the Pacific Ocean, and his willingness to use force to accomplish this aim.

Polk did much to provoke war with the Mexicans. He encouraged settlers in Mexico to occupy territory all the way to the Rio Grande River, which the Mexicans considered to be outside of the territory of Texas (Mexico considered the Nueces River, north of the Rio Grande, as the border between Texas and the rest of Mexico). Polk also wanted to buy territory from Mexico that would allow the United States to expand all the way to California. In October 1845, he offered the Mexican government $5 million for the territory between the Nueces and Rio Grande rivers, $25 million for California, and $5 million for other Mexican territory in the West. John Slidell, the diplomat sent to Mexico City with Polk's offer, was never even received by the Mexican government. Early in 1846, Polk sent an American force commanded by General Zachary Taylor to defend the territory between the Nueces and Rio Grande rivers. In early April, part of this force was ambushed by the Mexican army. Polk had to do little to convince the American Congress to issue a declaration of war against Mexico on May 13, 1846.

Many Whigs had hoped the conflict with Mexico could be peacefully negotiated; Abolitionists feared the conflict with Mexico was little more than a Southern ruse to expand slavery in the American territories. Texas had never achieved real prosperity since its independence from Mexico, and the Mexican government was riddled with corruption. President Polk had predicted that the Mexicans would refuse American efforts to purchase western territories; and he proceeded, through officials stationed there, to let Americans and Mexicans living in California know that if they rose in opposition to Mexican control of the area, the American army would protect them. Not coincidentally, American naval and infantry forces arrived in California in late 1845 as a show of American force. Shortly after the American declaration of war against Mexico, settlers rose up in revolt, supported by American infantry forces commanded by John C. Fremont. On July 4, 1846, the **Bear Flag Republic** was officially proclaimed in the California territory.

American troops also entered Mexico itself, easily defeating the Mexican army. Forces under Zachary Taylor were especially successful in winning battles over the Mexicans in late 1846 and early 1847. The Mexican government refused to surrender or negotiate with the Americans. President Polk then sent an American force under General Winfield Scott to Mexico to occupy Mexico City, the capital. Scott landed on Mexican territory at Veracruz on March 8, 1847, and was victorious in several battles against the Mexicans. Mexico still refused to settle for peace, and on September 13, 1847, Scott's army entered Mexico City. Mexican partisans continued guerrilla warfare well into 1848.

Effects of the Mexican War

The **Treaty of Guadalupe Hidalgo** was signed on February 2, 1848, and officially ended the Mexican-American War. Many who had favored war considered the treaty too generous to the defeated Mexicans. For $15 million the United States acquired the Texas territory north of the Rio Grande, New Mexico, and California (the exact territory they had previously offered to buy). The American government also assumed all claims of Americans against the Mexican government.

The territory of the United States increased by one-third as a result of this treaty, and the controversy over slavery in the new territories was immense. In 1846, David Wilmot, a Democratic representative from Pennsylvania, introduced an amendment to a bill authorizing funding for the Mexican-American War that stated slavery could not exist in any territory acquired from Mexico. The **Wilmot Proviso** was passed by the House of Representatives four times and rejected by the Senate each time. Nevertheless, each debate concerning the bill stirred up intense sectional differences concerning slavery in the territories. Southerners such as John C. Calhoun strenuously argued that the federal government had no right to outlaw something in an American territory that was legal in a number of American states. President Polk's compromise decision was to continue the line drawn by the **Missouri Compromise** out to the Pacific Ocean, with slavery allowed in territories south of the line and not allowed in territories north of the line.

To avoid being hurt by the controversies surrounding slavery, both the Democrats and the Whigs said little about it in the 1848 presidential election. Zachary Taylor ran as a Whig and was victorious, largely because of his war record in Mexico and because he made no comments whatsoever about the future of slavery in the territories. Some members of the Liberty party and defectors from the Whig and Democratic parties formed the **Free-Soil party**, whose main purpose was to oppose slavery in the newly acquired western territories. The Free-Soilers nominated former president Van Buren, who won 10 percent of the popular vote.

Political Challenges of the 1850s

The controversies of the 1850s largely centered around slavery and its status in the newly acquired American territories. Americans had been able to compromise on such issues in the first half of the nineteenth century. By the 1850s, the volatile nature of debate on the issue of slavery made compromise much harder to come by.

The discovery of gold in California in January 1848 caused a flood of "diggers" to enter the territory. Within a year, over 80,000 "forty-niners" entered the state. By the end of 1849, the territory's population swelled to over 100,000. Law enforcement and governmental controls were severely lacking in much of the territory. Zachary Taylor encouraged settlers in California and New Mexico to draft constitutions and to apply for statehood. By the end of 1849, California had adopted a constitution prohibiting slavery; New Mexico did the same six months later.

Taylor's proposal to allow California to enter the Union as a nonslave state infuriated many Southerners. Southern senators railed that much of the California territory was south of the Missouri Compromise line: shouldn't slavery be allowed in that part of California? A convention was called for representatives of Southern states to come together and discuss leaving the Union. John C. Calhoun captured the feeling of many Southerners when he said, "I trust we shall persist in our resistance until restoration of all our rights, or disunion, one or the other, is the consequence."

Henry Clay, the author of the Missouri Compromise, spoke forcefully against many of Calhoun's arguments and wrote the parts of the legislation that together would be called the **Compromise of 1850**. Both the North and the South got some of what they wanted in this compromise. Northerners were happy that the legislation allowed California to enter the Union as a free state, that the residents of the New Mexico and Utah territories would decide if these areas would be slave territories, and that slave trading was eliminated in Washington, DC. Southerners were satisfied over several provisions found in the legislation: provisions of the **Fugitive Slave Act** were toughened, Congress stated that it didn't have jurisdiction over interstate slave trade, and slavery was allowed to continue in Washington. Eight months of debate were needed to pass all provisions of the compromise. Senator Stephen A. Douglas of Illinois was the most effective spokesperson for the cause of the compromise. California entering the Union as a free state gave the free states a majority; in the future, that majority would grow, helping to explain the increased tensions between the North and the South between 1850 and 1860.

The presidential election of 1852 was another campaign devoid of much discussion of the slave issue. The Free-Soilers got half the votes they had received in the 1848 election. General Winfield Scott was the candidate of the Whigs. Like Zachary Taylor in 1848, he made few public statements on political issues. Franklin Pierce was another **dark horse candidate** who won the Democratic nomination and then the presidency.

Effects of the Compromise of 1850

The part of the Compromise of 1850 that most bothered Abolitionists in the North was the strengthening of the Fugitive Slave Act. Under the new provisions of the bill, judges in the North determined the fate of blacks accused of being escaped slaves. Accused runaways were denied jury proceedings and often were denied the right to testify in their own trials. Heavy financial penalties were imposed on Northerners who helped slaves escape or who hid slaves. Harriet Beecher Stowe's ***Uncle Tom's Cabin*** was written as a response to the Fugitive Slave Act. Stowe demonstrated the immorality of slavery in her novel, which sold nearly 275,000 copies in its first year of publication.

Presidency of Franklin Pierce

Pierce's foreign policy was proexpansionism. In 1853, he sent a naval force under Commodore Matthew Perry to Japan to open Japan to American trade and diplomatic contact. American diplomats negotiated the **Gadsden Purchase** with Mexico, which gave

America an additional southern route for trade (and territory for a proposed transcontinental railroad). Pierce also initiated efforts to purchase Cuba from the Spanish. When this effort proved unsuccessful, many in the Pierce administration favored the seizing of Cuba by force, which infuriated many in the North. Pierce's policies seemed to benefit Southern interests and were viewed with suspicion by many in the North.

This period also witnessed the decline of the Whig party. Many former Whigs became members of the American or **Know-Nothing party** that developed in response to the rising immigration from Ireland and Germany, which had begun in the late 1840s. The Know-Nothing party was **nativist** and especially anti-Catholic. They favored restrictions on further immigration and various schemes that would keep recent immigrants from voting. The fact that it was the second most powerful party in America during the first years of the Pierce administration demonstrates the weakness of the two-party system in this period.

Return of Sectional Conflict

The desire to organize settlements in Kansas and Nebraska brought tensions between the North and the South back to the forefront. According to the provisions of the Missouri Compromise, slavery would be banned in both of these territories. Stephen A. Douglas, sponsor of the bill that proposed the creation of the Kansas and Nebraska territories, wanted to create a large region free of Native Americans so that a transcontinental railroad could be built between Chicago and the West Coast. Douglas was pressured by Southern senators and included a provision in the bill that the existence of slavery in these territories would be decided by a vote of those who lived there. This **Kansas-Nebraska Act** infuriated many in the North. The bill was passed with the support of President Pierce.

The fury over the passage of the Kansas-Nebraska Act caused the creation of the **Republican party**. The party was an exclusively Northern one and was dedicated to the principle that slavery should be prohibited in all territories. Some former Democrats, Whigs, and Free-Soilers made up the base of the Republican party, which would quickly replace the Know-Nothings as the second most important political party in the United States.

"Bleeding Kansas": Slave or Free?

In preparation for elections that would be held in 1855, states and interests supporting and opposing slavery all were active in sending settlers into Kansas that would support their cause. Abolitionists financed the journey to Kansas of many settlers opposed to slavery; at the same time, many Southern states "encouraged" settlers to travel there. Conflicts, often involving bloodshed, erupted between the two sides. Many proslavery settlers flooded into Kansas from Missouri, thus ensuring the election of a proslavery legislature in 1855 by casting illegal ballots. The legislature enacted measures designed to protect slavery in the territory (the "Lecompton Constitution" made slavery legal in a constitutional sense). Free-Soilers proceeded to elect their own legislature and adopted equally harsh antislavery legislation. Violence continued in "**Bleeding Kansas**" in 1856: the free-soil settlement at Lawrence was attacked, and in response, Abolitionist John Brown and his followers killed five proslavery settlers. Fighting between supporters and opponents of slavery continued throughout the year.

Democrat James Buchanan won the presidential election of 1856. The opposition to him was split, with John C. Fremont running as a Republican and ex-president Millard Fillmore running as the Know-Nothing candidate. It should be noted that Fremont and Fillmore together gained nearly 55 percent of the popular vote.

Dred Scott Decision

The ***Dred Scott* case** finally made it to the Supreme Court docket in 1856. Many hoped it would decisively end the controversy over slavery in the territories. Dred Scott was a former slave who was suing for his freedom on the basis that his owner had taken him to stay first in a free state, Illinois, and then into a free territory, Wisconsin.

The final decision of the Supreme Court, in essence, supported the Southern position concerning slavery in the territories. The court ruled that Scott as a slave had no legal right to sue in federal court, that his time in a free state and a free territory did not make him a free man, and that Congress had no right to prohibit slavery in the territories, since the Constitution protected property rights and slaves were still considered property.

Instead of easing tensions between the North and South, the *Dred Scott* decision only made tensions between the sections worse. Southerners felt their position had been justified and felt little need to compromise with the North; Northerners were more convinced than ever that "slave interests" controlled all the branches of government.

President Buchanan further antagonized Northerners by recommending that Kansas be admitted to the Union as a slave state, even though the legislature in Kansas had been elected by largely illegal means (Kansas was finally admitted to the Union as a free state in 1861).

Lincoln-Douglas Debates

Stephen Douglas was opposed by Abraham Lincoln in the 1858 election for senator from Illinois. Lincoln had been a Whig but was now a Republican, having broken from the Whig party over slavery. Lincoln was a practicing attorney, had been in the U.S. Congress during the Mexican War, and had narrowly lost an earlier bid for the Senate in 1852. Douglas and Lincoln debated at seven locations throughout Illinois in the months leading up to the election. The issues of slavery and the territories dominated all of these debates. At a debate in Freeport, Lincoln asked Douglas how the residents of a territory could exclude slavery in light of the *Dred Scott* decision. Douglas responded with the **Freeport Doctrine**, which maintained that a territory could exclude slavery if the laws and regulations written made slavery impossible to enforce. Douglas won the Senate seat, but Lincoln was recognized by many as an up-and-coming force in the Republican party.

John Brown's Raid

Radical Abolitionist John Brown and 18 followers seized the federal arsenal at Harper's Ferry, Virginia, on the evening of October 16, 1859. Brown hoped to incite a slave uprising by his actions. It would later become known that Brown's actions had been financed by several wealthy Northern Abolitionists. Brown was captured, tried for treason, and hanged. The response to Brown's death further intensified the tensions between the North and the South. Henry David Thoreau was one of many Northerners to consider Brown as "the bravest and humanest man in all the country," while Southerners were outraged by Northern support of Brown's actions.

Presidential Election of 1860

The election of Abraham Lincoln as president in 1860 virtually ensured that some Southern states would leave the Union. Lincoln campaigned on the need to contain slavery in the territories. The Democratic party split at their nominating convention, with Stephen Douglas receiving the support of Northern Democrats and John Breckinridge getting the backing of Southern Democrats. Douglas stated that the slave issue in the territories should be decided by a vote of those residing in each territory; Breckinridge proposed that slavery should be legally protected in the territories. John Bell also received some ex-Whig support as he ran as a candidate of the Constitutional Union party. Lincoln received nearly 40 percent of the popular vote and easily won the Electoral College vote.

To many Southerners, the election was an insult. A man had been elected president who virtually no one in the South had voted for. Since free states outnumbered slaves states, it was only natural that their representatives would dominate Congress and the Electoral College. Lincoln had repeatedly stated that Republicans had no interest in disturbing slavery in the South, but many Southerners did not believe him.

South Carolina was the first state to leave the Union on December 20, 1860. In the next six weeks, legislatures in Mississippi, Georgia, Florida, Alabama, Texas, and Louisiana all voted to do the same. Representatives of these seven states met in February 1861 to create the **Confederate States of America**, with former moderate Jefferson Davis elected as president. The only question remaining was where and when the first shots between the North and the South would actually be fired.

Chapter Review

Rapid Review

To achieve the perfect 5, you should be able to explain the following:

- The concept of Manifest Destiny spurred American expansion into Texas and the far West.
- American settlers much more loyal to the United States than to Mexico entered Texas in large numbers and encouraged Texas to break away from Mexico and eventually become an American state.
- The issue of slavery in the territories came to dominate American political debate more and more in the 1840s and 1850s.
- California entered the Union as a free state under the Missouri Compromise, upsetting the balance between free and slave states and intensifying the conflict between them.
- The Kansas-Nebraska Act created violence in these territories as they "decided" on whether they would be slave or free; both Abolitionists and proslavery forces shipped in supporters to help sway the elections in these territories.

- The *Dred Scott* decision only intensified tensions between the North and the South.
- The election of 1860 was seen as an insult to many in the South, and after its results were announced, the secession of Southern states from the Union was inevitable.

Time Line

1836: Texas territory rebels against Mexico; independent republic of Texas created
1841: Beginning of expansion into Oregon territory
1844: James K. Polk elected president
1845: Texas becomes a state of the United States
1846: Oregon Treaty with Britain gives most of Oregon to United States
   War with Mexico begins
   Wilmot Proviso passed
1848: Gold discovered in California; beginning of California gold rush
   Treaty of Guadalupe Hidalgo
   Formation of Free-Soil party
   Zachary Taylor elected president
1850: Passage of Compromise of 1850
1852: Franklin Pierce elected president
   Uncle Tom's Cabin by Harriet Beecher Stowe published
1854: Kansas-Nebraska Act passed
   Formation of the Republican party
1856: Democrat James Buchanan elected president
   "Bleeding Kansas"
1857: *Dred Scott* decision announced
1858: Lincoln-Douglas debates
   Freeport Doctrine issued by Stephen Douglas
1859: Harper's Ferry raid of John Brown
1860: Abraham Lincoln elected president
   South Carolina secedes from the Union (December)

> Review Questions

1. Northerners approved all of the provisions of the Compromise of 1850 *except*
   A. the section of the document concerning slavery in California
   B. the section of the document concerning the Fugitive Slave Law
   C. the section of the treaty on slave trading in Washington, DC
   D. the section of the document concerning slavery in New Mexico

2. During the presidential election of 1860
   A. the Democratic party had split and was running two candidates.
   B. the new president was someone whom almost no one in the South had voted for.
   C. the issue of the future of slavery in the territories was a major issue.
   D. all of the above.

3. According to the concept of Manifest Destiny
   A. it was primarily economic factors that caused Americans to expand westward.
   B. it was primarily political factors that caused Americans to expand westward.
   C. westward expansion was the fulfillment of America's destiny.
   D. overpopulation on the eastern seaboard forced westward expansion.

4. American settlers first came to Mexico in the early 1830s
   A. to avenge the attack on the Alamo
   B. for political reasons; most who came were disenchanted with American policy toward Native Americans
   C. out of personal loyalty to Davey Crockett or Jim Bowie
   D. because they could receive a large plot of land for next to nothing

5. The political party of the era that supported nativist policies was the
   A. Free-Soil party
   B. Democratic party
   C. Know-Nothing party
   D. Whig party

> Answers and Explanations

1. **B.** In the Compromise of 1850, provisions of the Fugitive Slave Law were made tougher. California was to enter the Union as a free state, the residents of New Mexico and Utah could decide if they wanted to be slave or free, and slave trading was outlawed in Washington, DC.

2. **D.** All of the factors mentioned concerning the 1860 election are true.

3. **C.** The concept of Manifest Destiny stated that social, political, and economic factors all came together to encourage western expansion, and that western expansion was actually "God's plan" for America.

4. **D.** Settlers who came and became Mexican citizens and Catholics could receive very large plots of land for almost nothing. The incident at the Alamo did not occur until 1836.

5. **C.** The Know-Nothing party, a popular party in the early 1850s, supported a number of anti-immigrant and anti-Catholic policies.

CHAPTER 15

Union Divided: The Civil War (1861–1865)

IN THIS CHAPTER

Summary: The Civil War was the culmination of nearly 40 years of tensions between the North and the South. Northern Abolitionists looked forward to the war with great anticipation: victory over the South would finally allow the dreaded institution of slavery to be eliminated. Northern industrialists saw the war as an opportunity, at long last, to expand their control of American industry. The majority of Southerners rejoiced at the onset of war; they perceived that victory would allow the "Southern way of life" to continue without constant criticism from the North. As in many wars, politicians and generals on both sides predicted a quick victory. Newspapers in both the North and the South declared that the war would be over by Christmas of 1861.

To state that the Civil War was just about slavery is an oversimplification. Certainly, criticism by Northern Abolitionists of the "peculiar institution" of slavery, and Southern responses to that criticism, were important factors. However, other tensions between the North and the South also existed. The future of the American economy as seen by Northern industrialists differed drastically from the desires and needs of the leaders of Southern plantation societies. Most important, the Southern view of "states' rights" differed most dramatically from the view of the Union held in the North. By 1861, many political leaders in the South fervently espoused the views that John C. Calhoun had formulated decades earlier. It was up to the individual state to decide on the validity of any federal law or federal action for that state. This position was intolerable to President Lincoln and most political leaders in the North. If anything, it was debate over the state's rights issue that made the Civil War inevitable.

Other factors increased the animosity between the North and the South. By this point, slavery was synonymous with Southern identity; in Southern eyes, any attack on slavery was an attack on the South as a whole. The fact that this struggle between the North and the South had gone on for 40 years served to harden positions on both sides. In addition, by this point the population of the North was greater than the population of the South, and the number of free states was greater than the number of slave states. As a result, Southerners knew that Northern antislave interests would control the Congress (and the ability to influence Supreme Court appointments) and the Electoral College for the foreseeable future.

Keywords

First Battle of Bull Run (1861): early Civil War engagement ending in defeat for the Union army; this battle convinced many in the North that victory over the Confederacy would not be as easy as they first thought it would be.

Emancipation Proclamation: January 1, 1863, proclamation that freed slaves in Southern territories was controlled by the Union army; this executive proclamation by President Lincoln also committed the Union to the abolition of slavery.

Battle of Gettysburg (1863): bloodiest overall battle of the Civil War; many historians claim that the Southern defeat in this battle was the beginning of the end for the Confederacy.

Appomattox: Virginia courthouse where General Robert E. Lee surrendered Confederate forces on April 9, 1865.

Advantages of the North and South in the War

Many Southerners were very excited when the Civil War finally began, yet there were some harsh realities facing them as the war commenced. Most of the nation's wealth was situated in the North; the industrialization of the North would give Northerners an advantage in producing guns, bullets, and other materials needed for warfare. The Northern railway system was far superior to the existing railways in the South. Most influential banks and financial markets were located in the North. More people (by a nearly 3-to-1 margin) lived in the North. The South could at least say that they were larger than the North; conquering the South would be a formidable task. At the outset of the war, Southerners also felt that their officer corps, led by men such as Robert E. Lee, was superior to the officer corps of the Union, led by Winfield Scott.

Aftermath of Secession

As mentioned in the previous chapter, South Carolina, Mississippi, Florida, Louisiana, Texas, Georgia, and Alabama all voted to secede from the Union in late 1860 or early 1861. In February 1861, the **Confederate States of America** was officially created. States in the Upper South (such as Virginia and Kentucky) were not eager to join the secessionist movement (there were fewer slaves in these states). Leaders of Kentucky and Maryland proposed that Congress in Washington enact legislation that would protect slavery in any territory or state where it already existed; the desire of these leaders was the preservation of the Union. President James Buchanan did little to aid the situation. Buchanan stated in December

1860 that secession from the Union was illegal, but that nowhere in the Constitution was it stated that any state could be forced to remain in the Union.

Politicians in South Carolina and elsewhere in the South interpreted Buchanan's statement as, in essence, stating that he would do nothing to bring back the seceded states and that they were now independent. Leaders in South Carolina demanded the surrender of **Fort Sumter**, a federal fort located in Charleston harbor. To test the will of the leaders of South Carolina, Buchanan sent an unarmed merchant ship to bring supplies to the fort in January 1861. When the ship was fired on, Buchanan did not send the navy in (which many in South Carolina was sure he would do); "patriots" in South Carolina and elsewhere in the South now felt certain that independence was theirs.

As the crisis continued at Fort Sumter, Senator John Crittenden of Kentucky emerged with a compromise plan. The **Crittenden Plan** proposed that the federal government guarantee the existence of slavery in any state where it existed, and that the line of the Missouri Compromise be extended all the way to the Pacific, with territories to the north of the line being free from slavery and those south of the line having slavery. Republicans in Congress rejected this plan, since it went away from the concept of "free soil" that president-elect Lincoln had just been elected on.

Attack on Fort Sumter and the Beginning of the War

Abraham Lincoln had to walk a political tightrope upon his inauguration in March 1861. It was necessary to maintain the authority of the federal government, but at the same time to do nothing that would provoke war with the South. Many of Lincoln's advisors thought that negotiations could bring at least some of the states that had seceded back into the Union. In his inauguration speech, however, Lincoln stated that force would be used if necessary to preserve the Union.

The skill of Lincoln as president was immediately called upon. In April 1861, Lincoln sent another ship to supply Fort Sumter. The government of South Carolina was informed that the ship would be arriving and that no troops would land unless the delivery of these supplies was interfered with. Jefferson Davis and the Confederate government saw this as an opportunity to strike against the Union. Confederate guns bombed Fort Sumter for two days, and on April 14 the fort surrendered. Davis was hopeful that early victory would force states in the Upper South to turn to the Confederate cause; Confederates also hoped to obtain British and French assistance. Any thought of compromise between North and South ended with the attack on Fort Sumter.

Three days after the surrender of the fort, Virginia passed a resolution favoring secession. On the same day, Robert E. Lee rejected an offer to command the Union army, resigned from the Union army, and took control of the Confederate army. In the end, Lincoln was able to keep four of the states of the Upper South in the Union (Kentucky, Missouri, Maryland, and Delaware).

War Aims and Strategies

From the beginning of the war, the Southern defense of the slave system was unrelenting. This position greatly undermined the possibility of the Confederacy receiving aid from the French and the English. Economically, European support of the Confederacy would have made sense; European nations were dependent on cotton cultivated in the American

South. However, both France and England firmly opposed slavery and had outlawed it in their countries decades earlier. The South also overestimated the British need for Southern cotton; Britain soon proved that it could get cotton elsewhere.

Both sides began recruiting armies in the spring and early summer of 1861. Lincoln was able to summon support in the Northern states not from speeches on slavery but from the simple claim that the actions of the South was an attack on the very principles of the republican form of government. Both sides predicted early victory. The capital of the Confederacy was moved to Richmond, Virginia, after Virginia joined the Confederacy; cries of "On to Richmond!" filled the Northern newspapers. For political reasons, Lincoln pushed for an early attack against the South (Winfield Scott presented an alternative proposal, stating that the best policy for the North would be to blockade all Southern ports and starve the South into submission). A Union army advanced on Richmond. On July 21, 1861, at the **First Battle of Bull Run**, Union forces retreated in chaos back toward Washington. After this battle, Northern political leaders and generals conceded that victory in this war would not be as easy as they initially thought it might be.

Effects of Bull Run

The Battle of Bull Run showed both sides that new tactics would be necessary for victory. The plan proposed by Winfield Scott, now referred to as the **Anaconda Plan**, was reviewed more carefully by Abraham Lincoln. Lincoln had the United States Navy blockade Southern ports; as the war wore on, this became increasingly important. Industrial goods that the South had imported from the industrial North in earlier years now could not be obtained from Europe either. Later in the war, Confederate states could not export cotton to Europe for very badly needed currency. Another part of the Anaconda Plan called for Northern naval forces to control the Mississippi River. The Union made major headway with this part of the plan in April 1862 when a Union naval force captured New Orleans.

The Confederacy also made a major foreign trading mistake in early 1862. Cotton-producing states were convinced not to export cotton to England and France. Confederate leaders thought that textile factory owners in those countries would be so affected by this that they would pressure their governments to help the Confederacy and get their cotton back. Instead, Europeans turned elsewhere for cotton (especially India). As stated previously, when the South wanted to export cotton later in the war, they couldn't because of the naval blockade. It also became obvious that the organization of the South into a confederacy during a period of war was a disadvantage; individual state governments had the constitutional right to block critical tax programs and requisitions. The decision of the Confederacy to print paper money with no secure backing also would prove to be detrimental.

Union Triumphant in the West

The Confederacy won several more battles in 1862, including the **Second Battle of Bull Run**. General George McClellan was named commander of the Union army and began formulating a plan to attack the Confederacy from the west. In February 1862, forces commanded by General Ulysses S. Grant captured Fort Henry and Fort Donelson, in Tennessee. Forces on both sides realized the importance of these victories. Grant continued to conquer Southern territory from this position. On April 6, 1862, the incredibly bloody but inconclusive **Battle of Shiloh** was fought. Up until this point, it was the bloodiest battle ever fought in America. McClellan began to develop the reputation as a commander who was afraid to enter his troops into battle, even though the situation warranted it.

The Confederacy attempted to use technology to defeat the Northern naval blockade. In March 1862, they presented their very first **ironclad ship**, the *Merrimack*. Shortly after, the Union displayed the first Union ironclad, the *Monitor*. The two ironclads met once in battle, with neither ship able to do much damage to the other.

Developments in the South and in the North

Being a nation founded on the principle of **states' rights** was often a disadvantage for the Confederacy. Many Confederate soldiers who enlisted for one year in 1861 appeared ready to return home in 1862. General Robert E. Lee insisted that a system of **conscription** be introduced to ensure a steady supply of soldiers. In April 1862, the Confederate legislature passed laws requiring three years in the army for all white men from ages 18 to 35 (after the horrible losses of Antietam, this was extended to 45). Many advocates of states' rights violently objected to these regulations. Three Southern governors tried to block the conscription law in their states, saying that only the individual states had the right to make such laws. In some sections of the South, nearly 60 percent of available manpower never served in the army. The Confederacy also adopted a plan to pay plantation owners who released their slaves to serve in the army; this was largely resisted because it was economically harmful to slave owners.

By late 1862, severe shortages of food and other materials began to spread throughout the South. Prices skyrocketed. Many soldiers deserted the army to return home to help their families through these difficult times. Large numbers of deserters and those who had resisted the draft became a problem in some sections of the South. The Confederacy instituted an income tax in order to get needed income for the government. Under existing circumstances, the actual collection of this money was sometimes difficult.

Many similar tensions existed in the North. In 1863, a system of conscription was introduced, requiring service of all men from ages 20 through 45. As in the South, draft dodgers could be found in the North. A provision of the Northern draft law that was very unpopular with many allowed a drafted person to avoid service by hiring a substitute or by paying the government $300; many of the "replacement" soldiers were Irish immigrants. Draft riots took place in New York City in July 1863, with nearly 200 people dying in these protests. Many taking part in the riots were Irish Americans, and many of those killed were black. Draft offices and other buildings were destroyed; Irish Americans did not want to take part in a war that would free the slaves, whom they perceived would be their competitors for jobs.

The North also had trouble financing the war. In 1861, a federal income tax was instituted. Still short of money, the government began issuing "**greenbacks**" in 1862; this money, not backed by gold, was considered official legal tender until the end of the war.

In every wartime setting in American history, the power of the chief executive was expanded. This was certainly true in the Civil War. President Lincoln assumed powers that no previous president had even considered. By executive order, parts of Kentucky were placed under **martial law** for much of the war. Some Democrats in the North, nicknamed **Copperheads**, vigorously opposed the war, stating that it would lead to masses of freed slaves coming North and taking jobs. Copperheads were sometimes arrested, and three of them were actually deported from the North. Over 14,000 who opposed the war were imprisoned without trial. In several cases, Lincoln ordered the **writ of habeas corpus** suspended.

Emancipation Proclamation

When he was elected president, Abraham Lincoln had no thought whatsoever of freeing the slaves; he repeatedly stated that he had no constitutional right to do that. However, on a practical level Lincoln realized that the continued existence of slavery in the South would make Northern victory harder; the existence of slavery allowed Southern landowners to leave their fields and fight in the Confederate army.

The **Emancipation Proclamation** was issued on January 1, 1863. The timing of this was a brilliant political move. Support for the war in the North had been waning; the Emancipation Proclamation gave Northerners a moral justification to continue fighting. This measure was received by different groups in predictable ways. Northern blacks were heartened by it, Southerners condemned it, and in Southern territories controlled by the Union army, slaves were actually freed. Many in England agreed with the proclamation; any last hopes that England might enter the war to aid the Confederacy were dashed at this point. Some whites in the North feared that ex-slaves would end up taking their jobs, and as a result, in the 1862 congressional elections, Democrats picked up seats.

Blacks were not accepted into the Union army at the beginning of the war. After the Emancipation Proclamation, many ex-slaves from Southern territories and free blacks from the North joined the Union army. By 1865, blacks made up almost 10 percent of the entire Union army. Black soldiers traditionally served in all-black units with white officers. (The heroism of the 54th Massachusetts Infantry can be seen in the movie *Glory*.)

1863: The War Tips to the North

The darkest days of the war for the Union occurred in late 1862 and early 1863. The Union army suffered major defeats at the **Battle of Fredericksburg** (December 13, 1862) and at the **Battle of Chancellorsville** (May 1 to 3, 1863). Competent leadership of the Union army remained a major problem.

Yet, time was an enemy of the Confederate army. As commander, General Robert E. Lee found it increasingly difficult to get men and resources (the Northern naval blockade definitely was affecting Southern military efforts by this point). In June 1863, Lee decided to move the Confederate army out of Virginia into Pennsylvania. At the **Battle of Gettysburg** (July 1 to 3, 1863), Lee was defeated by the Union army, commanded by General George Meade. This was the bloodiest overall battle of the war, with 24,000 casualties suffered by the North and 28,000 by the South. Lee's army was forced to retreat to Virginia and would never again be able to mount an attack into Northern territory. Some military historians claim that the fate of the Confederate army was sealed by their defeat at Gettysburg.

The tide of the war continued to swing to the North as a result of several victories by armies commanded by Ulysses S. Grant. On July 4, 1863, Grant completed his victory at the **Battle of Vicksburg**, ending a siege of the city that lasted six weeks. Victory at Vicksburg gave the Union virtual control of the Mississippi River. In November, Grant was victorious at the Battle of Chattanooga (November 23 to 25, 1863). Abraham Lincoln's **Gettysburg Address** had been given four days earlier. In January 1864, Grant was made commander of the Union army. At the same time, some in the Confederate government began speaking of the need for peace negotiations with the North.

Grant and the army of the Potomac began to advance toward Richmond in the spring of 1864, while an army commanded by William T. Sherman began to advance toward Atlanta.

War Weariness in the North and the South

In both the North and the South, the pressures of a long war were obvious by 1864. To many in the South, it was clear that the Confederacy would be defeated. Severe food and material shortages continued. In the North, the presidential campaign of 1864 produced little excitement. Lincoln's Democratic opponent was General George McClellan. In early September 1864, Lincoln confided to friends that he thought he would lose the presidency. However, word arrived that General Sherman had taken the key Confederate city of Atlanta. That, along with any real enthusiasm for (and by) McClellan, allowed Lincoln to easily win reelection.

End of the Confederacy

Sherman employed a scorched earth policy as he marched from Atlanta to Savannah, Georgia, in November and December 1864. In early April 1865, General Lee took the Confederate army from Richmond and tried to escape to the South. The Union army caught up to him, and he finally surrendered on April 9, 1865, at the courthouse in **Appomattox**, Virginia. By the first week of June, all other Confederate forces also surrendered and began to return to oftentimes devastated homelands.

Lincoln only had time to begin to plan for what a post–Civil War America would look like. On April 14, 1865, he was assassinated by John Wilkes Booth at Ford's Theater. Booth was a pro-Southerner. He and a group of co-conspirators also planned to kill Vice President Andrew Johnson and other members of the Lincoln cabinet. Booth was hunted down several days later and was killed by gunfire; several others conspiring with him were found and, after trials by military tribunals, hanged. The incredibly difficult task of reconstruction would have to be handled by the new president, Andrew Johnson, a Tennessee Democrat whom Lincoln had chosen to be his vice president.

Chapter Review

Rapid Review

To achieve the perfect 5, you should be able to explain the following:

- By 1861, various social, political, economic, and cultural factors made conflict between the North and the South inevitable.
- The North had numerous industrial, transportation, and financial advantages that they utilized throughout the Civil War.
- The Confederate States of America was created in February 1861; the fact that these states were organized as a confederacy had several disadvantages that would become obvious as the war progressed.

- Success for the Confederacy depended on European aid; Southerners overestimated the dependence of Europe on Southern crops.
- Confederate generals proved much more competent than their Union counterparts in several key battles in the first years of the war.
- By late 1862, the war had produced severe effects on the home fronts; food shortages were occurring in the South, and President Lincoln imposed martial law in several locations and suspended the writ of habeas corpus in the cases of some of his political opponents.
- The Emancipation Proclamation provided a moral justification for Northerners to continue the war.
- The war shifted decisively in favor of the North in 1863, with the battles at Gettysburg and Vicksburg proving to be critical victories for the North.
- The surrender of the Confederacy in April 1865 was caused by a severe lack of morale, manpower, and economic stability in the South.

Time Line

1860: Lincoln elected president
South Carolina secedes from Union
1861: Confederate States of America created
Attack on Fort Sumter
First Battle of Bull Run
Union begins blockade of Southern ports
1862: New Orleans captured by Union navy
Battle of Shiloh
Conscription begins in Confederate states
Emancipation of slaves in Southern states begins
Battle of Antietam
British announce they will not aid the Confederacy in any substantial way
1863: Emancipation Proclamation
Conscription begins in the North; draftees may hire "replacements"
First black soldiers enlist in Union army
Crucial Union victory at Gettysburg
Crucial Union victory at Vicksburg
Draft riots in New York City
1864: Abraham Lincoln reelected
General Sherman carries out his "march to the sea"
Desertion becomes a major problem in the Confederate army
1865: General Lee surrenders at Appomattox
Abraham Lincoln assassinated

> Review Questions

1. The North held many advantages at the beginning of the Civil War *except*
   A. the North occupied more territory than the South.
   B. the North had more railroad lines.
   C. the North had more factories.
   D. the North had a larger population.

2. European states did not aid the Confederacy in the Civil War because
   A. there were alternative sources of cotton and other crops that they could turn to.
   B. they opposed the Confederacy's position on slavery.
   C. they did not believe that the Confederacy could win.
   D. all of the above.

3. The military draft was unpopular to many in the North because
   A. the draft allowed blacks to enter the armed forces.
   B. the draft allowed Irish-American immigrants to enter the army.
   C. the draft allowed those drafted to hire "replacements."
   D. martial law was needed in many locations to enforce the draft provisions.

4. The Battle of Vicksburg was an important victory for the Union because
   A. it reversed several Union defeats in the same year.
   B. it gave the Union a pathway to Atlanta.
   C. it gave the Union virtual control of the Mississippi River.
   D. it demonstrated that General Lee could, in fact, be beaten.

5. Copperheads were
   A. Democrats in the North who opposed the war
   B. Republicans in the North who suggested that Lincoln be replaced
   C. Democrats in the North who switched alliance to Lincoln
   D. Southern Democrats who wanted negotiations with the North as early as 1863

> Answers and Explanations

1. **A.** All of the others were major advantages for the Union war effort.

2. **D.** All of the reasons given helped convince the Europeans not to assist the Confederacy. The Confederacy's position on slavery proved to be especially troublesome, since slavery had long been outlawed in Europe.

3. **C.** The fact that replacement soldiers, usually immigrants, could be hired or that a payment of $300 to the government could get a man out of the draft made the system very unpopular to many.

4. **C.** The six-week Battle of Vicksburg occurred in 1863 and helped turn the war in the Union's favor. As a result of Vicksburg, the Mississippi River was virtually in the hands of the Union. Lee did not command the Confederate forces at Vicksburg.

5. **A.** Copperheads were Democrats in the North who claimed that the war would bring economic ruin to the North, with freed slaves taking jobs that whites now had. Some were arrested and deported.

CHAPTER 16

Era of Reconstruction (1865–1877)

IN THIS CHAPTER

Summary: Postwar plans for assimilating the South back into the Union provoked strong resentment among many white Southerners. In addition, the plans of President Abraham Lincoln, the Radical Republicans in the Congress, and President Andrew Johnson all contained significant differences. Policies enacted that improved the political and economic position of former slaves were opposed by many Southern whites. The impeachment of Andrew Johnson demonstrated the disagreements over Reconstruction policy between Johnson and the Radical Republicans. Congressional passage of the Thirteenth, Fourteenth, and Fifteenth Amendments outlawed slavery, established the rights of blacks, and defined the framework by which Southern states could rejoin the Union. Passage of these amendments, profits made by carpetbaggers and scalawags, and the increased economic and political power held by some Southern blacks all caused some elements of traditional Southern society to feel long-lasting anger and resentment. The Compromise of 1877 ended Reconstruction, bringing another reordering of the political, economic, and social structures of the South.

Keywords

Reconstruction Era (1865–1877): period after the Civil War during which Northern political leaders created plans for the governance of the South and a procedure for former Southern states to rejoin the Union; Southern resentment of this era lasted well into the twentieth century.

Radical Republicans: congressional group that wished to punish the South for its secession from the Union; pushed for measures that gave economic and political rights to newly freed blacks in the South and that made it difficult for former Confederate states to rejoin the Union.
Reconstruction Act (1867): act placing Southern states under military rule and barring former supporters of the Confederacy from voting.
Carpetbaggers: northerners who moved to the South during the Reconstruction Era; traditional elements of Southern society were deeply resentful of profits made by carpetbaggers during this period.
Scalawags: term of derision used in the South during the Reconstruction Era for white Southern Republicans.
Ku Klux Klan: this group was founded in Tennessee in 1866; its oftentimes violent actions during the Reconstruction Era represented the resentments felt by many Southern whites toward the changing political, social, and economic conditions of the Reconstruction Era.
Compromise of 1877: political compromise ending the disputed presidential election of 1876. By the terms of this compromise Republican candidate Rutherford B. Hayes was awarded the electoral votes of Florida, Louisiana, and South Carolina, thus giving him the presidency; in return, all federal troops were removed from the South and Congress promised to stop enforcing much Reconstruction Era legislation concerning the South.

"Some men are born great, some achieve greatness and others lived during the Reconstruction period"

—Paul Laurence Dunbar, 1903

Lincoln's Plans for Reconstruction

The preceding quote perfectly expresses the frustrations felt by many Americans during the **Reconstruction Era**. During this period, political leaders in the North had to decide how the former states of the Confederacy would be assimilated back into the Union. What should be done with former Confederate leaders? What should be done with former slaves? How much punishment (if any) should the former states of the Confederacy be made to endure? These were obviously incredibly complicated questions, and the results *had* to be imperfect in some manner.

Other factors increased the difficulty of Southern assimilation after the Civil War. It was only when defeated Confederate soldiers returned to their homes that the extent of the devastation of the South during the war became widely known. Virtually the entire Southern railway system and many farms and cities were destroyed by the war. In addition, nearly one-third of all adult males residing in Confederate states died or were wounded during the war. For those plantation owners whose plantations were not destroyed, laborers now had to be hired; many of these owners were now strapped for cash. Many freed blacks wandered the countryside looking for work, while many poorer white men with jobs lived in fear of being replaced by freed black men.

The problems of Reconstruction were compounded by the assassination of Abraham Lincoln at the very end of the Civil War. Lincoln had begun giving shape to a Reconstruction plan as early as mid-1863. Lincoln devised a plan for former Confederates to rejoin the Union, entitled the **Ten Percent Plan**. By the provisions of this plan, citizens of former Confederate states would be given the opportunity to swear allegiance to the government in Washington (high-ranking Confederate military and civilian authorities would not be offered this opportunity). When 10 percent of the registered voters in the state signed this pledge, the state was afforded the chance to form its own state government, which obviously had to be loyal to Washington.

Tennessee, Louisiana, and Arkansas all went through the appropriate procedures to form loyal state governments, yet their applications for renewed participation in the Union were not approved by the **Radical Republicans** who dominated the Congress. These men were determined to punish the Southern states in any way possible for their "betrayal" of the Union. This group, led by Thaddeus Stevens, included several who had been ardent Abolitionists in the years before the Civil War. They believed that power in the Southern states had to be totally reorganized in order for blacks to achieve equality. The Radical Republicans also saw the creation of Reconstruction policy as a constitutional issue, stating that it was the job of Congress and not the president to create this policy.

Radical Republicans felt that action was needed to counter the **Black Codes**, which had been passed by all Southern state legislatures in 1866. These sets of regulations limited movement by blacks, prohibited interracial marriage, and insisted that blacks obtain special certificates to hold certain jobs.

The Radical Republicans were insistent on immediate voting rights for blacks in the South; this desire was behind the **Wade-Davis Act**, which was passed by Congress in the summer of 1864. This bill stated that Congress would only authorize a state government in former Confederate states when the majority of voters took an "ironclad" oath, stating that they were not now disloyal to the Union nor had they ever been disloyal. Under these provisions, it would be impossible for any state to reenter the Union without a large number of black voters. President Lincoln killed this bill by a **pocket veto**.

Andrew Johnson's Plan for Reconstruction

Much to the disappointment of the Radical Republicans, the Reconstruction plan announced by Andrew Johnson was also a relatively lenient one. Johnson stated that the United States should offer "amnesty and pardon" to any Southerner who would swear allegiance to the Union and the Constitution. Like Lincoln, Johnson felt that ex-Confederate leaders should not be eligible for amnesty; he also opposed amnesty for individuals (almost always plantation owners) whose property was worth over $20,000. Johnson had been a small farmer from Tennessee before he entered politics, and he possessed the typical hatred that small farmers had for plantation owners. Johnson also created a fairly simple plan for Confederate states to reenter the Union.

All of the former Confederate states followed the proscribed procedures and elected members to the Congress of the United States that met in December 1865. However, the "loyalty" of the former Confederate states was still questioned by some in the North. Many former Confederate officials and military officers were elected in local and even congressional elections. The issues of blacks getting the vote or education for former slaves were not even considered in any state legislature in the months following the Civil War. The **Radical Republicans** of the North found this totally unacceptable.

Reconstruction Programs of the Radical Republicans

The Radical Republicans soon began to implement their own program for Reconstruction in the South. Although they differed on tactics, all agreed that their main goal in the South should be to advance the political, economic, and social position of the **freedmen**, or former slaves. In early 1865, Congress passed legislation creating the Freedmen's Bureau, which was designed to help ex-slaves get employment, education, and general assistance as they adjusted to their new lives. By 1866, large numbers of freedmen were back on their original plantations (often against the advice of the Freedmen's Bureau), working as **tenant farmers**. Under programs established by the Freedmen's Bureau, ex-slaves could receive "40 acres and a mule."

Some Radical Republicans, such as Charles Sumner of Massachusetts, stated that the ex-slave's position would improve the quickest in the South if they were given the vote. Thaddeus Stevens felt that black voters would be strongly influenced by wealthy landowners who oftentimes employed them, and stated that the first goal of the federal government should be to take land from former Confederate leaders and give it to the freedmen. A Joint Committee on Reconstruction first met in January 1866.

The Joint Committee proposed, and the Congress passed, a bill authorizing the continuation of the Freedmen's Bureau and a Civil Rights bill early in 1866. Johnson immediately vetoed both, stating they were unconstitutional and emphasizing the need to allow former Confederates to have more of a say in affairs in the South. It is at this point that tensions between Congress and the president began to increase severely. Johnson gave a Washington's Birthday speech where he claimed the Radical Republicans were traitors and actually wanted to kill him.

Congress eventually overrode the presidential veto of both of these bills. Johnson's actions and demeanor were causing many moderate Republicans to join forces with the radical branch of the party. The **Civil Rights Act of 1866** granted freedmen all the benefits of federal citizenship and promised that federal courts would uphold these rights. In cases where these rights were violated, federal troops would be used for enforcement. The Civil Rights Act also helped to enforce the **Thirteenth Amendment** to the Constitution, which had been ratified in December 1865 and outlawed slavery and other forms of involuntary servitude.

The **Fourteenth Amendment** was passed by Congress and sent to the states for ratification. The amendment declared that citizenship would be the same in all states, that states that did not give freedmen the vote would have reduced representation in Congress, and that former Confederate officials could not hold public office. Antiblack riots in New Orleans and Memphis in early 1866 caused the Radical Republicans to push for the passage of the Fourteenth Amendment even more forcefully. President Johnson publicly opposed the ratification of the Fourteenth Amendment. However, Radical Republicans won by large margins in the 1866 congressional elections. After these elections, the Radical Republicans began to dictate the course of Reconstruction in the South.

Period of Radical Reconstruction

With many Democrats and even moderate Republicans swept out of office in the 1866 congressional elections, Radical Republicans immediately put their plans for Reconstruction into action. The 1867 **Reconstruction Act** actually placed the Southern states under military rule, with the South being divided into five regions and a military general in control of each region. Former Confederate states were ordered to hold new constitutional conventions to form state constitutions that allowed qualified blacks to vote and provided them with equal rights. The legislation barred former supporters of the Confederacy from voting and required that the Fourteenth Amendment be passed in all former Confederate states. To guarantee the assistance of the United States Army in these efforts, Congress also passed the Army Act, which reduced the control of the president over the army. To ensure that Secretary of War Edwin Stanton (an ally of the Radical Republicans) would not be dismissed, Congress passed the **Tenure of Office Act**, which stated that the president could not dismiss any cabinet member without the approval of the Senate.

Impeachment of Andrew Johnson

In the fall of 1867, President Johnson tried to remove Edwin Stanton as secretary of war. Radical Republicans loudly proclaimed that Johnson had flouted the United States Constitution by directly violating the Tenure of Office Act, and began **impeachment** proceedings against him. The House of Representatives voted to impeach Johnson on February 24, 1868, making him the first president of the United States to be impeached (Bill Clinton was the second). The trial of Johnson in the Senate began in May. By the Constitution, two-thirds of the Senate had to vote to convict the president for him to be removed. Andrew Johnson escaped conviction by one vote (the deciding vote was a Republican from Kansas by the name of Edmund Ross, who was opposed to Johnson but felt there was insufficient evidence to actually remove him from office).

Johnson served the remainder of his term without incident. In the 1868 presidential election, Ulysses S. Grant, a hero of the Civil War with little political knowledge and few stated political opinions, led the Republican party to victory.

Radical Reconstruction Reinforced

With the election of Grant, Radical Republicans finally had an ally in the White House. In March 1870, the final Reconstruction amendment was ratified. The **Fifteenth Amendment** stated that no American could be denied the right to vote "on account of race, color, or previous condition of servitude." Elections in the South in 1870 were regulated by federal troops stationed there. In these elections, thousands of Southern blacks voted for the first time; predictably, many Southern whites did not vote in these elections and viewed the entire process with disgust.

In the 1870 elections, nearly 630 blacks were elected as representatives in Southern state legislatures. Sixteen blacks were elected to Congress, one to the United States Senate, and a black, P. B. S. Pinchback, was elected governor of Louisiana.

It would be impossible to overstate the resentment with which many Southern whites viewed the entire Reconstruction process. Reconstruction was oftentimes blamed on **carpetbaggers**, who were Northerners who moved to the South during the Reconstruction period, or on **scalawags**, a Southern term for white Southern Republicans.

Groups such as the **Ku Klux Klan** (founded in Tennessee in 1866) fueled white resentment into violence against blacks and their "outside" supporters in the South. The Klan's activities ranged from trying to intimidate blacks at polling places, to the burning of crosses, to torture and murder. Various federal laws were passed to limit the activities of the Klan, with thousands of members being arrested. The group and its activities persisted, however. In the 1920s, the Klan would reemerge as a major political force in several states.

End of Reconstruction

Grant won reelection in 1872, yet during his second term, federal and Northern interest in the affairs of the South began to wane. The reasons for this were numerous. By this time in history, many of the original Radical Republicans had died or no longer were active in government. There were numerous corruption scandals in the second Grant administration (some historians state that this was the most corrupt administration in American history). A recession in 1873 turned the interests of many Northerners to economic and not political and social issues. As a result, Northern troops were gradually removed from the South, allowing whites in Southern states to regain control of Southern governments. Many Reconstruction-style reforms made by earlier state legislatures were overturned.

The political event that "officially" ended Reconstruction was the **Compromise of 1877**. In the presidential election of 1876, Samuel Tilden, governor of New York, was the Democratic party candidate, running against Republican Rutherford B. Hayes. Tilden won the popular vote and was leading in the electoral vote, but he needed the electoral votes of Florida, Louisiana, and South Carolina, all still occupied by federal troops and under Republican control. Both sides claimed victory in these three states. A special congressional commission was created to resolve this situation. The commission had more Republicans than Democrats on it and was ready to hand the election to Hayes, even though evidence indicated that Tilden had won enough electoral votes to win. When Democrats in Congress stated that they would loudly and publicly protest the Commission's findings, the Compromise of 1877 was worked out. Hayes was named president; in return, the new president promised to remove all federal troops from the South and to stop the enforcement of much Reconstruction Era legislation concerning the South. As a result, blacks in the South were again reduced to the status of second-class citizens. In addition, Southern hatred of Reconstruction Era Republican policies would make the South solidly Democratic; white Southern support of the Democratic policy would last for nearly 100 years. It should be noted that whites who returned to power in state legislatures in the South in 1878 were called "the redeemers."

Chapter Review

Rapid Review

To achieve the perfect 5, you should be able to explain the following:

- Any plan to assimilate the Southern states back into the Union after the Civil War would have major difficulties; a problem was determining the appropriate postwar status of former supporters of the Confederacy.
- The plans for Reconstruction proposed by Abraham Lincoln, the Radical Republicans, and Andrew Johnson all varied dramatically.
- Radical Republicans instituted policies to improve the political and economic status of former slaves; this created great resentment in other segments of Southern society.
- The impeachment of Andrew Johnson went forward because of major disagreements over policy between Johnson and the Radical Republicans in Congress.

- The Thirteenth, Fourteenth, and Fifteenth Amendments outlawed slavery, established the rights of blacks, and established the framework by which Southern states could rejoin the union.
- Profits made by carpetbaggers and scalawags further angered the traditional elements of Southern society. Many in the South, including members of the Ku Klux Klan, felt great resentment toward the carpetbaggers and scalawags and toward the political and economic power now held by some Southern blacks.
- The Compromise of 1877 ended Reconstruction in the South; as Union troops left, blacks were again reduced to the status of second-class citizens.

Time Line

1865: Andrew Johnson institutes liberal Reconstruction plan
Whites in Southern legislatures pass Black Codes
Thirteenth Amendment ratified

1866: Civil Rights Act, Freedmen's Bureau Act approved by Congress (vetoed by Johnson)
Fourteenth Amendment passes Congress (fails to be ratified in Southern states)
Antiblack riots in New Orleans, Memphis
Republicans who favor Radical Reconstruction win congressional elections, in essence ending Johnson's Reconstruction plan
Ku Klux Klan founded

1867: Tenure of Office Act approved by Congress (Congress had to approve presidential appointments, dismissals)
Reconstruction Act approved by Congress (Southern states placed under military rule)
Constitutional conventions called by former Confederate states
Johnson tries to remove Edwin Stanton as secretary of war, leading to cries for his impeachment

1868: Impeachment of Andrew Johnson: Johnson impeached in the House of Representatives, not convicted in the Senate
Southern states return to Union under policies established by Radical Republicans
Final ratification of Fourteenth Amendment
Former Civil War General Ulysses S. Grant elected president

1870: Amendment ratified
Many blacks elected in Southern state legislatures

1872: Confederates allowed to hold office
Ulysses S. Grant reelected

1876: Disputed presidential election between Tilden, Hayes

1877: Compromise of 1877 awards election to Hayes, ends Reconstruction in the South

Review Questions

1. Radical Republicans favored all of the following *except*
   A. the governing of the South by military generals
   B. the impeachment of Andrew Johnson
   C. the return of former Confederate leaders to positions of power in the South
   D. the election of newly enfranchised blacks to positions in Southern state legislatures

2. The official reason for impeachment proceedings against Andrew Johnson was
   A. he had violated the Tenure of Office Act
   B. he had violated the Reconstruction Act
   C. his Reconstruction policies were much too lenient to the South
   D. he had failed to enforce the Civil Rights Act of 1866

3. Black Codes were instituted to
   A. increase black participation in Southern politics during Reconstruction
   B. increase the effectiveness of the Freedmen's Bureau
   C. prevent blacks from having certain jobs
   D. maintain slavery in some sections of the Deep South

4. Reconstruction ended as a result of the Compromise of 1877 because
   A. a presidential mandate ordered that Reconstruction end.
   B. by the provisions of the compromise, the U.S. Army was removed from Southern states.
   C. the new president, Rutherford B. Hayes, was strongly against the existing Reconstruction policy.
   D. many blacks were now in positions of power in the South, and Reconstruction policies were no longer needed.

5. The Fifteenth Amendment
   A. allowed Southern states to reenter the Union
   B. outlawed slavery
   C. stated that a person could not be denied the vote because of his color
   D. said that former Confederate officials could not hold public office

Answers and Explanations

1. **C.** All of the other choices were favored by Radical Republicans. The Reconstruction Act of 1867 placed the former Confederate states under military rule.

2. **A.** By attempting to remove Edwin Stanton as secretary of war, many in Congress stated that Johnson had knowingly violated the Tenure of Office Act, thus violating provisions of the U.S. Constitution.

3. **C.** Black Codes were adopted by Southern legislatures in 1866 and limited movement by blacks, prevented them from having certain jobs, and prohibited interracial marriage.

4. **B.** After Hayes was given the presidency by the Compromise of 1877, the U.S. Army left control of the South to the South. Without the army present to enforce Reconstruction policies, these policies ended. Blacks were soon second-class citizens again.

5. **C.** The Fifteenth Amendment stated that no American could be denied the right to vote "on account of race, color, or previous condition of servitude."

CHAPTER 17

Western Expansion and Its Impact on the American Character (1860–1895)

IN THIS CHAPTER

Summary: Settlers were encouraged to move westward after the Civil War by federal legislation such as the Homestead Act, which gave 160 acres of land to American citizens who were committed to settling on the land and who could pay the $10 registration fee. However, farming on the plains proved much more difficult than many settlers thought it would be. Thousands of blacks moved west after the Civil War to escape life in the South; mining, ranching, and lumbering also attracted settlers to the West. This westward expansion greatly affected the lives of Native Americans, who were removed to Oklahoma and South Dakota. Farmers in the West began to organize; Farmers' Alliances and the Grange were established to protect farmers' rights. The 1893 Turner Thesis (a well-known theory promulgated by a distinguished historian) proposed the idea that settlers had to become more adaptable and innovative as they moved westward and that these characteristics would slowly become ingrained into the very fabric of American society.

KEY IDEA

Keywords

Homestead Act (1862): bill that did much to encourage settlers to move west; 160 acres of land were given to any settler who was an American citizen or who had applied for citizenship, who was committed to farming the land for six months of the year, and who could pay the $10 registration fee for the land.

Massacre at Wounded Knee (1890): battle that was the last large-scale attempt by Native Americans to resist American settlement in the Great Plains region. Federal soldiers opened fire on Native Americans, killing more than 200.

Dawes Act (1887): act designed to break up Native American tribes by offering individual Native Americans land to be used for either farming or grazing.

Farmers' Alliances: organization that united farmers at the statewide and regional levels; policy goals of this organization included more readily available farm credits and federal regulation of the railroads.

Populist party: formed in 1892 by members of the Farmers' Alliances, this party was designed to appeal to workers in all parts of the country. Populists favored a larger role of government in American society, a progressive income tax, and more direct methods of democracy.

Turner Thesis (1893): thesis by the historian Frederick Jackson Turner suggesting that the innovations practiced by western settlers gradually became ingrained into the fabric of American society; democracy and self-improvement were also central to western expansion, Turner claimed. In short, Turner suggested that many of the characteristics of the "American character" were created by westward expansion. Later historians questioned parts of this thesis.

Federal Legislation Encourages Western Settlement

Adventurous Americans had settled west of the Mississippi and out to the Pacific in the decades prior to the Civil War. However, several acts passed by the federal government in 1862 set the stage for the massive movement westward that would take place after the Civil War.

The one act that gave land directly to settlers was the **Homestead Act**. This legislation allocated 160 acres to any settler who (1) was an American citizen, or who, in the case of immigrants, had at least filed for American citizenship; (2) was 21 years old and the head of a family; (3) was committed to building a house on the property and living there at least six months of the year; and (4) could pay a $10 registration fee for the land. After actively farming the land for five years, the farmer was given actual ownership of his 160-acre plot. By 1900, nearly 610,000 parcels of land had been given out under the provisions of the Homestead Act, allowing nearly 85 million acres of land to go over to private ownership.

A bill that indirectly gave land to settlers was the 1862 **Morrill Land-Grant Act**. To encourage the building of "land-grant" colleges in Western territories that had already been granted statehood, hundreds of thousands of acres of land were given to state governments. This land could be sold by the states to pay for these colleges. At 50 cents an acre (and sometimes less), settlers and **land speculators** received land from individual states.

The expansion of the railroad was closely tied to western expansion. In acts of 1862 and 1864, the Union Pacific and Central Pacific railroads received grants of land to extend their rail lines westward. Part of the legislation also gave the railroads 10 square miles on both sides of the track for every mile of track constructed. This land was sometimes sold to settlers as well, sometimes at exorbitant prices.

Farming on the Great Plains

In the ideology of Thomas Jefferson, the yeoman farmer was the central figure in the development of the American character. The abilities, fortitude, and luck of the yeomen were severely tested as they moved to the Great Plains. Many settlers who went west were immigrants with families (unlike the single male immigrants who lived in New York, Boston, and other Eastern cities).

The harshness of life on the plains was simply too much to bear for many settlers and their families. Temperatures ranged from over 100 degrees in the summer to bitter cold in the winter, and many of the sod houses built by settlers did little to keep out the heat or the cold. Having enough water was a constant problem, with some of the water collected in barrels or buckets carrying "prairie fever" (typhoid fever). In a single year, a settler and his land might be attacked by fierce blizzards, howling dust storms, and locusts or grasshoppers. The rosy picture of life on the Great Plains presented in recruitment brochures found in New York or in Currier & Ives prints popular in the East were a harsh contrast with reality. By 1900, two-thirds of the homestead farms failed, causing many ex-farmers to return to the East.

How did the settlers who survived on the Great Plains manage to do so? Survival on the plains largely depended on cooperation with other settlers who lived nearby. Groups of men would put up new barns and construct fences; women on the plains would get support from wives of other settlers. In short, successful farmers on the plains were no longer the individual yeomen envisioned by Jefferson.

Transformation of Agriculture on the Plains

More important, success on the plains became increasingly dependent on the use of technology and the introduction of business approaches to agriculture. The U.S. Department of Agriculture was established in 1862 and by late 1863 was distributing information to plains farmers on new farm techniques and developments. New plows and threshers (including some powered by steam) were introduced in the late 1860s and early 1870s.

Slowly, control of agricultural production on the plains was taken from individual farmers as large **bonanza farms** developed. While individual settlers were interested in producing enough for their families to survive, bonanza farms usually produced only one or two crops on them. Produce from these farms was sold to the Eastern United States or abroad. While individual settlers were being driven off the land because of the hardships of farming on the plains, bonanza farms were run as large businesses and had the technology and professional backing to be successful.

Bonanza farms were plentiful by the late 1870s and demonstrated the transformation that had taken place in agriculture. These farms were truly capitalistic; their success was dependent on the machinery that existed on the farms and on the railroad that would take their crops away for export. Farm production increased dramatically with the advent of bonanza farms. At the same time, the numbers of Americans involved in agriculture decreased (from nearly 60 percent in 1860 to 37 percent in 1900).

The new business techniques practiced by bonanza farms were successful in the short term, but created problems for both bonanza farms and individual farmers in the future. Several times in the 1880s and early 1890s, there was simply too much grain being produced on these farms, dropping the prices drastically. To remain economically successful, farmers proceeded to do the only logical thing: produce even more, which drove prices down even more. Many plains farmers in this period were unable to pay their mortgages, and farms were foreclosed. Bonanza farms usually had the technology for the production of only one or two crops and could not diversify; they too faced financial distress. Many farmers felt that federal policies had to do more to protect them, and thus started to organize to protect themselves.

Women and Minorities on the Plains

As stated previously, most settlers came to the plains as families (there were a tiny number of women who filed for land claims on their own). Diaries of many women who lived on the plains spoke of the loneliness of their existence, especially in the nonharvest periods when many men left for other work and women were left on the farms. Perhaps the greatest novel describing prairie life is *O Pioneers!* (1913) by Willa Cather. This book describes both the tremendous challenges and the incredible rewards found in life on the prairie. An equally compelling vision of prairie life is *Giants of the Earth* (1927) by O. E. Rolvaag. In this novel, the harshness of prairie life drives the wife of an immigrant settler to madness and eventual death.

It was in the Western states that the first American women received the vote. In 1887, two towns in Kansas gave women the vote (with one of them electing a woman mayor to a single term in office). The state constitution of Wyoming was the first to give women the vote on a statewide basis.

Thousands of blacks moved west after the Civil War to escape the uncertainty of life in the Reconstruction South. Many who ended up in the plains and elsewhere lacked the finances and farming abilities to be successful, and faced many of the same racial difficulties they had faced in the American South. However, some black farmers did emerge successfully as plains farmers. The most prominent of the Southern blacks who went west was the 1879 group, the **Exodusters** (modeling their journey after that of the Israelites fleeing Egypt to the Promised Land). Less than 20 percent of this group became successful farmers in the plains region.

Mining and Lumbering in the West

The rumors of gold at Pike's Peak, Nevada, silver at Comstock, Nevada, and other minerals at countless other locations drew settlers westward in the quest for instant riches (it should be noted that a large number of Californians traveled eastward for exactly the same reason). People of all backgrounds, including women and some Chinese who had left their jobs in railroad construction, all took part in the search for riches. Stories of the wild nature of many early mining towns are generally accurate; stories of the failure of most speculators to find anything to mine are almost always true. Most prospectors who did find something in the ground found it much too difficult to dig for and then to transport; often they sold their claims to Eastern mining companies such as the **Anaconda Copper Company** which did the work for them. For many of these companies, minerals such as tin and copper became just as profitable as gold and silver to mine.

Lumber companies also began moving into the Northwest in the 1870s to start to cut down timber. The lumber industry benefited greatly from the federal **Timber and Stone Act**, passed in 1878. This bill offered land in the Northwest that was unsuitable for farming to "settlers" at very cheap prices. Lumber companies hired seamen from port cities and others who had no interest in "settling" to buy the forest land cheaply and then to transfer the ownership of the land to the companies.

Ranching in the West

In Texas, the ranching industry was profitable long before either farming or mining was fully developed. Settlers there had learned cattle ranching from the Mexicans. Much of the romantic view many still have of the West comes from our vision of cowboys driving cattle on the "long drive" from Texas to either Kansas or Missouri (nearly one-third of the cowboys involved were either Mexicans or blacks).

The long drive was economically inefficient, and with the removal of Native Americans and buffalo from the Great Plains in the 1860s and 1870s (to be discussed in the next section), many cattle ranchers moved their herds northward, allowing them to be closer to the cattle markets of Chicago, Kansas City, and St. Louis.

However, conflicts between farmers and ranchers soon developed. Farmers often accused ranchers of allowing herds to trample their farmlands. The invention of barbed wire by Joseph Glidden in 1873 was the beginning of the end for the cattle industry; as farmers began to contain their farmlands, the open range began to disappear.

A critical blow to the cattle industry occurred during the very harsh winters of 1885, 1886, and 1887. Many cattle froze to death or starved during these years, with some ranchers losing up to 85 percent of their cattle. Those ranchers who survived turned to the same business techniques that had saved many plains farms; scientific methods of breeding, feeding, and fencing were now utilized. In reality, the independent cowboy present in our myths of the West also died during this transformation.

Plight of Native Americans

The westward stream of settlers in the mid-1800s severely disrupted the lives of Native Americans. The migration patterns of the buffalo, which the Native Americans depended on, were disrupted; settlers thought nothing of seizing lands that previous treaties had given to Native Americans. Some tribes tried to cooperate with the onrush of settlers, while others violently resisted. It is unlikely that anything would have saved Native American territories from the rush of American expansionism. The completion of the transcontinental railroad required that rail lines run through territories previously ceded to Native American tribes. A congressional commission meeting in 1867 stated the official policy of the American government on "Indian affairs": Native Americans would all be removed to Oklahoma and South Dakota, and every effort would be made to transform them from "savages" into "civilized" beings.

The tribe that resisted the onrush of settlement most fiercely was the **Sioux**. In 1865, the government announced their desire to build a road through Sioux territory; the following year, tribesmen attacked and killed 88 American soldiers. After negotiations in 1868, the Sioux agreed to move to a reservation in the Black Hills of South Dakota. Yet, in late 1874, miners searching for gold began to arrive in the Black Hills. The chief of the tribe, Sitting Bull, and others of the tribe left the Dakota reservation at this point. General George Custer was sent to round up Sitting Bull and the Sioux. He and his force of over 200 men were all killed at the **Battle of the Little Bighorn** in June 1876. This was the last major Native American victory against the American army. Large numbers of federal troops were brought into the region, returning the Sioux to their reservations.

Conflict with the federal army occurred again in 1890 after the death of Sitting Bull. Some Sioux again attempted to leave their reservation; these tribesmen were quickly apprehended by the federal army. As the male Sioux were handing in their weapons, a shot was fired by someone. The soldiers opened fire on the Native Americans, killing over 200 men, women, and children in the **Massacre at Wounded Knee**.

Other tribes such as the **Nez Perce** also initially resisted, only to be eventually driven to reservations. Nez Perce warriors ending up taking part in elaborate **Ghost Dances**, which were supposed to remove the whites from Native American territories, return the buffalo, and bring ancestors killed by the whites back to life. The Ghost Dances terrified white settlers who viewed them and served to bring more federal forces into territories nominally controlled by Native Americans.

The killing of herds of buffalo by white settlers for food, hides, and even for pure sport did much to destroy Native American life, since Native Americans depended on the buffalo for their very existence. A fatal blow to the remaining land owned by Native American tribes was the 1887 **Dawes Act**. This act was passed in the spirit of "civilizing" the Native Americans and was designed to give them their own plots of land to farm on. The real intent of the legislation was to attempt to destroy the tribal identities of Native Americans. Many Native Americans had little skill or interest in farming; many eventually sold "their" land to land speculators.

In 1889, there were still 2 million acres of unclaimed land in "Indian territory" in Oklahoma. On April 22, a mad rush took place by white settlers staking out claims on this territory (those who staked claims that day were called "boomers"; settlers who had entered Indian territory a day or more early to stake their claims were called "sooners").

By the end of the century, virtually all Native Americans had been placed on reservations. Many young Indians attempted to dress, talk, and act like white men in schools established by white reformers.

Organization of the American Farmer and Populism

As stated previously, American farmers from the West were in economic trouble by the mid-1880s. Many farmers from the South shared their plight. Several policies originated in Washington that farmers felt greatly hurt them economically. Congresses of this era favored high tariffs, which helped Eastern businessmen. Farmers felt they were hurt by the high tariff policy, as it kept foreigners from buying their produce. The issue that farmers were most upset about, however, concerned currency.

Issue of the Gold Standard

After the Civil War, federal budget officials enacted a "**tight money**" policy and took the paper money used during the Civil War out of circulation. In addition, the dollar during this period was for the first time put on the **gold standard**, meaning that every dollar in circulation had to be backed by a similar amount of gold held by the federal government. This action also served to limit the amount of money in circulation. These financial measures ensured that inflation would not occur, but Western farmers were convinced that depressed farm prices were largely a result of these policies. Several congressional acts to increase the coining and mining of gold and silver met with limited success and were opposed by the presidents of the era.

Beginning of Organization: The Grange and Farmers' Alliances

In 1867, the **Grange** organization was founded by Western farmers. By 1875, it boasted of over 800,000 members. Through the Grange, farmer cooperatives were formed, allowing farmers to buy in large quantities the products that they needed (and at lower prices). Farmers were also convinced that railroad rates were disadvantageous to them, and legislators in farm states began to receive communications from farmers urging regulation of railroad rates and policies. Some farmers supported the **Greenback party**, which supported getting more paper money into circulation, in the 1878 election. The Greenbacks managed to elect several congressmen from farm states but got little support elsewhere.

While the Grange organization largely operated on the local level, development of the **Farmers' Alliances** joined farmers at the statewide and even regional levels. By 1889, the Southern Alliance claimed 1 million members, while a separate Colored Farmers' National Alliance also had 1 million members on the books. Membership in the Farmers' Alliances on the Great Plains was nearly 2 million. The policies endorsed by the Farmers' Alliances included federal regulation of the railroad, putting more money into circulation, the establishment of a state department of agriculture in every state, and readily available farm credits. It was proposed that the federal government have large warehouses where farmers could store their grain and get credit for it if prices were low during harvest season. These measures were spelled out in detail at a national Alliance Convention held in 1890 in Ocala, Florida. The **Ocala Platform** stated the principles that motivated most political activity by farmers for the remainder of the century. Some federal policies did at least partially meet the demands of agricultural interests; the **Interstate Commerce Act** of 1887 stated that the federal government could regulate interstate railway rates, and the **Sherman Antitrust Act** of 1890 aimed to control the power of trusts and monopolies.

By 1890, some leaders of the Farmers' Alliances began to plan for political action on the national level. Alliance strength was particularly strong in the South, where four governors owed their elections to Alliance support. Forty-seven congressmen in the South were also strongly supported by the Alliance. In the plains states, Alliance candidates were successful on the local level. Alliance support extended to women as well; several women held important leadership positions at the top levels of the Farmers' Alliances.

Populist Campaign of 1892

On July 4, 1892, in a convention held in Omaha, Nebraska, a national convention of Farmers' Alliances created the People's party, whose followers soon became known as Populists. The **Populist party** was intended to appeal to workers of all parts of the country. Populists desired a much greater role of government in American society. The party platform expressed support for increasing the circulation of money, a progressive income tax (by which wealthy Eastern industrialists would pay the most and farmers would pay the least), government ownership of communication and transportation systems, and more direct methods of democracy (greater use of direct primaries, recall, referendum, etc.). To appeal to urban workers, the platform also supported an eight-hour workday. The Populists nominated James B. Weaver, a Union general from the Civil War, as their candidate.

Despite a spirited campaign by Populist supporters, the party only received 1 million popular votes and 22 electoral votes in the 1892 election. Few voters in the Northeast supported the Populists, and Democratic control of the electoral process in the South remained strong. Only in the western United States did Populism do well.

Populism in the 1890s

The reelection of Grover Cleveland angered the agricultural interests greatly, as he announced his continued support of the gold standard during his inauguration speech. A great depression hit America in 1893, with workers from all parts of the country being laid off (in some cities up to 25 percent of laborers were unemployed). Populist marchers joined with marchers from many groups protesting government financial policy in Washington in 1894.

In the 1896 presidential election, the Republican candidate was William McKinley, who followed Cleveland in his support of the gold standard. The Democratic candidate, endorsed by the Populists, was William Jennings Bryan, who campaigned on a policy of free silver and an expanded availability of currency, stating, "You shall not crucify mankind upon a cross of gold!". Many Populist leaders hit the campaign trail for Bryan, yet with little success. Bryan carried the South and the West, but was unable to garner support in the Midwestern or Northeastern states.

As the depression ended at the end of the decade, Populists and others in the agricultural sector began to recognize the massive changes that had taken place in the American economy since the end of the Civil War. The American economy was now a national economy and not a sectional one; the railroad had been largely responsible for this change. In addition, slowly, but surely, the United States was becoming an industrial nation and not an agricultural one.

Impact of the West on American Society

The myths we now associate with the frontier began to be created as early as the 1870s in dime-store novels by Edward L. Wheeler and others. Wheeler's story of *Deadwood Dick: The Prince of the Road* portrayed a Western America filled with gamblers, hard drinkers, and stagecoach robberies. The Wild West shows that began in 1883 and were promoted by Buffalo Bill Cody contributed to the myths begun by Wheeler: Spectators were shown log cabins, rodeos, and mock battles between cavalrymen and seemingly deadly Indians.

A different view of the West was presented by Frederick Jackson Turner, an academic who in 1893 published his "frontier thesis." The **Turner Thesis** stated that Americans were forced to adapt and innovate as they moved westward. The thesis also explained how western expansion helped to ingrain these characteristics into the fabric of American society. Turner stated that their frontier had created a society of men and women who were committed to self-improvement, who supported democracy, and who were socially mobile. In short, the Turner Thesis maintained that much of the nature of America came from their experiences in the West.

Each of these views was partially correct. The view of western expansion espoused (and later partially rejected) by Turner ignored the fact that not everyone who settled in the West were whites. In addition, the massacre of large numbers of Native Americans violated the basic principles of democracy. There was also some truth to Buffalo Bill's view of western settlement, yet his view ignored the cultural and material progress that took place in the West as a result of western expansion. In 1893, the Turner Thesis and Buffalo Bill's shows both drew incredible interest. During that year, it became clear that the Western frontier was closed, for all practical purposes, and Americans were attempting to make sense of what that actually meant for the country. Historians today still revisit this question on a regular basis.

Chapter Review

Rapid Review

To achieve the perfect 5, you should be able to explain the following:

- The Homestead Act and the Morrill Land-Grant Act encouraged thousands to go westward to acquire land for farming.
- Farming on the Great Plains proved to be very difficult and was oftentimes accomplished by help from one's neighbor; many farmers were not successful on the Great Plains.
- Bonanza farms were part of a transformation of agriculture that began in the late 1860s.
- Western states were the first states where women received the vote.
- Mining and lumbering also attracted many settlers to the West.
- Native American tribes were gradually forced off their lands because of American expansion to the West; some resistance to this by Native Americans did take place, such as at the Battle of the Little Bighorn and through the Ghost Dances.
- The 1887 Dawes Act did much to break up the remaining Native American tribal lands.
- American farmers organized beginning in the late 1860s through the Grange, through the Farmers' Alliances, and eventually through the Populist party.
- Dime-store novels of the era and the Turner Thesis presented contrasting views of western settlement and its overall impact on American society.

Time Line

1848: California Gold Rush
1859: Silver discovered in Comstock, Nevada
1862: Homestead Act, Morrill Land-Grant Act
    Department of Agriculture created by Congress
1867: Founding of the Grange
1869: Transcontinental Railroad completed
1870s: Popularity of *Deadwood Dick* stories by Edward L. Wheeler and other dime-store novels on the West
1874: Barbed wire invented by Joseph Glidden
1876: Battle of the Little Bighorn
1879: Exoduster movement leaves the South for the Great Plains
1880s: Large movement of immigrants westward
1883: "Buffalo Bill's Wild West Show" begins
1886: Beginnings of harsh weather that would help destroy the cattle industry
1887: Dawes Act
1889: Indian territories open for white settlement
1890: Massacre at Wounded Knee
    Wyoming women get the vote
    High point of political influence of the Farmers' Alliances
1893: Beginning of great depression of the 1890s
    Publication of the Turner Thesis
1896: William Jennings Bryan's "Cross of Gold" speech

> # Review Questions

1. Those farmers who were successful on the Great Plains
   A. came to the West as single men, without families
   B. utilized many farming techniques they had learned in the East
   C. personified the spirit of rugged individualism
   D. relied on the assistance of other settlers around them

2. Exodusters were
   A. newly arrived miners in Oregon
   B. Southern blacks who went west to settle
   C. those who "dusted" or cleaned crops on bonanza farms
   D. immigrants who went west to farm

3. The Dawes Act
   A. tried to turn Native Americans into farmers who would farm their own individual plots only
   B. protected Native American land from further encroachment
   C. broke up large Native American reservations into smaller ones
   D. made Ghost Dances illegal

4. The organization that expressed the views of farmers to the largest national audience was the
   A. Greenback party
   B. Populist party
   C. Grange
   D. Farmers' Alliances

5. The Turner Thesis
   A. agreed with accounts of the West in the dime-store novels of the 1870s concerning the character of western expansion.
   B. took into account the massacre of Native Americans.
   C. noted the impact of western expansion on the American character.
   D. emphasized the "hard living" that went on in many western settlements.

> # Answers and Explanations

1. **D.** Almost every diary from individuals who lived on the plains noted that rugged individualism was not enough to be successful.

2. **B.** This group went west to farm in 1879 and modeled their journey after the journey of the Israelites fleeing Egypt to the Promised Land.

3. **A.** The Dawes Act tried to "civilize" Native Americans and destroy their tribal lands.

4. **B.** The Populist party platform was intended to appeal to all workers in society, including those in the city. The policies of the Populist party were heard nationwide in the 1892 presidential election; however, because of the power of the Democratic party in the South, the Populist presidential candidate received only 1 million votes in the election.

5. **C.** Turner himself would later revise his thesis based on some of the characteristics of western expansion noted in the other possible answers.

CHAPTER 18

America Transformed into the Industrial Giant of the World (1870–1910)

IN THIS CHAPTER

Summary: During this era, there was massive industrial growth in the United States, making America the major industrial producer of the world. This growth was largely a product of the expansion of heavy industry; steel was an important component of this industrial growth. The development of the assembly line and Taylorism, which encouraged efficiency in the workplace, created a factory setting where skilled workmanship was de-emphasized. Horizontal and vertical integration allowed major American businesses such as Standard Oil and United States Steel to expand greatly. American workers began to unionize in this era through labor organizations such as the Knights of Labor, the American Federation of Labor, and the Industrial Workers of the World. "New" immigrants from eastern and southern Europe took unskilled jobs in many of the expanding factories but were not wanted by some labor organizations. The American city was also greatly transformed in this era. Political machines dominated many city governments, although efforts took place at the federal level to create a professional civil service system.

Keywords

Taylorism: following management practices of the industrial engineer Frederick Winslow Taylor, the belief that factories should be managed in a scientific manner, utilizing techniques that would increase the efficiency of the individual workers and the factory process as a whole.

Horizontal integration: strategy of gaining as much control over a single industry as possible, often by creating trusts and holding companies; this strategy was utilized by John D. Rockefeller and Standard Oil.

Vertical integration: strategy of gaining as much control over a single industry as possible by controlling the production, marketing, and distribution of the finished product. Andrew Carnegie and United States Steel are the best examples from the era of this approach.

"Gospel of Wealth": philosophy of Andrew Carnegie who believed that wealthy industrialists had an obligation to help local communities and philanthropic organizations.

Knights of Labor: established in the 1880s, this was the major union of that decade. It was made up of unions of many industries and accepted unskilled workers.

American Federation of Labor: national labor union formed by Samuel Gompers in 1886; original goal was to organize skilled workers by craft.

Industrial Workers of the World: more radical than the American Federation of Labor, this union was formed in 1905 and attempted to unionize unskilled workers not recruited by the AFL. Members of this union were called "Wobblies."

Gilded Age: depiction of late nineteenth-century America that emphasizes a surface of great prosperity hiding problems of social inequality and cultural shallowness.

Pendleton Civil Service Act (1883): federal act that established a civil service system at the federal level. For the first time, not all government jobs would be political appointments.

Tammany Hall: political machine that ran New York City Democratic and city politics beginning in 1870; became a model for other urban political machines in the late 1800s.

Growth of Industrial America

By 1894, the United States had become the largest manufacturing nation in the world. (Germany had been the world's industrial leader since the middle of the century.) Compared to industrial growth that had occurred in Europe earlier in the century, the economic growth that took place in America during this period was nearly beyond belief. Massive factories employed a very large number of workers. In 1860, nearly one out of every four Americans worked in manufacturing, while by 1900 this number increased to one out of every two. Radical transformations also took place in the approaches to work taken by former rural dwellers or immigrants who moved to the American city for factory work. Things such as time clocks, scheduled breaks, and the repetition of doing the same tasks over and over made work very different for those who came from rural settings.

The essential characteristics of this **Second Industrial Revolution** developed because of a combination of new developments in both technology and business organization. Initially, this growth was aided by the lack of government control over the affairs of business (laissez-faire capitalism was the dominant economic theory of the era).

Changing Nature of American Industry

The massive industrial growth of this period was largely based on the expansion of **heavy industry**. Prior to the Civil War, most American production was based on turning out materials that the American consumer would purchase, such as food products and textiles. These products continued to be produced, but during 1870 to 1910, rapid industrial growth was fueled by the production of steel, machinery, and petroleum products. Most of these products were designed *not* for the consumer, but for those who produced the goods. Heavy industry produced new machinery that a textile mill might install, or a stronger, more durable steel that a railroad line might use for a new stretch of tracks. Industrial expansion during this era spiraled; new machinery introduced in textile mills, for example, fueled a further expansion of textile manufacturing.

Another key component of the Second Industrial Revolution was the development of new and more efficient sources of power. In 1865, the majority of American industries were still dependent on water power. The discovery of anthracite coal (in Pennsylvania, West Virginia, and elsewhere) caused the price of coal to drastically drop and fueled the transformation in many American industries to steam power. By 1890, nearly 70 percent of American industries used steam.

Industry expanded in this era into geographic regions where it had scarcely existed before. In the **New South**, many former sharecroppers went to work in textile factories, which often utilized state-of-the-art machinery that had been produced in the North. The American Tobacco Company started to manufacture cigarettes by machine, and the steel mills found in Southern cities such as Birmingham, Alabama, made these cities start to resemble factory cities in the North.

Changes in the Workplace

Production methods changed in virtually every factory in America during this period, as the desire for more efficiently produced goods became paramount. Efficiency experts were utilized by many companies, and most championed the ideas of Frederick W. Taylor, a mechanical engineer who wrote popular treatises on efficiency and scientific management. **Taylorism** emphasized speed and efficiency in the workplace; factories found that paying workers "by the piece" made them produce more. Workers were timed, and factories sometimes redesigned to promote efficiency and greater production. One by-product of Taylorism was the elimination of some workers in the factory as other workers did their jobs "more efficiently."

Part of this move toward efficiency was the beginning of assembly line production methods. The application of Taylorism and the introduction of the assembly line best demonstrate the combination of technology and business organization that fueled much of the economic growth of the era. The Ford Motor Company was first established in 1903, and by 1910, it was producing nearly 12,000 cars per year. Henry Ford's factories first used assembly line production methods in 1913; during that year, Ford produced nearly 250,000 automobiles. Similar growth occurred in the chemical and electrical industries as new production methods were introduced.

How did the role of workers in the production process change in this era? Critics charged that the individual worker had merely become "one more cog in the machine"; in an automobile assembly line, the worker might, for example, put the left door on a whole series of identical automobiles all day long. The need for skilled craftsmen, so important in preindustrial America, drastically lessened as a result of the assembly line.

Many factory jobs could now be learned in several hours or less. The result of this on the nature of the workforce was immense. Immigrants with no previous training could perform the simple tasks associated with many industrial jobs. In addition, many women left their previous jobs as domestics to go to work in the textile mills (many women took clerical jobs in this era as well). Children could also do some of the more menial tasks associated with factory work and be paid a pittance of what adults were making. By 1900, nearly 20 percent of all children between 10 and 15 were employed, many in textile mills and shoe factories. During this period, some states began to pass laws regulating child labor, although these were often difficult to enforce.

Clear differences were present in this period between the pay offered to men and women in most factories. Skilled women factory workers made $5 a week, while unskilled male workers often made $8 per week. Women still preferred factory work to the very time-consuming and low-paying job of being a domestic worker. Some female workers turned to prostitution; there is some evidence that the number of prostitutes increased in industrial cities at the end of the nineteenth century.

Marriage usually ended a woman's work in the factory; doing all of the chores while the husband was away at work was a back-breaking exercise in this era. Some urban married women also added income to the household by doing knitting or sewing for others at home.

Consolidation of Businesses

John D. Rockefeller made millions through Standard Oil, as did Andrew Carnegie through United States Steel. During this period, these businessmen and others attempted to further control the industries in which they were invested. Many of these schemes did allow the rich to get richer, with little or no benefit to those working under them.

Some of these organizational schemes were quickly squashed by governmental intervention. Influential stockholders of companies of the same industry would sometimes agree to limit production, set prices, and even share profits. This type of activity was outlawed in 1887 by the **Interstate Commerce Act**. This bill was passed with the intent of regulating the railroads, but it generally was not enforced. The commission in charge of enforcement was made of former railroad executives and others who favored the interests of the railroads.

Another popular method of business organization was the creation of **trusts**, an organizational technique perfected by John D. Rockefeller and Standard Oil. At the time, state laws prohibited one corporation from holding stock in another. However, it was legal to create a trust, by which stockholders in a smaller oil company could be "persuaded" to give control of their shares in that company "in trust" to the board of trustees of Standard Oil. Using this technique, Standard Oil established a **horizontal integration** of the oil industry in the early 1880s, meaning that the board of trustees of Standard Oil also controlled many other oil-producing companies.

Standard Oil expanded in the late 1880s even further by becoming a **holding company**. In 1888, New Jersey passed new legislation allowing businesses incorporated there to own stock in other corporations. Standard Oil stockholders began to buy up shares in other companies as well; under the regulations for a holding company, management of various companies could be joint as well. Standard Oil stockholders became the majority holders in other oil companies, allowing Standard Oil management to run these companies also. By the early 1890s, Standard Oil had merged 43 oil-producing companies together under their control and produced nearly 90 percent of all oil in America. Standard Oil also achieved **vertical integration** when the company not only moved to control production but also the marketing and distribution of the finished product. Similar examples of vertical integration were found in many other companies (Gustavus Swift exhibited similar control over the meat-processing industry). Carnegie's steel operation, Carnegie Steel, is often cited as the best example of vertical integration in this era, along with its successor company, United States Steel.

Those at the very pinnacle of the economic pyramid were able to rationalize their incredible economic successes. American social philosopher William Graham Sumner wrote in this period about **Social Darwinism**, which proclaimed that God had granted power and wealth to those who most deserved it. Believers in Social Darwinism could thus justify any scheme that could bring more money to the Rockefellers and the Carnegies of America, since God had wanted them to have that economic power. Carnegie spoke and wrote about the "**Gospel of Wealth.**" According to this theory, the major role of America's industrialists was to act as the "guardians" of the wealth of America (and *not* to give this wealth out in the form of higher wages to the workers). Carnegie stated that it was the duty of the wealthy to return a large portion of their wealth to the community. To the credit of both Rockefeller and Carnegie, foundations they established have contributed over $650 million to various educational and artistic ventures since the time of their deaths. Observers with a less sympathetic view call the giants of business from this era "robber barons."

Growth of Labor Unions

Although craft unions existed in the period before the Civil War, the first major strike in American history was the large strike of railroad workers that began in July 1877. Railroad workers protested layoffs and the reduction of their wages. In various parts of the country, railroad property was destroyed and trains were derailed. In Pittsburgh, Pennsylvania, over 30 strikers were killed by militia forces loyal to the railroad companies. President Hayes finally sent in government troops to restore order and break up the strike, although he felt that steps should be taken to "remove the distress which afflicts laborers."

The major union to emerge from the 1870s was the **Knights of Labor**, which was founded in Philadelphia in 1869. Many earlier unions represented single crafts (shoemakers, for example). The Knights of Labor opened their doors to skilled *and* unskilled workers, and welcomed immigrants, blacks, and women as well. Membership in the Knights of Labor peaked around 750,000 in the mid-1880s. Brochures written by the Knights of Labor proposed a new, cooperative society, in which laborers would one day work for themselves and not for their industrial bosses. Unfortunately, this rhetoric failed to impress many bosses, and in several large strikes, ownership refused to even negotiate with representatives of the union, causing it to gradually lose members.

On May 1, 1886, a massive labor rally was held in Chicago, with nearly 100,000 workers turning out to support strikers at the nearby McCormick reaper plant. Chicago authorities were aware of the violent tactics practiced by many European Socialists at this time and vowed not to let that happen in Chicago. The next evening, a large worker's demonstration took place near **Haymarket Square** in downtown Chicago. Police and militia forces arrived to break up the demonstration. At that moment, a bomb went off. Seven people died, and nearly 70 were wounded. Eventually, eight anarchists were convicted of setting off the bomb. To many not involved in labor unions, the events at Haymarket Square hurt the labor movement; the press at the time drew little distinction between "hard-working union men" and "foreign" Socialists and anarchists. Police forces in cities across the country also increased their supplies of ammunition, guns, and men in preparation for the next outbreak of "anarchism." The Knights of Labor suffered a decline in membership as a result of Haymarket Square.

The **American Federation of Labor (AFL)** was the next major national labor organization to achieve national stature. The AFL was organized by crafts and made up almost exclusively of skilled workers. This helped its image, since in the eyes of the public, most anarchists and other radicals were unskilled workers. The union's first leader was Samuel Gompers. Unlike the idealistic philosophy of the Knights of Labor, the AFL bargained for "bread-and-butter issues" like higher wages and shorter hours. By 1917, the AFL had over 2.5 million members. Although the union used strike tactics on many occasions, it strenuously avoided the appearance of being controlled by radicals. Major strikes of the era included an 1892 strike against the Carnegie Steel Company in Homestead, Pennsylvania, and an 1894 strike by the American Railway Union against the Pullman Palace Car Company. The American Railway Union was founded by Eugene V. Debs, who would later run for president on the Socialist party ticket.

Miners in the West also were engaged in labor activity, and in late 1905 helped found the **Industrial Workers of the World (IWW)**. In spirit, this union was close to the old Knights of Labor, as it attracted both skilled and unskilled workers. Union literature spoke of class conflict, violence, and the desirability of socialism. IWW members were called "Wobblies" and included "Mother" Jones, who organized coal miners, and Big Bill Haywood of the Western Federation of Miners. The union was involved in many strikes, many of them bloody, and was destroyed during World War I when many of its leaders were jailed for "treasonous" activities.

Strikes by all of the unions mentioned in the preceding text clearly advanced the condition of the American worker during this era. Their wages had risen, and the hours they worked were less. However, the limitations of unions in this era must also be noted. The Knights of Labor and the IWW were the only unions that recruited women, blacks, and immigrants. The AFL vigorously rejected the recruitment of these groups, claiming that their acceptance in the workforce would depress the wages of all. Some women did form their own labor unions; the 1909 strike by the International Ladies Garment Workers Union in New York City was one of the largest strikes of the era.

Industrial bosses were able to scare some workers away from joining unions, and many continually suspected that unions were filled by anarchists and other agitators. The government supported industrial owners on several other occasions by sending in the military to end strikes. Pinkerton guards were also used against strikers. Unions had still not achieved widespread acceptance in this era. Even in 1915, only 12 percent of the workforce was unionized.

Improved Standard of Living?

Many history textbooks place great emphasis on the growth of a **consumer society** in America during this period. These textbooks would note that Americans could now afford things that previously had been luxuries of the upper classes such as tea and silk stockings. The texts would discuss the fact that average life expectancy increased by over six years between 1900 and 1920, and that things like flush toilets were now present in many houses. The growth of the department store would be emphasized to demonstrate all of the goods that the new consumer could buy.

It should be carefully noted, however, that large segments of American society did not share the newly created wealth found in the pockets and bank accounts of many upper-middle-class and upper-class Americans. Many Americans, especially newly arrived immigrants, experienced crushing poverty. Conveniences such as flush toilets were not available in most working-class houses until the late 1920s or 1930s. Wages may have gone up, yet in many parts of the country, increases in living costs were even more profound. Fresh fruits and clothing made out of new fabrics were now available, but with the wages that workers were being paid, actually purchasing any of these goods was absolutely out of the question for the vast majority of workers. For many in the growing middle class, however, families could now not just buy the goods and services that they needed; they could begin to buy merchandise and services that they wanted as well.

Impact of Immigration on American Society

Immigration patterns shifted dramatically in the late 1880s and 1890s. Before then, most European immigrants coming to the United States came from northern Europe, with large numbers coming from England, Ireland, and Germany. A large segment of these immigrants were English speakers; although assimilation into American society was difficult, the commonality of language made it less so. Starting in the late 1880s, most immigrants arrived from non-English-speaking areas, such as Eastern Europe, Russia, and Italy. Many of these "**new immigrants**" were poorer than those who had arrived in America earlier. This and the language barrier made their assimilation into American society more difficult.

From 1870 to 1920, nearly 28 million immigrants arrived in the United States (peak years for immigration were from 1900 to 1910). Ellis Island opened in 1892, and Europeans desiring to settle in America first had to undergo the physical, psychological, and political testing that was given there. In 1910, Angel Island in San Francisco was completed; this was the West Coast's version of Ellis Island.

Nearly 14,000 Chinese laborers had been recruited to build the transcontinental railroad. Many Chinese avoided racial hostilities by moving to sections of cities like Chinatown in San Francisco. The fear existed that Chinese workers would work for lower wages than "our" workers would, and the Chinese Exclusion Act of 1882 prohibited any new Chinese laborers from entering the country (those who were already here were permitted to stay). After the United States acquired Hawaii in 1898, many Japanese living in Hawaii came to California to work in vegetable and fruit fields there. The Japanese faced many of the same prejudices that the Chinese had faced. In 1906, the Board of Education in San Francisco ruled that separate schools would have to be established for white and Asian students. The 1913 California **Webb Alien Land Law** prohibited Asians who were not citizens from owning land anywhere in the state.

The majority of immigrants on both the West and East Coasts initially settled in coastal cities. Eastern and southern Europeans on the East Coast had come to America to escape oppressive governments, religious persecution, rising taxes, and declining production on their farms. The transformation for many from working in agriculture in Europe to working in a factory in America was massive. To survive, many clung to their old European customs, spoke their native languages at home, lived in neighborhoods dominated by their own ethnic groups (thus the development of Chinatown and Little Italy in New York City), became members of mutual benefit associations or other ethnic organizations, or sent their children to religious instead of public schools.

The initial intent of many of these immigrants was to come to America, make money, and then return to their homelands. Some did return, yet those who remained were a crucial component of the economic growth of the era. Eastern and southern Europeans worked in many factories on the East Coast but also provided the manpower for the economic growth of cities such as Milwaukee and Chicago as well. Some immigrants did become involved in agriculture; a small number of Europeans continued on to the mining towns of the West. The one part of the country where few immigrants went was the South; few jobs opened up for them there.

Transformation of the American City

The construction of new factories and the influx of immigrants from abroad and from the countryside helped force the radical transformation of many industrial cities in this era. Before the Civil War, cities were relatively small, with most people who lived within the city being able to easily walk to work. Almost all cities had poor sections in them before the Civil War. The rapid influx of poor immigrants turned many of these sections into horribly overcrowded slums.

New methods of transportation aided in the transformation of the industrial city. Elevated trains (first introduced in New York in 1867), cable cars (in San Francisco), electric trolleys, and subways (first founded in Boston in 1897) allowed middle- and upper-class citizens to move farther and farther away from the center of the city. In the early nineteenth century, the "best" houses were found in the middle of the city; residents of these houses were now relocating to **suburbia**. Businesses, banks, and offices became located in the business district, usually found in the center of the city. Little housing existed in this part of the city. Located in various sectors surrounding the business district were factories and other centers of manufacturing. Cheap housing for workers usually was located very close to each factory. The upper and lower classes physically lived much farther apart in the "modern" cities of the late 1800s than they had earlier in the century.

The conditions of working-class slums are well documented. Many workers lived in "apartments" that were created from residences formerly belonging to middle- and upper-class residents. Rooms in these buildings were divided and subdivided again so that large numbers of families could live in buildings that formerly housed one family. Tenement buildings were more cheaply constructed and were built to house as many families as possible. Outdoor bathrooms were still the rule in many slum areas. Even those who could receive water inside often emptied waste, human and otherwise, into back alleys (sewage systems proved to be woefully inadequate in almost every city). Poverty, disease, and crime were the central elements of life for many living in industrial slums, although in many cities somewhat better conditions were available for workers who were better off. Technology did bring some changes to life even in the slums after the turn of the century, as a few worker residencies started to have gas, electricity, and running water. In the later 1800s, cities such as New York also started to develop building codes for all new construction.

Office buildings in many cities became taller during this era. Before the Civil War the tallest buildings in most American cities were four or five stories high. The development of stronger and more durable **Bessemer steel** meant that steel girders could now support taller buildings, and the first elevators began to be installed in buildings in the early 1880s. The first actual "skyscraper" was the building of the Home Insurance Company in Chicago. Finished in 1885, this building was 10 stories high, with four separate elevators taking passengers to the top.

City officials in almost every industrial city realized the necessity for construction and city improvements. After the turn of the century, schools, public buildings, and even sewers began to be built at a rapid rate. However, lack of housing was a major problem that urban planners were unable to solve. Many urban reformers, who will be discussed in a later chapter, had other plans to improve the lives of the urban poor.

Politics of the Gilded Age

Mark Twain coined the term "**Gilded Age**" to refer to the period between 1875 and 1900. This is not a positive image of the era; it implies a thin layer of gold (symbolizing prosperity) covering all of the problems of the era, including grinding poverty in the time of incredible wealth and political corruption on a wide scale.

The irony of political life in this period was that many Americans were deeply involved in political activity. Large numbers of Americans were involved in party politics; nearly 75 percent of all registered voters voted in the presidential elections of the era, far more than had voted in any recent presidential election. Yet, at the same time, much of the political activity at the time was at a superficial level. Few elections of the era had two candidates who differed radically on the issues; most campaigns revolved around different personalities and not around issues. One observer noted that the American politicians of the period were the most "thoroughly ordinary" political leaders in the history of the United States. On top of all this, there was more corruption in the American political system during this period than in any other period of the nineteenth century.

During the 1870s, Congress exerted a greater power than the executive branch. This was largely caused by the weak Republican presidents who followed Abraham Lincoln (Andrew Johnson and Ulysses S. Grant). It was during this period that some reformers began to point out the evils of the **spoils system** to the American public. This system, which had been started by Andrew Jackson, allowed the victorious party in any election to reward their loyal supporters by giving them government jobs.

The lack of controversy or debate on issues during this period was partially because Republicans and Democrats each had roughly the same amount of support. As a result, neither party could risk alienating nor turning away anyone from their party ranks. One way to do this was not to talk about real issues. Republican support from bankers, industrialists, and farmers was balanced by Democratic support from immigrants (those who could vote), laborers, and farmers (especially from the West). Democrats of this era (as well as Democrats of today) have always made the claim that their party represents "the people."

President Rutherford B. Hayes, the successor to Grant, did make an attempt to reform the spoils system. After he won the election of 1876, Hayes refused to use the spoils system when he named officials for his new administration, and he removed some individuals from government positions who had been appointed to their positions by patronage, including Chester A. Arthur in New York, a future president.

What to do about the spoils system was an important issue in the 1880s, with Republicans themselves being divided on what to do with it. James Garfield, a congressman from Ohio, suggested that the system be reformed. Garfield was not a strong campaigner but emerged victorious in the presidential election, becoming the fourth consecutive Republican president. Garfield, ironically, was assassinated in July 1881 by a man who was outraged because he was passed over for a job that he thought he should have gotten through the spoils system.

After Garfield's assassination, many major newspapers and some politicians began to call for a thorough reform of the spoils system. Garfield's successor, Chester A. Arthur, urged Congress to pass legislation to that effect. The result was the **Pendleton Civil Service Act**, which went into effect in 1883. This act created a **Civil Service Commission**, which would test applicants and ensure that government jobs were given to those who were qualified to get them. The legislation also stated that government officials couldn't be required to contribute to political campaigns (a practice that had been relatively commonplace). As a result, a **professional bureaucracy** began to be created in both the legislative and executive branches. Aides to cabinet members and congressmen became indispensable to the operations of government. Some at the time suggested that this professional bureaucracy was important because it couldn't be voted out of office by the "rabble" who were increasingly being given the vote. As any observer of the American political system knows, however, the reforms of this era did not end corruption as a major influence on the system.

Perhaps the best example of politics focusing on the individual and not the issues was the presidential election of 1884. The regulation of business deserved serious discussion, as did the government's tariff policies (a fiercely debated topic at local political meetings across the nation), yet the campaign largely centered around whether Republican James Blaine had, when he was a congressman, accepted free railroad stock while voting to support bills favorable to the railroad industry. The second most important issue of the campaign was whether Grover Cleveland had fathered a child before he was married. When all was finished, Cleveland became the first Democrat since 1856 to be elected president.

The issue of tariffs remained a major one throughout the 1880s and into the 1890s, with Eastern business interests leading the charge for higher tariffs. As discussed in the previous chapter, a major depression began in 1893. Millions of Americans lost their jobs. Standard economic and government policy of the time was that it was not the job of the federal government to intervene. A Populist from Ohio named Jacob Coxey led a group of unemployed workers to Washington in 1894 and demanded that the government assist the unemployed of America. **Coxey's Army** did little to affect government policy in Washington, although it did demonstrate the distress felt by unemployed Americans.

The policies of the Populists in the 1890s and William Jennings Bryan and his defeat at the hands of William McKinley were discussed in Chapter 15. McKinley's rout of Bryan in the 1896 election signaled a major shift in American politics. As previously stated, both parties were nearly similar in strength for much of the period discussed in this chapter. The 1896 election ended this. The 1896 election cast the Republicans as a truly national party (Bryan's support was largely sectional). Republicans could claim they were the party of prosperity. Nearly as soon as they were elected, the effects of the depression began to end (a part of this was luck; gold was discovered in parts of Alaska in late 1892, thus increasing the national money supply). Republican domination of politics at the national level filtered down to the state and local levels as well. As a result, many local races were no longer close (increasingly Democrats even failed to challenge Republicans in a number of races). One result of this was a striking decrease in political participation and voting by supporters of both major parties. Some historians also argue that William McKinley was the first "modern" president, in that he amassed a large amount of power in the office of the presidency.

Political life in many of the major industrial cities was controlled by **political machines**. These political organizations were designed to keep a certain party, or in many cases a certain individual, in power. Favors, jobs, and in some cases money were promised to voters in return for political support. Many machines used the support of immigrants to remain in power, as newly arrived immigrants were often eager to receive the types of help that political machines could give them. Some machines did make positive reforms in local services and education. The most famous machine existed in New York City, where William Marcy Tweed ("Boss" Tweed) ran New York City through the political club located at **Tammany Hall** beginning in 1870. Tweed and his associates bilked the city treasury out of millions of dollars. The famous political cartoons of Thomas Nast helped to bring Tweed down and send him to jail, although Tammany Hall ran the politics of New York City for nearly 50 years. Politicians in other large cities copied the corrupt practices that existed in New York City.

Cultural Life in the Gilded Age

Many books written in the era present a critical view of America. *Looking Backward* (1888) by Edward Bellamy was a very popular book. This book looks ahead to Boston in 2000: in Bellamy's view, everyone works hard in efficient factories. A difference, however, was that in Bellamy's view of the future, cooperation between the workers and the bosses has replaced the ruthless capitalism that existed in Bellamy's time.

In 1890, Jacob Riis published *How the Other Half Lives*, a documentary account of slum life in New York City. This book was especially powerful because it also contained photographs he had taken of immigrants and the conditions they lived in. Finally, *The Jungle* (1906) by Upton Sinclair was written as an exposé of the meatpacking industry.

Chapter Review

Rapid Review

To achieve the perfect 5, you should be able to explain the following:

- The industrial growth that occurred in the United States during this era made the United States the major industrial producer of the world.
- The industrial growth was largely based on the expansion of heavy industry; the availability of steel was critical to this expansion.
- Taylorism and the assembly line created major changes in the workplace for factory workers.
- Horizontal and vertical integration allowed businesses to expand dramatically during this era; Standard Oil (John D. Rockefeller) and United States Steel (Andrew Carnegie) are the best examples of this type of expansion.
- Andrew Carnegie's "Gospel of Wealth" proclaimed it was the duty of the wealthy to return large amounts of their wealth back to the community.
- American workers began to unionize in this era by joining the Knights of Labor, the American Federation of Labor, and the Industrial Workers of the World. Because of intimidation by company bosses and the publicity that came from several unsuccessful strikes, union membership remained low, even into the twentieth century.
- The impact of the "new immigrants" from eastern and southern Europe on American cities and in the workplace was immense.
- The American city became transformed in this era, with new methods of transportation allowing many from the middle and upper class to move to suburbia and still work in the city.

- Political life at the state and city levels during this era was dominated by various political machines, although reforms were instituted at the federal level and in some states to create a professional civil service system.

Time Line

1869: Knights of Labor founded in Philadelphia
1870: Beginning of Tammany Hall's control over New York City politics
1879: Publication of *Progress and Poverty* by Henry George
1881: Assassination of President James Garfield
1882: Chinese Exclusion Act passed by Congress
1883: Pendleton Civil Service Act enacted
1885: Completion of Home Insurance Company building in Chicago, America's first skyscraper
1886: Haymarket Square demonstration and bombing in Chicago
1887: Interstate Commerce Act enacted
Major strike of railroad workers; President Hayes sends in government troops to break up strike in Pittsburgh
1888: New Jersey passes legislation allowing holding companies
Publication of *Looking Backward* by Edward Bellamy
1890: Publication of *How the Other Half Lives* by Jacob Riis
1892: Ellis Island opens to process immigrants on the East Coast
1893: Beginning of major depression in America
1894: March of Coxey's Army on Washington, DC
United States becomes world's largest manufacturing producer
1896: Decisive victory of Republican William McKinley breaks decades-long deadlock between Democrats and Republicans
America begins to recover from great depression of early 1890s
1897: America's first subway begins regular service in Boston
1901: Assassination of President William McKinley
1903: Ford Motor Company established
1905: Industrial Workers of the World formed
1906: Publication of *The Jungle* by Upton Sinclair
1909: Strike of International Ladies Garment Workers Union in New York City
1910: Angel Island opens to process immigrants on West Coast
Number of American children attending school nears 60 percent
1913: Webb Alien Land Law enacted, prohibiting aliens from owning farmland in California
Ford Motor Company begins to use assembly line techniques; 250,000 automobiles produced in one year

Review Questions

1. The practices championed by Frederick W. Taylor that were championed by many factory owners of the era
   A. made it easier for immigrant workers to assimilate into the American working class
   B. ensured that all workers would receive higher wages and conditions in the factories would improve
   C. emphasized the need for greater efficiency in factory operations
   D. reemphasized the need for extensive training before the worker could do almost any job in the factory

2. Many citizens became involved in the political process by actively supporting the Republican and Democratic parties for all of the reasons listed *except*
   A. The parades, rallies, and campaigns of the era provided an exciting entry into the American political system.
   B. The strength of the two parties was roughly identical in this era, thus creating close and interesting races.
   C. The expansion and spread of newspapers in this era made more people aware of political developments.
   D. Candidates for president from both parties in almost every race of this era were dynamic and very popular campaigners, thus energizing the forces of both parties.

3. An analysis of the march on Washington by Coxey's Army in 1894 demonstrates that
   A. large segments of the unemployed in America were willing to become involved politically to protest their situation.
   B. all classes in American society were deeply affected by the depression of the early 1890s.
   C. the policies of dealing with the depression in the 1890s were somewhat similar to policies championed by Herbert Hoover from 1929 to 1932.
   D. the march was extremely well covered by the press.

4. The following statements are true about the new industrial city of the late nineteenth century *except*
   A. The working class lived around the factories, usually somewhat near the center of the city.
   B. The factories of the city were almost always found near a source of water, since water power was common.
   C. The central area of the city usually consisted of offices, banks, and insurance buildings.
   D. Many saloons existed in working-class neighborhoods.

5. Evidence that the standard of living for the working class improved in this era could be found by carefully analyzing all of the following *except*
   A. a comparison of increased wages with increased living costs for factory workers
   B. an analysis of the increased diversity of foods available for purchase by factory workers
   C. an analysis of the growth of amusement parks, sporting events, and movie theaters in the major cities
   D. a comparison of the wages of most immigrant workers with the wages of workers who remained to work in the "old country"

Answers and Explanations

1. **C.** Taylorism made efficiency in the workplace a science and set the stage for assembly line production techniques.

2. **D.** Most of the presidential candidates—and presidential winners—of this era were nondescript men, thus allowing much power to go over to Congress.

3. **C.** The march had little effect on government policy. Coxey's Army was relatively small by the time it got to Washington. Official policy of the time was that it was not the job of the federal government to actively intervene during hard times, a policy similar to that supported by Herbert Hoover in the first years of the Great Depression.

4. **B.** By 1890, most American industry had converted to steam power.

5. **A.** Many diverse foods were available for purchase by factory workers, but few could afford them. For many workers, wages did go up in this period; however, increased living costs often outstripped higher wages.

CHAPTER 19

Rise of American Imperialism (1890–1913)

IN THIS CHAPTER

Summary: Beginning in the 1890s, the United States began to practice some of the same imperialistic policies that it had previously criticized major European powers for. Spurred on by sugar planters, America expanded its influence in Hawaii and in 1896 annexed the islands. Americans also pushed for an "Open Door" trading policy with China. Efforts to expand American influence abroad were motivated by economic, political, religious, and social factors; the "white man's burden" argument was influential in both Europe and the United States. There were also opponents to imperialism who often based their opposition on moral grounds. American imperialistic impulses flourished during the Spanish-American War; newly created American naval power was one important factor in the defeat of Spain. After contentious debate within the United States, America finally decided to annex the Philippines; it took three years for American forces to defeat Filipino rebels, who instead of fighting the Spanish now resisted their new occupiers, the Americans. Americans finished building the Panama Canal in 1914; the Roosevelt Corollary to the Monroe Doctrine further increased American influence in Latin America.

Keywords

Open Door policy: policy supported by the United States beginning in 1899 that stated that all major powers, including the United States, should have an equal right to trade with China.

Social Darwinism: philosophy that emerged from the writings of Charles Darwin on the "survival of the fittest"; this was used to justify the vast differences between the rich and the poor in the late nineteenth century as well as American and European imperialistic ventures.

Spanish-American War: war that began in 1898 against the Spanish over treatment of Cubans by Spanish troops that controlled the island. As a result of this war, the United States annexed the Philippines, making America a major power in the Pacific.

Yellow journalism: method of journalism that utilized sensationalized accounts of the news to sell newspapers. This approach helped to whip up nationalistic impulses that led to the Spanish-American War.

U.S.S *Maine*: U.S. naval ship that sank in Havana harbor in February 1898 following an explosion. The incident was used to increase calls for war against Spain. It was never definitively determined why or how the ship was sunk.

Panama Canal: canal across the Panama isthmus that was begun in 1904 and completed in 1914; its opening enabled America to expand its economic and military influence.

Roosevelt Corollary (1904): policy that warned Europeans against intervening in the affairs of Latin America and that claimed the right of the United States to intervene in the affairs of Latin American nations if "chronic wrongdoing" was taking place.

Dollar Diplomacy: foreign policy supported by President William Howard Taft and others that favored increased American investment in the world as a way of increasing American influence.

Period of Foreign Policy Inaction

In the years immediately after the Civil War, the United States aggressively sought out new territories to acquire or to economically control. In 1867, the United States purchased Alaska from the Russians. During the same year, the Midway Islands were also annexed, as the United States was also searching for potential bases in the Pacific Ocean.

The United States did not take part in imperialistic adventures until the 1890s. Several reasons can be cited for this. America was still expanding, but this expansion was still westward; the American frontier did not totally close until the last decade of the century. In addition, rapid industrial growth, urban growth, and a large influx of immigrants kept America occupied for much of the later nineteenth century. Another factor was that most of the men in power had been veterans of the Civil War or had intimate knowledge of it. These men had little stomach for further warfare, which imperialism was likely to bring.

The results of these factors were obvious. During the 1870s and early 1880s, the American State Department had fewer than 100 employees. The United States Army and Navy both would have been no match for the military forces of four or five European countries. Virtually no politician spoke of increased imperialistic adventures when campaigning in this era.

Sign of Things to Come: Hawaii

An initial indication that American attitudes toward the use of force abroad was first demonstrated by American actions in Hawaii. American missionaries had first come to Hawaii in the 1820s. The United States was, for obvious reasons, interested in Hawaii's sugar plantations. In 1887, a deal was struck allowing sugar from the islands to be imported into America duty-free. This stimulated the sugar trade in Hawaii. Sugar planters in Hawaii exerted tremendous economic and political power. During that same year, they forced King Kalakaua to accept a new constitution that took away some of his political power and put it in their hands.

In 1891, the king died, and his sister, Queen Liliuokalani, replaced him. By this point, planters in Hawaii, and some members of the U.S. Senate, saw the obvious economic advantages of turning Hawaii into a U.S. protectorate. Queen Liliuokalani vigorously rejected this; her goal was to greatly reduce the influence of foreign countries, especially the United States, in Hawaii. In 1893, pro-American sugar planters, assisted by American marines, overthrew the queen, declared Hawaii to be a republic, and requested Hawaii be annexed by the United States. This takeover was partially a reaction to U.S. tariff policies, which favored domestic producers. If Hawaii was annexed, then planters from Hawaii would be considered domestic producers.

Much debate took place on the floor of the Senate on the proper role of the United States in Hawaii. President Grover Cleveland sent a commission to Hawaii to determine the wishes of the citizens of Hawaii concerning their future. After the commission reported that most people interviewed supported Queen Liliuokalani, Cleveland announced that he was opposed to annexation but recognized the Republic of Hawaii. President McKinley had no such reservations after his election in 1896, stating that it was "**Manifest Destiny**" that the United States should control Hawaii. Congress soon approved annexation, largely on the promise that future military bases placed in Hawaii could cement America's strategic position in the Pacific.

It also should be noted that American economic interests required increased involvement in China during this period as well. The possibility of investment in China would cause Secretary of State John Hay to ask European leaders for an **Open Door policy** in China in 1899, which would allow all foreign nations, including the United States, to establish trading relations with China.

During this era, the desire for American expansion did not extend to the Middle East. American Christian missionaries were active in the region throughout the nineteenth century. American religious groups founded Robert College in Turkey in 1863 and the Syrian Protestant College in 1866; students in both schools were the sons of the local governmental and social elites. In the first years of the twentieth century, many fears were expressed in the Middle East about possible encroachment by the European "imperialist" powers; during these discussions, there was virtually no mention of the United States.

The 1890s: Reasons for American Imperialism

By the 1890s, many American leaders began to have new attitudes toward imperialistic adventures abroad. The reasons for this were also numerous. At the forefront of those pushing for an aggressive American policy abroad were various industrial leaders, who feared that the United States would soon produce more than it could ever consume. New dependent states could prove to be markets for these goods. Some in business also perceived that in the future, industries would need raw materials that could simply not be found in America (rubber and petroleum products, for example). In the future, America would need dependent states to provide these materials.

Other influential Americans stated that it was important for political reasons that America expand. Bases would be needed in the future in the Pacific, many claimed—thus the need to acquire strategic locations in that region. Many of those interested in reviving the American navy also were very interested in imperialistic adventures; the **Naval Act of 1900** authorized the construction of battleships that would be clearly offensive in nature. A major supporter of naval expansion was Captain Alfred T. Mahan, who in 1890 wrote *The Influence of Sea Power upon History*, which stated that to be economically successful America must gain new markets abroad; the navy would have to be expanded to accomplish this.

Several other factors accounted for the increased American interest in foreign frontiers in the 1890s. The concept of **Social Darwinism** was used by supporters of imperialism, as were ideas, many imported from Europe, about the racial superiority of the Anglo-Saxon race. *Our Country,* written in 1885 by Josiah Strong, stated that God had appointed the Anglo-Saxons to be their "brother's keepers." Some Americans believed in Kipling's **"White Man's Burden"** and felt it was their duty to civilize the "inferior races" of Africa and Asia. This was also the period when American missionaries felt the time was right to Christianize the "heathens" of these regions. Others, including Senator Albert J. Beveridge of Indiana, feared that the American spirit would be sapped by the closing of the frontier and suggested that adventures abroad might help offset this. It should also be remembered that a new generation of Americans, less affected by the horrors of the Civil War, was now in positions of power in Washington, DC.

Spanish-American War

Those who wanted American adventure abroad finally got their wish with the **Spanish-American War**. In this "splendid little war," America was able to fight against an insignificant European power with little military clout. The steps leading to this war began in 1868, when Cuban colonists revolted against the Spanish, who controlled the island. The Spanish made some efforts to control the efficiency of their operations in Cuba, but generally failed in their promises of allowing more self-government on the island. In 1895, an economic depression, caused by falling sugar and tobacco prices, hit the native population especially hard, and another revolt took place.

American investors, plantation owners, and government officials initially did not support the rebellion. The Spanish sent in a huge force of 150,000 troops and instituted a policy of **reconcentration**, which sent civilians, including women and children, who the Spanish thought might be potential allies of the rebels, into heavily guarded camps. Conditions in these camps were appalling; it was estimated that in two years up to 225,000 people died in them.

The Cuban exile community in the United States pressured America to intervene on the side of the rebels, yet both Presidents Cleveland and McKinley resisted these efforts. Pressure on McKinley to intervene increased when Cuban rebels started to destroy American economic interests in Cuba, such as sugar mills.

American public opinion began to swerve toward intervention in Cuba. It is often pointed out that the American press was more responsible for this than were the actual events in Cuba. Several American newspapers practiced the most lurid forms of **yellow**

journalism when dealing with events in Cuba. Stories of the rape of Cuban girls by Spanish soldiers and brutal torture and execution of innocent Cuban citizens were standard fare in the *New York World* (published by Joseph Pulitzer) and the *New York Morning Journal* (owned by William Randolph Hearst), both of which were competing for circulation in New York. Both papers sent numerous reporters and illustrators to Cuba, and editors in New York demanded sensationalized stories. Newspapers across the country reprinted the accounts published in these papers. As a result of these stories, **jingoism** developed in America; this combined an intense America nationalism with a desire for adventure abroad.

It became harder for McKinley to resist the calls for intervention in Cuba, especially after the sinking of the **U.S.S *Maine*** on February 15, 1898. The *Maine* had been sent to Havana harbor to protect American interests after violent riots broke out in Cuba in January. During the same month, a letter stolen from the Spanish ambassador to Washington, in which he called President McKinley "weak," was published in newspapers across the country, further inflaming public opinion. The sinking of the *Maine* was undoubtedly caused by an explosion on board, yet both New York newspapers in banner headlines called for Americans to "Remember the *Maine*!" An American commission sent to study the sinking of the *Maine* was never able to conclusively determine why or how the ship was sunk.

Outbreak of War

Theodore Roosevelt was the assistant secretary of the navy at the time, and a vigorous supporter of an increased American role abroad. On February 25 (without the approval of his boss), he cabled all of the commanders in the Pacific to be ready for immediate combat against the Spanish. When the existence of these cables was discovered, President McKinley ordered the content of all of them to be rescinded, except the one to Admiral George Dewey; McKinley reaffirmed that if war broke out in Cuba, Dewey should attack the Spanish fleet quartered in the Philippines.

The pressure on McKinley to go to war was enormous. It should be noted that at this point both American expansionists and those with humanitarian motives supported American intervention in Cuba. McKinley sent the Spanish a list of demands that had to be met to avoid war. The Spanish agreed to the vast majority of them, yet McKinley finally gave in to pressures at home. On April 11, 1898, he finally sent a message to Congress stating that he favored American intervention in Cuba. The next day Congress authorized the use of force against Spain.

It is still debated whether American disorganization or Spanish disorganization was more pronounced in the Spanish-American War. American efforts to organize an army to go to Cuba were woefully inefficient. Theodore Roosevelt resigned his position in the Naval Department to lead the "**Rough Riders**" up San Juan Hill in the most famous event of the war; his actual role in this battle has been debated. Americans lost 2,500 men in this war, the vast majority from malaria or food poisoning. Only 400 died in battle.

It was the American navy earlier championed by Captain (by now Admiral) Mahan that proved decisive in the American victory over the Spanish. In seven hours, Admiral Dewey destroyed the Spanish fleet in the Pacific; every ship of the Spanish Atlantic force was destroyed by the American navy. In the **Treaty of Paris** ending the war, Spain recognized the independence of Cuba and, for a payment of $20 million, gave the Philippines, Puerto Rico, and Guam over to the United States.

Role of America: Protector or Oppressor?

After victory over the Spanish, the United States was placed in a somewhat uncomfortable position. It had criticized Spain for the way it had controlled Cuba, yet many in America did not want Cuba to be totally free either. The dilemma facing Americans after victory was one that would be rethought throughout the twentieth century: how to combine imperialistic intentions with the deep-seated American beliefs in liberty and self-government.

Fearing that America would want to annex Cuba, supporters in Congress of Cuban independence had inserted the **Teller Amendment** in the original congressional bill calling for war against Spain. This amendment stated that America would not do this under any circumstances. Nevertheless, President McKinley authorized that the Cubans would be ruled by an American military government (which kept control until 1901). The military government did authorize the Cubans to draft a constitution in 1900 but also insisted that the Cubans agree to all of the provisions of the **Platt Amendment**. This document stated that Cuba could not enter into agreements with other countries without the approval of the United States, that the United States had the right to intervene in Cuban affairs "when necessary," and that America be given two naval bases on the Cuban mainland. The Platt Amendment remained in force in Cuba until the early 1930s.

Debate over the Philippines

The debate in America over what to do with the Philippines was a much more intense one. This debate took place on the floor of the Senate and in countless editorial pages across the country. An aggressive policy toward Cuba could be justified, since it was only 90 miles away and seemed important to the United States' position in the Western Hemisphere. Many had second thoughts, however, over controlling the Philippines; the Filipinos seemed a world away, and, after all, were not "like us." In addition, Americans became aware that Filipinos expected that after the Americans helped throw out the Spanish they would then help them achieve independence. What, indeed, should America's role in the Philippines be?

All of the most basic arguments on the merits of imperialism were debated in the aftermath of the Spanish-American War. Didn't the concept of ruling a territory by force violate everything that America stood for? An **Anti-Imperialist League** was formed in 1898 (with Mark Twain and William Jennings Bryan as charter members). The first brochures put out by this organization wondered if America didn't have too many problems at home to be involved abroad, and also expressed the fear that the armies needed for imperialistic adventures abroad might also be used to curb dissent at home.

Others pointed to the huge costs of imperialism and the fear that natives from newly acquired territories might take the jobs (or lower the wages) of American workers. Some pointed out the basic racism involved in American attitudes toward the Filipinos; some Southerners opposed imperialism because they feared it would bring people of the "inferior races" to America in greater numbers.

In the end, those arguing the political, strategic, and economic advantages that control of the Philippines would bring won the national argument. The American frontier *was* closing; wouldn't expansion abroad keep America vital and strong? In addition, religious figures noted that the acquisition of the Philippines would give the church the opportunity to convert Filipinos to Christianity.

In the end, President McKinley supported American control of the Philippines, stating that if the Americans didn't enter, civil war was likely there. He also proclaimed that the Filipinos were simply "unfit for self-government." The treaty authorizing American control of the Philippines was ratified in February 1899. It should be noted that American soldiers fought Filipino rebels for the next three years, with nearly 4,500 American soldiers killed in this fighting. The American army attacked Filipino rebels with a vengeance; by the end of the insurrection, 200,000 Filipinos had been killed. Many humanitarian groups in America, which had initially enthusiastically supported the Spanish-American War, were appalled. An American commission later criticized the U.S. military for its conduct when dealing with the rebel forces.

Connecting the Pacific and the Atlantic: The Panama Canal

After the Spanish-American War, most in America and in Europe regarded America as one of the major world powers. Theodore Roosevelt became president after the assassination of President McKinley and, as he had previously demonstrated, favored an aggressive foreign policy. (McKinley was killed during the first year of his second term as president by an anarchist; the next day, political boss Mark Hanna lamented "now that damned cowboy is president of the United States.") One of Roosevelt's most cherished goals was the construction of the **Panama Canal**, which would link the Pacific and the Atlantic oceans. The strategic and economic benefits of such a canal for America at the time were obvious.

A French building company had already acquired the rights to build such a canal in the region of Panama (which was controlled by Colombia). In 1902, the United States bought the rights from the company to construct the land, but this agreement was opposed by the Colombians. A "revolt" was organized in Panama by the French. U.S. warships sailed off the coast of Panama to help the "rebels." The United States was the first to recognize Panama as an independent country; newly installed Panamanian officials then gave America territory to build a canal. By the terms of the Hay-Bunau-Varilla Treaty of 1904, the United States received permanent rights and sovereignty over a 10-mile-wide area on which they planned to build the canal. In return, Panama was given $10 million. Construction of the canal began shortly afterward.

In the United States, there was much criticism of American actions in Panama, but as in the case of the Philippines, the practical benefits of having a canal won out. The canal was finally completed in 1914. American businesses could now ship their goods faster and cheaper, although the acquisition of the Panama Canal deepened the suspicions of many in Latin America toward the United States.

Roosevelt Corollary

Theodore Roosevelt's most famous quote was to "speak softly and carry a big stick." In 1904, he also announced the **Roosevelt Corollary** to the Monroe Doctrine to Congress, which stated that the United States had the right to intervene in any country in the Western Hemisphere that did things "harmful to the United States," or if the threat of intervention by countries outside the hemisphere was present. The Roosevelt Corollary strengthened American control over Latin America, justified numerous American interventions in Latin American affairs in the twentieth century, and increased the "Yankee go home" sentiment throughout the region. In Santo Domingo (now the Dominican Republic), the government went bankrupt, and European countries threatened to intervene to collect their money. Under the provisions of the Roosevelt Corollary, Roosevelt organized the American payment of Santo Domingan debt to keep the Europeans out.

In fairness, it should also be noted that Roosevelt won the Nobel Peace Prize for his mediation between the Japanese and the Russians after the Russo-Japanese War of 1904.

William Howard Taft, Roosevelt's successor, was not as aggressive in foreign policy as Roosevelt. He favored "dollars over bullets" and instituted a policy labeled by his critics as "**Dollar Diplomacy**," which stated that American investment abroad would ensure stability and good relations between America and nations abroad. This policy would also be hotly debated throughout the twentieth century.

Chapter Review

Rapid Review

To achieve a perfect 5, you should be able to explain the following:

- America became the economic and imperialistic equal of the major European powers by the beginning of the twentieth century.
- The United States acquired territory in the years immediately following the Civil War, but then entered a period where little foreign expansion took place.
- Americans and natives friendly to America increased the economic and political control of Hawaii by the United States, signaling a new trend in foreign policy.
- America desired trade in China; these desires were represented in John Hay's Open Door policy.
- Economic, political, and strategic motives pushed America to pursue imperialist goals in the 1890s.
- Many in this era also opposed imperialism, often on moral or humanitarian grounds.
- The Spanish-American War allowed American imperialistic impulses to flourish; religious figures also supported imperialism in this era.
- Spanish incompetence and the strength of the American navy were important factors in the American victory in the Spanish-American War.
- America was deeply conflicted but finally decided to annex the Philippines, with three years of fighting between Americans and Filipino rebels to follow.
- The Panama Canal was built by the United States for military, strategic, and economic reasons; its construction began in 1904 and was completed in 1914.
- The Roosevelt Corollary to the Monroe Doctrine increased American control over Latin America.

Time Line

1867: United States purchases Alaska from Russia
United States annexes Midway Islands
1871: Beginning of European "Scramble for Africa"
1875: Trade agreement between United States and Hawaii signed
1885: Publication of *Our Country* by Josiah Strong; book discusses role of Anglo-Saxons in the world
1890: Captain Alfred T. Mahan's *The Influence of Sea Power upon History* published
1893: Pro-American sugar planters overthrow Queen Liliuokalani in Hawaii

1895: Revolt against Spanish in Cuba; harsh Spanish reaction angers many in United States
1898: Explosion of U.S.S *Maine* in Havana harbor; beginning of Spanish-American War
Annexation of Hawaii receives final approval from Congress
Anti-Imperialist League formed
1899: Secretary of State John Hay asks European leaders for an Open Door policy in China
First fighting between American army forces and Filipino rebels in Manila
1900: Naval Act of 1900 authorizes construction of offensive warships requested by navy
1901: Assassination of President McKinley; Theodore Roosevelt becomes president
1904: Roosevelt Corollary to Monroe Doctrine announced
United States begins construction of Panama Canal
1905: Roosevelt mediates conflict between Japan, and Russia in Portsmouth, New Hampshire
1914: Completion of the Panama Canal

Review Questions

1. The intent of the Roosevelt Corollary to the Monroe Doctrine was
   A. to prevent European powers from becoming directly involved in affairs of the Western Hemisphere
   B. to allow the United States to "assist" countries in the area that demonstrated economic or political instability
   C. to allow the United States to remove "unfriendly governments" in the Western Hemisphere
   D. all of the above

2. Many humanitarians in the United States initially supported the Spanish-American War because
   A. they were appalled at the Spanish policy of reconcentration in Cuba
   B. they were able to ignore editorial comments found in most American newspapers
   C. they desired to assist the Filipino natives
   D. of American economic interests in Cuba

3. The major criticism that some Americans had concerning the construction of the Panama Canal was that
   A. the canal would force America to have a navy in both the Pacific and the Atlantic.
   B. the canal would be outlandishly expensive to build.
   C. the tactics that the Americans used to get the rights to build the canal were unsavory at best.
   D. American forces would have to be stationed indefinitely in Panama to guard the canal.

4. The United States was able to annex Hawaii because
   A. Queen Liliuokalani desired increased American investment in Hawaii.
   B. pro-American planters engineered a revolt in Hawaii.
   C. public opinion in Hawaii strongly favored annexation.
   D. Hawaii felt threatened by other Pacific powers.

5. American missionary leaders supported imperialism in this era because
   A. they thought their involvement would temper the excess zeal of other imperialists.
   B. they admired the "pureness of spirit" found in the Filipinos and other native groups.
   C. religious leaders in Europe favored imperialism.
   D. they saw imperialism as an opportunity to convert the "heathens" of newly acquired territories.

> Answers and Explanations

1. **D**. The Roosevelt Corollary allowed the United States to intervene in affairs of Latin American countries under several circumstances, but was also intended to keep the European powers out of Latin America.

2. **A**. The Spanish policy of placing civilians in camps horrified many Americans. Most American newspapers initially supported the war as well. Concern for the Filipinos only became an issue during the debate over whether or not the United States should annex the Philippines.

3. **C**. The United States acquired the rights to build the canal through the encouragement of a "revolt" by Panamanians against Colombia. The American navy wanted the canal.

4. **B**. The United States was able to annex Hawaii after pro-U.S. planters led a rebellion against Queen Liliuokalani, who had opposed U.S. influence.

5. **D**. Missionary leaders worked in conjunction with other imperialists in this era. Little admiration of the natives was demonstrated by missionary leaders; the possibility of conversions was the major reason for religious support for imperialism.

CHAPTER 20

Progressive Era (1895–1914)

IN THIS CHAPTER

Summary: Progressivism began in the 1890s as a movement that attacked the political, social, and political inequalities of the age. Many Progressives blamed capitalism for the evils of society. However, unlike the Socialists, who wanted to destroy the capitalist system, the Progressives wanted to fix that system. Many Progressives were tied to the Social Gospel movement of the Protestant church; others wanted to reform city governments, while still others desired to instill even more democracy in the electoral process (direct primaries, more use of the referendum, etc.). Many Progressives launched projects to aid the immigrant population that existed in America's cities. One example was Hull House, a settlement house that aided Chicago's poor. The high point of the Progressive movement was the "Square Deal" of the presidency of Theodore Roosevelt. Progressives did much to reform America's cities but were less effective in aiding America's farmers and minorities.

Keywords

Social Gospel movement: movement originating in the Protestant church that aimed to help the urban poor; many Progressives were influenced by this movement.

Muckrakers: writers who exposed unethical practices in both government and business during this era; newspaper editors discovered that these types of stories increased circulation.

Seventeenth Amendment (1913): U.S. Constitutional amendment that allowed voters instead of state legislatures to elect U.S. senators; this amendment had been championed by Progressives.

Initiative process: this Progressive-supported process allowed any citizen to propose a law. If enough supporters' signatures could be procured, the proposed law would appear on the next ballot.
Referendum process: this process allowed citizens (instead of legislatures) to vote on proposed laws.
Recall process: this process allowed voters to remove an elected official from office before his or her term expired.
Direct primary: this process allowed party members to vote for prospective candidates; previously most had been chosen by party bosses.
Hull House: Settlement house in Chicago founded by Jane Addams; Hull House became a model for settlement houses around the country.
National American Woman Suffrage Association: created in 1890 by a merger of two womens' suffrage organizations and led in its early years by Elizabeth Cady Stanton and Susan B. Anthony; was instrumental in demanding women's right to vote.
Triangle Shirtwaist Fire (1911): fire in New York City that killed 150 female factory workers. It was later found that the workers had been locked in the factory; as a result, many factory reforms were enacted.
The Jungle: Novel written by Upton Sinclair that highlighted numerous problems of the meatpacking industry and inspired the Pure Food and Drug Act and the Meat Inspection Act.

Origins of Progressivism

It should be emphasized that progressivism was not a unified movement in any way. There was never a unifying agenda or party; many "Progressives" eagerly supported one or two Progressive reforms without supporting any others. Thus, Progressive reforms could be urban or rural, call for more government or less government, and, on occasion, could even be perceived as being probusiness.

Progressivism has many sources of origin. Books mentioned in Chapter 16 such as *Progress and Poverty* by Henry George and *Looking Backward* by Edward Bellamy were read by most early Progressives. **Taylorism** (also discussed in Chapter 16) influenced many Progressives. Many felt that the efficiency that Taylor proposed for American industry could also be installed in American government, schools, and even in one's everyday life.

Progressive reforms also shared some of the same critiques of society that American Socialists were making at the time. Progressives and Socialists both were very critical of capitalism and wanted more wealth to get into the hands of the poor working class. However, as stated previously, Progressives were interested in reforming the capitalist system, while American Socialists wanted to end capitalism (by this point, by the ballot box). It should be noted that many Progressive reformers had knowledge of socialism, some attended Socialist meetings at some point in their careers, and a few Progressives remained Socialists throughout their careers. Upton Sinclair, author of *The Jungle,* was both a Progressive and a Socialist.

Progressivism was also influenced by religious developments of the era. During this era, the **Social Gospel movement** flourished; this movement had its origin in Protestant efforts to aid the urban poor. The Social Gospel movement emphasized the elements of Christianity that emphasized the need to struggle for social justice. Followers stated that this fight was much more important than the struggle to lead a "good life" on a personal level. Many

Progressive leaders (such as Jane Addams) had grown up in very religious homes and found in Progressive politics a place where they could put their religious beliefs into action. The Social Gospel movement was strictly a Protestant movement.

Finally, Progressives were deeply impacted by the **muckrakers**. Newspaper editors discovered that articles that exposed corruption increased circulation, and thus exposés of unethical practices in political life and business life became common in most newspapers. The term muckrakers was used in a negative way by Theodore Roosevelt, but writers using that title exposed much corruption in American society. *The Jungle* by Upton Sinclair attacked the excesses of the meatpacking industry. Ida Tarbell wrote of the corruption she found in the Standard Oil Trust company, while Lincoln Steffens exposed political corruption found in several American cities in *The Shame of the Cities*. Jacob Riis exposed life in the slums in *How the Other Half Lives*. Progressives wanted to act on the evils of society uncovered by the muckrakers.

Goals of Progressives

The fact that many in the Progressive movement were from the middle class greatly influenced the goals of progressivism. Progressives wanted to improve the life experienced by members of the lower classes; at the same time, most desired that the nature and pace of this improvement be dictated by them and not the workers themselves. Progressives greatly feared the potential for revolution found in Socialist and anarchist writings of the era; they proposed a series of gradual reforms. *Progressives, as stated previously, wanted to make existing institutions work better.* Factories, they felt, could be changed so that they would be concerned with the quality of life of their workers; governments could be altered so that they would act as protectors of the lower classes.

It should be noted that Progressive goals and programs were not universally popular. Progressive programs for the betterment of the poor often meant that the government would have more control over their lives; many in the lower class were vehemently opposed to this. In addition, Progressives wanted to crack down on urban political machines, which in many cases did much to aid the lives and conditions of the lower classes. As a result, the very people whom Progressive reforms were designed to help were often resentful of these reforms.

Historians debate the overall intent of the Progressive movement. Some maintain that social reformers of the era wanted to protect Americans from the evils of contemporary society. Others maintain that the real goal of progressivism was to control Americans so that they could be functioning members of that society.

Urban Reforms

Many of the early successes of progressivism were actions taken against urban political machines. Yet again, some reforms supported by Progressives put more power in the hands of those machines. Certain "reform mayors," such as Tom Johnson in Cleveland and Mark Fagan in Jersey City, were legitimately interested in improving the living and working conditions of the lower classes and improving education. In cities such as Cleveland, municipal utilities were taken over by the city to provide more efficient service. Some reform mayors also pushed citywide relief programs and established shelters for the homeless.

Other Progressive reformers wanted to professionalize the administrations of various cities and to enact measures so that mere "political hacks" could not get municipal jobs. It should be noted that some of these reforms appeared to be antidemocratic in nature. By attacking the system of political machines and ward politics, reformers were attacking a system that had given a degree of assistance and influence to the urban working classes. The new "professionals" who reformers envisioned getting municipal jobs would be almost exclusively from the middle class, the same class as the reformers themselves.

Progressives at the State Level

It was at the state level that some of the most important political work of the Progressives took place. Governors Robert La Follette from Wisconsin and Hiram Johnson from California introduced reforms in their states that would allow citizens to have a more direct role in the political process. These reforms included the following:

1. The adoption of the **Seventeenth Amendment**. Finally adopted in 1913, it allowed voters, instead of the state legislatures, to directly elect U.S. senators.
2. The adoption of the **initiative process**. This initiative allowed a citizen to propose a new law. If he or she got enough signatures, the proposed law would appear on the next ballot.
3. The adoption of the **referendum process**. Referendum allowed citizens to vote on a law that was being considered for adoption.
4. The adoption of the **recall process**, which allowed the voters to remove an elected official from office before his or her term was up.
5. The adoption of the **direct primary**, which allowed party members to vote for prospective candidates instead of having them handpicked by the party boss.

Women and Progressivism

Women played a major role in progressivism from the very beginning. In 1899, Florence Kelley founded the **National Consumers League**, an organization made up largely of women who lobbied at the state and national levels for legislation that would protect both women and children at home and in the workplace. Minimum wage laws for women were enacted in various states beginning in 1911; more stringent child labor laws began to be enacted in the states one year later.

Women also played a crucial role in the creation of **settlement houses**. In 1889, Jane Addams and Ellen Gates Starr founded **Hull House** in Chicago, which would become a model for settlement house construction in other cities. Found at Hull House (and at many other centers) were clubs for adults and children, rooms for classes, and a kindergarten. Settlement house workers also gave poor and immigrant women (and their husbands) advice on countless problems that they encountered in the city. Some settlement houses were more successful than others in actually helping lower-class families cope with urban life. Programs at settlement houses were multidimensional, stressing art, music, drama, and dance. Classes in child care, health education, and adult literacy could be found at most settlement houses.

Women differed greatly on how they felt the urban poor could be helped. Some pushed heavily for reforms in the workplace, while others joined organizations such as the

Anti-Saloon League, whose members felt that alcohol was the major cause for the woes of the lower classes. Still others became deeply involved in the suffrage movement, often attempting to get lower-class women interested in the vote as well. Women started to get the vote in individual Western states beginning with Idaho, Colorado, and Utah in the 1890s. In 1890, the **National American Woman Suffrage Association** was created by a merger of two women's suffrage groups. It was led in its early years by Elizabeth Cady Stanton and Susan B. Anthony. In 1916, Alice Paul founded the more radical **National Woman's Party**. Both organizations would be crucial in the final push for women's suffrage after World War I.

In addition, during this era, women in public meetings first began to discuss the topic of **feminism**. The word was first used by a group of women meeting in New York City in 1914. Feminists wanted to remove themselves from the restraints that society had placed on them because they were female. A radical feminist of the time was Margaret Sanger, who as a nurse in New York City observed the lack of knowledge that immigrant women had about the reproductive system. Sanger devoted herself to teaching the poor about birth control and opened the first birth control clinic in the United States.

Some laws were passed in the era to protect working women. In *Muller v. Oregon,* a case that went all the way to the Supreme Court in 1908, it was ruled constitutional to set limits on the number of hours a woman could work. The rationale given for this, which the Court agreed with, was that too much work would interfere with a woman's prime role as a mother.

Reforming the Workplace

Horrible events such as the **Triangle Shirtwaist Fire** convinced many Progressives to push for reforms of safety and health conditions in factories. Progressives lobbied hard for the creation of accident insurance programs for workers in New York and elsewhere. From 1910 to 1917, many states adopted legislation that would help to protect families of those killed or injured in workplace and mine accidents.

Progressives and labor unions often did not see eye to eye. However, one issue that some Progressives and unions did agree on was the need to restrict further European immigration, especially from southeastern Europe. Immigrants were not union supporters, and increased immigration would cause a larger supply of labor, thus driving down wages. By not bringing in more immigrants who were "unlike ourselves," supporters stated that city life and morale in the workplace would improve. To some, opposing immigration was a progressive reform. More than anything, this demonstrated that "progressivism" meant very different things to different people.

Square Deal of Theodore Roosevelt

Theodore Roosevelt's ascending to presidency in 1901 after the assassination of William McKinley brought to office a man unafraid to use the power of the government to address the evils of society. In 1902, Roosevelt helped mediate a strike between the United Mine Workers and the coal companies. Roosevelt stated that the agreement was a **"Square Deal"** for both sides. This term would be used throughout his time in office to emphasize that government intervention could help the plight of ordinary Americans.

Roosevelt was reelected in 1904, and, in 1906, Roosevelt supported legislation that was progressive in nature. He supported the Hepburn Act, which gave teeth to the **Interstate Commerce Act**, designed to further regulate interstate shippers, and the creation of the **Pure Food and Drug Act** and the **Meat Inspection Act**. The writings of many muckrakers, including Upton Sinclair's *The Jungle,* highlighted many of the problems of the food industry addressed in these bills.

Roosevelt also used the federal government to aggressively investigate and prosecute illegal **trusts** and **holding companies** (both described in Chapter 16). The **Sherman Antitrust Act** had been in place since 1890, yet neither President Cleveland nor President McKinley had ordered its enforcement on a regular basis. To many Americans, it appeared that a small group of Wall Street bankers controlled the entire American economy (this complaint would be echoed many times in the twentieth century). Roosevelt had the Justice Department sue Standard Oil, the American Tobacco Company, and the Northern Securities Company, a holding company that controlled many American railroads. All were partially broken up as a result of these government actions. By the end of his time in office, Roosevelt had taken on 45 major American corporations. It should be emphasized that Theodore Roosevelt was *not* antibusiness; however, he did strongly believe that corporations who abused their power should be punished.

Roosevelt also enacted other measures applauded by Progressives. In 1905, he created the **U.S. Forest Service**, which soon acted to set aside 200 million acres of land for national forests. The **Sixteenth Amendment**, enacted in 1913, authorized the collection of federal income taxes, which could be collected largely from the wealthy (the income of the federal government had been previously collected from tariffs. Progressives argued that to pay for them the prices of goods sold to the working classes were artificially high). In the end, the "Square Deal" was based on the idea of creating a level playing field. Roosevelt was not against trusts; he opposed trusts that were harmful to the economy. He supported Standard Oil, for example, because of the benefits he said it brought to America.

Progressivism under William Howard Taft

Many historians regard Taft as the real trustbuster. More antitrust lawsuits went to court when he was president than during the Roosevelt presidency, although some of them had begun during the Roosevelt administration. In the 1908 presidential election, William Howard Taft, Theodore Roosevelt's handpicked successor, defeated three-time candidate William Jennings Bryan. In the campaign, Bryan continually came across as supporting more progressive measures than Taft did. Taft did promise to follow Roosevelt's progressive legacy, and to some degree he followed through on this. During his presidency, the Sherman Antitrust Act was used against another 95 corporations.

However, Taft never had the personal magnetism that Roosevelt possessed, and totally unlike Roosevelt, he deferred on important issues to Congress. Taft was influenced by the conservative wing of the Republican party, which opposed additional Progressive reforms. His support of the Payne-Aldrich Tariff Act of 1909 further angered Progressives, who usually viewed tariffs as hurting the lower classes (since to pay for them the prices of goods were usually higher).

Progressives in the Republican party finally took action against Taft after the **Ballinger-Pinchot Affair**. Richard A. Ballinger was secretary of the interior under Taft and allowed private business interests to gain access to several million acres of land in Alaska. A close friend of Roosevelt, Gifford Pinchot, headed the Forest Service. When Pinchot protested against Ballinger's actions in front of a congressional committee, Taft proceeded to fire him. Progressives now labeled Taft as being antienvironment.

Progressive Republicans began to campaign against Taft and the "old guard" of pro-business Republicans. In the 1910 congressional primaries, Taft campaigned against several of these Progressives. Theodore Roosevelt, just back from an extended trip to Africa, campaigned for a number of these Republican Progressives. His speeches called for more Progressive reforms, especially in the workplace. Roosevelt called his program for reform the **New Nationalism**. Roosevelt called again and again for a greatly expanded role of the federal government. As a result of the 1920 congressional elections, Progressives dominated the U.S. Senate.

1912 Presidential Election

By early 1912, Theodore Roosevelt decided that the policies of President Taft were not progressive enough and announced he was running for president. The single event that several biographers say pushed Roosevelt to run was the decision of Taft to go after United States Steel because it had purchased Tennessee Coal and Iron back in 1907. Taft knew that Roosevelt had personally approved this deal. As might be expected, Taft's followers controlled the Republican party machinery, thus allowing Taft to easily win the 1912 Republican nomination.

Roosevelt's followers marched out of the Chicago convention site, proclaimed themselves to be the Progressive party, and nominated Roosevelt for president (with California's Progressive governor Hiram Johnson as his running mate). This party soon became known as the **Bull Moose party**. Its platform included many Progressive causes, including the elimination of child labor, suffrage for women, and an eight-hour workday. Many women supported the Bull Moose party; in several states where women had the vote, women ran for local offices as members of the party.

The beneficiary of the split in the Republican party was the Democratic candidate Woodrow Wilson, governor of New Jersey. Wilson also campaigned as a Progressive, although in his platform, called the **New Freedom policy**, he also cautioned against big government. Wilson argued that government was wrong to concentrate on regulating big monopolies; instead, government should be trying to break them up. Wilson won the election, but only received 42 percent of the popular vote. Roosevelt received 27 percent and Taft only 23 percent. It should also be noted that Eugene Debs ran as a candidate of the Socialist party and received 6 percent of the votes. The political will of the times is easily shown in this election: the three candidates openly calling for Progressive policies (Wilson, Roosevelt, and Debs) received 75 percent of the popular vote.

Progressive Legacy of Woodrow Wilson

Much legislation was enacted under Woodrow Wilson that pleased reformers. The Underwood Tariff Act of 1913 cut tariffs on imported goods. The **Clayton Antitrust Act** of 1914 was a continuation of the Sherman Antitrust Act, and outlawed certain specific business practices. A key element of this act also helped the labor movement by making strikes and other labor activities legal. In 1914, the **Federal Trade Commission** was established; the main job of this organization was to uniformly enforce the antitrust laws. Wilson also signed legislation creating the **Federal Reserve System**, which established 12 district reserve banks and the creation of Federal Reserve notes. This system was designed to protect the American economy against further panics such as had occurred in the early 1890s.

Did Progressivism Succeed?

Progressives had done much to improve the condition of American cities, the plight of factory workers, the support available for urban immigrants, and the democratic nature of the American political process. However, Progressive reforms did much less for migrant farmers and others outside of the city. Many blacks were disappointed that few alliances ever took place between black leaders and Progressives; Theodore Roosevelt met twice with Booker T. Washington but other than that did little to help the conditions of blacks during his presidency. Race riots occurred in Springfield, Illinois, in 1908. The antiblack message of D. W. Griffith's 1915 film ***Birth of a Nation*** was applauded by many; President Wilson stated that the film presented a "truthful" depiction of the Reconstruction Era. In 1909, the **National Association for the Advancement of Colored People (NAACP)** was founded to further the fight of blacks for political equality in America.

The outbreak of World War I in Europe turned the interests of many away from political reform. Only those reformers concerned with women's suffrage relentlessly pursued their cause during the war years.

Chapter Review

Rapid Review

To achieve the perfect 5, you should be able to explain the following:

- Political, economic, and social inequities and problems existed in America in the late 1890s, and the Progressive movement developed to attempt to address some of those problems.
- The Progressive movement did not have a unifying set of goals or leaders.
- Progressives shared some of the same critiques of American society as the Socialists, but wished to reform and not attack the American system.
- Progressive reformers were closely tied to the Social Gospel movement of the Protestant church; progressivism and religious fervor often marched hand in hand.
- Muckraking magazines and newspapers of the era often created and published the Progressive agenda.
- Many Progressives were determined to reform city government and the services provided by city government.
- Progressive political reforms included the initiative, the referendum, and the recall processes, and the direct primary.
- Hull House was an example of a settlement house copied by reformers across the country.
- The presidency of Theodore Roosevelt was a high point of progressivism; Roosevelt's "Square Deal" included many progressive measures.
- Progressive policies were sometimes challenged by Roosevelt's successor, William Howard Taft; the advent of World War I blunted the Progressive reform impulse for many.
- Progressivism succeeded in achieving some of its goals but fell short in aiding farmers and minorities in America.

Time Line

1879: *Progress and Poverty* by Henry George published
1888: *Looking Backward* by Edward Bellamy published
1889: Formation of National Consumers League
1890: National American Woman Suffrage Association founded
1901: Theodore Roosevelt becomes president after the assassination of William McKinley
Progressive Robert La Follette elected as governor of Wisconsin
Progressive Tom Johnson elected as mayor of Cleveland, Ohio
1903: Founding of Women's Trade Union League
1904: *The Shame of the Cities* by Lincoln Steffens published
1905: IWW (Industrial Workers of the World) established
Establishment of U.S. Forest Service
1906: *The Jungle* by Upton Sinclair published
Meat Inspection Act enacted
Pure Food and Drug Act enacted
1908: William Howard Taft elected president
1909: Foundation of the NAACP
1910: Ballinger-Pinchot controversy
1911: Triangle Shirtwaist Company fire
1912: Progressive party (Bull Moose party) founded by Theodore Roosevelt
Woodrow Wilson elected president
Establishment of Industrial Relations Committee
1913: Establishment of Federal Reserve System
Ratification of Sixteenth Amendment, authorizing federal income tax
Ratification of Seventeenth Amendment, authorizing direct election of senators
1914: Clayton Antitrust Act ratified
Outbreak of World War I in Europe
1915: First showing of D. W. Griffith's film *Birth of a Nation*

> Review Questions

1. Successful reforms initiated by the Progressives included all but which of the following:
   A. Governments became more efficient in American cities such as Cleveland.
   B. Health and safety conditions improved in some large factories.
   C. The conditions of migrant farmers improved to some degree.
   D. The federal government began to collect a national income tax.

2. Theodore Roosevelt ran for president in 1912 because
   A. the policies of William Howard Taft's administration were almost exclusively antiprogressive.
   B. he desired to split the Republican party and give the election to the Democrats.
   C. he was appalled by the results of the Ballinger-Pinchot Affair.
   D. of the Taft administration's decision to apply the Sherman Antitrust Act to United States Steel.

3. American blacks were discouraged by their lack of racial progress during the Wilson administration. Which of the following is *not* true?
   A. The film *Birth of a Nation* presented a positive view of blacks in Reconstruction states after the Civil War.
   B. Black and Progressive leaders forged tight political bonds during the Wilson administration and battled for many of the same causes.
   C. Booker T. Washington and Theodore Roosevelt developed close political ties after their two meetings together.
   D. All of the above.

4. Many Progressives agreed with Socialists that
   A. capitalism had created massive inequality in America
   B. the American factory system had to be fundamentally altered
   C. labor unions were inherently evil
   D. revolutionary tactics were needed to reform the economic and social systems

5. Which of the following was *least* likely to be a Progressive in this era?
   A. A member of the Protestant Social Gospel movement
   B. A large stockholder in United States Steel
   C. A follower of Eugene Debs
   D. A member of the Bull Moose party

› Answers and Explanations

1. **C.** Progressives did much less for workers in the agricultural sector than they did for factory workers.

2. **D.** The Taft administration enacted many important progressive measures. Roosevelt considered the actions against United States Steel to be a personal affront to him.

3. **D.** D. W. Griffith's film presented a very negative view of blacks during Reconstruction. Progressives and black leaders never worked closely together. Theodore Roosevelt met twice with Booker T. Washington but did little to help the conditions of blacks.

4. **A.** Progressives and Socialists were both critical of the effects of capitalism in the United States. Progressives, however, were intent on reforming that system.

5. **B.** Progressives were insistent that corporations like United States Steel be made to reform. Members of the Social Gospel movement and Socialist followers of Eugene Debs shared goals with the Progressives.

CHAPTER 21

United States and World War I (1914–1921)

IN THIS CHAPTER

Summary: The United States was officially neutral in the first two years of World War I. In 1916, one of President Woodrow Wilson's campaign slogans was "he kept us out of war." However, America was soon drawn into this conflict on the side of the British and French against the Germans (and the Austro-Hungarians). The 1915 sinking of the British passenger ship the *Lusitania* infuriated many Americans, as did the publication of the Zimmerman Note, in which Germany tried to entice Mexico to go to war against the United States. In January 1917, Germany announced a policy of unrestricted submarine warfare, and several American ships were sunk. These events caused President Wilson to call for a declaration of war against Germany. American entry into the war was a tremendous psychological lift for the British and the French. On the American home front, the government imposed unprecedented controls on the economy and on the spreading of news. The war ended with an armistice in November 1918. At the subsequent Paris Peace Conference, Wilson attempted to convince the Allies to accept his peace plan, called the "Fourteen Points." Britain and France were generally not enthusiastic about Wilson's proposals, but they did support the creation of a League of Nations. However, the League was opposed by isolationist members of the U.S. Senate, and the United States never became a member of the League. Instead, U.S. foreign policy became isolationist and remained largely so through the 1930s.

Keywords

American Expeditionary Force: American force of 14,500 men that landed in France in June 1917 under the command of General John J. Pershing. Both women and blacks served in the American army during the war, although black units were segregated and usually had white officers.

War Industries Board: board that regulated American industry during World War I; it attempted to stimulate war production by allocating raw materials to factories that aided the war effort.

Committee on Public Information: agency created during the war whose mission was to spread pro-Allied propaganda through the press and through newsreels; newspapers were asked to print only articles that were helpful to the war effort.

Fourteen Points: plan for the postwar world that Woodrow Wilson brought to the Paris Peace Conference; Wilson's plan proposed open peace treaties, freedom of the seas, arms reductions, and a League of Nations. Britain and France were openly suspicious of these plans, but they supported the creation of a League of Nations.

League of Nations: world body proposed by Woodrow Wilson as part of his 14-point peace plan. The League was created but without the participation of Germany, the Soviet Union, and the United States (isolationists in the Senate ensured that the treaty creating the League was never signed). As a result, the League remained a relatively ineffective body throughout its existence.

American Response to the Outbreak of War

The assassination of Archduke Franz Ferdinand by Bosnian nationalists on June 28, 1914, set off the series of events that would lead to World War I. Tensions between European powers had been building, with almost all of the major powers undergoing rapid military buildup in the years immediately prior to 1914. These conflicts were caused by increasing nationalism throughout Europe, the competition of imperialism, and the complicated system of alliances that wove together the fates of most European nations. When the war actually began in earnest in August 1914, France, Russia, and Great Britain were the major **Allied Powers**, while Germany, Austria-Hungary, and Italy made up the **Central Powers**.

Many Americans felt deeply connected to the events of World War I, as over one-third of the American population was a first- or second-generation immigrant. However, not every American supported Great Britain and France. A large number of German immigrants lived throughout the United States. President Wilson and others personally supported the cause of the Allied Powers, especially when reports of the alleged barbarism of the German soldiers in the battles of 1914 appeared in American newspapers.

On August 4, 1914, President Wilson issued an official proclamation of American neutrality in the war. Even though most Americans were sympathetic to the cause of the Allied Powers, economic common sense dictated that America remain neutral; America in 1914 desired to continue to trade with both sides. After English ships interfered with American trade with Germany and German submarines interfered with American trade with England, America issued a series of diplomatic protests.

Increasing American Support for the Allied Powers

American sympathies and practical considerations dictated that American trade with the Allies increase as the war progressed. By 1916, American trade with the Central Powers was down to near zero, whereas trade with the Allied powers had increased nearly 400 percent. Many who traded with Great Britain urged Washington to begin to prepare the United States for eventual war against Germany. A private **National Security League** was founded in late 1914 to instill patriotism in Americans and to psychologically prepare Americans for war. By the summer of 1915, Congress was taking the first steps to prepare the American army for actual combat in Europe. It should also be noted that peace movements existed in many major American cities, with women making up a large part of the membership of these organizations.

It was the actions of German U-boats that angered many Americans and caused them to favor entering the war against the "**Hun**." According to existing international law, if one ship were to sink another, it first had to board the ship and offer all on board "safe passage" before sinking it. The advantage a U-boat had was that it glided underwater undetected and fired at other ships without warning.

Americans were outraged when a German U-boat sank a British passenger ship, the *Lusitania*, in the Atlantic Ocean on May 7, 1915; all 128 Americans on board perished. President Wilson issued a strong protest, but it should be noted that the ship was carrying weapons meant to help the Allied cause (which made it technically legal for the Germans to sink the ship). In addition, Germany had placed advertisements in major American newspapers warning Americans not to travel on the ship that day.

In August, the *Arabic*, another passenger liner, was sunk by the Germans. President Wilson again forcefully protested; in response, the Germans issued the "Arabic pledge," in which they promised to stop sinking passenger ships without warning as long as the crews of the ships allowed the Germans to search the ships.

Official American concern about the actions of the U-boats continued. On March 24, 1916, a French ship called the *Sussex* was attacked by a U-boat; seven Americans on board were badly injured. The United States threatened to entirely cut diplomatic ties with Germany over this incident. In the **Sussex Pledge**, the Germans promised to sink no more ships without prior warning. The actions described above all caused public opinion in the United States to increasingly favor military support of the Allied Powers.

America Moves Toward War

Woodrow Wilson won the 1916 presidential election over his Republican opponent Charles Evans Hughes by stating that the Republicans were the party of war. "He kept us out of war" was the popular slogan of Wilson's supporters. This was a promise, however, that Wilson could not keep for long. On January 31, 1917, Germany announced a policy of **unrestricted submarine warfare**, stating that any ship from any country attempting to enter the ports of Allied nations would be sunk. Historians believe that the Germans knew that eventually the United States would enter the war; by beginning this policy at this time, the Germans were gambling that they could win the war before the United States was truly involved. On February 3, Wilson officially broke off American diplomatic relations and suggested to Congress that American merchant ships be armed.

American public opinion became increasingly enraged when they heard about the **Zimmermann Telegram** (also called the Zimmermann Note in some textbooks). This was an intercepted message between Arthur Zimmermann, the German foreign minister, and German officials in Mexico, suggesting that when Germany went to war with the United States, the Mexicans should be persuaded to attack the United States as well. As a reward, the Mexicans would receive Texas, New Mexico, and Arizona after the United States was defeated.

Between March 16 and March 18, three more American ships were sunk by German vessels. On April 2, President Wilson formally asked Congress for a declaration of war; this declaration was enthusiastically passed the following day. Wilson was motivated to declare war by the legitimate danger to American shipping that existed and by his belief that American entry into the war would help shorten it. Some critics claim that American arms makers exerted pressure to persuade Wilson to get involved in the war.

America Enters the War

By the time the Americans entered the war in April 1917, the English and the French were desperate for American assistance. The Russian army had suffered crushing defeats since 1916, and the removal of the tsar from power in March 1917 threw into doubt the entire Russian commitment to the war effort. Without Russia in the war, the Germans could place virtually their entire army in the western front.

The initial **American Expeditionary Force** that landed in France in June 1917 under the command of General John J. Pershing consisted of 14,500 men; its main psychological effect was to help boost the morale of the Allies. Volunteers were recruited to serve in the army, but a Selective Service Act was passed in May 1917. The ages of those originally drafted were between 21 and 30; this was later extended to between 17 and 46.

Both women and blacks were in the armed forces during the war. Some 11,500 women served, primarily as nurses and clerks, and over 400,000 blacks served. Black units were kept segregated and almost always had white officers.

American shipping to Europe became increasingly disrupted by German U-boats after the formal American declaration of war. Starting in May 1917, all American shipping to Europe traveled in a **convoy system**. The navy developed special torpedo boats that were able to destroy submarines. These techniques drastically decreased the damage done by German U-boats and other ships; only two troop transports were sunk from this point onward, and losses suffered by the merchant marine were much fewer.

Impact of the American Expeditionary Force

The size of the American Expeditionary Force (AEF) expanded to over 2 million by November 1918, and they were definitely needed. Lenin and the Bolsheviks took over in Russia in November 1917 and pulled the Russians out of the war. With only one front to worry about, by March 1918, the Germans had almost all of their troops on the western front, and were less than 50 miles from Paris in early June.

American soldiers played a major role in preventing the Germans from taking Paris. The Americans held firm at the **Battle of Chateau-Thierry**, preventing the Germans from crossing the Marne and advancing toward Paris. Americans were also involved in a major offensive against the Germans in July and decisively defeated the Germans at the Battle of St. Mihiel. Over 1 million AEF forces took part in the final **Meuse-Argonne Offensive** of late September 1918, which cut the supply lines of the German army and convinced the German general staff that victory was impossible.

The armistice ending the war was signed on November 11, 1918. Nearly 115,000 Americans died in this war, a mere pittance compared to the nearly 8 million European soldiers who died in battle. American military heroes from World War I included fighter pilot Eddie Rickenbacker and Corporal Alvin York, who single-handedly shot 32 German soldiers and captured another 132.

Home Front During World War I

Despite the fact that America was far removed from the physical fighting of World War I, much had to be done to prepare America for the war effort. Americans were encouraged to buy **Liberty Bonds** to support the war; movie stars of the era such as Charlie Chaplin made speeches and short films extolling the virtues of Liberty Bonds.

Poor harvests in 1916 and 1917 made it necessary to regulate food production and consumption during the war years. In August 1917, Congress passed the **Lever Food and Fuel Control Act**; almost immediately, the government began to regulate food consumption. The Food Administration was headed by future president Herbert Hoover, who attempted to increase production and decrease consumption. Hoover's approach to problems was centered around voluntary cooperation, as "Wheatless Mondays" and "Meatless Tuesdays" became commonplace. Harvests greatly improved in 1918 and 1919 as well. The introduction of daylight saving time allowed farmers more time in the evenings to work in the fields and also served to save electricity.

Industry was also regulated by the **War Industries Board**, headed by Wall Street financier Bernard Baruch. This board attempted to stimulate production for the war effort by strictly allocating raw materials and by instituting strict production controls. A Fuel Administration also acted to preserve coal and gasoline; "Fuelless Mondays" and "Gasless Sundays" also existed in 1917 and 1918.

Some historians make the point that World War I was actually the high point of **progressivism**. The government regulated the economy in positive ways that could have only been dreamed about in the days of Theodore Roosevelt. Business leaders loudly claimed they were supporting the war effort (many of them were). As a result, the Sherman Antitrust Laws were largely forgotten during World War I.

Keeping America Patriotic

Another new agency created in 1917 was the **Committee on Public Information**, headed by George Creel. The job of this agency was to spread anti-German and pro-Allied propaganda through newsreels and lectures, and through the cooperation of the press. Germans were portrayed as beastlike Huns wherever possible. Liberty Leagues were established in communities across America; members of these organizations were encouraged to report suspicious actions by anyone (especially foreigners) to their local authorities. George Creel asked newspapers to voluntarily censor themselves and to print only articles that would be helpful to the war effort.

A fine line between patriotism and oppression existed during much of World War I. The **National Security League** convinced Congress to insist on a literacy test for all new immigrants. German language instruction, German music, and even pretzels were banned in some cities. In April 1918, a German-born American citizen was lynched outside of St. Louis; ironically, an investigation found that he had recently attempted to enlist in the American navy.

Most Americans felt they were fighting the war to help the spread of democracy, yet many critics lamented some of the actions taken by the government during the war era. The 1917 **Espionage Act** made it illegal to obstruct the draft process in any way and stated that any material that was sent through the mail that was said to incite treason could be seized. The Sedition Act of 1918 stated that it was illegal to criticize the government, the Constitution, the U.S. Army, or the U.S. Navy. Prominent Socialist Eugene Debs received a three-year prison term for speaking against militarism; movie producer Robert Goldstein was even sentenced to three years in prison for showing the American colonists fighting the British in a Revolutionary War film. Radical labor unions such as the IWW were also harassed during the war years. Over 1,000 Americans were found guilty of violations of either the Espionage Act or the Sedition Act.

The war did provide a measure of social mobility for blacks and women. With large numbers of men fighting in Europe and no immigrants entering the country, northern factories needed workers, and encouraged blacks to move north to take factory jobs. This move north was called the **Great Migration**; during the war, nearly 600,000 blacks moved north. Many women were able to find jobs on farms or in factories for the very first time during the war. After the war, men would replace them in the labor market and force them to return to the "women's sphere."

Woodrow Wilson and the Treaty of Versailles

The Paris Peace Conference began on January 12, 1919, and had the very difficult task of creating lasting European peace. The conference was dominated by the "Big Four": the representatives of England, France, Italy (which had switched sides in the middle of the war), and the United States.

Woodrow Wilson was treated as a hero when he arrived in Paris, yet it was obvious in the initial sessions of the peace conference that the leaders of the victorious countries had very different goals. The suffering of England and especially France during the war was horrific; the goal of the French delegation was clearly to punish Germany as much as possible. Woodrow Wilson, on the other hand, came to France supporting his **Fourteen Points**, which called for open peace treaties, freedom of the seas, free trade, arms reduction, a gradual reduction of colonial claims, and some sort of a world organization to ensure peace. Wilson's plan was coolly received in France; the French, as stated previously, were mainly interested in what they could get out of the Germans. It was also coolly received in the United States by those who were opposed to continued American involvement in European affairs.

Wilson's Fourteen Points were largely opposed by the other members of the Big Four. Wilson called for a reduction of colonial claims: England and France had every intention of taking Germany's colonies after the war. When the treaty was finally signed, Wilson got only a fraction of what he initially wanted. Germany was held responsible for the war and was made to pay reparations. The **League of Nations** was created, although initially without Germany and the Bolshevik-led Soviet Union. Wilson believed that this was the most important of the Fourteen Points, so he did not leave Paris totally discouraged.

United States and the Middle East

During the initial two decades of the twentieth century, the United States became increasingly interested in Middle Eastern affairs. Theodore Roosevelt brokered a settlement to the Moroccan crisis between France and Germany in 1905 to 1906 (both countries desired to be dominant in the region: the conference eventually supported French claims in the region). It was World War I, however, that drew the attention of many in the United States, including President Woodrow Wilson, to the region.

Turkey joined the war on the side of the Central Powers (Germany and Austria-Hungary) in late 1914, thus causing the war to spread to the Middle East. The Ottoman Empire, which controlled much of what we call the "Middle East" today, had been gradually collapsing for over a century. World War I completed this collapse. Residents of the Ottoman Empire, including Jews, suffered from disease and famine during the war. To support the Jews in the region, many Jews in the United States gave moral and financial backing to various factions of the Zionist movement, which was dedicated to creating a homeland in Palestine for Jews from around the world (the Zionist movement had its origins in Europe in the nineteenth century). In 1917, the British issued the Balfour Declaration, which supported, at least in principle, the creation of a Jewish state in Palestine. President Wilson announced his support of this policy.

The tragedy of the Armenian Massacre also caused many in the United States to become more interested in Middle Eastern affairs. Caught up in the war between the Turks and the Russians, the Armenians revolted in 1915 against the Turks, who had occupied their homeland. The Turks brutally suppressed this uprising, with thousands of Armenians being executed (to this day, the Turks have failed to take responsibility for this event). American missionaries and aid workers were already present in Armenia (Armenians were Christians), and some of these Americans witnessed the slaughter.

In 1916 and 1917, there were countless rallies organized by Armenian immigrants and church organizations in the United States to protest the killing of the Armenians and to raise money for Armenian relief efforts.

At the end of the war, Woodrow Wilson's Fourteen Points called for the breakup of the Austro-Hungarian and the Ottoman Empires and stated that residents of these areas should be encouraged to move toward "autonomous political development." At the same time, in the immediate aftermath of World War I, the British and the French sought to increase their colonial holdings in the region. The Paris Peace Conference authorized the United States to establish the **King-Crane Commission**, whose members went into areas that the Europeans were trying to control to determine what political structure the residents of these areas desired.

The King-Crane Commission found that many in the region wanted independence; if that could not be attained, almost all were opposed to French or British control. If anyone was going to have a mandate over the region, public opinion said it should be the Americans, who were seen as having no desire to exploit the people or the lands of the region. The commission recommended against the creation of a Jewish state in Palestine, since vast numbers of non-Jews already living in Palestine would have to be displaced to establish this state. The commission supported the creation of a single state in the region that would be under the control of the Americans. Predictably, the British and the French saw to it that this report was never formally presented at the Paris Peace Conference, as it was directly against their interests. In the end, the Balfour Declaration was issued, the British received mandates over Palestine, Iraq, and Transjordan, France received mandates over Syria and Lebanon, and the only country to experience "self-determination" was Saudi Arabia, which was given independence.

Treaty of Versailles and the U.S. Senate

Woodrow Wilson had not appointed a Republican member of the Senate in the United States delegation to the Paris Peace Conference. This proved to be a huge political mistake. Wilson returned from Paris, needing Senate confirmation of the Treaty of Versailles. Many Republicans in the Senate had huge reservations about the treaty; all of them centered around American commitment to the League of Nations. A dozen senators were "**irreconcilables**," opposed to American membership in the League under any circumstances. Another large group, led by Henry Cabot Lodge, were called "**reservationists**" and wanted restrictions on American membership in the League. Lodge, for example, wanted it stated that Congress would have to approve any American action on behalf of the League, and that provisions of the Monroe Doctrine remain in place even if the League of Nations opposed them.

To win national support for the Versailles Treaty, Wilson began a national speaking tour on September 3, 1919. On October 2, he suffered a severe stroke and never totally recovered. Lodge stated that he would support passage of the Versailles Treaty with certain reservations; Wilson rejected the reservations, and the treaty never got the two-thirds majority necessary for its passage. Many politicians both at home and abroad urged Wilson to compromise with congressional leaders and to get America into the League of Nations. Wilson was never willing to do this; his chief biographer maintains that his stroke impeded his judgment during this era. In 1921, the United States formally ended the war with Germany, but the United States never entered the League of Nations.

Consequences of American Actions After the War

The failure of the United States to join the League of Nations greatly affected European affairs in the succeeding decades. The League of Nations was never the organization it could have been with American involvement. Many European leaders felt that the United States could have been the "honest broker" in the League, and that with U.S. involvement, the League could have had more substance. In addition, Europeans expected the United States to be a major player in European and world affairs in the years following the war. Led by the Senate, the United States backed off from the commitment, and entered a period of isolationism that would last through the 1930s. It was only after World War II in 1945 that America finally took the role that many thought it would take in 1920.

Chapter Review

Rapid Review

To achieve the perfect 5, you should be able to explain the following:

- World War I greatly impacted the American mindset and America's role in world affairs; this was the first time that America became directly involved in affairs taking place on the European continent.
- Many Americans expressed support for the Allied Powers from the beginning of the war; German U-boat attacks solidified American support for Britain and France.

- The sinking of the *Lusitania* and the Zimmermann Telegram did much to intensify American anger against Germany.
- Germany's decision to utilize unrestricted submarine warfare caused President Wilson to call for war in 1917; Wilson claimed that this policy violated America's rights as a neutral power.
- The American Expeditionary Force did much to aid the Allied war effort, both militarily and psychologically.
- The federal government did much to mobilize the American population at home for the war effort; Liberty Bonds were sold, voluntary rationing took place, and propaganda was used to encourage Americans to oppose the "Hun" however possible.
- Many blacks moved to northern cities to work in factories during World War I; this migration would continue through the 1920s.
- Woodrow Wilson's Fourteen Points met with opposition from French and English leaders at the Paris Peace Conference; many of them had to be abandoned to secure the creation of the League of Nations.
- The Treaty of Versailles was opposed by U.S. senators who felt that America should pursue an isolationist policy after the war. As a result, the treaty was never signed by the United States and the United States never joined the League of Nations.
- Many European leaders expected America to be active as a leader in world affairs after World War I. Instead, America adopted neo-isolationist policies that lasted until America entered World War II.

Time Line

1914: Outbreak of World War I in Europe
Woodrow Wilson officially proclaims American neutrality in World War I
National Security League founded to prepare America for war

1915: Sinking of the *Lusitania* by German U-boat

1916: Germany torpedoes *Sussex*, then promises to warn merchants ships if they are to be attacked
Woodrow Wilson reelected with campaign slogan of "He kept us out of war"

1917: Zimmermann Telegram
Germany declares unrestricted submarine warfare
United States enters World War I, stating that U.S. rights as a neutral had been violated
Russian Revolution; Russian-German peace talks
Conscription begins in United States
War Industries Board formed to create a war economy
Espionage Act passed
American Expeditionary Force lands in France

1918: Military success by American Expeditionary Force at Chateau-Thierry
Sedition Act passed; free speech limited (illegal to criticize government or American military forces)
Wilson announces the Fourteen Points
Armistice ends World War I (November 11)

1919: Paris Peace Conference creates Treaty of Versailles
Race riots in Chicago
Wilson suffers stroke during speaking tour promoting Treaty of Versailles
Senate rejects Treaty of Versailles; United States does not join the League of Nations

Review Questions

1. All of the following events prepared America for war against Germany *except*
   A. the Sussex Pledge
   B. German policy concerning use of U-boats in 1917
   C. the sinking of the *Lusitania*
   D. the Zimmermann Telegram

2. The French were opposed to many of Wilson's Fourteen Points because
   A. they were fundamentally opposed to the creation of a world body such as the League of Nations.
   B. they were angry that Wilson had insisted that the Germans not take part in the creation of the treaty.
   C. French diplomats had little respect for Wilson and his American counterparts.
   D. the Fourteen Points disagreed fundamentally with what the French felt should be contained in the Treaty of Versailles.

3. After America declared war in 1917
   A. ration cards were issued to all families
   B. camps were set up to detain "troublesome" Americans of German background
   C. drills took place in American cities to prepare Americans for a possible attack
   D. movie stars and other celebrities helped sell Liberty Bonds to the American public

4. Some critics maintained that the United States had no right to be outraged over the sinking of the *Lusitania* because
   A. the *Lusitania* was carrying contraband, which meant that it could legally be sunk.
   B. the Germans had sunk passenger ships before.
   C. the Germans had placed advertisements in American newspapers warning Americans not to travel on the *Lusitania*.
   D. all of the above.

5. Many senators were opposed to American entry into the League of Nations because
   A. they feared that the United States would end up financing the organization.
   B. they feared the U.S. Army would be sent into action on "League of Nations business" without congressional authorization.
   C. American opinion polls demonstrated that the American public was almost unanimously opposed to American entry into the League.
   D. they feared that the Germans and Russians would dominate the League.

Answers and Explanations

1. **A.** In the Sussex Pledge, the Germans actually promised not to sink American merchant ships without warning. All of the other choices deeply angered many in America.

2. **D.** While Wilson saw the treaty as a chance to create a democratic world free of old diplomatic entanglements, the French saw it as an opportunity to punish the Germans, as much of the fighting of the war had taken place on French territory.

3. **D.** Charlie Chaplin and others appeared at rallies and urged Americans to buy Liberty Bonds. Rationing during World War I was voluntary.

4. **D.** Many maintain that the advertisements the Germans put in American newspapers were strong enough warnings that the ship was going to be sunk.

5. **B.** A major fear was that U.S. entry into the League would cause Congress to lose its right to declare war and approve American military actions. Germany and the Soviet Union were not initially members of the League of Nations.

CHAPTER 22

Beginning of Modern America: The 1920s

IN THIS CHAPTER

Summary: During the 1920s, Americans created a consumer culture in which automobiles, home appliances, and other goods were purchased at an unprecedented rate. Advertising helped to fuel this desire to purchase, and the popularity of radio and motion pictures helped to create a more uniform national culture. However, many small-town and rural Americans never felt totally comfortable with the values of the consumer-oriented, more urban "modern" America that they saw threatening their way of life. The conflict between urban and small-town American values was manifested in numerous ways: many in small-town America supported the Prohibition amendment banning alcohol, while many in America's cities tried to get around it. Many in small-town America feared immigration, while many American cities contained immigrant enclaves. Many in small-town America still opposed the teaching of evolution, while many urban newspapers mocked their views. The flapper and a more relaxed sense of morality were symbols of the Jazz Age; generally, these symbols were harder to find in small-town America. All Americans did rally around the two heroes of the age: aviator Charles Lindbergh and home run hitter Babe Ruth.

KEY IDEA

Keywords

Teapot Dome: major scandal in the scandal-ridden administration of President Warren Harding; Secretary of the Interior Albert Fall had two oil deposits put under the jurisdiction of the Department of the Interior and leased them to private companies in return for large sums of money.
Red Scare: after World War I, the fear of the spread of communism in the United States.

Palmer Raids: as part of the Red Scare, in these 1919 to 1920 raids thousands of Americans not born in the United States were arrested, and hundreds were sent back to their countries of origin. Today many view the raids as a gross violation of the constitutional rights of American citizens.

National Origins Act (1924): anti-immigration federal legislation that took the number of immigrants from each country in 1890 and stated that immigration from those countries could now be no more than 2 percent of that. In addition, immigration from Asia was halted. The act also severely limited further immigration from eastern and southern Europe.

Scopes Trial (1925): trial of teacher John Scopes of Dayton, Tennessee, for the teaching of evolution. During this trial, lawyers Clarence Darrow and William Jennings Bryan squared off on the teachings of Darwin versus the teachings of the Bible.

Jazz Age: image of the 1920s that emphasized the more relaxed social attitudes of the decade; F. Scott Fitzgerald's *The Great Gatsby* is seen by many as the novel that best depicts this view.

Flapper: "new woman" of the 1920s, who was pictured as having bobbed hair, a shorter skirt, makeup, a cigarette in her hand, and somewhat liberated sexual attitudes. Flappers would have been somewhat hard to find in small-town and rural America.

"Lost Generation": group of post–World War I writers who in their works expressed deep dissatisfaction with mainstream American culture. *A Farewell to Arms* by Ernest Hemingway is a novel that is representative of the works of these writers.

Harlem Renaissance: 1920s black literary and cultural movement that produced many works depicting the role of blacks in contemporary American society; Zora Neale Hurston and Langston Hughes were key members of this movement.

Decade of Prosperity

By the middle of the 1920s, many of the dire predictions of the effects of capitalism that had been preached by Progressives 15 years earlier seemed like no more than ancient history. Business opportunities were plentiful. The prosecution of trusts, which took up much of the Justice Department's time in World War I, were few in the 1920s. New opportunists with capital could challenge corporations like United States Steel and make profits. Nevertheless, certain industries, such as the automobile industry, were virtually impossible to crack; by 1929, Ford, General Motors, and Chrysler controlled nearly 85 percent of all auto sales. Socialist predictions that the plight of the workers was getting worse seemed to be negated by statistics published in 1924 stating that industrial workers were making nearly double what they had made 10 years earlier.

Strikes and union activities were plentiful in the two years immediately following the end of World War I, but diminished greatly after that (many factory owners realized that paying their workers a decent wage would make them less likely to listen to speeches made by union "agitators").

By the mid-1920s, products made in American factories were available to Americans and also in many European and other world markets. The assembly line of Henry Ford continued to be perfected to the point that by 1925 a **Model T** was being produced in a

Ford plant every 24 seconds. During the decade, the ideas of "scientific management" first proposed by Frederick W. Taylor (see Chapter 16) were utilized in businesses and factories across the country. Production was now being done more efficiently; this ultimately lowered the cost of production and the cost to the consumer.

Many other consumer products, such as vacuum cleaners, refrigerators, and radios, were also churned out by American factories at record rates. Many of the products also were produced by assembly line techniques, and the stream of workers who continued to enter the cities from rural America could get work doing one of the monotonous jobs involved in assembly line production. For the consumer, products that were impossible to even dream about 10 years earlier could now be purchased with the installment plan. For 36 or 48 "easy" payments, a middle-class family in the 1920s could have an automobile, a refrigerator, and a vacuum cleaner. Some economists saw danger in the fact that by 1928 nearly 65 percent of all automobiles were being purchased on credit. Most Americans saw little problem with this, since they could not foresee a time when Americans would be unable to make payments on these goods.

The decade of the 1920s can certainly be seen as the beginning of the **advertising age**. Consumers were warned that if they wanted to live the "good life," they *had* to have the latest model refrigerator or automobile. People living in urban, suburban, and rural areas all saw the same advertisements for products that had been placed in both national and local publications by advertising men. As stated previously, this helped create a universal national culture. Advertisements showed the farmer in Kansas and the suburbanite in Connecticut that they *had* to have exactly the same product.

Republican Leadership in the 1920s

Throughout the 1920s, the Republican party was truly dominant at the national level. Both houses of Congress were under Republican control, the three presidents of the decade (Warren G. Harding, Calvin Coolidge, and Herbert Hoover) were all Republicans, and for most of the decade the Supreme Court was dominated by Chief Justice (and ex-president) William Howard Taft. Government policies throughout the decade were almost exclusively probusiness; Republican candidates at all levels during this decade *had* to be acceptable to the business community. Presidents in this era were largely engaged in domestic issues.

Presidency of Warren G. Harding

Many presidential scholars claim that Warren G. Harding was one of the least qualified men ever nominated for the presidency by a major party in America. Harding, a senator from Ohio, was not even mentioned as a possible candidate before the Republican convention of 1920. Harding finally became the Republican nominee after the party bosses determined that he would be a candidate they could control. He was opposed in the national election by Governor James Cox of Ohio. Harding ran on a platform of low taxes, high tariffs, farmer's assistance, and opposition to the League of Nations.

Where Governor Cox (and his running mate, Assistant Secretary of the Navy Franklin D. Roosevelt) ran a strong and aggressive campaign, Harding was generally content to campaign from his own back porch. He ended up winning 61 percent of the national vote. Americans found something they liked in both the message and style of Harding: his message was essentially that it was time to pull back from "schemes" to change the world (the postwar plans of Woodrow Wilson) and "social experiments" (all of the programs of the Progressives). Harding's call for a period of "normalcy" struck a chord with Americans and seemed to put the final nail in the coffin of progressivism in American thought.

During the presidency of Harding, efforts were made to prevent America from having any involvement with the League of Nations or any other provision of the Versailles Treaty. One of the outstanding appointments made by Harding was the naming of former Supreme Court Justice Charles Evans Hughes as secretary of state. Hughes's major accomplishment as secretary of state took place at the **Washington Conference** of 1921. At this meeting, diplomats from the United States, Japan, China, the Netherlands, Belgium, Portugal, France, Great Britain, and Italy met to discuss the possible elimination of further naval development and affairs in China and the rest of Asia. All nine nations agreed to respect the independence of China (and maintain the Open Door in China), a major goal of American business interests. The United States, Britain, France, Japan, and Italy all agreed to halt the construction of naval vessels (Hughes did not realize at the time that this gave naval superiority in the Pacific to the Japanese).

Another notable appointment by Harding was the naming of Andrew Mellon, the "richest man in America," as secretary of the treasury. Mellon firmly believed in the traditional Republican tenet that very low taxes would ultimately encourage business investment and ensure economic prosperity. To do this, Mellon sought to reduce government spending in any way possible, and to reduce taxes, especially for the wealthier business classes. To cut expenses, Harding opposed bonus payments to World War I veterans in 1921; some benefits for veterans were authorized by Congress. In the Revenue Act of 1921, the administration proposed large reductions in the amounts of taxes that the wealthiest Americans would have to pay (protests from some Republicans from farm states caused these reductions to be less than what Mellon desired). In the end, many of Mellon's policies increased the economic pain of the working class while benefiting the rich.

To assist American business interests, Mellon also wanted large tariff increases on imported industrial goods. The **Fordney-McCumber Tariff** of 1922 did increase the tariffs on industrial products. However, to appease Republicans from farm states, the largest tariff increases were on imported farm products.

Little was done in the Harding administration to assist organized labor. Many court decisions of the decade took the side of management, including several court decisions that overturned lower-court rulings making child labor illegal. It was clear in this decade that the interests of farmers and the interests of industrial workers were very dissimilar.

Scandals of the Harding Administration

The Harding administration may have been the most scandal-ridden administration in American political history. No principle whatsoever was involved in these scandals; the participants were only interested in money. There is no knowledge that Harding participated in any way in these scandals; his biggest sin was probably appointing political cronies from his Ohio days to important government positions in his administration and not supervising them.

The scandals of the Harding administration were numerous. Charles Forbes, the director of the Veteran's Bureau, stole or horribly misused nearly $250 million of government money; he was indicted for fraud and bribery concerning government hospital supply contracts. Harding allowed Forbes to go abroad and to resign, although he eventually did go to jail. Attorney General Harry Daugherty had taken bribes from businessmen, bootleggers, and many others. Daugherty failed to go to jail when a hung jury was unable to convict him.

The worst of the scandals was the **Teapot Dome Scandal**. Secretary of the Interior Albert Fall maneuvered to have two oil deposits put under the jurisdiction of the Department of the Interior; one of these was a reserve in Wyoming called Teapot Dome. Fall then leased these reserves to private companies and got large sums of money from them for doing it. Fall was convicted and finally sent to prison in 1929.

The revelation of these scandals greatly bothered Harding, who died of a stroke on August 2, 1923. He was replaced by his vice president, Calvin Coolidge of Vermont.

Presidency of Calvin Coolidge

American business leaders could have had no better friend in the White House than Calvin Coolidge. His credo was that "the business of the United States is business." Coolidge did little as president, but this was largely intentional; he was convinced that the major decisions affecting American society should be made by businessmen. Like Harding, Coolidge believed in increased tax cuts for the wealthy and favored policies that would help promote American business.

Several decisions made during Coolidge's presidency demonstrate the administration's thinking. Coolidge proposed that a dam constructed at Muscle Shoals, Alabama, on the Tennessee River by the government during World War I be turned over to private interests; this plan was defeated by Congress (the dam would become a crucial part of the Tennessee Valley Authority in the 1930s). In the Revenue Act of 1926, large tax cuts were given to the wealthiest members of society. Finally, on the grounds that the government couldn't afford it, Coolidge vetoed payments to World War I veterans (Congress passed the legislation over the president's veto).

Election of 1928

Coolidge made the announcement "I do not choose to run" several months before the 1928 presidential election. The Republicans nominated Secretary of Commerce Herbert Hoover. Hoover was a seemingly perfect candidate for the mood of the era. He was a self-made man, had worked his way through Stanford, had made his first million in business before he was 40, and had run relief efforts in Belgium and the Commerce Department with tremendous, although unsmiling, efficiency. Hoover's campaign speeches emphasized the achievements of past Republican administrations that had created prosperity and the possibilities for success achievable through rugged individualism.

The Democratic candidate was New York Governor Al Smith, an opponent of Prohibition and a Catholic. Many Southern Democrats had obvious suspicions about him; Smith's supporters received their support by promising that the Democratic platform would say nothing about the repeal of Prohibition. The election was a landslide for Hoover, with Smith only winning eight states. Nevertheless, the fact that many people living in the large cities of America voted for Smith showed the divisions that existed in American society in the 1920s.

Urban vs. Rural: The Great Divide of the 1920s

As stated previously, the 1920s was the decade that the United States, population-wise, became an urban country. Tremendous resentment existed in rural and small-town America against the growing urban mindset that was increasingly permeating America. Many citizens who did not live in America's cities felt that the values associated with urban life needed to be opposed. From these sentiments came many of the great cultural battles that were at the center of American life in the 1920s.

Many in the North and the South shared resentment against black Americans in the years immediately after World War I. A number of blacks had come North during the war to take factory jobs in urban centers; now that the war was over, many Northerners saw them as competitors for prime industrial employment. In 1919, large race riots took place in Washington, DC, and in many other Northern cities; antiblack riots in Chicago lasted nearly two weeks. Press reports of these riots often noted the participation of white veterans.

During the postwar years, violence against blacks intensified in the South as well. Lynchings increased dramatically in the postwar years; over 70 blacks were lynched in 1919 alone. The response by some blacks was to think of leaving the United States altogether; beginning in 1920, sign-ups began for the **Universal Negro Improvement Association**, headed by Marcus Garvey. Garvey called on blacks to come with him to Africa to create a new empire (with him on the throne). By 1925, nearly half a million people had expressed interest in Garvey's scheme. In the end, the Garvey program was a failure, since few blacks actually went to Africa, and many of those who did go ended up returning to the United States. Garvey was later arrested and jailed for fraud, but the fact that his plan attracted so many black supporters demonstrated the plight of black Americans during the period.

The **Ku Klux Klan** grew tremendously during the early 1920s; by 1925, the Klan's membership was over 5 million. Unlike the Klan of the Reconstruction era, membership in the Klan was not entirely from the South, although it was almost entirely from rural and small-town America (Indiana was a huge hotbed of Klan activity in the 1920s). Blacks continued to be a target of the Klan, as were other groups who appeared to be "enemies" of the rural way of life, such as Catholics and immigrants. The Klan had tremendous political power in several states, although terror tactics such as lynchings and cross burnings remained a dominant part of Klan activity.

The Klan began to lose its popularity in 1925 with revelations of scandals involving Klan members, including the murder conviction of the leader of the Klan in Indiana. Many historians see the popularity of the Klan in the 1920s as a symbol of the intolerance prominent in much of American society; several see it as an American version of totalitarianism, which took control in Germany, the Soviet Union, and Italy during this period.

Many Americans in the years following World War I were also terrified of bolshevism. America, to no avail, gave military aid and actual manpower to forces attempting to overthrow Lenin and the bolsheviks in the years immediately following the Russian Revolution of 1917. Much about bolshevism (soon to be called communism) was in opposition to mainstream American thought. Communism taught that capitalism was evil, and that worker's revolutions would soon break out in highly industrialized countries like the United States. As a result, a **Red Scare** developed in America in 1919. Many historians maintain that Americans were not just opposed to the ideas of communism, but that many Americans began to see everything wrong in American society as a creation of the "Reds."

Beginning in November 1919, Attorney General Mitchell Palmer carried out raids in the homes and places of employment of suspected radicals. As a result of the **Palmer**

Raids, thousands of Americans were arrested, in many cases for no other crime than the fact that they were not born in the United States. Hundreds of former immigrants were sent back to their countries of origin, even though it was never proven (or, in most cases, even charged) that they were political radicals. The Red Scare demonstrated the nativism present in America during the period. This was also one of the worst examples in American history of the trampling of the constitutional rights of American citizens.

Nativism probably also accounts for the results of the case of Sacco and Vanzetti. Both were Italian immigrants, and were charged with the murder of two employees of a shoe company in Massachusetts in 1920. Although there was little evidence against them, they were convicted and finally executed in 1927.

American nativism also was displayed in immigration legislation that was passed in the early 1920s. Many in small-town America blamed the problems of America on the continued inflow of immigrants to the country; pseudoscientific texts published in the first part of the decade claimed that white Americans were naturally superior to Southern and Eastern Europeans as well as blacks, but warned that these groups had to be carefully controlled to prevent them from attempting to dominate the country.

Congress passed the **Emergency Quota Act** of 1921, which limited immigration to 3 percent of the number of persons each country had living in the United States in 1910. This act limited the immigration of Eastern and Southern Europeans, and cut immigration in 1922 to roughly 40 percent of its 1921 totals. A real blow to immigration was the **National Origins Act** of 1924. This legislation took that number of immigrants from each foreign country living in the United States in 1890, and stated that immigration to the United States from these countries could now be no more than 2 percent of that; the bill also stated that no more than 150,000 new immigrants could come from outside the Western Hemisphere. In addition, all immigration from Asia was halted. The intent and the effect of this legislation was obvious. Immigration from countries such as Italy and Poland was virtually halted.

Another area where urban and rural/small-town interests clashed was over the issue of Prohibition. Statistics from 1924 indicated that 95 percent of citizens in Kansas were obeying the Prohibition law, while the figure was close to 5 percent in New York State. For many small-town observers, alcohol, immigrants, and urban life were viewed together as one giant evil. Many small-town preachers spoke of alcohol as an "instrument of the devil" and were outraged that the law was not enforced in places like New York City.

However, the enforcement of Prohibition in a city like New York would have been virtually impossible. Neither the citizenry nor elected officials favored enforcement (it was reported that Warren Harding had a huge collection of bootlegged alcohol that he served to guests). **Speakeasies** were frequented by police officers and city officials in many locations; "bathtub gin," some of it good and some of it absolutely atrocious, was also consumed by thousands eager for some form of alcohol during the Prohibition era. Bootlegging of alcohol allowed many famous gangsters of the 1930s to get their feet wet in the world of organized crime. Al Capone in Chicago became the king of the bootleggers, with judges, newspapers, and elected government officials all eventually under his control.

The final area where urban and rural/small-town mindsets drastically differed was over religion and evolution. Many in small-town America felt vaguely threatened by the changes that science had brought about, and clung to the literal interpretation of the Bible as a defense. William Jennings Bryan and others led the charge against the teachings of Darwin in the postwar years. In 1925, Bryan assisted a group in Tennessee in drafting a bill that would outlaw the teaching of evolution in the state. The American Civil Liberties Union offered to assist any teacher who would challenge this law, and John Scopes of

Dayton, Tennessee, volunteered. For several weeks in 1925, the **Scopes Trial** (or "monkey trial") riveted the nation.

One of America's finest lawyers Clarence Darrow assisted Scopes, while Bryan was retained to work with prosecutors who wanted to convict Scopes. Scopes was found guilty and fined (this was later overturned on a technicality), but the real drama of the trial was when Darrow questioned Bryan, who took the stand as an "expert on the Bible." Bryan seriously discredited the entire cause of **creationism** when he admitted on the stand that he personally did not take every fact found in the Bible literally.

Culture in the 1920s

Vast numbers of Americans were attracted to the culture of business that so permeated American life in the 1920s. It was possible, it was felt, that an individual could start with nothing and become a millionaire (a few buying land in Florida and elsewhere did exactly that). It is no surprise that individual heroes were worshipped in the press, on the radio, and on street corners. Sports heroes such as Babe Ruth were perceived as hardly mortal (members of the press had to cover up the excesses found in the personal lives of Ruth and many other heroes). Newspapers delighted in reporting incidents such as those involving Ruth visiting children's hospitals and promising countless home runs for sick children.

Other heroes of the decade included other athletes such as boxer Jack Dempsey, and movie stars Rudolph Valentino, Charlie Chaplin, Clara Bow, and Mary Pickford. No hero, however, was lionized more than Charles Lindbergh after he became the first person to fly solo across the Atlantic Ocean in 1927. Incredible numbers of songs and newspaper headlines were devoted to Lindbergh for several years after this historic flight.

The Jazz Age

Many Americans rejected the values of business civilization adopted in the decade. These people, both men and women, decided that pleasure and private expression were more important than the virtues of Taylorism. Those associated with the **Jazz Age** adopted more open attitudes toward sex, and adopted jazz music as another symbol of their rejection of traditional society. Rural/small-town America (and some in the cities) saw jazz as "the devil's music," as black music, and as music that helped to promote lewd dancing and sexual contact. For many who went to jazz clubs in Harlem in the early 1920s, these were probably the very reasons why they listened to it.

The typical symbol of the Jazz Age was the **flapper**, a young girl with short hair, a short hemline, a cigarette in her hand, and makeup (all of these things were frowned on in rural/small-town America and in pre–World War I urban America). The number of actual flappers in American cities was always relatively small. Many advertisements of the 1920s portrayed women as sex objects; as a result, in the eyes of many Americans, women lost their respected position as moral leaders of the family.

Statistics do show that both sexual promiscuity and the consumption of alcohol increased among the young during this decade. This revolution was greatly aided by the availability of the automobile, which allowed young people to get away from the prying eyes of parents. Margaret Sanger and others promoted the increased availability and usage of birth control during this period. The behavior of flappers and their male counterparts was looked down on by some urban and by almost all rural observers. It should be noted that this "freer" behavior by young people would be drastically reduced by the massive economic difficulties of the Great Depression and World War II, but would again become pronounced in the 1950s (with critics voicing many of the same concerns as they had in the 1920s). By the 1950s, rock 'n' roll had replaced jazz as the "devil's music."

After the passage of the Nineteenth Amendment in 1920, which gave women the right to vote, many female leaders thought that women would come to have a pronounced role in American political life. Much to their disappointment, this did not occur in the 1920s. Women did not vote in a block "as women." Yet, the overall position of women did increase in the decade. Divorces increased throughout the decade, showing that more women (and men) were leaving unhealthy married relationships. The number of women working during the decade also increased, although working women were usually single. Restrictions remained, however. Women seldom received the same pay for doing the same work as men, and women were almost never put into management positions. Most women still worked in clerical jobs, as teachers, or as nurses.

Rise of Radio and Motion Pictures

As stated previously, as more and more people read newspapers, listened to the radio, and watched movies, a truly universal mass culture was being created. Movie attendance rose rapidly during the 1920s; in 1922, about 35 million people a week saw movies. By 1929, this figure was up to 90 million people per week. In 1927, **The Jazz Singer**, starring Al Jolson, became the first "talking" motion picture, a trend that would create new movie stars and ruin the careers of others who had been stars in the silent era.

Nothing created a more national mass culture than did the radio. Station KDKA in Pittsburgh was the first station to get a radio station license in 1920. Radio networks began to form (the National Broadcasting Company being the first in 1926) and brought listeners across the country news, variety shows, and (at first) recreated sporting events.

The Lost Generation

Many novels were written during the 1920s that supported the business culture of the decade. The most famous of these was Bruce Barton's 1925 *The Man Nobody Knows*, which portrayed Christ as a businessman. Most famous novelists of the era, however, wrote of deep feelings of alienation from mainstream American culture. These writers, called by Gertrude Stein members of the "**Lost Generation**," turned their backs on the business culture and the Republican political culture of the era. Some of these writers ended up in Paris, while others congregated in Greenwich Village in New York City.

The goal of these writers seemed to be to attack the notion of America that they had either physically or spiritually left behind. In novels such as *Main Street* and *Babbit*, Sinclair Lewis attacked the materialism and narrow thinking of middle-class business types in small-town America. Sherwood Anderson's *Winesburg, Ohio* was another novel of alienation in small-town America.

F. Scott Fitzgerald was both a celebrant of the Jazz Age and a brilliant commentator on it; his novel *The Great Gatsby* dissects the characters of typical Jazz Age figures. Ernest Hemingway in works such as *A Farewell to Arms* expresses a deep dissatisfaction with American values, especially concerning war. Perhaps none was more direct in his criticisms of American society than journalist H. L. Mencken, who called the American people an "ignorant mob" and was especially disdainful of the "booboisie," his term for the American middle class.

It should also be remembered that black cultural expression in the 1920s was being celebrated in a cultural movement called the **Harlem Renaissance**. Writers of this movement, including Langston Hughes and Zora Neale Hurston, wrote on the role of blacks in contemporary American society; the theme of blacks "passing" into the white world and the importance of black expression were common among writers of the Harlem Renaissance. Many in the Harlem Renaissance studied African folk art and music and anthropology. The goal of many in the movement was reconciling the notions of being black and being American (and also to reconcile the notions of being black and being intellectual). Jazz was the music of the movement, with Louis Armstrong and Duke Ellington playing this "primitive music" in clubs across Harlem.

When Herbert Hoover was inaugurated in early 1929, America looked to the 1930s with eager anticipation. The stock market was at an all-time high, and Hoover had continually promised during the campaign that the Republican goal was to wipe out poverty once and for all. All of this would make the events that would begin to unfold in the fall of 1929 even more cruel and devastating.

Chapter Review

Rapid Review

To achieve the perfect 5, you should be able to explain the following:

- A consumer economy was created in the 1920s on a level unprecedented in American history.
- Advertising, newspapers, radio, and motion pictures provided new forms of entertainment in the 1920s and helped create a uniform national culture.
- The changes of the 1920s were resisted by many in small-town/rural America, creating many of the cultural conflicts of the decade.
- Assembly line techniques and the ideas of scientific management of Frederick W. Taylor helped make industrial production in the 1920s quicker and more efficient, ultimately creating cheaper goods.
- Installment buying helped fuel consumer buying in the 1920s.
- The Republican party controlled the White House, Congress, and the Supreme Court in the 1920s, generally sponsoring government policies friendly to big business.
- The scandals of the Harding administration were among the worst in history.
- Resentment against blacks existed in both the American South and North in the years after World War I, resulting in race riots in the North and lynchings and the rebirth of the Ku Klux Klan in the South.
- The Red Scare of 1919 and 1920 resulted in the suspension of civil liberties and deportation of hundreds of immigrants, the vast majority of whom had committed no crime.
- Nativist fears also resulted in restrictive quota legislation passed in the early 1920s.
- Cultural conflicts between urban and rural America also developed over the issues of Prohibition and the teaching of evolution in schools (resulting in the Scopes Trial).
- During the Jazz Age, many Americans rejected the prominent business values of the decade and turned to jazz, alcohol, and looser sexual mores for personal fulfillment.
- The flapper was the single most prominent image of the Jazz Age.
- Writers of the Lost Generation expressed extreme disillusionment with American society of the era; writers of the Harlem Renaissance expressed the opinions of American blacks concerning American culture.

Time Line

1917: Race riots in East St. Louis, Missouri
1918: Armistice ending World War I
1919: Race riots in Chicago
  Major strikes in Seattle and Boston
  Palmer Raids
1920: Warren Harding elected president
  First broadcast of radio station KDKA in Pittsburgh
  Publication of *Main Street* by Sinclair Lewis
  Arrest of Sacco and Vanzetti
  Prohibition takes effect
1921: Immigration Quota Law passed
  Disarmament conference held
1922: Fordney-McCumber Tariff enacted
  Publication of *Babbitt* by Sinclair Lewis
1923: Teapot Dome scandal
  Death of Harding; Calvin Coolidge becomes president
  Duke Ellington first performs in New York City
1924: Election of Calvin Coolidge
  Immigration Quota Law enacted
  Ku Klux Klan reaches highest membership in history
  Women governors elected in Wyoming and Texas
1925: Publication of *The Man Nobody Knows* by Bruce Barton
  Publication of *The Great Gatsby* by F. Scott Fitzgerald
  Scopes Trial held in Dayton, Tennessee
1926: Publication of *The Sun Also Rises* by Ernest Hemingway
1927: *The Jazz Singer*, first movie with sound, released
  Charles Lindbergh makes New York to Paris flight
  Execution of Sacco and Vanzetti
  15 millionth car produced by Ford Motor Company
  $1.5 billion spent on advertising in United States
  Babe Ruth hits 60 home runs
1928: Election of Herbert Hoover
1929: Nearly 30 million Americans have cars
  Stock market crash

Review Questions

1. Many in rural/small-town America would support legislation that
   A. increased immigration from Eastern Europe
   B. mandated the teaching of creationism in schools
   C. lessened the penalties for those who sold illegal alcohol
   D. made it harder to deport immigrants who might have "Red" ties

2. The novel that supported the business philosophy of the 1920s most definitively was
   A. *Main Street*
   B. *The Great Gatsby*
   C. *The Man Nobody Knows*
   D. *Babbitt*

3. In 1928, in most Eastern cities, one could find
   A. a speakeasy
   B. a continual flow of immigrants from Northern, Southern, and Eastern Europe
   C. large numbers of supporters of the Ku Klux Klan
   D. the first bread lines

4. Republican leaders of the 1920s believed all of the following *except*
   A. "the business of government is business"
   B. the government should do as little as possible
   C. labor unions should be strengthened through legislation
   D. immigration should continue to be restricted

5. The election of Herbert Hoover in 1928 demonstrated all of the following *except*
   A. Most Americans believed that Republican policies had been responsible for the prosperity of the 1920s.
   B. Fewer divisions existed between the urban and rural populations than had existed at the beginning of the decade.
   C. Prohibition was still a "hot-button issue" for many Americans.
   D. America was not ready for a Catholic president.

› Answers and Explanations

1. **B.** All of the other "causes"—more immigration, the lessening of Prohibition, and the lessening of methods to deport potential Communists—were vehemently opposed by most in small-town America. They would, however, support the elimination of the teaching of evolution, and the continued teaching of creationism in American schools.

2. **C.** All of the other novels are unsympathetic to the world of business—both A and D are by Sinclair Lewis. In *The Man Nobody Knows*, Jesus Christ is portrayed as a businessman.

3. **A.** The influx of immigrants had been greatly reduced by immigration legislation passed in the first half of the decade. Supporters of the KKK were largely not city dwellers; the KKK had also lessened in importance by 1928. Bread lines were not found until the beginning of the Great Depression.

4. **C.** All of the other answers are solid beliefs of Republican leaders of the 1920s. Republicans did very little for labor unions in the decade.

5. **B.** Hoover's overwhelming election demonstrated the appeal of his business background and the fact that many Americans credited the Republicans for prosperity. The fact that Al Smith was defeated in this election demonstrated that his anti-Prohibition statements definitely hurt him. However, many in urban centers voted for him; this demonstrated that the divisions between urban and rural America were still wide at the end of the decade.

CHAPTER 23

Great Depression and the New Deal (1929–1939)

IN THIS CHAPTER

Summary: The Great Depression had a monumental effect on American society, and its effects are still felt today. Franklin Roosevelt, the architect of the New Deal, is considered by many to be one of America's greatest presidents, and he was the model for activist presidents who desired to utilize the power of the federal government to assist those in need. The origins of the Great Depression can be found in economic problems in America in the late 1920s: "installment buying" and buying stocks "on the margin" would come back to haunt many homeowners and investors. The stock market crash of 1929 was followed by bank failures, factory closings, and widespread unemployment. President Herbert Hoover believed that voluntary action by business and labor interest could pull America out of its economic doldrums. Franklin Roosevelt was elected president in 1932 with the promise of a "New Deal" for the American people. During his first hundred days in office, Roosevelt acted forcefully to restore confidence in the banks, stabilize prices, and give many young people work through the establishment of the Civilian Conservation Corps. During the Second New Deal later in the 1930s, measures such as the Social Security Act were enacted to provide a safety net for Americans in need. Some critics of the New Deal branded it socialism; others said it didn't go far enough to fight poverty in America. New Deal policies never ended the Great Depression; America's entry into World War II did.

KEY IDEA

Keywords

Hoovervilles: settlements of shacks found on the outskirts of many American cities beginning in the early 1930s.

Dust Bowl: name given in the 1930s to regions of Oklahoma, Kansas, Nebraska, Colorado, and Texas, where severe drought and poor farming practices caused massive dust storms. By the end of the decade, nearly 60 percent of all farms there were either ruined or abandoned. Many from the Dust Bowl ended up moving westward in search of jobs.

Hawley-Smoot Tariff (1930): tariff act that imposed severe tariffs on all incoming goods; European countries responded with their own high tariffs. Most historians say this tariff did little to help the American economy.

Federal Deposit Insurance Corporation (FDIC): federal agency established during the "First Hundred Days" of the New Deal in 1933 in an effort to halt panic over bank closings. The FDIC insures the bank deposits of individual citizens.

Civilian Conservation Corps (CCC): also established in 1933, the CCC eventually provided jobs for 2.5 million young Americans in forest and conservation programs.

National Industry Recovery Act: New Deal legislation requiring owners and labor unions in various industries to agree upon hours, wages, and prices; as a result, wages did go up for many workers but so did prices.

Tennessee Valley Authority: agency created in the New Deal to oversee the construction of dams, providing electricity and flood control for many in the Tennessee River Valley; for many in the region, this was the first time their homes had electricity.

Works Progress Administration (WPA): New Deal program that employed nearly 8 million Americans; WPA projects included the construction of schools and roads. Unemployed artists and musicians were also employed by the WPA.

Wagner Act: critical piece of New Deal legislation that protected the right of workers to form unions and utilize collective bargaining.

Social Security Act (1935): New Deal legislation providing pensions for workers reaching retirement age. Both workers and employers pay into the fund that provides this benefit. Initially, farm workers and domestic workers were not covered by Social Security.

New Deal Coalition: The political coalition created by Franklin Roosevelt that, by and large, kept the Democratic Party in power from the 1930s through the 1960s. This coalition consisted of workers in American cities, voters in the South, labor unions, and blacks.

Scottsboro Boys: nine black defendants in a famous 1931 case; they were accused of raping two white women on a train, and despite the lack of evidence, eight were sentenced to death. The American Communist party organized their defense.

American Economy of the 1920s: Roots of the Great Depression

The vast majority of Americans in 1929 foresaw a continuation of the dizzying economic growth that had taken place in most of the decade. In his inauguration speech, newly elected president Herbert Hoover reemphasized his campaign promise that it was the goal of the Republican party to permanently wipe out poverty in America. In early September 1929, the average share of stock on the New York Stock Exchange stood near 350, a gain of nearly 200 points in a little over a year.

However, careful observers of the American economy noticed several disturbing trends that only seemed to be increasing. These included the following:

1. *Agricultural problems.* Farm prices were at a record high during World War I, dropped after the war, and never recovered. Many farmers were unable to pay back bank loans they had acquired to purchase land, tractors, and other equipment; many farms were foreclosed, and, in farm states, over 6,200 banks were forced to close. Legislation to help farmers had been passed by Congress, but bills to help the farmers were vetoed by President Coolidge on two occasions.
2. *Installment buying.* As stated in the previous chapter, large numbers of Americans purchased automobiles, refrigerators, vacuum cleaners, and similar household products on credit. Many Americans simply did not have anywhere near enough cash to pay for all they had purchased. The money of many families was tied up making installment payments for three or four big-ticket items; this prevented them from purchasing many other items available for sale. In 1928 and 1929, new goods continued to be produced, but many people simply could not afford to buy them. As a result, layoffs began occurring in some industries as early as 1928.
3. *Uneven division of wealth.* America was wealthy in the 1920s, but this wealth did not extend to all segments of society. The gains made by wealthy Americans in the 1920s far outstripped gains made by the working class. By the time of the stock market crash, the upper 0.2 percent of the population controlled over 40 percent of the nation's savings. On the other hand, over three-quarters of American families made less than $3,000 a year. Problems that could develop from this situation were obvious. The bottom three-quarters of families were too poor to purchase much to help the economy to continue to flourish. Furthermore, at the early signs of economic trouble, many of the wealthiest Americans, fearing the worst, curtailed their spending.
4. *The stock market.* There were cases in the late 1920s of ordinary citizens becoming very wealthy by purchasing stock. Some of these people were engaged in **speculation**, meaning that they would invest in something (like the previously mentioned Florida lands) that was very risky, but that they could potentially "make a killing" on. Another common practice in the late 1920s was buying shares of stock "**on the margin.**" A stockbroker might allow a buyer to purchase stock for only a percentage of what it was worth (commonly as low as 10 percent); the rest could be borrowed from the broker. As long as stock prices continued to rise, investors would have no trouble paying brokers back for these loans. After the stock market crash, brokers wanted payment for these loans. Countless numbers of investors had no way to make these payments.

Stock Market Crash

The prices of stock crested in early September 1929. The price of stock fell very gradually during most of September and early October. Some investors noted that some factories were beginning to lay workers off; whispers were heard around Wall Street that perhaps the price of stock *was* too high, and that it might be good to sell before prices began to fall.

The first signs of panic occurred on Wednesday, October 23, when in the last hour of trading, the value of a share of stock dropped, on average, 20 points. On October 24 a massive amount of stock was sold, and prices again fell dramatically. Stockbrokers told nervous investors not to worry; Herbert Hoover announced that the stock market and the economy "is on a sound and prosperous basis."

A group of influential bankers and brokers pooled resources to buy stock, but this was unable to stop the downward trend. Prices fell again on Monday, October 28, and on the following day, Black Tuesday, the bottom fell out of the market. Prices fell by 40 points that day; it is estimated that total losses to investors for the day was over $20 million. Stockbrokers and banks frantically attempted to call in their loans; few investors had the money to pay even a fraction of what they owed.

How the Stock Market Crash Caused the Great Depression

In the weeks immediately following the crash, important figures from the banking world and President Hoover all assured the American people that America was still economically sound, and that the crash was no worse than other stock downturns that had had little long-term effect on the economy. In retrospect, it can be seen that through both direct and indirect means, the stock market crash was a fundamental cause of the Great Depression. As a result of the crash:

1. *Bank closings increased.* As stated previously, many banks in rural America had to close when farmers couldn't repay loans. The exact same thing happened to many city banks after 1929 when investors could not repay their loans. In addition, the news of even a single bank closing had a snowball effect; thousands of people went to banks across the country to withdraw their life savings. Banks did not have this kind of money (it had been given out to investors as loans); soon urban banks began to fail as well. It is estimated that by 1932 approximately 5,000 banks fell, with the life savings of over 5 million Americans gone forever

2. *Income fell for industrialists.* Many large industrialists invested heavily in the stock market. They had less available cash, and some started to close or reduce the scale of their factory operations. Workers were laid off or made much less money; as a result, they were able to buy fewer products made in other industrial plants, causing layoffs there as well. By 1933, nearly 25 percent of the labor force was out of work.

3. *Effect on the world.* Many European countries, especially Germany, utilized loans from American banks and investment houses in the 1920s and 1930s to remain viable. When American financial institutions were unable to supply these loans, instability occurred in these countries. Some historians make the argument that, perhaps indirectly, the American stock market crash opened the door for Hitler to come to power in Germany.

Social Impact of the Great Depression

Many Americans felt a huge sense of uprootedness in the 1930s. By late 1932, virtually all sectors of American society were affected in some way by the depression. Both professional men and common laborers lost their jobs. It was not uncommon during the depression for two people to share a job, or for a man who had lost his job to continue to put his suit on every morning and pretend to go to work, somehow averting the shame he felt for being unemployed. Women and minorities were often the first to lose their jobs, although women in certain "female" occupations (such as domestic work) were almost never uprooted by men. "Respectable" white men were willing to take jobs that had been previously seen as fit only for minorities. Many behaviors of the 1920s, such as buying on credit, were forgotten practices by 1932.

Many private agencies established soup kitchens and emergency shelters in the early 1930s, but many more were needed. Many couples postponed marriage and having children. Those with nowhere to live in cities often ended up in **Hoovervilles**, which were settlements of shacks (made from scrap metal or lumber) usually located on the outskirts of cities. Many unemployed young people, both men and women, took to the road in the 1930s, often traveling in empty railroad cars.

The greatest human suffering of the depression era might have existed in the **Dust Bowl**. For most of the decade, massive dust storms plagued the residents of Oklahoma, Kansas, Nebraska, Colorado, and Texas; farm production in this area fell drastically for much of the decade. A severe drought was the major cause of the dust storms, although poor farming practices (stripping the soil of any topsoil) also contributed to them. By the decade's end, nearly 60 percent of all farms in the Dust Bowl were either ruined or abandoned. Many Dust Bowlers traveled to California to get agricultural jobs there, and discovered that if an entire family picked grapes from sunup to sundown, it might barely scrape by. (John Steinbeck's book *The Grapes of Wrath*, as well as the film version, are highly recommended for further study of Dust Bowlers and their move to California, as are the recordings of Woody Guthrie entitled "Dust Bowl Ballads" and the depression-era photos taken by Dorothea Lange.)

The behavior and attitudes of many who lived through the depression changed forever. Many would *never* in their lives buy anything on credit; there are countless stories of depression-era families who insisted on paying for everything, including automobiles, with cash. Depression-era shortages led many in later life to be almost compulsive "savers" of everything and anything imaginable. Many who lived through the depression and had children in the 1950s were determined to given their kids all that they had been deprived of in the 1930s.

Hoover Administration and the Depression

To state that Herbert Hoover did nothing to stem the effects of the Great Depression is not entirely accurate. Nevertheless, he did believe that this crisis could be solved through **voluntarism**. Hoover urged Americans to donate all they could to charities, and held several conferences with business leaders where he urged them not to reduce wages or lay off workers. When it became obvious that these measures were not enough, public opinion quickly turned against Hoover.

The Hoover administration did take several specific measures to offset the effects of the depression. Even before the stock market crash, the **Agricultural Marketing Act** created a Federal Farm Board that had the ability to give loans to the agricultural community and buy crops to keep farm prices up. By 1932, there was not enough money to keep this program afloat. In 1930, Congress enacted the **Hawley-Smoot Tariff**, which to this day is the highest import tax in the history of the United States. In response, European countries drastically increased their own tariffs as well; some historians maintain that this legislation did little to improve the economy of the United States, but that its effects did much to ensure that the American Depression would be a worldwide one.

Hoover did authorize more money for public works programs, and, in 1932, he authorized the creation of the **Reconstruction Finance Corporation**. This agency gave money to banks, who were then authorized to loan this money to businesses and railroads. Another bill authorized loans to banks to prevent them from failing. To many in America, these bills were merely signs that Hoover was only interested in helping those at the top of society and that he cared little about the common person. Hoover vetoed legislation authorizing a federal relief program, although in 1932 he did sign legislation authorizing federal loans to the states; states could then administer relief programs with this money.

Those Americans who felt that Hoover was unconcerned about the plight of the common man had their views seemingly confirmed by federal actions against the **Bonus Army** that appeared in Washington in the summer of 1932. This group of nearly 17,000 unemployed World War I vets came to ask the federal government to give them the bonuses that they were supposed to get in 1945 immediately. At Hoover's urging, the Senate rejected legislation authorizing this. Most of the Bonus Army then went home, but a few thousand stayed, living in shacks along the Anacostia River. Hoover ordered them removed; military forces led by Douglas MacArthur used tear gas and cleared the remaining bonus marchers from their camp and burned down the shacks they had been living in.

1932 Presidential Election

The two candidates in the 1932 presidential election could not have been more different in both content and style. In a joyless convention, the Republicans renominated Herbert Hoover. In newsreels seen by Americans across the country, Hoover came across as unsmiling and utterly lacking in warmth. He insisted that his policies would eventually lead America out of the depression, stating that history demonstrated that lulls in the American economy are always followed by upturns. Hoover warned against "mindless experimentation" in the creation of government policies. It should be noted that Hoover was echoing the standard economic and political theory of the era.

Hoover's opponent in the election was the governor of New York, Franklin Delano Roosevelt. Roosevelt was a man of wealth. After serving as assistant secretary of the navy under Woodrow Wilson, Roosevelt unsuccessfully tried to get the vice presidential nomination in 1920. During the summer of 1921, he came down with polio, which left him unable to walk for the rest of his life. Several of Roosevelt's biographers maintain that the mental and physical anguish caused by his polio made Roosevelt much more sensitive to the sufferings of others.

Franklin Roosevelt married a distant cousin, Eleanor Roosevelt, in 1905. While Franklin spent much of the 1920s attempting to recover from polio in Warm Springs, Georgia, Eleanor became a tireless worker in New York state politics, pushing for governmental reform and better conditions for working women. The role that Eleanor Roosevelt played during the presidency of Franklin Roosevelt cannot be overestimated. FDR (this shortening of his name was done by a reporter in 1932) often stated that Eleanor served as his "legs," visiting miners, schools, and countless other groups. Eleanor also discussed policy with Roosevelt and continually urged him to do more to offset the effects of the depression.

As governor of New York during the first years of the Great Depression, Roosevelt instituted relief programs that became models for others across the country. During his campaign Roosevelt promised the "**New Deal**" for the American people; unlike Hoover, he also promised to experiment to find solutions to America's problems. Roosevelt's broad smile and personal demeanor contrasted drastically with the public image of Herbert Hoover; Americans were convinced that Roosevelt cared (this would be demonstrated during his presidency by the hundreds of letters that both Roosevelt and his wife received during the presidency, asking for things such as small loans, money to pay doctors, and old clothes; it should also be noted that many Americans had a picture of Franklin Roosevelt on display somewhere in their living quarters during the depression).

The 1932 presidential election was easily won by Roosevelt, who won by over 7 million votes. Hoover's only strength was in the Northeastern states. In addition, the Democrats won control of both houses of Congress. Some had feared (or hoped) that the depression would radicalize the American working class, yet the Socialist candidate for president, Norman Thomas, received considerably less than 1 million votes.

First Hundred Days

Franklin Roosevelt's inauguration speech in 1933 was one of optimism; the most quoted line of this speech is ". . . so first of all let me assert my firm belief that the only thing we have to fear is fear itself." Within a week of taking office, Roosevelt gave the first of his many **fireside chats**. During these radio addresses, Roosevelt spoke to the listening audience as if they were part of his family; Roosevelt would usually explain the immediate problems facing the country in these speeches and outline the reasons for his decided solutions.

Roosevelt surrounded himself with an able cabinet, as well as a group of unofficial advisors called Roosevelt's "brain trust." In dealing with the problems of the depression, Roosevelt urged his advisors to experiment. Some programs thus failed, some were continually reformed, and several conflicted with each other. The key, insisted Roosevelt, was to "do something."

During the first **Hundred Days** of the Roosevelt administration, countless programs were proposed by the administration and passed by Congress that attempted to stimulate the American economy and provide relief and jobs. A very popular act, for psychological reasons if nothing else, was the repeal of Prohibition, which was actually voted on by Congress in February 1933.

Roosevelt's economic advisor told him that his first priority should be the banking system. On March 5, 1933, he officially closed all banks for four days and had the federal government oversee the inspection of all banks. By March 15, most banks were reopened; this cooling-off period gave people a renewed confidence in the banks, and slowly people started putting back into banks instead of taking out. The Banking Act of 1933 created the **Federal Deposit Insurance Corporation (FDIC)**, which insured the bank deposits of individual citizens.

During the hundred days, large amounts of federal money were handed down to local relief agencies, and a Federal Emergency Relief Administration (led by Harry Hopkins) was also established. Efforts were also made to help people find work. Thousands were hired from funds distributed to states by the Public Works Administration; many schools, highways, and hospitals were built under this program.

The **Civilian Conservation Corps (CCC)** was founded during this period and would eventually employ over 2.5 million young men. Under this program, forest and conservation programs were undertaken. CCC workers were only paid a small amount (this money was actually sent to their families), but in a period where little work was available, many veterans of CCC programs later perceived the program as a godsend.

Roosevelt considered the bolstering of the industrial sector of the American economy to be a top priority. Falling prices had caused layoffs and the failure of many businesses. The **National Industrial Recovery Act (NIRA)** was established to try to stop falling prices in industry. Under this act, committees of both owners and union leaders in each industry would meet to set commonly agreed-on prices, wages, working hours, and working expectations. Unions and collective bargaining were accepted in industry as a result of the NIRA. Wages in many industries rose as a result of this; the thinking in the creation of the NIRA was that as wages rose, workers would then buy more, stimulating the economy and stopping the fall of industrial prices. The goals of this program were not largely met; as wages rose so did prices. As a result, many workers did not buy more, negating any benefit that rising wages were supposed to have.

Another body created by the NIRA was the National Recovery Administration (NRA), which was supposed to enforce the decisions of the NIRA. The entire process of the NIRA was declared unconstitutional in the 1935 Supreme Court case *Schechter v. United States*, although the agency had largely lost its effectiveness by then.

Two other important programs developed during the first hundred days. The **Agricultural Adjustment Administration (AAA)** attempted to stop the sharp decline in farm prices by paying farmers *not* to produce certain crops and livestock. It was hoped that this would cause the prices of these goods to rise. The **Tennessee Valley Authority** authorized the construction of a series of dams that would ultimately provide electricity and flood control to those living in the Tennessee River Valley. Thousands who had not had electricity in their homes now did.

The hundred days and the months that followed it provided some relief to those affected by the depression, but by no means solved the basic economic problems facing the United States. The 1934 midterm congressional elections showed that most Americans favored FDRs policies, yet even in 1935 some 20 percent of all Americans were still out of work.

Second New Deal

Many wealthy members of American society were appalled by the actions that Roosevelt took during his first year in office; he was called a traitor to his class, a Communist, and far worse. Other elements of Roosevelt's brain trust (as well as his wife Eleanor) were advising Roosevelt to do even more to help the unemployed of America. As a result, the **Second New Deal**, beginning in 1935, included another flurry of legislation.

It was obvious that even more dramatic measures were needed to help farmers; many farms were still being foreclosed on because farmers could not make necessary payments on their lands. The **Resettlement Administration**, established in May 1935, offered loans to small farmers who faced foreclosure. In addition, migrant farmers had not been affected by previous New Deal measures dealing with agriculture; funds to help them find work were included under the Resettlement Administration.

One of the outstanding achievements of the Second New Deal was the creation of the **Works Progress Administration (WPA)**. The WPA took people who were on relief and employed them for 30 or 35 hours a week. On average, 2 million people per month were employed by the WPA. By 1941, well over 8 million people had worked for the WPA. WPA workers were usually engaged in construction projects, building schools, hospitals, and roads across the country. In addition, unemployed musicians, artists, and actors were all employed by the WPA. WPA artists painted many of the murals found in public buildings, concerts were given for both urban and rural audiences, and plays were performed for audiences who had never seen one before.

Another important piece of legislation from this period was the **Wagner Act**, which reaffirmed the right of workers to organize and to utilize collective bargaining. These rights had been guaranteed by provision 7a of the NIRA guidelines, but when the NIRA was declared to be unconstitutional, additional legislation protecting workers was needed. The Wagner Act also listed unfair labor practices that were outlawed and established the **National Labor Relations Board (NLRB)** to enforce its provisions.

The most important legislation passed during the Second New Deal was the 1935 **Social Security Act**. The critical provision of this act was the creation of a retirement plan for workers over 65 years old. Both workers and employers paid into this retirement fund; the first payments were scheduled to be made in January 1942. It should be noted that the initial social security legislation did not cover agricultural and domestic workers.

Other provisions of this act established a program that provided unemployment insurance for workers who had lost their jobs; this was paid for by a payroll tax that was imposed on all employers with more than eight workers. The federal government also provided financial support to programs at the state level that provided unemployment insurance. The federal government also gave money to the states to provide aid programs for dependent children, for the blind, and for the physically challenged.

As stated previously, some Americans were exempt from the provisions of the Social Security Act. Nevertheless, this act fundamentally changed the relationship of the federal government with American citizens. At the root of the Social Security Act was the concept that it was the job of the federal government to take care of those who couldn't take care of themselves. This was a fundamentally new role for the federal government to have, and it justified the worst fears of many opponents of the Roosevelt administration.

Presidential Election of 1936

The 1936 election was the first true national referendum of the presidency of Franklin Roosevelt. In his campaign speeches, Roosevelt often railed against the business class; according to Roosevelt, they opposed many of his policies only so they could continue to get rich. The Republicans nominated Governor Alfred Landon of Kansas as their presidential candidate. Landon never actually repudiated the programs of the New Deal, but he stated that a balanced budget and less expensive government programs should be top priorities.

The election was one of the most one-sided in American history. Roosevelt won the electoral college 523 to 8, with Landon only winning the states of Maine and Vermont. Roosevelt was able to craft a **New Deal Coalition**, which made the Democrats the majority party in America throughout the rest of the 1930s and all the way into the 1980s. The fact that white urban dwellers supported the Democrats in large numbers was noted during the 1928 defeat of Smith; whites in the Solid South had largely voted Democratic since the nineteenth century. The two groups that joined the Democratic coalition in this era were labor unions and blacks (this was a dramatic shift, as most blacks had voted Republican since the period of Emancipation). Roosevelt enjoyed support in the agricultural community as well.

Opponents of Franklin Roosevelt and the New Deal

Despite the overwhelming electoral success of Franklin Roosevelt, many Americans vehemently disagreed with his programs. Some wealthy Americans called him a traitor to his class, while some businessmen called him a Socialist or a Communist. To others, the programs of Roosevelt were perceived as being designed to benefit the business interests of America and never truly addressed the human suffering of the country. Some of these Americans felt that neither the Democratic nor the Republican parties were really concerned with helping the average American, and perceived socialism as the only viable solution. Many idealistic Americans dabbled with socialism in the 1930s; for some the one- or two-party meetings they attended became career-threatening during the McCarthy era of the 1950s.

One group that thought the New Deal had gone too far was the **American Liberty League**. This group was led by former presidential candidate Al Smith and several very influential business figures, including prominent members of the Du Pont family. The membership of this organization was largely relatively wealthy Republicans; they were particularly incensed by the **Revenue Act of 1935**, which considerably increased the tax rate for those making over $50,000. The American Liberty League equated the New Deal with "bolshevism" in much of their literature.

The majority of those opposing the New Deal felt that it didn't go far enough. Dr. Francis Townsend of California proposed an **Old Age Revolving Pension Plan**; under this plan, a national sales tax would pay for a pension of $200 per month for all retired Americans. Townsend maintained that the benefit would be that more and more money would be put into circulation. In 1934, Upton Sinclair, author of *The Jungle*, ran for governor of California on the Democratic ticket and announced his "End Poverty in California" (EPIC) plan. Under this plan, California factories and farms would be under state control. Sinclair was defeated by the Republican candidate and was also sabotaged by members of his own party; the Democratic smear campaign against Sinclair was approved of by Franklin Roosevelt.

The two most vicious opponents of the New Deal were Father Charles Coughlin and Louisiana senator Huey Long. Millions of people listened to Coughlin on the radio. Originally a supporter of Roosevelt, by the mid-1930s he told his listeners that Roosevelt was a "liar" and "the great betrayer." By the late 1930s, Coughlin was praising Mussolini and Hitler on his broadcasts, and making increasingly anti-Semitic statements. By order of the church, Coughlin was pulled off the air during World War II.

As governor and later senator from Louisiana, Huey Long instituted many New-Deal-type programs in Louisiana, and also developed the most effective and ruthless political machine in the entire South. By 1934, Long felt that Franklin Roosevelt was not committed to doing enough to end the depression. Long called for a true redistribution of wealth in his "Share the Wealth" program, which would have allowed no American to make over a million dollars a year (the rest would be taken in taxes). From these taxes, Long proposed to give every American family $5,000 immediately and an annual income of $2,000. Long talked of running against Roosevelt in 1936, but was assassinated by the relative of a Louisiana political enemy in 1935.

Last Years of the New Deal

Franklin Roosevelt was frustrated that the United States Supreme Court had struck down several New Deal programs. In early 1937, he proposed the **Justice Reorganization Bill**, which would have allowed him to appoint an additional Supreme Court justice for every justice over 70 years old (nothing in the Constitution stated that there had to be only nine Supreme Court justices). Roosevelt would have been able to appoint six new judges under this scheme. Roosevelt claimed that the purpose of this plan was to help the older judges with their workload, but many Republicans and Democrats in Congress believed that Roosevelt was altering the balance of power between branches of government just to get his ideas enacted into law. Newspaper editorial writers and cartoonists compared Roosevelt to the dictators of Europe, Hitler and Mussolini. Many Southern Democrats joined with the Republicans to defeat this bill; the aftereffects seriously damaged Roosevelt's relationship with Congress. Ironically, without the bill, several justices retired in the next two years, allowing Roosevelt to appoint justices who would approve his programs anyway.

Any hopes that the New Deal was actually ending the depression were dashed by a fairly large recession that occurred in mid-1937. Once again, factories began major layoffs. Critics of the New Deal blamed Roosevelt's programs for this recession. Many in the administration were worried that the national debt was too high, and urged Roosevelt to cut programs. The WPA was drastically scaled back, putting some that had worked for it out of work. In addition, a part of every worker's salary was now deducted to be put into the Social Security fund; critics charged that this money would have been better utilized if it was actually being spent on goods and services. By 1940, the administration restored some of the cutbacks made to government programs, slightly improving the economy again.

Effects of the New Deal

The Wagner Act and other New Deal legislation permanently legitimized labor unions and collective bargaining. Some unions became emboldened by the Wagner Act, and several **sit-down strikes** occurred in the late 1930s. The most famous occurred at the General Motors plant in Flint, Michigan, in December 1936. Workers refused to leave the plant; by February, management had to give in to the worker's demands. Other strikes of the era turned bloody; in a 1937 strike at Republic Steel in Chicago, 10 strikers were killed. Nevertheless, union membership rose dramatically in the 1930s.

Another development was the creation of the **Congress of Industrial Organizations (CIO)**. The American Federation of Labor, founded in the 1880s, was made up mostly of skilled workers. The first president of the CIO was John L. Lewis; the goal of this union was to organize and represent unskilled factory and textile workers. By 1938, this organization represented over 4 million workers. CIO members were on the front lines of the strikes mentioned in the previous paragraph.

The burden on women and blacks was great during the New Deal. As men lost their jobs, more and more women were forced to take meager jobs to support their families (despite the fact that women workers were often criticized for "stealing" the jobs of men). It should be noted that Francis Perkins was the secretary of labor during the 1930s; Roosevelt employed a number of women in influential roles during his presidency.

Blacks were especially oppressed during the New Deal. Often, they were the first to be fired from a factory or business; relief programs in Southern states sometimes excluded blacks from receiving benefits. Lynchings continued in the South throughout the 1930s;

Roosevelt never supported an antilynching bill for fear of alienating Southern Democrats. The **Scottsboro Boys** trial received national attention. In 1931, nine black young men were accused of raping two white women on a train. Without any real evidence, eight of the nine were sentenced to die. It is ironic that the American Communist party organized the appeals of the Scottsboro Boys; in the end, some of their convictions were overturned.

Nevertheless, blacks did support Franklin Roosevelt, as they felt that he was generally supportive of their cause. Roosevelt did hire blacks for several policy posts in his New Deal administration. Mary McLeod Bethune, founder of the National Council of Negro Women, was appointed in 1936 as director of the Division of Negro Affairs of the National Youth Administration. Bethune lobbied Roosevelt on the concerns of blacks, and also worked to increase the support of influential black leaders for the New Deal.

New Deal Culture

Many authors attempted to capture the human suffering that was so pronounced in the 1930s. Zora Neale Hurston wrote *Their Eyes Were Watching God* about growing up black in a small Florida town. *Studs Lonigen* by James T. Farrell depicted the lives of the Irish in Chicago. The previously mentioned *The Grapes of Wrath* by John Steinbeck tells the story of Dust Bowlers moving to California for survival, while Erskine Caldwell's *Tobacco Road* describes the suffering of sharecroppers in Georgia. *Gone with the Wind* by Margaret Mitchell offered a romanticized tale of survival from another period of crisis, the Civil War.

Most Americans of the 1930s got their entertainment through radio. Radio in the 1930s offered soap operas, comedies, and dramas. Americans were also offered "high culture" on most radio stations, as symphonic music and operas were standard fare. The response to H. G. Well's dramatization of "War of the Worlds" demonstrated the power of radio in American life.

Going to the movies provided a way for Americans to escape the sufferings of their daily lives; by 1939, nearly 70 percent of all adults went to the movies at least once a week. Lavish sets and dancing in movies such as *The Gold Diggers of 1933* allowed people to leave their cares behind, at least for a couple of hours. Shirley Temple charmed millions, and movies such as *Mr. Smith Goes to Washington* showed audiences that in the end, justice would prevail. Promoters attempted to make movie-going itself a special event in the 1930s; theaters were designed to look like palaces, air conditioning was installed, and dishes and other utensils were often given away as theater promotions.

Chapter Review

Rapid Review

To achieve the perfect 5, you should be able to explain the following:

- The Great Depression had numerous long-lasting effects on American society.
- Franklin Roosevelt was the first activist president of the twentieth century who used the power of the federal government to help those who could not help themselves.
- The Great Depression's origins lay in economic problems of the late 1920s.
- The 1929 stock market crash was caused by, among other things, speculation on the part of investors and buying stocks "on the margin."

- The stock market crash began to affect the economy almost immediately, and its effects were felt by almost all by 1931.
- Herbert Hoover did act to end the depression, but believed that voluntary actions by both business and labor would lead America out of its economic difficulties.
- Franklin Roosevelt won the 1932 election by promising the New Deal to the American people and by promising to act in a decisive manner.
- Suffering was felt across American society; many in the Dust Bowl were forced to leave their farms.
- During the first hundred days, Roosevelt restored confidence in the banks, established the Civilian Conservation Corps, stabilized farm prices, and attempted to stabilize industry through the National Industrial Recovery Act.
- During the Second New Deal, the WPA was created and the Social Security Act was enacted; this was the most long-lasting piece of legislation from the New Deal.
- Roosevelt was able to craft a political coalition of urban whites, Southerners, union members, and blacks that kept the Democratic party in power through the 1980s.
- The New Deal had opponents from the left who said it didn't do enough to alleviate the effects of the depression and opponents from the right who said that the New Deal was Socialist in nature.
- Roosevelt's 1937 plan to pack the Supreme Court and the recession of 1937 demonstrated that New Deal programs were not entirely successful in ending the Great Depression.
- Many Americans turned to radio and the movies for relief during the depression.

Time Line

1929: Stock market crash
1930: Hawley-Smoot Tariff enacted
1931: Ford plants in Detroit shut down
Initial trial of the Scottsboro Boys
1932: Glass-Steagall Banking Act enacted
Bonus marchers routed from Washington
Franklin D. Roosevelt elected president
Huey Long announces "Share Our Wealth" movement
1933: Emergency Banking Relief Act enacted
Prohibition ends
Agricultural Adjustment Act enacted
National Industrial Recovery Act enacted
Civilian Conservation Corps established
Tennessee Valley Authority formed
Public Works Administration established
1934: American unemployment reaches highest point
1935: Beginning of the Second New Deal
Works Progress Administration established
Social Security Act enacted
Wagner Act enacted
Formation of Committee for Industrial Organization (CIO)
1936: Franklin Roosevelt reelected
Sit-down strike against GM begins
1937: Recession of 1937 begins
Roosevelt's plan to expand the Supreme Court defeated
1939: *Gone with the Wind* published
The Grapes of Wrath published

Review Questions

1. Which of the following was *not* a cause of the stock market crash?
   A. Excessive American loans to European countries
   B. Uneven division of wealth
   C. Installment buying
   D. Purchasing of stocks "on the margin"

2. Wealthy businessmen who objected to the New Deal programs of Franklin Roosevelt claimed that
   A. they unfairly aided the many who did not deserve it.
   B. New Deal programs smacked of "bolshevism."
   C. New Deal programs unfairly regulated businesses.
   D. all of the above.

3. The purpose of the Federal Deposit Insurance Corporation (FDIC) was to
   A. ensure that poor Americans had something to fall back on when they retired
   B. inspect the financial transactions of important businesses
   C. insure bank deposits of individual citizens
   D. increase governmental control over the economy

4. One group of women who were able to keep their jobs during the Great Depression were
   A. schoolteachers
   B. clerical workers
   C. domestic workers
   D. government employees

5. The popularity of Huey Long and Father Coughlin in the mid-1930s demonstrated that
   A. most Americans felt that the New Deal had gone too far in undermining traditional American values.
   B. more Americans were turning to religion in the 1930s.
   C. most Americans favored truly radical solutions to America's problems.
   D. many Americans felt that the government should do more to end the problems associated with the depression.

Answers and Explanations

1. **A.** All of the others were major underlying reasons for the crash. American loans to Europe benefited both European countries and American banking houses until the crash.

2. **D.** All of the criticisms listed were heard throughout the 1930s.

3. **C.** The FDIC was established after the bank holiday to insure individual accounts in certified banks and to increase confidence in the banking system. Americans began to put money back into banks after its institution.

4. **C.** In the other occupations, women were often fired before men, or had their hours drastically reduced. Those women who were employed as domestic workers were relatively safe, as this was one occupation that men, as a whole, rejected.

5. **D.** Many Americans wanted more New Deal–style programs and felt that Roosevelt should have gone even further in his proposed legislation. Many may have listened to Long and Coughlin, but when the time to vote came, cast their ballots for Roosevelt—thus negating answer C. The idea that the New Deal went too far in destroying American capitalism was popular in the business community, but was not widely shared in mainstream America.

CHAPTER 24

World War II (1933–1945)

IN THIS CHAPTER

Summary: Throughout the 1930s the United States followed a foreign policy based on isolationism, which emphasized noninvolvement in European affairs. After Adolph Hitler became the Nazi dictator of Germany, some Americans believed that he was a reasonable man who could serve as a European bulwark against Stalin and the Soviet Union. After World War II began in Europe, President Roosevelt sensed that America would eventually be drawn into it and began Lend-Lease and other measures to help the British. The December 7, 1941, Japanese attack on Pearl Harbor mobilized American public opinion for war. Americans fought on two fronts during the war: against the Germans and the Italians in Europe and against the Japanese in the Pacific. In Europe, U.S. forces and their British and Soviet Allies eventually invaded Germany and crushed the Nazis. In the Pacific, superior American air and sea power led to the defeat of the Japanese. The decision to drop the atomic bomb on two Japanese cities is still considered controversial by some historians today. At the time, President Truman decided to drop the bomb based on calculations of the human cost of an American invasion of Japan. Americans contributed greatly to the war effort at home through rationing, working extra shifts, and the purchase of war bonds. As a result of World War II, the United States and the Soviet Union emerged as the two major world powers.

KEY IDEA

Keywords

Isolationism: American foreign policy of the 1920s and 1930s based on the belief that it was in the best interest of the United States not to become involved in foreign conflicts that did not directly threaten American interests.

Yalta Conference: meeting held at Yalta in the Soviet Union between President Roosevelt, British Prime Minister Winston Churchill, and Soviet leader Joseph Stalin in February 1945; at this meeting critical decisions on the future of postwar Europe were made. At Yalta it was agreed that Germany would be divided into four zones, that free elections would take place after the war in Eastern Europe, and that the Soviet Union would join the war against Japan.

Bataan Death March: after the Japanese landed in the Philippines in May 1942, nearly 75,000 American and Filipino prisoners were forced to endure a 60-mile march; during this ordeal, 10,000 prisoners died or were killed.

Manhattan Project: secret project to build an atomic bomb that began in Los Alamos, New Mexico, in August 1942; the first successful test of a bomb took place on July 16, 1945.

Rosie the Riveter: figure that symbolized American working women during World War II. After the war, women were expected to return to more traditional roles.

Double V campaign: campaign popularized by American black leaders during World War II emphasizing the need for a double victory: over Germany and Japan and also over racial prejudice in the United States. Many blacks who fought in World War II were disappointed that the America they returned to still harbored racial hatreds.

Internment camps: mandatory resettlement camps for Japanese Americans from America's West Coast, created in February 1942 during World War II by executive order of President Franklin Roosevelt. In 1944, the Supreme Court ruled that the camps were legal.

American Foreign Policy in the 1930s

As Italy, Germany, and Japan all expanded their empires in the 1930s, most Americans favored a continuation of the policy of **isolationism**. An Isolationist group, the **America First Committee**, attracted nearly 820,000 members by 1940. Isolationists believed that it was in America's best interests to stay out of foreign conflicts that did not directly threaten American interests. A congressional committee led by Senator Gerald Nye investigated the origins of America's entry into World War I and found that bankers and arms manufacturers did much to influence America's entry into the war. On a practical level, Americans were consumed with the problems of the Great Depression and were generally unable to focus on overseas problems.

Congressional legislation passed in the period attempted to keep America out of future wars between other powers. The **Neutrality Act of 1935** stated that if countries went to war, the United States would not trade arms or weapons with them for six months; in addition, any nonmilitary goods sold to nations at war would have to be paid for up front and would have to be transported in non-American ships (this was called "cash-and-carry").

German expansionism in Europe convinced Franklin Roosevelt that the United States, at some point, would *have* to enter the war on the side of Great Britain (even though public opinion strongly opposed this). On September 1, 1939, Germany invaded Poland, and two days later England and France declared war on Germany. Within three weeks, Roosevelt asked Congress to pass the **Neutrality Act of 1939**, which would allow the cash-and-carry sale of arms to countries at war (this legislation was designed to facilitate the sale of American arms to Britain and France). The bill passed on a party-line vote.

News of rapid German advances in Europe began to change American attitudes, with more and more people agreeing with Roosevelt that the best course of action would be to prepare for eventual war. The rapid defeat of France at the hands of the Nazis was stunning to many Americans. In September of 1940, Roosevelt gave Great Britain 50 older American destroyers in return for the rights to build military bases in Bermuda and Newfoundland.

United States and the Middle East in the Interwar Era

In the 1920s, the United States rejected Woodrow Wilson's vision of the United States as an active leader on the world stage and instead turned to a twenty-year period of isolationism. As a result, American political involvement in the Middle East became minimal, leaving France and Great Britain to exert tremendous influence in the region. As previously noted, France had a mandate to control Syria and Lebanon, while the British controlled Iraq, Transjordan, and Palestine. In 1932, the British granted Iraq independence, although the British continued to have major influence on government officials and their actions in Iraq.

In the 1920s, the Middle East remained a romantic and idealized region of the world to most Americans. They became fascinated with the adventures of T. E. Lawrence ("Lawrence of Arabia") leading and uniting Arab tribesmen against the Turks in World War I and went in droves to see romantic movies set in the deserts of the region, starring Rudolph Valentino. The appeal of Zionism for many American Jews waned in the post–World War I years as stories of the sufferings of Jews that were so widespread in the World War I era declined.

However, the concern among Jews in the United States for the plight of European Jews increased with the ascension of Adolf Hitler to power in Germany in 1933. With the increased persecution of the German Jews in the mid-1930s, pressure began to be exerted on European countries as well as on the United States to allow more German Jews to immigrate. In the 1930s, there was increased hope that a Jewish homeland could be established in Palestine, but this hope was dashed by a White Paper issued by the British government in 1939, which seriously limited the number of Jews who could immigrate to Palestine.

There are historians who are very critical of the conscious decision of the United States in the 1930s not to allow more Jewish refugees into the country. These critics state that if the United States had opened its shores to more Jews in the 1930s, their lives could have been saved. Provisions of the National Origins Act of 1924 limited the number of Germans who could enter the country to slightly over 25,000 per year. In addition, immigrants from all countries were refused admission if they could not prove that they could support themselves once they arrived in the United States, thus further limiting the number of Jewish immigrants who could settle in the United States. As a result, an average of fewer than 9,000 Jews from Germany entered the United States annually during the 1930s.

It should be noted that American public opinion in the decade was decidedly against allowing more immigrants to enter the country, especially immigrants who were Jewish. America was in the midst of the Great Depression; editorial page writers, politicians, and many average citizens stated that under these circumstances the last thing America needed was immigrants competing for precious jobs that existed there. Unfortunately, anti-Semitism did not exist only in Germany; anti-Semitic sentiment in the United States strongly opposed allowing any more Jewish immigrants into the country.

The one resource from the Middle East that attracted great interest from American investors in the 1920s and 1930s was oil. As more and more Americans began to drive automobiles in the 1920s, reliable sources of petroleum products were needed outside of the United States. In 1928, British, French, Dutch, and American oil companies agreed to the Red Line Agreement, in which they agreed to act together to export oil from the region; as a result, America began to export oil from Iraq in late 1928.

In 1933, the King of Saudi Arabia granted Standard Oil of California the right to export Saudi Arabian oil. Five years later, geologists working for Standard Oil of California discovered major oil reserves in Saudi Arabia.

During World War II, the United States would have to move to actively protect its oil reserves in Saudi Arabia from attack by the Axis powers. Thus began the trend, which has lasted into the twenty-first century, of the United States depending on the Middle East region for oil and using its military to protect its oil interests there.

Presidential Election of 1940 and Its Aftermath

No president in American history had ever served more than two consecutive terms. Just before the Democratic National Convention, Roosevelt quietly stated that if he was nominated, he would accept. Roosevelt was quickly nominated; his Republican opponent was Wendell Wilkie, an ex-Democrat. Roosevelt emerged victorious, but by a smaller margin than in his two previous victories. A number of those who voted against Roosevelt did so as a protest against the widespread poverty and unemployment that still existed in America.

Roosevelt interpreted his victory as a mandate to continue preparations for the eventual U.S. entry into World War II. By early 1941, Roosevelt proposed giving the British aid for the war effort without getting cash in return (it was stated that payment could be made after the war). By the terms of the **Lend-Lease Act**, Congress gave the president the ability to send immediate aid to Britain; Roosevelt immediately authorized nearly $7 billion in aid. As Roosevelt had stated in a 1940 speech, the United States had become an "arsenal of democracy."

In August 1941, Roosevelt secretly met with British Prime Minister Winston Churchill off the coast of Newfoundland. The two agreed that America would, in all probability, soon be in the war and that the war should be fought for the principles of democracy. Roosevelt and Churchill authorized the publication of their commonly held beliefs in a document called the **Atlantic Charter**. In this document, the two leaders proclaimed that they were opposed to territorial expansion for either country, and they were for free trade and self-determination. They also agreed that another world organization would have to be created to replace the League of Nations and that this new world body would have the power to guarantee the "security" of the world. Roosevelt also agreed that the United States would ship lend-lease materials bound for Britain as far as Iceland; this brought the United States one step closer to full support for the Allied cause.

Attack on Pearl Harbor

The Japanese desire to create an Asian empire was the prime motivation behind their invasion of Manchuria in 1931, attacks on eastern China in 1937, and the occupation of much of French Indochina in 1941. As a result of Japanese actions in Southeast Asia, Roosevelt froze all Japanese assets in the United States, cut off the sale of oil to Japan, and closed the Panama Canal to Japanese ships.

From July 1941 until the beginning of December, near-constant negotiations took place between diplomats of Japan and the United States. The Japanese desperately wanted to regain normal trade relations with the United States, but American diplomats insisted that the Japanese leave China first, which the Japanese were unwilling to do. Most Japanese military and civilian leaders were convinced that the Japanese could never achieve their goal of a Pacific empire as long as the United States was militarily active in the region. By December 1, the planning was complete for the Japanese attack on Pearl Harbor.

A few revisionist historians believe that Franklin Roosevelt knew of the impending attack on Pearl Harbor. These historians maintain that Roosevelt was acutely aware that many Americans were still opposed to American entry into war, but that an event such as Pearl Harbor would put the entire country squarely behind the war effort. The vast majority of historians believe that American intelligence knew the Japanese were going to attack somewhere, but didn't know that the attack would be at Pearl Harbor; many in American military intelligence believed the Dutch East Indies would be the next target of the Japanese. The "Roosevelt Knew" thesis might be good for a documentary film or two but little else.

On Sunday morning, December 7, 1941, 190 Japanese warplanes attacked the American Pacific fleet anchored at Pearl Harbor. When the attack was done, 150 American airplanes were destroyed (most of them never left the ground), six battleships were sunk, as were a number of smaller ships, and nearly 2,400 Americans were killed. Luckily for the American navy, the aircraft carriers based at Pearl Harbor were out at sea on the morning of the attack.

The next day Roosevelt asked Congress for a declaration of war, stating that December 7 was "a date which will live in infamy." On December 11, Germany and Italy (who had signed a Tripartite Pact with Japan in 1940) declared war on the United States.

America Enters the War

In September of 1940, the President had authorized the creation of a system for the **conscription** of men into the armed forces; in the months immediately after Pearl Harbor, thousands were drafted and countless others volunteered for service. Soldiers in World War II called themselves "**GIs**"; this referred to the "Government Issued" stamp that appeared on the uniforms, tools, weapons, and everything else the government issued to them. A Council for National Defense had also been created in 1940; this body worked rapidly to convert factories over to war production. Additional legislation was also needed to prepare the country for war. In early 1942, the General Maximum Price Regulation Act immediately froze prices and established the rationing system that was in place for most of the war. The **Revenue Act of 1942** greatly expanded the number of Americans who had to pay federal income tax, thus increasing the amount of federal revenue.

America was forced to fight a war in Europe and a war in the Pacific. In the European theater of war, American naval forces first engaged the Germans as they attempted to protect convoys of ships taking critical food and supplies to Great Britain. These convoys were often attacked by German submarines. In this **Battle of the Atlantic**, German torpedoes were dreadfully accurate (even though sonar was being used by the Americans). Between January and August 1942, over 500 ships were sunk by German submarines.

American infantrymen were first involved in actual fighting in North Africa. American and British forces joined to defeat French North Africa in late 1942. American troops also played a role in the battles that eventually forced General Rommel's Africa Korps to surrender in May 1943. American and British soldiers also began a difficult offensive into Sicily and Italy two months later; by June 1944, Rome had surrendered.

Ever since 1941, the Soviet Union had been the only power to consistently engage the Nazi army (the Soviet Union lost 20 million people in World War II). Stalin had asked on several occasions that a second front be opened in Western Europe; by early 1944, an invasion of France by water was being planned by Dwight D. Eisenhower, commander of all Allied forces (who would become president in 1953).

The D-Day invasion took place on the morning of June 6, 1944. The initial Allied losses on Omaha Beach were staggering, yet the D-Day invasion was the beginning of the end for Nazi Germany. By the end of July, over 2 million Allied soldiers were on the ground in France, and the final squeeze of Nazi Germany began. American and British forces liberated French cities and towns as they moved eastward; at the same time, Russian troops were rolling westward. By August, Paris had been liberated.

The last major German offensive of the war was the **Battle of the Bulge**. Nearly 85,000 American soldiers were killed, wounded, or captured in this battle. The German attack moved the Allied lines back into Belgium, but reinforcement led by General George S. Patton again forced the Germans to retreat. When the German general staff learned that they had not been victorious at the Battle of the Bulge, most admitted that Germany would soon be defeated. American and British bombings did much to destroy several German cities.

Advancing American, British, and Russian troops were horrified to find concentration camps or the remnants of them. These camps were integral parts of Nazi Germany's **Final Solution** to the "Jewish problem." Between 1941 and 1945, over 6 million Jews were killed in the event now referred to as the **Holocaust**. Historians maintain that if the war continued for another two years, all of European Jewry might have been eliminated. Advancing troops were outraged at what they saw in these camps, and on several occasions shot all of the Nazi guards on the spot. Why the Holocaust occurred, and why it was endorsed by so many Germans, is the subject of hundreds of books and articles in scholarly journals.

Some historians are critical of the diplomatic and military actions of the United States both before and during the Holocaust. During the mid- to late 1930s, the State Department made it very difficult for European Jews to immigrate to the United States; with alarming unemployment figures in the United States because of the Great Depression, American decision makers felt it unwise to admit large numbers of immigrants to the country. Franklin Roosevelt knew of the existence of the concentration camps as early as late 1943, yet chose not to bomb them (which many in the camps say they would have welcomed). Roosevelt maintained that the number one priority of America had to be winning the war. Nevertheless, historians note that concern for the plight of the Jews caused a number of world leaders to support the creation of the state of Israel in the years immediately following the war.

In March 1945, Allied troops crossed the Rhine River, and met up with advancing Russian troops at the Elbe River on April 25. After a fierce battle, the Russians took Berlin. Deep in his bunker, Hitler committed suicide on May 1, and Germany unconditionally surrendered one week later. Celebrations for V-E Day (Victory in Europe Day) were jubilant in London and Paris, but were more restrained in American cities, as the United States still had to deal with the Japanese.

In February 1945, Roosevelt, Stalin, and Churchill met at the **Yalta Conference**. Franklin Roosevelt had been elected to a fourth term in 1944, but photos revealed him to be very ill at Yalta (he would live only another two months). At Yalta, the three leaders made major decisions concerning the structure of postwar Europe. It was agreed that Germany would be split into four zones of occupation (administered by England, France, the United States, and the Soviet Union), and that Berlin, located in the Soviet zone, would also be partitioned. Stalin promised to allow free elections in the Eastern European nations he had freed from Nazi control, and said that the Soviets would join the war against Japan after the surrender of Germany. Many historians consider the decisions made at the Yalta Conference (and the failure of the Soviet Union to totally adhere to them) to be major reasons for the beginning of the cold war.

Some historians are critical of Franklin Roosevelt for "giving in" to Stalin at Yalta. It should be remembered that, at the time of this meeting, Roosevelt had only two months to live. In addition, in February 1945, the atomic bomb was not yet a working weapon. American planning for the defeat of Japan was for a full attack on the Japanese mainland; in Roosevelt's eyes, Soviet participation in this attack was absolutely crucial (in return for this support, Roosevelt made concessions to Stalin on Eastern Europe and supported the Soviet acquisition of ports and territories in Korea, Manchuria, and Outer Mongolia). Winston Churchill had strong reservations about the ultimate goals and conduct of Stalin and the Soviet Union at Yalta; these reservations would later intensify, and were articulated by Churchill in his "iron curtain" speech of March 1946.

Role of the Middle East in World War II

The Middle East played an important strategic role in Allied military planning during World War II. Some historians argue that this is the first time American political leaders appreciated the true significance of the region in world affairs. The Americans and the British both thought it absolutely crucial that oil resources in the region not fall into German hands, and that these resources continue to be available for the Allied war effort. In addition, there were fears that the Germans and the Japanese might link up and cut off British access to India; control of the Middle East would be central to this plan.

Many of the efforts to maintain control of the Middle East for the strategic interests of the Allies fell on the Americans. The United States established diplomatic relations with Saudi Arabia and gave the Saudis large amounts of economic aid to ensure the continued flow of Saudi oil supplies. American diplomats in both Washington and Turkey worked to convince the Turks to stay neutral in the war, which would allow the Allies continued access to the Mediterranean Sea. In addition, American and British forces landed in Morocco and Algeria in 1942. Military planners placed Allied troops in the region to prepare for an eventual invasion of Italy. In 1943, British and American forces occupied Tunisia (which was controlled by the Germans), and from there began their assault on Sicily and eventually Italy itself.

American Lend-Lease efforts extended aid to both Great Britain and the Soviet Union by late 1941, and American efforts to assist the Soviet war effort also went through the Middle East. The Americans established large port facilities in Iran, where the parts for trucks, airplanes, weapons, and other war material were landed, assembled, and then sent by train to the Soviet armies fighting the Germans on the Eastern front. History of the war between Germany and the Soviet Union points to this assistance being absolutely indispensable for the eventual Soviet victory over the Nazis. The thousands of Iranians employed by the Americans in this effort were thankful for the additional income these jobs provided them, but sometimes complained about the arrogance and total disregard for local manners and customs exhibited by their employers and the majority of American soldiers stationed in Iran.

War Against Japan

In the aftermath of the attack on Pearl Harbor, Japan advanced against British controlled islands and territories in the Pacific. By April 1942, Hong Kong and Singapore were both in Japanese hands. General Douglas MacArthur controlled a large American and Filipino force in the Philippines. A large Japanese force landed there, and in March MacArthur was forced to abandon his troops and go to Australia. On May 6, 1942, Americans holding out on the Bataan Peninsula were finally forced to surrender. About 75,000 American and Filipino prisoners were forced to endure the 60-mile **Bataan Death March**, during which over 10,000 prisoners were executed or died from weakness (it was several years before Washington became aware of this march).

Just two days later, the Americans won their first decisive victory at the **Battle of the Coral Sea**. American airplanes launched from aircraft carriers were able to stop the advance of several large Japanese troop transports. Troops on these ships were to be used for an attack on Australia. After this defeat, the Japanese could never again mount a planned attack there. American airplanes also played a crucial role in the **Battle of Midway**. This battle took place in early June 1942; in it, the Japanese lost 4 aircraft carriers and over 200 planes. Many military historians consider the battle to be the turning point of the Pacific War; after this, Japan was never able to launch a major offensive. By mid-1942, American industrial might became more and more of a factor; the Americans could simply produce more airplanes than the Japanese could.

The Japanese were again halted at the **Battle of Guadalcanal**, which began in August 1942 and continued into the following year. American marines engaged in jungle warfare and even hand-to-hand combat. On many occasions Japanese units would fight nearly until the last man. Beginning in 1943, the Allies instituted a policy of **island-hopping**; by this policy, key Japanese strongholds would be attacked by air and sea power as American marines would push on around these strongholds. By late 1944, American bombers were able to reach major Japanese cities, and unleashed massive bombing attacks on them.

By 1944, the war had clearly turned against the Japanese. In late October, General MacArthur returned to the Philippine island of Leyte (although the city of Manila was not totally liberated until the following March). The Japanese began to use **kamikaze pilots** in a desperate attempt to destroy Allied ships. Several more bloody battles waited ahead for American forces. America suffered 25,000 casualties at the Battle of Iwo Jima, and another 50,000 at the Battle of Okinawa. After these battles, however, nothing was left to stop an Allied invasion of Japan.

Decision to Drop the Atomic Bomb

The incredibly bloody battles described in the preceding section greatly concerned military officials who were planning for an invasion of Japan. Japanese resistance to such an attack would have been fanatical. Franklin Roosevelt had suddenly died in April 1945; the new president, Harry Truman, was then informed about the atomic bomb. The actual planning for this bomb was the purpose of the **Manhattan Project**, begun in August 1942. Construction of this bomb took place in Los Alamos, New Mexico, under the direction of J. Robert Oppenheimer. The bomb was successfully tested in the New Mexico desert on July 16, 1945.

Much debate had taken place over the American decision to drop the atomic bomb on Japanese cities. For Harry Truman, this was not a difficult decision. Losses in an invasion of Japan would have been large; Truman later admitted that what had happened at Pearl Harbor and on the Bataan Death March also influenced his decision. Some historians also claim that some in both the State Department and the War Department saw the Soviet Union as the next potential enemy of the United States and wanted to use the atomic bomb to "show them what we had." After the atomic bombs were dropped, American public opinion was incredibly supportive of Truman's decision. It should be noted that movies, newsreels, and even comic books made the eventual decision to drop the bomb easier by turning the war against the Japanese into a race war. The Japanese, referred to as "Japs," were portrayed with crude racial stereotypes, and were seen as sneaky and certainly not to be trusted (it is interesting to note that the war against Germany was usually portrayed as a war against "Hitler" or against "the Nazis" and almost never as a war against the German people).

On August 6, 1945, the airplane **Enola Gay** dropped a bomb on the city of Hiroshima. Over 75,000 were killed in the attack. Three days later another bomb was dropped on Nagasaki. Some historians are especially critical of the dropping of the second bomb; there is evidence that the Japanese were pursuing a surrender through diplomatic circles on the day of the attack. Japan surrendered one day later, and V-J celebrations took place in many American cities the following day.

Home Front During the War

As previously stated, the federal government took action even before the war began, to prepare the American economy for war. Thousands of American businessmen also went to Washington to take on jobs relating to the war effort. These were called "dollar-a-year" men, as almost all still received their regular salary from wherever they worked.

The demand for workers increased dramatically during the war years, thus increasing wages for workers as well. Union membership increased during the war; unions generally honored "no-strike" agreements that were made in the weeks after Pearl Harbor. Beginning in 1943, some strikes did occur, especially in the coal mines.

The government needed money to finance the war effort. As stated previously, more money was raised by expanding greatly the number of Americans who had to pay income taxes. In addition, America followed a policy begun in World War I and sold **war bonds**.

During both wars, various celebrities made public appearances to encourage the public to buy these bonds.

Average Americans were asked to sacrifice much during the war. Goods such as gasoline, rubber, meat, sugar, and butter were rationed during the war; American families kept **ration cards** to determine which of these goods they could still buy during any given period. Recycling was commonplace during the war, and many had to simply do without the goods they desired. Women, for example, were desperate for silk stockings; some took to drawing a line up the back of their legs to make it appear that they had stockings on.

City dwellers had to take part in "blackouts," where they would have to lower all shades to make any enemy airplane attacks more difficult. Men and boys both took turns at lookout stations, where the skies were constantly scanned for enemy bombers. Many high schools across the country eliminated vacations during the year; by doing this, school could end early and students could go off and do essential work. Many workers stayed for extra shifts at work, called "victory shifts."

Popular culture also reflected the necessities of war. Many movies during the war were light comedies, designed to keep people's minds off the war. Other movies, such as *Casablanca,* emphasized self-sacrifice and helping the war effort. "White Christmas" (sung by Bing Crosby) was a favorite during the war, evoking nostalgia in both soldiers abroad and those on the home front. Professional baseball continued during the war, but rosters were made up of players who had been classified 4-F by local draft boards (unfit for military service). The All-American Girls' Baseball League was founded in 1943 and also provided a wartime diversion for thousands of fans.

Women also entered the American workforce in large numbers during the war. Many women working in "traditional women's jobs" moved to factory jobs vacated when men went off to fight. The figure of **Rosie the Riveter** symbolized American working women during the war. In the 1930s, women were discouraged from working (the argument was that they would be taking jobs from men); during World War II, many posters informed women that it was their patriotic duty to work. Problems remained for women in the workplace, however. For many jobs, even in the defense industry, they were paid less than men. It is also ironic that when the war ended, women were encouraged that it was now their "patriotic duty" to return home and become housewives.

Discrimination During the War

Many blacks also took important factory jobs and eagerly signed up for military service. However, discrimination against blacks continued during the war. Black military units were strictly segregated and were often used for menial chores instead of combat. Some American blacks at home began the **Double V campaign**. This pushed for the defeat of Germany and Japan but also the defeat of racial prejudice. CORE (the Congress for Racial Equality) was founded in 1942, and organized the very first sit-ins and boycotts; these actions would become standard tactics of the civil rights movement in the 1950s and 1960s.

Many on the West Coast feared that the Japanese who lived there were sympathizers or even spies for the Japanese cause (even though many had been born and brought up in the United States). On February 19, 1942, Franklin Roosevelt signed Executive Order 9066, which ordered Japanese Americans to **internment camps**. American public officials told the Japanese that this was being done for their own protection; however, many Japanese noted when they got to their camps that the guns guarding these relocation centers were pointed inward and never outward. Many businesses and homes were lost by Japanese citizens.

Influential Japanese Americans were outraged by these actions, and a legal challenge was mounted against the internment camps. In a 1944 decision, *Korematsu v. United States,* the Supreme Court ruled that the internment camps were legal, since they were based "on military necessity." In 1988, the United States government formally apologized to those who had been placed in camps and gave each survivor $20,000. It should be noted that

American units of soldiers of Japanese descent were created during the war, and that they fought with great bravery in the campaign against Hitler.

Chapter Review

Rapid Review

To achieve the perfect 5, you should be able to explain the following:

- War production for World War II pulled America out of the Great Depression.
- World War II turned America into one of the two major world powers.
- America continued to pursue a foreign policy of isolationism throughout the 1930s.
- Lend-Lease and other measures by Franklin Roosevelt brought America into the war on the side of England one year before America actually entered the war.
- The Pearl Harbor attack was part of an overall Japanese strategy, and it mobilized American public opinion for war.
- Battles fought by American GIs in Africa, Italy, and Western Europe were crucial in creating a "second front" and important in the eventual defeat of Hitler.
- Decision made at the Yalta Conference did much to influence the postwar world.
- Superior American air and sea power ultimately led to the defeat of the Japanese in the Pacific.
- The decision to drop the atomic bomb was based on the calculations of the human cost of an American invasion of Japan and as retaliation for Japanese actions during the war.
- Americans sacrificed greatly during the war and contributed to the Allied victory through rationing, extra work, and the purchase of war bonds.
- American women contributed greatly to the war effort, especially by taking industrial jobs that had been held by departed soldiers.
- Blacks continued to meet with discrimination both in and out of the armed services, as did the Japanese. Japanese citizens from the West Coast were forced to move to internment camps. The American government in 1988 issued a formal apology for these actions.

Time Line

1933: Hitler comes to power in Germany
1935: Neutrality Act of 1935
1938: Hitler annexes Austria, Sudetenland
1939: Nazi-Soviet Pact
   Germany invades Poland/beginning of World War II
1940: Roosevelt reelected for third term
   American Selective Service plan instituted
1941: Lend-Lease assistance begins for England
   Japanese attack on Pearl Harbor/United States officially enters World War II
   Germany declares war on United States
1942: American troops engage in combat in Africa
   Japanese interment camps opened
   Battle of Coral Sea, Battle of Midway
   Casablanca released

1943: Allied armies invade Sicily
United Mine Workers strike
1944: D-Day Invasion
Roosevelt defeats Thomas Dewey, elected for fourth term
Beginning of Battle of the Bulge
1945: Yalta Conference
Concentration camps discovered by Allied forces
FDR dies in Warm Springs, Georgia; Harry Truman becomes president
Germany surrenders unconditionally
Atomic bombs dropped on Hiroshima and Nagasaki
Japan surrenders unconditionally

> Review Questions

1. The internment of Japanese Americans began for all of the reasons listed *except*
   A. It was felt that Japanese living in California had divided loyalties when war began.
   B. Newspapers on the West Coast reported incidents of Japanese Americans aiding the Japanese military effort.
   C. Japanese Americans needed protection, and the camps would provide it for them.
   D. The portrayal of the Japanese in American films and magazines.

2. Which was *not* a reason for the hatred many felt toward the Japanese during the war?
   A. The bombing of Pearl Harbor.
   B. The fact that they were physically different in appearance from most Americans.
   C. The outrage over the Bataan Death March as soon as Americans first learned of it in late 1941.
   D. The portrayal of the Japanese in American films, magazines, and newspapers.

3. Many observers would later be critical of the Yalta Conference for all of the following *except*
   A. At the conference the Soviet Union was given control over more of Germany than the other Allied powers.
   B. The Soviet Union did not promise to join the war against Japan immediately.
   C. Franklin Roosevelt was near death at the time of the conference.
   D. All of the countries liberated by the Soviet Union would remain at least temporarily under Soviet control.

4. The United States did little to stop the spread of Hitler and Nazi Germany in the 1930s because
   A. the United States was much more concerned with diplomatic and political affairs in the Pacific than in Europe in the 1930s.
   B. the United States was more interested in solving domestic problems in the 1930s.
   C. the findings of the Nye commission did much to sour Americans on future military involvement.
   D. B and C

5. Americans continued to crave diversions during World War II and went in large numbers to see all of the following *except*:
   A. Auto racing
   B. Professional baseball
   C. Movies
   D. Big band concerts

Answers and Explanations

1. **C.** Although this was the official reason given at the time, the other reasons listed were the actual reasons. California newspapers reported fabricated stories of Japanese Americans assisting the Japanese war effort.

2. **C.** The Bataan Death March did not occur until 1942, and most Americans did not know about it until 1945.

3. **A.** At the conference, the Soviet Union, England, France, and the United States were all to administer parts of Germany; the Soviets did not get more than anyone else. Criticism existed because by the decisions made at Yalta, the Soviet Union joined the war against Japan only days before Japan was defeated. In addition, "temporary" Soviet control over Eastern Europe allowed Communist governments to be set up there. Other historians question the decisions Franklin Roosevelt made at Yalta; many wonder if his physical and mental condition were adequate for such a conference.

4. **D.** American policies in the 1930s were largely concerned with solving the problems of the Depression, and the Nye commission reported that arms manufacturers, looking for profits, were largely responsible for pushing America into World War I.

5. **A.** Because of shortages of gasoline and rubber for tires, auto racing was almost totally eliminated for much of the war.

CHAPTER 25

Origins of the Cold War (1945–1960)

IN THIS CHAPTER

Summary: Even before the end of World War II, strains began to develop in the wartime alliance between Great Britain, the United States, and the Soviet Union. At the Yalta conference, Soviet leader Joseph Stalin had promised free elections in eastern European countries the Soviet Union liberated from nazism; in the months after the war it became obvious that these elections would not take place. British Prime Minister Winston Churchill warned that the Soviet Union was creating an "iron curtain" between Eastern and Western Europe; the United States began to follow a policy of containment to stop the spread of communism. Through the Marshall Plan, the United States spent millions to rebuild Western Europe after the war. Stalin tested Western will by enforcing a blockade of Berlin in 1948. Western anxieties increased in 1949 when the Soviets announced that they had an atomic bomb and when Communist forces led by Mao Zedong took power over mainland China. The cold war had a major impact at home; the House Un-American Activities Committee (HUAC) began to search for Communists in the entertainment industry, State Department official Alger Hiss was accused of being a Communist spy, and Julius and Ethel Rosenberg were executed for giving atomic secrets to the Soviet Union. During the Korean War, United Nations and American forces were severely tested as they attempted to "contain communism" in Korea. Senator Joseph McCarthy claimed knowledge of Communists in the State Department, the army, and in other branches of government. Both the United States and the Soviet Union built up their military arsenals in the 1950s; by the end of the decade, President Eisenhower warned of the spreading "military-industrial complex."

Keywords

Satellite countries: Eastern European countries that came under the control of the Soviet Union after World War II; the Soviets argued that they had liberated these countries from the Nazis and thus they had a right to continue to influence developments there.

Iron Curtain: Term coined by British Prime Minister Winston Churchill in a March 1946 speech in Fulton, Missouri; Churchill forcefully proclaimed that the Soviet Union was establishing an "iron curtain" between the free countries of Western Europe and the Communist-controlled countries of Eastern Europe.

Containment Policy: policy devised by American diplomat George F. Kennan; Kennan believed that the United States needed to implement long-term military, economic, and diplomatic strategies in order to "contain" the spread of communism. Kennan's ideas became official U.S. government policy in the late 1940s.

Truman Doctrine: articulated in 1947, this policy stated that the United States would support any democratic nation that resisted communism.

Marshall Plan: American plan that spent $12 billion for the rebuilding of Western Europe after World War II; the plan produced an economic revival and helped stave off the growth of Communist influence.

Berlin Airlift: American effort that flew in supplies to West Berlin after the Soviet Union and the East German governments blocked the roads to that city beginning in June 1948; American airplanes flew in supplies for 15 months, causing the Soviet Union to call off the blockade.

NATO: North Atlantic Treaty Organization, a military alliance between the United States and Western European countries that was formed in April 1949.

Warsaw Pact: military pact formed in 1955 between the Soviet Union and its Eastern European satellite countries.

HUAC: House Un-American Activities Committee; in 1947 this committee began to investigate the entertainment industry for Communist influences.

Blacklist: list created by HUAC and various private agencies indicating individuals in the entertainment industry who might be Communists or who might have been influenced by Communists in the past; many individuals named in the blacklist could not find work in the industry until the 1960s.

McCarthyism: term used to describe the accusations by Wisconsin Senator Joseph McCarthy and his supporters in the early 1950s that certain people in government, academia, and the arts were secret Communists. McCarthy's charges were largely unsubstantiated.

Domino theory: theory that if one country in a region fell under Communist rule, then other countries in the region would follow; this theory would be used to justify American involvement in Vietnam.

Sputnik: first artificial satellite, launched in 1957 by the Soviet Union; the fact that the Soviets launched a satellite before the United States shocked many in the American scientific community.

Winning the **cold war** was the central goal of the United States from 1945 all the way until the fall of communism in 1990 to 1991. Almost all domestic and foreign policy decisions made in this era related in some way to American efforts to defeat the Soviet Union and their Allies. A large part of the success of many sectors of the American economy in the post–World War II era was related to defense and defense-related contracts. Some politicians lost their careers in this era if they were perceived to be "soft on communism."

Exactly whose fault was the cold war? Hundreds of books and articles have been written about that very subject. American historians assigned blame to the Soviet Union for aggressive actions on their part in the period immediately following the end of World War II. "**Revisionist**" American historians have claimed that the Soviets were forced into these actions by the perceived aggressiveness of the United States and its Allies. What actually happened in those years immediately following World War II is the subject of this chapter.

First Cracks in the Alliance: 1945

The alliance that proved victorious in World War II began to show strains even before the end of the war. In the preceding chapter, it was mentioned that tough decisions were made at the **Yalta Conference**, including allowing elections in Eastern European nations. Stalin was especially reluctant to allow free elections in Poland; as Hitler demonstrated, it provided a perfect invasion route into Soviet territory.

The United States would be somewhat handicapped diplomatically by the death of Franklin Roosevelt in April 1945. Roosevelt had excellent personal relations with Winston Churchill and felt that he could at least "understand" Stalin. When Harry Truman took over the presidency, he had little experience in foreign affairs, and Roosevelt had met with him only a few times, sharing little about the appropriate way to deal with America's wartime allies.

Truman met Soviet diplomats for the first time at the initial session of the United Nations, which was held in San Francisco two weeks after he took over as president. His first face-to-face meeting with Stalin took place at the **Potsdam Conference**, held at the end of July 1945. Truman, Stalin, and Clement Atlee (who had just replaced Churchill as prime minster) represented the United States, the Soviet Union, and Great Britain, respectively, at this meeting. Again, the future of Eastern Europe was discussed. It was also decided to hold war-crimes trials for top Nazi leaders (the most famous of these would be known as the Nuremberg Trials). At this meeting, Truman announced to Stalin the existence of the atomic bomb (ironically, Stalin had learned of it some two weeks earlier from Soviet spies in the United States).

Great philosophical differences between the two sides were apparent at this meeting. Truman expressed the view that free elections should be held in all Eastern European countries. Stalin, on the other hand, expressed the desire to have Eastern European **satellite countries** that would act as buffers to potential future invasions of the Soviet Union.

The Iron Curtain

During 1946 and 1947, the Soviet Union tightened its hold on Eastern Europe (Romania, Hungary, Bulgaria, Poland, Czechoslovakia, and East Germany). Promised elections in Europe did not actually take place for two years. In some cases, Communists backed by Stalin forced non-Communists, who had been freely elected, out of office.

In March 1946, Winston Churchill made a speech at a college in Fulton, Missouri, where he noted that the Soviet Union had established an **iron curtain** that divided the Soviet Union and its Eastern European satellites from the independent countries of Europe. This speech is often viewed as the symbolic beginning of the cold war.

Another key document from this era was written by American diplomat and expert in Soviet affairs, George F. Kennan. Kennan wrote an anonymous article in *Foreign Affairs* magazine in July 1947 (the author was only identified as "Mr. X"), stating his opinion that Soviet policymakers were deeply committed to the destruction of America and the American way of life. The article maintained that the USSR felt threatened by the United States and felt that it had to expand for self-preservation. Kennan stated that a long-range and long-term **containment policy** to stop communism was needed. According to Kennan, if communism could be contained, it would eventually crumble under its own weight. The policy of containment was central to most American policy toward the Soviet Union for the next 45 years.

If President Truman was looking for an opportunity to apply the containment policy, opportunities soon presented themselves in Turkey and Greece. The Soviets desperately desired to control the Dardanelles Strait; this Turkish-controlled area would allow Soviet ships to go from the Black Sea into the Mediterranean. In addition, Communists were threatening the existing government in Greece. In February 1947, the British (still suffering severe economic aftershocks from World War II) stated that they could no longer financially assist the Turkish and Greek governments, and suggested that the United States step in (some historians maintain that this symbolically ended Great Britain's great power status and demonstrated that now the United States was one of the two major players on the world stage). In March 1947, the president announced the **Truman Doctrine**, which stated that it would become the stated duty of the United States to assist all democratic nations of the world who resisted communism. Congress authorized $400 million in aid for Greece and Turkey. The policies outlined in the Truman Doctrine and in George Kennan's article can be found embedded in American foreign policy all the way through the 1980s.

Marshall Plan

Most Americans applauded Truman's decision to help countries resisting communism. Others wanted to see a much larger American role in Europe in the postwar era. Several observers stated that Hitler was able to rise to power because of the lack of stability in both the German government and economy in the era following World War I, and that such a situation should never be allowed to develop again.

Many felt that it was the duty of the United States to rebuild the devastated countries of Europe after World War II; it was felt that, in the long run, this would bring both political and economic benefits to the Western world.

By the terms of the **Marshall Plan**, the United States provided nearly $12 billion in economic aid to help rebuild Europe. This assistance was of a strictly nonmilitary nature, and was designed, in large measure, to prevent Western Europe from falling into economic collapse. Seventeen Western European nations received aid under the Marshall Plan; several of them became valuable trading partners of the United States by the early part of the 1950s. The Soviet Union was invited to apply for aid from the Marshall Plan. Stalin refused and ordered the Soviet satellite countries to do the same.

Berlin: The First Cold War Crisis

In 1948, the Americans, French, and British announced that they were to combine their areas of occupation in Germany and create the Federal Republic of Germany. West Berlin (located within the eastern zone of Germany) was supposed to join this Federal Republic. Berlin was already a "problem city" for Communist authorities. Many residents of East Berlin (and other residents of Eastern Europe) escaped communism by passing from East Berlin to West Berlin.

In June 1948, Soviet and East German military units blocked off transportation by road into West Berlin. Historians of Soviet foreign policy note that this was the first real test by Stalin of Western cold war resolve. Truman authorized the institution of the **Berlin Airlift**; for nearly 15 months, American and British pilots flew in enough food and supplies for West Berlin to survive. The Americans and British achieved at least a public relations victory when Stalin ordered the lifting of the blockade in May 1949. Shortly afterward, the French, English, and American zones of occupation were joined together into "West Germany," and the Americans stationed troops there to guard against further Soviet actions.

One month earlier, the United States, Canada, and 10 Western European countries had announced the formation of **NATO (North Atlantic Treaty Organization)**. The main provision of the NATO treaty was that an attack on one signatory nation would be considered an attack on all of them. The NATO treaty placed America squarely in the middle of European affairs for the foreseeable future. NATO would expand in the early 1950s, and, as a response to NATO, the Soviet Union and its satellite countries created the **Warsaw Pact** in 1955.

1949: A Pivotal Year in the Cold War

In 1949, two events occurred that rocked American postwar confidence. In September, the Soviets announced that they had exploded an atomic bomb. The potential threat of nuclear annihilation was an underlying fear for many Americans throughout the 1950s. Truman quickly gave authorization for American scientists to begin work on the **hydrogen bomb**, a bomb much more powerful than the atomic bombs dropped on Hiroshima and Nagasaki.

An equally horrifying event occurred shortly after the successful Soviet atomic test. Since 1945, the United States had been a major financial backer of Nationalist China, led by Chiang Kai-shek. Communist guerrilla forces under Mao Tse-tung were able to capture much of the Chinese countryside. In 1949, Mao's forces captured Peking, the capital city. The People's Republic of China was established by Mao. Nationalist forces were forced to flee to Formosa (now Taiwan). From Formosa, Chiang Kai-shek and the Nationalists maintained that they were the "true" government of China, and continued to receive a very sizable aid package from the United States. The question of "who lost China" would be repeatedly asked over the next 10 years in the United States, usually to attack the president, Harry Truman, and the Democratic party, who were in power when Nationalist China fell.

Middle East in the Early Years of the Cold War

In the years immediately after World War II, the United States continued to take a back seat to the British in terms of influencing leaders and events in the Middle East. It was the 1947 decision by the British to stop assisting the Turks and Greeks (followed by the articulation of the Truman Doctrine by the president) that drastically increased the role of the United States in the region.

Since the 1920s, a major reason for American interest in the region was oil: this certainly did not decline in the cold war era. It should be noted that in the late 1940s and early 1950s, the United States itself was not dependent on oil from the region; however, two regions that the United States was trying to rebuild, Western Europe and Japan, desperately needed Middle Eastern oil. In the late 1940s, the Truman administration cemented relations with Saudi Arabia, America's major trading partner for oil since the 1930s. Tax policies encouraged American oil companies to do business with the Saudis, and the Americans pledged to assist Saudi Arabia if it was attacked by the Soviets. The fact that the United States was establishing a seemingly close relationship with a completely undemocratic regime was largely unnoticed by American commentators at the time; observers today note that in their quest for oil, Americans have developed these same "close relationships" with countless despotic kings and other authoritarian rulers in the region.

In addition, sections of the Middle East were very close to the U.S. new enemy, the Soviet Union. American planners and decision makers wanted to: (1) ensure that the region would not be vulnerable to potential attacks by the Soviets and (2) utilize the region as a staging point for potential military advances against the Soviet Union (American missiles placed in Turkey were as close to some of their targets as Soviet missiles in Cuba were to their targets in the 1962 Cuban Missile Crisis).

Role of the United States in the Creation of Israel

The entire dynamic of the Middle East was changed by the establishment of the state of Israel in 1948. The United States played a key role in this pivotal event. The pressure for the creation of a Jewish state in Palestine increased enormously as a result of the Holocaust in Europe. Great Britain had governed Palestine by mandate since the 1920s, but stated in 1947 that the United Nations should decide the future of the region. The UN announced its support for a plan that would divide Palestine into Jewish and Arab sections.

The Arab states unanimously rejected this plan, noting that countless non-Jewish residents of Palestine would be uprooted if it were implemented. The U.S. State Department opposed the partition plan, noting that it went against long-standing American support of the principle of "self-determination" in regions such as this. Nevertheless, President Truman announced his support of the plan and instructed American diplomats to "twist some arms" to get other countries to support it.

After the United Nations narrowly supported the plan, fighting began between Jews and Arabs living in Palestine. Countless Arabs were forced to flee the Jewish-controlled regions. Throughout the Arab world, the United States began to be blamed for the bloodshed in Palestine; President Truman and others in the American government were perceived as the ones who had forced this "solution" through the United Nations. In 1948, the independent state of Israel was proclaimed and was immediately recognized by the United States (some historians maintain that the main reason for this was to recognize Israel before the Soviets could). The Arab states surrounding Palestine immediately attacked the new state of Israel, but were defeated.

Conflict between Israel and its neighbors has remained a constant ever since, with Israel winning two more major wars with its neighbors. Another constant is the "special relationship" that will continue to exist between the United States and Israel. Israel's strongest backer in virtually every crisis has been the United States. Americans have given millions of dollars of military aid to the Israelis. There have been situations where virtually the entire world has condemned the Israelis for its actions against its neighbors; in almost every case, the United States has continued to back Israel. There are countless reasons why the United States and Israel have developed this special relationship. However, this relationship is also the reason for the animosity that exists in much of the Arab world toward the United States.

United States and the Shah of Iran

When Dwight Eisenhower became president in 1953, he faced a new and potentially more volatile force in the Middle East: Arab nationalism. In an early press conference, Eisenhower stated that he favored political independence for the peoples of the region. Nevertheless, he stated, this could not be done "too quickly," as a power vacuum might develop that would allow the Soviets an opportunity to expand into the region.

In 1951, Prime Minister Mohammed Mossadeq of Iran announced a plan to nationalize the British oil facilities in the country. Many in Iran viewed him as a hero for opposing British imperialism in the region. The British imposed an oil embargo on Iranian oil and proposed military action against Mossadeq (which was opposed by the United States). The Shah of Iran, who was actually in charge of the government, was a favorite of American officials; Washington became increasingly concerned when Mossadeq began to quietly question the Shah's relationship with the United States.

With Eisenhower's approval, the CIA went to Iran and financed anti-Mossadeq demonstrations, which eventually led to his downfall. Mossadeq was replaced by a prime minister who was loyal to the Shah (and not opposed to American influence in the country). In the long run, the American role in the removal of Mossadeq from power would prove detrimental to the image of the United States in the region. After the events of 1953, the Shah ruled as a brutal autocrat; the perception was that the Shah's actions were sanctioned by the United States. When the American embassy in Tehran was occupied by Islamic militants in 1979, the actions by the CIA in Iran in 1953 were long-forgotten by virtually everyone in the United States; to many Iranians, the effects of American actions in Iran in 1953 were still very much alive.

As this section demonstrates, anti-American sentiment in the Middle East did not begin with the Iranian hostage crisis or with Saddam Hussein. In reality, resentment of the United States began to brew in the early years of the cold war and intensified over the years as countless American officials have been pictured smiling and shaking hands with rulers in the region who have little or no regard for the people whom they govern.

Cold War at Home

During 1949 and 1950, many Americans felt a sense that the tides of the cold war were somehow shifting over in favor of the Soviet Union. Many felt that the Soviet Union could never do this alone, and that they *had* to have a large number of spies within the United States helping them. Thus, under President Truman and later under President Eisenhower, there was a tremendous effort made to rid the United States of a perceived internal "Communist menace."

As stated in Chapter 21, on the depression, many idealists had dabbled in communism in the 1930s; this "dabbling" would now come back to haunt them.

The Truman administration began by jailing the leaders of the American Communist party under the provisions of the 1940 Smith Act. This document stated that it was illegal to advocate the overthrow by force of the American government. When some Republicans claimed that the Truman administration was "soft on communism," Truman ordered the creation of a **Loyalty Review Board**, which eventually had the legal jurisdiction to investigate both new and experienced federal workers. Three or four million federal workers were examined by the board; as a result of these investigations, slightly over 100 workers were removed from their jobs. Investigations revealed that some of those investigated were homosexuals, who were often hounded out of office as well.

While the Truman administration was investigating the executive branch of government, Congress decided to investigate Communists in the government and in the entertainment industry. The congressional committee overseeing these investigations was the **HUAC (House Un-American Activities Committee)**. In 1947, the HUAC began to investigate the movie industry in earnest. Committee investigators relentlessly pursued actors, directors, and writers who had attended Communist party meetings in the past. Directors of movies made during World War II who cast the Soviet Union in a favorable light (such as *Mission to Moscow* and *North Star*) were brought in for questioning. Dozens of writers, actors, and directors were called in to testify about their political orientation. The Hollywood Ten was an influential group of writers and directors who refused to answer questions posed to them by members of the HUAC in an open congressional session. Members of the Hollywood Ten were all sentenced to jail time.

The effects on Hollywood were major. Some Hollywood movies of the late 1940s dealt directly with the problems of society (such as *The Best Years of their Lives*). As a result of pressure from the HUAC, Hollywood movies became much more tame. In addition, a **blacklist** was made of actors, directors, and writers who were potentially Communist and whom the major studios should *not* hire. Many Hollywood careers were ruined by the blacklist; some writers wrote under false names or had "fronts" turn in their screenplays for them. Some of those blacklisted were unable to get work until the early 1960s.

On the Senate side, Senator Pat McCarran sponsored several bills to "stop the spread of communism" in the United States. The **McCarran Internal Security Act** was enacted in 1950; under this bill, all Communist or Communist-front organizations had to register with the government, and members of these organizations could not work in any job related to the national defense. The **McCarran-Walter Act** of 1952 greatly limited immigration from Asia and Eastern Europe; this would hopefully limit the "influx of communism" into the United States. President Truman vetoed both these bills, but Congress passed both of them over the president's veto.

Were There Spies in America?

The trials of Alger Hiss and the Rosenbergs indicated to many Americans that there just might be Communist spies infiltrating America. In 1948, the HUAC began an investigation of Hiss, a former official in the State Department and an advisor to Franklin Roosevelt at the Yalta Conference. An editor of *Time* magazine, Whitaker Chambers, had previously been a Communist and testified to the HUAC that Hiss had been a Communist too. After several trials, Hiss was finally convicted for perjury and spent four years in jail. To this day, the guilt or innocence of Alger Hiss is still debated.

In 1950, Julius and Ethel Rosenberg were charged with passing atomic secrets to the Soviet Union. The government had much more evidence on Julius than on his wife, but they were both found guilty of espionage in 1952 and executed. Considerable debate has also taken place on the guilt of the Rosenbergs, although materials released from the Soviet archives after the fall of communism strongly implicated Ethel. Material from these archives demonstrated that some Communists in the United States had closer ties to Moscow than was previously believed.

Heating of the Cold War: Korea

After World War II, Korea was divided into a Communist North Korea and a non-Communist and pro-American South Korea, divided along the **38th parallel**. In late June 1950, North Korea invaded the south. The Security Council of the United Nations voted to send in a peacekeeping force (the Soviet Union was protesting the UN's decision not to allow Communist China in as a member and failed to attend the Security Council session when this was discussed). Douglas MacArthur was appointed to lead the UN forces, and the **Korean War** began.

UN forces under MacArthur drove northward into North Korea. In late November, forces from Communist China forced MacArthur's troops to retreat, yet by March 1951, his troops were on the offensive again. MacArthur was very critical of President Truman's handling of the war, demanding a greatly intensified bombing campaign and suggesting that Truman order the Nationalist Chinese to attack the Chinese mainland. In April 1951, Truman finally fired MacArthur for insubordination. Armistice talks to end the war dragged on for nearly two years; in the end, it was decided to divide North and South Korea along the 38th parallel (along virtually the same line that divided them before the war!). More than 57,000 Americans died in this "forgotten war."

Rise of McCarthyism

The seeming inability of America to decisively defeat communism both abroad and at home led to the meteoric rise of Senator Joseph McCarthy of Wisconsin. In a speech in Wheeling, West Virginia, on February 9, 1950, McCarthy announced that he had a list of 205 known Communists who were working in the State Department. McCarthy's list was sometimes longer and sometimes smaller, and often also included prominent diplomats, scholars, and Defense Department and military figures. **McCarthyism** was the ruthless searching out of Communists in the government that took place in this period, largely without any real evidence.

For four years, McCarthy reigned supreme in Washington, with few in power or in the news media being willing to challenge him. McCarthy offered a simple reason why the United States was not conclusively winning the cold war: because of Communists in the government. The Republican party was a semireluctant supporter of McCarthy in this era; a number of Republicans were skeptical of many of McCarthy's charges, but realized that anticommunism was a "winner" for Republicans politically. McCarthy even accused Harry Truman and former Secretary of State Marshall of being "unconscious" agents of the Communist conspiracy.

In March 1954, McCarthy claimed in a lengthy speech that the U.S. Army was full of Communists as well. It was at this point that McCarthy began to run into major opposition; Republican President Eisenhower (a former general) stated privately that it was definitely time for McCarthy to be stopped. Tensions between the army and McCarthy increased when it was announced that McCarthy had asked for special privileges for an aide of his that had been drafted.

The **Army-McCarthy Hearings** appeared on network television, and thousands found themselves riveted to them on a daily basis. Over the course of the hearings, it was discovered that McCarthy *had* asked for special favors for his aide, had doctored photographs, and had used bullying tactics on a regular basis. The end was clearly in sight for McCarthy when Joseph Welch, attorney for the army, received loud applause when he asked McCarthy if he had any "sense of decency" and when reporter Edwin R. Murrow went on CBS News with a negative report about McCarthy and his tactics. In late 1954, McCarthy was formally censured by the Senate. His power gone, McCarthy died only three years later. The McCarthy era is now remembered as one in which attack by innuendo was common and where, during the investigations to "get at the truth" about communism, the civil rights of many were violated. It should be noted that several biographies have been published in the last few years exonerating McCarthy and his tactics.

Cold War Policies of President Eisenhower

Foreign policy decisions of the Eisenhower administration were often crafted by the Secretary of State, John Foster Dulles. Dulles felt that the policy of containment was not nearly aggressive enough; instead of merely containment, Dulles often spoke of "**massive retaliation**" against Communist advances anywhere in the world. Dulles also spoke of the need to use nuclear weapons if necessary. At one press conference, Dulles stated that instead of containing communism, the goal of the United States should be to "make communism retreat" whenever and wherever possible.

Eisenhower hoped that the death of Stalin in 1953 would allow a "new understanding" between the United States and the Soviet Union. In some ways, Nikita Khrushchev was different from Stalin, speaking about the possibilities of "peaceful coexistence" with the United States. However, when Hungary revolted in 1956, Khrushchev ordered this to be brutally stopped by the Soviet army.

The fate of the Hungarian leader Irme Nagy was sealed when the United States failed to assist the anti-Soviet rebellion of his government. Despite the tough talk of John Foster Dulles, who had boldly proclaimed that the United States would come to the aid of any in Eastern Europe who wanted to "liberate" themselves from communism, it was determined that U.S. forces could not be used to help the Hungarian rebels (despite the fact that the CIA operatives in Hungary had promised Nagy this aid), because this might provoke war with the Soviets. Eisenhower was also reluctant to get militarily involved in Southeast Asia, even though he believed in the **domino theory**, which proclaimed that if one country in Southeast Asia fell to the Communists, others would follow. In 1954, French forces in Vietnam were being overrun by nationalist forces under the control of Ho Chi Minh. The French desperately asked for aid. Despite segments of the American military who pushed for assisting the French, Eisenhower ultimately refused.

As a result, the French were finally defeated at the **Battle of Dien Bien Phu**. After they left, an international conference took place and the **Geneva Accords** established a North Vietnam under the control of Ho Chi Minh and a South Vietnam under the control of the Emperor, Bao Dai. From the beginning, the United States supplied military aid to South Vietnam. By the terms of the Geneva Accords, a national election was scheduled for 1956 on the potential unification of the entire country. However, a coup in South Vietnam overthrew the emperor and sabotaged the election plans. Nevertheless, the United States continued to support South Vietnam.

The major Middle Eastern crisis during the era was the Suez Canal crisis. The United States had helped Egyptian leader Colonel Gamal Abdul Nasser build the Aswan Dam. The Egyptians wanted to purchase arms from the United States as well. When the Americans refused, the Egyptians went to the Soviets with the same request. When the United States (and Great Britain), in response, totally cut off all loans to Egypt, Nasser nationalized the British-owned Suez Canal. The British and the French attacked Egypt. In response to Soviet threats that they might join the conflict on the side of the Egyptians, the Americans got the British and French to retreat from Egypt.

Eisenhower and Dulles desperately wanted to prevent the spread of communism in the Middle East. In January 1957, the **Eisenhower Doctrine** was formally unveiled, which stated that Americans arms would be used in the region to prevent Communist aggression. The Americans invoked the Eisenhower Doctrine when they landed troops in Beirut, Lebanon, in mid-1958 to put down a rebellion against the government.

The Americans were equally concerned with the spread of communism in Latin America, where America had numerous economic interests. A defensive alliance of most nations of the Western Hemisphere was signed as the **Rio Pact** in 1947. Critics would argue that the United States was never shy about throwing its weight around in the region. In 1954, the CIA helped orchestrate the overthrow of the president of Guatemala on the grounds that his administration was too friendly with the Soviet Union; during this coup, property that had been seized from American businesses was restored to American hands.

In 1959, Fidel Castro orchestrated the removal of dictator Fulgencio Batista from power. Castro soon seized American businesses located in Cuba and began trade negotiations with the Soviet Union. Thus, beginning in late 1960, the United States cut off trade with Cuba, and eventually cut off diplomatic relations with the island (a situation that still exists today).

Dangerous Arms Buildup

During the Eisenhower administration, both the United States and the Soviet Union built up their nuclear arsenals to dangerously high levels. By August 1953 both countries had exploded hydrogen bombs, which made the bomb used at Hiroshima look primitive in comparison. Both countries carried out nuclear tests, although in 1958 Eisenhower and Khrushchev both agreed to suspend further atomic tests in the atmosphere.

The Soviets concentrated on building up their missile capabilities in this period, causing some Americans to fear that they were falling behind, and that a "missile gap" was developing. The startling fact that the Soviets might be ahead in technology was demonstrated by their 1957 launching of *Sputnik*, the first man-made satellite that could orbit the earth. Americans were shocked as they could look up in the sky and see the satellite whiz by (in the next two years, many American high schools and colleges increased the number of math and science courses students had to take so that Americans could "keep up" with the Soviets). Even more troubling was the fact that American tests to create a man-made satellite had failed.

A final humiliation for the United States came in May 1960, when the Russians shot down an American **U-2** spy plane. The pilot, Francis Gary Powers, was captured and taken prisoner by Soviet forces. For several days, the Americans refused to admit that an American plane had even been shot down; Eisenhower eventually took full responsibility for the incident.

Toward the end of his term in office, Eisenhower warned of the extreme challenge to peace posed by the massive "military-industrial complex" that existed in America in the 1950s. The size of the military-industrial complex would certainly not decline in the 1960s.

Chapter Review

Rapid Review

To achieve the perfect 5, you should be able to explain the following:

- Winning the cold war was the central goal of American policy for 45 years.
- Economic impact of the cold war on American industry was enormous; many plants continued making military hardware throughout the cold war era.
- Debate over who "started" the cold war has occupied the minds of historians since 1945.
- Decisions made at the Yalta and Potsdam conferences ushered in cold war tensions between the World War II victors.
- Concept of the "iron curtain" was first articulated by Winston Churchill in 1946.
- American strategy of containment motivated many foreign policy decisions in the cold war era.
- The Truman Doctrine, the Marshall Plan, and NATO united America and Western Europe both militarily and economically against the Soviet Union and its satellites.
- America's resolve to oppose communism was tested during the Berlin Crisis and the Korean War.
- 1949 was a critical year in the cold war, as the Soviet Union got the atomic bomb and mainland China turned Communist.
- Some Americans feared that Communists had infiltrated the American government and the entertainment industry; investigations by the House Un-American Activities Committee and Senator Joseph McCarthy were dedicated to "rooting out" Communists in America.
- Under President Dwight Eisenhower, Secretary of State John Foster Dulles formulated an aggressive foreign policy that would not just contain communism but also attempt to roll communism back whenever possible.
- During the Eisenhower administration, crises in Southeast Asia, the Middle East, and Latin America further tested American resolve.
- Both the Soviet Union and the United States built up their nuclear arsenals to dangerous levels in this era.

Time Line

1945: Yalta Conference
Harry Truman becomes president
Potsdam Conference
1946: Winston Churchill gives "iron curtain" speech
Article by George Kennan on containment
1947: HUAC begins probe into movie industry
Introduction of Federal Employee Loyalty program
President Truman articulates Truman Doctrine

1948: Berlin Airlift
Implementation of Marshall Plan
Creation of nation of Israel
Alger Hiss implicated as a Communist
1949: NATO established
Soviet Union successfully tests atomic bomb
Mainland China turns Communist
1950: Joseph McCarthy gives speech on Communists in the State Department
Alger Hiss convicted of perjury
McCarran Internal Security Act enacted
Beginning of Korean War
1952: Dwight Eisenhower elected president
1953: CIA orchestrates return of Shah of Iran to power
Death of Joseph Stalin
Execution of the Rosenbergs
1954: Army-McCarthy hearings
Government in Guatemala overthrown
French defeated at Dien Bien Phu
Geneva Conference
1955: Creation of the Warsaw Pact
1956: Hungarian Revolt suppressed by Soviet Union
Suez crisis
1957: *Sputnik* launched by Soviet Union
1959: Castro comes to power in Cuba; United States halts trade with Cuba
1960: U-2 incident
John Kennedy elected president

> Review Questions

1. The Army-McCarthy hearings proved
   A. that Americans were largely uninterested in the issue of communism.
   B. that Eisenhower would support McCarthy at any cost.
   C. that McCarthy had little proof for his claims.
   D. the massive popularity of Joseph McCarthy.

2. The policy of containment stated that
   A. America should go out and attempt to dislodge Communist leaders wherever possible.
   B. America should hold firm against Communist encroachment in all parts of the world.
   C. America should not hesitate to use atomic weapons against the Soviet Union.
   D. the United States should depend on its Western European Allies for help against the Soviet Union.

3. America was especially interested in stopping Communist expansion in Latin America because
   A. the United States had many economic interests in the region.
   B. both presidents Truman and Eisenhower were close to many of the Latin American leaders.
   C. the Soviet Union expressed a special interest in expanding in this region.
   D. the CIA had repeatedly failed in operations in Latin America in the past.

4. When the HUAC began their investigation of the movie industry, they looked with suspicion at writers, actors, and directors who
   A. attended Communist party meetings in the 1930s
   B. wrote or appeared in World War II–era films that were sympathetic to the Soviet Union
   C. invoked the Fifth Amendment when testifying before the HUAC
   D. all of the above

5. Republicans claimed that the Democrats were "soft on communism" for all of the following reasons *except*
   A. During the Truman administration mainland China had gone Communist.
   B. Alger Hiss was an advisor to Franklin Roosevelt at Yalta.
   C. The Truman administration failed to establish a system to check on the possibility of Communists working for the federal government.
   D. Decisions made by Roosevelt and Truman at the end of World War II made it easier for the Soviet Union to control Eastern Europe.

› Answers and Explanations

1. **C.** The hearings did much to discredit McCarthy. By this point, Eisenhower had broken from McCarthy, and many Americans watched these hearings from beginning to end.

2. **B.** Containment emphasized stopping communism whenever it attempted to expand; containment did not emphasize attacking communism where it already existed.

3. **A.** The United States had factories in and active trade relationships with many Latin American countries, and feared that communism would destroy American economic interests in the region. The CIA had actually been quite successful in their operations in the region in the past—witness their role in Guatemala.

4. **D.** As a result of the HUAC hearings, the American movie industry changed dramatically.

5. **C.** All of the other three were used by Republicans to say that the Democrats were indeed "soft on communism." Truman instituted a Loyalty Review Board to verify that nearly 4 million federal workers were "true Americans."

CHAPTER 26

Prosperity and Anxiety: The 1950s

IN THIS CHAPTER
Summary: In the 1950s, many middle-class, white American families experienced a prosperity they had never known before. Many young couples moved to the suburbs and purchased their first home (for veterans, this could be partially financed by the GI Bill). Observers noted that Dwight Eisenhower was the perfect president for the seemingly placid 1950s. Many commentators wrote on the conformity of American suburban life in the period. However, there were also many Americans pushing for change. Proponents of civil rights for black Americans were heartened by the 1954 *Brown v. Board of Education* Supreme Court decision outlawing segregation in public schools, yet found that their struggles would continue throughout this decade and all through the next. Many women felt frustrated in the role of housewife that they were expected to play in suburban America. Many teenagers rebelled in the decade as well, by emulating the "rebellious" movie star James Dean, by dabbling in Beat poetry, or by listening to the new rock 'n' roll music.

Keywords
***Brown v. Board of Education* (1954):** Supreme Court decision stating that "separate but equal" schools for white and black students were unconstitutional and that school districts across America must desegregate with "all deliberate speed"; controversy over enforcement of this decision was to last for more than a decade.

Montgomery bus boycott (1955): effort by blacks in Montgomery, Alabama, to have the local bus company end discriminatory seating and hiring policies. The movement started with the arrest of Rosa Parks for refusing to give up her bus seat to a white man; the boycott was later led by the Rev. Martin Luther King, Jr.

Baby boom: from 1947 to 1962 Americans married and had children at a record pace; the "high point" of the baby boom was 1957.
The Feminine Mystique: book written by Betty Friedan describing the frustration felt by suburban women in the 1950s; this book was a landmark for feminists of the 1960s and 1970s.
James Dean: young actor whose character in the film *Rebel Without a Cause* inspired many rebellious young people of the 1950s.
Beat Generation: literary movement of the 1950s; writers of this movement rejected the materialistic American culture of the decade. Jack Kerouac, Allen Ginsberg, and William Burroughs were key writers of this movement.

Economic Growth and Prosperity

Some economists feared that the ending of World War II would lead to economic recession. Instead, the American economy enjoyed tremendous growth in the period between 1945 and 1960. In 1945, the American gross national product (GNP) stood at just over $200 billion; by 1960, the GNP had grown to over $500 billion.

A significant reason for this growth was the ever-growing spending on defense during the cold war era. The "military-industrial complex" (a term coined by Dwight D. Eisenhower) was responsible for billions of dollars of new spending during the 1950s (and far beyond). Millions were spent on technological research throughout the era.

Other significant factors were responsible for the economic growth of the era. Consumers had accumulated significant amounts of cash during World War II, but had little to spend it on, as the production of consumer goods was not emphasized in the war era. With the war over, consumers wanted to spend. Credit cards were available to consumers for the first time; Diner's Club cards were issued for the first time in 1950. Two industries that benefited from this were the automobile industry and the housing industry.

Many American households had never owned a new automobile since the 1920s, and in the postwar era, demand for cars was at a record high. If consumers needed assistance in deciding on which automobile to buy, they could receive assistance from the advertisers who were working for the various automobile companies (advertising reached levels in the 1950s equal to the 1920s). As the 1950s wore on, consumers could buy cars with bigger and bigger fins and fancier and fancier interiors. President Eisenhower and Congress encouraged America's reliance on the automobile when they enacted legislation authorizing the massive buildup of the interstate highway system (at the expense of the construction of an effective mass transit system). The highway system was a by-product of national defense plans of the cold war; planners thought they would be ideal for troop movements and that airplanes could easily land on the straight sections of them.

The other industry that experienced significant growth in the postwar era was the housing construction business. There was a dire shortage of available housing in the immediate postwar era; in many cities, two families living in an apartment designed for one was commonplace. Housing was rapidly built in the postwar era, and the demand was insatiable. The **GI Bill** of 1944 authorized low-interest mortgage loans for ex-servicemen (as well as subsidies for education).

William Levitt helped ease the housing crises when he built his initial group of dwellings in Levittown, New York. Several other **Levittowns** were constructed; homes were prefabricated, were built using virtual assembly line practices, and all looked remarkably the same. Nevertheless, William Levitt and developers like him began the move to the suburbs, the most significant population shift of the postwar era.

The economy was also spurred by the mass of appliances desired by consumers for their new homes in the suburbs. Refrigerators, televisions, washing machines, and countless other appliances were found in suburban households; advertising helped ensure that the same refrigerator and television would be found in homes across the nation. Economist John Kenneth Galbraith noted that, by the 1950s, America had become an "**affluent society.**" It should be noted, however, that even though the economy of the era enjoyed tremendous growth, the wages of many workers lagged behind spiraling prices. For many workers, real income declined; this led to labor unrest in the postwar era.

Political Developments of the Postwar Era

It would have been difficult for anyone to follow Franklin Roosevelt as president, and Harry Truman, in the opinion of many, definitely suffered in comparison. Although Truman stated that "the buck stops here" when decisions were made, many critics felt that he had no consistent set of beliefs to guide him as he decided policy. Truman was considered antiunion by much of organized labor, yet he vetoed a key piece of legislation designed to take power away from labor unions. There were many strikes in 1946 and 1947, and the **Taft-Hartley Act** was passed by Congress in 1947 over the president's veto (several biographers claim that Truman's veto was primarily symbolic and was done for political reasons). This bill stated that if any strike affected the health and safety of the country, the president could call for an 80-day cooling off period, during which negotiations could take place and workers would go back to work, that the union contributions of individuals could not be used in federal elections, and that union leaders had to officially declare they were not Communists. Unions were furious at these and other restrictions the bill imposed on them.

Truman declared a **Fair Deal** policy, in which he tried to expand the principles of the New Deal. Included in Truman's Fair Deal were plans for national health care and civil rights legislation; Truman also wanted to repeal the Taft-Hartley Act and increase government spending for public housing and education. In early 1948, he sent a civil rights bill to Congress (the first civil rights bill sent to Congress by a president since the Reconstruction). Nevertheless, Truman's popularity in early 1948 was low. Republicans rallied behind second-time candidate Thomas Dewey (who had been defeated by Franklin Roosevelt in 1944) and felt that victory would be theirs. Truman's chances seemed especially dim when Strom Thurmond also ran as a Dixiecrat candidate (in opposition to a civil rights plank in the 1948 Democratic platform) and Henry Wallace, Truman's secretary of commerce, ran as a Progressive. The highlight of Truman's political career was his eventual victory over Dewey; Truman's success is attributed to the fact that he campaigned more against the "do-nothing" Republican Congress than he did against Dewey. Truman could never capitalize on his 1948 victory; in the years after this victory, charges of being "soft on communism" plagued the administration.

Truman decided not to seek reelection in 1952, and former general Dwight D. Eisenhower defeated Adlai Stevenson in the general election. As president, Eisenhower saw his role as a crafter of compromise, and not as a creator of new policies. He tried to oversee a scaling back of government shift of power to the courts and to Congress. Eisenhower also shifted much of the power traditionally held by the president to his cabinet and other advisors. He was similar to the Republican presidents of the 1920s in that he was extremely friendly to business interests; most members of his cabinet were businessmen. At many levels, Dwight Eisenhower was the perfect president for the 1950s.

Eisenhower's vice president was Richard Nixon, a former member of the House of Representatives and U.S. Senate from California. Nixon had first made a political name for himself in the Alger Hiss case, and his role in the 1952 campaign was largely as an anti-Communist hatchet man. Midway through the campaign, it was charged that supporters had set up an illegal campaign fund for his personal use. Candidate Eisenhower gave Nixon the opportunity to give a public speech to try to save himself. During the **Checkers Speech**, Nixon declared that he had done nothing wrong, that his wife Pat wore a "very respectable Republican cloth coat," and the only thing given to him had been a dog, Checkers. Nixon remained on the ticket, thus saving a political career that would make him one of the most dominant figures in American politics for the next 25 years.

Civil Rights Struggles of the Postwar Period

Many black veterans who had gone overseas to fight for democracy were appalled to find that conditions for blacks had remained largely unchanged during the war years. After speaking to many leaders from NAACP and CORE in early 1948, Truman outlawed discrimination in the hiring of federal employees and ordered the end to segregation in the armed forces. Change in both the federal government and the armed forces was slow.

Black athletes had often been heroes for large segments of the black population. In the 1930s and early 1940s, it had been Joe Louis; starting in 1947, Jackie Robinson became the first black to play major league baseball, wearing the uniform of the Brooklyn Dodgers. Robinson had to endure threats and racial slurs throughout his first season. Nevertheless, Robinson maintained his dignity and was named National League Rookie of the Year in 1947.

Black leaders had long wanted to strike down the 1896 *Plessy v. Feguson* case, which stated that as long as black and white schools or facilities were "equal," it was not unconstitutional that they were separate. In reality, schools in many districts were separate, but they were in no way equal; white schools would get 80 or 85 percent of the financial allocations in some Southern cities and towns. The case that challenged the 1896 law came from Oliver Brown from Topeka, Kansas, who sued the Topeka school district because his daughter had to walk by an all-white school to get to the bus that took her to an all-black school on the other side of town.

The case made it all the way to the Supreme Court and was argued there by NAACP lawyer Thurgood Marshall (later a U.S. Supreme Court justice). The case was heard by a court presided over by Earl Warren, former governor of California and appointed chief justice by Eisenhower in 1953. By a unanimous decision, the 1954 ***Brown v. Board of Education*** decision stated that "separate but equal" was unconstitutional, and that local districts should desegregate with "all deliberate speed." Parents, government officials, and students in many districts in the South responded: "2, 4, 6, 8. We don't want to integrate!" Earl Warren was chief justice from 1953 to 1969, during which the Court practiced "judicial activism," making important decisions on topics such as the rights of the accused and prayer in schools.

The main battlefield for civil rights in 1955 was in Montgomery, Alabama. Rosa Parks, a secretary for the Montgomery NAACP, refused to give up her seat for a white man to sit in, and was arrested. Civil rights leaders in Montgomery began the **Montgomery bus**

boycott, during which blacks in the city refused to ride the city buses; instead, they carpooled or walked. The bus company refused to change its policies; finally, the Supreme Court stepped in again and stated that segregation on city buses (like in schools) was unconstitutional. A 27-year-old minister by the name of Martin Luther King, Jr., became the main spokesperson for the blacks of the city.

Another major battle for civil rights took place in Little Rock, Arkansas, in 1957. A small number of black students were set to enroll in Central High School in Little Rock in the fall of 1957. The governor of Arkansas, Orval Faubus, sent the National Guard to Central High School to keep the black students out. President Eisenhower had personally been opposed to the *Brown v. Board of Education* decision, but saw this as a direct challenge to a Supreme Court decision and to the authority of the federal government. Eisenhower sent in federal troops and federalized the National Guard; under armed guard, the black students attended Central High School in Little Rock, Arkansas, that year. Decisions by the federal courts outlawing various forms of segregation, and federal troops in Southern states enforcing these federal court orders, would become an increasingly common sight in the early 1960s.

Conformity of the Suburbs

Many young people who had grown up during the Great Depression and had come of age during World War II decided in the postwar era to move to the suburbs and to have families. It was decided by many that **domesticity** would be the avenue to happiness in the postwar world. As a result, the **baby boom** ensued, during which the birthrate soared beyond all expectations. The baby boom lasted from 1945 until 1962; during the peak of the baby boom, 1957, nearly 4.5 million babies were born.

The perfect place for large numbers of newly married couples to have these families was, as stated previously, in the suburbs. Many critics of the time noted the conformity of the suburbs: the houses looked much the same, everyone watched the same shows on TV, and because of TV advertising, everyone pretty much used the same appliances and wore the same clothes. Life (especially for women) was centered around their children, as there were endless rounds of PTA meetings, Little League practices, and Boy Scout meetings to get to. Social historians state that young people were using the comfort of the family and home as a buttress against any return to the disruptions they had felt earlier in their lives. William H. Whyte's *The Organizational Man*, written in 1956, analyzed the conformity and conservatism of suburban life.

Many men felt dissatisfaction with their lives in the postwar years. Many who had served in the "good war," World War II, found it difficult to return to civilian life. Many felt civilian jobs to be largely unrewarding. As the book and film **The Man in the Gray Flannel Suit** emphasized, a man who had fought in combat in World War II might find a 9-to-5 job in an office utterly unrewarding. Many men took on hunting and fishing as hobbies; here, they could at least symbolically duplicate the war experience. For men, the most popular magazines of the 1950s were *Field and Stream* and Hugh Hefner's *Playboy*.

Women felt equal frustration during this era. Many continued to work; yet women's magazines and other publications carried the clear message that now it was the woman's patriotic duty to return to the home and remain a housewife. Doris Day was the star of many films of the decade; she had a "girl-next-door" type of appeal, which was attractive to many women and men of the period. Women saw college as an avenue to meet potential husbands; many dropped out immediately after finding one. Many women *did* find fulfillment as mothers and by doing volunteer work in the community. Yet, to others, family life was terribly unsatisfying. Women who felt dissatisfaction with their role in suburban life were routinely told by their doctors that they were neurotics; the sale of tranquilizers to women skyrocketed. Many, many suburban women experienced discontent with their lives in the 1950s and early 1960s. Betty Friedan in **The Feminine Mystique** maintained that the lack of fulfillment experienced by many housewives was the genesis of the feminist revolution of the 1960s. Friedan would found NOW (National Organization for Women) in 1966.

Stereotypically, 1950s teenagers were seen as the "silent generation," interested in only hot rod cars, school mixers, and panty raids. There is a great deal of truth to this characterization. Teenagers in this era were the first teen generation to be targeted by advertisers; many teens wore the same styles and had similar tastes, as a result. Adults spent a great deal of time in ensuring that teenagers did nothing in any way rebellious. Educational films in schools taught students to obey authority, to fit in with the group, to control one's emotions, and to not even think about sex. Popular television shows of the era such as *Ozzie and Harriet* showed young people who acted in exactly that manner.

However, there was a youth rebellion in the 1950s. A few brave students would show it in their attitude and attire, using the main character played by James Dean in **Rebel Without a Cause** or Marlon Brando in *The Wild One* as models. Jackson Pollock and other artists were also at the vanguard of another form of cultural rebellion; the significance of their giant "abstract expressionist" painting moved the center of the art world to New York City. Other young people would attempt to copy the writings and attitudes of the **Beat Generation**, a group of writers and artists who rejected an American society obsessed with the atomic bomb and with material culture. In rejecting conventional society, many Beats and their followers enjoyed jazz and drugs, and studied Eastern religious thought. Key works of the Beats include Jack Kerouac's *On the Road*, in which the main characters travel simply for the joy of traveling, and *Howl*, a poem by Allen Ginsberg that outlines in graphic detail the evils of modern society and what that society does to those attempting to live decent lives in it. It should be emphasized that few young people were actual members of the Beat Generation; a larger number went to coffeehouses, dabbled in writing poetry, and sympathized with the plight of Holden Caufield in *Catcher in the Rye*.

The main form of 1950s rebellion for young people was through rock 'n' roll. To many adults, rock 'n' roll was immoral, was the "devil's music," and caused juvenile delinquency; a few even charged that it was sent to America by the Communists as part of their plot to conquer the United States. Nevertheless, those who listened and danced to rock 'n' roll were, at some level, rejecting the core values of 1950s America. Young people were told to "control their emotions"; it was very hard to do that while listening to "Good Golly Miss Molly" sung by Little Richard.

The connection in the minds of many adults between rock 'n' roll blackness accounts for the reaction of many to Elvis Presley. To many, Elvis was very, very dangerous. He covered many black songs, and exuded sex during his live and television performances. For many who feared rock 'n' roll, the best thing that could have possibly happened was when Elvis went into the army in 1958. By the end of the decade, rock had lost much of the ferocity it possessed in 1956 to 1957.

The legacy of the cultural rebels of the 1950s would certainly have tremendous influence in the 1960s. The behavior of members of the Beat Generation would be copied by the hippies. In addition, the rules that were so carefully taught to 1950s teenagers would be very intentionally broken by many teens in the 1960s.

Chapter Review

Rapid Review

To achieve the perfect 5, you should be able to explain the following:

- The 1950s is viewed by some as a decade of complacency and by others as a decade of growing ferment.
- Large-scale economic growth continued throughout the 1950s, spurred by cold war defense needs, automobile sales, housing sales, and the sale of appliances.
- The advertising industry did much to shape consumer desires in the 1950s.
- The GI Bill gave many veterans low-income mortgages and the possibility of a college education after World War II.
- Many families moved to suburbia in the 1950s; critics maintain that this increased the conformity of American society.
- During the baby boom, the birthrate drastically increased; the baby boom lasted from 1945 to 1962.
- Presidents Truman and Eisenhower were both dwarfed by the memory of the personality and the policies of Franklin Roosevelt.
- Jackie Robinson did much to advance the cause of rights in the postwar era.
- *Brown v. Board of Education* was a tremendous victory for those pushing for school integration in the 1950s.
- The Montgomery bus boycott and the events at Central High School in Little Rock, Arkansas, demonstrated the techniques that would prove to be successful in defeating segregation.
- Many men and many women felt great frustration with suburban family life of the 1950s.
- 1950s teenagers are often called the "silent generation," although James Dean, the Beat Generation writers, and Elvis Presley attracted followers among young people who did rebel in the 1950s.

Time Line

1944: GI Bill enacted
1947: Taft-Hartley Act enacted
   Jackie Robinson first plays for Brooklyn Dodgers
1948: Truman elected president in stunning upset
   Truman orders desegregation of armed forces
1950: Diner's Club credit card offered
1951: Publication of *Catcher in the Rye* by J. D. Salinger
1952: Dwight D. Eisenhower elected president
1953: Defense budget at $47 billion
   Allen Freed begins to play rock 'n' roll on the radio in Cleveland, Ohio
1954: *Brown v. Board of Education* Supreme Court decision
1955: First McDonald's opens
   Rebel Without a Cause released
   Bus boycott in Montgomery, Alabama

1956: Interstate Highway Act enacted
Majority of U.S. workers hold white-collar jobs
Howl by Allen Ginsberg first read
1957: Baby boom peaks
Publication of *On the Road* by Jack Kerouac
Resistance to school integration in Little Rock, Arkansas
1960: Three-quarters of all American homes have a TV set

> Review Questions

1. Consumer spending increased in the 1950s because of all of the following *except*
   A. Many Americans were once again purchasing stock.
   B. Many families were buying automobiles.
   C. Many Americans were buying homes.
   D. Advertising had a major impact on the American consumer.

2. The policies of the presidency of Dwight D. Eisenhower are most similar to the policies of the presidency of
   A. Franklin Roosevelt
   B. William Howard Taft
   C. Calvin Coolidge
   D. Theodore Roosevelt

3. How did their experiences in the Great Depression and World War II affect the generation who began to raise families in the postwar era?
   A. They turned inward to family for comfort.
   B. They were likely to want to give their children many of the things they had not been able to have.
   C. Interested in consumer goods, they would be likely to buy many things on credit.
   D. A and B above.

4. The most important impact of television on viewers of the early 1950s was that
   A. it provided them with comedies that allowed them to forget the difficult years of the 1950s.
   B. it allowed them to receive the latest news of the day.
   C. it imposed a sense of conformity on American society.
   D. it fostered a growing youth culture.

5. Many Americans were especially fearful of rock 'n' roll in the 1950s because
   A. many of the musicians who played it were black.
   B. Elvis Presley and many of the early performers of rock 'n' roll came from a decidedly lower-class background.
   C. Elvis Presley and many other early rock 'n' roll performers came from the American South.
   D. the messages found in early rock 'n' roll supported communism.

› Answers and Explanations

1. **A.** Americans were buying consumer goods in the postwar era. Many had money but not goods to buy in World War II. The purchase of stock would become pronounced only after this post–World War II buying spree ended.

2. **C.** Although each was somewhat different in style, Coolidge and Eisenhower were both friends of big business, believed in a balanced budget, and believed in a smaller role for the federal government and the presidency.

3. **D.** Many of those who lived through the depression were never comfortable with the idea of buying on credit; some never got credit cards at any point in their lives. Some historians say that this generation of parents spoiled their children, forming the expectations that some of these children would have as young adults in the 1960s.

4. **C.** TV viewers could get comedies and news on the radio. There was little on television in the early 1950s that specifically appealed to youth.

5. **A.** Elvis, Carl Perkins, Jerry Lee Lewis, and others were of lower-class backgrounds and were from the South, but the main objection to rock 'n' roll was its connection to black culture—for instance, Fats Domino, Chuck Berry, and Little Richard. No known early rock 'n' roll song supported communism.

CHAPTER 27

America in an Era of Turmoil (1960–1975)

IN THIS CHAPTER

Summary: The events and consequences of the 1960s still have the ability to provoke contentious debate. Many claim the changes that came out of the decade have had a positive long-term effect on American society; for example, women's rights and protection of the environment became popular causes during this period. Others point to destructive consequences of the decade, including the loosening of morality and excessive drug use, as more emblematic of the 1960s. The election of John Kennedy as president in 1960 caused many in America to feel optimistic about the future. But for some, Kennedy's assassination in 1963 was a sign of the violence that would consume America later in the decade. The construction of the Berlin Wall, the Cuban Missile Crisis, and the Vietnam War were the major foreign policy issues of the decade; opposition to the Vietnam War eventually drove President Lyndon Johnson from the White House. Blacks made many civil rights gains during the decade, but a number of younger blacks now called for "black power" rather than integration into white society. College and high school students became increasingly empowered in the decade; hundreds of thousands protested against the Vietnam War. While a number of students were increasingly involved in political affairs, other young people supported cultural instead of political revolution and became members of a widespread counterculture.

Keywords

New Frontier: group of domestic policies proposed by John Kennedy that included Medicare and aid to education and urban renewal; many of these policies were not enacted until the presidency of Lyndon Johnson.

Great Society: overarching plan by President Lyndon Johnson to assist the underprivileged in American society; it included the creation of the Department of Housing and Urban Affairs and the Head Start and Medicare programs. Some Great Society programs were later reduced because of the cost of the Vietnam War.

Civil Rights Act of 1964: major civil rights legislation that outlawed racial discrimination in public facilities, in employment, and in voter registration.

Black power: philosophy of some younger blacks in the 1960s who were impatient with the slow pace of desegregation; its advocates believed that blacks should create and control their own political and cultural institutions rather than seeking integration into white-dominated society.

Roe v. Wade (1973): Supreme Court decision that made abortion legal (with some restrictions).

Gulf of Tonkin Resolution: congressional resolution passed in August 1964 following reports that U.S. Navy ships had been fired on by North Vietnamese gunboats off the Vietnam coast; in essence it gave the president the power to fight the Vietnam War without approval from Congress. Many historians doubt if any attack on U.S. ships actually took place.

Students for a Democratic Society (SDS): radical, activist student organization created in 1960 that advocated a more democratic, participatory society. SDS was one of the major student organizations opposing the Vietnam War.

Counterculture: movement by young people in the 1960s who rejected political involvement and emphasized the need for personal instead of political revolution. Many members of the counterculture wore long hair and experimented with various drugs, with sex, and with unconventional living arrangements.

Kent State University: campus in Ohio where four students who were part of a 1970 protest against U.S. involvement in Cambodia were shot and killed by National Guardsmen.

1960 Presidential Election

Many Americans perceived the election of John Kennedy over Richard Nixon in 1960 as the beginning of a new age for America. His statement during his inauguration speech "Ask not what your country can do for you—ask what you can do for your country" is remembered by millions today. At age 43, Kennedy appeared young and vigorous (especially when flanked by his wife, Jacqueline). Kennedy was the son of a former ambassador to Britain and had served as a congressman and senator from Massachusetts. He was also a Roman Catholic.

Some voters considered Richard Nixon to be "too tied to the past"; as previously mentioned, he was the vice president under Dwight D. Eisenhower. Historians note that this was the first election greatly affected by television; in four presidential debates, Nixon appeared nervous and tired. Ironically, those who heard the debates on the radio didn't feel that Nixon lost them. Some historians argue that the television image projected by Nixon actually cost him the election. The 1960 popular vote was one of the closest in history; Nixon lost by only 120,000 votes (out of nearly 34 million votes cast).

Domestic Policies under Kennedy and Johnson

Early in his administration, John Kennedy stated that America was on the brink of entering into a **New Frontier**. The press from this point on dubbed his domestic policies "New Frontier" policies. Kennedy had plans to stimulate the economy and to seriously attack poverty in America (*The Other America* by Michael Harrington was published in 1962; this book outlined the plight of America's poor and had a great effect on Kennedy and his circle). Kennedy supported several important domestic programs, including a Medicare program (later approved during the administration of Lyndon Johnson) and substantial federal aid to education and to urban renewal.

Very little of Kennedy's domestic agenda was adopted by Congress. His plans to cut taxes and to increase spending on education never even got out of the congressional committee. One of Kennedy's domestic successes was to convince Congress to raise the minimum wage from $1.00 per hour to $1.25. Kennedy also established a Peace Corps program, in which young men and women volunteered to help residents in developing countries around the world.

One program that was considered a top priority by both Kennedy and Congress was the space program. Kennedy was barely in office when Soviet cosmonaut Yuri Gagarin became the first human to travel in space. In early May 1961, America put its first man in space (Alan Shepard), and in February 1962 John Glenn (later a U.S. senator) became the first American astronaut to orbit the earth. During this era, Kennedy also made the bold promise that America would land a man on the moon by the end of the 1960s.

The New Frontier programs ended permanently when John Kennedy was assassinated in Dallas, Texas, on November 22, 1963. Kennedy was in Texas to heal wounds in the local Democratic party and to rally support for the 1964 presidential election. Kennedy was riding in a motorcade through downtown Dallas when he was killed. An ex-marine named Lee Harvey Oswald was arrested and charged with Kennedy's death. Oswald never went to trial because he was shot and killed by a Dallas nightclub owner, Jack Ruby, two days later. The **Warren Commission** was formed to investigate the assassination; the report of this committee firmly supported those who said that Oswald acted alone. To this day, there are those who maintain that a conspiracy was responsible for Kennedy's death.

Vice President Lyndon Johnson was sworn into office shortly after Kennedy's assassination. In the year after Kennedy's death, Johnson was able to get much of Kennedy's domestic policy plans through Congress. Johnson had been the Senate majority leader before becoming vice president, and in early 1964 was easily able to maneuver the previously rejected Kennedy tax cut through Congress.

Johnson ran for reelection against Senator Barry Goldwater in the 1964 presidential election. Goldwater was a conservative from Arizona who was too far to the right for mainstream America to accept. He spoke of using nuclear weapons in Vietnam and famously stated that "extremism in the defense of liberty is no vice." Lyndon Johnson won nearly 62 percent of the popular vote and was able to institute his own economic plans in 1965; in a speech early in that year, Johnson stated that his goal was to create a **Great Society** in America.

In speech after speech, Johnson stated that it would be possible to truly end poverty in America. The Department of Housing and Urban Affairs was created as a cabinet-level department. In 1964, Johnson had begun the **VISTA (Volunteer in Service to America)** program, which organized volunteers who worked in the poorest communities of the United States. In 1965, Congress passed Johnson's Housing and Urban Development Act, which organized the building of nearly 250,000 new housing units in America's cities and authorized over $3 billion for further urban development. Johnson's major initiatives in education authorized grants to help schools in the poorest sections of America and established **Head Start**, a program to help disadvantaged preschool students. In 1965, Johnson established a **Medicare** system, which provided hospital insurance and medical coverage for America's senior citizens, and Medicaid, which assisted Americans of any age who could not afford health insurance.

The Great Society programs of Lyndon Johnson positively impacted the lives of thousands of Americans, but frustration set in when it appeared that, despite massive government efforts, a large number of Americans still lived in poverty. In addition, the cost of Great Society programs put a strain on American taxpayers. However, it should be noted that the number of those living in poverty was cut by at least 40 percent by Great Society programs. Many of these programs ended up being reduced or eliminated because of the expense of America's war in Vietnam.

Struggle of Black Americans: From Nonviolence to Black Power

As was noted in the previous chapter, Martin Luther King, Jr., emerged as a key leader of the civil rights movement during the Montgomery, Alabama, bus boycott. King and other Southern clergymen founded the Southern Christian Leadership Conference (SCLC), which taught that civil rights could be achieved through nonviolent protest. SCLC leaders taught that violence could never be utilized to achieve their goals, no matter what the circumstance.

Many younger blacks were eager for the fight for civil rights to develop at a quicker pace. In 1960, the Student Nonviolent Coordinating Committee (SNCC) was formed; its leaders were not ministers, and they demanded immediate, not gradual, change. During the first years of its existence, SNCC attracted both black and white members; many of the whites were college students from Northern universities.

An effective technique utilized by the civil rights movement in the early 1960s was the **sit-in**. Blacks were not allowed to eat at the lunch counters of many Southern stores, even though blacks could buy merchandise at these stores. Black and white civil rights workers would sit down at these lunch counters; when they were denied service, they continued to sit there (preventing other paying customers from taking their spaces). Picketers would often march outside the store in question. Those participating in sit-ins received tremendous verbal and physical harassment from other whites, yet the tactic of the sit-in helped to integrate dozens of Southern establishments in the first several years of the 1960s.

In May 1961, the Congress for Racial Equality sponsored the **Freedom Rides**. During the previous year, the Supreme Court had ruled that bus stations and waiting rooms in these stations had to be integrated. On the Freedom Rides, both black and white volunteers started in Washington and were determined to ride through the South to see if cities had complied with the Supreme Court legislation. In Anniston, Alabama, a white mob greeted the bus, beating many of the Freedom Riders and burning the bus. Freedom Rides continued throughout the summer; almost all riders experienced some violence or were arrested.

The Freedom Rides introduced an important influence into the civil rights struggle in the South: the public opinion of the rest of the country. Many Americans were horrified at the violence they witnessed; many called their representatives in Congress to urge that the federal government do more to support the Freedom Riders. By the end of the summer, marshals from the Justice Department were in every city the Freedom Ride buses passed through to ensure a lack of violence.

Under Attorney General Robert Kennedy, the federal government became much more involved in enforcing federal civil rights guidelines and court rulings. In September 1962, President Kennedy nationalized the Alabama National Guard and sent in federal marshals to suppress protesters and allow James Meredith to be the first black to take classes at the University of Mississippi. In Birmingham, Alabama, city officials turned fire hoses and trained dogs on civil rights protesters; the broadcast of these events to the entire nation again created a widespread outrage against those in the South who were opposing court-ordered integration.

President Kennedy went very slowly on civil rights issues, but in the summer of 1963, he presented to Congress a wide-ranging civil rights bill that would have withheld large amounts of federal funding from states that continued to practice segregation. To muster support for this bill, civil rights leaders organized the August 28, 1963, **March on Washington**. More than 200,000 people showed up to protest for civil rights legislation; it was at this rally that Martin Luther King, Jr., made his very famous "I have a dream" speech.

In 1964, Lyndon Johnson presented to Congress the most wide-ranging civil rights bill since Reconstruction. The **Civil Rights Act of 1964** stated that the same standards had to be used to register white and black voters, that racial discrimination could not be used by employers to hire workers, that discrimination was illegal in all public locations, and that an Equal Employment Opportunity Commission would be created. The Voting Rights Act of 1965 outlawed measures such as literacy tests, which had been used to prevent blacks from voting. Passage of this bill was aided by the public sentiment that followed the revelation that three civil rights workers had been killed the previous summer while attempting to register voters in Mississippi. Television reports of violence against civil rights workers, such as was seen during Martin Luther King's march in Selma, Alabama, in 1965, convinced many Americans that additional civil rights legislation was necessary.

Many blacks who lived in poverty in Northern cities believed that the civil rights movement was doing little or nothing for them. In August 1965, riots broke out in the Watts section of Los Angeles; Chicago, Newark, and Detroit soon experienced similar riots. The **Kerner Commission** was authorized to investigate the cause of these riots, and stated that black poverty and the lack of hope in the black urban communities were the major causes of these disturbances. The Kerner Commission reported that two societies existed in America, one white and rich, and the other poor and black.

One group that preached opposition to integration was the **Nation of Islam**. This organization (also called the Black Muslims) preached that it was to the benefit of white society to keep blacks poor and in ghettoes, and that for blacks to improve their position they would have to do it themselves. Malcolm X would become the most famous representative of this group, preaching **black nationalism**. Eventually, Malcolm X rejected the more extreme concepts of the Nation of Islam, and he was killed in February 1965.

The ideas of black nationalism exerted a great deal of influence on many of the younger members of SNCC. One, Stokely Carmichael, began to urge blacks to take up arms to defend themselves against whites; Carmichael also orchestrated the removal of all whites from SNCC. In addition, Carmichael began to urge SNCC members to support **black power**; this concept stated that blacks should have pride in their history and their heritage, and that blacks should create their own society apart from the all-controlling white society.

The most visible group supporting black power were the **Black Panthers**. This San Francisco group, founded by Bobby Seale and Huey Newton, had a militarist image. Several members died after vicious gun battles with police. At the same time, the Black Panthers set up programs that gave food to the poorest members of San Francisco's black population and established schools to teach black history and culture to the children in the community. However, the image of this organization was greatly damaged by its violent reputation.

Rise of Feminism

Another group that fought for additional freedoms in the 1960s were women. As discussed in the previous chapter, many women felt extreme frustration with their lives in the 1950s. Some college-aged women were active in the civil rights movement in the early 1960s, but often felt frustrated when they were always the ones asked to make the coffee or do the typing.

In the mid-1960s, even women in suburbia began to notice that the frustrations they had were shared by many of the women living around them. Women's support groups became common on both college campuses and in suburban communities. A pivotal book that helped bolster this growing **feminist movement** was *The Feminine Mystique* by Betty Friedan.

In 1966, **NOW (National Organization for Women)** was founded by Friedan. NOW was a decidedly middle-class organization and was dedicated to getting equal pay for women at work and to ending images in the media that objectified women. In 1972, Gloria Steinem founded the feminist magazine **Ms.** The key Supreme Court decision of the era concerning women was the 1973 **Roe v. Wade** ruling, which, with some restrictions, legalized abortion. Many feminists pushed for the passage of an Equal Rights Amendment, but this amendment was never ratified by enough states to become part of the Constitution. Some opponents to the amendment stated that its passage would eventually lead to other "unacceptable" actions, such as gay marriage.

Other groups protested for equal rights during this period. The **American Indian Movement (AIM)** wanted Native Americans to be knowledgeable about their heritage, and also influenced various tribes to mount legal battles to get back land that had been illegally taken from them. A standoff between AIM members and government authorities took place at Wounded Knee, South Dakota, in 1973; as a result, legislation passed in the 1970s gave Native Americans more autonomy in tribal matters.

Latino groups also began to protest for rights in this era. A large number of Latinos were employed as migrant farm workers in California; Cesar Chavez organized the **United Farm Workers** against farmers (especially grape growers) in California. Environmental groups also became active in this era. *Silent Spring* by Rachel Carson came out in 1962 and warned about the dangers of DDT. Many also protested throughout the decade against the dangers of nuclear power.

Cold War in the 1960s

Cold war tensions and fears continued to dominate in the early 1960s. The fear of the bomb continued unabated; movies such as *Fail-Safe* and *Dr. Strangelove* explored a world in which an "accident" with the bomb might occur. Both the United States and the Soviet Union openly tested nuclear weapons during 1961 and 1962.

A plan to liberate Cuba from Castro had actually been formulated during the Eisenhower administration; by this plan, the CIA would train Cubans living in America to invade Cuba, and the United States would provide air cover. This operation, called the **Bay of Pigs**, took place in April 1961 and was a complete fiasco, with virtually the entire invasion force killed or captured by Castro's forces. The Bay of Pigs was a major embarrassment for the Kennedy administration in its first months in office.

In Berlin, refugees from the East continued to try to escape to West Berlin on a daily basis; in August 1961, the East Germans and the Soviets constructed the concrete **Berlin Wall**, dividing the two halves of the city. The issue that almost brought the world to World War III was not in Europe, however; it was in Cuba. In mid-October 1962, American reconnaissance flights over Cuba indicated Soviet-made missile sights under construction. In the **Cuban Missile Crisis**, President Kennedy established a naval blockade of Cuba and told Soviet leader Nikita Khrushchev to remove the missiles from Cuba. Khrushchev backed down and removed the missiles, averting the potential of world war. It is known now that if American forces had landed in Cuba, Soviet authorities were seriously contemplating the use of tactical nuclear weapons against them. Luckily, effective diplomacy prevented the outbreak of a potentially catastrophic crisis. Shortly afterward, the United States and the Soviet Union signed a Limited Test Ban Treaty, and a "hot line" was installed, connecting the White House and the Kremlin so that future crises could be dealt with quickly.

Vietnam War and Its Impact on American Society

Since the 1950s, the United States had supported non-Communist South Vietnam against the North, led by Communist and nationalist Ho Chi Minh. The South Vietnamese government also had to fight the **Vietcong**, Communist guerrillas who lived in South Vietnam but supported the North. During the Kennedy administration, the number of American advisors in Vietnam increased. American officials became increasingly suspicious of the effectiveness of South Vietnamese president Diem; in the fall of 1963, these officials supported (or orchestrated, depending on which historian you read) the assassination of Diem.

Shortly after becoming president, Lyndon Johnson decided that to achieve victory, the war in Vietnam had to be intensified. In August 1964, Johnson announced to the nation that light North Vietnamese gunboats had fired on American destroyers in the Gulf of Tonkin, which is in international waters. Some historians are skeptical that these events ever took place. Nevertheless, Congress passed the **Gulf of Tonkin Resolution,** which gave the president the power to "prevent further aggression" in Vietnam; this resolution allowed the president to control the war without the necessity of consulting Congress.

Throughout 1965, 1966, and 1967, America continued to increase its commitment in Vietnam; by early 1968 nearly 540,000 American soldiers were stationed in Vietnam. Beginning in 1965, bombing campaigns against North Vietnam became commonplace. American soldiers in Vietnam became increasingly frustrated by the jungle tactics used by their enemies, by the fact that one's friend by day might be one's enemy by night, and by the seeming lack of effectiveness of the South Vietnamese army.

A key battle of the war was the **Tet Offensive**, which began on January 30, 1968. During the first day of the Vietnamese new year, the Vietcong initiated major offensives in cities across South Vietnam. Even Saigon, the capital, was attacked, and the Vietcong held the American embassy for several hours. In the end, the Vietcong and North Vietnamese suffered major losses as a result of the Tet Offensive. Nevertheless, this was the battle that began to conclusively turn American public opinion against the war. The sights on television of American forces trying to recapture their own embassy certainly made many question the idea that "victory was just around the corner," which is what was being told to the American people by military and civilian officials.

The Vietnam War drove Lyndon Johnson from the White House. Diaries of several in Johnson's inner circle show that he was consumed by the war. In February 1968, Johnson began his reelection bid by taking on Senator Eugene McCarthy of Minnesota, who was running on a peace ticket, in the New Hampshire presidential primary. Johnson won, but got only 48 percent of the total votes to 42 percent for McCarthy. Johnson considered this a humiliation, and one month later pulled out of the presidential race. Johnson endorsed Vice President Hubert Humphrey for president. By this point, Robert Kennedy had also announced his candidacy.

Throughout 1968, support for the Vietnam War continued to fade in America. The Republican candidate for president, Richard Nixon, gained support when he proclaimed that he had a "secret plan" to end the war. Reports of the brutality of the war also shocked many Americans. Many were disturbed to find that Americans were using **napalm**, a substance that sticks to the skin and burns, on civilian villages. The story of the 1968 **My Lai Massacre**, in which more than 300 Vietnamese women, children, and elderly men were murdered by American soldiers, horrified many Americans. Some Americans began to wonder what the United States was doing in Vietnam, and what the war was doing to the United States.

The student protest movement also began to furiously campaign against the war. Student activists had previously been active in the civil rights movement. In 1960, the **Students for a Democratic Society (SDS)** organization was formed. The *Port Huron Statement* was the founding document of this organization, and called for a less materialistic society that encouraged "participatory democracy." SDS would become one of the major student organizations opposing the war.

The **Free Speech Movement** had grown at the University of California at Berkeley in 1964 when school officials refused to allow political materials to be distributed on campus. Campus buildings were occupied, as students demanded college courses more relevant to their lives. Tactics used by Berkeley students were copied by students at colleges across the country.

The Vietnam War greatly expanded the student protest movement in America. Many students were passionately opposed to the war on moral grounds; to be fair, others were part of the movement because they didn't want to be drafted. Television pictures of young men burning their draft cards were commonplace. Antiwar demonstrations that had attracted a few hundred people in 1964 were now attracting thousands; a 1967 antiwar rally drew 500,000 people to Central Park in New York.

The year 1968 saw the protests grow, both in number and in intensity. Events of 1968 convinced many young people that getting involved in mainstream politics (as Eugene McCarthy had tried to get them to do) was fruitless. Martin Luther King and Robert Kennedy were killed in the spring of that year; to many, that left the presidential race between two representatives of the old guard, Richard Nixon and Hubert Humphrey. What, many students asked, was the point of even getting involved in politics if the candidates that they could choose from all ended up being traditional politicians? In the spring of 1968, major protests broke out at Columbia University; in August, as protesters chanted "the whole world is watching," Chicago police officers brutally beat students and others who had shown up to protest at the Democratic National Convention. By 1969, disputes over how much violence is acceptable began to tear SDS apart as well.

Another group of revolutionaries in the 1960s rejected political involvement and supported cultural revolution instead. Members of the **counterculture** rejected America and its values as much as antiwar protesters did, but believed that personal revolution was most vital. These "hippies," or countercultural rebels, often had little to do with members of SDS; the revolution of the hippies consisted of growing one's hair long, listening to the "right" music, and partaking of psychedelic drugs. Timothy Leary and other proponents of LSD implored young people to "tune in, turn on, and drop out." Sexual freedom was also commonplace in the counterculture. A birth control pill had been approved by the federal government in 1960; a button worn by many in the 1960s stated "If It Feels Good, Do It!" The Mecca for many of these rebels in 1967 was San Francisco, where the music and lifestyle of groups such as the Grateful Dead personified the counterculture of the 1960s. The **Woodstock Music Festival** of 1969 was the most outward manifestation of the "peace and love" rebels of the 1960s. For members of the counterculture, personal rebellion was a much more valid form of rebellion than political rebellion; it should be remembered that Pete Townshend of The Who threw radical political organizer Abbie Hoffman off the stage at Woodstock.

Richard Nixon was elected in November 1968, and soon announced his policy of **Vietnamization** of the war, which consisted of training the South Vietnamese army and gradually pulling American forces out. By 1972, American forces in Vietnam only numbered 24,000 (as the numbers of soldiers in Vietnam decreased, so did the antiwar protests). In April 1970, however, Nixon announced that to support the South Vietnamese government, massive bombing of the North was needed and that the war needed to be extended into Cambodia to wipe out Communist bases there. College campuses across the country, for one last time, joined together in massive protest. At **Kent State University** four students were killed by National Guardsmen who opened fire on the protesters; two students were killed at Jackson State University in Mississippi. American public opinion at this point was deeply divided on the war; two days after Kent State, nearly 100,000 construction workers marched in New York City for the war.

In 1971, the **Pentagon Papers** were leaked by a former Department of Defense employee, Daniel Ellsburg. The Pentagon Papers revealed that the government had deceived the American public and Congress about Vietnam as early as 1964. By this point, most Americans awaited the end of American involvement in the war.

America was involved in negotiations with the North Vietnamese in Paris. Negotiations intensified in December 1972 when President Nixon ordered the heaviest bombing of the war against North Vietnam. In January 1973, it was announced that American forces would leave Vietnam in 60 days, that all American prisoners would be returned, and that the boundary between North and South Vietnam would be respected. On March 29, 1973, the last American soldiers left Vietnam; 60,000 Americans had died there. On April 30, 1975, the North Vietnamese captured Saigon, the capital of South Vietnam, ending the Vietnam War. The last Americans had left the country one day earlier.

Chapter Review

Rapid Review

To achieve the perfect 5, you should be able to explain the following:

- The events that dramatically altered America including protests and cultural rebellion in the 1960s are seen by some in a positive light and others in a negative light.
- John Kennedy projected a new image of presidential leadership, although few of his domestic programs were actually passed by Congress.
- The Cuban Missile Crisis was the critical foreign policy crisis of the Kennedy administration, and may have brought the world close to world war.
- After Kennedy's death, Lyndon Johnson was able to get Congress to pass his Great Society domestic programs, which included Head Start and Medicare.
- Nonviolence remained the major tactic of the civil rights movement throughout the 1960s, although some black leaders began to advocate "black power."
- Women strove to achieve equal rights in the 1960s through the National Organization for Women (NOW) and consciousness-raising groups.
- Lyndon Johnson determined early in his presidency that an escalation of the war in Vietnam would be necessary, and more materials and men went to Vietnam from 1965 to 1968.
- The military in Vietnam was frustrated by the military tactics of the enemy and by faltering support at home.
- The Tet Offensive did much to turn American public opinion against the war.
- Student protesters held increasingly large demonstrations against the war; SDS was the main organization of student activists.
- Members of the counterculture advocated a personal and not a political rebellion in this era.
- Richard Nixon removed American troops from Vietnam through the policy of Vietnamization; the South Vietnamese government fell two years after American troops departed.

Time Line

1960: John Kennedy elected president
    Sit-ins began
    Students for a Democratic Society (SDS) formed
    Student Nonviolent Coordinating Committee (SNCC) formed
1961: Freedom Rides
    Bay of Pigs invasion
    Construction of Berlin Wall
    First American travels in space
1962: James Meredeth enters University of Mississippi
    SDS issues *Port Huron Statement*
    Silent Spring by Rachel Carson published
    Cuban Missile Crisis
    The Other America by Michael Harrington published
1963: John Kennedy assassinated; Lyndon Johnson becomes president
    Civil rights march on Washington
    The Feminine Mystique by Betty Friedan published
    President Diem ousted in South Vietnam

1964: Beginning of Johnson's War on Poverty programs
Civil Rights Act enacted
Free Speech Movement at Berkeley begins
Tonkin Gulf Resolution
Johnson reelected
1965: Elementary and Secondary Education Act passed
Johnson sends more troops to Vietnam
Voting Rights Act passed
Murder of Malcolm X
Watts riots burn sections of Los Angeles
1966: Stokely Carmichael calls for "black power"
Formation of Black Panther party
Formation of National Organization for Women (NOW)
1967: Riots in many American cities
Antiwar demonstrations intensify
1968: Martin Luther King assassinated
Robert Kennedy assassinated
Student protests at Columbia University
Battle between police and protesters at Democratic National Convention
Richard Nixon elected president
American Indian Movement (AIM) founded
Tet Offensive
My Lai Massacre
1969: Woodstock Music Festival
1970: United States invades Cambodia
Killings at Kent State, Jackson State
1971: *Pentagon Papers* published by the *New York Times*
1972: Nixon reelected
1973: Vietnam cease-fire announced; American troops leave Vietnam
Roe v. Wade decision
1975: South Vietnam falls to North Vietnam, ending the Vietnam War

> Review Questions

1. The initial fate of the Freedom Riders demonstrated that
   A. Southerners had largely accepted Northern orders to integrate bus stations and other public facilities.
   B. state governments were at the forefront in the enforcement of civil rights laws.
   C. television news broadcasts had a powerful hold on the American public.
   D. by 1961 the federal government was committed to vigorously protecting the civil rights of all citizens.

2. The Tet Offensive demonstrated that
   A. American forces were fairly close to a decisive victory in Vietnam.
   B. military and civilian officials had been less than candid with the American people on the progress of the war.
   C. the Vietcong could defeat American soldiers in the battlefield.
   D. cooperation between Americans and the South Vietnamese army was improving.

3. The membership rolls of Students for a Democratic Society were at an all-time high when
   A. the struggles of the civil rights movement in the South were shown on national television.
   B. Nixon invaded Cambodia.
   C. Nixon intensified the bombing to its highest levels of the war in 1972.
   D. more young men were being sent to Vietnam between 1965 and 1967.

4. Some Northern blacks were attracted to the call for "black power" for all of the following reasons *except*
   A. Martin Luther King and others in the civil rights movement seemed more interested in improving the position of Southern blacks.
   B. Ghetto sections of Northern cities remained poor, and many residents there felt little hope.
   C. Malcolm X and Stokely Carmichael evoked powerful images of black pride.
   D. Vast numbers of Northern blacks had joined the Nation of Islam.

5. Highlights for feminist leaders of this era included all of the following *except*
   A. the founding of *Ms.*
   B. the formation of NOW
   C. the drive for passage of the Equal Rights Amendment
   D. the increased awareness of "women's issues" in society

› Answers and Explanations

1. **C.** The images of burned buses and beaten Freedom Riders horrified many Americans. At this point, neither the federal nor state governments protected the rights of Freedom Riders.

2. **B.** The Tet Offensive was a military defeat for the Vietcong. However, it did prove that victory was not "around the corner," which is what many military officials were publicly claiming.

3. **D.** By the time of the invasion of Cambodia and the massive bombing at the end of the war, SDS had split into factions. The civil rights movement attracted a relatively small number of new members to SDS.

4. **D.** All of the other reasons caused some Northern blacks to abandon Martin Luther King's call for integration. Only a small proportion of blacks ever joined the Nation of Islam.

5. **C.** After a long struggle, the drive to get the ERA into the Constitution was finally abandoned when it became obvious that not enough state legislatures would ever pass it.

CHAPTER 28

Decline and Rebirth (1968–1988)

IN THIS CHAPTER

Summary: Some historians claim that the accomplishments of the presidency of Richard Nixon are often overlooked. Nixon opened diplomatic relations with China, improved relations with the Soviet Union, and began to break the Democratic stranglehold on politics in the South that had existed since the New Deal. Despite these developments, Richard Nixon will always be associated with the Watergate scandal. Watergate began a period when faith in the national government sharply declined; this lasted through the presidencies of Gerald Ford and Jimmy Carter. With the election of Ronald Reagan, many Americans began to "have faith in America again." Just as Nixon began a new relationship with China, under Reagan, America entered into a more positive relationship with its formal rival, the Soviet Union.

Keywords

Southern Strategy: political strategy implemented by President Richard Nixon to win over Southern whites to the Republican party; the strategy succeeded through administration policies such as delaying school desegregation plans.

Détente: foreign policy of decreasing tensions with the Soviet Union; began in the first term of the Nixon administration.

Watergate: series of events beginning with the break-in at the Democratic party headquarters in the Watergate complex in Washington, DC, that led to the downfall of President Richard Nixon; Nixon resigned as the House of Representatives was preparing for an impeachment hearing.

OPEC: Organization of Petroleum Exporting Countries; the group of twelve countries that produce most of the world's oil and, by determining production quantities, influence worldwide oil prices.

Camp David Accords (1978): peace agreement between Israel and Egypt that was mediated by President Jimmy Carter; many consider this the highlight of the Carter presidency.

Iranian Hostage Crisis: diplomatic crisis triggered on November 4, 1979, when Iranian protesters seized the U.S. embassy in Tehran and held 66 American diplomats hostage for 444 days. President Carter was unable to free the hostages despite several attempts; to many this event symbolized the paralysis of American power in the late 1970s.

Religious right: right-leaning evangelical Christians who increasingly supported Republican candidates beginning with Ronald Reagan.

Iran-Contra Affair: scandal that erupted during the Reagan administration when it was revealed that U.S. government agents had secretly sold arms to Iran in order to raise money to fund anti-Communist "Contra" forces in Nicaragua. Those acts directly contravened an ongoing U.S. trade embargo with Iran as well as federal legislation limiting aid to the Contras. Several Reagan administration officials were convicted of federal crimes as a result.

Presidency of Richard Nixon

Richard Nixon's election to the presidency in 1968 capped one of the greatest comeback stories in American political history. Nixon's political obituary had been written after successive defeats in 1960 (when he was defeated by John Kennedy for the presidency) and in 1962 (after being defeated by Pat Brown for governor of California; he informed the press on election night that "you won't have Nixon to kick around anymore," as he was resigning from politics).

Nixon was one of the most interesting men to be elected to the presidency in the twentieth century. He was never comfortable with large groups of people, and even in staged photo events sometimes appeared uncomfortable and out of place (such as the time he was pictured walking "informally" along the beach in dress shoes). Nixon was convinced that large numbers of the news media and many members of Congress were his enemies. He relied on a small group of close-knit advisors, including H. R. Haldeman, his chief of staff, and John Ehrlichman, his advisor for domestic affairs.

Nixon's Domestic Policies

As mentioned in the previous chapter, the Vietnam War took up large amounts of Nixon's time and energies. However, other potentially crucial crises also existed. As Nixon entered office in 1969, inflation was growing rapidly, unemployment was rising, the gross national product was exhibiting a lack of growth, and the United States had a rather substantial trade deficit. Some of these economic problems can be attributed to the administration of Lyndon Johnson; paying for Great Society programs and the Vietnam War at the same time created serious strains on the federal budget.

At first, Nixon tried to raise taxes and cut government spending; this policy only worsened the economy. The president then imposed a 90-day freeze on prices and wages; after these measures, he also established mandatory guidelines for wage and price increases. By 1971, Nixon also directed that a program of **deficit spending** begin. This was somewhat similar to the approach utilized by Franklin Roosevelt in attacking the economic problems of the Great Depression.

"Southern Strategy" of Richard Nixon

Southern whites had voted firmly Democratic since the Reconstruction Era. In the 1968 presidential election, cracks in this relationship between the Democratic party and the South began to show. George Wallace, former governor of Alabama, broke from the party and ran for president as a candidate of the American Independence Party in 1968. He picked up 13.5 percent of the popular vote (a large percentage of these from the South); this aided Richard Nixon in his victory over Hubert Humphrey.

Richard Nixon decided to take decisive measures to appeal to these Southern whites and win them over to the Republican party. Nixon's "**Southern Strategy**" included delaying school desegregation plans (that had been ordered by a federal court) in Mississippi and attempting to block an extension of the Voting Rights Act of 1965. Nixon also attempted to block school integration by busing after the Supreme Court had endorsed busing as a method to achieve integration. Under Nixon, the Supreme Court also became much more conservative, especially with Warren Burger as the new chief justice (nevertheless, it should be remembered that in *Roe v. Wade* this court outlawed state legislation opposing abortion).

Nixon's Foreign Policy

The greatest achievements of the Nixon presidency were undoubtedly in the area of foreign affairs. In formulating foreign policy, Nixon was aided by former Harvard professor Henry Kissinger, his national security advisor and, beginning in 1973, his secretary of state. Kissinger had conducted many of the negotiations with the North Vietnamese that allowed American troops to leave Vietnam in 1973. Nixon greatly trusted the judgment of Kissinger on foreign policy affairs.

Nixon's greatest accomplishments included better relationships with both the Soviet Union and China. Nixon had been a fierce anti-Communist in the 1950s, but during his first term in office, he instituted a policy of "**détente**" with the Soviet Union. The reduced tensions that this policy created were a welcome relief from the fierce anti-Communist rhetoric that had existed through most of the Kennedy and Johnson administrations.

In addition, Nixon realized the foolishness of continued **nuclear proliferation**. He visited the Soviet Union in 1972 and, during discussions with Soviet Premier Leonid Brezhnev, agreed to halt the continued buildup of nuclear weapons. The **SALT I** treaty (Strategic Arms Limitation Talks) was historic, since this was the first time the two superpowers agreed not to produce any more nuclear ballistic missiles and to reduce their arsenals of antiballistic missiles to 200 per side.

A journey that Nixon took earlier in 1972 was even more significant. During much of the 1950s and 1960s, Nixon spoke about the need to support Nationalist China (the non-Communist state established on the island of Taiwan) and the need to be vigilant against the expansion of "Red" China (the Communist state on the Chinese mainland). Henry Kissinger was an admirer of **realpolitik** and convinced Nixon that a new approach to Communist China was necessary. Kissinger maintained that it was foolish to think that the Communist Chinese would ever be overthrown, and that it would be to America's advantage to recognize that fact. In addition, Nixon felt that a friendlier China could be used as a wedge to get future concessions from the Soviet Union.

In February 1972, Nixon and Kissinger made a historic trip to Communist China. Meetings were held with Chinese leader Mao Zedong and other officials. At these meetings, it was decided that trade talks between the two countries would begin, and that cultural exchanges would start almost immediately. Most importantly, Nixon agreed to support the admission of Communist China to the United Nations (going against what had been traditional U.S. policy for the entire cold war period).

Watergate Affair

As a result of his foreign policy successes, Nixon's ratings in public opinion polls were extremely high as the presidential election of 1972 approached. Nixon's opponent was Democrat George McGovern, who campaigned for a faster pullout from Vietnam. Nixon's victory in 1972 was truly staggering; in the Electoral College he won 521 to 17.

The one-sided nature of the 1972 election made the desires of Richard Nixon and his campaign associates for the events leading up to the **Watergate Affair** difficult to understand. Nixon's paranoid view of the American political system colored the decisions that he and his aides made in the months leading up to the 1972 campaign. In 1971, Nixon created an "enemies list" and suggested various forms of harassment that could be used on everyone on the list (wiretaps, investigating income tax records, etc.). On this list were politicians (Senator Edward Kennedy), newsmen (Daniel Schorr of CBS News), and even sports personalities (New York Jets quarterback Joe Namath).

After the Pentagon Papers were released in the spring of 1971 by Daniel Ellsburg, a former employee of the State Department, a special unit to "plug" leaks was formed by the White House. This unit was known as the **Plumbers**, and included Howard Hunt, a former member of the CIA, and Gordon Liddy, a former agent of the FBI. One of the first actions of the Plumbers was to break into Daniel Ellsburg's psychiatrist's office to try to find incriminating information about Ellsburg. Other aides working for CREEP (the Committee to Reelect the President) performed various "dirty tricks" on political opponents. In the 1972 Democratic primaries, CREEP operatives on two occasions ordered 200 pizzas delivered to an opposing campaign office unannounced, "canceled" political rallies for opponents without the opponents knowing it, and, with no basis whatsoever, charged that Democratic Senator Edmund Muskie had made negative remarks about French Canadians living in New Hampshire.

On the night of June 16, 1972, James McCord, an assistant in the office of security of CREEP, led four other men into Democratic National Committee headquarters at the Watergate Hotel in Washington, DC. The goal of this group was to photocopy important files and to install electronic surveillance devices in the Democratic offices. The five were caught and arrested; money they had on their person could be traced back to CREEP. This was the beginning of the chain of events that came to be called Watergate or the Watergate scandal.

Five days later, Nixon became part of the illegal cover-up of the Watergate break-in. On that day, he publicly announced that the White House had absolutely nothing to do with the break-in. More importantly, on the same day Nixon contacted friendly CIA officials and tried to convince them to call the FBI and tell the FBI to cease its investigation of Watergate. This was the first illegal action taken by Nixon in the Watergate Affair.

In the months before the 1972 presidential election, "hush money" was paid to the Watergate burglars, and several officials of CREEP committed perjury by denying under oath that Nixon had any knowledge of the break-in.

The Watergate story most assuredly would have died if not for the efforts of reporters Carl Bernstein and Bob Woodward of the *Washington Post*. Despite threats from the White House and other political operatives, the two reporters continued to follow the story. They were aided by a secret source named "Deep Throat," who provided them with valuable background information about the case. It was revealed in 2005 that "Deep Throat" was Mark Felt, former associate director of the FBI.

James McCord and the other Watergate burglars were found guilty in their January 1973 trial; no mention of White House involvement was made by any of the defendants. It later became known that Nixon personally approved the payment of hush money to one of the defendants during the trial. In February, the Senate Select Committee on Presidential Campaign Activities began to investigate the Watergate Affair. During these hearings, White House attorney John Dean testified that Nixon was involved in the cover-up and another aide revealed the existence of a taping system in the Oval Office that recorded all conversations held by the president. H. R. Haldeman, John Ehrlichman, and Attorney General Richard Kleindienst all resigned in an attempt to save the presidency of Richard Nixon. Nixon's public approval ratings began to fall.

In an effort to quell the firestorm building around him, Nixon appointed a **special prosecutor** to investigate the Watergate Affair. Almost immediately after being appointed, Archibald Cox demanded that the White House hand over the tapes of all taped conversations.

After losing a court argument that the tapes should be exclusive property of the president, Nixon ordered the new Attorney General to fire Cox. Richardson refused, as did his assistant, William Ruckelhaus, and both resigned. Solicitor General Robert Bork (who would later be an unsuccessful Supreme Court nominee) finally fired Cox. All of these events took place on October 20, 1973, and are referred to as the "**Saturday Night Massacre**."

After these events, the president's approval rating dipped dramatically. The Judiciary Committee of the House of Representatives began to discuss the formal procedures for impeaching a president. Nixon turned over heavily edited transcripts of most of the tapes to Leon Jaworski, Cox's replacement; many of the vulgar comments made by Nixon on the tapes shocked both opponents and supporters. Also, during this period, it was revealed that Spiro Agnew, Nixon's vice president, had taken bribes as an elected official in Maryland before he was vice president. Agnew resigned in October 1973, and it was two months before his appointed successor, Congressman Gerald Ford of Michigan, was approved as the new vice president.

During the following months, the calls for Nixon's resignation increased. In April 1974, Nixon released more, but not all, of the tapes requested by the special prosecutor. In July, the House Judiciary Committee formally approved three articles of impeachment, stating that the president had ignored their subpoenas, had misused presidential power, and had obstructed justice. Debate was to begin in the full House on impeachment; Nixon's supporters admitted that Nixon would have been impeached.

Before House hearings could begin, the White House finally complied with a Supreme Court order to release all remaining tapes. One had an 18½-minute gap on it; another was the "smoking gun" that Nixon's opponents had been looking for. Nixon had always denied that he had known about the cover-up, yet a tape made one week after the break-in demonstrated that Nixon was actually participating in the cover-up at that point.

With no support left, Nixon finally resigned on August 9, 1974. Gerald Ford took over as president and announced that "our long national nightmare is over." In retrospect, the Watergate Affair was one of the low points of American political history in the twentieth century, rivaled only by the scandals of the presidency of Warren G. Harding.

Presidency of Gerald Ford

As described previously, Gerald Ford came to the presidency under the worst of circumstances. To his advantage, he was incredibly well liked in Washington and totally free of any hint of scandal. However, during his time in office, Ford seemed to lack a grand "plan" for what he wanted to accomplish. Several historians note that Ford's presidency was doomed from September 8, 1974, when he pardoned Richard Nixon for any crimes that he might have committed. This soured many Americans on Ford; his later explanation was that up until that point virtually his entire time in office was spent dealing with Watergate-related affairs, and that the only way to move past that was to pardon the former president. The public expressed their opinion in the fall congressional elections, when many Democrats were swept into office.

Ford became the second American president to visit China, and the first to visit Japan. It should be remembered it was during the Ford administration that South Vietnam fell to the North Vietnamese and the Vietcong. The last American troops had left in 1973; by 1975, the North Vietnamese army began to occupy several major South Vietnamese cities. Ford toyed with the idea of sending in troops to aid the South Vietnamese, but ended up asking Congress for a major aid package for South Vietnam. By this point, the vast majority of Americans wanted nothing to do with the situation in Southeast Asia, and Congress defeated Ford's request. In late April, the North Vietnamese were closing in on Saigon; some of the most gripping photographs of the era were photos of American helicopters evacuating Americans and Vietnamese who had worked for them from the roof of the American embassy in Saigon one day before the city was captured by the North Vietnamese.

The major problem that Ford's presidency faced was the economy. During the Ford administration, the economy suffered from both unemployment and inflation. This economic situation was termed **stagflation**. Critics of Ford claimed that his tactics were no different from those of Herbert Hoover, as he tried to restore confidence in the economy by asking people to wear "WIN" buttons ("Whip Inflation Now") and to voluntarily spend less to lessen the effects of inflation. Ford pushed for tax cuts and for less government spending; despite these various approaches, by 1975, unemployment in America stood near 10 percent and inflation remained a problem. On several occasions, Ford fell or tripped in public settings, which did not improve the image of the presidency.

In the race for the Republican presidential nomination, in 1976, President Ford was able to fend off the campaign of former governor of California and actor Ronald Reagan. In the election, Ford faced the former governor of Georgia, Jimmy Carter. During the campaign, Carter continually stressed that he would be an outsider in Washington, and not tied to any of the messes that had gone on in Washington since 1968; to many in a post-Watergate America, this message sold perfectly. In addition, Ford did not help himself in the campaign by making several misstatements, such as claiming in one debate that Eastern Europe was not controlled by the Soviet Union. Carter won the presidency by a fairly narrow margin by keeping the New Deal Democratic coalition together. Some Southerners who had voted for Nixon in 1968 and 1972 returned to vote Democrat in 1976 because of Carter's Southern roots.

Presidency of Jimmy Carter

Jimmy Carter discovered that coming into the presidency as an outsider had some advantages but also some definite drawbacks. One of the weaknesses of the Carter presidency was his inability to find "insiders" in Congress with whom he could successfully work to get legislation passed. Carter hired many women and minorities for his White House staff and did away with some of the pomp and circumstance traditionally associated with the presidency (he sometimes wore sweaters when giving addresses to the nation). To Carter's critics, these were signs that he was not really up to the responsibilities of the presidency.

Domestic problems continued to exist in the Carter presidency. Unemployment and inflation remained as major problems. As Ford had done, Carter asked the American people to voluntarily refrain from spending and excessive energy use to bring down inflation. He then tried to cut government spending to cool the economy, and angered many liberal Democrats by cutting social programs. Another approach tried by the administration was to have the Federal Reserve Board tighten the money supply, hoping this would stop inflation; the resulting high interest rates served to depress the economy. Unfortunately, none of these policies worked, and confidence in Carter's abilities to solve economic problems began to wane; by the end of his term, unemployment still stood near 8 percent, with inflation over 12 percent.

Other domestic measures undertaken by Carter included the granting of amnesty to those who had left America to avoid the draft during the Vietnam era and measures for the federal cleanup of chemical waste dumps. Pressures from **OPEC** drove the price of gasoline higher during the Carter presidency; in 1978, the National Energy Act was passed, which taxed cars that were not energy efficient and deregulated the prices of domestic oil and gasoline. During the Carter administration, a cabinet-level Department of Energy was created.

On foreign policy, Carter's early speeches stated that the goal of America should be the spreading of basic human rights around the world. Critics maintained that Carter's idealism blinded him to the real interests of America at the time. Conservatives were very critical of his treaty that gave the Panama Canal back to Panama (this would not actually take place until 1999). Critics also attacked his decision to officially recognize the People's Republic of China as the government of China (thus reducing America's support of Taiwan) and his continued negotiations with the Soviets to limit nuclear weapons (critics stated that America's military might should not be limited). Conservatives were cheered by his response to the 1979 Soviet invasion of Afghanistan. Carter cut aid programs to the Soviet Union and refused to allow the athletes to compete in the 1980 Moscow Summer Olympics.

One of the high points of the Carter presidency was the September 1978 negotiations between Menachem Begin of Israel and Anwar Sadat of Egypt, which produced the **Camp David Accords**. These negotiations were mediated by Carter; as a result of these talks, Israel promised to return occupied land to Egypt in return for official recognition of Israel's right to exist by Egypt. Carter was unable to negotiate a solution to the problem of Palestinian refugees (a problem that still exists today).

The nadir of the Carter presidency was the **Iranian Hostage Crisis**. Iran had been governed by the repressive Shah of Iran, who was propped up by arms and economic aid from the United States. In 1978, a revolution of Fundamentalist Muslims forced the Shah to leave the country; the Ayatollah Khomeini, a Fundamentalist Muslim leader, became leader of Iran. In October 1979, the exiled Shah was suffering from cancer, and Carter allowed him into the United States for treatment. This outraged the Iranians; on November 4, protesters stoned and then seized the American embassy in Tehran, Iran, taking 66 Americans who worked there hostage.

The Americans were kept hostage for 444 days. Some were kept in solitary confinement, while others were not; most were moved around on a regular basis to discourage rescue attempts. Carter tried various attempts to win the release of the hostages, including freezing Iranian assets in America, stopping trade with Iran, and negotiating through third parties. A 1980 attempt to rescue the hostages ended in a military embarrassment when helicopters sent to rescue them either crashed or could not fly because of heavy sand. Carter had been criticized for being ineffectual on domestic programs; as the hostage crisis wore on, he increasingly was seen as ineffectual in the diplomatic sphere as well. The hostages were finally released in January 1981, but only after Carter had left office and Ronald Reagan was sworn in as president.

Election of 1980

Carter was able to win the 1980 Democratic nomination for president despite a challenge from Edward Kennedy. Ronald Reagan, portraying himself as the spokesperson for the conservatives of America, won the Republican nomination. Carter was forced to campaign on his record, which was a very difficult thing to do. Reagan promised while campaigning to build up the military; at the same time, he promised to cut taxes. He promised strong leadership from Washington and also pledged to take power from Washington and give it to the states. Reagan also pledged support for a renewed emphasis on family and patriotism. Reagan won the election by a decisive margin.

The 1980 election was the first totally successful assault on the New Deal Democratic coalition. Social issues of the era, such as the increasing rights of women, sexual freedom, and **affirmative action**, drew many blue-collar workers away from the Democrats and into the Republican camp. (Conservatives successfully convinced many Americans that the Democrats were the cause of the declining image of America abroad and the reason for the decline in traditional morality at home.) Members of the **religious right** supported the Republicans in large numbers (and would continue this pattern in elections that followed). Many Southerners saw the Republicans and Reagan representing their interests more than Jimmy Carter; others perceived Carter to be "soft on communism." As a result of these factors, the **New Right** had become a major force in American politics; besides electing Reagan, they had also pushed the Republicans to the majority in the Senate in 1980.

Presidency of Ronald Reagan

Admirers and detractors of Ronald Reagan both agree that he was a true master of politics (Bill Clinton studied the techniques Reagan used to achieve political success). Reagan used his previously honed skills as an actor to set the right tone and present the right messages at meetings and speeches throughout his presidency. Reagan also used his staff well; on many occasions, he would set the general policy and allow staff people to set up the details.

Upon becoming president, Reagan instituted traditional conservative economic practices. In 1981, federal taxes were cut by 5 percent, and then cut by another 10 percent in 1982 and 1983. Reagan and his economic staff believed in **"supply-side economics,"** which stated that if more money was put in the hands of wealthy Americans by cutting taxes, they would invest it in the economy, thus creating more jobs and additional growth (and eventually additional tax revenue). Capital gains taxes were reduced, also with the intent of encouraging investment.

Political battle lines were drawn early in the Reagan administration. As a result of the tax cuts, the government was taking in less money, causing many domestic programs to be cut, including aid to education, to urban housing programs, and to the arts and the humanities. Liberals were outraged over the fact that, at the same time that social programs were being cut, Reagan increased the defense budget by nearly $13 billion. Reagan also pushed for funding for a Strategic Defense Initiative (SDI; nicknamed "Star Wars") program. As envisioned, this system could shoot down enemy missiles from outer space. Reagan also pushed to give more power back to the states at the expense of the federal government. Reagan called this plan the **New Federalism**. Under this program, how federal money was spent by states was determined by the states and not by the federal government. During the Reagan administration, the policy of deregulation was intensified; industries such as the energy industry and the transportation industry were freed from "cumbersome" regulations imposed by previous administrations (supporters of these regulations would maintain that they were in the interest of the consumers). In addition, funding for the Environmental Protection Agency was greatly reduced during the Reagan presidency. Many perceived the Reagan administration to be antiunion as well; in 1981, the government actively destroyed the union for the air traffic controllers, and striking controllers were fired.

In response to the perceived foreign policy weakness of America in the Carter years, Reagan worked hard to build up America's image in the world. On a small scale, the American army successfully invaded the island of Grenada in 1983. On a much larger scale, Reagan ended the friendlier relations between the United States and the Soviet Union of the détente era. He put new cruise missiles in Europe and referred to the Soviet Union as the "evil empire." Reagan's harsh rhetoric won him much support in the United States. Reagan's popularity also had gone up after the attempt on his life by John Hinckley in 1981.

Reagan ran for reelection in 1984 against Walter Mondale (Mondale's running mate was Geraldine Ferraro, a congresswoman from New York). Mondale criticized Reagan on economic issues; the supply-side approach had not produced as much growth, and as much income from taxes, as its proponents had said it would. However, Reagan's tough cold war rhetoric and support of conservative social issues allowed him to continue to break up the Democratic New Deal coalition; Reagan got nearly 60 percent of the popular vote in 1984. Critics who said that the major beneficiaries of Reagan's economic policies who were the very rich were still very much in the minority.

Reagan continued to practice conservative policies during his second term. The **Tax Reform Act of 1986** dramatically reduced federal tax rates; the tax the wealthiest Americans had to pay on their income, for example, was reduced from 50 percent to 28 percent. In 1986 and 1987, both unemployment and inflation declined. Under Reagan, the Supreme Court also became more conservative, as William Rehnquist became chief justice and Antonin Scalia was one of the new justices on the court. Reagan also nominated Sandra Day O'Connor to be the first woman to serve on the Supreme Court. Most women's groups, however, strongly disapproved of the Reagan administration, citing actions such as efforts during Reagan's second term to cut food stamps and the federal school lunch program.

During Reagan's second term, serious economic problems also developed. On October 19, 1987, known as "Black Monday," the average price for a share of stock fell nearly 20 percent. During Reagan's second term, federal government deficits grew drastically; this occurred because less income was coming into the government because of the previously enacted tax cuts and because of a large increase in defense spending. In addition, for the first time since World War I the United States began to import more than it exported.

Nevertheless, Reagan's foreign policy remained incredibly popular. In April 1986, the United States bombed Libyan air bases after Muammar al-Gadhafi, the leader of Libya, ordered Libyan gunboats to challenge American ships sailing close to Libya. Reagan and the new leader of the Soviet Union, Mikhail Gorbachev, established a close personal relationship and held meaningful negotiations on the reduction of nuclear weapons. Reagan also supported anti-Communist forces fighting in Nicaragua and El Salvador.

Many critics of Reagan had claimed since 1980 that he was unaware of what was being done by others working for him. This view seemed to be validated by the **Iran-Contra Affair** of 1986 and 1987. Apparently without the knowledge of the president, National Security Advisor John Poindexter, Lieutenant Colonel Oliver North, and several others devised an "arms for hostages plan." By this plan, the United States sold arms to Iran, hoping that it could use Irani influence to help free American hostages held in Lebanon. The problem with this plan was that at this point America had an official trade embargo with Iran and had persuaded several European countries to support this. The money for this sale was to be used to fund anti-Communist fighters in Nicaragua, called the "Contras." Again, a problem existed: Congress had passed legislation carefully regulating how much funding could go to the Contras. Congressional and legal hearings were held on the Iran-Contra Affair; as a result, nearly a dozen officials of the Reagan administration were forced to resign.

Many Americans felt (and continue to feel) that the political hero of the modern era was Ronald Reagan. Many supporters felt he restored pride to America, stood up to our enemies abroad, restored the economy of America, and reasserted "traditional" American values. Critics of Reagan maintain that the economic policies of the Reagan administration only benefited the wealthiest Americans; they point out that the gap between the richest Americans and the poorest Americans dramatically increased under Reagan, with the real income of middle- and lower-class Americans actually receding. Critics stated that the Iran-Contra Affair proved the fact that Reagan was dangerously out of touch on many policy decisions. Nevertheless, Reagan's vice president, George H. Bush, would certainly have a tough act to follow as he ran for president on his own in 1988.

Chapter Review

Rapid Review
To achieve the perfect 5, you should be able to explain the following:

- One of the low points of American political life in the twentieth century was the Watergate Affair.
- Richard Nixon's greatest accomplishments were in the field of foreign policy, as he crafted new relationships with both China and the Soviet Union.
- The Watergate Affair developed from the paranoid view of American politics held by Richard Nixon and several of his top aides.
- Gerald Ford's presidency was tainted from the beginning by his pardoning of Richard Nixon.
- Ford faced huge economic problems as president; during his presidency, America suffered from both inflation and unemployment.
- Jimmy Carter and many politicians of the post-Watergate era emerged victorious by campaigning as outsiders.

- President Carter's outsider status hurt him, especially in terms of getting legislation passed in Congress.
- Carter demonstrated his diplomatic skills by helping Egypt and Israel bridge their differences through the Camp David Accords; he was unable to negotiate a release of the American hostages in Iran, and this may have cost him the presidency.
- Ronald Reagan was elected as a conservative and restored the pride of many Americans in America.
- Reagan practiced "supply-side" economics, which benefited the American economy but which also helped create large deficits.
- Under Reagan, the gap between the wealthiest Americans and the poorest Americans increased.
- Reagan reinstituted cold war rhetoric, but later created cordial relations with leaders of the Soviet Union.
- Reagan's lack of direct control over the implementation of presidential policies was demonstrated by the Iran-Contra Affair.

Time Line

1968: Richard Nixon elected president
1971: Nixon imposes wage and price controls
       Pentagon Papers released
1972: Nixon visits China and Soviet Union
       Nixon reelected
       SALT I signed
       Watergate break-in
1973: Watergate hearings in Congress
       Spiro Agnew resigns as vice president
       "Saturday Night Massacre"
1974: Inflation peaks at 11 percent
       Nixon resigns; Gerald Ford becomes president
       Ford pardons Richard Nixon
       WIN economic program introduced
1975: South Vietnam falls to North Vietnam, ending Vietnam War
1976: Jimmy Carter elected president
1977: Carter signs Panama Canal treaty
       Carter issues Vietnam-era draft amnesty
1978: Camp David Accords
1979: Americans taken hostage in Iran
1980: Ronald Reagan elected president
1981–1982: Major recession
       Assassination attempt on Reagan
1981–1983: Major tax cuts instituted
1983: Reagan proposes "Star Wars"
       Americans victorious in Grenada
1984: Reagan reelected
1985: Gorbachev assumes power in Soviet Union
1986: Additional tax reform measures passed
       Iran-Contra Affair
1987: "Black Monday"
1988: George Bush elected president

Review Questions

1. What tactic was *not* used by supporters of Richard Nixon in the 1972 presidential campaign?
    A. Breaking into private offices
    B. Reviewing income tax records of suspected "enemies"
    C. Falsifying war records of opposing presidential candidates
    D. Attempting to halt official investigations of actions of campaign officials

2. According to supply-side economics, when wealthy Americans received tax cuts, they would proceed to do all but which of the following:
    A. Invest heavily in the economy
    B. Open new factories
    C. Purchase stocks
    D. Increase their savings dramatically

3. Which of the following did *not* help create the deficits of the second term of the Reagan years?
    A. Reduction of federal tax rates
    B. Desperately needed increases in funding for education
    C. Increases in military spending
    D. Changes in the tax code that favored wealthier Americans

4. Critics of Ronald Reagan would most emphasize
    A. the effects of the 1981–1983 tax cuts
    B. the U.S. response to threats from Libya
    C. the effects of Reagan's economic policies on the middle and lower classes
    D. his public image and political skills

5. Gerald Ford's WIN program demonstrated to many Americans that Ford
    A. had no real grasp of economic issues
    B. had the uncanny knack of knowing how to inspire the American public
    C. was still under the shadow of Richard Nixon
    D. understood sophisticated foreign policy issues

Answers and Explanations

1. **C.** Of all of the "dirty tricks" practiced by the Republicans in 1972, this was not one of them.

2. **D.** The key to supply-side economics is that when tax cuts give individuals large amounts of money, they will reinvest that money in the economy.

3. **B.** Even though education advocates were saying that funding had to be drastically increased in many urban school districts, funding for education declined during the Reagan era.

4. **C.** The 1981 to 1983 tax cuts did help bring down inflation; at this same time, employment possibilities increased. Compared to the wealthiest Americans, the middle and lower classes experienced little benefit from Reagan's economic policies, especially from the tax cuts of the second term.

5. **A.** Many Americans saw the WIN program as a public relations gimmick, demonstrating that Ford did not truly understand the economic problems of America; many equated WIN to some of the public pronouncements of Herbert Hoover in 1930 and 1931.

CHAPTER 29

Prosperity and a New World Order (1988–2000)

IN THIS CHAPTER

Summary: For much of the post–World War II era, the popularity of a president was largely determined by his success in foreign policy and in handling foreign crises. With the ending of the cold war at the end of the 1980s, skills in handling domestic issues became equally important for presidents and their staffs. Presidents Bush (I) and Clinton are perfect examples of this: Bush's popularity was sky-high after his Desert Storm victory, yet he ended up being defeated by Bill Clinton largely because of economic problems that developed in the closing years of his term. Despite a mountain of personal and ethical issues that surrounded him, President Clinton was able to keep high approval ratings because of a continuing successful economy.

Keywords

New Right: conservative movement that began in the 1960s and supported Republican candidates into the twenty-first century; many voters from the South and from the middle class were attracted by the New Right's emphasis on patriotism and strict moral values.

Operation Desert Storm (1991): military action by the United States and a coalition of Allied nations against Iraq and its leader Saddam Hussein after Iraq had invaded Kuwait; this operation was a resounding success, although the decision was made not to force Saddam Hussein from power.

Whitewater: series of real estate dealings in Arkansas involving Bill Clinton long before he became president; Republicans accused Clinton of associated financial improprieties, but no charges were ever proven. The Whitewater affair was one of several accusations that eventually led to Clinton being impeached by the House of Representatives but acquitted by the Senate.

Contract with America: list of conservative measures proposed by Republicans after winning control of the House of Representatives in 1994; it included term limits and promises to balance the federal budget and to reduce the size of the federal government. Republican supporters of the Contract were led by Speaker of the House Newt Gingrich.

1988 Election

Republican advertisements in 1988 touted George H. Bush as "the most qualified man of our times" to be president. Bush had served as a congressman, as the American ambassador to the United Nations, and as the director of the CIA. The **New Right** had never been entirely comfortable with Bush during his eight years as Reagan's vice president; to appease them, he nominated Senator Dan Quayle, a staunch Conservative, as his vice presidential nominee.

The Democrats nominated Massachusetts Governor Michael Dukakis as their candidate. Dukakis campaigned on his experience as a governor, touting the "Massachusetts miracle" that had pulled the state out of its economic doldrums. Televisions during the 1988 campaign were glutted with negative advertisements, the most notable being one that linked Dukakis to Willie Horton, a black man who had raped a woman while taking advantage of a furlough program established in Massachusetts by the governor. Bush won the election rather handily, despite being behind Dukakis in early polls.

Presidency of George H. Bush

Conservative suspicions of Bush increased during the first months of this presidency. Many considered his stated desires for a "kinder, gentler America" as a heretical attempt to distance himself from the social policies of former president Reagan. Bush's major domestic problem was an ever-growing federal deficit. To broker a deal with Congress to lower the deficit, Bush broke his campaign promise of "no new taxes" and, in 1990, signed a bill authorizing tax increases. Many Conservatives never forgave him for this decision. During Bush's term, few substantive domestic programs were instituted; some commentators complained of the **gridlock** created by a Republican president and a Democratic congress.

During the presidency of George Bush, the 45-year-old cold war ended. In late 1988, Soviet leader Mikhail Gorbachev admitted to Communist party leaders that the vast portion of the Soviet economy that was devoted to military spending and to "protecting" the satellite countries was preventing economic growth of any type from taking place. In 1989, the Soviets began to withdraw support from the satellite states; many in Moscow naively believed that Communist leaders in the satellite states could remain in power without being propped up by the Soviet Union. In Poland, Solidarity, the non-Communist labor party, removed the Communist government from power; throughout late 1989, Communists were removed from power in all of the satellite nations. Many of the republics of the Soviet Union also desired independence. In December 1991, Russian President Boris Yeltsin announced the abolition of the Soviet Union and the creation of 11 independent republics.

A large amount of American aid was pumped into Russia and the other Eastern European states. American academics rushed to Moscow and other major centers in the region, explaining to leaders how capitalism could be introduced in the shortest period of time.

American aid was also sent to help several of the former Soviet republics dismantle the nuclear missiles that had been placed there in the cold war era. The meaning of the cold war is still being debated by academics; whether the United States won the cold war or whether the Soviet Union lost is still a topic of numerous books and historical papers.

The central crisis of the Bush presidency began on August 2, 1990, when the army of Iraq invaded Kuwait. Fears that Saddam Hussein's next target would be Saudi Arabia, the largest exporter of oil to the United States, pushed the United States into action. Almost immediately, in **Operation Desert Shield**, large numbers of American troops were sent to protect Saudi Arabia.

Encouraged by the United States, member states of the United Nations condemned the Iraqi aggression and authorized the creation of a multinational military force to remove Saddam Hussein from Kuwait. The high point of the Bush presidency was the personal diplomacy undertaken by the presidency to get almost all of the states of the Middle East to support military action against Iraq. On February 24, 1991, a ground offensive, termed **Operation Desert Storm**, was mounted against Iraq. Iraqi casualties were over 40,000, while the Americans (who made up most of the troops of the UN international force) lost 150 soldiers in battle. Iraqi soldiers surrendered by the hundreds as they retreated from Kuwait. In a decision that would later be questioned, American forces did not move into Iraq and force Saddam Hussein from power. It should be noted that this was *not* part of the United Nations mandate, and that such an action would have definitely created division in the Middle Eastern coalition so carefully crafted by Bush.

Bush's popularity was at an all time high after Desert Storm. However, problems soon arose that his administration seemed incapable of solving. A recession and continued economic difficulties hit the United States in early 1992. In addition, the end of the cold war brought new difficulties in several states formerly controlled by the Soviet Union. In former Yugoslavia, Serbs began to practice "ethnic cleansing" against Bosnian Muslims. Critics of Bush claimed that he lacked any "vision" of what the role of the United States should be in a post–cold war world.

1992 Election

George Bush and Bill Clinton ran against each other in 1992. The buzzword of politics in 1992 was "change," and both candidates claimed they were prepared to offer it. At the 1992 Republican National Convention, speakers of the New Right spoke about the need for "family values" and that a "religious war" against the Democrats was needed.

The former governor of Arkansas, Bill Clinton, had the political sense to realize that Americans in the early 1990s were interested in economic rather than social issues, and pledged that as president he would overhaul the health care system and work for the preservation of the Social Security system. Clinton campaigned as a "**New Democrat**," stating that he was not another typical big-spending advocate of big government. During his presidency, Clinton on occasion took Republican concepts and claimed them as his own; right-wing critics such as Rush Limbaugh maintained that he would say or do anything if it meant his position would be improved in the polls.

A third candidate in the 1992 race was Texas multibillionaire Ross Perot. Perot spent a lot of money on campaign ads, complaining in these ads about how the politicians in Washington were beholden only to special interests, and that if elected he would bring "common sense" back to the White House. However, the charts depicting the American economy that he used on his advertisements were understood by few people.

Clinton won the 1992 election fairly easily. Many from the New Deal Democratic coalition that had deserted the Democrats for Reagan came back to vote for Clinton in 1992. Bush appeared oddly out of touch at several points during the campaign; at one point, he was caught looking at his watch in the middle of a presidential debate. Nearly 19 million Americans supported Perot; analysts maintain that the support for Perot hurt Bush more than it did Clinton.

Presidency of Bill Clinton

From the beginning, Clinton strove to create an administration different from the one that had preceded it. He appointed minorities and women to his cabinet. During his first term, there were several legislative successes, such as the Brady bill, which created a waiting period for handgun purchases, and the anticrime bill (officially known as the Violent Crime Control and Law Enforcement Act of 1994), which provided federal funds to hire more police officials. However, several issues that Clinton attempted to tackle during his first term drew the ire of many. His attempt to legislate the proper status of gays in the military caused many in all branches of the military service to distrust him. His attempt to legislate a national health insurance plan was defeated by a combination of effective lobbying by the American Medical Association and intense advertising paid for by the healthcare industry. In addition, the fact that Hillary Rodham Clinton was actively involved in the formulation of healthcare policy caused debate over the proper role of a First Lady.

Many also began to question the Clintons concerning their financial dealings. Investments in a failed savings and loan company and in a land development called **Whitewater** caused much controversy; in August 1994, Kenneth Starr became the independent counsel in charge of investigating the Whitewater Affair. Many Clinton supporters felt that Starr moved too vigorously and was out to "get" the Clintons.

The 1994 Congressional elections appeared to be a sweeping rejection of the presidency of Bill Clinton. Republicans, led by new Speaker of the House Newt Gingrich, supported the **Contract with America**, and promised to get rid of many social programs long supported by liberals. Republicans soon learned that the political skills of Bill Clinton were formidable, however. In an attempt to lessen the size of the federal government, there were brief shutdowns of the federal government in 1995 and 1996; on each occasion, public opinion polls stated that the American public strongly sided with the president in his argument that all of this was the fault of the Republicans.

Clinton's popularity rose further as the economy improved steadily in 1995 and 1996. The values of stocks rose, economic growth continued at a steady rate, and inflation remained low (many credited Alan Greenspan, chairman of the Federal Reserve, for his ability to skillfully maneuver interest rates to keep inflation low and growth high).

Clinton's role as a "New Democrat" was again demonstrated when he supported passage of the Personal Responsibility and Work Opportunity Reconciliation Act of 1996. This legislation more carefully regulated the welfare system, cut the food stamp program, and gave power to the states to organize their own "welfare-to-work" programs. This program, which ended "welfare as we know it," was hailed by Clinton supporters as a sign of his pragmatism; many liberals were appalled that he so easily "sold them out."

In foreign policy, Clinton faced some of the same criticisms as Bush. Many claimed that the United States still did not have a post–cold war foreign policy "focus." Many debated the appropriate role of the U.S. military. A humanitarian mission to Somalia led to the death of 18 American soldiers in 1992. The U.S. military was sent in to restore the government of Jean-Bertrand Aristide in Haiti; Clinton also supported NATO air and military efforts to protect Muslims from the "ethnic cleansing" policies of President Slobodan Milosevic of Serbia. Americans remain as peacekeepers in Bosnia to this day.

President Clinton also favored the continued **globalization** of the economy, which included the lowering of tariffs and the expansion of global markets. Clinton worked with many Republicans to secure the passage of **NAFTA (North American Free Trade Agreement)** in Congress. The goal of NAFTA was to gradually remove all trade barriers between the United States, Canada, and Mexico. As with welfare reform, a segment of the traditional Democratic base was infuriated by one of Clinton's policies. In this case, it was the labor unions who felt betrayed.

In 2000, Clinton unsuccessfully attempted to broker peace between the Palestinians and Israel. He increasingly became aware of the threats of Fundamentalist Muslims against the United States. In 1993, bombings took place at the World Trade Center in New York City; American embassies were bombed in Tanzania and Kenya in 1998, and a United States naval ship docked in Yemen was bombed in 2000. Clinton attempted several bombing missions in response to these terrorist attacks, and in one instance came fairly close to killing Osama bin Laden, leader of the Al Qaeda terrorist network.

Campaigning on the continued strength of the American economy, Clinton became the first Democrat since Franklin Roosevelt to win back-to-back terms when he defeated long-time Senator Robert Dole of Kansas in the 1996 presidential election. Early in Clinton's second term, the era of gridlock appeared to be over, as both parties joined in passing legislation to reduce the federal budget. Yet, it was the Whitewater Affair that consumed the most political energy in Washington during the last years of Clinton's second term.

As was stated previously, Kenneth Starr and the Whitewater investigation was originally charged with analyzing the financial dealings of the Clintons in Arkansas. However, the investigation soon delved into other areas of the president's life. It was revealed that he had an affair with a White House intern, Monica Lewinsky. Clinton boldly proclaimed on television that he had never had "sexual relations with that woman." In a lawsuit brought against the president by Paula Jones (for alleged sexual harassment when Clinton was governor of Arkansas), Clinton denied, under oath, having an affair with Lewinsky. Physical evidence obtained from Lewinsky seemed to prove otherwise. Talk show hosts and other opponents stated that the case had long gone beyond merely the matter of the president having an affair; he had actually lied under oath about it.

Clinton's approval ratings remained high throughout his second term; his approval was especially strong in black districts across the country. In the 1996 congressional elections, the Republicans lost five seats in the House of Representatives. Congressional calls for impeachment began; others wondered whether the actions of the president were actually the "high crimes and misdemeanors" that the Constitution stated were grounds for impeachment. On December 19, 1998, the House of Representatives passed two articles of impeachment (obstruction of justice and perjury), thus preparing the way for a trial in the Senate. Two-thirds of the Senators had to vote for an article of impeachment in order to remove him from office. Senate voting took place on February 12, 1999; neither article of impeachment received the necessary two-thirds vote. Many Clinton supporters that spoke during the congressional proceedings noted that despite millions of dollars being spent and years of investigation, the special prosecutor was unable to uncover any illegal actions by the president or his wife. Popular support for the president remained high, and economic prosperity and expansion continued.

2000 Presidential Election

Excitement for the candidates in the 2000 presidential election was very low. The Democrats nominated Al Gore, Clinton's vice president, who often appeared wooden when giving speeches and stirred little emotion, even among long-time Democrats. George W. Bush, son of the former president, was the Republican nominee; in several early interviews, he appeared to lack the knowledge of critical issues that might be expected of a presidential candidate. Ralph Nader ran as a candidate of the Green Party.

When the final results were tabulated, Al Gore actually received some 500,000 votes more than Bush (Nader received less than 3 million votes). However, Gore surprisingly lost his home state of Tennessee, and the winner in the Electoral College would be the winner of the popular vote in Florida. Several recounts were held there, with Bush holding on to a tiny lead. Blacks in several parts of Florida (who voted heavily for Gore) complained that in parts of the state they had been prevented from voting. Further recounts were planned in contested counties. By a 5-to-4 vote on December 9, 2000, the Supreme Court of the United States temporarily halted all recounts. On December 12, the court ruled, again by a 5-to-4 margin, that recounts in contested counties only was a violation of the constitution, thus securing the election of George W. Bush. In the first months of his presidency, Bush concentrated much of his effort on domestic affairs; the events of September 11, 2001, would dramatically change the course of his presidency.

Chapter Review

Rapid Review

To achieve the perfect 5, you should be able to explain the following:

- The ability to manage domestic issues were critical for a president's political success in the post–cold war era.
- George Bush alienated many conservatives, especially when he broke his "no new taxes" pledge.
- The end of the cold war can be attributed to American policy decisions and to weaknesses in the infrastructure of the Soviet Union.
- George Bush skillfully managed the Desert Storm operation against Iraq.
- Bill Clinton presented himself as a "New Democrat" and focused on economic issues in the 1992 presidential campaign; these were important factors in his victory.
- Clinton's failure on national health insurance helped pave the way for large Republican gains in the 1994 congressional elections.
- Clinton and Newt Gingrich were formidable opponents in the budget battles of the mid-1990s.
- The Whitewater scandal and investigations of the personal life of Bill Clinton were the defining political events of the second term of Clinton's presidency.
- George W. Bush's election demonstrated the difficulties of arriving at a "final tally" in any election and was finally secured by the intervention of the U.S. Supreme Court.

Time Line

1988: George Bush elected president
Solidarity replaces Communist government in Poland
1989: Berlin Wall opened, Communist governments fall in Eastern Europe
1991: Persian Gulf War
Breakup of the Soviet Union
Beginnings of economic recession
1992: Election of Bill Clinton
American troops killed in Somalia
1993: NAFTA ratified by Senate
Terrorist bombings at World Trade Center
1994: Republicans sweep congressional elections
U.S. military enters Haiti
Kenneth Starr becomes Whitewater independent counsel
1996: Clinton reelected
1998: Federal budget surplus announced
Articles of impeachment passed in House of Representatives
1999: Clinton acquitted in impeachment trial in U.S. Senate
2000: George W. Bush elected president

> Review Questions

1. A defining characteristic of the Clinton presidency was his
   A. strict adherence to traditional Democratic values
   B. pragmatic policy making
   C. close alliance with liberals in the Democratic party
   D. unprecedented alliance with labor unions

2. George H. Bush alienated many conservative Republicans by
   A. appointing the relatively inexperienced Dan Quayle as vice president
   B. continuing to urge the tearing down of the Berlin Wall
   C. signing the 1990 agreement with the Democrats to reduce the deficit
   D. pursuing policies against Iraq

3. Critics accused Bush of lacking "vision" because
   A. he failed to articulate a successful policy to end the economic deficit.
   B. he failed to remove Saddam Hussein from power.
   C. he failed to sign an arms treaty with Mikhail Gorbachev.
   D. he failed to explain his perception of America's role in the post–cold war world.

4. All of the following were reasons for the end of the cold war *except*
   A. the United States military buildup under Ronald Reagan
   B. the fact that many producers of military weaponry in the United States did not want to continue to produce this weaponry
   C. the weaknesses of the Soviet economy
   D. the cold war rhetoric of both Ronald Reagan and George Bush

5. Bill Clinton was a formidable political opponent for the Republicans for all of the following reasons *except*
   A. his ability to eventually win over former Republicans of the New Right
   B. his support in the black community
   C. his ability to take Republican positions and make them appear to be his own
   D. his ability to withstand political scandal

› Answers and Explanations

1. **B.** In claiming to be a "New Democrat," Clinton sometimes adopted traditional Republican ideas as his own. To many critics, the pragmatism of the Clinton White House masked the fact that President Clinton had few principles that he actually believed in.

2. **C.** This was the agreement where Bush broke his "no new taxes" pledge and broke with traditional Republican policy.

3. **D.** Several historians state that a weakness of both Bush and Clinton was that they were unable to articulate a coherent post–cold war foreign policy.

4. **B.** Most manufacturers had no desire to stop producing weaponry for the cold war. When the cold war finally ended, many of these companies were forced to lay off workers, and some that could not diversify were forced to close.

5. **A.** The New Right was the group that came to despise Bill Clinton the most. Members of the New Right interested in social issues were among Clinton's most passionate detractors during the Whitewater scandal.

CHAPTER 30

Threat of Terrorism, Increase of Presidential Power, and Economic Crisis (2001–2014)

IN THIS CHAPTER

Summary: The threat of terrorism following the September 11, 2001, attack on the World Trade Center in New York City revived the historic conflict between the need for a strong central authority during wartime and the need to maintain civil liberties. President Bush and Congress enacted the Patriot Act, giving the federal government wide powers to investigate terrorists in the United States. The administration argued that policies such as wiretapping the telephones of suspected terrorists without warrants were necessary for security. Civil libertarians stated that the president's actions were unauthorized and probably illegal.

U.S. forces attacked terrorist strongholds in Afghanistan in late 2001. In 2003, U.S. and Allied forces invaded Iraq and toppled the regime of Saddam Hussein. The Bush administration claimed that Iraq was a military threat and a potential terrorist ally. Critics disputed these claims.

At home, America remained politically divided. When sectarian violence broke out in Iraq, public opinion questioned the rationale for the invasion and the continued American military presence there. Social issues such as abortion and gay marriage also caused huge divides in American society.

In the 2006 congressional elections, Democrats regained control of both the Senate and the House of Representatives. National debate continued over the war in Iraq and decisions made by the Bush administration. The presidential election of 2008 took place just as the U.S. economy entered a severe downturn. In the voting, Democratic Senator Barack Obama defeated Senator John McCain for the presidency, and Democrats solidified their control over Congress.

Continued foreign policy debates and severe economic problems challenged the Obama administration from day one. Efforts to revive the economy and to lower the unemployment rate had only mixed results. In Iraq, U.S. military efforts brought some stability, and in 2010, U.S. troops were withdrawn from that country. However, ongoing combat against guerrilla fighters in Afghanistan proved frustrating. At home, there were battles over immigration issues and an effort by the administration to expand health care insurance. There was also a rise in antigovernment sentiment led by the so-called "Tea Party" movement. The result was Democratic losses in the 2010 congressional elections.

In the 2012 presidential elections, President Obama won a second term, defeating the Republican candidate, former governor Mitt Romney. Obama was supported by a diverse coalition that included large numbers of younger voters, women, minorities, and working class Americans.

KEY IDEA

Keyword
Neoconservatism: modern American political philosophy that opposes big-government approaches to domestic issues yet favors an interventionist and aggressive foreign policy; most neoconservatives advocated American intervention in Iraq in 2003.

9/11 and Its Aftermath

On September 11, 2001, Saudi Arabian terrorists hijacked four American commercial airliners. Two slammed into the World Trade Center, one crashed into the Pentagon, and the fourth slammed into a field near Pittsburg (after passengers attempted to seize control of the plane from the terrorists). World opinion stood firmly on the side of the United States in the immediate aftermath of 9/11. It soon became known that Osama bin Laden, living in Afghanistan and protected by the Taliban government there, had helped mastermind the terrorist attack. On September 20, President Bush addressed a joint session of Congress, stating that the United States would prevail in this conflict and that Osama bin Laden would be brought to justice.

The United States and its allies began a military assault on Afghanistan in November 2001; within two weeks, resistance to the American and allied attacks ended, with many members of the Taliban and their supporters fleeing to the mountains between Afghanistan and Pakistan. It was later reported that Secretary of Defense Donald Rumsfeld began to plan for a military invasion of Iraq during this same period. Secretary Rumsfeld and others in the administration followed the policies advocated by an influential group of American thinkers called **neoconservatives** (or neocons), who wanted to use American might to remake the Middle Eastern region into a democracy. Neocons firmly believed that, to accomplish this, Sadaam Hussein had to be removed from power in Iraq.

Events Leading Up to the American Invasion of Iraq

During his State of the Union address in January 2002, President W. Bush stated that Iraq, Iran, and North Korea were all part of an "Axis of Evil," and that Iraq possessed weapons of mass destruction (and was close to developing a nuclear weapon). Vice President Dick Cheney urged the president to act quickly and forcefully against Iraq during this period, while

Secretary of State Colin Powell suggested a more cautious approach. It was also revealed that, during the months before the attack, both the CIA and FBI had information on the activities of the Al Qaeda terrorists who flew the airplanes on 9/11, but that some of it was not acted upon. President Bush announced the creation of the new Department of Homeland Security, which would attempt to reorganize America's intelligence-gathering organizations as a result of the **Homeland Security Act of 2002** being signed into law.

In his 2003 State of the Union address, President Bush stated that a war against Iraq was not inevitable, and that Saddam Hussein should reveal his weapons programs to United Nations inspectors. At the same time, plans were being developed in the United States military establishment for the invasion of Iraq. During Operation Desert Storm, President Bush's father was successful in creating a strong coalition of nations (including several in the Middle Eastern region) that supported the invasion of Iraq; fewer nations enthusiastically supported American claims that Iraq might have to be invaded again. In his State of the Union address, President Bush stated that he had learned from the British that Iraq had attempted to obtain uranium from Niger, an African country. (Uranium is necessary for nuclear development.) This claim would later become controversial when it would become known that the CIA had already discredited it. The fact that North Korea might possess a nuclear weapon was another very thorny international issue facing the Bush administration.

Operation Iraqi Freedom

On March 18, 2003, American and British forces invaded Iraq and faced only minor resistance as they moved toward Baghdad. (By April 11, most of the city was occupied by American and British army units.) Many Americans viewed with pride the televised scene of Iraqis cheering the pulling down of a statue of Saddam Hussein. Secretary of Defense Rumsfeld had led the move in the Defense Department toward an emphasis on smaller, more mobile military units; initial successes in Iraq seemed to vindicate this new approach.

Looting and violence took place in Baghdad and other Iraqi cities in the aftermath of the fall of Saddam Hussein and continued unabated for several weeks. American efforts to bring running water and electricity to citizens in Baghdad and other cities were a very slow process; some Iraqis began to resent the Americans because of this. From the very beginning, Americans attempted to rebuild schools and the basic infrastructure of Iraq; news broadcasts around the world emphasized the violence that became a daily feature of Iraqi life as Kurds, Shiites, and Sunnis (the three major groups in Iraq) began to attack each other. These attacks would only intensify in the ensuing years. In addition, Americans were unable to locate the weapons of mass destruction in Iraq that had been the major justification for the invasion in the first place, and firm connections between Al Qaeda and Saddam Hussein remained elusive.

Effects of the War at Home

After the initial euphoria of victory in Iraq wore off, an intense debate developed in the United States over the justification and purpose of American efforts in Iraq. President Bush and others in the administration portrayed the war in Iraq as a crucial part of America's worldwide attack on terrorism; critics of the administration said the war had sidetracked America from its mission of fighting terrorism. Additionally, in July, unnamed officials in the administration were accused of illegally revealing the identity of CIA agent Valerie Plame in order to discredit her husband Joseph Wilson; Wilson had cast doubt on the administration's account of Iraq purchasing uranium from Niger. Eventually, I. Lewis

"Scooter" Libby, Vice President Cheney's chief of staff, was indicted on charges related to this case, and, by 2006, it was suggested that the president himself had authorized the release of this information.

Continued violence in Iraq, the cost of the war, and claims by several former administration officials that President Bush was preparing for war against Iraq even as he was taking office dominated the presidential elections of 2004. Supporters of American efforts in Iraq were cheered by the fact that an interim Iraqi government took power on June 28, 2004; however, the authority of this government remained uncertain. Evidence of American torture of Iraqi prisoners caused many to further question American efforts in Iraq. Many observers stated that photographs of American soldiers humiliating Iraqis at the Abu Ghraib prison seriously undermined the American mission in Iraq.

Democrats chose Senator John Kerry of Massachusetts to oppose President Bush in November. Many Democrats felt that Kerry was the perfect choice as a candidate, since he was a decorated veteran of the Vietnam War and could thus credibly attack the war policies of the president. As the campaign wore on, however, many were unable to comprehend the nature of Senator Kerry's opposition to the war in Iraq, since he had voted to support the resolutions authorizing American efforts in Iraq. (Kerry responded that he opposed the war that was being conducted.) In addition, what each candidate had done during the Vietnam conflict (some 35 years earlier) became a focus of the campaign. Charges that had been lodged against President Bush in 2000 questioning his service in the National Guard resurfaced. A group of "swift boat veterans," several of whom had served with Senator Kerry in Vietnam, questioned the nature of the medals he had won and the nature of the wounds he had received in Vietnam; in addition, they were deeply critical of Kerry's attack on American efforts in Vietnam when he returned home after the war. President Bush also emphasized moral values in his campaign, thus winning the strong support of the **"religious right"** in America. As a result, President Bush was victorious in the 2004 presidential election; Republican majorities in both the House and the Senate also increased as a result of this election.

Victory of Conservatism in the Bush Era

Many policy initiatives that Conservatives had long desired were either discussed or enacted by the Bush administration and Congress during this era. Gay marriage was a campaign issue in 2004, and, in many states where the president was victorious in the November election, ballot initiatives to allow gay marriage were convincingly defeated. (At the same time, the state of Massachusetts was making gay marriage legal.) In 2004, the president supported and signed legislation expanding the legal rights of human fetuses; prochoice supporters saw this as part of the Conservative agenda to slowly chip away at abortion rights. In 2005, President Bush nominated two new justices to the Supreme Court, John Roberts and Samuel Alito, who were both considered Conservative; those opposing abortion were hopeful that the Supreme Court might be in a position to overturn the *Roe v. Wade* case in the near future. In the 2005 Terri Schiavo case, many Conservatives stated that the feeding tube should not be removed from this seemingly brain-dead woman, even though she had reportedly expressed the desire not to be kept alive in such a condition some 10 years earlier (well before she had gone into a coma). In an extraordinary development, Congress passed, and the president signed, a bill authorizing the federal courts to review her case. (Federal courts had previously refused to order the feeding tube be reinserted, as did this federal court.)

Conservatives had long desired a decrease in the size of the federal budget and a decrease in taxes; under the Bush administration, these goals were partially achieved. A 2004 bill authorized a sweeping reform of corporate tax law, giving businesses tax breaks that the president stated were necessary to ensure economic prosperity. Taxes on income were also decreased during the Bush administration; the administration stated that all Americans would benefit from this, although critics stated that these tax cuts largely benefited the wealthy.

Congress and the Bush administration were unable to find significant ways to decrease government spending; as a result, federal deficits skyrocketed. The administration argued that the war in Iraq and the war on terrorism created a necessary increase in spending on the military and on items related to internal security. Those cuts that were enacted included reductions in farm subsidies, benefits for veterans, and spending on education and the environment. Large-scale reform of the Social Security system, which President Bush had stated to be a top priority on several occasions, was not enacted during his presidency.

Another difficult problem facing the United States during this period was the balance between environmental concerns and the needs of the American economy. President Bush stated in his 2006 State of the Union address that "America is addicted to oil" and that this issue had to be addressed. But proposals to drill for oil in Alaska worried many **environmentalists**, who were concerned with the impact on presently pristine land, and American car manufacturers were slow in developing hybrid automobiles. President Bush was attacked by environmentalists for a number of his policies, which they claimed served American business interests at the expense of the environment. Ironically, some suggested that after the United States "won" in Iraq, we could import a substantial amount of oil from that country. However, Iraqi oil production remained far below what it had been before the American invasion.

The ultimate success or failure of America's decision to invade Iraq remained uncertain. Certainly, the goal of the neoconservatives to have Iraq serve as a model of democracy in the Middle East was far from being achieved. Public attitudes toward the president were at an all-time low in mid-2006. Much of this concerned the war in Iraq, but it also came from the perceived failure of the administration to deal effectively with the level of devastation caused in 2005 by Hurricane Katrina. Many Americans recall viewing the utter destruction caused by the hurricane in New Orleans and the perception that the administration was horribly slow to respond to the crisis.

Several influential Republicans in Congress were also damaged by their alleged ties with influential lobbyists in Washington; at least two members of Congress resigned as a result of investigations into the influence of such lobbyists, the most famous being Tom DeLay from Texas, the former majority leader of the House of Representatives. By 2006, Republicans controlled the presidency, both branches of Congress, and the Supreme Court. In the fall of 2006 congressional elections, Democrats won control of both the House of Representatives and the Senate for the first time since 1994.

United States in Transition: 2007–2008

Democratic gains in the 2006 congressional elections demonstrated the dissatisfaction felt by many with the policies of the Bush administration and the Republican Congress that supported the vast majority of those policies. One day after the election, President Bush announced the resignation of Defense Secretary Donald Rumsfeld, the major architect of American policy in Iraq. In the new Congress, California Democratic Representative Nancy Pelosi became the first female Speaker of the House of Representatives.

At the same time, President Bush announced a new policy in Iraq: a "surge" of an additional 20,000 troops were sent to Baghdad to reduce sectarian fighting between Sunnis and Shiites. On a military level, this policy was a success: from 2007 to 2009 violence was dramatically reduced in Iraq, as were American casualties.

Other problems continued to damage the credibility of the Bush administration in 2007. It was found that returning veterans were receiving inadequate military care at the Walter Reed Army Medical Center. Lewis "Scooter" Libby, former chief of staff to Vice President Dick Cheney, was found guilty of lying to a grand jury over the issue of who leaked the name of a covert CIA agent to the press; the agent, Valerie Plame, was married to former ambassador Joseph Wilson, who had questioned President Bush's claim that Saddam Hussein was developing a nuclear weapons program in Iraq. In congressional hearings, it was charged that seven U.S. attorneys had been fired in late 2006 for purely political reasons; ultimately, Attorney General Alberto Gonzales was forced to resign over this issue. In January 2008, it was reported that CIA videotapes of the use of "harsh interrogation techniques" on Al Qaeda suspects had been inappropriately destroyed.

Primary elections for the 2008 presidential election began in February 2008. Senator John McCain of Arizona emerged as the Republican candidate, but many Conservative Republicans remained unconvinced that McCain was "Conservative enough" to truly represent the party. Senators Barack Obama and Hillary Clinton battled for the Democratic nomination. Signs of economic distress intensified. In January 2008, the economy lost jobs for the first time in 52 months, and in February, General Motors announced the largest ever loss for one of the major automakers in a single quarter.

Barack Obama won the Democratic nomination for president, making him the first African American to be selected to be the nominee for president of a major party. Obama chose Senator Joseph Biden as his vice-presidential nominee. At the Republican National Convention, John McCain officially became the nominee of his party. McCain surprised many by choosing Governor Sarah Palin from Alaska as his choice for vice president; Palin had little exposure at the national level.

As the American economy continued to deteriorate, financial and economic issues began to dominate the American presidential campaign. Barack Obama claimed that a major cause of the economic downturn was the deregulation of business championed by many Republicans during the Bush administration; McCain countered that Obama favored much more government spending and an increase in taxes. A huge financial crisis broke in September, leading Congress to pass a major bailout package for financial institutions; the crisis may have influenced the outcome of the election. Obama eventually won the presidential election, with Democrats increasing their control over both houses of Congress. Severe economic woes continued: the stock market continued to fall, unemployment continued to increase, and additional bailout plans for various financial institutions were discussed. By the end of the year many economic commentators began making comparisons with the Great Depression of the 1930s.

Obama Presidency

President Obama and his administration found that many of the issues confronting them were incredibly difficult to tackle. The economy, ongoing wars in Iraq and Afghanistan, healthcare, and immigration were all complicated ones. In Iraq, a civilian government had taken office in 2006, and despite ongoing incidents of sectarian violence, by 2010 the situation was stable enough to permit the withdrawal of U.S. troops. However, in Afghanistan, U.S. forces were engaged in continuing military operations against Taliban guerrilla fighters who were attempting to topple the U.S.-backed civilian government. After much debate, the president authorized a troop buildup in Afghanistan, although many inside and outside the administration questioned whether it would really be possible to "win" in Afghanistan. The administration enacted economic bailout plans that saved many jobs—and saved banks, the auto industry, and AIG (a large insurance and financial services company) from bankruptcy—while Republican opponents criticized the cost of these measures and the lack of progress in bringing down the unemployment rate, which remained near 10 percent. The issue of jobs was on the minds of most Americans; when it appeared that the president's policies didn't appear to be creating enough of them, his approval ratings fell. President Obama pressed hard to have Congress pass comprehensive healthcare legislation but some supporters of reform said that the bill didn't go far enough, while others believed that the bill was unconstitutional and resulted in "socialized medicine."

Other issues created political controversy during the period. A British Petroleum (BP) oil well in the Gulf of Mexico exploded and spilled huge amounts of oil into the sea, and for several months it appeared that neither private industry nor the government could contain the human and environmental damage. Some compared Obama's reaction to the oil spill to President Bush's inadequate response to Hurricane Katrina. A fear of illegal immigration grew in the southwestern United States and spread to other parts of the nation, with increased calls to place a fence or wall on the border with Mexico and to increase penalties on undocumented immigrants. There were also signs of an increase in anti-Islamic sentiment in the United States; a proposal to construct an Islamic center in the vicinity of the World Trade Center site in New York City generated loud debate. A number of Americans continued to state in opinion polls that they believed that President Obama was either a Muslim or was born outside the United States.

In this climate the so-called "Tea Party" movement developed. There was no unified set of beliefs that members of the Tea Party movement followed but, as a whole, Tea Party members favored a scaling down of the size of government and a reduction in taxes; some also favored the elimination or reduction of government "entitlement" programs. To many in the movement, President Obama and "political insiders" in Washington were the embodiment of all that was wrong with America. Tea Party members were also critical of "establishment" members of the Republican Party; in primaries leading up to the 2010 congressional elections a number of candidates supported by the Tea Party defeated "mainstream" Republicans.

On election day 2010, the Republican Party was able to win control of the House of Representatives and gain seats in the Senate. A number of Republican candidates supported by the Tea Party were victorious (although several prominent Republican Party candidates supported by the Tea Party were not).

The last two years of President Obama's first term were contentious ones. Republicans and Democrats fiercely battled on issues surrounding the budget and on the legitimacy of "Obamacare," President Obama's plan for many more American citizens to have healthcare insurance. Critics of Republicans argued that Republicans in Washington (especially those in the House of Representatives) refused to cooperate with the President on budgetary issues for purely political reasons. Republican Senate President Mitch McConnell stated that Republicans' main agenda during this period should be the defeat of President Obama. Critics of the President argued that he never legitimately attempted to achieve compromise with the Republicans on a multitude of issues, and that he lacked the political skills to do so. Many Americans were surprised when in the spring of 2012 the Supreme Court, by a 5-to-4 vote, validated most of the president's healthcare initiative.

Election of 2012

The 2012 presidential election pitted President Obama against Mitt Romney, former governor of Massachusetts. Both candidates agreed that the nation faced serious economic issues. President Obama emphasized his desire to increase taxes on the wealthiest Americans and to protect the middle class. Mitt Romney and his vice-presidential nominee, Congressman Paul Ryan, emphasized the need for fiscal responsibility and the need to reform "entitlement programs" (Social Security, Medicare, and Medicaid). The candidates generally focused on domestic affairs during the course of the campaign.

On election day 2012, President Obama was returned to office, defeating former Governor Romney in the Electoral College by a sizable 322 to 206 majority; Democrats also (surprisingly) increased their majority in the United States Senate and slightly increased their numbers in the House of Representatives. President Obama won all but one of the important "swing states" in the election; his winning coalition included many younger voters, women, Hispanic Americans, African Americans, and, especially in the Midwest, working class Americans. Governor Romney won the majority of white Americans and senior citizens.

There were numerous reasons for the Democratic victory in this election. Governor Romney was perceived as being supportive of wealthy Americans at the expense of the rest of American citizens; the Democratic campaign message was that the Romney/Ryan ticket favored the upper "1 percent" of Americans. Republicans were also perceived as being out of touch with mainstream America on social issues, especially those relating to women's rights. Remarks made by several Republican senatorial candidates on the issue of abortion alarmed a number of Americans. During the Republican primaries, Governor Romney took a very harsh stance on immigration issues; during the election this caused many Hispanic Americans to vote for President Obama. In analyzing the election numbers one thing was clear: the demographic nature of America was gradually changing; receiving the votes of a majority of white American voters alone would no longer be enough to ensure victory in any national political election. Both major political parties would have to recognize that fact as they planned their policies and platforms for the future.

Chapter Review

Rapid Review

To achieve the perfect 5, you should be able to explain the following:

- The 9/11 attacks on the World Trade Center had a huge impact on America and its perceived role in the world, and affected policy decisions.
- The need for unity and strength in time of war versus the desire for individual liberty has created major divisions in public opinion during the period of the Iraqi war.
- The overall agenda of the neoconservatives greatly influenced the decision of the administration to go to war in Iraq.
- "Winning" the war in Iraq proved to be much more difficult than many of the supporters of the war initially imagined.
- Failure to find weapons of mass destruction and failure to establish a link between Al Qaeda and Iraq caused many in the United States to question the overall purpose of American efforts in Iraq.
- An effective emphasis on social issues and the failure of John Kerry to truly distance himself from President Bush on Iraq were factors in President Bush's victory in the 2004 presidential elections.
- Several Conservative policy positions concerning social issues and taxation were enacted during the presidency of George Bush.
- Public attitudes toward George Bush, his policies, and the war in Iraq were sharply divided during his presidency.
- The efforts of the Bush administration in countering the devastation of Hurricane Katrina caused many to doubt the effectiveness of that administration in confronting serious disasters.

- Continued dissatisfaction with Republican policies and a desire for new leadership helped lead to the election of Barack Obama in 2008.

Time Line

2001: Terrorist attack on World Trade Center and the Pentagon
American and British troops invade Afghanistan
Planning for military operations against Iraq begins

2002: President Bush terms Iran, Iraq, and North Korea the "Axis of Evil"
Creation of Department of Homeland Security
Homeland Security Act signed into law

2003: President Bush warns of possible war with Iraq in State of the Union address
Operation Iraqi Freedom: U.S. and British invasion of Iraq
"Outing" of CIA agent Valerie Plame
Violence in Iraq between Kurdish, Shiite, and Sunni factions
Controversy develops as weapons of mass destruction are not found in Iraq

2004: President Bush proposes budget with $521 billion deficit
Photographs show American soldiers torturing Iraqi prisoners at the Abu Ghraib prison
Provisional government with limited authority comes into power in Iraq
George Bush defeats John Kerry in presidential elections; Republicans increase their control of the House and the Senate

2005: Presidential budget proposes deep cuts in social programs
Violence between Sunnis and Shiites in Iraq increases dramatically
John Roberts becomes Supreme Court chief justice
Hurricane Katrina devastates New Orleans
I. Lewis "Scooter" Libby, Vice President Cheney's chief of staff, indicted on obstruction of justice concerning the Valerie Plame case
Samuel Alito becomes Supreme Court justice

2006: In an effort to deal with federal deficit, President Bush proposes reduction of many government programs
Controversy develops over secret wiretapping program by the federal government
Under investigation regarding his connections with a lobbyist, Tom DeLay, Republican majority leader of the House of Representatives, resigns

2007: Nancy Pelosi of California becomes first female Speaker of the House

2008: Barack Obama becomes first African American elected to the U.S. presidency
Severe economic downturn affects U.S. financial institutions

2009: Unemployment in the United States remains near 10 percent
President Obama announces "troop surge" in Afghanistan

2010: BP oil spill clogs Gulf of Mexico
Healthcare legislation passes
Tea Party candidates win some seats in midterm elections

2012: President Obama elected to a second term
Gunman murders 20 children and 6 staff members at Sandy Hook Elementary School in Connecticut
Supreme Court upholds the legality of most provisions of the Affordable Care Act

2013 Former National Security Agency contractor Edward Snowden leaks information about NSA surveillance practices
Supreme Court strikes down the Defense of Marriage Act, which limited federal benefits to marriages between a man and a woman
Budget dispute between Congressional Republicans and President Obama leads to a partial shutdown of government for 16 days

Healthcare.gov website for purchasing Affordable Care Act health plans starts up but suffers many glitches
2014 U.S.-Russia relations deteriorate because of Russian takeover of Crimea
Supreme Court strikes down limits on biennial donations to politicians by individuals

> Review Questions

1. Major reasons stated by President Bush for the war in Iraq included all but which of the following?
   A. Iraq possessed weapons of mass destruction.
   B. Saddam Hussein had tried to assassinate the president's father.
   C. Iraq had links to terrorism.
   D. Saddam Hussein had killed his own people in the past.

2. Which of the following was not a major policy goal of the religious right?
   A. have a constitutional amendment banning gay marriage
   B. limit abortions in the United States
   C. cut the income tax of wealthy Americans
   D. take steps to save the life of Terri Schiavo

3. Which of the following developments that occurred during the Bush administration will potentially have the longest-lasting impact on American society?
   A. the creation of the Department of Homeland Security
   B. the passage of the Patriot Act
   C. the president's opposition to gay marriage
   D. the appointment of John Roberts and Samuel Alito to the Supreme Court

4. All of the following hurt John Kerry in his bid for the presidency in 2004 *except*:
   A. his statements on the Vietnam War when he returned home after the war
   B. his voting record on the Iraqi war
   C. his performance in the 2004 debates
   D. the fact that questions on social issues (gay marriage, etc.) appeared on the ballots in many states

5. In his expressed desire to expand democracy to the Middle East, President Bush can be equated with which twentieth century president who wanted to expand American concepts of freedom and democracy to Europe and other parts of the world?
   A. Woodrow Wilson
   B. Franklin Roosevelt
   C. Dwight Eisenhower
   D. Lyndon Johnson

> Answers and Explanations

1. **B.** All of the other three were given by administration officials as reasons for war. The president noted in several speeches that Saddam Hussein had tried to kill his father, but this was not used by the administration as a major reason for war.

2. **C.** Many fiscal Conservatives supported the reduction of income taxes in the United States. This was not an issue that was important to the socially Conservative members of the religious right.

3. **D.** The appointments of two Conservative justices to the Supreme Court caused the entire court to swing to the Conservative side; rulings from such a court on issues such as abortion might fundamentally alter American society.

4. **C.** Many Vietnam War veterans were deeply offended by Senator Kerry's statements when he returned home after the war. Many voters were never sure where Kerry actually stood on the issue of the Iraqi war. President Bush portrayed himself as the "moral" candidate; questions on any ballot dealing with morality served to help him. In reality, Senator Kerry did quite well in the 2004 debates.

5. **A.** Several observers have noted the similarity between President Bush's desire to spread democracy in the Middle East with Woodrow Wilson's Fourteen Points, which proposed the creation of a more democratic and freer Europe, and world, after World War I.

CHAPTER 31

Contemporary America: Evaluating the "Big Themes"

IN THIS CHAPTER

Summary: The current events and debates of today become the history of tomorrow. People's actions and opinions are affected by their knowledge and memories of the past. As students of history, you should remember to look at the connections running back and forth in time as we examine some important current issues.

KEY IDEA

Keywords
Economic crisis
United States and the world
Big vs. little government
Individual rights in "wartime"
Presidential power
Religion and government
Immigration

Americans in every period in U.S. history have evaluated the past in comparison to the time in which they lived. Many Americans in the 1980s viewed the 1960s in a negative light and maintained that a "better" America existed back in the 1950s. Many American writers in the 1920s noted that they were in a new era that was decidedly different from the America that existed before World War I. This chapter is being written in 2010, as some people are comparing and contrasting the present economic crisis with the Great Depression of the 1930s. Indeed, as this is being written, many central questions about American identity and the American experience are under scrutiny. What are the big themes of American history that have relevance today, and what central characteristics of the American identity are being questioned during the first years of the Obama presidency?

To help you study, think of the following both in terms of present-day events and historical context. "History is in the past, period," a professor of mine once told me. However, one can sometimes get a richer interpretation of the past by viewing prior events through the lens of the present. Major themes to evaluate in this manner might include:

(1) **What should the role of the government be in the economic affairs of the nation?** This was a question that was being asked at the beginning of the Obama administration. Many commentators maintained there was very little regulation of big business and the banking industry as a result of Republican policies during the Bush administration; to offset this, the Obama administration authorized a stimulus package worth billions of dollars. In supporting this program, government officials emphasized that with big business and the banking industry in poor shape the only institution left to "prime the pump" of the economy was the federal government. When those in Congress voted on the stimulus package, only three Republican senators voted for the legislation; every other Republican in Congress voted against it.

This debate about whether government should be a "pump-primer" of the economy was a replica of economic debates that have gone on in the past about the role of government in the economy. "Free market" Conservatives (in recent decades, mainly Republicans) are generally opposed to government intervention in the economy (although some argued that the 2009 economic crisis was so severe that government intervention was necessary). Many would argue that the appropriate government response to economic downturns should be to cut taxes: Conservatives believe this will put money in the pockets of millions of consumers, who will do all the "pump-priming" that is necessary. Others would argue that, when they are left to their own devices, business interests are only interested in profits; supporters of this view would state that the sheer greed of business and banking interests led to the banking and housing crises besetting the country in 2009. These critics would argue that it is the job of government to regulate the economy and to have an active role in economic affairs, despite the uncertainty of success of the actual stimulus package that was passed by Congress.

During the first years of the Great Depression, Herbert Hoover did exactly what many "sensible" economists of the time said he should do: wait out the downturn and rely on state, local, and voluntary agencies to deal with the impact of the stock market crash and subsequent business failures. To many economists of the time, active government intervention in the economy would be nothing short of "socialism" (a charge that some made when discussing the policies of Barack Obama). Franklin Roosevelt responded with the New Deal, which turned the federal government into a major engine of economic growth.

The controversy over the role of the federal government in economic affairs goes back to the differing views of America held by Thomas Jefferson and Alexander Hamilton. It appears that the federal government will continue to be a major player in the economic affairs of the nation for the foreseeable future, although members of the "Tea Party" and other critics claim that government's role in the economy must be sharply curtailed.

(2) **What should the role of the United States be in world affairs?** Americans have asked this central question since the foundation of the republic. George Washington warned the nation to stay out of world affairs that are not of immediate concern to us. Many in the 1920s and 1930s agreed, pushing the United States to a position of

severe isolationism. However, if America is to call itself a world leader, do we not have the responsibility to truly lead the world? If we are utterly convinced that democracy is the best form of government on the face of the earth, don't we have a responsibility to spread that form of government abroad?

This was the view of Woodrow Wilson as he tried to get Americans to support the Versailles Treaty after World War I, and it was the view of George Bush and the neoconservatives leading up to the latest invasion of Iraq. Those who support this view are forced to ponder the thorny possibility that parts of the world that we may want to transform may be opposed to some of the changes that we are proposing for their country or region. Which is more important: promoting self-determination (another stated American goal) or promoting the American way? These are fundamental issues that Americans have wrestled with in the past and are still concerned with today.

(3) **What should be the impact of the federal government be on the lives of American citizens?** This is another question that Americans have wrestled with, especially in the last 80 years. It is connected to the issue of the role of the federal government in the economy. Before the New Deal policies of Franklin Roosevelt, the role of the federal government in the lives of citizens was minimal. However, the New Deal created a radically new role for the federal government: it was now the responsibility of the federal government to take care of those who could not take care of themselves. The Social Security Act is perhaps the most famous example of a New Deal policy exemplifying this new thinking. The Great Society programs sponsored by Lyndon Johnson in the 1960s followed the New Deal spirit of assisting those who are unable to assist themselves.

During the past 30 years, there has been an effort by Conservative Republicans to roll back some of these "liberal policies"; a famous statement of this "end big government" philosophy was the 1992 Republican Contract with America. Many conservatives maintain that Americans act most nobly when they stand up and act independently and are not burdened with regulations, rules, and excessive taxation handed down by the federal government. However, it would be extremely hard to credibly argue that there was anything noble about the way that American business interests acted during the Bush years when concerted efforts *were* made to "get the government off the backs of the people."

A "New Deal liberal" would say that we need government to take care of those who can't take care of themselves, while many Conservatives would say that we need government to help people take care of themselves. However, during the economic crises of late 2008 and 2009 most public opinion polls stated that the majority of Americans felt that we needed a government that was strong enough to successfully handle domestic crises such as Hurricane Katrina or economic turmoil. Now some members of the Tea Party and others call for a reduction or elimination of Social Security benefits and the elimination of some government agencies such as the Department of Education and the Office of Environmental Protection.

(4) **How many of our individual rights should we be willing to give up when fighting a foreign enemy?** This is another difficult issue that Americans have debated since the founding of the nation. John Adams passed the Alien and Sedition Acts, Abraham Lincoln promoted censorship of the press during the Civil War, and dissidents who spoke against military intervention were jailed during World War I. Historians today still debate whether these actions were justified.

Debate on this issue flared again during the War on Terror: many Americans wondered how invasive the government should be when "protecting us" during major crises? Many maintained that if government officials wanted to look through their phone logs and e-mail messages to help defeat terrorism, so be it; others wondered about the impact of government actions such as these on individual freedoms. Also, how much freedom should the press have in times of crises? Many maintained that the freedom of the press should also be curtailed during times of crisis, while others argued that such restrictions were overly likely to be abused, whether from good intentions or to deliberately protect or benefit those in power.

(5) **Should the power of the three branches remain equal, or should the power of the executive branch expand in times of crisis?** This is another question that commentators and politicians have discussed over time. Critics complained that Abraham Lincoln, Franklin Roosevelt, George Bush, and even Barack Obama have acted as if the other branches of government didn't exist. But isn't there a need for a strong executive branch in times of crisis? During the latest Bush administration, the president and his supporters justified the expansion of the executive branch as being essential in the battle against terrorism; critics maintained that President Bush and Vice President Cheney used terrorism as an excuse to increase the power of the executive branch (at the expense of congressional power). In the past, there has been an ebb and flow of power between the executive and the legislative branches. Critics fear that some of the measures of recent years will make the increase in power of the executive branch permanent.

(6) **What connections should exist between religion and government?** This is another question that has been a topic of discussion since the earliest days of the republic. Historians point out that religion has always been an issue in American politics. Many voted against presidential candidate Al Smith in 1928 because he was a Catholic. John Kennedy faced many questions concerning his Catholicism when he ran for president in 1960; Joseph Lieberman had to state what he could do and not do on the Sabbath (he is an Orthodox Jew) when he ran for vice president in 2000. Since the 1980s some critics have voiced concern over the increasing role of the religious right in the Republican party. Ministers from the religious right urged congregations to support President Bush's reelection in 2004 because he was a "man of God" and the war in Iraq because it had "God's blessing." Yet in recent years, other diverse voices, even from within the religious right, have been heard. The religious right had always been keenly interested in issues such as abortion and homosexuality; some members of that community have recently maintained that the environment and helping America's homeless are equally important issues. Several Christian ministers have recently noted that Christianity can be liberal as well, reminding followers that Christian ministers were among the first supporters of the civil rights movement in the South in the 1960s.

(7) **What should American policy toward immigration be?** Recent American debates on illegal immigration mirror debates that have occurred on numerous occasions in American history. The words of those who wish to severely restrict immigration today somewhat match the pronouncements of nineteenth-century "Know-Nothings" or nativists of the 1920s; in each case, the work ethic, educational background, and moral character of those attempting to enter the United States has been questioned. Recent plans to build fences on the Mexican border were matched by demands in the 1920s to send immigrants back to Eastern and Southern Europe. Congressional debates in the early 1920s produced legislation that reduced immigration to a trickle. Passions concerning this issue are just as high in the early twenty-first century.

There are other major issues that have been continually redebated and reanalyzed throughout American history, including the question of the nature of the American dream. When studying American history and studying for this exam, I would encourage you to compare how key issues such as these were seen in the past compared to how they are perceived today. If you do this, past historical trends will make more sense to you; this approach will also help you write historical essays, and it certainly makes the historical material that you are studying much more interesting!

STEP 5

Build Your Test-Taking Confidence

AP U.S. History Practice Exam 1
AP U.S. History Practice Exam 2

PRACTICE EXAM 1

Answer Sheet For Multiple-Choice Questions

1.1 Ⓐ Ⓑ Ⓒ Ⓓ
1.2 Ⓐ Ⓑ Ⓒ Ⓓ
1.3 Ⓐ Ⓑ Ⓒ Ⓓ
1.4 Ⓐ Ⓑ Ⓒ Ⓓ
2.1 Ⓐ Ⓑ Ⓒ Ⓓ
2.2 Ⓐ Ⓑ Ⓒ Ⓓ
2.3 Ⓐ Ⓑ Ⓒ Ⓓ
2.4 Ⓐ Ⓑ Ⓒ Ⓓ
3.1 Ⓐ Ⓑ Ⓒ Ⓓ
3.2 Ⓐ Ⓑ Ⓒ Ⓓ
3.3 Ⓐ Ⓑ Ⓒ Ⓓ
3.4 Ⓐ Ⓑ Ⓒ Ⓓ
4.1 Ⓐ Ⓑ Ⓒ Ⓓ
4.2 Ⓐ Ⓑ Ⓒ Ⓓ
4.3 Ⓐ Ⓑ Ⓒ Ⓓ

4.4 Ⓐ Ⓑ Ⓒ Ⓓ
5.1 Ⓐ Ⓑ Ⓒ Ⓓ
5.2 Ⓐ Ⓑ Ⓒ Ⓓ
5.3 Ⓐ Ⓑ Ⓒ Ⓓ
5.4 Ⓐ Ⓑ Ⓒ Ⓓ
6.1 Ⓐ Ⓑ Ⓒ Ⓓ
6.2 Ⓐ Ⓑ Ⓒ Ⓓ
6.3 Ⓐ Ⓑ Ⓒ Ⓓ
6.4 Ⓐ Ⓑ Ⓒ Ⓓ
7.1 Ⓐ Ⓑ Ⓒ Ⓓ
7.2 Ⓐ Ⓑ Ⓒ Ⓓ
7.3 Ⓐ Ⓑ Ⓒ Ⓓ
7.4 Ⓐ Ⓑ Ⓒ Ⓓ
8.1 Ⓐ Ⓑ Ⓒ Ⓓ
8.2 Ⓐ Ⓑ Ⓒ Ⓓ

8.3 Ⓐ Ⓑ Ⓒ Ⓓ
8.4 Ⓐ Ⓑ Ⓒ Ⓓ
9.1 Ⓐ Ⓑ Ⓒ Ⓓ
9.2 Ⓐ Ⓑ Ⓒ Ⓓ
9.3 Ⓐ Ⓑ Ⓒ Ⓓ
9.4 Ⓐ Ⓑ Ⓒ Ⓓ

AP U.S. HISTORY PRACTICE EXAM 1

Section I

Part A (Multiple Choice)

Time: 35 minutes

Directions: Each of the following questions refers to a historical source. These questions will test your knowledge about the historical source and require you to make use of your historical analytical skills and your familiarity with historical themes. For each question select the *best* response and fill in the corresponding oval on your answer sheet.

Questions 1.1-1.4 refer to the following quotation:

At a meeting of working girls held at Hull House during a strike in a large shoe factory, the discussions made it clear that the strikers who had been most easily frightened, and therefore the first to capitulate, were naturally those girls who were paying board and were afraid of being put out if they fell too far behind. After a recital of a case of peculiar hardship one of them exclaimed: "Wouldn't it be fine if we had a boarding club of our own, and then we could stand behind each other in a time like this?" After that events moved quickly. We ... discussed all the difficulties and fascinations of such an undertaking, and on the first of May, 1891, two comfortable apartments near Hull House were rented and furnished. The Settlement was responsible for the furniture and paid the first month's rent, but beyond that the members managed the club themselves. ... At the end of the third year the club occupied all of the six apartments which the original building contained, and numbered fifty members.

—Jane Addams, *Twenty Years at Hull House*, 1912

1.1 Which of the following *best* reflects the perspective of Jane Addams in the passage above?
   A. Poor people need the leadership of reformers like herself.
   B. Poor people need support in helping themselves.
   C. Poor people don't need outside help.
   D. Poor people don't deserve help.

1.2 Settlement houses like Hull House expressed a desire of reformers to do which of the following?
   A. Convert immigrants to Christianity
   B. Prevent political radicalism
   C. Provide cheap labor for industry
   D. Improve conditions in urban neighborhoods

1.3 A settlement house worker was most likely to be motivated by which of the following?
   A. The Social Gospel
   B. Social Darwinism
   C. Communism
   D. The support of an urban political machine

1.4 The perspective of the passage above would most directly support which of the following political goals?
   A. Women's suffrage
   B. Trust-busting
   C. Greater rights for unions
   D. Weakening political machines

Question 2.1 refers to the following image:

> TO BE SOLD on board the Ship *Bance-Island*, on tuesday the 6th of *May* next, at *Ashley-Ferry*, a choice cargo of about 250 fine healthy NEGROES, just arrived from the Windward & Rice Coast.—The utmost care has already been taken, and shall be continued, to keep them free from the least danger of being infected with the SMALL-POX, no boat having been on board, and all other communication with people from *Charles-Town* prevented.
>
> *Austin, Laurens, & Appleby.*
>
> N. B. Full one Half of the above Negroes have had the SMALL-POX in their own Country.

Advertisement, Charleston, South Carolina, 1780s

2.1 Which of the following *best* reflects the perspective of the above image?
   A. Slaves represent a public health threat.
   B. The importation of slaves is a legitimate enterprise.
   C. The importation of slaves needs to be halted.
   D. Smallpox is a major danger to Charleston.

2.2 During the 1780s, which of the following was the most widespread crop cultivated by slaves in North America?
   A. Wheat
   B. Sugar
   C. Tobacco
   D. Cotton

2.3 Following the American Revolution, many Founding Fathers believed which of the following?
   A. Slavery would gradually disappear in the United States.
   B. The freeing of slaves should be outlawed.
   C. Slavery would be the foundation of the American economy.
   D. Freed slaves deserved government reparations for their suffering.

2.4 Which of the following was a reference to slavery in the Constitution?
   A. The banning of slavery in the Northwest Territory.
   B. Slavery was outlawed above the Mason-Dixon Line.
   C. Slavery could not be outlawed.
   D. A prohibition for 20 years of any law banning the importation of slaves.

Questions 3.1-3.4 refer to the following quotation:

Those who came before us made certain that this country rode the first waves of the industrial revolutions, the first waves of modern invention, and the first wave of nuclear power, and this generation does not intend to flounder in the backwash of the coming age of space. We mean to be a part of it—we mean to lead it. For the eyes of the world now look into space, to the moon, and the planets beyond, and we have vowed that we shall not see it governed by a hostile flag of conquest, but by a banner of freedom and peace. We have vowed that we shall not see space filled with weapons of mass destruction, but with instruments of knowledge and understanding. ... We choose to go to the moon. We choose to go to the moon in this decade and do the other things, not because they are easy, but because they are hard, because that goal will serve to organize and measure the best of our energies and skills, because that challenge is one that we are willing to accept, one we are unwilling to postpone, and one which we intend to win, and the others, too.

—John F. Kennedy, September 12, 1962

3.1 John F. Kennedy in this passage is urging his fellow Americans to emulate which of the following?
   A. The pioneers
   B. Progressive reformers
   C. Captains of industry
   D. The Green Berets

3.2 Kennedy's statement *best* reflects which of the following?
   A. American unease in a time of troubles
   B. American confidence in a time of prosperity
   C. A liberal concern for social justice
   D. A conservative fear of big government

3.3 Kennedy's speech can *best* be compared to which of the following?
   A. Dwight Eisenhower's speech on the "military-industrial complex"
   B. George Washington's Farewell Address
   C. Abraham Lincoln's Gettysburg Address
   D. Franklin D. Roosevelt's "Arsenal of Democracy" speech

3.4 Kennedy's speech most directly led to which of the following?
   A. The Vietnam War
   B. The Mutually Assured Destruction (MAD) nuclear strategy
   C. The Apollo space program
   D. The Great Society social programs

Questions 4.1–4.4 refer to the following quotation:

I appeal to any white man to say, if ever he entered Logan's cabin hungry, and he gave him not meat: if ever he came cold and naked, and he clothed him not? During the course of the last long and bloody war, Logan remained idle in his cabin, an advocate for peace. Such was my love for the whites, that my countrymen pointed as they passed, and said, "Logan is the friend of the white man." I had even thought to have lived with you but for the injuries of one man. Colonel Cresap, the last spring, in cold blood and unprovoked; murdered all the relations of Logan, not even sparing my women and children. There runs not a drop of my blood in the veins of any living creature. This called on me for revenge. I have sought it: I have killed many; I have fully glutted my vengeance. For my country, I rejoice at the beams of peace. But do not harbor a thought that mine is the joy of fear. Logan never felt fear. He will not turn on his heel to save his life. Who is there to mourn for Logan? Not one.

—Address attributed to Logan, an Indian leader, 1774

4.1 Which of the following *best* expresses the perspective of Logan in the passage above?
   A. Logan believes the expansion of British settlements must be stopped
   B. Logan laments the loss of his family
   C. Logan opposes a new peace treaty
   D. Logan believes that Indians need to find strength in unity

4.2 Which of the following most directly expresses why Logan's Address became very popular in the early United States?
   A. Many Americans believed that the Indians had been treated badly.
   B. Many Americans believed that the only good Indian was a dead Indian.
   C. Many Americans believed that Indians were a noble people who were disappearing.
   D. Many Americans believed that Indians should abandon their way of life.

4.3 Which of the following in later years would be most likely to see themselves in Logan's position?
   A. An opponent of big government in the 1930s
   B. An opponent of consumerism in the 1950s
   C. A supporter of liberalism in the 1960s
   D. A supporter of feminism in the 1970s

4.4 A sympathetic reader of Logan's Address in the early years of the United States would be most likely to support which of the following Indian policies?
   A. Exterminating all Indians
   B. Respecting Indian territory and sovereignty
   C. Encouraging Indians to migrate to Canada and Mexico
   D. Building reservations and encouraging Indians to change their ways

Questions 5.1–5.2 refer to the following cartoon:

BORN TO COMMAND.

OF VETO MEMORY.

HAD I BEEN CONSULTED.

KING ANDREW THE FIRST.

Political cartoon, 1832

5.1 Which of the following groups would be most likely to support the perspective of the cartoon?
  A. Democrat supporters of Andrew Jackson
  B. Whig opponents of Andrew Jackson
  C. Know-Nothing opponents of immigration
  D. Anti-Masonic opponents of special privilege

5.2 The cartoon most likely refers to which of the following policies of Andrew Jackson?
  A. The "war" against the Bank of the United States
  B. Opposition to nullification threats in South Carolina
  C. Indian removal
  D. Support for the spoils system

5.3 Though a supporter of "strict construction" of the Constitution, Jackson was notable for which of the following?
  A. Weakening the presidency
  B. Spending on internal improvements
  C. Strengthening the presidency
  D. Weakening the party system

5.4 Andrew Jackson saw himself as a champion of which of the following continuities in United States history?
  A. The struggle for civil rights for all
  B. Government assistance for the underprivileged
  C. The cooperation of government and big business
  D. The democratization of American life

Questions 6.1-6.4 refer to the following quotation:

The 1980s have been born in turmoil, strife, and change. This is a time of challenge to our interests and our values and it's a time that tests our wisdom and skills.

At this time in Iran, 50 Americans are still held captive, innocent victims of terrorism and anarchy. Also at this moment, massive Soviet troops are attempting to subjugate the fiercely independent and deeply religious people of Afghanistan. These two acts—one of international terrorism and one of military aggression—present a serious challenge to the United States of America and indeed to all the nations of the world. Together we will meet these threats to peace. …

Three basic developments have helped to shape our challenges: the steady growth and increased projection of Soviet military power beyond its own borders; the overwhelming dependence of the Western democracies on oil supplies from the Middle East; and the press of social and religious and economic and political change in the many nations of the developing world, exemplified by the revolution in Iran.

Each of these factors is important in its own right. Each interacts with the others. All must be faced together, squarely and courageously. We will face these challenges, and we will meet them with the best that is in us. And we will not fail.

—Jimmy Carter, State of the Union Address, January 23, 1980

6.1 Which of the following has some of its roots in the conditions discussed by Jimmy Carter in this passage?
   A. The War on Terror
   B. High unemployment
   C. Tensions with China
   D. High budget deficits

6.2 The problems that Carter faced in 1980 can *best* be compared to those of which of the following?
   A. Abraham Lincoln in the 1860s
   B. Theodore Roosevelt in the 1900s
   C. Warren Harding in the 1920s
   D. Franklin D. Roosevelt in the 1930s

6.3 The situation Carter described led most directly to which of the following?
   A. The creation of the North Atlantic Treaty Organization (NATO)
   B. Carter's defeat in the next presidential election
   C. An American invasion in the Middle East
   D. Carter's victory in the next presidential election

6.4 Which of the following *best* expresses Carter's approach to foreign policy in the passage above?
   A. Isolationism
   B. Appeasement
   C. Containment
   D. A call for war

Questions 7.1–7.4 refer to the following advertisement:

Ford advertisement, 1952
Used with permission of Ford Motor company.

7.1 Which of the following *best* expresses the message of the advertisement?
   A. Ford cars are for the well-off
   B. Ford cars are great work vehicles
   C. Ford cars are for the whole family
   D. Ford cars are for the lower classes

7.2 The advertisement most directly reflects which of the following?
   A. The growing prosperity and leisure of Americans in the 1950s
   B. The materialistic excesses of the rich in the 1950s
   C. A push for social conformity in the 1950s
   D. The recreational limits imposed by a poor economy in the 1950s

7.3 The American embrace of the automobile in the twentieth century most directly reflects which continuity in U.S. history?
   A. A desire for social justice
   B. A desire for economic equality
   C. A desire for higher social status
   D. A desire for more personal freedom

7.4 In the 1950s the widespread availability of the automobile most directly helped make possible which of the following?
   A. The rise of international corporations
   B. The rapid growth of suburbs
   C. The prevalence of stay-at-home moms
   D. The baby boom generation

Questions 8.1–8.4 refer to the following quotation:

Let us not, I beseech you sir, deceive ourselves. Sir, we have done everything that could be done, to avert the storm which is now coming on. We have petitioned; we have remonstrated; we have supplicated; we have prostrated ourselves before the throne, and have implored its interposition to arrest the tyrannical hands of the ministry and Parliament. Our petitions have been slighted; our remonstrances have produced additional violence and insult; our supplications have been disregarded; and we have been spurned, with contempt, from the foot of the throne. In vain, after these things, may we indulge the fond hope of peace and reconciliation. There is no longer any room for hope. … It is in vain, sir, to extenuate the matter. Gentlemen may cry, Peace, Peace, but there is no peace. The war is actually begun! The next gale that sweeps from the north will bring to our ears the clash of resounding arms! Our brethren are already in the field! Why stand we here idle? What is it that gentlemen wish? What would they have? Is life so dear, or peace so sweet, as to be purchased at the price of chains and slavery? Forbid it, Almighty God! I know not what course others may take; but as for me, give me liberty or give me death!

—Patrick Henry, March 23, 1775

8.1 The sentiments expressed by Patrick Henry led most directly to which of the following?
   A. The Declaration of Independence
   B. The Albany Plan
   C. The Boston Tea Party
   D. The Constitution of the United States

8.2 In this passage, Henry expresses an abiding American concern about which of the following?
   A. No entangling alliances with foreign countries
   B. The dangers of standing armies
   C. Self-government
   D. The separation of church and state

8.3 Which of the following nineteenth-century groups most directly saw themselves as following in the tradition of Patrick Henry?
   A. Supporters of Manifest Destiny
   B. Members of the Republican Party
   C. Abolitionists
   D. Southern secessionists

8.4 The "storm" that Henry refers to was most directly the result of which of the following?
   A. American efforts to trade with Spain and France
   B. British efforts to shrink a budget deficit after the French and Indian War
   C. British unwillingness to fight Indian tribes on the frontier
   D. British impressments of American sailors and interference with American trade

Questions 9.1–9.4 refer to the following quotation:

Of all the band of adventurous cavaliers, whom Spain, in the sixteenth century, sent forth on the career of discovery and conquest, there was none more deeply filled with the spirit of romantic enterprise than Hernando Cortes. Dangers and difficulties, instead of deterring, seemed to have a charm in his eyes. ... He conceived, at the first moment of his landing in Mexico, the design of its conquest. When he saw the strength of its civilization, he was not turned from his purpose. ... This spirit of knight-errantry might lead us to undervalue his talents as a general, and to regard him merely in the light of a lucky adventurer. But this would be doing him injustice; for Cortes was certainly a great general, if that man be one, who performs great achievements with the resources which his own genius has created. There is probably no instance in history, where so vast an enterprise has been achieved by means apparently so inadequate. ... He brought together the most miscellaneous collection of mercenaries who ever fought under one standard: adventurers from Cuba and the Isles, craving for gold; hidalgos, who came from the old country to win laurels; ... wild tribes of the natives from all parts of the country, who had been sworn enemies from their cradles, and who had met only to cut one another's throats, and to procure victims for sacrifice; men, in short, differing in race, in language, and in interests, with scarcely anything in common among them. Yet this motley congregation was assembled in one camp, compelled to bend to the will of one man, to consort together in harmony, to breathe, as it were, one spirit, and to move on a common principle of action!

—William Hickling Prescott, *History of the Conquest of Mexico*, 1843

9.1 Given the perspective of the passage above, William Hickling Prescott believed which of the following about the conquest of the Aztec Empire?
   A. The actions of Hernando Cortes were irrational.
   B. The conquest of Mexico was a racist atrocity.
   C. Cortes was chiefly motivated by a desire for wealth.
   D. The Aztec Empire had to give way to the superior civilization of Spain.

9.2 As Prescott makes clear in the passage above, an important reason for Cortes's military success was which of the following?
   A. The advantage of superior numbers
   B. The superior military skill of mercenaries
   C. Taking advantage of divisions among the Indians
   D. Effective use of European artillery

9.3 The Spanish in America were interested in which of the following?
   A. Escaping oppression at home
   B. Expanding territories under Spanish control
   C. Seeking religious freedom for themselves
   D. Creating independent principalities for themselves

9.4 Prescott's interpretation of the conquest of Mexico resembles which contemporary nineteenth-century American political movement?
   A. Support for Manifest Destiny
   B. Support for Southern secessionism
   C. Support for abolitionism
   D. Support for Know-Nothingism

Part B (Short Answer)

Time: 50 minutes

Directions: Answer the following four questions. Carefully read and follow the directions for each question. Some will refer to historical sources. These questions will require you to make use of your historical analytical skills and your familiarity with historical themes. These questions do *not* require you to develop a thesis in your responses.

Question 1 is based on the following passages:

The problem lay buried, unspoken, for many years in the minds of American women. It was a strange stirring, a sense of dissatisfaction, a yearning that women suffered in the middle of the twentieth century in the United States. Each suburban wife struggled with it alone. As she made the beds, shopped for groceries, matched slipcover material, ate peanut butter sandwiches with her children, chauffeured Cub Scouts and Brownies, lay beside her husband at night—she was afraid to ask even of herself the silent question—"Is this all?"

—Betty Friedan

It is my belief, based on working with this movement for quite a number of years, that the movement is having an adverse effect on family life, that it is a major cause of divorce today, and that it is highly detrimental to our country and to our families. ... Motherhood must be a self-sacrificing role. The mother must be able to subordinate her self-fulfillment and her desire for a career to the well-being of her children so she can answer her child's call any hour of the day or night. This is what marriage and motherhood are all about.

—Phyllis Schlafly

1. Based on the two interpretations of feminism in the 1960s and 1970s, complete the following three tasks.
   A. Briefly explain the main point made by Passage 1.
   B. Briefly explain the main point made by Passage 2.
   C. Explain how one of the perspectives above influenced American politics in the 1960s and 1970s. Provide at least *one* piece of evidence to support your explanation.

2. At different times in U.S. history Americans have been concerned about internal subversion.
   A. Choose *one* of the following and explain how it reflected American concerns about internal subversion. Provide at least *one* piece of evidence to support your explanation.
   - Haymarket Square Riot
   - First Red Scare
   - Second Red Scare
   B. Explain how the event you chose affected American politics. Provide at least *one* piece of evidence to support your explanation.

3. Supreme Court decisions played a key role in defining the civil rights of African Americans.
   A. Choose *one* of the following and explain its importance for African Americans. Provide at least *one* piece of evidence to support your explanation.
   - *Dred Scott v. Sanborn*
   - *Plessy v. Ferguson*
   - *Brown v. Board of Education of Topeka, Kansas*
   B. Explain how the Supreme Court's attitude toward African-American civil rights changed over time. Provide at least *one* piece of evidence to support your explanation.

Question 4 is based on the following image:

Railroad schedule, 1840s

4. Use the image and your knowledge of U.S. history to answer parts A, B, and C.
   A. Briefly explain the transportation situation in the United States before the advent of railroads. Provide at least *one* piece of evidence to support your explanation.
   B. Briefly explain the transportation advantage of railroads. Provide at least *one* piece of evidence to support your explanation.
   C. Briefly explain how railroads influenced American economic, political, or military history. Provide at least *one* piece of evidence to support your explanation.

END OF SECTION I

Section II

Part A (Document-Based Question)

Time: 60 minutes

Directions: This question asks you to write a well-constructed essay making use of the following documents and your broader knowledge of U.S. history. You will need to make use of your historical analytical skills and your familiarity with historical themes. You must develop a thesis that answers the question, supporting it with evidence drawn from the documents and from evidence and information outside the documents.

At the turn of the century, several nations were competing for international empires. After the Spanish-American War, the U.S. government sought to extend and solidify its influence in the Western Hemisphere. Analyze the effects of American foreign policy in Latin America in the period 1899 to 1917.

Document A
Source: Platt Amendment, May 22, 1903

> *Article III. The Government of Cuba consents that the United States may exercise the right to intervene for the preservation of Cuban independence, the maintenance of a government adequate for the protection of life property, and individual liberty, and for discharging the obligations with respect to Cuba imposed by the Treaty of Paris on the United States, now to be assumed and undertaken by the Government of Cuba.*

Document B
Source: Hay-Bunau-Varilla Treaty, November 18, 1903

> *The Republic of Panama grants to the United States in perpetuity, the use, occupation and control of a zone of land and land under water for the construction . . . of said canal. . . . The Republic of Panama further grants to the United States in perpetuity, the use, occupation and control of any other lands and waters outside the zone . . . which may be necessary and convenient for the construction . . . and protection of the said Canal.*

Document C
Source: Theodore Roosevelt, Annual Message to Congress, December 6, 1904

> *If a nation shows that it knows how to act with reasonable efficiency and decency in social and political matters, if it keeps order and pays its obligations, it need fear no interference from the United States. Chronic wrongdoing, or an impotence which results in a general loosening of the ties of civilized society, may . . . ultimately require intervention by some civilized nation, and in the Western Hemisphere the adherence of the United States to the Monroe Doctrine may lead the United States, . . . in flagrant cases of such wrongdoing or impotence, to exercise an international police power.*

Document D
Source: W. A. Rogers, "The Full Dinner Pail," *Harper's Weekly,* April 13, 1907; courtesy of Theodore-Roosevelt.com.

Document E
Source: William Howard Taft, Fourth Annual Message to Congress, December 3, 1912

The diplomacy of the present administration has sought to respond to modern ideas of commercial intercourse. This policy has been characterized by substituting dollars for bullets. . . . It is an effort frankly directed to the increase of American trade upon the axiomatic principle that the government of the United States shall extend all proper support to every legitimate and beneficial American enterprise abroad.

Document F
Source: Erving Winslow, "Aggression in South America," excerpt from Report of the Thirteenth Annual Meeting of the Anti-Imperialist League, 1912

It is proposed that in the Honduras and Nicaragua . . . the United States government should be authorized to secure the collection and disbursement of the revenue in the interest of American capitalists who contemplate making loans to those countries. This involves serious risk of complications which may lead to further interferences and ultimate control.

The delicacy of these and other foreign relations of the United States is such as should put our citizens upon their guard and confirm their determination to treat with justice all their neighbors and to recognize generally their independent right to govern (or misgovern) their own countries.

Document G

Source: Woodrow Wilson, Address to Congress, April 20, 1914

> A series of incidents have recently occurred which cannot but create the impression that the representatives of General Huerta were willing to go out of their way to show disregard for the dignity and rights of this government, . . . making free to show in many ways their irritation and contempt.
>
> I, therefore, come to ask your approval that I should use the armed forces of the United States in such ways . . . as may be necessary to obtain from General Huerta and his adherents the fullest recognition of the rights and dignity of the United States, even amidst the distressing conditions now unhappily obtaining in Mexico.

Part B (Long Essay)

Time: 35 minutes

Answer *one* of the following questions. Develop a thesis and support it with appropriate historical evidence. This question will require you to make use of your historical analytical skills and your familiarity with historical themes.

1. Some historians have argued that the development of differing economies shaped differing social structures in the English colonies in North America. Support, modify, or refute this contention using specific evidence.

2. Some historians have argued that the development of the West from 1763 to 1820 profoundly influenced American politics. Support, modify, or refute this contention using specific evidence.

END OF SECTION II

ANSWERS TO PRACTICE EXAM 1

Multiple Choice

1.1 B	3.2 B	5.3 C	7.4 B
1.2 D	3.3 D	5.4 D	8.1 A
1.3 A	3.4 C	6.1 A	8.2 C
1.4 C	4.1 B	6.2 D	8.3 D
2.1 B	4.2 C	6.3 B	8.4 B
2.2 C	4.3 A	6.4 C	9.1 D
2.3 A	4.4 D	7.1 C	9.2 C
2.4 D	5.1 B	7.2 A	9.3 B
3.1 A	5.2 A	7.3 D	9.4 A

Explanations for the Multiple-Choice Questions

1.1. **B.** Poor people need support in helping themselves *best* reflects the perspective of Jane Addams in the passage. Jane Addams was a pioneering social worker who became famous for her work with the poor. She was a leader in the settlement house movement, which established social centers in disadvantaged urban neighborhoods. Addams founded Hull House in Chicago.

1.2. **D.** Settlement houses like Hull House expressed a desire of reformers to improve conditions in urban neighborhoods. Settlement houses provided a variety of social services such as childcare for working mothers and English language classes. Settlement house workers also helped the people in their neighborhoods lobby government for better living conditions and city services.

1.3. **A.** A settlement house worker was most likely to be motivated by the Social Gospel. The Social Gospel was a liberal strain of American Protestantism that called on the church to battle injustices in society and to work for social betterment as a way of saving souls.

1.4. **C.** The perspective of the passage would most directly support greater rights for unions. In the passage, Jane Addams helps young women workers find secure communal housing so they can safely strike for better working conditions. Settlement house workers often helped immigrants and the poor organize to protect their rights in their working places and elsewhere.

2.1. **B.** The image reflects the perspective that the importation of slaves is a legitimate enterprise. The image is a notice for a slave auction in Charleston, South Carolina, in the 1780s. Slavery was believed to be crucial to South Carolina's plantation economy.

2.2. **C.** During the 1780s, the most widespread crop cultivated by slaves in North America was tobacco. Cotton did not become the chief cash crop in the South until after Eli Whitney's invention of the cotton gin in the 1790s.

2.3. **A.** Following the American Revolution, many Founding Fathers believed that slavery would gradually disappear in the United States. Economically, tobacco was losing some of its importance as new sources appeared elsewhere in the world. Also the human rights ideals of the Revolution seemed to be at odds with the institution of slavery. The 1787 Northwest Ordinance banned slavery in the Northwest Territory. The Constitution, while recognizing the existence of slavery for representation purposes, ended the importation of slaves from Africa after 1807. What the Founding Fathers did not anticipate was the cotton gin, the cotton boom, and the renewed economic importance of slavery.

2.4. **D.** A ban on the importation of slaves after 20 years was a reference to slavery in the Constitution. This was part of the growing consensus in the years after the Revolution that slavery was a weakening institution, for both economic and ideological reasons. Slavery was gradually outlawed in the Northern states. George Washington and others freed their slaves upon their deaths. Then the invention of the cotton gin made slavery highly profitable again in the South.

3.1. **A.** President John F. Kennedy in this passage is urging his fellow Americans to emulate the pioneers. Kennedy ran for the presidency on a program that he termed the New Frontier. He wanted Americans to emulate their pioneer forebears and surmount a number of challenges, from domestic problems to the cold war. Taking the lead in the space race with the Soviets and landing the first men on the moon would be a dramatic way of demonstrating this pioneering spirit.

3.2. **B.** Kennedy's statement best reflects American confidence in a time of prosperity. The early 1960s were a time of prosperity that had endured since the end of World War II. Kennedy and his successor, Lyndon B. Johnson, believed that the United States could achieve any task it set out to accomplish, whether it was landing a man on the moon, ending poverty in the United States, or winning a war in Vietnam.

3.3. **D.** Kennedy's speech can *best* be compared to Franklin D. Roosevelt's "Arsenal of Democracy" speech. In the "Arsenal of Democracy" speech, Roosevelt also set a challenge for the American people, producing weapons and supplies for the nations resisting Axis aggression during World War II.

3.4. C. Kennedy's speech most directly led to the Apollo space program. The Apollo space missions focused on landing men on the moon. *Apollo 8* circled the moon in December 1968. The *Apollo 11* mission set a lunar module down on the moon. Neil Armstrong and Edwin "Buzz" Aldrin became the first and second men to walk on the moon.

4.1. B. In the passage, Logan laments the loss of his family. Logan was an Indian war chief. After members of his family were murdered by settlers, Logan led a series of retaliatory raids. This began Lord Dunmore's War in 1774, named after the Governor of Virginia. Logan refused to attend the talks that led to a peace treaty but sent the message in the passage instead.

4.2. C. Logan's Address became very popular in the early United States because many Americans believed that Indians were a noble people that were disappearing. As Indians became perceived as a minor and fading threat, many Americans expressed sympathy for their plight. They were sometimes portrayed as "noble savages" free of the corruptions of society. A good example of this is the character of Uncas in James Fenimore Cooper's novel *The Last of the Mohicans* (1825).

4.3. A. In later years, an opponent of big government in the 1930s would be most likely to sympathize with Logan. Like Logan, an opponent of big government during the years of the New Deal and the rapid expansion of the welfare state would feel as if events were moving in the wrong direction.

4.4. D. A reader of Logan's Address in the early years of the United States would most likely support building reservations and encouraging Indians to change their ways. Thomas Jefferson believed that the only hope for Indians was for them to adopt American culture. Until they did so, he thought that they should be moved away from the settlements, giving them time to "civilize" themselves. The consensus of American policymakers during the nineteenth century was that the key to Indian survival was a combination of reservations and eventual assimilation into American society.

5.1. B. Whig opponents of Andrew Jackson would be most likely to support the perspective of the cartoon. The Whigs saw Jackson as an overbearing and tyrannical chief executive, most notably for his veto of the rechartering of the Bank of the United States. Hence, the portrayal of Jackson in the cartoon as "King Andrew."

5.2. A. The cartoon most likely refers to the "war" against the Bank of the United States. President Jackson believed that the privately run Bank of the United States had too much power over the nation's finances. He thought its power was undemocratic. When Henry Clay and Bank supporters passed a rechartering bill through Congress, Jackson vetoed it. He also pulled federal funds from the Bank of the United States, depositing the money in state banks that came to be known as "pet banks." These banks soon began issuing large amounts of paper money. Hoping to rein in inflation, Jackson issued the Specie Circular, requiring gold or silver coins in payment for public lands. This spurred a financial panic and depression in 1837.

5.3. C. Though a supporter of "strict construction" of the Constitution, Jackson was notable for strengthening the presidency. While philosophically a believer in limited government, temperamentally, Jackson could not resist vigorously using the powers of his office in instances as varied as his defiance of the Supreme Court over Indian removal or taking a strong stand against advocates of nullification in South Carolina. Jackson's veto of the recharter of the Bank of the United States because he thought this would be bad policy was unprecedented. Previous presidential vetoes had been based on the perceived unconstitutionality of bills. Jackson here expanded the range of presidential prerogative.

5.4. D. Andrew Jackson saw himself as the champion of the democratization of American life. Jackson portrayed himself as the representative of the common man. During the period of his political ascendancy in the 1820s and 1830s most property qualifications for voting disappeared. The emergence of a vigorous two-party political system encouraged politicians to court and celebrate ordinary Americans. Historians use the term "Jacksonian Democracy" to describe this new era.

6.1. A. The War on Terror has some of its roots in the conditions discussed by President Jimmy Carter in this passage. The difficulties with revolutionary Iran and the Iranian hostage crisis, as well as concerns about the free flow of Middle Eastern oil, spurred increased American involvement in the region. Resentment of this American role played a part in motivating the Al Qaeda attacks on September 11, 2001.

6.2. D. The problems that Carter faced in 1980 can *best* be compared to Franklin D. Roosevelt in the 1930s. Roosevelt also had to deal with great powers, such as Japan, Italy, and Germany launching wars of aggression, and the resulting international instability. Carter was responding to the Soviet Union's invasion of Afghanistan and the problems caused by the new revolutionary regime in Iran. Within a few months, Saddam Hussein's Iraq would start a long and bloody war with Iran.

6.3. B. The situation Carter described led most directly to his defeat in the next presidential election. Carter's inability to secure the release of the Americans held hostage in Iran and the perception that American foreign policy was ineffective contributed to his defeat by Ronald Reagan in the 1980 election.

6.4. C. Containment *best* expresses Carter's approach to foreign policy in the passage. The containment of the Soviet Union and the spread of communism had been a centerpiece of American foreign policy since the late 1940s. Carter's determination to confront the Soviet Union over the invasion of Afghanistan was consistent with the policy of containment.

7.1. C. Ford cars are for the whole family *best* expresses the message of the advertisement. The 1950s were a time of general prosperity. The baby boom was underway, and popular culture celebrated family togetherness. The Ford ad addresses this by showing a family vacationing in their new Ford convertible.

7.2. A. The advertisement most directly reflects the growing prosperity and leisure of Americans in the 1950s. The United States was enjoying a postwar economic boom. This prosperity and government programs such as the G.I. Bill facilitated the movement of many Americans to new levels of affluence. Family vacations such as that pictured in the advertisement became an attainable reality for millions of Americans.

7.3. D. The American embrace of the automobile in the twentieth century most directly reflects a desire for more personal freedom. From the beginning, Americans desired the easy and affordable mobility provided by automobiles. As early as 1929, there was one automobile for every five Americans, more cars than in all the rest of the world. By the 1950s, cars symbolized the prosperity and openness of American society.

7.4. B. In the 1950s, the widespread availability of the automobile most directly helped make possible the rapid growth of suburbs. The rapid spread of new roads, facilitated in part by the 1956 Interstate Highway Act, encouraged developers like the Levitt brothers to create extensive suburban housing developments outside cities. Suburbanites could enjoy the amenities of single family dwellings in attractive surroundings while using their automobiles to commute to work in the cities.

8.1. A. The sentiments expressed by Patrick Henry led most directly to the Declaration of Independence. Speaking in March 1775, shortly before the outbreak of the Revolutionary War in April, Henry pointed out the unwillingness of the British authorities to compromise with the American colonists. Once fighting began, the British continued to show little inclination to address American concerns. This led more and more Americans to contemplate independence. On June 7, 1776, Richard Henry Lee of Virginia submitted a resolution to the Second Continental Congress calling for independence.

8.2. C. In this passage, Henry expresses an abiding American concern for self-government. Unlike the Spanish and French colonies, the English colonies had been largely self-governing from the time of their founding. The Virginia House of Burgesses dated back to 1619. That meant that by the 1770s some of the American colonies had been governing themselves for close to 150 years. This tradition of self-governance led the American colonists to resent new British taxation after 1763 and to stand up for what they believed were their rights as Englishmen.

8.3. D. The nineteenth-century group of Americans that most directly saw themselves in the tradition of Patrick Henry were Southern secessionists. The secessionists of 1860–1861 saw themselves as people whose states' rights were being threatened by a federal government headed by a man that they regarded as a "radical" Republican. They saw their secession from the Union as equivalent to the American colonies withdrawing from the British Empire.

8.4. B. The "storm" that Henry refers to was most directly the result of British efforts to shrink a budget deficit after the French and Indian War. Faced with enormous debts after the expensive war with the French, the British government looked to the American colonies as a new revenue source, leading Parliament to pass a series of taxes on the Americans. The American colonists resented this "taxation without representation," provoking a series of political crises that ended with a war.

9.1. D. Given the perspective of the passage, William Hickling Prescott believed that the Aztec Empire had to give way to the superior civilization of Spain. Prescott, like most nineteenth-century Americans, was convinced that the European conquest of America was part of the upward march of human progress. He saw Hernando Cortes as a hero whose actions were justified by history.

9.2. C. As Prescott makes clear in the passage, an important reason for Cortes's military success was taking advantage of divisions among the Indians. Cortes never had enough Spanish troops to overthrow the Aztec Empire. He built a coalition with other Indian peoples who resented the rule of the Aztecs. This provided him with the manpower to achieve victory.

9.3. B. The Spanish in America were interested in expanding territories under Spanish control. This was a major goal of Cortes and other conquistadors. They were also anxious to spread the Christian religion and win riches for themselves. But whatever they conquered became part of the Spanish Empire, under the rule of the Spanish king.

9.4. A. Prescott's interpretation of the conquest of Mexico resembles the contemporary nineteenth-century support for Manifest Destiny Just as Prescott believed that the Spanish conquest of Mexico represented human progress and demonstrated the superiority of European civilization, the supporters of Manifest Destiny argued that the inevitable spreading of American settlement to the Pacific Ocean and beyond was a measure of the glorious role that the United States would play in the future.

Explanations for the Short-Answer Questions

1. A. This is a passage from Betty Friedan's *The Feminine Mystique* (1963), a major work of the "Second Wave" feminism that emerged in the 1960s. Friedan argued that women were facing an existential crisis in the "comfortable concentration camp" of their homes and could not find personal fulfillment in their role as housewives. She believed women needed to express themselves outside the home. Inspired by the African-American civil rights movement of the 1960s, "Second Wave" feminists (to distinguish them from the "First Wave" feminists who fought for the vote) worked to ensure equality for women in all fields of life from the workplace to politics. Inspired by these ideas and by changing economic circumstances, millions of women entered the workforce in the 1960s and 1970s.
B. Phyllis Schlafly headed the conservative Eagle Forum. She defended the importance of the traditional role of women as mothers and housewives. She argued that modern feminists were "bitter women" who were inflicting their personal maladjustment on everyone else. She believed that feminism was hurting children and weakening the family. Schlafly led the successful opposition to the Equal Rights Amendment.

C. Betty Friedan helped found the National Organization of Women (NOW) in 1966. NOW became a major political force lobbying for feminist issues. In 1972, Title IX of the Educational Amendments prohibited discrimination by sex in any educational institution that received federal funding. This revolutionized women's athletics, opening up unprecedented options for female athletes. The 1973 Supreme Court decision *Roe v. Wade* guaranteed women a right to an abortion. Abortion became a polarizing political issue for decades to come. Congress passed an Equal Rights Amendment (ERA) to the Constitution in 1972. This amendment would have mandated that equality of rights could not be limited by sex. Within a short time 28 states ratified the ERA. At the same time, opposition to the ERA grew in strength. Conservative critics of the ERA argued that such a sweeping amendment would lead to such things as the drafting of women into the military and same-sex bathrooms. As the momentum of the ERA stalled, Congress in 1979 extended the deadline for ratification. The opponents of the ERA, led by Phyllis Schlafly, redoubled their efforts, and by 1982 the campaign to ratify the ERA had failed.

2. A. In early May 1886 labor disturbances rocked Chicago, Illinois. Two strikers were killed by police at the McCormick Harvester Company. On May 4, a meeting was called at Haymarket Square to protest police brutality. When a phalanx of police arrived to disperse the gathering, someone threw a bomb into their ranks. The police responded by shooting into the crowd. Members of the crowd fired back. In this violent episode 7 policemen were killed and 70 others were wounded. Four other people died, and many more were injured. The Haymarket Square bombing was blamed on anarchists. These anarchists were radicals who called for the violent overthrow of the government. Many were foreign born. Eight anarchists were arrested and charged with the crime. All were convicted. Five were sentenced to death; one of these committed suicide in prison, and the other four were hanged. The Haymarket Square Riot and its legal aftermath convinced many people that bloody-minded anarchists threatened American institutions.

During World War I the federal government took action to stifle dissent with the Espionage Act of 1917 and the Sedition Act of 1918. The government also worked to suppress political radicalism, with federal agents rounding up activists of the International Workers of the World (IWW). Eugene Debs, the head of the Socialist party, was sent to prison for criticizing the war. Concerns about radical subversion intensified after the Bolshevik Revolution in Russia late in 1917. In 1919, rapid demobilization led to labor unrest and fears of "Bolshevik" uprisings. A series of terrorist bombings in the spring and early summer, including the explosion of a bomb at the home of Attorney General A. Mitchell Palmer, heightened fears of radicals unleashing a systematic campaign of revolutionary violence. Attorney General Palmer launched a series of raids in November 1919 that arrested hundreds of political radicals. In December, 249 detained aliens, including the famous anarchist writer Emma Goldman, were put on a ship bound for the Soviet Union. More raids followed in 1920. Altogether, around 6,000 people were arrested. The First Red Scare began to die down after a predicted May 1, 1920, Communist outbreak failed to materialize. A terrorist bomb exploded on September 16 on Wall Street, killing 33 people and wounding over 100. Hostility toward political radicals, especially if they were foreign born, continued into the 1920s, playing a role in the Sacco and Vanzetti case.

The Second Red Scare emerged with the cold war following World War II. Former Communists like Elizabeth Bentley declared that Soviet spy rings were operating in the U.S. government. The writer Whitaker Chambers accused Alger Hiss, a distinguished former government official, of having spied for the Soviet Union. Congressman Richard Nixon of the House Committee on Un-American Activities (HUAC) pursued the case, and Hiss was eventually convicted of perjury. It was learned that Soviet agents had stolen atomic bomb secrets. For participating in this, Julius and Ethel Rosenberg were convicted of espionage in 1951, and executed in 1953. To address the security issue in the federal government, President Harry Truman created the Loyalty Review Board to screen federal employees. Anyone who belonged to a politically suspect organization, or who was thought to be a security risk because of behaviors such as alcoholism or homosexuality, was removed from public service. Altogether about 3,000 federal employees were fired or resigned.

B. The Haymarket Square Riot decisively weakened the Knights of Labor, the leading labor union in the United States, and the group that had sponsored the strikes in Chicago. Many people assumed that the Knights of Labor were associated with the anarchists. Unfairly labeled a radical organization, the Knights of Labor rapidly lost members. John P. Altgeld, the Democratic governor of Illinois, investigated the Haymarket bombing and was troubled enough by the way the trial of the anarchists was conducted to pardon the three remaining defendants. Public opinion was outraged by this decision, and Altgeld's political career was ruined.

The First Red Scare led to a deep and long-standing hostility to political radicalism in the United States during the 1920s. Attorney General A. Mitchell Palmer hoped to use his crusade against radicalism as a platform to launch a presidential campaign. His overselling the threat led to the frustration of his political hopes. Weariness with the upheaval associated with the First Red Scare played a role in the election of Republican Warren G. Harding in the 1920 presidential election, with his promise of a "return to normalcy." The popular identification of political radicalism with immigrants contributed to the postwar restriction of immigration. In 1921, immigration was limited to 350,000 a year. The 1924 National Origins Act cut this number to 150,000 and set national quotas based on the 1890 census, which reduced the number of people who could enter the United States from southern and eastern Europe.

The Second Red Scare became a major political issue as fears grew of Communist infiltration of the federal government and other American institutions. Both parties worked to burnish their anti-Communist credentials. The HUAC not only worried about Communists in the government but also conducted investigations of Hollywood because of concerns that Communist messages might be inserted into movies and other forms of entertainment. Ten Hollywood writers and directors with Communist ties refused to cooperate in the investigation and went to jail. Leftists in Hollywood and the entertainment industry were blackballed and saw their careers derailed. In 1950, Congress passed the McCarran Act, which forced Communists to register with the government and gave authorities new powers to detain suspect aliens. In 1950, Senator Joseph McCarthy of Wisconsin claimed to have a list of Communists in the federal government. For the next four years, McCarthy launched a series of high-profile investigations in the Senate that made him a popular anti-Communist hero. He rarely could substantiate his accusations, but that did not matter to his supporters, and senators who publically criticized him suffered politically. Finally, in 1954, after holding televised hearings on communism in the army, during which he appeared to be a bully, McCarthy was censured by the Senate. Though McCarthy's power waned, anticommunism continued to be a force in the United States.

3. A. Dred Scott was a slave in Missouri whose masters had taken him to live in the free state of Illinois and the Wisconsin Territory for several years. Scott went to court to ask for his freedom, arguing that residence in free territory had made him free. In 1857, the Supreme Court in *Dred Scott v. Sanborn* ruled that as a black slave, Scott could not be a citizen and therefore could not sue in the courts. The court also ruled that since Scott was the property of his masters, residence in a free state did not make him free; private property could not be taken from citizens without due process. This reasoning led the court to rule the Missouri Compromise unconstitutional, opening up the possibility of slaveholders freely taking their slaves anywhere in the country. The *Dred Scott* decision outraged many Northerners and intensified sectional differences in the 1850s.

Following the end of Reconstruction in 1877, Southern states began to institutionalize discrimination against African Americans. Measures such as poll taxes and literacy laws were enacted to keep African Americans from voting. Jim Crow laws segregated whites and blacks in public and private facilities. The 1896 Supreme Court decision in *Plessy v. Ferguson* responded to a challenge against segregation in railroad accommodations in Louisiana. The court held that segregation was lawful as long as the segregated accommodations were "separate but equal." This decision helped institutionalize segregation in the South; the stipulation that segregated facilities should be equal was ignored.

Overturning *Plessy v. Ferguson* became a long-standing goal of the National Association for the Advancement of Colored People (NAACP). The NAACP and its lead lawyer, Thurgood Marshall, took the case of Oliver Brown to the Supreme Court. Brown was unhappy that his daughter could not attend a local school in Topeka, Kansas, but was instead bussed to an all-black school. In 1954, the Supreme Court in *Brown v. Board of Education of Topeka, Kansas* unanimously ruled that segregated schools were "inherently unequal," and thus unconstitutional. This effectively overruled *Plessy v. Ferguson* and overturned the legal foundations of racial segregation in the United States.

B. Over time, the attitude of the Supreme Court moved from hostility to African-American rights to support for the African-American civil rights movement. In *Dred Scott v. Sanborn*, Chief Justice Roger Taney and the majority of the court were Southerners. Instead of making a narrow, technical ruling in the case, they intentionally attempted to mount a constitutional defense of slavery. Though Taney had freed his own slaves, he argued that blacks were so inferior to whites they had no claim to the rights of citizens.

The Supreme Court in the aftermath of Reconstruction helped Southerners establish the Jim Crow regime in the South. In the 1883 *Civil Rights Cases*, the court struck down the 1875 Civil Rights Act that had given African Americans equal access to accommodations like hotels and restaurants. The court argued that African Americans were only accorded Fourteenth Amendment protections against discrimination in public facilities; privately owned businesses could constitutionally discriminate in choosing their customers. *Plessy v. Ferguson* continued the process of narrowing the social gains made by African Americans during Reconstruction by offering a constitutional defense of segregation.

For years the NAACP chipped away at *Plessy v. Ferguson* in the courts. A victory came in 1944, when in *Smith v. Allwright* the Supreme Court declared all-white political primaries unconstitutional. This was an opening in the effort to end segregation. Earl Warren, who became chief justice in 1953, after being nominated by President Dwight Eisenhower, was determined to take a stand against legalized discrimination. He played a leading role in organizing a unanimous decision in *Brown v. Board of Education*. From this point on, the Supreme Court was a supporter of African-American civil rights. Fittingly, Thurgood Marshall, who argued the *Brown* case, joined the Supreme Court in 1967, becoming the first African-American Supreme Court justice.

4. A. Before railroads, transportation in the United States was often very difficult. Roads were poor and often badly maintained. Some roads, like the Lancaster Turnpike, completed in Pennsylvania in the 1790s, were exceptions to this rule, and economically important. Opposition to federal road construction on states' rights constitutional grounds limited road building. The best way to travel and transport goods was by water, by sea along the coast, and by river in the interior. The Ohio and Mississippi Rivers were major transportation routes, especially after the invention of the steamboat, which allowed movement both up- and downstream. By 1860, over a thousand steamboats were operating in the Mississippi River Valley. Canals offered a way to bring waterways to areas not blessed with a convenient river. New York governor DeWitt Clinton's Erie Canal, completed in 1825, connected the Hudson River and New York City to the Great Lakes. This inaugurated a canal-building craze. By 1840, over 3,300 miles of canals had been constructed.

B. The advantage of railroads was that they were cheaper to build than canals, and tracks could be laid across almost any type of terrain. The first railroad was constructed in 1828, and by the 1830s railroads were spreading rapidly. In the next two decades the gauges for tracks were standardized, making possible a national railway network. Safety devices improved. In 1859, the Pullman sleeper car appeared, providing a new level of comfort for travelers. Increasingly speedy, safe, and economical, by the 1850s, railroads were becoming the dominant transportation mode in the United States.
C. Before 1840, most Midwestern grain was shipped south down the Mississippi River to the port of New Orleans. With the rise of a thriving railroad network in the Northeast and Northwest, Midwestern grain was increasingly shipped to the big cities of the East. The West and East became increasingly economically interdependent. The growing economic ties between West and East would prove decisive in the Civil War.

American expansionists dreamed of a railroad connection between the settled areas of the United States and the Pacific Coast. Senator Stephen Douglas of Illinois wanted a transcontinental railroad to start west from Chicago. This northern transcontinental route would have to run through the Kansas and Nebraska Territories. Kansas and Nebraska would have to be organized politically to facilitate railroad construction. The only way that Douglas could win Southern votes for this in the Senate was to overturn the Missouri Compromise, which banned slavery in these territories. Douglas's 1854 Kansas-Nebraska Act provided for the settlers in Kansas and Nebraska to decide the issue of slavery in their territories through popular sovereignty. The Kansas-Nebraska Act outraged many people in the North, who saw it as potentially allowing slavery into what should have been free territory. Popular sovereignty in Kansas devolved into violence as proslavery and antislavery settlers fought each other. Douglas's scheme to promote a railroad helped bring on the Civil War.

During the Civil War, railroads were often vital lines of communication and supply. Occasionally troops were shipped from one front to another by railroad. As the war went on, the Northern advantage in miles of railroad became increasingly important as the growing industrial might of the North was mobilized for the Union war effort. Railroads became strategic targets during the war. Atlanta, Georgia, was vital to the South as an industrial center and railroad hub. This made it a key target for Union General William Tecumseh Sherman in 1864. When Sherman left Atlanta for his famous march to the sea, his troops made sure to destroy railroad tracks along the way. The Confederacy lacked the industrial capacity to replace these tracks.

Explanation for the Document-Based Question

Students might begin the essay with a brief discussion of the Treaty of Paris (1898) and its impact on Cuba. American military occupation under General Leonard Wood followed ratification of the treaty. Wood oversaw the construction of infrastructure, revamped Cuba's political administration, and pioneered health reforms. However, the United States violated the Teller Amendment by not affording Cuba complete independence. Congress retained the right to intervene in Cuban affairs and curbed Cuban autonomy in the Platt Amendment (Document A). Students may note that the United States sent troops into Cuba in 1906 and 1912 to quell rebellions and maintained a naval base at Guantanamo. Students may also refer to "dollar diplomacy" by discussing how American corporations came to dominate the oil, railroad, and, most importantly, sugar industries. Some might compare American involvement in Cuba to a different policy toward Puerto Rico (Foraker Act of 1900, Jones Act of 1917). Students should identify the policies of Theodore Roosevelt, William H. Taft, and Woodrow Wilson. They should examine how the Venezuela crisis (1902) precipitated the announcement of the "Roosevelt Corollary" to the Monroe Doctrine (Document C). Students will apply their knowledge of this policy to American intervention in the Dominican Republic in 1905. Some might note that U.S. control of Dominican customs undermined the nation's independence. Students might speculate on the results of involvement in the internal affairs of nations. A discussion of American interests in constructing an isthmian canal should include Secretary of State John Hay and overtures to Colombia. Students may discuss Philippe Bunau-Varilla, the USS *Nashville*, and Panamanian Revolution. Students will note how Panama reacted to the Hay-Bunau-Varilla Treaty (Document B). They might argue that the Hay-Bunau-Varilla Treaty enabled the United States to direct Panamanian affairs. An examination of "dollar diplomacy" under Taft (Document E) may touch upon his Secretary of State Philander C. Knox. Students will note how the growing influence of American mining companies in Nicaragua resulted in military intervention in 1909. Others might note that American banks financed and owned Nicaraguan railroads. American troops returned in 1912 to help maintain the government of Adolfo Diaz. Students might state that Document D reflects the belief that the United States used its military to open or preserve economic opportunities. Some might point to future problems with the Sandinistas or Contras. Students may use Document F to indicate that American imperialism did not enjoy universal support in the United States. Students could observe how the United States continued its involvement in the Dominican Republic and Nicaragua (Bryan-Chamorro Treaty, 1914) under Wilson. They may also touch upon how intervention in Haiti in 1915 paralleled involvement with its neighbor. Most students will discuss Wilson's relationship with Mexico. Some might begin with the transfer of power from Porfirio Diaz to Francisco Madero to General Victoriano Huerta and Wilson's refusal to recognize the Huerta regime. Students might observe that American businesses wanted to promote stability in Mexico in order to establish favorable trade. Students should examine the instability related to conflicts between Huerta and Venustiano Carranza. Students should discuss the effects of the Tampico affair (Document G) and seizure of Veracruz. Students should also refer to the tenuous relationship between Wilson and Carranza and the issue of recognition. Some may touch upon Pancho Villa and raids in the American Southwest that caused Wilson to send General John Pershing and an expeditionary force across the border. Students will note that the United States and Mexico approached war and should speculate about the long-term effects of American policy.

Explanations for the Long-Essay Questions

1. You can construct an argument making use of information that can include the following:

The English colonies in the South were dominated by a plantation economy sustained through the production of staple crops for the market. In the Chesapeake Bay colonies of Virginia and Maryland, the chief cash crop was tobacco. In South Carolina, it was rice. These crops were labor intensive, and early plantations required more labor than could be supplied by the planter and his family. Virginia and Maryland encouraged the importation of indentured servants from Britain through the "headright" system. Planters received 50 acres of land for every laborer they brought into the colony. By 1700, over 100,000 indentured servants were brought into the Chesapeake Bay colonies. Indentured servants worked for their masters for a given term of years, then were released from service and provided with supplies and possibly a piece of land. However, indentured servants could not meet the labor needs in the Southern colonies, where the hot and humid climate took a high toll on the new arrivals.

Planters looked for other sources of workers. There were efforts to enslave Indians, but the susceptibility of Native Americans to European diseases and the relative ease of escape to the frontier made them an unreliable labor source. The first African slaves arrived in Virginia aboard a Dutch ship in 1619. At first, African slaves were too expensive to be bought in large numbers. Over time, their numbers grew. Coming from a tropical climate, Africans were believed to be more adaptable to the Southern climate. At the end of the seventeenth century, greater competition in the slave trade led to a larger supply of slaves. At the same time, improving economic conditions in Britain limited the number of potential indentured servants. By the early eighteenth century, African slaves were becoming the major source of labor on Southern plantations. Within 50 years African slaves outnumbered white settlers in South Carolina and comprised almost half the population of Virginia. At the same time that African slavery was establishing itself, a small number of large landowners were coming to dominate an increasingly hierarchical Southern society. These planters played a disproportionate role in politics and the economy. In Virginia, leading families like the Lees and Fitzhughs formed an informal landed aristocracy. Most white settlers were small farmers, who owned few, if any, slaves. The plantation economy precluded the settlement and growth of many towns. The South was rapidly developing the agrarian model centered on slave-worked plantations that it would carry into the nineteenth century. In the Northern colonies, the climate discouraged the growth of a plantation economy.

In contrast, the North was dominated by small farms and a more mixed economy. Although indentured servants and slaves were found in the North, farms were more likely to be worked by the members of a family. The temperate climate in New England and elsewhere proved healthier for immigrants from Britain, and the population grew rapidly. Towns and cities played an important role in the more densely populated North. A thriving commercial economy developed, with merchants in Boston, New York, Philadelphia, and elsewhere trading with Europe and the other colonies. American merchants played a key role in the triangular trade between the American colonies, Africa, and the West Indies. The wealth of American seaports supported prosperous artisans and businessmen. Benjamin Franklin's print shop in Philadelphia and Paul Revere's silversmith shop in Boston are examples of the businesses that flourished in the rich Northern towns. Many Northerners made their living at sea, either working for the large numbers of merchantmen sailing across the Atlantic, or as fisherman, catching and then drying fish for the European market. Abundant sources of timber provided lumber for export and for an extensive shipbuilding industry. An upper class of wealthy merchants and landowners were very influential in the North, but their power was checked to a degree by a larger middle class that existed in the South. A more dynamic economy made for a more egalitarian society.

2. You can construct an argument making use of information that can include the following:

Following the defeat of the French in the French and Indian War, the Ottawa chief Pontiac, unhappy at the prospect of British control of the Ohio Valley, led an uprising in 1763 that destroyed many British outposts in the West. The uprising was eventually suppressed, but British officials in London were alarmed at the prospect of expensive warfare on the frontier. They issued the Proclamation of 1763, outlawing settlement west of the Appalachian Mountains. The proclamation was intended to avert war with the western Indians, but it outraged many Americans who hoped to move west. Settlers were already beginning to filter into the Indian lands. The Proclamation of 1763 was one of the laws that began to strain relations between the American colonies and Great Britain.

The 1774 Quebec Act also angered Americans looking west. The main purpose of the Quebec Act was to reconcile the French inhabitants of Quebec to British rule by protecting their Catholic religion and traditional form of government. The act also extended the boundary of the Province of Quebec into the Ohio Valley. To Americans this seemed to be another attempt to block settlement in the West, reviving the influence of their traditional French opponents in a region from which they had been expelled in the French and Indian War.

During the American Revolution, the successful campaigns of George Rogers Clark established an American claim to the trans-Appalachian West. The Treaty of Paris, which ended the Revolutionary War, made the Mississippi the western frontier of the United States.

The Northwest Ordinance of 1787 laid down the steps by which a territory could become a state. It also prohibited slavery in the Northwest Territory. This kept slavery out of the states formed above the Ohio River.

The American government had great difficulty exerting its control over the Northwest Territory. The British retained influence in the region and even built Fort Miami near what is now Toledo, Ohio. The British supported the local Indians who formed a Western Confederacy, which defeated American forces under General Josiah Harmar in 1790, and General Arthur St. Clair in 1791. A better organized and more formidable army under General Anthony Wayne won a decisive victory over the Indians on August 20, 1794, at Fallen Timbers, near Fort Miami. The British failed to assist the Indians. At the 1795 Treaty of Greenville, Wayne forced the Indians to surrender extensive lands, including much of what eventually became the state of Ohio. John Jay negotiated a treaty with Great Britain that called for the removal of the remaining British garrisons in the Northwest Territory. They were soon gone, though the British in Canada remained potential allies for the western Indians and a threat to American settlers.

In 1795, Thomas Pinckney negotiated a treaty with Spain that reopened the Mississippi River and New Orleans to American trade, an economic boon for western farmers. Napoleon's France acquired Louisiana from Spain in 1800. In 1802, Spanish authorities in Louisiana placed restrictions on American trade in

New Orleans. This and the prospect of an aggressive French regime on the border of the United States convinced President Thomas Jefferson to send James Monroe to join Robert Livingston in Paris. The mission of the American envoys was to buy New Orleans. By 1803, Napoleon realized that he would soon be at war with Great Britain and would probably lose Louisiana because of the strength of the British navy. Napoleon surprised the American diplomats by offering to sell the whole of Louisiana for $15 million, and the United States gained lands that doubled the size of the country. Many Federalist politicians opposed the acquisition of lands where the future population would probably end up voting Democratic-Republican. Jefferson himself had constitutional scruples, unsure whether he had the authority to make such a purchase. In the end, the Senate supported the Louisiana Purchase and Jefferson dispatched the Lewis and Clark Expedition to explore the new territory.

The renewed war between Napoleon's France and Great Britain led to growing tensions as the British navy interfered with American trade and sometimes impressed American sailors to serve on its ships. Settlers in the West believed that the British were once again providing support to the Indians. The Shawnee warrior Tecumseh and his brother Tenskwatawa, the religious visionary known as The Prophet, were urging the western Indian tribes to unite in resisting the expansion of American settlements. In 1811, the governor of the Indiana Territory, General William Henry Harrison, defeated the Indians inspired by the Prophet at the Battle of Tippecanoe. Despite this victory, tensions remained high. Western War Hawks like Henry Clay believed that one benefit of war with Great Britain in 1812 would be the conquest of Canada and the elimination of British aid to the Indians. The United States failed to conquer Canada in the War of 1812, but the power of the western Indians was broken. In the North, William Henry Harrison defeated the British and Indians at the Battle of Thames River in 1813. Tecumseh was killed in this battle. In the South, General Andrew Jackson crushed the Creek Indians and later defeated the British at the Battle of New Orleans on January 8, 1815.

Western expansion sparked the first major political crisis over slavery. In 1819, Missouri applied to join the Union as a slave state. Many Northerners opposed adding another slave state, giving slave states the majority in the Senate. Southerners worried about the North's booming population and the growing Northern majority in the House of Representatives. After complex political maneuvering, Henry Clay worked out a compromise. Missouri was admitted as a slave state, and Maine was admitted as a free state. A line was drawn west from the southern border of Missouri. North of that line, territories would be organized as free states, and south of it as slave states. The 1820 Missouri Compromise endured until the Kansas-Nebraska Act of 1854.

PRACTICE EXAM 2

Answer Sheet for Multiple-Choice Questions

1.1 Ⓐ Ⓑ Ⓒ Ⓓ
1.2 Ⓐ Ⓑ Ⓒ Ⓓ
1.3 Ⓐ Ⓑ Ⓒ Ⓓ
1.4 Ⓐ Ⓑ Ⓒ Ⓓ
2.1 Ⓐ Ⓑ Ⓒ Ⓓ
2.2 Ⓐ Ⓑ Ⓒ Ⓓ
2.3 Ⓐ Ⓑ Ⓒ Ⓓ
2.4 Ⓐ Ⓑ Ⓒ Ⓓ
3.1 Ⓐ Ⓑ Ⓒ Ⓓ
3.2 Ⓐ Ⓑ Ⓒ Ⓓ
3.3 Ⓐ Ⓑ Ⓒ Ⓓ
3.4 Ⓐ Ⓑ Ⓒ Ⓓ
4.1 Ⓐ Ⓑ Ⓒ Ⓓ
4.2 Ⓐ Ⓑ Ⓒ Ⓓ
4.3 Ⓐ Ⓑ Ⓒ Ⓓ

4.4 Ⓐ Ⓑ Ⓒ Ⓓ
5.1 Ⓐ Ⓑ Ⓒ Ⓓ
5.2 Ⓐ Ⓑ Ⓒ Ⓓ
5.3 Ⓐ Ⓑ Ⓒ Ⓓ
5.4 Ⓐ Ⓑ Ⓒ Ⓓ
6.1 Ⓐ Ⓑ Ⓒ Ⓓ
6.2 Ⓐ Ⓑ Ⓒ Ⓓ
6.3 Ⓐ Ⓑ Ⓒ Ⓓ
6.4 Ⓐ Ⓑ Ⓒ Ⓓ
7.1 Ⓐ Ⓑ Ⓒ Ⓓ
7.2 Ⓐ Ⓑ Ⓒ Ⓓ
7.3 Ⓐ Ⓑ Ⓒ Ⓓ
7.4 Ⓐ Ⓑ Ⓒ Ⓓ
8.1 Ⓐ Ⓑ Ⓒ Ⓓ
8.2 Ⓐ Ⓑ Ⓒ Ⓓ

8.3 Ⓐ Ⓑ Ⓒ Ⓓ
8.4 Ⓐ Ⓑ Ⓒ Ⓓ
9.1 Ⓐ Ⓑ Ⓒ Ⓓ
9.2 Ⓐ Ⓑ Ⓒ Ⓓ
9.3 Ⓐ Ⓑ Ⓒ Ⓓ
9.4 Ⓐ Ⓑ Ⓒ Ⓓ

AP U.S. HISTORY PRACTICE EXAM 2

Section I

Part A (Multiple Choice)

Time: 35 minutes

Directions: Each of the following questions refers to a historical source. These questions will test your knowledge about the historical source and require you to make use of your historical analytical skills and your familiarity with historical themes. For each question select the *best* response and fill in the corresponding oval on your answer sheet.

Questions 1.1–1.4 refer to the following quotation:

One of the rights which the freeman has always guarded with most jealous care is that of enjoying the rewards of his own industry. Realizing that the power to tax is the power to destroy and that the power to take a certain amount of property or of income is only another way of saying that for a certain proportion of his time a citizen must work for the government, the authority to impose a tax on the people has been most carefully guarded. ... A government which lays taxes on the people not required by urgent necessity and sound public policy is not a protector of liberty, but an instrument of tyranny. It condemns the citizen to tyranny. One of the first signs of the breaking down of free government is a disregard by the taxing power of the right of the people to their own property. ... Unless the people can enjoy that reasonable security in the possession of their property, which is guaranteed by the Constitution, against unreasonable taxation, freedom is at an end. ... With us economy is imperative. It is a full test of our national character. ... It is always the people who toil that pay.

—Calvin Coolidge, "Economy in the Interest of All," June 30, 1924

1.1. Which of the following political ideas *best* reflects the perspective of Calvin Coolidge in the passage above?
A. Taxation is an effective means of redistributing wealth.
B. Government should be limited.
C. A bigger government can ensure social justice.
D. Government has the final say on what people do with their property.

1.2. Which of the following presidents would be most likely to share Coolidge's sentiments?
A. Franklin D. Roosevelt
B. Lyndon B. Johnson
C. Ronald Reagan
D. Barack Obama

1.3. The ideas expressed above were influenced by which of the following?
A. Widespread prosperity in the 1920s
B. Widespread economic hardship in the 1920s
C. The rapid growth of the welfare state in the 1920s
D. Highly publicized antitrust prosecutions

1.4. In the passage above Coolidge is reacting against which of the following?
A. The economic policies of his predecessor Warren G. Harding
B. The growing strength of radical politics in America following the Russian Revolution
C. Populist agitation in the West
D. The governmental policies of the Progressive Era

Questions 2.1–2.4 refer to the following image:

Theodor de Bry, "The Natives of Florida Worship the Column Erected by the Commander on His First Voyage," *Grand Voyages*, 1591

2.1. Which of the following most directly reflects the perspective of de Bry in the image above?
A. The natives of Florida are primitive and superstitious.
B. The natives of Florida are highly religious.
C. The Europeans are unjustly exploiting the natives of Florida.
D. Conflict is inevitable between the natives of Florida and the Europeans.

2.2. The image above is an expression of which of the following?
A. European fear of native peoples
B. European religious fervor
C. European doubts about the value of exploration
D. European curiosity about the wider world

2.3. The column erected by the commander signified which of the following?
A. European intentions to convert the Indians to Christianity
B. European desires for trade and new products
C. European desires to establish political control over new territories
D. European interest in sharing the culture of the Indians

2.4. European rivalries would lead to the French depicted above being driven from Florida by which of the following?
A. The natives of Florida
B. The Spanish
C. The English
D. The Dutch

Questions 3.1–3.4 refer to the following quotation:

Here is the case of a woman employed in the manufacturing department of a Broadway house. It stands for a hundred like her own. She averages three dollars a week. Pay is $1.50 for her room; for breakfast she has a cup of coffee; lunch she cannot afford. One meal a day is her allowance. This woman is young, she is pretty. She has "the world before her." Is it anything less than a miracle if she is guilty of nothing less than the "early and improvident marriage," against which moralists exclaim as one of the prolific causes of the distresses of the poor? Almost any door might seem to offer a welcome escape from such slavery as this. "I feel so much healthier since I got three square meals a day," said a lodger in one of the Girls' Homes. Two young sewing-girls came in seeking domestic service, so that they might get enough to eat. They had been only half-fed for some time, and starvation had driven them to the one door at which the pride of the American-born girl will not permit her to knock, though poverty be the price of her independence.

—Jacob Riis, *How the Other Half Lives*, 1890

3.1. Which of the following would be *most* likely to support the perspective expressed by Riis in the passage above?
A. A supporter of Social Darwinism
B. A Progressive
C. A businessman
D. An opponent of immigration

3.2. The situation faced by the young women in the passage above is *most* directly comparable to which of the following?
A. American revolutionaries in the 1770s
B. Slaves in the antebellum South
C. Populist farmers in the 1890s
D. Detroit autoworkers in the 1930s

3.3. Concerns like those expressed by Riis in the passage above led *most* directly to which of the following?
A. Laws regulating the working conditions of women
B. Restrictions on immigration
C. Women's suffrage
D. Antitrust legislation

3.4. Riis's work as an investigator of the lives of the poor can *most* directly be associated with which of the following?
A. Yellow Journalism
B. Abolitionism
C. The muckrakers
D. Socialism

Questions 4.1–4.4 refer to the following quotation:

It is natural, it is a privilege, I will go farther, it is a right, which all free men claim, that they are entitled to complain when they are hurt. They have a right publicly to remonstrate against the abuses of power in the strongest terms, to put their neighbors upon their guard against the craft or open violence of men in authority, and to assert with courage the sense they have of the blessings of liberty, the value they put upon it, and their resolution at all hazards to preserve it as one of the greatest blessings heaven can bestow. ... But to conclude: The question before the Court and you, Gentlemen of the jury, is not of small or private concern. It is not the cause of one poor printer, nor of New York alone, which you are now trying. No! It may in its consequence affect every free man that lives under a British government on the main of America. It is the best cause. It is the cause of liberty. And I make no doubt but your upright conduct this day will not only entitle you to the love and esteem of your fellow citizens, but every man who prefers freedom to a life of slavery will bless and honor you as men who have baffled the attempt of tyranny, and by an impartial and uncorrupt verdict have laid a noble foundation for securing to ourselves, our posterity, and our neighbors, that to which nature and the laws of our country have given us a right to liberty of both exposing and opposing arbitrary power (in these parts of the world at least) by speaking and writing truth.

—Andrew Hamilton, concluding argument, libel trial of newspaper editor John Peter Zenger, August 4, 1735

4.1. Which of the following *best* describes the significance of the Zenger Trial?
  A. An important incident in opposing British taxation policy
  B. An early attack on the institution of slavery
  C. A landmark case concerning voting rights
  D. A landmark case concerning freedom of expression

4.2. Andrew Hamilton assumes which of the following?
  A. Americans have more freedoms than people in other countries.
  B. People in other countries have more rights than Americans.
  C. Natural rights are merely ideas that don't really exist.
  D. Rights are granted by the government.

4.3. The Zenger Case can *best* be compared to which of the following?
  A. Abraham Lincoln's suspension of habeas corpus during the Civil War
  B. Government efforts to prevent the publication of the Pentagon Papers in 1971
  C. The trial of the accused Haymarket Square bombers in 1886
  D. The *Brown v. Board of Education* Supreme Court decision of 1954

4.4. Hamilton's success in the Zenger case *most* directly reflects which of the following?
  A. American desires for independence from Great Britain
  B. American rejection of Enlightenment ideals
  C. A long tradition of self-rule in the American colonies
  D. The weakening of economic ties between America and Great Britain

Questions 5.1–5.4 refer to the following cartoon:

Thomas Nast, "The Union as It Was / The Lost Cause, Worse Than Slavery," *Harper's Weekly,* October 24, 1874

5.1. Which of the following *best* expresses the perspective of Thomas Nast in the cartoon above?
  A. The Reconstruction of the South is going well.
  B. The government is not adequately protecting freed slaves.
  C. White people in the South need to stand together.
  D. The Reconstruction of Southern society was a bad idea.

5.2. The situation described in the cartoon above *most* directly resulted in which of the following?
  A. The passage of the Fifteenth Amendment
  B. The passage of the Homestead Act offering settlers free land in the West
  C. Efforts to create an industrialized New South
  D. The *Plessy v. Ferguson* Supreme Court decision

5.3. The Southerners in the cartoon above wanted a "Union" characterized by which of the following?
A. Sovereignty centered in the federal government.
B. An "American System" of internal improvements.
C. Sovereignty centered in the states.
D. The anti-nullification nationalism of Andrew Jackson.

5.4. The ideas in the cartoon above *most* directly reflect which of the following continuities in U.S. history?
A. Debates about civil rights
B. Debates about the use of military power
C. Debates about gun control
D. Debates about the role of political parties

Questions 6.1–6.4 refer to the following quotation:

Tonight, the daughter of a woman whose highest goal was a future for her children talks to our nation's oldest political party about a future for us all. Tonight, the daughter of working Americans tells all Americans that the future is within our reach, if we're willing to reach for it. Tonight, the daughter of an immigrant from Italy has been chosen to run for (vice) president in the new land my father came to love. ... Americans want to live by the same set of rules. But under this administration, the rules are rigged against too many of our people. It isn't right that every year the share of taxes paid by individual citizens is going up, while the share paid by large corporations is getting smaller and smaller. ... It isn't right that young couples question whether to bring children into a world of 50,000 nuclear warheads. That isn't the vision for which Americans have struggled for more than two centuries. ... Tonight, we reclaim our dream. We're going to make the rules of American life work for all Americans again. ... The issue is not what America can do for women, but what women can do for America.

—Geraldine Ferraro, Vice Presidential Nomination Acceptance Address, July 19, 1984

6.1. The nomination of Geraldine Ferraro for vice president was most directly a continuation of which of the following?
A. The successful assimilation of immigrants to the United States
B. The struggle for civil rights for ethnic minorities
C. Increased economic and political opportunities for women
D. The increasing democratization of the political nomination process

6.2. The political ideas expressed by Ferraro in the passage above *most* directly reflect those of which of the following?
A. Colonial opponents of British taxation in the 1760s and 1770s
B. Abolitionists of the antebellum period
C. Republicans of the 1920s
D. New Dealers of the 1930s

6.3. The ideas expressed in the passage above would *most* directly have strengthened which of the following during the 1980s?
A. Opposition to the administration's arms buildup
B. Efforts to deregulate many industries
C. Efforts to reform the welfare system
D. Support for the administration's cold war policies

6.4. Geraldine Ferraro can be most directly compared to which of the following women?
A. Abigail Adams
B. Sandra Day O'Connor
C. Jane Addams
D. Rosa Parks

Questions 7.1–7.4 refer to the following quotation:

These were the first emigrants that we had overtaken, although we had found abundant and melancholy traces of their progress throughout the whole course of the journey. Sometimes we passed the grave of one who had sickened and died on the way. The earth was usually torn up and covered thickly with wolf-tracks. Some had escaped this violation. One morning a piece of plank, standing upright on the summit of a grassy hill, attracted our notice, and riding up to it we found the following words very roughly traced upon it, apparently by a red-hot piece of iron:

MARY ELLIS DIED MAY 7th, 1845
Aged two months.

Such tokens were of common occurrence, nothing could speak more for the hardihood, or rather infatuation, of the adventurers, or the sufferings that await them upon their journey. ... We were late in breaking up our camp on the following morning, and scarcely had we ridden a mile when we saw, far in advance of us, drawn against the horizon, a line of objects stretching at regular intervals along the level edge of the prairie. An intervening swell soon hid them from sight, until, ascending it a quarter of an hour after, we saw close before us the emigrant caravan, with its heavy white wagons creeping on in their slow procession, and a large drove of cattle following behind. ... Many were murmuring against the leader they had chosen, and wished to depose him. ... The women were divided between regrets for the homes they had left and apprehension of the deserts and savages before them. ... As we left the ground, I saw a tall slouching fellow with the nasal accent of "down east," contemplating the contents of his tin cup, which he had just filled with water.
"Look here, you," he said: "it's chock full of animals!"
The cup, as he held it out, exhibited in fact an extraordinary variety and profusion of animal and vegetable life.
—Francis Parkman, *The Oregon Trail: Sketches of Prairie and Rocky-Mountain Life*, 1849

7.1. The situation described in the passage above led *most* directly to which of the following?
  A. Passage of the Homestead Act
  B. Passage of the Northwest Ordinance
  C. The *Dred Scott* Supreme Court decision
  D. Passage of the Indian Removal Act

7.2. The actions of the people in the passage above *most* directly reflect the influence of which of the following political ideals?
  A. Popular sovereignty
  B. Jacksonian Democracy
  C. Manifest Destiny
  D. Progressivism

7.3. The experiences of the people encountered by Francis Parkman can be *most* directly compared to those of which of the following?
  A. The Spanish conquistadors
  B. The Pilgrims
  C. The Apollo astronauts
  D. Cowboys on the first cattle drives of the 1860s

7.4. Which of the following had *most* directly anticipated and desired the movement described by Parkman?
  A. Benjamin Franklin
  B. James Madison
  C. Alexander Hamilton
  D. Thomas Jefferson

Questions 8.1–8.4 refer to the following quotation:

Our leaders talk about stopping aggression from the north, but this was a struggle among groups of Vietnamese until we intervened. We seem bent upon saving the Vietnamese from Ho Chi Minh even if we have to kill them and demolish their country to do it. As the native people survey bombed-out villages, women and children burned by napalm, rice crops destroyed and cities overrun with our military personnel, they are doubtless saying secretly of the Vietcong guerilllas and of the American forces, "A plague on both your houses." . . . Stop the bombing, north and south, end search and destroy offensive sweeps, and confine our military action to holding operations on the ground. Bombing the north has failed to halt or seriously check the flow of troops to the south and may, in fact, have prompted a much greater war effort by Hanoi.

—Senator George McGovern, "The Lessons of Vietnam," April 25, 1967

8.1. Which of the following opinions from the 1960s *most* directly reflects the perspective of George McGovern's speech?
A. Americans must maximize their technological edge in Vietnam.
B. American bombing in Vietnam is step by step leading to progress in the war.
C. American bombing in Vietnam is a failure.
D. America must not give in to defeatism about the war in Vietnam.

8.2. The sentiments expressed in the speech above *most* directly influenced which of the following?
A. The passage of the War Powers Act of 1973
B. The Tet Offensive of 1968
C. The resignation of Richard Nixon in 1974
D. The emergence of a youth counterculture

8.3. The sentiments expressed in the speech *most* directly reflect which popular attitude that became widespread in the 1960s?
A. The United States should embrace isolationism.
B. The United States should use force to spread American ideals abroad.
C. American commanders were not being given enough weapons in Vietnam.
D. Government statements about Vietnam could not be trusted.

8.4. Political discord during the Vietnam War most closely resembled the political dissensions during which of the following?
A. The Spanish-American War
B. The Mexican War
C. World War I
D. World War II

Questions 9.1–9.4 refer to the following quotation:

On Being Brought from Africa to America

'Twas mercy brought me from my Pagan land,
Taught my benighted soul to understand
That there's a God, that there's a Saviour too;
Once I redemption neither sought nor knew.
Some view our sable race with scornful eye,
"Their colour is a diabolic die."
Remember, Christians, Negroes, black as Cain,
May be refin'd, and join th' angelic train.

—Phillis Wheatley, *Poems on Various Subjects, Religious and Moral*, 1773

9.1. The ideas expressed in Phillis Wheatley's poem *most* directly reveal the influence of which of the following?
A. The First Great Awakening
B. The natural rights theory of John Locke
C. British ideas about social hierarchy
D. Eighteenth century scientific racism

9.2. The sentiments expressed in Wheatley's poem *most* directly reflect which of the following continuities in U.S. history?
A. Debates over religious freedom
B. Debates over social justice
C. Debates over immigration
D. Debates over freedom of expression

9.3. The literary success of Phillis Wheatley led *most* directly to questions about which of the following?
A. The granting of political rights to women
B. The harsh treatment of pro-British Loyalists
C. The moral justification of slavery
D. The legitimacy of established churches in the states

9.4. The point of Wheatley's poem can *best* be compared to which of the following?
A. The Declaration of Independence
B. Jonathan Edwards's sermon "Sinners in the Hands of an Angry God"
C. The Seneca Falls Declaration of Rights and Sentiments
D. Martin Luther King, Jr.'s "I Have a Dream" speech

Part B (Short Answer)

Time: 50 minutes

Directions: Answer the following four questions. Carefully read and follow the directions for each question. Some will refer to historical sources. These questions will require you to make use of your historical analytical skills and your familiarity with historical themes. These questions do *not* require you to develop a thesis in your responses.

Question 1 is based on the following passages:

The following are among the principal advantages of a bank: First. The augmentation of the active or productive capital of a country. Gold and Silver, when they are employed merely as the instruments of exchange and alienation, have been not improperly denominated dead Stock; but when deposited in Banks, to become the basis of a paper circulation, which takes their character and place, as the signs or representatives of value, they then acquire life, or, in other words, an active and productive quality. ... It is evident, for instance, that the money which a merchant keeps in his chest, waiting for a favourable opportunity to employ it, produces nothing, {'}till that opportunity arrives. But if instead of locking it up in this manner, he either deposits it in a Bank, or invests in the Stock of a Bank, it yields a profit, during the interval.

—Alexander Hamilton

If the American people ever allow private banks to control the issue of their currency, first by inflation, then by deflation, the banks and corporations that will grow up around them will deprive the people of all property until their children wake up homeless on the continent their Fathers conquered. ... I believe that banking institutions are more dangerous to our liberties than standing armies. ... The issuing power should be taken from the banks and restored to the people, to whom it properly belongs.

—Thomas Jefferson

1. Based on these passages concerning the creation of the Bank of the United States in 1791, complete the following three tasks.
   A. Briefly explain the main point made by Passage 1.
   B. Briefly explain the main point made by Passage 2.
   C. Explain how one of the perspectives above reflected debates about the Constitution in the 1790s. Provide at least *one* piece of evidence to support your explanation.

2. U.S. historians have argued that an industrial revolution transformed American life in the late nineteenth century.
   A. Choose *one* of the following and explain how he influenced industrialization in the United States during the late nineteenth century. Provide at least *one* piece of evidence to support your explanation.
   - John D. Rockefeller
   - Andrew Carnegie
   - J. Pierpont Morgan
   B. How did the business success of your choice help change the life of ordinary Americans? Provide at least *one* piece of evidence to support your explanation.

3. The twentieth century witnessed an expansion in rights for women and minorities in the United States.
   A. Choose *one* of the following and explain how this group gained in rights and status during the twentieth century. Provide at least *one* piece of evidence to support your explanation.
   - Women
   - African Americans
   - Mexican Americans
   B. Explain how your choice influenced or was influenced by *one* of the other options above. Provide at least *one* piece of evidence to support your explanation.

Question 4 is based on the following image:

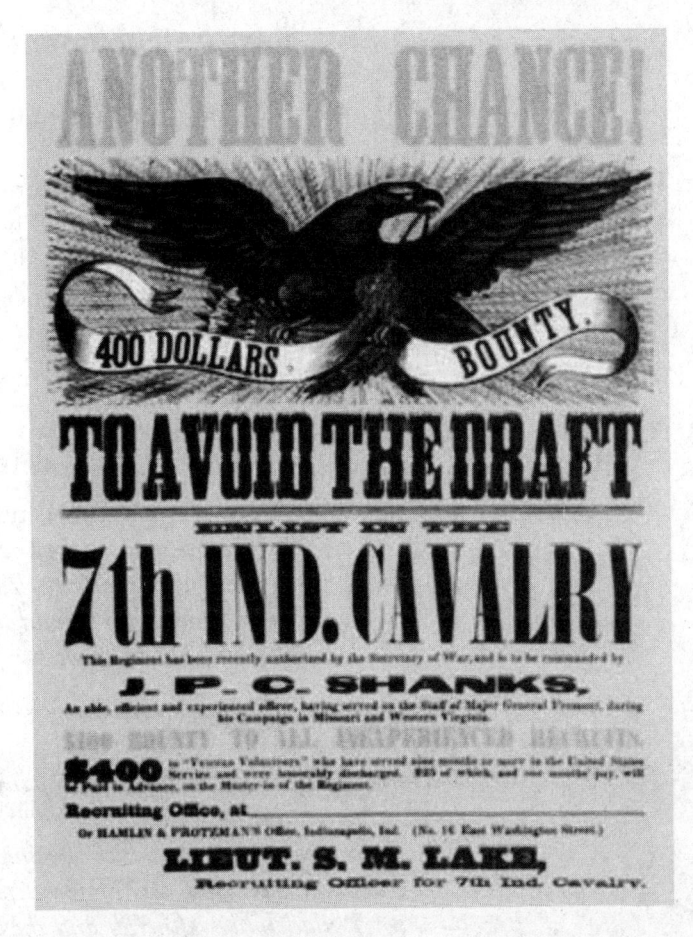

Civil War recruiting poster

4. Use the image and your knowledge of U.S. history to answer parts A, B, and C.
   A. Briefly explain the issue addressed by the image. Provide at least *one* piece of evidence to support your explanation.
   B. Why did the government need to take such measures to raise troops? Provide at least *one* piece of evidence to support your explanation.
   C. Briefly explain the perspective of someone opposed to the government's recruiting efforts. Provide at least *one* piece of evidence to support your explanation.

END OF SECTION I

Section II

Part A (Document–Based Question)

Time: 60 minutes

Directions: This question asks you to write a well-constructed essay making use of the following documents and your broader knowledge of U.S. history. You will need to make use of your historical analytical skills and your familiarity with historical themes. You must develop a thesis that answers the question, supporting it with evidence drawn from the documents and from evidence and information outside the documents.

To what extent did the Supreme Court advance or inhibit Progressive regulation of corporations in the period 1885 to 1920?

Document A
Source: U.S. v. Debs, et al., 1894 (response to the Pullman Strike)

> That the original design [of the Sherman Antitrust Act] to suppress trusts and monopolies . . . is clear; but it is equally clear that further and more comprehensive purpose came to be entertained. . . . Combinations are condemned, not only when they take the form of trusts, but in whatever form found, if they be in restraint of trade.

Document B
Source: U.S. v. E. C. Knight Company, 1895

> Congress did not attempt . . . to make criminal the acts of persons in the acquisition and control of property which the states of their residence or creation sanctioned or permitted.
>
> The contracts and acts of the defendants related exclusively to the acquisition of the Philadelphia refineries and the business of sugar refining in Pennsylvania, and bore no direct relation to commerce between states or with foreign countries. The object was manifestly private gain in the manufacture of the commodity, but not through the control of interstate or foreign commerce.

Document C
Source: Smyth v. Ames, 1898

> By the 14th Amendment it is provided that no state shall deprive any person of property without the due process of law nor deny to any person within its jurisdiction the equal protection of laws. That corporations are persons within this amendment is now settled.
>
> [The Court] adjudged that the enforcement of the schedules of rates established by the [Nebraska law reducing railroad rates] . . . would deprive the railroad companies of the compensation they were legally entitled to receive.

Document D
Source: Lochner v. New York, 1905

> The act [state law limiting maximum hours of bakers] is not . . . a health law, but is an illegal interference with the rights of individuals, both employers and employees, to make contracts regarding labor upon such terms as they may think best. . . . Statutes of the nature of that under review, limiting the hours in which grown and intelligent men may labor to earn their living, are meddlesome interferences with the rights of the individual, and they are not saved from condemnation by the claim that they are passed upon the subject of the health of the individual whose rights are interfered with.

Document E

Source: *Muller v. Oregon*, 1908

> The two sexes differ in structure of body, . . . in the amount of physical strength in the capacity for long-continued labor, . . . the influence of vigorous health upon the future well-being of the race, . . . and in the capacity to maintain the struggle for subsistence. This difference justifies a difference in legislation.
>
> For these reasons, and without questioning in any respect the decision in Lochner v. New York, we are of the opinion that it cannot be adjudged that the [state law limiting the hours women may work] is in conflict with the Federal Constitution, so far as it respects the work of a female in a laundry.

Document F

Source: *Standard Oil Company of New Jersey v. United States*, 1911

> The public policy has been to prohibit . . . contracts or acts entered into with the intent to wrong the public and which unreasonably restrict competitive conditions, limit the rights of individuals, restrain the free flow of commerce, or bring about public evils such as the enhancement of prices.
>
> The combination of the defendants in this case is an unreasonable and undue restraint of trade in petroleum and its products moving in interstate commerce, and falls within the prohibitions of the [Sherman Antitrust Act].

Document G

Source: *Wilson v. New*, 1917

> The effect of the [Adamson Act] is not only to establish permanently an eight-hour standard for work and wages as between the [railroad] carrier and employees affected, but also to fix a scale of minimum wages for the eight-hour day and proportionately for overtime.
>
> Viewed as an act establishing an eight-hour day as the standard of service by employees, the statute is clearly within the power of Congress under the commerce clause.
>
> Viewed as an act fixing wages, the statute merely illustrates the character of regulation essential, and hence permissible, for the protection of the public right.

Part B (Long Essay)

Time: 35 minutes

Directions: Answer *one* of the following questions. Develop a thesis and support it with appropriate historical evidence. This question will require you to make use of your historical analytical skills and your familiarity with historical themes.

1. Some historians have argued that reform movements played an important role in shaping American society from 1820 to 1860. Support, modify, or refute this contention using specific evidence.

2. Some historians have argued that an upsurge in democracy shaped American politics in the first half of the nineteenth century. Support, modify, or refute this contention using specific evidence.

END OF SECTION II

ANSWERS TO PRACTICE EXAM 2

Multiple Choice

1.1 B	3.2 D	5.3 C	7.4 D
1.2 C	3.3 A	5.4 A	8.1 C
1.3 A	3.4 C	6.1 C	8.2 A
1.4 D	4.1 D	6.2 D	8.3 D
2.1 A	4.2 A	6.3 A	8.4 B
2.2 D	4.3 B	6.4 B	9.1 A
2.3 C	4.4 C	7.1 A	9.2 B
2.4 B	5.1 B	7.2 C	9.3 C
3.1 B	5.2 D	7.3 B	9.4 D

Explanations for the Multiple-Choice Questions

1.1. B. The political idea that *best* reflects the perspective of President Calvin Coolidge in the passage is that government should be limited. A limited government would be an inexpensive government. Hence Coolidge opposed heavy taxes on citizens. He believed overtaxation hurt taxpayers, took money out of the private economy, and encouraged wasteful government spending.

1.2. C. The president most likely to share Coolidge's sentiments would be Ronald Reagan. President Reagan also worked to limit the size of government and cut taxes. Reagan admired Coolidge and prominently displayed a portrait of him in the White House.

1.3. A. The ideas expressed by Coolidge were influenced by the widespread prosperity in the 1920s. Coolidge believed that the growing prosperity of most Americans was the result of keeping government out of the way of business and allowing people to keep more of their money by reducing taxes. His ideas proved popular with voters. Taking office after the death of President Warren Harding in 1923, he won election to the presidency in his own right in 1924. His Republican party kept control of Congress throughout the 1920s.

1.4. D. In the passage, Coolidge is reacting against the governmental policies of the Progressive Era. The Progressives greatly expanded the role of the government in the economy and in American life. This culminated in the policies of President Woodrow Wilson during World War I, when the government coordinated much of the economy and monitored what people said about the war. Following the war, there was a reaction against such control. Warren Harding successfully appealed to this sentiment with his call for a "return to normalcy" in 1920. Coolidge was Harding's vice president and continued his policies.

2.1. A. de Bry in the image reflects the perspective that the natives of Florida are primitive and superstitious. The image shows the Indians worshipping a column erected by the French explorers, indicating that they thought the Europeans possessed special powers. The Europeans tended to regard the natives of America as heathens who had to be Christianized and subjected to the tutelage of their more advanced civilization.

2.2. D. The image is an expression of European curiosity about the wider world. This illustration is one of many that de Bry made picturing the peoples of the New World. In addition to looking for lands to conquer and new sources of trade, Europeans were interested in learning more about the world. This desire for learning was inspired by the Renaissance and the Scientific Revolution.

2.3. C. The column erected by the French commander signified European desires to establish political control over new territories. The European powers competed to acquire new territories in the New World, which they hoped would be rich sources of valuable goods and trade.

2.4. B. European rivalries would lead to the French being driven from Florida by the Spanish. In 1564, French Protestants, called Huguenots, built Fort Caroline, near modern-day Jacksonville. The following year Spanish forces from St. Augustine destroyed the settlement. The French retaliated with an attack of their own but were never able to reestablish themselves in Florida.

3.1. B. A Progressive would be most likely to support the perspective expressed by Riis in the passage. The Progressives were middle-class reformers interested in addressing the problems created by the rapid industrialization and urbanization of the United States during the first two decades of the twentieth century. Many Progressives worked to ameliorate labor conditions for workers.

3.2. D. The situation faced by the young women in the passage is most directly comparable to that of Detroit autoworkers in the 1930s. The autoworkers also needed better wages and working conditions. They staged famous sit-down strikes in 1936 and 1937 to win recognition of the United Auto Workers (UAW) union.

3.3. A. Concerns like those expressed by Riis in the passage led most directly to laws regulating the working conditions of women. During the Progressive Era, laws were passed to protect women in the workplace. The great lawyer Louis Brandeis persuaded the Supreme Court to uphold a law mandating an eight-hour workday for women in *Muller v. Oregon* (1908).

3.4. C. Riis's work as an investigator of the lives of the poor can most directly be associated with the muckrakers. Muckrakers were Progressive Era journalists who exposed corruption and social injustice in American life. Examples of muckrakers were Lincoln Steffens, who wrote about urban political machines, Ida Tarbell, who documented the history of John Rockefeller's Standard Oil, and Ray Stannard Baker, who explored the living conditions of African Americans.

4.1. D. The Zenger Trial was a landmark case concerning freedom of expression. Zenger was a newspaper editor who had published criticisms of the royal governor of New York. Brought to trial for seditious libel, the judge instructed the jury that the truth or falsity of what Zenger wrote was immaterial; the law held that printing unflattering commentary on a royal governor was enough to declare the defendant guilty. The defense lawyer Andrew Hamilton appealed to the jurors' love of liberty and asked them to oppose governmental tyranny. The jury voted to acquit Zenger. This case helped ensure freedom of the press and freedom of speech in colonial America.

4.2. A. Andrew Hamilton assumes that Americans have more freedoms than people in other countries. Hamilton appeals to the natural rights enjoyed by free men and to the liberties accorded to British subjects. He urges the jurors to vindicate these rights against arbitrary power "in these parts of the world at least," indicating a sense that Americans are freer than people living elsewhere.

4.3. B. The Zenger case can best be compared to government efforts to prevent the publication of the Pentagon Papers in 1971. Daniel Ellsberg, a former Defense Department official, leaked a secret Pentagon study of the origins of the Vietnam War to the *New York Times*. The Nixon administration went to court to stop the newspaper from publishing these documents. Ultimately, the Supreme Court upheld the right of the newspaper to publish the Pentagon Papers in *New York Times Co. v. United States* (1971). This decision was a strong affirmation of First Amendment protections for a free press.

4.4. C. Hamilton's success in the Zenger case most directly reflects a long tradition of self-rule in the colonies. Hamilton's argument to the jury assumed a lack of deference on the part of the jurors toward established authority. This reflected a century during which the colonies had been largely self-governing. Hamilton correctly expected that the jurors knew that they had rights and would feel free to defend them. This tradition of self-government would be very important during the political crisis leading to American independence.

5.1. B. The perspective of Thomas Nast's cartoon is that the government is not adequately protecting freed slaves. Nast was worried that Southern whites working through organizations like the Ku Klux Klan were returning the South to places where African Americans were oppressed. He notes that in some ways the situation is worse than it was under slavery, with the terroristic Klan lynching freedmen and burning schools.

5.2. D. The situation described in the cartoon most directly resulted in the *Plessy v. Ferguson* Supreme Court decision. *Plessy v. Ferguson* (1896) ruled that separate but equal facilities for whites and African Americans were constitutional. This court case reflected a retreat on the part of the government in protecting African-American rights in the South that began with the end of Reconstruction in 1877. Many in the North grew tired of trying to force Southern whites to accept African-American rights. While *Plessy v. Ferguson* paid lip service to equality, in reality Southern whites were able to impose Jim Crow laws on African Americans.

5.3. C. The Southerners in the cartoon wanted a "Union" characterized by sovereignty centered in the states. The doctrine of states' rights had been used before the Civil War to protect the institution of slavery. Following the end of Reconstruction, Southerners would invoke states' rights to justify the enforcement of Jim Crow laws.

5.4. A. The ideas in the cartoon reflect continuities in debates about civil rights. Thomas Nast, at a late stage in Reconstruction, was worried about African-American rights. His cartoon was a plea for the enforcement of laws passed to protect African Americans, including the Thirteenth, Fourteenth, and Fifteenth Amendments to the Constitution.

6.1. C. The nomination of Geraldine Ferraro for vice president was most directly a continuation of increased economic and political opportunities for women. The women's movement of the 1960s was remarkably successful in altering people's expectations for women. Large numbers of women entered the workforce in the 1970s and 1980s and flourished in fields that had previously been largely closed to them. Ferraro's nomination was an emblematic first for women in politics.

6.2. D. The political ideas expressed by Ferraro in the passage most directly reflect those of New Dealers of the 1930s. Ferraro was a liberal Democrat. Like the New Dealers of Franklin Roosevelt's day, she believed that government could be used to help the ordinary in a country dominated by the wealthy and big business. She opposed President Ronald Reagan's efforts to limit the size of government and deregulate business.

6.3. A. The ideas expressed by Ferraro would have most directly strengthened opposition to the administration's arms buildup. During the 1980s, President Ronald Reagan increased the size of the American military to carry on the cold war with the Soviet Union from a position of strength. Like many liberal Democrats, Ferraro opposed the size of this increase in military spending, preferring to spend money on domestic social programs.

6.4. B. Geraldine Ferraro can most directly be compared to Sandra Day O'Connor. In 1981, O'Connor became the first woman to serve on the Supreme Court, after being nominated by President Ronald Reagan. Like O'Connor, Ferraro was blazing new trails for women in the 1980s.

7.1. A. The situation described in the passage led most directly to the Homestead Act. Like the people Parkman met on the Oregon Trail, many Americans regarded the West as a land of opportunity. In 1862, Congress passed the Homestead Act. This law encouraged western settlement, giving people title to 160 acres of land if they lived on it for five years and made improvements.

7.2. C. The actions of the people in the passage most directly reflect the influence of Manifest Destiny. During the 1840s publicists popularized the idea of Manifest Destiny, that Americans would spread their democratic institutions across the North American continent. This idea helped justify the Mexican War. It also helped inspire American settlement in the Oregon Territory, where the United States disputed a boundary line with Great Britain. Thousands of settlers followed the Oregon Trail to the Oregon Territory.

7.3. B. The experiences of the people encountered by Francis Parkman can most directly be compared to the Pilgrims. The people Parkman met suffered many hardships as they traveled west. The Pilgrims also suffered a great deal, including a starving time, before their colony began to prosper.

7.4. D. Thomas Jefferson had most directly anticipated and desired the movement described by Parkman. Jefferson wanted to see a United States dominated by independent farmers. Land was necessary to fulfill this vision, so Jefferson was intensely interested in the West. Jefferson swallowed his constitutional scruples to purchase the Louisiana Territory in 1803 and then sent Lewis and Clark on an epic journey to explore it.

8.1. C. The perspective of Senator George McGovern's speech reflects the opinion that American bombing in Vietnam was a failure. Operation Rolling Thunder began in 1965 as a carefully calibrated bombing campaign designed to pressure the North Vietnamese regime to halt its support for its war against the South Vietnamese government. By 1967, it was becoming increasingly clear that bombing would not dissuade the North Vietnamese from carrying on the war. The American intervention into the war with a growing number of troops on the ground led the North Vietnamese to match this with a buildup of their own forces in South Vietnam.

8.2. A. The sentiments expressed in the speech most directly influenced the passage of the War Powers Act of 1973. Congress passed this law over the veto of President Richard Nixon. Hoping to prevent another situation like Vietnam where presidents involved the United States in a war without direct approval by Congress, this act required the president to notify Congress within two days of sending troops into combat. Unless Congress authorized the action, these troops would have to be withdrawn after 60 days.

8.3. D. The sentiments expressed in the speech most directly reflected the widespread popular attitude of the 1960s that government statements about Vietnam could not be trusted. As the war ground on without resolution, despite optimistic statements coming from the administration of President Lyndon Johnson, some commentators began to talk about a "credibility gap." Evoking memories of John F. Kennedy's political campaigning about a perceived "missile gap" with the Soviet Union, some now pointed to a gap between what the administration said and the truth.

8.4. B. Political discord during the Vietnam War most closely resembled the political dissensions during the Mexican War. Just as with Vietnam, there was significant opposition to the Mexican War. Many Americans thought it was an unjust war of aggression, and some thought it was intended to open up new territories to slavery. Prominent Americans who opposed the Mexican War included Congressman Abraham Lincoln and writer Henry David Thoreau.

9.1. A. The ideas expressed in Phillis Wheatley's poem most directly reflect the influence of the First Great Awakening. The First Great Awakening was a revival of religious fervor in the American colonies during the middle of the eighteenth century. It emphasized the need for salvation and a direct personal relationship with God. This religious movement spread to many slaves. Wheatley in her poem expresses her gratitude for her conversion to Christianity.

9.2. B. The continuity in American history most directly reflected in Wheatley's poem is debates over social justice. Wheatley makes a gentle case for human rights in her poem. She reminds her readers, almost exclusively white, that Africans can become Christians. The equality of all races in Christ could be a radical message in the 1770s.

9.3. C. The literary success of Phillis Wheatley led most directly to questions about the moral justification of slavery. Wheatley's critically acclaimed poetry contradicted racist assumptions that Africans were intellectually inferior. Wheatley, a slave who benefitted from an education, and who wrote poetry modeled on the best English forms, demonstrated that Africans, even slaves, possessed the same potential as white Europeans.

9.4. D. The point of Wheatley's poem can best be compared to Martin Luther King, Jr.'s "I Have a Dream" speech. Like King's speech, Wheatley's poem emphasizes the essential equality of all people and reminds readers that skin color should not be a barrier to unity. Just as King wanted all Americans to join together in equal enjoyment of their constitutional rights, so Wheatley urged all people to come together in Christian harmony.

Explanations for the Short-Answer Questions

1. **A.** Alexander Hamilton was the first secretary of the treasury. He saw the creation of a Bank of the United States as a crucial step in his program of strengthening the new central government and establishing a firm foundation for the new nation's finances. A Bank of the United States would allow depositors and investors to derive income from money that would otherwise be unproductive if simply locked away in a strongbox. The Bank would support business through loans. It would also be able to stimulate the economy though issuing properly secured paper money. Hamilton believed that in addition to facilitating commerce, the Bank of the United States would provide a secure place for the government to place its funds; paper money issued by the Bank would make it easier for citizens to pay financial obligations to the government, and for the government to carry out its own financial transactions.

   B. A planter from Virginia, Thomas Jefferson, the first secretary of state, was suspicious of Alexander Hamilton's efforts to support commercial interests. Hamilton's Bank of the United States was modeled on the Bank of England, and Jefferson feared that, as in Britain, a powerful central bank would play an outsized political role because of its ability to provide financial favors to lawmakers. Jefferson associated banks with financial speculators, who made money by manipulating the currency. He believed such speculations impoverished the people dependent upon a secure and reliable currency, something he identified with gold and silver money. As an agrarian who believed farmers were the backbone of a free republic, Jefferson saw banks and their financial operations as an opening to urban corruption.

   C. Jefferson believed in limited government. He argued that the Constitution should be strictly interpreted, and that the federal government could only exercise powers explicitly granted to it. Since there is nothing in the Constitution about the federal government creating banks, he believed that the chartering of banks was a power reserved to the states. Hamilton supported a strong central government. He argued that the Constitution should be loosely interpreted, and that the federal government could exercise "implied" powers not expressly forbidden. In defending the chartering of the Bank of the United States, Hamilton made the case that the clause in the Constitution that gave Congress the authority to "make laws necessary for carrying out the enumerated powers" of the federal government allowed the creation of a bank. The federal government had to collect taxes and engage in other financial transactions. A bank would facilitate this governmental business; therefore it was constitutional to establish one. President George Washington was convinced by Hamilton's argument and backed Hamilton's bank legislation. In 1791, Congress created the first Bank of the United States, chartering it for 20 years.

2. **A.** John D. Rockefeller entered the oil refining business in Cleveland, Ohio, during the 1860s. In 1870, Rockefeller and his partners formed the Standard Oil Company. Rockefeller practiced horizontal integration in the oil refining business, expanding his business by either acquiring or driving out of business competing oil companies. Rockefeller used ruthless methods against business rivals who refused to cooperate with him, including forcing railroads to pay him rebates for transporting his product, allowing Standard Oil to undersell the competition. By the late 1870s, Rockefeller controlled more than 90 percent of the oil refining industry. Rockefeller's legal advisor Samuel C. T. Dodd invented an innovative legal mechanism to allow Rockefeller to control his business empire. The companies owned by Rockefeller surrendered their stock in "trust" to a single board of directors. The "trust" form of business organization was outlawed by the Sherman Antitrust Act of 1890. By this time New Jersey, in 1889, had passed legislation allowing corporations to own other corporations. Standard Oil of New Jersey was reorganized as a "holding company" in 1899, a corporation that owned all the companies in Rockefeller's massive portfolio.

Andrew Carnegie immigrated to the United States from Scotland as a boy. His first job was working in a textile mill. He eventually found a job at the Pennsylvania Railroad, and worked his way up, becoming a successful executive. He diversified his business interests, and in 1875 entered the steel business. Carnegie practiced vertical integration, attempting to control every aspect of the production of steel. In addition to his steel plants and blast furnaces, he owned much of the Mesabi Range, from which iron ore was extracted, fleets of ships, railroads, coal mines, and coke ovens. Eventually, Carnegie also expanded horizontally, buying up other steel companies. By 1900, Carnegie's holdings produced more steel than Great Britain.

J. P. Morgan was a Wall Street investment banker. His business was providing funding for businesses, and he used his financial power to reorganize and consolidate firms in a wide range of industries. Morgan liked order and predictability in business, and he attained this by forming large industrial combinations. He merged a number of railroads and helped create such powerful and well-known firms as General Electric (GE), American Telephone and Telegraph (AT&T), and International Harvester. Morgan's most ambitious combination came in 1901. Morgan persuaded Andrew Carnegie to sell his steel company for $400 million. To this he added eight other steel companies and formed the United States Steel Corporation. Morgan's U.S. Steel was capitalized at $1.4 billion dollars and was the most prodigious industrial enterprise yet seen in the world. Morgan and his bank kept a degree of control over his handiworks by placing partners on these firms' boards of directors, creating an elaborate system of "interlocking directorates."

B. The business success of Rockefeller, Carnegie, and Morgan changed the lives of Americans in a variety of ways. They and their fellow "robber barons" of the late nineteenth century pioneered the transformation of the United States from an agrarian republic to a predominantly urban and industrialized nation. Increasingly, Americans lived in cities and more and more worked for large businesses. The transition from rural life to the city was wrenching for many. Working conditions in the new industries could be harsh and the hours long. Workers made efforts to unionize, though at Carnegie's steel mill at Homestead, Pennsylvania, in 1892 a union-led strike was violently crushed. The ready availability of industrial jobs in the United States stimulated immigration, and millions of people entered the country in the late nineteenth century, many coming from southern and eastern Europe, changing the ethnic composition of the American population.

Despite the hardships suffered by many working in the new industries, the general standard of living in the United States rose in these years. Industrialists like Rockefeller provided good products at reasonable prices. In an era before a central bank, Morgan and fellow Wall Street bankers played a key role in the economy. Following the panic of 1893, the gold reserves of the United States fell precipitously. In 1895, President Grover Cleveland turned to Morgan, who organized a consortium of bankers to lend the federal government gold and stabilize the currency. Morgan also helped settle conditions following the panic of 1907.

Many Americans resented the power wielded by businessmen like Rockefeller, Carnegie, and Morgan. They believed that the trusts exploited consumers through monopolistic control of markets, and corrupted politics because of their economic influence. The Interstate Commerce Act of 1887 was an early effort to regulate the railroads. The Sherman Antitrust Act of 1890 outlawed trusts but initially proved ineffective. The Progressive Era of the early twentieth century saw the government take on a regulatory role toward big business. President Theodore Roosevelt put teeth into the Sherman Act through such actions as his prosecution of Morgan's Northern Securities Company, a railroad holding corporation. Under President Woodrow Wilson, Congress passed the Clayton Antitrust Act of 1914 and the Federal Trade Commission Act of 1914. In 1913, Congress passed the Federal Reserve Act, giving the government greater control over the currency, reducing the role played by bankers like Morgan. Big business remained big, but the federal government now actively regulated it.

3. A. The big battle for women at the beginning of the twentieth century was the struggle for suffrage. Carrie Chapman Catt led the mainstream National America Woman Suffrage Association. Alice Paul led the more radical Congressional Union. A number of states began to allow women to vote in state elections. The efforts of women to assist in the war effort during World War I overcame the last resistance to blocking women's suffrage. Congress passed a women's suffrage amendment, which was ratified as the Nineteenth Amendment in 1920.

Most women in the 1920s, such as the youthful flappers, focused on personal self-fulfillment rather than politics, though women such as Jeanette Rankin, the first female elected to Congress, Nellie Ross of Wyoming and Miriam Ferguson of Texas, elected governors in 1924, and Frances Perkins, the first female cabinet secretary, made notable contributions to public affairs. Alice Paul lobbied for an Equal Rights Amendment, though without success.

Also, many women made important contributions to victory by working in war industries. During World War II, "Rosie the Riveter" became a celebrated image. After the war, many women left these jobs as men returned from military service. Popular culture celebrated the woman as homemaker during the 1950s. Despite this, by the end of the 1950s, about 40 percent of women were working outside the home. This was a continuation of a growing trend in women's employment that had begun early in the century.

In 1963, Betty Friedan published *The Feminine Mystique*, which argued that women needed to liberate themselves from the role of housewife. In 1966, Friedan helped found the National Organization of Women (NOW), launching what is now called "Second Wave" feminism, which worked to increase the influence of women in all aspects of society. The women's movement quickly saw many victories. Title IX of the Education Amendments in 1972 opened up unprecedented opportunities for female athletes at schools receiving federal money. The Supreme Court decision *Roe v. Wade* made abortion a right. Women rapidly moved into the workforce, a trend that was accelerated by economic problems in the 1970s. One defeat for the women's movement involved the Equal Rights Amendment, which passed Congress in 1972. At first seemingly assured of ratification in the states, it ultimately failed because of the opposition of conservative activists like Phyllis Schlafly, who argued that it would lead to drafting women into the military and unisex public restrooms. Despite this, women achieved many firsts in the 1980s. Sandra Day O'Connor became the first female Supreme Court justice in 1981. Sally Ride became the first American woman in space in 1983. Geraldine Ferraro received the Democratic nomination for vice president in 1984.

African Americans at the turn of the twentieth century faced Jim Crow laws and legalized segregation in the South and discrimination elsewhere in the United States. Booker T. Washington, the president of the Tuskegee Institute, argued that African Americans should focus on education and economic self-empowerment instead of immediately challenging segregation. He believed that increased economic power would eventually lead to full civil rights. W. E. B. Du Bois, a Harvard University trained historian, disagreed with Washington and wrote that African Americans should strive for full social equality. In 1910, he was one of the founders of the National Association for the Advancement of Colored People (NAACP), which would become one of the most important and effective civil rights organizations.

Around the time of World War I, many African-Americans left the South in the Great Migration to northern cities, looking for work in war industries. This led to social tensions that sometimes erupted in race riots like those in Chicago in 1919. These new centers of African-American settlement also became the sources of cultural creativity, such as the Harlem Renaissance of the 1920s. Writers such as Langston Hughes and Zora Neale Hurston and musicians such as Duke Ellington won respect across racial lines.

During World War II, more African Americans moved to the North and West seeking employment in rapidly expanding industrial plants. African Americans faced discrimination in war industries. A. Philip Randolph, leader of the Brotherhood of Sleeping Car Porters, threatened a march on Washington in 1941 to protest these conditions. President Franklin Roosevelt avoided this by creating the Fair Employment Practices Commission (FEPC) to ensure that African Americans were not subject to discrimination in the military and in defense work. The FEPC could not eliminate all discrimination, but it was an important precedent. During the war, many African Americans supported the "Double V" campaign—victory over the enemy overseas and against racism in the United States.

The NAACP kept up a legal campaign against Jim Crow laws in the South. The 1944 Supreme Court decision *Smith v. Allwright* declared all-white political primaries unconstitutional. In 1948, President Harry Truman, anxious to win African-American support in that year's presidential election, ordered the integration of the U.S. military. The 1950s saw the African-American civil rights movement make great strides. Thurgood Marshall, chief counsel for the NAACP, argued crucial cases before the Supreme Court. In 1950, the Supreme Court in *Sweatt v. Painter* ruled against segregated professional schools. In 1954, in *Brown v. Board of Education of Topeka, Kansas* the Supreme Court declared that segregated schools were "inherently unequal" and therefore unconstitutional, overruling the 1896 *Plessy v. Ferguson* decision and removing the legal basis of segregation.

In 1955, Rosa Parks and the Reverend Martin Luther King, Jr., led a successful campaign to integrate the buses in Montgomery, Alabama. The Montgomery bus boycott made Martin Luther King, Jr., a nationally known civil rights leader. In 1957, when African-American students were prevented from enrolling at Central High School in Little Rock, Arkansas, President Dwight D. Eisenhower sent federal troops to protect them. Civil Rights Acts were passed in 1957 and 1960. These established a Civil Rights Commission and attempted to protect African-American voting rights. Martin Luther King, Jr., founded the Southern Christian Leadership Conference (SCLC) in 1957. Other civil rights organizations followed, such as the Student Nonviolent Coordinating Committee (SNCC) in 1960. In 1960, students in Greensboro, North Carolina, started the "sit-in" movement, sitting at a whites-only Woolworths lunch counter. Groups of black and white "Freedom Riders" rode buses into the South in an attempt to desegregate bus terminals. Many were attacked, and the Kennedy administration had to intervene to protect them. President John F. Kennedy also had to protect James Meredith as he attempted to enroll at the University of Mississippi.

The August 1963 March on Washington, with Martin Luther King, Jr.'s "I Have a Dream" speech, attempted to rally support for a new civil rights bill. Efforts to desegregate Birmingham, Alabama, were met with violent action by police chief "Bull" Connor, who unleashed dogs and fire hoses on protestors. Episodes like this helped turn public opinion against the segregationists. President Lyndon B. Johnson pushed the Civil Rights Act of 1964 through Congress. This outlawed discrimination in public facilities and employment. The next year, the Voting Rights Act of 1965 made literacy tests illegal and put the power of the federal government behind registering African-American voters. The legal basis for discriminating against African Americans was overthrown by these laws. In the late 1960s, radical "Black Power" groups like the Black Panther party promoted African-American militancy and pride but alienated many whites.

By the 1920s, the Mexican-American population in the United States doubled in size as people fled the violence of the Mexican Revolution or looked for work in the United States. In the depths of the Great Depression, some Mexican Americans were deported as local authorities in the Southwest attempted to protect jobs for white Americans. During World War II, demand increased for Mexican-American labor. Many Mexican Americans found work in war industries. The Bracero Program brought Mexican contract laborers into the United States to work in agriculture. Tensions between Mexican Americans and whites in Los Angeles, California, boiled over in the 1943 "Zoot Suit" Riots. After reports that Latino youths wearing gaudy "zoot suits" had insulted men in uniform, sailors from a nearby navy base surged into Mexican-American neighborhoods and beat up young men wearing the distinctive clothing. The Mexican-American population continued to grow. In 1954, the government launched "Operation Wetback" and rounded up and deported up to a million illegal immigrants. In 1960, Mexican-American leaders formed the Mexican-American Political Association (MAPA) to increase their political influence. Soon Mexican Americans were being elected to a variety of local, state, and federal offices. In 1965, Cesar Chavez formed the United Farm Workers to improve conditions for Mexican-American farm workers. His efforts brought the plight of poor Mexican Americans to national attention.

B. Early feminists were influenced by the gains African Americans made during Reconstruction. They argued that if African-American men had the vote, white women should have it as well. The feminist movement was also influenced by the struggles of African Americans during the civil rights movement. Some female members of the civil rights movement joined the feminist movement. Feminists staged protests and marches modeled on those of the civil rights movement. The Equal Rights Amendment was an effort to gain a statutory victory akin to the Civil Rights Act of 1964. Cesar Chavez and Chicano activists were also inspired by the civil rights movement. Like Martin Luther King, Jr., Cesar Chavez emphasized nonviolence in his strikes and boycotts. Some Mexican-American activists imitated the African-American exponents of greater militancy and ethnic pride. Reies Tijerina led a group that occupied the Kit Carson National Forest to protest historic wrongs against Hispanics in the Southwest. "Brown Panthers" were modeled on the Black Panthers. *La Raza Unida* (The Race United) was founded to promote Hispanic interests.

4. A. The poster recruited soldiers into the Seventh Indiana Cavalry by reminding men that a draft had been enacted. By joining the unit, the men avoided the draft. They also made themselves eligible for a generous bounty of $400. Congress passed a federal draft law in 1863. A drafted man could pay a substitute to take his place, or purchase exemption by paying the government $300. If a draftee could not afford these options, he had to serve. Men of little means, but worried about being drafted, would find the financial inducement of the recruiting poster tempting.

B. The federal government resorted to the draft in 1863 because fewer men were volunteering for service in the army. It was well known that battle casualties had been heavy and that disease in army encampments was a real threat. The draft was an attempt to stimulate recruiting. The draft itself did not bring overwhelming numbers into the army. Only about 10 percent of federal troops were draftees. But the threat of the draft added to the attractiveness of recruiting efforts like that represented by the poster. To encourage enlistments, federal, state, and local authorities offered bounties to soldiers who volunteered. As in the poster, these bounties could be quite substantial, the equivalent of a year's wages for a laborer. Some unscrupulous "bounty jumpers" volunteered to collect their bonus, and then promptly deserted.

C. Opponents of the war, popularly termed Copperheads, denounced the draft. They saw the draft as one more example of tyranny from a government that, in addition to attacking the secessionists in the South, had arrested large numbers of Southern sympathizers, and on occasion suspended the right to habeas corpus. Many people regarded the provisions of the draft law as unfair, because wealthy men could buy exemption or hire a substitute. In July 1863 groups of mostly Irish workmen in New York City rioted over the law. Mobs attacked government officials and African Americans. The rioters were suppressed by federal troops fresh from the Battle of Gettysburg. Over 70 people were killed in the rioting.

Explanation for the Document-Based Question

Students should begin with a discussion of the Interstate Commerce Act (1887) and Sherman Antitrust Act (1890). The Interstate Commerce Act attempted to regulate railroad companies. It required railroads to submit their fare schedules with the federal government and publicize their rates. The act created an Interstate Commerce Commission (ICC) to monitor the industry. The Sherman Act declared illegal all combinations "in restraint of free trade." It empowered the Justice Department to bring suit and break up such monopolies. However, these acts would have to pass the scrutiny of the Supreme Court. Students might comment upon the composition of the Court during the period. They might explain how a conservative Court could thwart the efforts of reformers. Students should discuss the labor movement during the Progressive Era. Several strikes occurred in this period, including the Great Railway Strike (1877), Haymarket Affair (1886), and the Homestead Strike (1892). Students must examine the Pullman Strike (1894), in which railroad workers and the American Railway Union, led by Eugene Debs, crippled traffic in several states and territories. Many governors sided with the railroad companies by employing state troops to disperse the strikers. One notable exception was John Peter Altgeld, governor of Illinois. Railroad operators in Chicago appealed to President Cleveland and Attorney General Richard Olney to intercede on their behalf. The president ordered 2,000 federal troops to break up the strike. The Supreme Court further solidified the position of the railroad corporations by applying the Sherman Antitrust Act against unions that threatened free trade (Document A). In *E. C. Knight Company v. U.S.*, the Court further inhibited efforts to regulate corporations by putting manufacturing companies outside the purview of the Sherman Act (Document B). Thus, companies continued to form monopolies in various industries that fixed prices without competition. The Court undermined the Interstate Commerce Commission's authority to determine fair railroad rates by applying the "due process" clause of the Fourteenth Amendment to corporations (Document C). Progressives seeking to limit the hours of labor met with mixed results. In *Holden v. Hardy* (1898) the Court affirmed the right of state legislatures to regulate maximum hours in the interests of workers' health. Seven years later, the Court again reinterpreted the Fourteenth Amendment to cast aside a state law. The Lochner decision asserted that legislation not directly related to health concerns violated the rights of workers (Document D). However, reformers gained a partial victory in *Muller v. Oregon* (1908), which sustained the legislature's authority to pass regulatory legislation to protect women's health (Document E). Students might comment upon the double standard applied to men and women in the early twentieth century. Students might refer to the Elkins (1903) and Hepburn (1906) Acts, which intended to further the federal government's ability to regulate railroads. Others might explain how presidential leadership advanced the cause of reform by briefly discussing Theodore Roosevelt, William Howard Taft, or Woodrow Wilson. Some students might touch upon how the Roosevelt administration implemented the Sherman Act in *Northern Securities Company v. United States* (1904) to set the stage for an examination of the decentralization of monopolies.
The Court furthered its position by ordering the Standard Oil Company to break up its monopoly of the oil refining industry (Document F). Students may compare the decision with the Court's response to Swift and American Tobacco. To conclude the essay, students might discuss how the Court endorsed the Adamson Act, which established an eight-hour day for interstate railway workers (Document G).

Explanations for the Long-Essay Questions

1. A variety of reform movements flourished in the United States in the period from 1820 to 1860. You can construct an argument making use of information that can include the following:

    The Second Great Awakening began in Kentucky in the early 1800s. Initially a phenomenon of enthusiastic frontier camp meetings, this new religious revival soon spread across the country. The preachers of the Second Great Awakening fostered a vibrant evangelical Protestantism that emphasized the importance of personal conversion and an intense, often more openly emotional relationship with God. One of the most famous evangelists of the Second Great Awakening was Charles Grandison Finney, a brilliant orator who abandoned a career in the law after being "saved." Many people touched by the Second Great Awakening found spiritual homes in the Baptist and Methodist churches, but new religious groupings also appeared, such as the Millerites, or Adventists, who expected the imminent arrival of Jesus Christ. The Church of Jesus Christ of Latter-day Saints, or Mormons, founded by the visionary Joseph Smith, emerged during this period of religious enthusiasm, though it was deemed heretical by more orthodox Christian churches. Facing increasing hostility, the Mormons began moving to Utah in 1846. They were led by Brigham Young after Joseph Smith was murdered by a mob. The Second Great Awakening intensified the religious character of people in the United States. By 1840, nearly half of the population was formally connected to a church. Women played a prominent role in the Second Great Awakening, making up the majority of congregations and actively supporting a growing range of charitable organizations. A "Benevolent Empire" of such organizations attempted to spread the Christian message by supporting moral reforms or missionary activity at home and abroad. The American Bible Society (1816) and the American Tract Society (1825) were typical manifestations of the "Benevolent Empire," distributing bibles and other religious writings everywhere in the United States.

    The temperance movement combined some of the religious fervor of the Second Great Awakening with a more strictly secular concern about the social cost of heavy drinking. The American Temperance Society appeared in 1826. The politician and businessman Neal S. Dow was the sponsor of the 1851 Maine law that prohibited the sale and manufacture of liquor in that state. Prohibition remained a political issue throughout the nineteenth century.

    In this period, educational reform was spurred by the efforts of Horace Mann, who promoted public education for all children. Educators like Catharine Beecher established private schools designed for girls and young women. William H. McGuffey began publishing his phenomenally popular *McGuffey's Readers* in the 1830s. Large numbers of colleges, usually associated with religious denominations, appeared across the country. Oberlin College in Ohio began educating women as well as men in 1837.

    Efforts in these years were made to improve conditions in prisons. Alexis de Tocqueville, the French author of *Democracy in America* (two volumes, 1835 and 1840), first visited the United States to study its prisons. Dorothea Dix became famous for her work to reform the treatment of the mentally ill in asylums.

    Various utopian communities sprang up in the United States. In 1825, Robert Owen founded a communal society at New Harmony in Indiana. The Oneida Community established in New York in 1848, scandalized people by experimenting with "free love" and eugenics.

Lucretia Mott and Elizabeth Cady Stanton began the women's rights movement by calling for women's suffrage. They helped organize a conference at Seneca Falls, New York, in 1848 that issued a famous "Declaration of Sentiments" that demanded equal rights and the vote for women.

Abolitionism grew in strength in the 1820s and 1830s. William Lloyd Garrison began publishing his Abolitionist paper *The Liberator* in 1831. In 1833, Garrison, Lewis Tappan, and Theodore Weld founded the American Anti-Slavery Society. Abolitionists began an increasingly vocal campaign against slavery, infuriating many Southerners. Abolitionism was concentrated in the North, but some Southerners, such as the South Carolinian sisters Angelina and Sarah Grimke, spoke out against the institution of slavery. African Americans like the escaped slave Frederick Douglass also joined the cause. In addition to agitating against slavery, Abolitionists organized the Underground Railroad to help slaves make their way to freedom. The former slave Harriet Tubman helped "conduct" many African Americans along the Underground Railroad. Abolitionists were often very unpopular, even in the North. Garrison was attacked by a Boston mob in 1835, and in 1837 the Abolitionist editor Elijah Lovejoy was murdered in Alton, Illinois. Despite this, the Abolitionists succeeded in making slavery a major political issue, exemplified by the creation of the Liberty party in 1844 and the Free Soil party in 1848. Political abolitionism would set the stage for the emergence of the Republican party in the 1850s.

2. You can construct an argument making use of information that can include the following:

By the early 1820s, American politics was becoming increasingly democratic, reflecting an egalitarian ethos that differentiated the United States from Europe. At the founding of the nation, most states had property qualifications for voting. In 1824, only four states retained this. The country was rapidly moving toward universal white male suffrage. By 1832, only South Carolina maintained the practice of state legislators choosing presidential electors. Everywhere else the voters chose electors.

Voter participation soared as democratization spread. In 1824, there was a 27 percent voter participation rate in that year's presidential election. In the 1840 presidential election, the voter participation rate was 78 percent. This robust participation in the political process was spurred by the development of party politics in what scholars call the Second Party System. In these years party politics became a vibrant part of American culture.

The person most closely associated with this upsurge in democracy is Andrew Jackson. Historians talk of "Jacksonian Democracy" and the "Jacksonian Era." Andrew Jackson was a westerner from Tennessee and a military hero of the War of 1812. He had been a notable Indian fighter and had defeated the British at the Battle of New Orleans in 1815. He was associated with American expansionism and identified himself with ordinary men attempting to better themselves in a burgeoning national economy.

Jackson ran for president in 1824, competing in a four-way field that also included Secretary of State John Quincy Adams, Secretary of the Treasury William H. Crawford, and the Speaker of the House, Henry Clay. Jackson easily won the popular vote but did not win a majority in the Electoral College. This meant that the election would be decided by a vote in the House of Representatives. Here Clay threw his support to Adams, making possible Adams's election as president on the first ballot. Jackson was infuriated at the way that he was denied the presidency. When Adams later appointed Clay secretary of state, Jackson's supporters denounced this as the result of a "corrupt bargain."

The election of 1828 was a rematch between Jackson and Adams. Jackson had by this time laid the foundation for a new party—the Democrats. A new popular style of politics was emerging. Jackson was nicknamed "Old Hickory" by his supporters, who planted hickory poles as emblems of their candidate. Adams's supporters countered by associating the president with the stalwart oak tree. Both sides freely resorted to invective in their descriptions of the opposition. When Jackson's wife Rachel died a month after the election, he was convinced it was a result of the campaign's vicious name-calling. Despite this, Jackson easily won the election. After his inauguration, ordinary people surged into the presidential mansion to congratulate him. President Jackson continued to encourage the democratic political revolution in American politics. He embraced the spoils system, replacing officeholders with his political supporters. When critics argued that the new appointees were less qualified to do these jobs, Jackson replied that any American could carry out these public tasks.

In 1832, Jackson was renominated for the presidency by the first party political convention. Jackson's policies as president, such as the removal of eastern Indian tribes and the destruction of the Second Bank of the United States, were intended to further the fortunes of the common man. The opponents of Andrew Jackson, led by figures like Henry Clay, Daniel Webster, and William Henry Harrison, organized themselves. By 1836, they had created the Whig party. The Whigs embraced Henry Clay's "American System" of government support for internal improvements and policies to strengthen the market economy. They defended this as a better way of helping ordinary men make their way in the world than the policies of Jackson and the Democrats. Andrew Jackson's political heir Martin Van Buren prevailed in the election of 1836. But when he took office, he found himself overwhelmed by the panic of 1837, and a major depression, brought on in part by the killing of the Second Bank of the United States and Jackson's Specie Circular, which required that public lands be purchased with gold or silver.

The Whigs looked to the election of 1840 with optimism. Taking a page from the Democrats, they nominated William Henry Harrison for president, a military hero of the 1811 Battle of Tippecanoe and the War of 1812 who was associated with the West. For crossover appeal, they nominated John Tyler, a former Democrat, for vice president. This ticket provided a brilliant slogan: "Tippecanoe and Tyler too!" The Whigs did not bother to publish a party platform; instead they focused on campaign theatrics. They concocted the myth that Harrison lived in an ordinary log cabin, and soon portrayals of log cabins were everywhere. Harrison was also described as drinking hard cider like a common man. In Philadelphia, a distiller named E. C. Booz passed out samples of hard cider to Harrison voters. Harrison supporters rolled enormous balls across the countryside until he was elected, giving posterity the expression, "keep the ball rolling!" All this hoopla worked. Harrison easily defeated Van Buren. With the election of 1840, the new style of popular party politics was firmly established.

GLOSSARY

Abolitionist movement Movement dedicated to the abolition of slavery that existed primarily in the North in years leading up to the Civil War and consisted of both white and black members.

advertising age Term first used to describe America's consumer culture of the 1920s, when advertising began to influence the choices of purchasers.

affirmative action Policies that began in the 1970s to make up for past discrimination and give minorities and women advantages in applying for certain jobs and in applying for admission to certain universities.

affluent society Term used by economist John Kenneth Galbraith to describe the American economy in the 1950s, during which time many Americans became enraptured with appliances and homes in the suburbs.

Agricultural Adjustment Administration (AAA) Established by the Agricultural Act of 1932, a New Deal bureau designed to restore economic position of farmers by paying them *not* to farm goods that were being overproduced.

Agricultural Marketing Act of 1929 Act championed by Herbert Hoover that authorized the lending of federal money to farmer's cooperatives to buy crops to keep them from the oversaturated market; program hampered by lack of adequate federal financial support.

Albany Congress (1754) Meeting of representatives of seven colonies to coordinate their efforts against French and Native American threats in the Western frontier regions.

Alien and Sedition Acts Proposed and supported by John Adams, gave the president the power to expel aliens deemed "dangerous to the country's well-being" and outlawed publication and public pronouncement of "false, scandalous, and malicious" statements about the government.

Allied Powers Coalition of nations that opposed Germany, Italy, and Japan in World War II; led by England, the Soviet Union, and the United States. In World War I, the coalition consisted of France, Russia, and Great Britain. This group opposed the Central powers (Germany, Austria-Hungary, and Italy).

America First Committee Isolationist group in America that insisted that America stay out of World War II; held rallies from 1939 to 1941; argued that affairs in Europe should be settled by Europeans and not Americans and stated that the Soviet Union was a greater eventual threat than Nazi Germany.

American Colonization Society Formed in 1817, stated that the best way to end the slavery problem in the United States was for blacks to emigrate to Africa. By 1822, a few American blacks emigrated to Liberia. Organization's views were later rejected by most abolitionists.

American Expeditionary Force Official title of American army sent to Europe to aid England and France after United States entered World War I; army was commanded by General John J. Pershing.

American Federation of Labor (AFL) National labor union founded by Samuel Gompers in 1886; original goal was to organize skilled workers by craft. Merged with Congress of Industrial Organizations (CIO) in 1955.

American Indian Movement (AIM) Native American organization founded in 1968 to protest government policies and injustices suffered by Native Americans; in 1973 organized armed occupation of Wounded Knee, South Dakota.

American Liberty League Formed in 1934 by anti-New Deal politicians and business leaders to oppose policies of Franklin Roosevelt; stated that New Deal policies brought America closer to fascism.

American System Economic plan promoted by Speaker of the House Henry Clay in years following the War of 1812, which promoted vigorous growth of the American economy and the use of protective tariffs to encourage Americans to buy more domestic goods.

Anaconda Copper Company Large mining syndicate typical of many companies involved in mining in the western United States in the 1860s and 1870s; used heavy machinery and professional engineers. Many prospectors who found gold, silver, or copper sold their claims to companies such as this.

Anaconda Plan Critical component of initial Union plans to win the Civil War; called for capture of critical Southern ports and eventual control of the Mississippi River, which would create major economic and strategic difficulties for the Confederacy.

Antifederalists Group that opposed the ratification of the proposed Constitution of the United States in 1787; many feared that strong central government would remove the processes of government "from the people" and replicate the excesses of the British monarchy.

Anti-Imperialist League Organization formed in 1898 to oppose American annexation of the Philippines and American imperialism in general; focused the public on the potential financial, military, and especially moral costs of imperialism.

Anti-Saloon League Organization founded in 1893 that increased public awareness of the social effects of alcohol on society; supported politicians who favored prohibition and promoted statewide referendums in Western and Southern states to ban alcohol.

Appomattox In the courthouse of this Virginia city Robert E. Lee surrendered his Confederate army to Ulysses S. Grant on April 9, 1865.

Army-McCarthy hearings 1954 televised hearings on charges that Senator Joseph McCarthy was unfairly tarnishing the U.S. Army with charges of Communist infiltration into the armed forces; hearings were the beginning of the end for McCarthy, whose bullying tactics were repeatedly demonstrated.

Articles of Confederation Ratified in 1781, this document established the first official government of the United States; allowed much power to remain in the states, with the federal government possessing only limited powers. Articles replaced by the Constitution in 1788.

astrolabe Instrument that enabled navigators to calculate their latitude using the sun and the stars; allowed more accuracy in plotting routes during the Age of Discovery.

Atlantic, Battle of the Began in spring 1941 with the sinking of an American merchant vessel by a German submarine. Armed conflict between warships of America and Germany took place in September 1941; American merchant vessels were armed by 1942.

Atlantic Charter Fall 1941 agreement between Franklin Roosevelt and Winston Churchill, stating that America and Great Britain would support a postwar world based on self-determination and would endorse a world body to ensure "general security." U.S. agreement to convoy merchant ships across part of Atlantic inevitably drew America closer to conflict with Germany.

Aztecs Advanced Indian society located in central Mexico; conquered by Spanish conquistador Cortes. The defeat of the Aztecs was hastened by smallpox brought to Mexico by the Spanish.

baby boom Large increase in birthrate in United States that began in 1945 and lasted until 1962; new and larger families fueled the move to suburbia that occurred in the 1950s and produced the "youth culture" that would become crucial in the 1960s.

Ballinger-Pinchot Affair Crisis that occurred when William Howard Taft was president, further distancing him from Progressive supporters of Theodore Roosevelt. Richard Ballinger, Taft's secretary of the interior, allowed private businessmen to purchase large amounts of public land in Alaska. Forest Service head Gifford Pinchot (a Roosevelt supporter) protested to Congress and was fired by Taft.

Bank War Political battles surrounding the attempt by President Andrew Jackson to greatly reduce the power of the Second Bank of the United States. Jackson claimed the bank was designed to serve special interests in America and not the common people.

Bataan Death March Forced march of nearly 75,000 American and Filipino soldiers captured by the Japanese from the Bataan Peninsula in early May 1942; over 10,000 soldiers died during this one-week ordeal.

Bay of Pigs Failed 1961 invasion of Cuba by United States–supported anti-Castro refugees designed to topple Castro from power; prestige of the United States, and of the newly elected president, John Kennedy, was damaged by this failed coup attempt.

Bear Flag Republic Declaring independence from Mexican control, this republic was declared in 1846 by American settlers living in California. This political act was part of a larger American political and military strategy to wrest Texas and California from Mexico.

Beat Generation Literary movement of the 1950s that criticized the conformity of American society and the ever-present threat of atomic warfare; *On the Road* by Jack Kerouac, *Howl* by Allen Ginsberg, and *Naked Lunch* by William Burroughs were key works of the Beat Generation.

Berlin Airlift American and British pilots flew in food and fuel to West Berlin during late 1948 and early 1949 because the Soviet Union and East Germany blockaded other access to West Berlin (which was located in East Germany); Stalin ended this blockade in May 1949. Airlift demonstrated American commitment to protecting Western Allies in Europe during the early cold war period.

Berlin Wall Concrete structure built in 1961 by Soviets and East Germany physically dividing East and West Berlin; to many in the West, the Wall was symbolic of Communist repression in the cold war era. The wall was finally torn down in 1989.

Bessemer steel First produced in 1856 in converter (furnace) invented by Henry Bessemer; was much more durable and harder than iron. Steel was a critical commodity in the Second Industrial Revolution.

bias No historical writing can be totally objective; observers are always influenced by either conscious or unconscious bias. Conscious bias might be a flattering biography of Lincoln written by an abolitionist in 1865, or an unflattering biography of Lincoln written by a southerner in the same year. Unconscious bias may be created by one's education, predispositions toward the subject, or even one's race or gender.

bicameral legislature A legislative structure consisting of two houses, this was adopted by the authors of the U.S. Constitution; membership of the states in one house (the House of Representatives) is determined by population, while in the other house (the Senate) all states have equal representation.

Bill of Rights Added to the Constitution in 1791, the first 10 amendments protected freedom of speech, freedom of the press, the right to bear arms, and other basic rights of American citizens.

Birth of a Nation Epic movie released in 1915 by director D. W. Griffith; portrayed the Reconstruction as a period when Southern blacks threatened basic American values, which the Ku Klux Klan tried to protect. The film was lauded by many, including President Woodrow Wilson.

Black Codes Laws adopted by the Southern states in the Reconstruction era that greatly limited the freedom of Southern blacks. In several states blacks could not move, own land, or do anything but farm.

black nationalism Spurred by Malcolm X and other black leaders, a call for black pride and advancement without the help of whites; this appeared to be a repudiation of the calls for peaceful integration urged by Martin Luther King, Jr. Race riots in Northern cities in mid-1960s were at least partially fueled by supporters of black nationalism.

Black Panthers Group originally founded in Oakland, California, to protect blacks from police harassment; promoted militant black power; also ran social programs in several California cities. Founded by Bobby Seale and Huey P. Newton.

black power Movement of black Americans in the mid-1960s that emphasized pride in racial heritage and black economic and political self-reliance; term coined by black civil rights leader Stokely Carmichael.

blacklist Prevented persons accused of being Communists from getting work in entertainment and other industries during the period of anti-Communist fervor of the late 1940s and early 1950s; some entertainers waited until the mid-1960s before working publicly again.

"Bleeding Kansas" As a result of the Kansas-Nebraska Act of 1854, residents of Kansas territory could decide if territory would allow slavery or not. As a result, both pro and antislavery groups flooded settlers into Kansas territory. Much violence followed very disputed elections in 1855.

bonanza farms Large farms that came to dominate agricultural life in much of the West in the late 1800s. Instead of plots farmed by yeoman farmers, large amounts of machinery were used, and workers were hired laborers, often performing only specific tasks (similar to work in a factory).

Bonus Army Group of nearly 17,000 veterans who marched on Washington in May 1932 to demand the military bonuses they had been promised; this group was eventually driven from their camp city by the United States Army. This action increased the public perception that the Hoover administration cared little about the poor.

Boston Massacre Conflict between British soldiers and Boston civilians on March 5, 1770. After civilians threw rocks and snowballs at the soldiers, the soldiers opened fire, killing five and wounding six.

Boston Tea Party In response to the Tea Act and additional British taxes on tea, Boston radicals disguised as Native Americans threw nearly 350 chests of tea into Boston Harbor on December 16, 1773.

Brown v. Board of Education 1954 Supreme Court decision that threw out the 1896 *Plessy v. Ferguson* ruling that schools could be "separate but equal." The ruling began the long and painful process of school desegregation in the South and other parts of America.

Bulge, Battle of the December 1944 German attack that was the last major offensive by the Axis powers in World War II. Germans managed to push forward into Belgium but were then driven back. Attack was costly to the Germans in terms of material and manpower.

Bull Moose party Name given to the Progressive party in the 1912 presidential campaign. Bull Moose candidate ex-president Theodore Roosevelt ran against incumbent president William Howard Taft and Democrat Woodrow Wilson, with Wilson emerging victorious.

Bull Run, First Battle of July 21, 1861 Confederate victory over Union forces, which ended in Union forces fleeing in disarray toward Washington. This battle convinced Lincoln and others in the North that victory over the Confederates would not be as easy as they initially thought.

Bull Run, Second Battle of Decisive victory by General Robert E. Lee and Confederate forces over the Union army in August 1862.

Bunker Hill, Battle of In June 1775, the British attacked colonial forces at Breed's Hill outside Boston; despite frightful losses, the British emerged victorious in this battle.

Calvinism Protestant faith that preached salvation "by faith alone" and predestination; desire by Calvinists in England to create a "pure church" in England was only partially successful, thus causing Calvinist Puritans to come to the New World starting in 1620.

Camp David Accords Treaty between Egypt and Israel brokered by President Jimmy Carter and signed in early 1979; Israel agreed to give back territory in the Sinai Peninsula to Egypt, while Egypt agreed to recognize Israel's right to exist as a nation.

carpetbaggers Term used by Southerners to mock Northerners who came to the South to gain either financially or politically during the Reconstruction era.

Central Powers The alliance of Germany, Austria-Hungary, the Ottoman Empire, and Bulgaria that opposed England, France, Russia, and later the United States in World War I.

Chancellor of the Exchequer During the era prior to and during the Revolutionary War, this was the head of the department in the British government that issued and collected taxes. Many acts issued by the Chancellor of the Exchequer created great resentment in the American colonies.

Chancellorsville, Battle of Brilliant Confederate attack on Union forces led by Stonewall Jackson and Robert E. Lee on May 2 to 3, 1863. Union defeat led to great pessimism in the North and convinced many in the South that victory over the North was indeed possible.

Chateau-Thierry, Battle of One of the first 1918 World War I battles where soldiers of the American Expeditionary Force fought and suffered severe casualties.

Checkers Speech Speech made by Richard Nixon on national television on September 23, 1952, where he defended himself against charges that rich supporters had set up a special expense account for his use; by the speech Nixon saved his spot on the 1952 Republican ticket (he was running for vice president, with Eisenhower running for president) and saved his political career.

Cherokee Nation v. Georgia **(1831)** Supreme Court case in which the Cherokee tribe claimed that Georgia had no right to enforce laws in Cherokee territory, since Cherokees were a sovereign nation. This ruling by John Marshall stated that Cherokees were a "domestic dependent nation" and had no right to appeal in federal court.

Church of England Also called the Anglican church, this was the Protestant church established by King Henry VIII; religious radicals desired a "purer" church that was allowed by monarchs of the early seventeenth century, causing some to leave for the Americas.

Circular Letter In reaction to the 1767 Townshend Acts, the Massachusetts assembly circulated a letter to the other colonies, asking that they work together and jointly issue a petition of protest. Strong-willed response of British authorities to the letter influenced the colonial assemblies to work together on a closer basis.

Civil Rights Act of 1866 Act that struck down Black Codes and defined the rights of all citizens; also stated that the federal government could act when civil rights were violated at the state level. Passed by Congress over the veto of President Andrew Johnson.

Civil Rights Act of 1964 Key piece of civil rights legislation that made discrimination on the basis of race, sex, religion, or national origin illegal; segregation in public restrooms, bus stations, and other public facilities also was declared illegal.

Civil Service Commission Created by the Pendelton Civil Service Act of 1883, this body was in charge of testing applicants and assigning them to appropriate government jobs; filling jobs on the basis of merit replaced the spoils system, in which government jobs were given as rewards for political service.

Civilian Conservation Corps (CCC) New Deal program that began in 1933, putting nearly 3 million young men to work; workers were paid little, but worked on conservation projects and maintaining beaches and parks. CCC program for young women began in 1937.

Clayton Antitrust Act of 1914 Act designed to strengthen the Sherman Antitrust Act of 1890. Certain activities previously committed by big businesses, such as not allowing unions in factories and not allowing strikes, were declared illegal.

cold war Period between 1945 and 1991 of near-continuous struggle between the United States and its Allies and the Soviet Union and its Allies; cold war tensions were made even more intense by the existence of the atomic bomb.

colonial assemblies Existed in all of the British colonies in America; House of Burgesses in Virginia was the first one. Members of colonial assemblies were almost always members of the upper classes of colonial society.

Columbian Exchange The exchange of crops, animals (as well as diseases), and ideas between Europe and the Western Hemisphere that developed in the aftermath of the voyages of Columbus.

Committee on Public Information Created by Woodrow Wilson during World War I to mobilize public opinion for the war, this was the most intensive use of propaganda until that time by the United States. The image of "Uncle Sam" was created for this propaganda campaign.

Committees of Correspondence First existed in Massachusetts, and eventually in all of the colonies. Leaders of resistance to British rule listed their grievances against the British and circulated them to all of the towns of the colony.

Common Sense Very popular 1776 publication in the colonies written by Englishman Thomas Paine, who had come to America in 1774; repudiated the entire concept of government by monarchy. After publication of this document, public sentiment in the colonies turned decisively toward a desire for independence.

Compromise of 1850 Complex agreement that temporarily lessened tensions between Northern and Southern political leaders, and prevented a possible secession crisis; to appease the South, the Fugitive Slave Act was strengthened; to appease the North, California entered the Union as a free state.

Compromise of 1877 Political arrangement that ended the contested presidential election of 1876. Representatives of Southern states agreed not to oppose the official election of Republican Rutherford B. Hayes as president despite massive election irregularities. In return, the Union army stopped enforcing Reconstruction legislation in the South, thus ending Reconstruction.

Concord, Battle of Occurred on April 19, 1775, between British regulars and Massachusetts militiamen. Almost 275 British soldiers were wounded or died; as a result, a wider conflict between the colonies and the British became much more probable.

Confederate States of America Eventually made up of 11 former states with Jefferson Davis as its first and only president; was unable to defeat the North because of lack of railroad lines, lack of industry, and an inability to get European nations to support their cause.

Congress of Industrial Organizations (CIO) Group of unions that broke from the AFL in 1938 and organized effective union drives in automobile and rubber industries; supported sit-down strikes in major rubber plants. Reaffiliated with the AFL in 1955.

conscription Getting recruits for military service using a draft. This method was used by the American government in all of the wars of the twentieth century. Conscription was viewed most negatively during the Vietnam War.

consumer society Many Americans in the 1950s became infatuated with all of the new products produced by technology and went out and purchased more than any prior generation. Consumer tastes of the decade were largely dictated by advertising and television.

containment policy Formulated by George Kennan, a policy whereby the United States would forcibly stop Communist aggression whenever and wherever it occurred; containment was the dominant American policy of the cold war era, and forced America to become involved in foreign conflicts such as Vietnam.

Continentals Soldiers in the "American" army commanded by George Washington in the Revolutionary War. Victory at the Battle of Trenton on December 16, 1776, did much to raise the morale of the soldiers (and convince many of them to reenlist). Also a term used for paper money printed in 1781 that was soon made worthless by inflation.

Contract with America (1994) Pledge by Republican candidates for House of Representatives; led by Newt Gingrich, candidates promised to support term limits, balancing the budget, and lessening the size of the federal government. In 1994 Congressional elections, Republicans won both houses of Congress for the first time in 40 years.

convoy system System used to protect American ships carrying materials to Great Britain in 1940 and 1941; merchant ships were protected by American warships. Firing took place between these ships and German submarines, with American losses. Also used in World War I by the navy to allow American shipping to Europe.

Copperheads Democrats in Congress in the first years of the Civil War who opposed Abraham Lincoln and the North's attack on the South, claiming that the war would result in massive numbers of freed slaves entering the North and a total disruption of the Northern economy.

Coral Sea, Battle of the May 1942 American naval victory over the Japanese; prevented Japanese from attacking Australia. First naval battle where losses on both sides came almost exclusively from bombing from airplanes.

counterculture Youth of the 1960s who espoused a lifestyle encompassing drug use, free love, and a rejection of adult authority; actual "hippies" were never more than a small percentage of young people.

Coxey's Army Supporters of Ohio Populist Jacob Coxey who in 1894 marched on Washington, demanded that the government create jobs for the unemployed; although this group had no effect whatsoever on policy, it did demonstrate the social and economic impact of the Panic of 1893.

creationism Belief in the biblical account of the origin of the universe and the origin of man; believers in creationism and believers in evolution both had their day in court during the 1925 Scopes Trial.

Crittenden Plan (1860) Compromise proposal on the slavery issue designed to defuse tension between North and South; would have allowed slavery to continue in the South and would have denied Congress the power to regulate interstate slave trade. On the advice of newly elected President Lincoln, Republicans in Congress voted against it.

Crusades From these attempts to recapture the Holy Land, Europeans acquired an appreciation of the benefits of overseas expansion and an appreciation of the economic benefits of slavery.

Cuban Missile Crisis (1962) Conflict between the United States and the Soviet Union over Soviet missiles discovered in Cuba; Soviets eventually removed missiles under American pressure. Crisis was perhaps the closest the world came to armed conflict in the cold war era.

Currency Act of 1764 British act forbidding the American colonies to issue paper money as legal tender; act was repealed in 1773 by the British as an effort to ease tensions between themselves and the colonies.

dark horse candidate A candidate for office with little support before the beginning of the nomination process. James K. Polk was the first dark horse candidate for president in 1844.

Dawes Act of 1887 Act designed to break up Native American tribes, offered Native American families 160 acres of farmland or 320 acres of land for grazing. Large amounts of tribal lands were not claimed by Native Americans, and thus were purchased by land speculators.

Declaration of Neutrality Issued by President Woodrow Wilson after the outbreak of World War I in Europe in 1914, stating that the United States would maintain normal relations with and continue to trade with both sides in the conflict; factors including submarine warfare made it difficult for America to maintain this policy. Also declared by George Washington in 1793 to allow American merchants to trade with those on both sides of the French Revolution.

Declaration of Rights and Grievances (1774) Measure adopted by the First Continental Congress, stating that Parliament had some rights to regulate colonial trade with Britain, but that Parliament did not have the right to tax the colonies without their consent.

Declaratory Act of 1766 British law stating that the Parliament had absolute right to tax the colonies as they saw fit and to make laws that would be enacted in the colonies. Ironically, issued at the same time as the repeal of the Stamp Act.

deficit spending Economic policy whereby government spends money that it "doesn't have," thus creating a budget deficit. Although "conventional" economic theory disapproves of this, it is commonplace during times of crisis or war (e.g., the New Deal; post–September 11, 2001).

Democratic party Had its birth during the candidacy of Andrew Jackson; originally drew its principles from Thomas Jefferson and advocated limited government. In modern times many Democrats favor domestic programs that a larger, more powerful government allows.

Democratic-Republicans Believed in the ideas of Thomas Jefferson, who wrote of the benefits of a limited government and of a society dominated by the values of the yeoman farmer. Opposed to the Federalists, who wanted a strong national state and a society dominated by commercial interests.

détente The lessening of tensions between nations. A policy of détente between the United States and the Soviet Union and Communist China began during the presidency of Richard Nixon; the architect of policy was National Security Advisor Henry Kissinger.

Dien Bien Phu, Battle of (1954) Victory of Vietnamese forces over the French, causing the French to leave Vietnam and all of Indochina; Geneva Peace Accords that followed established North and South Vietnam.

direct primary Progressive-era reform adopted by some states that allowed candidates for state offices to be nominated by the rank-and-file party members in statewide primaries instead of by the party bosses, who had traditionally dominated the nominating process.

Dollar Diplomacy Foreign policy of President William Howard Taft, which favored increased American investment in the world as the major method for increasing American influence and stability abroad; in some parts of the world, such as in Latin America, the increased American influence was resented.

domesticity Social trend of post–World War II America; many Americans turned to family and home life as a source of contentment. Emphasis on family as a source of fulfillment forced some women to abandon the workforce and achieve "satisfaction" as homemakers.

Dominion of New England Instituted by King James II in 1686. Sir Edmund Andros governed the colonies of Massachusetts, Connecticut, Rhode Island, New York, Plymouth, and New Hampshire as a single entity without an elective assembly; Andros was finally overthrown by militiamen in Boston in April 1689 (after the Glorious Revolution).

domino theory Major tenet of cold war containment policy of the United States held that if one country in a region turned Communist, other surrounding countries would soon follow; this theory convinced many that to save all of Southeast Asia, it was necessary to resist Communist aggression in Vietnam.

Double V campaign World War II "policy" supported by several prominent black newspapers, stating that blacks in America should work for victory over the Axis powers but at the same time work for victory over oppression at home; black leaders remained frustrated during the war by continued segregation of the armed forces.

Dred Scott case Supreme Court case involving a man who was born a slave but had then lived in both a nonslave state and a nonslave territory and was now petitioning for his legal freedom; in 1857 the Court ruled that slaves were not people but were property, that they could not be citizens of the United States, and thus had no legal right to petition the Court for anything. Ruling also stated that the Missouri Compromise, which banned slavery in the territories, was unconstitutional.

Dust Bowl Great Plains region that suffered severe drought and experienced massive dust storms during the 1930s. Because of extreme conditions many who lived in the Dust Bowl left their farms and went to California to work as migrant farmers.

Eisenhower Doctrine Policy established in 1957 that promised military and economic aid to "friendly" nations in the Middle East; the policy was established to prevent communism from gaining a foothold in the region. The policy was first utilized later that year when the United States gave large amounts of aid to King Hussein of Jordan to put down internal rebellion.

Electoral College Procedure outlined in the Constitution for the election of the president; under this system, votes of electors from each state, and not the popular vote, determine who is elected president. As was demonstrated in 2000 presidential election, this system allows a person to be elected president who does not win the nationwide popular vote.

Emancipation Proclamation Edict by Abraham Lincoln that went into effect on January 1, 1863, abolishing slavery in the Confederate states. The proclamation did not affect the four slave states that were still part of the Union (so as not to alienate them).

Embargo of 1807 Declaration by President Thomas Jefferson that banned all American trade with Europe. As a result of the war between England and Napoleon's France, America's sea rights as a neutral power were threatened. Jefferson hoped the embargo would force England and France to respect American neutrality.

Emergency Quota Act Also called the Johnson Act, this 1921 bill limited immigration from Southern and Eastern Europe by stating that in a year, total immigration from any country could only equal 3 percent of the number of immigrations from that country living in the United States in 1910.

encomienda system American natives were given over to Spanish colonists, who in exchange for their labor, promised to "protect" them.

enlightenment Eighteenth-century European intellectual movement that attempted to discover the natural laws that governed science and society and taught that progress was inevitable in the Western world. Americans were greatly influenced by the Enlightenment, especially by the ideas of John Locke, who stated that government should exist for the benefit of the people living under it.

Enola Gay The name of the American bomber that on August 6, 1945, dropped the first atomic bomb on the city of Hiroshima, thus initiating the nuclear age.

environmentalists They broadly support the goals of environmentalism—a broad philosophy, ideology, and social movement that advocates preservation, restoration, and/or improvement of the natural environment by, in part, controlling pollution and protecting plant and animal diversity.

Era of Good Feelings Term used by a newspaper of the period to describe the years between 1816 and 1823, when after the end of the War of 1812 the United States remained generally free of foreign conflicts and when political strife at home was at a bare minimum (because of the collapse of the Federalist party).

Espionage Act World War I era regulation passed in 1917 that ordered severe penalties for citizens who criticized the war effort or the government. Mandatory prison sentences were also proclaimed for those who interfered with the draft process. Nearly 700 Americans were arrested for violating this act.

Essex Junto Group of Massachusetts Federalists who met to voice their displeasure with the policies of Thomas Jefferson during Jefferson's second term, and proposed that the New England states and New York secede from the Union.

Exodusters Large number of Southern blacks who left the South and moved to Kansas for a "better life" after Reconstruction ended in 1877; many failed to find satisfaction in Kansas because of lack of opportunities and open hostility from Kansas residents.

Fair Deal A series of domestic programs proposed to Congress by President Harry Truman that included a Fair Employment Practices Act, a call for government construction of public housing, an extension of Social Security, and a proposal to ensure employment for all American workers.

Farmers' Alliances After the decline of Grange organizations, these became the major organizations of farmers in the 1880s; many experimented with cooperative buying and selling. Many local alliances became involved in direct political activity with the growth of the Populist party in the 1890s.

Federal Deposit Insurance Corporation (FDIC) Passed during the first Hundred Days of the administration of Franklin Roosevelt, this body insured individual bank deposits up to $2,500 and helped to restore confidence in America's banks.

Federal Reserve System Established by the Federal Reserve Act of 1913, this system established 12 district reserve banks to be controlled by the banks in each district. In addition, a Federal Reserve Board was established to regulate the entire structure. This act improved public confidence in the banking system.

Federal Trade Commission Authorized after the passage of the Clayton Antitrust Act of 1914, it was established as the major government body in charge of regulating big business. The FTC investigated possible violations of antitrust laws.

Federalists During the period when the Constitution was being ratified, these were the supporters of the larger national government as outlined in the Constitution; the party of Washington and John Adams, it was supported by commercial interests. Federalists were opposed by Jeffersonians, who favored a smaller federal government and a society dominated by agrarian values. Federalist influence in national politics ended with the presidential election of 1816.

Feminine Mystique, The Betty Friedan's 1963 book that was the bible of the feminist movement of the 1960s and 1970s. Friedan maintained that the post–World War II emphasis on family forced women to think of themselves primarily as housewives and robbed them of much of their creative potential.

feminist movement Movement dedicated to the belief that women should have the same rights and benefits in American society that men do. Feminism gained many supporters during the Progressive Era, and in the 1960s drew large numbers of supporters. The National Organization for Women (NOW) was established in 1966 by Betty Friedan and had nearly 200,000 members in 1969.

Fifteenth Amendment Ratified in 1870, this amendment stated that a person could not be denied the right to vote because of the color of their skin or whether or not they had been a slave. This extended the rights of blacks to vote to the North (which the Emancipation Proclamation had not done); some in the women's movement opposed the amendment on the grounds that it did nothing for the rights of women.

Final Solution The plan of Adolf Hitler and Nazi Germany to eliminate Jewish civilization from Europe. By the end of the war in 1945, nearly 6 million Jews had been executed. The full extent of Germany's atrocities was not known in Europe and the United States until near the end of World War II.

fireside chats Broadcasts on the radio by Franklin Roosevelt addressed directly to the American people that made many Americans feel that he personally cared about them. FDR did 16 of these in his first two terms. Many Americans in the 1930s had pictures of Roosevelt in their living rooms. In addition, Roosevelt received more letters from ordinary Americans than any other president in American history.

First Continental Congress A 1774 meeting in Philadelphia at which colonists vowed to resist further efforts to tax them without their consent.

First Great Awakening A religious revival in the American colonies that lasted from the 1720s through the 1740s; speakers like Jonathan Edwards enraptured speakers with sermons such as "Sinners in the Hands of an Angry God." Religious splits in the colonies became deeper because of this movement.

flapper A "new woman" of the 1920s, who wore short skirts and bobbed hair and rejected many of the social regulations that controlled women of previous generations.

Force Act of 1832 Legislation that gave President Andrew Jackson the power to invade any state if that action was necessary to enforce federal law. The bill was in response to nullification of federal tariff regulation by the legislature of South Carolina.

Fordney-McCumber Tariff of 1922 Act that sharply increased tariffs on imported goods. Most Republican leaders of the 1920s firmly believed in "protectionist" policies that would increase profits for American businesses.

Fort Sumter Federal fort located in Charleston, South Carolina, that was fired on by Confederate artillery on April 12, 1861; these were the first shots actually fired in the Civil War. A public outcry immediately followed across the Northern states, and the mobilization of a federal army began.

Fourteen Points Woodrow Wilson's view of a post–World War I that he hoped the other Allied powers would endorse during the negotiations for the Treaty of Versailles. Wilson's vision included elimination of secret treaties, arms reduction, national self-determination, and the creation of a League of Nations. After negotiations, only the League of Nations remained (which the United States never became part of).

Fourteenth Amendment Ratified in 1868, this amendment stated that "all persons born or naturalized in the United States" were citizens. In addition, all former Confederate supporters were prohibited from holding office in the United States.

Franciscans Missionaries who established settlements in the Southwestern United States in the late 1500s; at their missions Christian conversion was encouraged, but at the same time Native Americans were used as virtual slaves. Rebellions against the missions and the soldiers sent to protect them began in 1598.

Fredericksburg, Battle of Battle on December 13, 1862, where the Union army commanded by General Ambrose Burnside suffered a major defeat at the hands of Confederate forces.

Free Speech Movement Protests at the University of California at Berkeley in 1964 and 1965 that opposed the control that the university, and "the establishment" in general, had over the lives of university students. Protesters demanded changes in university regulations and also broader changes in American society.

free trade The philosophy that trade barriers and protective tariffs inhibit long-term economic growth; this philosophy was the basis for the 1994 ratification by the United States of the North American Free Trade Agreement (NAFTA), which removed trade restrictions between the United States, Mexico, and Canada.

freedmen Term used for free blacks in the South after the Civil War. Freedmen enjoyed some gains in terms of education, the ability to hold office, and economic well-being during the Reconstruction era, although many of these gains were wiped out after the Compromise of 1877.

Freedom Rides Buses of black and white civil rights workers who in 1961 rode on interstate buses to the Deep South to see if Southern states were abiding by the 1960 Supreme Court ruling banning segregation on interstate buses and in waiting rooms and restaurants at bus stations. Buses met mob violence in numerous cities; federal marshals were finally called in to protect the freedom riders.

Freeport Doctrine Introduced by Stephen Douglas in the Lincoln-Douglas debates, the idea that despite the *Dred Scott* Supreme Court decision, a territory could still prevent slavery by electing officials who were opposed to it and by creating laws and regulations that would make slavery impossible to enforce.

Free-Soil party Political party that won 10 percent of the vote in the 1848 presidential election. They were opposed to the spread of slavery into any of the recently acquired American territories. Free-Soil supporters were mainly many former members of the Whig party in the North.

French and Indian War Called the Seven Years' War in European textbooks. In this war, the British and the French fought for the right to expand their empire in the Americas. Colonists and Native Americans fought on both sides, and the war eventually spread to Europe and elsewhere. The English emerged victorious, and in the end received all of French Canada.

Fugitive Slave Act Part of the Compromise of 1850, this legislation set up special commissions in Northern states to determine if an accused runaway slave really was one. According to regulations, after the verdict, commissioners were given more money if the accused was found to be a runaway than if he or she was found not to be one. Some Northern legislatures passed laws attempting to circumvent the Fugitive Slave Act.

Gadsden Purchase Strip of territory running through Arizona and New Mexico that the United States purchased from Mexico in 1853. President Pierce authorized this purchase to secure that the southern route of the transcontinental railroad (between Texas and California) would be in American territory.

Geneva Accords After the French were defeated in Vietnam, a series of agreements made in 1954 temporarily divided Vietnam into two parts (along the 17th parallel) and promised nationwide elections within two years. To prevent Communists from gaining control, the United States installed a friendly government in South Vietnam and saw that the reunification elections never took place.

Gettysburg Address Speech made by Abraham Lincoln at dedication ceremony for a cemetery for Union soldiers who died at the Battle of Gettysburg. In this November 19, 1863 speech Lincoln stated that freedom should exist in the United States for *all* men, and that "government of the people, by the people, for the people, shall not perish from the earth."

Gettysburg, Battle of The most important battle of the Civil War, this July 1863 victory by Union forces prevented General Robert E. Lee from invading the North. Defeat at Gettysburg, along with defeat at the Battle of Vicksburg during the same month, turned the tide of war firmly in the direction of Union forces.

Ghent, Treaty of (1814) Treaty between the United States and Great Britain ending the War of 1812; treaty restored diplomatic relations between the two countries but did nothing to address the issues that had initially caused the war.

Ghost Dances Religion practiced by Lakota tribesmen in response to repeated incursions by American settlers. Ghost dancers thought that a Native American messiah would come and banish the whites, return the buffalo, and give all former Native American land back to the Native Americans. Worried territorial officials had Sitting Bull arrested (he was later killed under uncertain circumstances) and killed another 240 Lakota at Wounded Knee Creek.

GIs Popular term for an American servicemen during World War II; refers to the fact that virtually anything worn or used was "government issued."

GI Bill Officially called the Serviceman's Readjustment Act of 1944, this legislation gave many benefits to returning World War II veterans, including financial assistance for veterans wanting to go to college or enter other job training programs, special loan programs for veterans wanting to buy homes or businesses, and preferential treatment for veterans who wished to apply for government jobs.

Gilded Age, The Some historians describe the late nineteenth century in this manner, describing it as an era with a surface of great prosperity hiding deep problems of social inequity and shallowness of culture. The term comes from the title of an 1873 Mark Twain novel.

globalization Belief that the United States should work closely with other nations of the world to solve common problems; this was the foreign policy approach of President Clinton. Policies that supported this approach included the ratification of NAFTA, the United States working more closely with the United Nations, and "nation building" abroad. Many policies of globalization were initially rejected by Clinton's successor, George W. Bush.

Glorious Revolution English revolution of 1688 to 1689 when King James II was removed from the throne and his Protestant daughter Mary and her Dutch husband William began to rule. Reaction to this in the American colonies was varied: There was a revolt against appointed Catholic officials in New York and Maryland, and in Massachusetts the governor was sent back to England with the colonial demand that the Dominion of New England be disbanded.

gold standard Economic system that based all currency on gold, meaning that all paper currency could be exchanged at a bank for gold. Business interests of the late nineteenth century supported this. William Jennings Bryan ran for president three times opposing the gold standard, and supported the free coinage of silver instead.

"Gospel of Wealth" The philosophy of steel magnate Andrew Carnegie, who stated that wealthy industrialists had an obligation to create a "trust fund" from their profits to help their local communities. By the time of his death, Carnegie had given over 90 percent of his wealth to various foundations and philanthropic endeavors.

Grange Initially formed in 1867, the Grange was an association of farmers that provided social activities and information about new farming techniques. Some local Grange organizations became involved in cooperative buying and selling.

Great Compromise Plan drafted by Roger Sherman of Connecticut that stated one house of the U.S. Congress would be based on population (the House of Representatives), while in the other house all states would be represented equally with two representatives per state (the Senate). This compromise greatly speeded the ratification of the Constitution.

Great Migration Migration of large numbers of American blacks to Midwestern and Eastern industrial cities that began during World War I and continued throughout the 1920s. Additional workers were needed in the North because of the war and during the 1920s because of immigration restrictions. Blacks were willing to leave the South because of continued lynchings there and the fact that their economic situation was not improving.

Great Society Aggressive program announced by President Lyndon Johnson in 1965 to attack the major social problems in America; Great Society programs included the War on Poverty, Medicare and Medicaid programs for elderly Americans, greater protection for and more legislation dealing with civil rights, and greater funding for education. Balancing the Great Society and the war in Vietnam would prove difficult for the Johnson administration.

Greenback party Political party of the 1870s and early 1880s that stated the government should put more money in circulation and supported an eight-hour workday and female suffrage. The party received support from farmers but never built a national base. The Greenback party argued into the 1880s that more greenbacks should be put in circulation to help farmers who were in debt and who saw the prices of their products decreasing annually.

"greenbacks" Paper money issued by the American government during and immediately after the Civil War that was not backed up by gold or silver.

gridlock Situation when the president is a member of one political party and the U.S. Congress is controlled by the other party, causing a situation where little legislation is actually passed. This is how some describe the situation with President Clinton and the Republican-controlled Congress after the 1994 congressional elections.

Guadalcanal, Battle of Battle over this Pacific island lasted from August 1942 through February 1943. American victory against fierce Japanese resistance was the first major offensive victory for the Americans in the Pacific War.

Guadalupe Hidalgo, Treaty of Treaty ending the war with Mexico that was ratified by the Senate in March 1848 and for $15 million gave the United States Texas territory to the Rio Grande River, New Mexico, and California.

Gulf of Tonkin Resolution (1964) Congressional resolution that gave President Johnson the authority to "take all necessary measures to repel" attacks against American military forces stationed in Vietnam. Later, critics would charge, this resolution allowed the president to greatly expand the Vietnam War without congressional oversight.

Harlem Renaissance Black literary and artistic movement centered in Harlem that lasted from the 1920s into the early 1930s that both celebrated and lamented black life in America; Langston Hughes and Zora Neale Hurston were two famous writers of this movement.

Hartford Convention Meeting of New England Federalists in the closing months of the War of 1812 where they threatened that New England would secede from the United States unless trade restrictions imposed by President Madison were lifted. American victory in the war made their protests seem pointless.

Hawley-Smoot Tariff In response to the initial effects of the Great Depression, Congress authorized this tariff in 1930; this established tariff rates on imported goods at the highest level of any point in U.S. history. Some American companies benefited in the short term, although the effect on world trade was disastrous, as many other countries erected tariff barriers on American imports.

Haymarket Square Location in Chicago of labor rally called by anarchists and other radical labor leaders on May 2, 1886. A bomb was hurled toward police officials, and police opened fire on the demonstrators; numerous policemen and demonstrators were killed and wounded. Response in the nation's press was decidedly antiunion.

Head Start One of Lyndon Johnson's War on Poverty programs that gave substantial funding for a nursery school program to prepare children of poor parents for kindergarten.

heavy industry The production of steel, iron, and other materials that can be used for building purposes; great increase in heavy industry fueled the massive industrial growth that took place in the last half of the nineteenth century.

Hessians German troops who fought in the Revolutionary War on the side of Great Britain; Hessian troops were almost all paid mercenaries.

Historiography The study of history and how it is written. Students of historiography would analyze various historical interpretations and the viewpoints of historians. This field is not as concerned with historical events themselves as it is with how these events are interpreted.

holding company A company that existed to gain monopoly control over an industry by buying large numbers of shares of stock in as many companies as possible in that industry. The best example in American history was John D. Rockefeller's Standard Oil corporation.

Holocaust Historical term used for the extermination of 6 million Jewish victims by Nazi Germany during World War II. Much has been written on the reasons for the Holocaust and why it occurred in Germany.

Homeland Security Act of 2002 States that it is the mission of the Department of Homeland Security to prevent terrorist attacks within the United States, reduce the vulnerability of the United States to terror, and minimize the damage and assist in the recovery from a terrorist attack that might occur in the United States.

Homestead Act of 1862 Enactment by Congress that gave 160 acres of publicly owned land to a farmer who lived on the land and farmed it for two years. The provisions of this bill inspired hundreds of thousands of Americans to move westward in the years after the Civil War.

Hoovervilles Groups of crude houses made of cardboard and spare wood that sprang up on the fringes of many American cities during the first years of the Great Depression. These shacks were occupied by unemployed workers; the name of these communities demonstrated the feeling that President Hoover should have been doing more to help the downtrodden in America.

horizontal integration The strategy of gaining as much control over an entire single industry as possible, usually by creating trusts and holding companies. The most successful example of horizontal integration was John D. Rockefeller and Standard Oil, who had at one point controlled over 92 percent of the oil production in the United States.

HUAC (House Un-American Activities Committee) Committee of the House of Representatives that beginning in 1947 investigated possible Communist infiltration of the entertainment industry and, more importantly, of the government. Most famous investigations of the committee were the investigation of the "Hollywood Ten" and the investigation of Alger Hiss, a former high-ranking member of the State Department.

Huguenots Protestants in France, who by the 1630s were believers in Calvinism. Few Huguenots ended up settling in the Americas, as French officials feared they would disrupt the unity of colonial settlements.

Hull House Established by Jane Addams and Ellen Gates Starr in Chicago in 1889, this was the first settlement house in America. Services such as reading groups, social clubs, an employment bureau, and a "day care center" for working mothers could be found at Hull House. The Hull House model was later copied in many other urban centers.

"Hun" Term used in Allied propaganda during World War I to depict the German soldier; Germans were portrayed as bloodthirsty beasts. World War I was the first war where propaganda was used on a widespread scale.

Hundred Days The period from March through June 1933; the first 100 days of the New Deal presidency of Franklin Roosevelt. During this period programs were implemented to assist farmers, the banks, unemployed workers, and businessmen. In addition, Prohibition was repealed.

hunter-gatherers Early civilizations that existed not by farming but by moving from region to region and taking what was necessary at the time from the land; some early Native American tribes in northern New England lived as hunter-gatherers.

hydrogen bomb Atomic weapons much more powerful than those used at Hiroshima and Nagasaki; these were developed and repeatedly tested by both the United States and the Soviet Union in the 1950s, increasing dramatically the potential danger of nuclear war.

impeachment The process of removing an elected public official from office. During the Progressive Era several states adopted measures making it easier to do this. Presidents Andrew Johnson and William Jefferson Clinton were both impeached by the House of Representatives, but neither was convicted by the U.S. Senate (the procedure outlined in the Constitution of the United States).

impressment British practice of forcing civilians and ex-sailors back into naval service. During the wars against Napoleon. The British seized nearly 7,500 sailors from American ships, including some that had actually become American citizens. This practice caused increased tensions between the United States and Great Britain and was one of the causes of the War of 1812.

Inca empire Advanced and wealthy civilization centered in the Andes mountain region; aided by smallpox, Francisco Pizarro conquered the Incas in 1533.

indentured servants Legal arrangement when an individual owed compulsory service (in some cases only 3 years, in others up to 10) for free passage to the American colonies. Many of the early settlers in the Virginia colony came as indentured servants.

Industrial Workers of the World (IWW) Established in 1905, this union attempted to unionize the unskilled workers who were usually not recruited by the American Federation of Labor. The IWW included blacks, poor sharecroppers, and newly arrived immigrants from Eastern Europe. Members of the union were called "Wobblies," and leaders of the union were inspired by Marxist principles.

Influence of Sea Power upon History, The Very influential 1890's book by Admiral Alfred Thayer Mahan, which argued that throughout history the most powerful nations have achieved their influence largely because of powerful navies. Mahan called for a large increase in the size of the American navy, the acquisition of American bases in the Pacific, and the building of the Panama Canal.

initiative process Procedure supported by the Populist party in the 1890s by which any proposed law could go on the public ballot as long as a petition with an appropriate number of names is submitted beforehand supporting the proposed law.

internment camps Controversial decision was made after the bombing of Pearl Harbor to place Japanese Americans living on the West Coast in these camps. President Roosevelt authorized this by Executive Order #9066; this order was validated by the Supreme Court in 1944. In 1988 the U.S. government paid compensation to surviving detainees.

Interstate Commerce Act Passed in 1887, the bill created America's first regulatory commission, the Interstate Commerce Commission. The task of this commission was to regulate the railroad and railroad rates, and to ensure that rates were "reasonable and just."

Intolerable Acts Term used by anti-British speakers across the colonies for the series of bills passed in Great Britain to punish the Massachusetts colony for the Boston Tea Party of December 1773. These including the closing of Boston harbor, prohibiting local meetings, and mandatory quartering of troops in the homes of Massachusetts residents.

Iran-Contra Affair During the second term of the Reagan administration, government officials sold missiles to Iran (hoping that this would help free American hostages held in Lebanon); money from this sale was used to aid anti-communist Contra forces in Nicaragua. Iran was a country that was supposed to be on the American "no trade" list because of their taking of American hostages, and congressional legislation had been enacted making it illegal to give money to the Contras. A major scandal for the Reagan administration.

Iranian Hostage Crisis On November 4, 1979, Islamic Fundamentalists seized the American embassy in Tehran, Iran, and took all Americans working there hostage. This was a major humiliation for the United States, as diplomatic and military efforts to free the hostages failed. The hostages were finally freed on January 20, 1981, immediately after the inauguration of Ronald Reagan.

iron curtain In a March 5, 1946, speech in Fulton, Missouri, Winston Churchill used this term to describe the division that the Soviet Union had created between itself and its Eastern European Allies and Western Europe and the United States. Churchill emphasized the need for the United States to stand up to potential Soviet aggression in the future.

ironclad ship Civil War-era ships that were totally encased in iron, thus making them very difficult to damage; the ironclad of the Confederate army was the *Virginia* (it had been the *Merrimac* when it was captured from the Union), whereas the Union ship was the *Monitor*. The two ships battled each other in March 1862, with both being badly damaged.

"irreconcilables" After World War I, a group of U.S. senators who were opposed to a continued U.S. presence in Europe in any form. This group was influential in preventing the passage of the Versailles Treaty in the Senate.

island-hopping A successful American military tactic in the Pacific in 1942 and 1943 of taking strategic islands that could be used as staging points for continued military offensives. Increasing American dominance in air power made this tactic possible.

isolationism A policy of disengaging the United States from major world commitments and concentrating on the U.S. domestic issues. This was the dominant foreign policy of the United States for much of the 1920s and the 1930s.

Jay's Treaty of 1794 Treaty between the United States and Great Britain designed to ease increasing tensions between the two nations. The British did make some concessions to the Americans, including abandoning the forts they occupied in the interior of the continent. However, Britain refused to make concessions to America over the rights of American ships. Tensions over this issue would eventually be a cause of the War of 1812.

Jazz Age Term used to describe the image of the liberated, urbanized 1920s, with a flapper as a dominant symbol of that era. Many rural, fundamentalist Americans deeply resented the changes in American culture that occurred in the "Roaring 20s."

Jazz Singer, The 1927 film starring Al Jolson that was the first movie with sound. Story of the film deals with a young Jewish man who has to choose between the "modern" and his Jewish past.

Jesuits Missionary group who established settlements in Florida, New Mexico, Paraguay, and in several areas within French territory in North America. Jesuits were organized with military precision and order.

jingoism American foreign policy based on a strident nationalism, a firm belief in American world superiority, and a belief that military solutions were, in almost every case, the best ones. Jingoism was most evident in America during the months leading up to and during the Spanish-American War.

judicial review In the 1803 *Marbury v. Madison* decision, Chief Justice John C. Marshall stated that the U.S. Supreme Court ultimately had the power to decide on the constitutionality of any law passed by the U.S. Congress or by the legislature of any state. Many had argued that individual states should have the power to do this; the *Marbury* decision increased the power of the federal government.

Judiciary Act of 1801 Bill passed by the Federalist Congress just before the inauguration of President Thomas Jefferson; Federalists appointed by this bill attempted to maintain control of the judiciary by reducing the number of Supreme Court judges (so Jefferson probably wouldn't be able to name a replacement) and by increasing the number of federal judges (who President Adams appointed before he left office). Bill was repealed by new Congress in 1802.

Justice Reorganization Bill Franklin Roosevelt's 1937 plan to increase the number of Supreme Court justices. He claimed that this was because many of the judges were older and needed help keeping up with the work. In reality he wanted to "pack the court" because the Court had made several rulings outlawing New Deal legislation. Many Democrats and Republicans opposed this plan, so it was finally dropped by Roosevelt.

kamikaze pilots 1945 tactic of Japanese air force where pilots flew at American ships at full speed and crashed into them, in several cases causing ships to sink. This tactic showed the desperate nature of the Japanese military situation at this time. By July 1945, kamikaze attacks were no longer utilized, as Japan was running out of airplanes and pilots.

Kansas-Nebraska Act of 1854 Compromise legislation crafted by Stephen Douglas that allowed the settlers in the Kansas and Nebraska territories to decide if those territories would be slave or free. Bill caused controversy and bloodshed throughout these territories; in the months before the vote in Kansas, large numbers of "settlers" moved in to influence the vote, and after the vote (won by proslavery forces), violence between the two sides intensified.

Kent State University Site of May 1970 antiwar protest where Ohio National Guardsmen fired on protesters, killing four. To many, this event was symbolic of the extreme political tensions that permeated American society in this era.

Kentucky and Virginia Resolves Passed by the legislatures in these two states, these resolutions maintained that the Alien and Sedition Acts championed through Congress by John Adams went beyond the powers that the Constitution stated belonged to the federal government. These resolves predated the later Southern argument that individual states could "nullify" federal laws deemed unconstitutional by the states.

Kerner Commission Established in 1967 to study the reason for urban riots, the commission spoke at length about the impact of poverty and racism on the lives of urban blacks in America, and emphasized that white institutions created and condoned the ghettoes of America.

King-Crane Commission The American commission that went into various regions of the Middle East immediately after World War I to discover what political future was desired by residents of the region. It was determined that many did not want to be controlled by Britain and France, and saw the United States in a favorable light. Predictably, the British and French saw to it that the findings of the commission were largely kept quiet.

King William's War Colonial war against the French that lasted from 1689 to 1697; army from New England colonies attacked Quebec, but were forced to retreat because of the lack of strong colonial leadership and an outbreak of smallpox among colonial forces.

Kitchen Cabinet An informal group of advisors, with no official titles, who the president relies on for advice. The most famous Kitchen Cabinet was that of Andrew Jackson, who met with several old political friends and two journalists for advice on many occasions.

Knights of Labor The major labor union of the 1880s; was not a single large union, but a federation of the unions of many industries. The Knights of Labor accepted unskilled workers. Publicity against the organization was intense after the Haymarket Square riot of 1886.

Know-Nothing party Political party developed in the 1850s that claimed that the other political parties and the entire political process were corrupt, that immigrants were destroying the economic base of America by working for low wages, and that Catholics in America were intent on destroying American democracy. Know-Nothings were similar in many ways to other nativist groups that developed at various points in America's history.

Korean War (1950 to 1953) War in which American and other UN forces fought to stop Communist aggression against South Korea. U.S. entry into the Korean War was totally consistent with the U.S. cold war policy of containment. Negotiated settlement divided Korea along the 38th parallel, a division that remains today.

Ku Klux Klan Organization founded in the South during the Reconstruction era by whites who wanted to maintain white supremacy in the region. The KKK used terror tactics, including murder. The Klan was revitalized in the 1920s; members of the 1920s Klan also opposed Catholics and Southern and Eastern European immigrants. The KKK exists to this day, with recent efforts to make the Klan appear to be "respectable."

labor movement The drive that began in the second half of the nineteenth century to have workers join labor unions. Divisions existed in nineteenth-century unions as to whether unions should focus their energies on political gains for workers or on "bread and butter" issues important to workers. In the twenty-first century, unions have broad political powers, as most endorse and financially support candidates in national and statewide elections.

laissez-faire economic principles Economic theory derived from eighteenth-century economist Adam Smith, who stated that for the economy to run soundly the government should take a hands-off role in economic matters. Those who have favored policies such as high import tariffs do *not* follow laissez-faire policies; a policy like NAFTA has more support among the "free market" supporters of Adam Smith.

land speculation The practice of buying up land with the intent of selling it off in the future for a profit. Land speculation existed in the Kentucky territory in the 1780s, throughout the West after the Homestead Act, and in Florida in the 1920s, when hundreds bought Florida swampland hoping to later sell it for a profit.

League of Nations International body of nations that was proposed by Woodrow Wilson and was adopted at the Versailles Peace Conference ending World War I. The League was never an effective body in reducing international tensions, at least partially because the United States was never a member of it.

Lend-Lease Act Legislation proposed by Franklin Roosevelt and adopted by Congress in 1941, stating that the United States could either sell or lease arms and other equipment to any country whose security was vital to America's interest. After the passage of this bill, military equipment to help the British war effort began to be shipped from the United States.

Letters from a Farmer in Pennsylvania A 1767 pamphlet by Pennsylvania attorney and landowner John Dickinson, in which he eloquently stated the "taxation without representation" argument, and also stated that the only way that the House of Commons could represent the colonies in a meaningful way would be for actual colonists to be members of it.

Lever Food and Fuel Control Act August 1917 measure that gave President Wilson the power to regulate the production and consumption of food and fuels during wartime. Some in his administration argued for price controls and rationing; instead, Wilson instituted voluntary controls.

Levittown After World War II, the first "suburban" neighborhood; located in Hempstead, Long Island, houses in this development were small, looked the same, but were perfect for the postwar family that wanted to escape urban life. Levittown would become a symbol of the post–World War II flight to suburbia taken by millions.

Lewis and Clark Expedition (1804 to 1806) Mission sent by Thomas Jefferson to explore and map the newly acquired Louisiana territory and to create good relations with various Native American tribes within the territory. Reports brought back indicated that settlement was possible in much of the region, and that the Louisiana territory was well worth what had been paid for it.

Lexington Massachusetts town where the first skirmish between British troops and colonial militiamen took place; during this April 19, 1775, "battle," eight colonists were killed and another nine were wounded.

Liberator, The The radical abolitionist journal of William Lloyd Garrison that was first published in 1831. Garrison and his journal presented the most extreme abolitionist views during the period leading up to the Civil War.

Liberty Bonds Sold to United States civilians during World War I. A holder who paid $10 for a bond could get $13 back if the holder held on to the bond until it matured. Bonds were important in financing the war effort, and celebrities such as Charlie Chaplin made short films encouraging Americans to buy them.

Little Bighorn, Battle of the (1876) Montana battle where Colonel George Custer and more than 200 of his men were killed by a group of Cheyenne and Lakota warriors. This was the last major victory by Native American forces over a U.S. army unit.

London Company In 1603 King James I gave the London Company a charter to settle the Virginia territory. In April 1607, the first settlers from this company settled at Jamestown.

"Lost Generation" Group of American intellectuals who viewed America in the 1920s as bigoted, intellectually shallow, and consumed by the quest for the dollar. Many became extremely disillusioned with American life and went to Paris. Ernest Hemingway wrote of this group in *The Sun Also Rises*.

Louisiana Purchase The 1803 purchase of the huge Louisiana territory (from the Mississippi River out to the Rocky Mountains) from Napoleon for $15 million. This purchase made eventual westward movement possible for vast numbers of Americans.

Lowell System Developed in the textile mills of Lowell, Massachusetts, in the 1820s. In these factories as much machinery as possible was used, so that few skilled workers were needed in the process, and the workers were almost all single young farm women who worked for a few years and then returned home to be housewives. Managers found these young women were the perfect workers for this type of factory life.

Loyalists Individuals who remained loyal to Great Britain during the years up to and during the Revolutionary War. Many who were Loyalists were from the higher strata of colonial society; when war actually broke out and it became apparent that the British were not going to quickly win, almost all went to Canada, the West Indies, or back to Great Britain.

Loyalty Review Board This were established in 1947 in an effort to control possible Communist influence in the American government. These boards were created to investigate the possibility of "security risks" working for the American government, and to determine if those "security risks" should lose their jobs. Some employees were released because of their affiliation with "unacceptable" political organizations or because of their sexual orientation.

Lusitania British passenger liner with 128 Americans on board that was sunk off the coast of Ireland by a German U-boat on May 7, 1915. This sinking caused outrage in the United States and was one of a series of events that drew the United States closer to war with Germany.

Man in the Gray Flannel Suit, The Early 1950s book and movie that compares the sterility, sameness, and lack of excitement of postwar work and family life with the vitality felt by many World War II veterans during their wartime experiences.

Manhattan Project Program begun in 1942 to develop an atomic weapon for the United States. The project was aided by German scientists added to the research team who had been working on a similar bomb in Germany. First test of the bomb took place in New Mexico on July 16, 1945.

Manifest Destiny Term first used in the 1840s, the concept that America's expansion westward was as journalist John O'Sullivan said, "the fulfillment of our Manifest Destiny to overspread the continent allotted by Providence for the free development of our yearly multiplying millions."

Marbury v. Madison **(1803)** Decision of this case written by Chief Justice John Marshall established the principle of judicial review, meaning that the Supreme Court ultimately has the power to decide if any federal or state law is unconstitutional.

March on Washington Over 200,000 came to Washington for this August 1963 event demanding civil rights for blacks. A key moment of the proceedings was Martin Luther King's "I have a dream" speech; the power of the civil rights movement was not lost on Lyndon Johnson, who pushed for civil rights legislation when he became president the following year.

Marshall Plan Plan announced in 1947 whereby the United States would help to economically rebuild Europe after the war; 17 Western European nations became part of the plan. The United States introduced the plan so that communism would not spread across war-torn Europe and bring other European countries into the Communist camp.

martial law During a state of emergency, when rule of law may be suspended and government is controlled by military or police authorities. During the Civil War, Kentucky was placed under martial law by President Lincoln.

Massacre at Wounded Knee December 28, 1890, "battle" that was the last military resistance of Native Americans of the Great Plains against American encroachment. Minneconjou Indians were at Wounded Knee Creek. American soldiers attempted to take their arms from them. After shooting began, 25 American soldiers died, along with more than 200 men, women, and children of the Indian tribe.

massive retaliation Foreign policy officials in the Eisenhower administration believed the best way to stop communism was to convince the Communists that every time they advanced, there would be massive retaliation against them. This policy explains the desire in this era to increase the nuclear arsenal of the United States.

McCarran Internal Security Act Congressional act enacted in 1950 that stated all members of the Communist party had to register with the office of the Attorney General and that it was a crime to conspire to foster communism in the United States.

McCarran-Walter Act of 1952 Bill that limited immigration from everywhere except Northern and Western Europe and stated that immigration officials could turn any immigrant away that they thought might threaten the national security of the United States.

McCarthyism Named after Wisconsin Senator Joseph McCarthy, the title given for the movement that took place during the late 1940s and early 1950s in American politics to root out potential Communist influence in the government, the military, and the entertainment industry. Harsh tactics were often used by congressional investigations, with few actual Communists ever discovered. This period is seen by many today as an era of intolerance and paranoia.

Meat Inspection Act Inspired by Upton Sinclair's *The Jungle*, this 1906 bill established a government commission that would monitor the quality of all meat sold in America and inspect the meatpacking houses for safety and cleanliness.

Medicare Part of Lyndon Johnson's Great Society program, this program acted as a form of health insurance for retired Americans (and disabled ones as well). Through Medicare, the federal government would pay for services received by elderly patients at doctor's offices and hospitals.

mercantilism Economic policy practiced by most European states in the late seventeenth century that stated the power of any state depended largely on its wealth; thus it was the state's duty to do all that it could to build up wealth. A mercantilist country would not want to import raw materials from other countries; instead, it would be best to have colonies from which these raw materials could be imported.

Merrimack Union ironclad ship captured by Confederates during the Civil War and renamed the *Virginia*.

Meuse-Argonne Offensive American forces played a decisive role in this September 1918 Allied offensive, which was the last major offensive of the war and which convinced the German general staff that victory in World War I was impossible.

Mexican-American War War fought over possession of Texas. The settlement ending this war gave the United States the northern part of Texas territory and the territories of New Mexico and California.

Middle Passage The voyage across the Atlantic Ocean taken by slaves on their way to the Americas. Sickness, diseases, and death were rampant as slave ships crossed the Atlantic; on some ships, over 20 percent of slaves who began the journey were dead by the time the ship landed.

"midnight appointments" Judicial or other appointments made by an outgoing president or governor in the last hours before he or she leaves office. The most famous were the judicial appointments made by John Adams in the hours before Thomas Jefferson was inaugurated as president.

Midway, Battle of June 4, 1942, naval battle that crippled Japanese offensive capabilities in the Pacific; American airplanes destroyed four aircraft carriers and over 200 Japanese planes. After Midway, Japanese military operations were mainly defensive.

Missouri Compromise In a continued effort to maintain a balance between free and slave states,

Henry Clay proposed this 1820 compromise, which admitted Maine to the Union as a free state, Missouri to the Union as a slave state, and stated that any part of the Louisiana Territory north of 36 degrees, 30 minutes would be nonslave territory.

Model T Automobile produced by Ford Motor Company using assembly line techniques. The first Model Ts were produced in 1907; using the assembly line, Ford produced half of the automobiles made in the world between 1907 and 1926.

Molasses Act In the early 1700s colonists traded for molasses with the French West Indies. British traders wanted to reduce trade between the colonies and the French; in 1733 they pressured Parliament to pass this act, which put prohibitively high duties on imported molasses. Colonists continued to smuggle French molasses into the Americas in spite of British efforts to prevent this.

Monitor Union ironclad ship utilized during the Civil War; fought one battle against the *Virginia*, the South's ironclad ship, and never left port again.

Monroe Doctrine President James Monroe's 1823 statement that an attack by a European state on any nation in the Western Hemisphere would be considered an attack on the United States; Monroe stated that the Western Hemisphere was the hemisphere of the United States and not of Europe. Monroe's statement was scoffed at by certain European political leaders, especially those in Great Britain.

Montgomery bus boycott Year-long refusal by blacks to ride city buses in Montgomery, Alabama, because of their segregation policies. Boycott began in December 1955; Supreme Court finally ruled that segregation on public buses was unconstitutional. Rosa Parks began the protest when she was arrested for refusing to give up her seat for a white man, and Martin Luther King was a young minister involved in organizing the boycott.

Morrill Land-Grant Act (1862) Federal act designed to fund state "land-grant" colleges. State governments were given large amounts of land in the western territories; this land was sold to individual settlers, land speculators, and others, and the profits of these land sales could be used to establish the colleges.

Ms. Founded in 1972 by Gloria Steinem, this glossy magazine was aimed at feminist readers.

muckrakers Journalists of the Progressive era who attempted to expose the evils of government and big business. Many muckrakers wrote of the corruption of city and state political machines. Factory conditions and the living and working conditions of workers were other topics that some muckrakers wrote about.

My Lai Massacre In 1968 a unit under the command of Lieutenant William Calley killed over 300 men, women, and children in this small Vietnamese village. The antiwar movement took the attack as a symbol of the "immorality" of U.S. efforts in Vietnam.

NAFTA (North American Free Trade Agreement) Ratified in 1994 by the U.S. Senate, this agreement established a free trade zone between the United States, Mexico, and Canada. Critics of the agreement claim that many jobs have been lost in the United States because of it.

napalm Jellylike substance dropped from American planes during the Vietnam conflict that horribly burned the skin of anyone who came into contact with it. On several occasions, napalm was accidentally dropped on "friendly" villages.

Nation of Islam Supporters were called Black Muslims; this group was founded by Elijah Muhammad and preached Islamic principles along with black pride and black separatism. Malcolm X was a member of the Nation of Islam.

National American Woman Suffrage Association The major organization for suffrage for women, it was founded in 1890 by Susan B. Anthony and Elizabeth Cady Stanton. It supported the Wilson administration during World War I and split with the more radical National Woman's Party, which, in 1917, began to picket the White House because Wilson had not forcefully stated that women should get the vote.

National Association for the Advancement of Colored People (NAACP) Formed in 1909, this organization fought for and continues to fight for the rights of blacks in America. The NAACP originally went to court for the plaintiff in the *Brown v. Board of Education* case, and Thurgood Marshall, the NAACP's chief counsel and later a Supreme Court justice, was the main attorney in the case.

national bank Planned by Alexander Hamilton to be similar to the Bank of England, this bank was funded by government and private sources. Hamilton felt a national bank would give economic security and confidence to the new nation. Republicans who had originally opposed the bank felt the same way in 1815 when they supported Henry Clay's American System.

National Consumers League Formed in 1899, this organization was concerned with improving the working and living conditions of women in the workplace.

national culture When a general unity of tastes and a commonality of cultural experience exist in a nation; in a general sense, when a country starts to "think the same." This occurred in America for the first time in the 1920s; as many people saw the same movies, read the same magazines, and heard the same things on the radio, a national culture was born.

National Industrial Recovery Act (NIRA) (1933) New Deal legislation that created the Works Progress Administration (WPA) that created jobs to put people back to work right away and the National Recovery Administration (NRA), who worked in conjunction with industry to bolster the industrial sector and create more long-lasting jobs.

National Labor Relations Board (NLRB) Part of the 1935 Wagner Act, which was a huge victory for organized labor. The NLRB ensured that factory owners did not harass union organizers, ensured that collective bargaining was fairly practiced in labor disputes, and supervised union elections. The NLRB was given the legal "teeth" to force employers to comply with all of the above.

National Origins Act Very restrictive immigration legislation passed in 1924, which lowered immigration to 2 percent of each nationality as found in the 1890 census. This lowered immigration dramatically and, quite intentionally, almost eliminated immigration from Eastern and Southern Europe.

National Security League Organization founded in 1914 that preached patriotism and preparation for war. In 1915, they successfully lobbied government officials to set up camps to prepare men for military life and combat. The patriotism of this group became more strident as the war progressed. In 1917, they lobbied Congress to greatly limit immigration into the country.

National Woman's Party Formed by Alice Paul after women got the vote, this group lobbied unsuccessfully in the 1920s to get an Equal Rights Amendment for women added to the Constitution. Desire for this amendment would return among some feminist groups in the 1970s.

nativist Nativist sentiment was especially strong in the 1920s. Nativism states that immigration should be greatly limited or banned altogether, since immigrants hurt the United States economically and also threaten the social well-being of the country. Nativist groups and parties have developed on several occasions in both the nineteenth and the twentieth centuries.

NATO (North Atlantic Treaty Organization) Collective alliance of the United States and most of the Western European nations that was founded in 1949; an attack of one member of NATO was to be considered an attack on all. Many U.S. troops served in Europe during the cold war era because of the NATO alliance. To counter NATO, the Soviet Union created the Warsaw Pact in 1955.

Naval Act of 1900 Legislation that authorized a large increase in the building of ships to be used for offensive purposes; this measure helped ensure the creation of a world-class American navy.

Navigation Acts of 1660 Measures passed by Charles II that were designed to increase the dependence of the colonies on England for trade. Charles mandated that certain goods produced in the colonies, such as tobacco, should be sold only to England; that if the colonies wanted to sell anything to other countries it had to come through England first; and that all trade by the colonies to other countries would have to be done in English ships. These measures could have been devastating to the colonies; however, British officials in the colonies did not enforce them carefully.

Neoconservativism Modern American political philosophy that opposes big-government approaches to domestic issues yet favors an interventionist and aggressive foreign policy; most neoconservatives advocated American intervention in Iraq in 2003.

Neoconservatives (neocons) Group who wanted to use American might to remake the Middle Eastern region into a democracy. Neocons believed that to accomplish this, Saddam Hussein had to be removed from power in Iraq.

Neutrality Act of 1935 To prevent the United States from being drawn into potential European conflicts, this bill said that America would not trade arms with any country at war, and that any American citizen traveling on a ship of a country at war was doing so at his or her own risk.

Neutrality Act of 1939 Franklin Roosevelt got Congress to amend the Neutrality Act of 1935; new legislation stated that England and France could buy arms from the United States as long as there was cash "up front" for these weapons. This was the first military assistance that the United States gave the Allied countries.

New Deal Series of policies instituted by Franklin Roosevelt and his advisors from 1933 to 1941 that attempted to offset the effects of the Great Depression on American society. Many New Deal policies were clearly experimental; in the end it was the onset of World War II, and not the policies of the New Deal, that pulled the United States out of the Great Depression.

New Deal Coalition The coalition of labor unions and industrial workers, minorities, much of the middle class, and the Solid South that carried Franklin Roosevelt to victories in 1936 and 1940 and that was the basis of Democratic victories on a national level until this coalition started to break up in the late 1960s and early 1970s. A sizable number of this group voted for Ronald Reagan in the presidential elections of 1980 and 1984.

New Democrat Term used to describe Bill Clinton and his congressional supporters during his two terms in office. A New Democrat was pragmatic, and not tied to the old Democratic belief in big government; New Democrats took both Democratic and Republican ideas as they crafted their policies. Some in the Democratic party maintained that Clinton had actually sold out the principles of the party.

New Federalism A series of policies during the administration of Ronald Reagan that began to give some power back to the states that had always been held by the federal government. Some tax dollars were returned to state and local governments in the form of "block grants"; the state and local governments could then spend this money as they thought best.

New Freedom policy An approach favored by Southern and Midwestern Democrats, this policy stated that economic and political preparation for World War I should be done in a decentralized manner; this would prevent too much power falling into the hands of the federal government. President Wilson first favored this approach, but then established federal agencies to organize mobilization.

New Frontier The program of President John Kennedy to revitalize America at home and to reenergize America for continued battles against the Soviet Union. Kennedy asked young Americans to volunteer for programs such as the Peace Corps; as he said in his inaugural speech: "Ask not what your country can do for you—ask what you can do for your country."

"new immigrants" Immigrants that came from Southern and Eastern Europe, who made up the majority of immigrants coming into the United States after 1900. Earlier immigrants from Britain, Ireland, and Scandinavia appeared to be "like" the groups that were already settled in the United States; the "new immigrants" were very different. As a result, resentment and nativist sentiment developed against this group, especially in the 1920s.

New Jersey Plan As the U.S. Constitution was being debated and drafted, large and small states each offered proposals on how the legislature should be structured. The New Jersey Plan stated that the legislature should have a great deal of power to regulate trade, and that it should consist of one legislative house, with each state having one vote.

New Nationalism The series of Progressive reforms supported by Theodore Roosevelt as he ran for president on the Progressive or Bull Moose ticket in 1912. Roosevelt said that more had to be done to regulate big business and that neither of his opponents were committed to conservation.

New Right The conservative movement that began in the 1960s and triumphed with the election of Ronald Reagan in 1980. The New Right was able to attract many middle-class and Southern voters to the Republican party by emphasizing the themes of patriotism, a smaller government, and a return to "traditional values."

New South Concept promoted by Southerners in the late 1800s that the South had changed dramatically and was now interested in industrial growth and becoming a part of the national economy. A large textile industry did develop in the South beginning in the 1880s.

Nez Perce Plains Native American tribe that attempted to resist reservation life by traveling 1,500 miles with American military forces in pursuit. After being tracked and suffering cold and hardship, the Nez Perce finally surrendered and were forced onto a reservation in 1877.

Non-Intercourse Act In response to the failure of France and Britain to respect the rights of American ships at sea, President Madison supported this legislation in 1809, which authorized trade with all countries except Britain and France, and stated that trade exist with those countries as soon as they respected America's rights as a neutral power. The British and the French largely ignored this act.

Northwest Ordinances Bills passed in 1784, 1785, and 1787 that authorized the sale of lands in the Northwest Territory to raise money for the federal government; these bills also carefully laid out the procedures for eventual statehood for parts of these territories.

NOW (National Organization for Women) Formed in 1966, with Betty Friedan as its first president. NOW was at first interested in publicizing inequalities for women in the workplace; focus of the organization later turned to social issues and eventually the unsuccessful effort to pass an Equal Rights Amendment for women.

nuclear proliferation The massive buildup of nuclear weapons by the United States and the Soviet Union in the 1950s and into the 1960s; in the United States this was fostered in the belief that the threat of "massive retaliation" was the best way to keep the Soviet Union under control. The psychological effects of the atomic bomb on the populations of the Soviet Union and the United States were also profound.

nullification The belief that an individual state has the right to "nullify" any federal law that the state felt was unjust. Andrew Jackson was able to resolve a Nullification Crisis in 1832, but the concept of nullification was still accepted by many Southerners, and controversy over this was a cause of the Civil War.

Ocala Platform Platform of the Farmer's Alliances, formulated at an 1890 convention held in Ocala, Florida. This farmer's organization favored a graduated income tax, government control of the railroad, the unlimited coinage of silver, and the direct election of U.S. senators. Candidates supporting the farmers called themselves Populists and ran for public offices in the 1890s.

Old Age Revolving Pension Plan Conceived by California doctor Francis Townsend in 1934, this plan would give every retired American $200 a month, with the stipulation that it would have to be spent by the end of the month; Townsend claimed this would revitalize the economy by putting more money in circulation. A national tax of 2 percent on all business transactions was supposed to finance this plan. A large number of Townsend clubs were formed to support this plan.

"on the margin" The practice in the late 1920s of buying stock and only paying in cash 10 percent of the value of that stock; the buyer could easily borrow the rest from his or her stockbroker or investment banker. This system worked well as long as investors could sell their stocks at a profit and repay their loans. After the 1929 stock market crash, investors had to pay these loans back in cash.

OPEC Acronym for Organization of Petroleum Exporting Countries, this organization sets the price for crude oil and determines how much of it will be produced. The decision of OPEC to raise oil prices in 1973 had a dramatic economic impact in both the United States and the rest of the world.

Open Door policy The policy that China should be open to trade with all of the major powers, and that all, including the United States, should have equal rights to trade there. This was the official American position toward China as announced by Secretary of State John Hay in 1899.

Operation Desert Shield After Iraq invaded Kuwait on August 2, 1990, President Bush sent 230,000 American troops to protect Saudi Arabia.

Operation Desert Storm February 1991 attack on Iraqi forces in Kuwait by the United States and other allied forces; although Iraq was driven from Kuwait, Saddam Hussein remained in power in Iraq.

Oregon Trail Trail that took settlers from the Ohio River Valley through the Great Plains and the Rocky Mountains to Oregon. Settlers began moving westward along this trail in 1842; by 1860 over 325,000 Americans had traveled westward along the trail.

Oregon Treaty Both the United States and Great Britain claimed the Oregon territory; in 1815 they agreed to jointly control the region. In 1843 the settlers of Oregon declared that their territory would become an independent republic.

Palmer Raids Part of the Red Scare, these were measures to hunt out political radicals and immigrants who were potential threats to American security. Organized by Attorney General A. Mitchell Palmer in 1919 and 1920 (and carried out by J. Edgar Hoover), these raids led to the arrest of nearly 5,500 people and the deportation of nearly four hundred.

Panama Canal Crucial for American economic growth, the building of this canal was begun by American builders in 1904 and completed in 1914. The United States had to first engineer a Panamanian revolt against Colombia to guarantee a friendly government in Panama that would support the building of the canal. In 1978 the U.S. Senate voted to return the Panama Canal to Panamanian control.

panic of 1837 The American economy suffered a deep depression when Great Britain reduced the amount of credit it offered to the United States. American merchants and industrialists had to use their available cash to pay off debts, thus causing businesses to cut production and lay off workers.

Paris, Treaty of The treaty ending the Revolutionary War, and signed in 1783. By the terms of this treaty, the United States received the land between the Appalachian Mountains and the Mississippi River. The British did keep their Canadian territories.

Pendleton Civil Service Act of 1883 Act that established a civil service system. There were a number of government jobs that were filled by civil service examinations and not by the president appointing one of his political cronies. Some states also started to develop professional civil service systems in the 1880s.

Pentagon Papers A government study of American involvement in Vietnam that outlined in detail many of the mistakes that America had made there. In 1971, a former analyst for the Defense Department, Daniel Ellsberg, released these to the *New York Times*.

Platt Amendment For Cuba to receive its independence from the United States after the Spanish-American war, it had to agree to the Platt Amendment, which stated that the United States had the right to intervene in Cuban affairs if the Cuban government could not maintain control or if the independence of Cuba was threatened by external or internal forces.

Plumbers A group of intelligence officials who worked for the committee to reelect Richard Nixon in 1972; the job of this group was to stop leaks of information and perform "dirty tricks" on political opponents of the president. The Plumbers broke into the office of Daniel Ellsberg's psychiatrist, looking for damaging information against him and totally discredited the campaign of Democratic hopeful Edmund Muskie.

pocket veto A method a president can use to "kill" congressional legislation at the end of a congressional term. Instead of vetoing the bill, the president may simply not sign it; once the congressional term is over, the bill will then die.

political machine An organization that controls the politics of a city, a state, or even the country, sometimes by illegal or quasi-legal means. A machine employs a large number of people to do its "dirty work," for which they are either given some government job or are allowed to pocket government bribes or kickbacks. The "best" example of a political machine was the Tammany Hall organization that controlled New York City in the late nineteenth century.

Populist party Party that represented the farmers who scored major electoral victories in the 1890s, including the election of several members of the U.S. House of Representatives and the election of one U.S. senator. Populist candidates spoke against monopolies, wanted government to become "more democratic," and wanted more direct government action to help the working classes.

Port Huron Statement The manifesto of Students for a Democratic Society, a radical student group formed in 1960. The *Port Huron Statement* called for a greater role for university students in the nation's affairs, rejected the traditional role of the university, and rejected the foreign policy goals that America was embracing at the time.

Postmodernism A recent trend in cultural and historical study that doubts the existence of absolute historical certainties. It is impossible to know, for example, what "really happened" in the past; therefore, how individuals observe and interpret the past becomes a valuable source of analysis. Postmodernists would also reject statements such as "democracy is best for all nations of the world," and would emphasize the study of various historical viewpoints.

Potsdam Conference July 1945 conference between new president Harry Truman, Stalin, and Clement Atlee, who had replaced Churchill. Truman took a much tougher stance toward Stalin than Franklin Roosevelt had; little substantive agreement took place at this conference. Truman expressed reservations about the future role of the Soviet Union in Eastern Europe at this conference.

Powhatan Confederacy Alliance of Native American tribes living in the region of the initial Virginia settlement. Powhatan, leader of this alliance, tried to live in peace with the English settlers when they arrived in 1607.

primary source Actual documents or accounts from an era being studied, these are invaluable to historians. Almost all true historical research involves analysis of primary source documents. Examples would be a letter written by Napoleon, an account of someone who knew Napoleon personally, or a newspaper account from Napoleon's time.

professional bureaucracy Government officials that receive their positions after taking competitive civil service tests; they are not appointed in return for political favors. Many government jobs at the state and national level are filled in this manner beginning in the 1880s.

progressivism A movement that desired political and social reform, and was most influential in America from the 1890s up until World War I. Most popular Progressive causes included reforming city government, better conditions for urban workers, the education of newly arrived immigrants, and the regulation of big businesses.

proportional representation The belief that representation in a legislature should be based on population; the states with the largest populations should have the most representatives. When the Constitution was being formulated, the larger states wanted this; the smaller states favored "one vote per state." The eventual compromise, termed the Connecticut plan, created a two-house legislature.

proprietorships Settlements in America that were given to individuals who could govern and regulate the territory in any manner they desire. Charles I, for example, gave the Maryland territory to Lord Baltimore as a proprietorship.

Pure Food and Drug Act of 1906 Bill that created a federal Food and Drug Administration; example of consumer protection legislation of the Progressive Era, it was at least partially passed as a result of Upton Sinclair's novel *The Jungle*.

Puritans Group of religious dissidents who came to the New World so they would have a location to establish a "purer" church than the one that existed in England. The Puritans began to settle the Plymouth Colony in 1620 and settled the Massachusetts Bay Colony beginning in 1630. Puritans were heavily influenced by John Calvin and his concept of predestination.

putting-out system The first textile production system in England, where merchants gave wool to families who, in their homes, created yarn and then cloth. The merchants would then buy the cloth from the families and sell the finished product. Textile mills made this procedure more efficient.

Quartering Act of 1765 British edict stating that to help defend the empire, colonial governments had to provide accommodations and food for British troops. Many colonists considered this act to be the ultimate insult; they perceived that they were paying for the troops that were there to control the colonies.

Queen Anne's War (1702 to 1713) Called the War of the Spanish Succession in European texts, pitted England against France and Spain. Spanish Florida was attacked by the English in the early part of this war, and Native Americans fought for both sides in the conflict. The British emerged victorious and in the end received Hudson Bay and Nova Scotia from the French.

Radical Republicans Group of Republicans after the Civil War who favored harsh treatment of the defeated South and a dramatic restructuring of the economic and social systems in the South; favored a decisive elevation of the political, social, and economic position of former slaves.

ratifying conventions In late 1787 and in 1788 these were held in all states for the purpose of ratifying the new Constitution of the United States. In many states, approval of the Constitution was only approved by a small margin; in Rhode Island ratification was defeated. The Founding Fathers made an intelligent decision in calling for ratifying conventions to approve the Constitution instead of having state legislatures do it, since under the system proposed by the Constitution, some of the powers state legislatures had at the time would be turned over to the federal government.

ration cards Held by Americans during World War II, these recorded the amount of rationed goods such as automobile tires, gasoline, meat, butter, and other materials an individual had purchased. Where regulation in World War I had been voluntary, consumption in World War II was regulated by government agencies.

realpolitik Pragmatic policy of leadership, in which the leader "does what he or she has to do" in order to be successful. Morality has no place in the mindset of a leader practicing realpolitik. The late nineteenth-century German chancellor Otto von Bismarck is the best modern example of a leader practicing realpolitik.

Rebel Without a Cause 1955 film starring James Dean exploring the difficulties of family life and the alienation that many teenagers felt in the 1950s. Juvenile delinquency, and the reasons for it, was the subtext of this film, as well as the source of countless other 1950s-era movies aimed at the youth market.

recall process One of a number of reforms of the governmental system proposed by progressive-era thinkers. By the process of recall, the citizens of a city or state could remove an unpopular elected official from office in midterm. Recall was adopted in only a small number of communities.

reconcentration (1896) Spanish policy designed to control the Cuban people by forcing them to live in fortified camps; American outrage over this led some politicians to call for war against Spain.

Reconstruction Act Plan of Radical Republicans to control the former area of the Confederacy and approved by Congress in March 1867. The former Confederacy was divided into five military districts, with each controlled by a military commander (Tennessee was exempt from this). Conventions were to be called to create new state governments (former Confederate officials could not hold office in these governments).

Reconstruction Era The era following the Civil War where Radical Republicans initiated changes in the South that gave newly freed slaves additional economic, social, and political rights. These changes were greatly resented by many Southerners, causing the creation of organizations such as the Ku Klux Klan. Reconstruction ended with the Compromise of 1877.

Reconstruction Finance Corporation Established in 1932 by Herbert Hoover to offset the effects of the Great Depression; the RFC was authorized to give federal credit to banks so that they could operate efficiently. Banks receiving these loans were expected to extend loans to businesses providing jobs or building low-cost housing.

Red Scare Vigorous repression of radicals, "political subversives," and "undesirable" immigrants groups in the years immediately following World War I. Nearly 6,500 "radicals" were arrested and sent to jail; some sat in jail without ever being charged with a crime, while nearly 500 immigrants were deported.

referendum process One of a series of progressive-era reforms designed to improve the political system. According to this referendum, certain issues would not be decided by elected representatives, but voters are called upon to approve or disapprove specific government programs. Consistent with populist and progressive era desire to return government "to the people."

religious right Primarily Protestant movement that greatly grew beginning in the 1970s and pushed to return "morality" to the forefront in American life. The religious right has been especially active in opposing abortion, and since the 1980s has extended its influence in the political sphere by endorsing and campaigning for specific candidates (e.g., during the 2004 campaign of President George W. Bush).

Removal Act of 1830 Part of the effort to remove Native Americans from "Western" lands so that American settlement could continue westward, this legislation gave the president the authorization (and the money) to purchase from Native Americans all of their lands east of the Mississippi, and gave him the money to purchase lands west of the Mississippi for Native Americans to move to.

***Report on the Public Credit* (1790)** Report by Secretary of the Treasury Alexander Hamilton, in which he proposed that the federal government assume the entire amount of the nation's debt (including state debt), and that the federal government should have an increased role in the nation's economy. Many of America's early leaders vigorously opposed the expansion of federal economic power in the new republic and the expansion of American industry that Hamilton also promoted.

Republican party Formed in 1854 during the death of the Whig party, this party attracted former members of the Free-Soil party and some in the Democratic party who were uncomfortable with the Democratic position on slavery. Abraham Lincoln was the first Republican president. For much of the twentieth century, the party was saddled with the label of being "the party of big business," although Richard Nixon, Ronald Reagan, and others did much to pull middle class and Southern voters into the party.

"reservationists" This group in the United States Senate was led by Henry Cabot Lodge and was opposed to sections of the Versailles Treaty when it was brought home from Paris by President Woodrow Wilson in 1919. Reservationists were especially concerned that if the United States joined the League of Nations, American troops would be used to conduct League of Nations military operations without the approval of the Congress.

Resettlement Administration In an attempt to address the problems of Dust Bowlers and other poor farmers, this 1935 New Deal program attempted to provide aid to the poorest farmers, resettle some farmers from the Dust Bowl, and establish farm cooperatives. This program never received the funding it needed to be even partially successful, and in 1937 the Farm Security Administration was created to replace it.

Revenue Act of 1935 Tax legislation championed by Franklin Roosevelt that was called a "soak the rich" plan by his opponents. Under this bill, corporate, inheritance, and gift taxes went up dramatically; income taxes for the upper brackets also rose. By proposing this, Roosevelt may have been attempting to diffuse the popularity of Huey Long and others with more radical plans to redistribute wealth.

Revenue Act of 1942 Designed to raise money for the war, this bill dramatically increased the number of Americans required to pay income tax. Until this point, roughly 4 million Americans paid income tax; as a result of this legislation, nearly 45 million did.

"revisionist" history A historical interpretation not found in "standard" history books or supported by most historians. A revisionist history of the origins of the cold war, for example, would maintain that the aggressive actions of the United States forced the Soviet Union to seize the territories of Eastern Europe for protection. Historical interpretations that may originally be revisionist may, in time, become standard historical interpretation.

revival meetings Religious meetings consisting of soul-searching, preaching, and prayer that took place during the Second Great Awakening at the beginning of the nineteenth century. Some revival meetings lasted over one week.

Rio Pact (1947) Treaty signed by the United States and most Latin American countries, stating that the region would work together on economic and defense matters and creating the Organization of American States to facilitate this cooperation.

Roe v. Wade (1973) Supreme Court decision that made abortion legal (except in the last months of pregnancy). Justices voting in the majority in this 5-to-2 decision stated that a woman's right to privacy gave her the legal freedom to choose to have an abortion. Abortion has remained one of the most hotly debated social issues in America.

Roosevelt Corollary An extension of the Monroe Doctrine, this policy was announced in 1904 by Theodore Roosevelt. It firmly warned European nations against intervening in the affairs of nations in the Western Hemisphere, and stated that the United States had the right to take action against any nation in Latin America if "chronic wrongdoing" was taking place. The Roosevelt Corollary was used to justify several American "interventions" in Central America in the twentieth century.

Rosie the Riveter Image of a woman factory worker drawn by Norman Rockwell for the *Saturday Evening Post* during World War II. Women were needed to take on factory jobs that had been held by departing soldiers; by 1945 women made up nearly 37 percent of the entire domestic workforce.

"Rough Riders" A special unit of soldiers recruited by Theodore Roosevelt to do battle in the Spanish-American War. This unit was composed of men from many backgrounds, with the commanding officer of the unit being Roosevelt (after he resigned as assistant secretary of the navy). The most publicized event of the war was the charge of the Rough Riders up San Juan Hill on July 1, 1898.

Salem Witch Trials 120 men, women, and children were arrested for witchcraft in Salem, Massachusetts, in 1692; 19 of these were executed. A new governor appointed by the Crown stopped additional trials and executions; several historians note the class nature of the witch trials, as many of those accused were associated with the business and/or commercial interests in Salem, while most of the accusers were members of the farming class.

SALT I (Strategic Arms Limitation Talks) 1972 treaty signed by Richard Nixon and Soviet premier Leonid Brezhnev limiting the development of additional nuclear weapon systems and defense systems to stop them. SALT I was only partially effective in preventing continued development of nuclear weaponry.

"salutary neglect" British policy announced at the beginning of the eighteenth century stating that as long as the American colonies remained politically loyal and continued their trade with Great Britain, the British government would relax enforcement of various measures restricting colonial activity that were enacted in the 1600s. Tensions between the colonies and Britain continued over British policies concerning colonial trade and the power of colonial legislatures.

satellite countries Eastern European countries that remained under the control of the Soviet Union during the cold war era. Most were drawn together militarily by the Warsaw Pact. Satellite nations that attempted political or cultural rebellion, such as Hungary in 1956 or Czechoslovakia in 1968, faced invasion by Soviet forces.

"Saturday Night Massacre" October 20, 1973, event when Richard Nixon ordered the firing of Archibald Cox, the special investigator in charge of the Watergate investigation. Attorney General Elliot Richardson and several others in the Justice Department refused to carry out this order and resigned. This event greatly damaged Nixon's popularity, both in the eyes of the public and in the Congress.

scalawags Term used by Southerners in the Reconstruction era for fellow Southerners who either supported Republican Reconstruction policies or gained economically as a result of these policies.

Scopes Trial of 1925 Tennessee trial where teacher John Scopes was charged with teaching evolution, a violation of state status. The American Civil Liberties Union hired Clarence Darrow to defend Scopes, while the chief attorney for the prosecution was three-time presidential candidate William Jennings Bryan. While Scopes was convicted and ordered to pay a small fine, Darrow was able to poke holes in the theory of creationism as expressed by Bryan.

Scottsboro Boys Nine black young men who were accused of raping two white women in a railway boxcar in Scottsboro, Arizona, in 1931. Quick trials, suppressed evidence, and inadequate legal council made them symbols of the discrimination that faced blacks on a daily basis during this era.

Scramble for Africa The competition between the major European powers to gain colonial territories in Africa that took place between the 1870s and the outbreak of World War I. Conflicts created by competing visions of colonial expansion increased tensions between the European powers and were a factor in the animosities that led to World War I.

secession A single state or a group of states leaving the United States of America. New England Federalists threatened to do this during the first administration of Thomas Jefferson. Southern states did this in the period prior to the Civil War.

Second Continental Congress Meeting of delegates from the American colonies in May 1775. During the sessions some delegates expressed hope that the differences between the colonies and Britain could be reconciled, although Congress authorized that the Continental army be created and that George Washington be named commander of that army.

Second Great Awakening Religious revival movement that began at the beginning of the nineteenth century. Revivalist ministers asked thousands of worshippers at revival meetings to save their own souls. This reflected the move away from predestination in Protestant thinking of the era.

Second Industrial Revolution The massive economic growth that took place in America from 1865 until the end of the century that was largely based on the expansion of the railroad, the introduction of electric power, and the production of steel for building. By the 1890s America had replaced Germany as the major industrial producer in the world.

Second National Bank Bank established by Congress in 1816. President Madison had called for the Second Bank in 1815 as a way to spur national economic growth after the War of 1812. After an economic downturn in 1818, the bank shrank the amount of currency available for loans, an act that helped to create the economic collapse of 1819.

Second New Deal Beginning in 1935, the New Deal did more to help the poor and attack the wealthy. One reason Roosevelt took this path was to turn the American people away from those who said the New Deal wasn't going far enough to help the average person. Two key legislative acts of this era were the Social Security Act of May 1935 and the June 1935 National Labor Relations Act (also called the Wagner Act), which gave all Americans the right to join labor unions. The Wealth Tax Act increased the tax rates for the wealthiest Americans.

secondary source A historical account written after the fact; a historian writing a secondary source would analyze the available primary sources on his/her topic. Examples would be a textbook, a biography written today of Napoleon, or a new account of the Black Death.

Separatists Religious group that opposed the Church of England. This group first went to Holland, and then some went on to the Americas.

settlement houses Centers set up by progressive-era reformers in the poorest sections of American cities. At these centers, workers and their children might receive lessons in the English language or citizenship; while for women, lessons in sewing and cooking were often held. The first settlement house was Hull House in Chicago, established by Jane Addams in 1889.

Seventeenth Amendment Ratified in 1913, this amendment allowed voters to directly elect U.S.

senators. Senators had previously been elected by state legislatures. This change perfectly reflected the spirit of progressive-era political reformers who wanted to do all they could to put political power in the hands of the citizenry.

Sherman Antitrust Act of 1890 Congressional legislation designed to break up industrial trusts such as the one created by John D. Rockefeller and Standard Oil. The bill stated that any combination of businesses that was "in the restraint of trade" was illegal. Because of the vagueness of the legislation and the lack of enforcement tools in the hands of the federal government, few trusts were actually prosecuted as a result of this bill.

Shiloh, Battle of Fierce Civil War battle in Tennessee in April 1862. Although the Union emerged victorious, both sides suffered a large number of casualties in this battle. Total casualties in this battle were nearly 25,000. General Ulysses S. Grant commanded the Union forces at Shiloh.

Sioux Plains tribe that tried to resist American westward expansion; after two wars, the Sioux were resettled in South Dakota. In 1876, Sioux fighters defeated the forces of General Custer at the Battle of the Little Bighorn. In 1890, almost 225 Sioux men, women, and children were killed by federal troops at the Massacre at Wounded Knee.

sit-down strikes A labor tactic where workers refuse to leave their factory until management meets their demands. The most famous sit-down strike occurred at the General Motors plant in Flint, Michigan, beginning in December 1936. Despite efforts by company guards to end the strike by force, the workers finally saw their demands met after 44 days.

sit-in Tactic used by the civil rights movement in the early 1960s; a group of civil rights workers would typically occupy a lunch counter in a segregated establishment in the South and refuse to leave, thus disrupting normal business (and profits) for the segregated establishment. During sit-ins civil rights workers often suffered physical and emotional abuse. The first sit-in was at the Woolworth's store in Greensboro, North Carolina, on February 1, 1960.

Sixteenth Amendment (1913) Amendment that instituted a federal income tax. In debate over this measure in Congress, most felt that this would be a fairer tax than a national sales tax, which was proposed by some.

Smith-Connally Act of 1943 Legislation that limited the nature of labor action possible for the rest of the war. Many in America felt that strikes, especially those organized in the coal mines by the United Mine Workers, were detrimental to the war effort.

Social Darwinism Philosophy that evolved from the writings of Charles Darwin on evolution that stated people inevitably compete with each other, as do societies; in the end the "survival of the fittest" would naturally occur. Social Darwinism was used to justify the vast differences between the rich and the poor in the late nineteenth century, as well as the control that the United States and Europe maintained over other parts of the world.

Social Gospel movement Late nineteenth-century Protestant movement preaching that all true Christians should be concerned with the plight of immigrants and other poor residents of American cities and should financially support efforts to improve the lives of these poor urban dwellers. Progressive-era settlement houses were often financed by funds raised by ministers of the Social Gospel movement.

Social history The field of history that analyzes the lives and beliefs of common people in any historical era. In American history, this field has grown dramatically since the 1960s. Social historians believe that we can get a more accurate view of the civil rights movement, by for example, studying the actions of civil rights workers in Mississippi than we can by studying the actions and pronouncements of leaders of the civil rights movement who were active on the national stage.

Social Security Act Considered by many to be the most important act passed during the entire New Deal, this 1935 bill established a system that would give payments to Americans after they reached retirement age; provisions for unemployment and disability insurance were also found in this bill. Political leaders of recent years have wrestled with the problem of keeping the Social Security system solvent.

Sons of Liberty Men who organized opposition to British policies during the late 1760s and 1770s. The Sons of Liberty were founded in and were most active in Boston, where in response to the Stamp Act they burned the local tax collector in effigy and burned a building that he owned. The Sons of Liberty also organized the Boston Tea

Party. Samuel Adams was one of the leaders of this group.

"Southern Strategy" Plan begun by Richard Nixon that has made the Republican party dominant in many areas of the South that had previously voted Democratic. Nixon, Ronald Reagan, and countless Republican congressional candidates had emphasized law and order and traditional values in their campaigns, thus winning over numerous voters. Support from the South had been part of the New Deal Democratic coalition crafted by Franklin Roosevelt.

Spanish-American War War that began in 1898 and stemmed from furor in America over treatment of Cubans by Spanish troops that controlled the island. During the war the American navy led by Admiral Dewey destroyed the Spanish fleet in the Pacific, the American ship the U.S.S *Maine* was sunk in Havana harbor, and Teddy Roosevelt led the Rough Riders up San Juan Hill. A major result of the war was the acquisition by the United States of the Philippines, which made America a major power in the Pacific.

speakeasies Urban clubs that existed in the 1920s where alcohol was illegally sold to patrons. The sheer number of speakeasies in a city such as New York demonstrated the difficulty of enforcing a law such as prohibition.

special prosecutor An official appointed to investigate specific governmental wrongdoing. Archibald Cox was the special prosecutor assigned to investigate Watergate, while Kenneth Starr was the special prosecutor assigned to investigate the connections between President Clinton and Whitewater. President Nixon's order to fire Cox was the beginning of the famous 1973 "Saturday Night Massacre."

speculation The practice of purchasing either land or stocks with the intent of selling them for a higher price later. After the Homestead Act and other acts opened up the western United States for settlement, many speculators purchased land with no intent of ever settling on it; their goal was to later sell the land for profit.

spoils system Also called the patronage system, in which the president, governor, or mayor is allowed to fill government jobs with political allies and former campaign workers. Political reformers of the 1880s and 1890s introduced legislation calling for large numbers of these jobs to be filled by the merit system, in which candidates for jobs had to take competitive examinations. President Andrew Jackson began the spoils system.

Sputnik First man-made satellite sent into space, this 1957 scientific breakthrough by the Soviet Union caused great concern in the United States. The thought that the United States was "behind" the Soviet Union in anything worried many, and science and mathematics requirements in universities across the country increased as a result.

Square Deal The philosophy of President Theodore Roosevelt; included in this was the desire to treat both sides fairly in any dispute. In the coal miner's strike of 1902 he treated the United Mine Workers representatives and company bosses as equals. This approach continued during his efforts to regulate the railroads and other businesses during his second term.

stagflation A unique economic situation faced political leaders in the early 1970s, where inflation and signs of economic recession occurred at the same time. Previously, in times of inflation, the economy was improving, and vice versa. Nixon utilized wage and price controls and increased government spending to address this problem.

Stamp Act To help pay for the British army in North America, Parliament passed the Stamp Act in 1765, under which all legal documents in the colonies had to be issued on officially stamped paper. A tax was imposed on all of these documents, as well as on all colonial newspapers. The resistance to the Stamp Act was severe in the colonies, and it was eventually repealed.

Stamp Act Congress Representatives of nine colonies went to this meeting held in New York in October 1765; the document produced by this congress maintained the loyalty of the colonies to the Crown but strongly condemned the Stamp Act. Within one year the Stamp Act was repealed.

states' rights The concept that the individual states, and not the federal government, have the power to decide whether federal legislation or regulations are to be enforced within the individual states. The mantle of states' rights would be taken up by New England Federalists during the presidency of Thomas Jefferson, by many Southern states in the years leading up to the Civil War, and by some Southern states again in response to federal legislation during the civil rights era of the 1960s.

Stono Rebellion of 1739 Slave rebellion in South Carolina where over 75 slaves killed white citizens and marched through the countryside with captured guns. After the rebellion was quashed, discipline imposed by many slave owners was much harsher. This was the largest slave rebellion of the 1700s in the colonies.

Students for a Democratic Society (SDS) Founded in 1960, this group was part of the "New Left" movement of the 1960s. SDS believed in a more participatory society, in a society that was less materialistic, and in university reform that would give students more power. By 1966 SDS concentrated much of its efforts on organizing opposition to the war in Vietnam. The *Port Huron Statement* was the original manifesto of SDS and was written by SDS founder Tom Hayden.

suburbia The area outside of the cities where massive numbers of families flocked to in the 1950s and 1960s. Suburban parents often still worked in the cities, but the suburban lifestyle shared little with urban life. Critics of 1950s suburbia point to the sameness and lack of vitality noted by some suburban residents and to the fact that suburban women often had to forget past dreams to accept the role of "housewife."

Suffolk Resolves These were sent from Suffolk County, Massachusetts, to the meeting of the First Continental Congress in September 1774 and called for the citizens of all of the colonies to prepare to take up arms against the British. After much debate, the First Continental Congress adopted the Suffolk Resolves.

Sugar Act Another effort to pay for the British army located in North America, this 1764 measure taxed sugar and other imports. The British had previously attempted to halt the flow of sugar from French colonies to the colonies: By the Sugar Act they attempted to make money from this trade. Another provision of the act harshly punished smugglers of sugar who didn't pay the import duty imposed by the British.

supply-side economics Economic theory adopted by Ronald Reagan stating that economic growth would be best encouraged by lowering the taxes of wealthy businessmen and investors; this would give them more cash, which they would use to start more businesses, make more investments, and in general stimulate the economy. This theory of "Reaganomics" went against economic theories going back to the New Deal that claimed to efficiently stimulate the economy, more money needed to be held by consumers (who would in turn spend it).

Sussex Pledge A torpedo from a German submarine hit the French passenger liner the *Sussex* in March 1916, killing and injuring many (including six Americans). In a strongly worded statement, President Wilson demanded that the Germans refrain from attacking passenger ships. In the Sussex Pledge the Germans said that they would temporarily stop these attacks, but that they might have to resume them in the future if the British continued their blockade of German ports.

Taft-Hartley Act of 1947 Congressional legislation that aided the owners in potential labor disputes. In key industries the president could declare an 80-day cooling off period before a strike could actually take place; the bill also allowed owners to sue unions over broken contracts, and forced union leaders to sign anti-Communist oaths. The bill was passed over President Truman's veto; Truman only vetoed the bill for political reasons.

Tammany Hall Political machine that ran New York City Democratic and city politics beginning in 1870, and a "model" for the political machines that dominated politics in many American cities well into the twentieth century. William Marcy "Boss" Tweed was the head of Tammany Hall for several years and was the most notorious of all of the political bosses.

Tariff of 1816 An extremely protectionist tariff designed to assist new American industries in the aftermath of the War of 1812. This tariff raised import duties by nearly 25 percent.

Tax Reform Act of 1986 The biggest tax cut in American history, this measure cut taxes by $750 billion over five years and cut personal income taxes by 25 percent. Tax cuts were consistent with President Reagan's belief that more money in the hands of the wealthy would stimulate the economy. Critics of this tax cut would argue that the wealthy were the ones that benefited from it, as little of the money that went to the hands of the rich actually "trickled down" to help the rest of the economy. Critics would also argue that the national deficits of the late 1980s and early 1990s were caused by these tax cuts.

Taylorism Following the management practices of Frederick Winslow Taylor, the belief practiced by many factory owners beginning in 1911 (when Taylor published his first book) that factories should be managed in a scientific manner, with everything done to increase the efficiency of the individual worker and of the factory process as a whole. Taylor describes the movements of workers as if they were machines; workers in many factories resisted being seen in this light.

Tea Act of 1773 Act by Parliament that would provide the American colonies with cheap tea, but at the same time would force the colonists to admit that Parliament had a right to tax them. The Sons of Liberty acted against this measure in several colonies, with the most dramatic being the Boston Tea Party. Parliament responded with the harsh Coercive Acts.

Teapot Dome Scandal One of many scandals that took place during the presidency of Warren G. Harding. The Secretary of the Interior accepted bribes from oil companies for access to government oil reserves at Teapot Dome, Wyoming. Other cabinet members were later convicted of accepting bribes and using their influence to make millions. The Harding administration was perhaps the most corrupt administration in American political history.

Teller Amendment As Americans were preparing for war with Spain over Cuba in 1898, this Senate measure stated that under no circumstances would the United States annex Cuba. The amendment was passed as many in the muckraking press were suggesting that the Cuban people would be better off "under the protection" of the United States.

temperance movement Movement that developed in America before the Civil War that lamented the effect that alcohol had on American society. After the Civil War, members of this movement would become especially concerned about the effect of alcohol on immigrants and other members of the urban poor. Out of the temperance movement came the drive for nationwide prohibition.

Ten Percent Plan Abraham Lincoln's plan for Reconstruction, which would have offered full pardons to persons living in Confederate states who would take an oath of allegiance to the United States (former Confederate military officers and civilian authorities would not be offered this possibility). Once 10 percent of the citizens of a state had taken such an oath, the state could take steps to rejoin the Union. Radical Republicans in the U.S. Senate felt that this plan was much too lenient toward the South.

tenant farmers In the Reconstruction South, a step up from sharecropping. The tenant farmer rented his land from the landowner, freeing him from the harsh supervision that sharecroppers suffered under.

Tennessee Valley Authority Ambitious New Deal program that for the first time provided electricity to residents of the Tennessee Valley; the TVA also promoted agricultural and industrial growth (and prevented flooding) in the region. In all, residents of seven states benefited from the TVA.

Tenure of Office Act (1867) Congressional act designed to limit the influence of President Andrew Johnson. The act took away the president's role as commander in chief of American military forces and stated that Congress had to approve the removal of government officials made by the president. In 1868, Johnson attempted to fire Secretary of War Stanton without congressional approval, thus helping set the stage for his impeachment hearings later that year.

Tet Offensive January 1968 attack launched on American and South Vietnamese forces by North Vietnamese and Vietcong soldiers. Although Vietcong troops actually occupied the American embassy in Vietnam for several hours, the end result was a crushing defeat for the anti-American forces. However, the psychological effect of Tet was exactly the reverse: Vietcong forces were convinced they could decisively strike at South Vietnamese and American targets, and many in America ceased to believe that victory was "just around the corner."

Thirteenth Amendment (1865) Amendment abolishing slavery in the United States and all of its territories (the Emancipation Proclamation had ended slavery only in the Confederate states). Final approval of this amendment depended on ratification by newly constructed legislatures in eight states that were former members of the Confederacy.

38th parallel The dividing line between Soviet-supported North Korea and U.S.-backed South Korea both before and as a result of the Korean War. American forces have been stationed on the southern side of this border continually since the Korean War ended in 1953.

Three-Fifths Compromise As the new Constitution was being debated in 1787, great controversy developed over how slaves should be counted in determining membership in the House of Representatives. To increase their representation, Southern states argued that slaves should be counted as people; Northerners argued that they should not count, since they could not vote or own property. The compromise arrived at was that each slave would count as three-fifths of a free person.

"tight money" Governmental policy utilized to offset the effects of inflation. On numerous occasions the Federal Reserve Board has increased the interest rate on money it loans to member banks; these higher interest rates are passed on to customers of member banks. With higher interest rates, there are fewer loans and other business activity, which "slows the economy down" and lowers inflation.

Timber and Stone Act of 1878 Bill that allowed private citizens to purchase forest territory in Oregon, Washington, California, and Nevada. Although the intent of the bill was to encourage settlement in these areas, lumber companies purchased large amounts of these land claims from the individuals who had originally purchased them.

Townshend Acts of 1767 Parliamentary act that forced colonists to pay duties on most goods coming from England, including tea and paper, and increased the power of custom boards in the colonies to ensure that these duties were paid. These duties were despised and fiercely resisted in many of the colonies; in Boston resistance was so fierce that the British were forced to occupy Boston with troops. The acts were finally repealed in 1770.

Trail of Tears Forced march of 20,000 members of the Cherokee tribe to their newly designated "homeland" in Oklahoma. Federal troops forced the Cherokees westward in this 1838 event, with one out every five Native Americans dying from hunger, disease, or exhaustion along the way.

Trenton, Battle of December 26, 1776, surprise attack by forces commanded by George Washington on Hessian forces outside of Trenton, New Jersey. Nearly 950 Hessians were captured and another 30 were killed by Washington's forces; three Americans were wounded in the attack. The battle was a tremendous psychological boost for the American war effort.

Triangle Shirtwaist Fire March 1911 fire in New York factory that trapped young women workers inside locked exit doors; nearly 50 ended up jumping to their death, while 100 died inside the factory. Many factory reforms, including increasing safety precautions for workers, came from the investigation of this incident.

triangular trade system The complex trading relationship that developed in the late seventeenth century between the Americas, Europe, and Africa. Europeans purchased slaves from Africa to be resold in the Americas, raw materials from the Americas were exported to European states, while manufactured products in Europe were sold throughout the Americas.

Truman Doctrine Created in response to 1947 requests by Greece and Turkey for American assistance to defend themselves against potentially pro-Soviet elements in their countries. This policy stated that the United States would be ready to assist any free nation trying to defend itself against "armed minorities or . . . outside pressures." This would become the major American foreign policy goal throughout the cold war.

trusts Late nineteenth-century legal arrangement that allowed owners of one company to own stock in other companies in the same industry. By this arrangement, John D. Rockefeller and Standard Oil were able to buy enough stock to control other oil companies in existence as well. The Sherman Antitrust Act and the Clayton Antitrust Act were efforts to "break up" the numerous trusts that were created during this period.

Turner Thesis Published by Frederick Jackson Turner in 1893, "The Significance of the West in American History" stated that western expansion had played a fundamental role in defining the American character, and that the American tendencies toward democracy and individualism were created by the frontier experience.

Twelfth Amendment of 1804 Amendment that established separate balloting in the Electoral College for president and vice president. This amendment was passed as a result of the electoral deadlock of the 1800 presidential election, when Thomas Jefferson and his "running mate" Aaron Burr ended up with the same number of votes in the Electoral College; the House of Representatives finally decided the election in favor of Jefferson.

U-2 American reconnaissance aircraft shot down over the Soviet Union in May 1960. President Eisenhower initially refused to acknowledge that this was a spy flight; the Soviets finally produced pilot Francis Gary Powers, who admitted the purpose of the flight. This incident created an increase in cold war tensions at the end of the Eisenhower presidency.

Uncle Tom's Cabin 1852 novel by Harriet Beecher Stowe that depicted all of the horrors of Southern slavery in great detail. The book went through several printings in the 1850s and early 1860s and helped to fuel Abolitionist sentiment in the North.

unicameral legislature A governmental structure with a one-house legislature. As written in the Articles of Confederation, the United States would have a unicameral legislature, with all states having equal representation.

United Farm Workers Organized by Cesar Chavez in 1961, this union represented Mexican-Americans engaged in the lowest levels of agricultural work. In 1965 Chavez organized a strike against grape growers that hired Mexican-American workers in California, eventually winning the promise of benefits and minimum wage guarantees for the workers.

U.S. Forest Service Created during the presidency of Theodore Roosevelt, this body increased and protected the number of national forests and encouraged through numerous progress the efficient use of America's natural resources.

Universal Negro Improvement Association Black organization of the early 1920s founded by Marcus Garvey, who argued that, however possible, blacks should disassociate themselves from the "evils" of white society. This group organized a "back to Africa" movement, encouraging blacks of African descent to move back there; independent black businesses were encouraged (and sometimes funded) by Garvey's organization.

unrestricted submarine warfare The German policy announcement in early 1917 of having their U-boats attack all ships attempting to land at British or French ports, despite their origin or purpose. Because of this policy, the rights of the United States as a neutral power were being violated, stated Woodrow Wilson in 1917, and America was forced to declare war on Germany.

U.S.S *Maine* American ship sent to Havana harbor in early 1898 to protect American interests in period of increased tension between Spanish troops and native Cubans. On February 15 an explosion took place on the ship, killing nearly 275 sailors. Later investigations pointed to an internal explosion on board, but all of the muckraking journals of the time in the United States blamed the explosion on the Spanish, which helped to develop intense anti-Spanish sentiment in the United States.

Valley Forge Location where General Washington stationed his troops for the winter of 1777 to 1778. Soldiers suffered hunger, cold, and disease: nearly 1,300 deserted over the course of the winter. Morale of the remaining troops was raised by the drilling and discipline instilled by Baron von Steuben, a former Prussian officer who had volunteered to aid the colonial army.

vertical integration Type of industrial organization practiced in the late nineteenth century and pioneered by Andrew Carnegie and United States Steel. Under this system all of the various business activities needed to produce and sell a finished product (procuring the raw materials, preparing them, producing them, marketing them, and then selling them) would be done by the same company.

Vicksburg, Battle of After a lengthy siege, this Confederate city along the Mississippi River was finally taken by Union forces in July 1863. This victory gave the Union virtual control of the Mississippi River and was a serious psychological blow to the Confederacy.

Vietcong During the Vietnam war, forces that existed within South Vietnam that were fighting for the victory of the North Vietnamese. Vietcong forces were pivotal in the initial successes of the Tet Offensive, which did much to make many in America question the American war effort in Vietnam and played a crucial role in the eventual defeat of the South Vietnamese government.

Vietnamization The process begun by Richard Nixon of removing American troops from Vietnam and turning more of the fighting of the Vietnam war over to the South Vietnamese. Nixon continued to use intense bombing to aid the South Vietnamese efforts as more American troops were being pulled out of Vietnam. In 1973, a peace treaty was finally signed with North Vietnam, allowing American troops to leave the country and all American POWs to be released. In March 1975, North Vietnamese and Vietcong forces captured Saigon and emerged victorious in the war.

Virginia Plan A concept of government crafted by James Madison and adopted by delegates to the convention that created the U.S. Constitution; this plan proposed a stronger central government than had existed under the Articles of Confederation to prevent too much power being placed in the hands of one person or persons. The plan also proposed that the powers of the federal government be divided among officials of executive, judicial, and legislative branches.

VISTA (Volunteer in Service to America) Program instituted in 1964 that sent volunteers to help poor Americans living in both urban and rural settings; this program was sometimes described as a domestic peace corps. This was one of many initiatives that were part of Lyndon Johnson's War on Poverty program.

voluntarism The concept that Americans should sacrifice either time or money for the well-being of their country. A sense of voluntarism has permeated America during much of its history, especially during the Progressive Era and during the administration of John Kennedy ("ask not what your country can do for you—ask what you can do for your country"). President George W. Bush called for a renewed sense of voluntarism in the aftermath of the attacks of September 11, 2001.

Wade-Davis Act Congress passed this bill in 1864 in response to the "10 Percent Plan" of Abraham Lincoln; this legislation set out much more difficult conditions than had been proposed by Lincoln for Southern states to reenter the Union. According to Wade-Davis, all former officers of the Confederacy would be denied citizenship; to vote, a person would have to take an oath that he had never helped the Confederacy in any way, and half of all white males in a state would have to swear loyalty to the Union before statehood could be considered. Lincoln prevented this from becoming law by using the pocket veto.

Wagner Act Also called the National Labor Relations Act, this July 1935 act established major gains for organized labor. It guaranteed collective bargaining, prevented harassment by owners of union activities, and established a National Labor Relations Board to guarantee enforcement of its provisions.

war bonds Also called Liberty Bonds, these were sold by the United States government in both World War I and World War II and used by the government to finance the war effort. A person purchasing a war bond could make money if he or she cashed it in after 5 or 10 years; in the meantime, the government could use the money to help pay its bills. In both wars, movie stars and other celebrities encouraged Americans to purchase war bonds.

War of 1812 War between the British and Americans over British seizure of American ships, connections between the British and Native-American tribes, and other tensions. Treaty ending war restored diplomatic relations between the two countries.

War Industries Board Authorized in 1917, the job of this board was to mobilize American industries for the war effort. The board was headed by Wall Street investor Bernard Baruch, who used his influence to get American industries to produce materials useful for the war effort. Baruch was able to increase American production by a staggering 22 percent before the end of the war.

Warren Commission The group that carefully investigated the assassination of John F. Kennedy. After hearing much testimony, the commission concluded that Lee Harvey Oswald acted alone in killing the president. Even today many conspiracy theorists question the findings of the Warren Commission, claiming that Oswald was part of a larger group who wanted to assassinate the president.

Warsaw Pact Defensive military alliance created in 1955 by the Soviet Union and all of the Eastern European satellite nations loyal to the Soviet Union; the Warsaw Pact was formed as a reaction against NATO and NATO's 1955 decision to invite West Germany to join the organization.

Washington Conference of 1921 Conference where the United States, Japan, and the major European powers agreed not to build any no more warships for 10 years. In addition, the nations agreed not to attack each other's territories in the Pacific. This treaty came from strong post–World War I sentiment that it was important to avoid conflicts between nations that might lead to war.

Watergate Affair The break-in into Democratic campaign headquarters was one of a series of "dirty tricks" carried out by individuals associated with the effort to reelect Richard Nixon president in 1972. Extensive efforts were also made to cover up these activities. In the end, numerous government and campaign officials spent time in jail for their role in the Watergate Affair, and President Nixon was forced to resign in disgrace.

Webb Alien Land Law (1913) California law that prohibited Japanese who were not American citizens from owning farmland in California. This law demonstrates the nativist sentiment found in much of American society in the first decades of the twentieth century.

Webster-Hayne Debate (1830) Senate debate between Senator Daniel Webster of Massachusetts and Senator Robert Hayne of South Carolina over the issue of state's rights and whether an individual state has the right to nullify federal legislation. Webster skillfully outlined the dangers to the United States that would be caused by the practice of nullification; this debate perfectly captured many of the political divisions between North and South that would increase in the 1830s through the 1860s.

Whig party Political party that came into being in 1834 in opposition to the presidency of Andrew Jackson. Whigs opposed Jackson's use of the spoils system and the extensive power held by President Jackson; for much of their existence, however, the Whigs favored an activist federal government (while their opponents, the Democrats, favored limited government). William Henry Harrison and Zachary Taylor were the two Whigs elected president. The Whig party dissolved in the 1850s.

Whiskey Rebellion Many settlers in Western frontier territory in the early 1790s questioned the power that the federal power had over them. In 1793 settlers in the Ohio territory refused to pay federal excise taxes on whiskey and attacked tax officials who were supposed to collect these taxes; large numbers of "whiskey rebels" threatened to attack Pittsburgh and other cities. In 1794 President Washington was forced to send in federal troops to put down the rebellion.

"White Man's Burden" From the poem of the same name by Rudyard Kipling, this view justified imperialism by the "white man" around the world, but also emphasized the duty of the Europeans and Americans who were occupying new territories to improve the lives of those living in the newly acquired regions.

Whitewater The name of the scandal that got President Bill Clinton impeached but not convicted. Whitewater was the name of a real-estate deal in Arkansas that Clinton and his wife Hillary Rodham Clinton were both involved in; opponents claimed the actions of the Clintons concerning Whitewater were illegal, unethical, or both. Independent Counsel Kenneth Starr expanded the investigation to include the suicide of Clinton aide Vincent Foster, missing files in the White House, and the relationship of President Clinton with a White House intern, Monica Lewinsky.

Wilmot Proviso In the aftermath of the war with Mexico, in 1846 Representative David Wilmot proposed in an amendment to a military bill that slavery should be prohibited in all territories gained in the treaty ending that war. This never went into law, but in the debate over it in both houses, Southern representatives spoke passionately in defense of slavery; John C. Calhoun even suggested that the federal government had no legal jurisdiction to stop the existence of slavery in any new territory.

Woodstock Music Festival (1969) Event that some perceive as the pinnacle of the 1960s counterculture. 400,000 young people came together for a weekend of music and a relative lack of hassles or conflict. The difficulty of mixing the 1960s counterculture with the radical politics of the era was demonstrated when Peter Townshend of the Who kicked Abbie Hoffman off the Woodstock stage.

Works Progress Administration (WPA) New Deal program established in 1935 whose goal was to give out jobs as quickly as possible, even though the wages paid by the WPA were relatively low. Roads and public buildings were constructed by WPA work crews. At the same time, WPA authors wrote state guidebooks, artists painted murals in newly constructed public buildings, and musicians performed in large cities and small towns across the country.

writ of habeas corpus Allows a person suspected of a crime not to simply sit in jail indefinitely. Such a suspect must be brought to court and charged with something, or he or she must be released from jail. Abraham Lincoln suspended the right of habeas corpus during the Civil War so that opponents of his policies could be contained.

Yalta Conference Meeting between Stalin, Churchill, and Roosevelt held two months before the fall of Nazi Germany in February 1945. At this meeting Stalin agreed to assist the Americans against the Japanese after the Germans were defeated; it was decided that Germany would be divided into zones (each controlled by one of the victors), and Stalin promised to hold free elections in the Eastern European nations the Soviet army had liberated from the Nazis. Critics of the Yalta agreement maintain that Roosevelt (he was only months from his own death) was naïve in his dealings with Stalin at this meeting, and that Churchill and Roosevelt essentially handed over control of Eastern Europe to Stalin.

yellow journalism This method uses accounts and illustrations of lurid and sensational events to sell newspapers. Newspapers using this strategy covered the events in Cuba leading up to the Spanish-American War, and did much to shift American opinion toward desiring war with Spain. Some critics maintain that many tactics of yellow journalism were used during the press coverage of the Whitewater investigation of Bill Clinton.

Yorktown, Battle of The defeat of the forces of General Cornwallis in this battle in October 1781 essentially ended the hopes of the British for winning the Revolutionary War. American and French troops hemmed the British in on the peninsula of Yorktown, while the French navy located in Chesapeake Bay made rescue of the British troops by sea impossible.

Zimmermann Telegram January 1917 telegram sent by the German foreign minister to Mexico suggesting that the Mexican army should join forces with the Germans against the United States. When the Germans and Mexicans were victorious, the Mexicans were promised most of the southwestern part of the United States. The British deciphered the code of this telegram and turned it over to the United States; the release of its content caused many in America to feel that war against the Germans was essential.

BIBLIOGRAPHY

To get the "perfect 5" on the AP exam you should read this study guide thoroughly. In addition, read all of the assignments your teacher gives you from the textbook. She/he will undoubtedly give you primary source readings and additional readings; these are also critical to your success. Remember, the more you read about American history, the more prepared you will be for the exam!

On this page, we have also included a number of topics that you will study in an AP U.S. History course and books that have been helpful to us in studying each particular topic. This is a totally subjective list; your teacher would probably recommend other books for some of the topics. Nevertheless, if you feel weak in a particular subject (or if you want to learn more about it) read all or a part of the books we have recommended. We are confident that you will not be disappointed.

The Age of Jackson: *Waking Giant: America in the Age of Jackson* by David S. Reynolds (Harper, 2008).

America and World War I: *The Illusion of Victory: America in World War I* by Thomas Fleming (Basic Books, 2004).

The American Revolution: *The American Revolution: A History* by Gordon S. Wood (Modern Library, 2003).

The Civil Rights Movement: *Eyes on the Prize: America's Civil Rights Years, 1954–1965* by Juan Williams (Penguin, 1988).

The Civil War: *Battle Cry of Freedom: The Civil War Era* by James M. McPherson (Oxford University Press USA, 2003).

The Clinton Era: *The Natural: The Misunderstood Presidency of Bill Clinton* by Joe Klein (Broadway, 2003).

The Cold War: *The Cold War: A History* by Martin Walker (Holt Paperbacks, 1995).

Colonial Settlement and the Environment: *Changes in the Land: Indians, Colonists, and the Ecology of New England* by William Cronon (Hill and Wang, 2003).

The Constitution: *A Brilliant Solution: Inventing the American Constitution* by Carol Berkin (Harvest Books, 2003).

Early Industrialization: *What Hath God Wrought: The Transformation of America, 1815–1848* by Daniel Walker Howe (Oxford University Press USA, 2007).

George Washington: *His Excellency: George Washington* by Joseph J. Ellis (Vintage, 2005).

The Gilded Age: *America in the Gilded Age* by Sean Cashman (NYU Press, 1993).

The Great Depression: *The Forgotten Man: A New History of the Great Depression* by Amity Shlaes (Harper Perennial, 2008).

Imperialism: *A People's History of American Empire* by Howard Zinn, Mike Konopacki, and Paul Buhle (Metropolitan Books, 2008).

1920s: *New World Coming: The 1920s and the Making of Modern America* by Nathan Miller (Da Capo Press, 2004).

1950s: *The Fifties* by David Halberstam (Ballantine Books, 1994).

1960s: *The Sixties: Years of Hope, Days of Rage* by Todd Gitlin (Bantam, 1993).

1970s: *It Seemed Like Nothing Happened: America in the 1970s* by Peter N. Carroll (Rutgers University Press, 1990).

Origins of the Civil War: *The Impending Crisis, 1848–1861* by David M. Potter (Harper Perennial, 1977).

Progressivism: *A Fierce Discontent: The Rise and Fall of the Progressive Movement in America, 1870–1920* by Michael McGerr (Oxford University Press USA, 2005).

The Reagan Era: *Transforming America: Politics and Culture During the Reagan Years* by Robert M. Collins (Columbia University Press, 2006).

The Reconstruction Era: *Reconstruction: America's Unfinished Revolution, 1863–1877* by Eric Foner (Harper Perennial Modern Classics, 2002).

The Settlement of the American Colonies: *American Colonies: The Settling of North America* by Alan Taylor (Penguin, 2002).

Slavery: *Slavery and the Making of America* by James Oliver Horton and Lois E. Horton (Oxford University Press USA, 2006).

Thomas Jefferson: *Thomas Jefferson: Author of America* by Christopher Hitchens (Eminent Lives, 2005).

The 2008 Elections: *The 2008 Elections and American Politics* by James W. Ceaser, Andrew E. Busch, and John J. Pitney (Rowman & Littlefield Publishers, 2009).

The War on Terror: *The Dark Side: The Inside Story of How the War on Terror Turned into a War on American Ideals* by Jane Mayer (Anchor, 2009).

Westward Expansion: *The American West: A New Interpretive History* by Robert V. Hine and John Mack Faragher (Yale University Press, 2000).

World War II: *The American People in World War II: Freedom from Fear, Part Two* by David M. Kennedy (Oxford University Press USA, 2003).

WEBSITES

There are literally thousands of sites on the web where you can get valuable information on aspects of American history. Historical figures, historical events, and historic sites all have websites with specific information; in addition, there are hundreds of websites with a vast variety of information and resources on topics of U.S. history. If you want to start somewhere, we would recommend two sites. One is a University of Delaware Library site, entitled "Internet Resources for U.S. History." This is found at http://www2.lib.udel.edu/subj/hist/ushist/internet.

Another excellent site is the Internet Public Library site. This is located at http://www.jpl.org/div/subject/browse/hum30.55.85.30.

Do some more exploring, and you will be utterly amazed at what you can find. In addition, go to your state and local historical society sites; here you will find information about the connections between the history of your town and state and the larger historical themes that you have studied in your AP U.S. History class.

Prepare for Success at Every Step in Your AP* Journey!

AP*

Prepare for Upcoming AP Classes →

McGraw-Hill
ONboard™
FOR ADVANCED PLACEMENT*

This online, interactive program builds the skills & background knowledge you'll need to succeed in upcoming AP coursework and beyond.

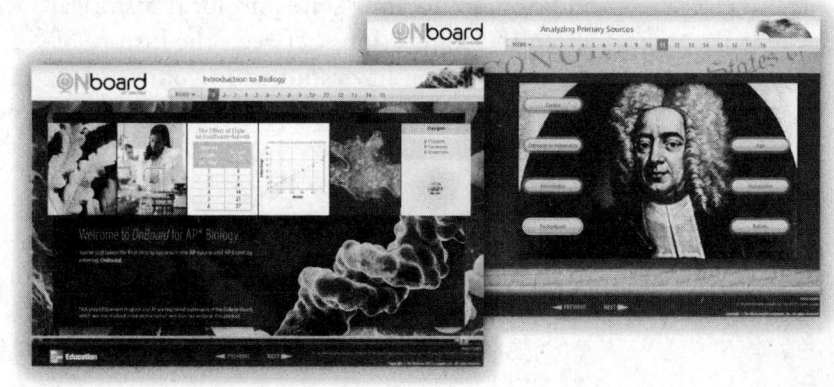

Prepare for the AP Exam →

McGraw-Hill
SCOREboard™
FOR AP* TEST PREP

This online, adaptive, diagnostic AP Test Prep series includes 4 complete AP practice exams and personalized study plans to help you maximize your time leading up to the exam.

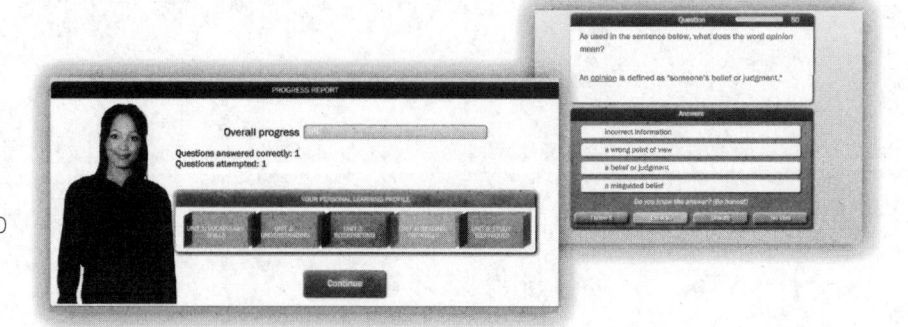

McGraw Hill Education

To learn more or to purchase, visit
MHEonline.com/advancedplacement

* Advanced Placement program and AP are registered trademarks of the College Board, which was not involved in the production of, and does not endorse, these products.